W9-ACH-749

Fahrenheit **Celsius**

Fahrenheit	Celsius
240	110
230	
220	100
210	
200	90
190	
180	80
170	
160	70
150	
140	60
130	
120	50
110	
100	40
90	30
80	
70	20
60	
50	10
40	
30	0
20	
10	−10
0	
−10	−20
−20	−30
−30	
−40	−40
−50	
−60	−50
−70	
−80	−60

Metric to English

Approximate Conversions from Metric Measures

Symbol	When You Know	Multiply by	To Find	Symbol
Length				
mm	millimeters	0.04	inches	in
cm	centimeters	0.4	inches	in
m	meters	3.3	feet	ft
m	meters	1.1	yards	yd
km	kilometers	0.6	miles	mi
Area				
cm²	square centimeters	0.16	square inches	in²
m²	square meters	1.2	square yards	yd²
km²	square kilometers	0.4	square miles	mi²
ha	hectares (10,000 m²)	2.5	acres	
Mass/Weight				
g	grams	0.035	ounces	oz
kg	kilograms	2.2	pounds	lb
t	tonnes (1000 kg)	1.1	short tons	
Volume				
ml	milliliters	0.03	fluid ounces	fl oz
l	liters	2.1	pints	pt
l	liters	1.06	quarts	qt
l	liters	0.26	gallons	gal
m³	cubic meters	35	cubic feet	ft³
m³	cubic meters	1.3	cubic yards	yd³
Temperature (Exact)				
°C	Celsius temperature	9/5 (then add 32)	Fahrenheit temperature	°F

Centimeters   **Inches**

1 2 3 4 5 6 7 8 9 10 11 12 13 14 15

1 2 3 4 5 6

SCIENCE IN ELEMENTARY EDUCATION

EIGHTH EDITION

SCIENCE IN ELEMENTARY EDUCATION

Peter C. Gega

Professor Emeritus
San Diego State University

Joseph M. Peters

Professor
The University of West Florida

Merrill
an imprint of Prentice Hall

Upper Saddle River, New Jersey   Columbus, Ohio

Cover photo: © Mugshots/The Stock Market
Editor: Bradley J. Potthoff
Production Editor: Louise N. Sette
Copy Editor: Margaret C. Gluntz
Photo Coordinator: Anthony Magnacca
Design Coordinator: Julia Zonneveld Van Hook
Text Designer: John Edeen
Cover Designer: Brian Deep
Production Manager: Deidra M. Schwartz
Director of Marketing: Kevin Flanagan
Marketing Manager: Suzanne Stanton
Advertising/Marketing Coordinator: Julie Shough

This book was set in Galliard and Helvetica by The
Clarinda Company and was printed and bound by
R.R. Donnelley & Sons Company. The cover was
printed by Phoenix Color Corp.

© 1998 by Prentice-Hall, Inc.
Simon & Schuster/A Viacom Company
Upper Saddle River, New Jersey 07458

Earlier editions © 1994, 1990, 1986 by Macmillan
Publishing Company, © 1982, 1977, 1970, 1966 by
John Wiley & Sons, Inc.

Printed in the United States of America

10 9 8 7 6 5 4

ISBN: 0-13-613852-7

Prentice-Hall International (UK) Limited, *London*
Prentice-Hall of Australia Pty. Limited, *Sydney*
Prentice-Hall of Canada, Inc., *Toronto*
Prentice-Hall Hispanoamericana, S. A., *Mexico*
Prentice-Hall of India Private Limited, *New Delhi*
Prentice-Hall of Japan, Inc., *Tokyo*
Simon & Schuster Asia Pte. Ltd., *Singapore*
Editora Prentice-Hall do Brasil, Ltda., *Rio de Janeiro*

Library of Congress Cataloging-in-Publication Data

Gega, Peter C.
  Science in elementary education / Peter C. Gega,
Joseph M. Peters.—8th ed.
    p.   cm.
  Includes bibliographical references and index.
  ISBN 0-13-613852-7
  1. Science—Study and teaching (Elementary)
I. Peters, Joseph M.   II. Title.
LB1585.G4   1998
372.3'5'044—dc21   97-3542
                                                     CIP

PHOTO CREDITS

Chapters 1–5 openers: Anthony Magnacca/Merrill
Figure 5–2: Barbara Schwartz/Merrill
Figure 5–3: Courtesy of Cannon Visual
    Communications
Chapter 6 opener: Anthony Magnacca/Merrill
Figure 6–7: Copyright Optical Data Corporation
Chapters 7–8 openers: Anthony Magnacca/Merrill
Chapter 9 opener: Anne Vega/Merrill
Figure 9–3: U.S. Department of Energy
Chapter 10 opener: Anthony Magnacca/Merrill
Figure 10–2: Spencer Grant/Stock Boston
Figure 10–3: American Museum of Natural History
Chapters 11–14 openers: Anthony
    Magnacca/Merrill
Figure 14–5: High Spencer
Figure 14–6: Bruce Roberts/Photo Researchers
Chapter 15 opener: Barbara Schwartz/Merrill
Figure 15–1: Tumblebrook Farms, Inc.
Figure 15–4: Runck Shoenburger/Grant Heilman
Figure 15–5: American Museum of Natural History
Figure 15–6: Carolina Biological Supply Co.
Figure 15–8: American Museum of Natural History

Figure 15–13: Carolina Biological Supply
Figure 15–14: Runck Shoenburger/Grant Heilman
Chapter 16 opener: Anthony Magnacca/Merrill
Chapter 17 opener: AP Wide World Photos
Figure 17–1: General Biological Supply House
Figure 17–3: USDA Soil Conservation Service
Figure 17–4: U.S. Department of Agriculture
Table 17–1: Pumice: H.Stearns/U.S. Geological
    Survey; volcanic brecca: Mackay School of Mines,
    University of Nevada; obsidian: C. Milton/U.S.
    Geological Survey; basalt, granite, conglomerate,
    sandstone, slate, quartzite: Courtesy Department
    of Library Services, American Museum of Natural
    History; shale: W. Bradley/U.S. Geological
    Survey; limestone: F. Calkins/U.S. Geological
    Survey; marble: A. Heitanen/U.S. Geological
    Survey
Chapter 18 opener: Anthony Magnacca
Figure 18–3: ESSA (a and b), NOAA (c).
Figure 18–5: Courtesy of Qualimetrics, Inc.,
    Sacramento, CA
Chapter 19 opener: Courtesy of NASA

This book is dedicated to Willard Korth, Science Education, The University of Pittsburgh, who has been an inspiration and mentor for countless students and colleagues.

PREFACE

Elementary school teaching is a challenging and exciting career. Professional educators have the responsibility to meet the future demands and challenges of society, and this—the elementary classroom—is where it all begins. The lifelong attitudes of elementary students toward science learning will be shaped, for the most part, before they finish fifth grade. Along with this comes the desire to seek out new information about the world around us and to apply this knowledge in the form of technology. It is our job to build the skills, content knowledge, and desire for inquiry that will allow these students to function in a society which we know will be highly scientific and technologically developed. Teachers will need to be lifelong learners and researchers in their own classrooms. This text serves as a guide to start the elementary professional educator on this pathway.

New in This Edition

The eighth edition of *Science in Elementary Education* demonstrates a strengthening of earlier editions with the inclusion of some new features. First, the reader will notice that a graphic organizer accompanies the beginning of each chapter. Second, Chapters 1–7 now include a vignette and a reflection in addition to the summary, references, and additional readings. Third, samples of the National Research Council *Science Education Standards* and American Association for the Advancement of Science *Benchmarks for Science Literacy* are cited throughout the text when applicable. Internet

links have been added, where appropriate, for the growing number of readers with electronic access. Finally, Chapter 7 has been rewritten, solely on the topic of assessment.

Organization of the Text

You will find that this book combines practical methods, subject matter, and activities on how to teach science to elementary through early middle-level learners. It has two complementary parts.

Part I centers on why science education is basic to children's schooling and explains the foundations that give it form and substance. Each of its seven chapters develops a broad competency or a cluster of related teaching skills through step-by-step descriptions and use of many real-life examples. The examples reflect our personal teaching experiences or ongoing first-hand observations with elementary school children. The chapters and several of the included follow-up exercises should enable you to:

- decide what areas of science are basic, useful, and learnable for children;
- recognize and assess differences in children's thinking;
- use closed-ended and open-ended teaching activities in planning and implementing lessons and units;
- improve children's scientific skills;
- locate and use a variety of resources to teach science;

- arrange and manage learning centers, micro-computer center, and projects; and

- assess science teaching.

Part II has 12 chapters of subject matter, broad investigations, and activities. The activities have been updated where necessary. Part II is designed with three purposes in mind. First, it helps you to apply the skills developed in Part I. For example, the questioning methods and the open-ended and closed-ended strategies in the early chapters are shown in hundreds of in-context examples. This is also true of suggested thinking processes. Early sections on learning centers and projects show how to quickly and easily convert many investigations in Part II for those uses. Following through on these and other methods is strongly emphasized.

Second, Part II gives you numerous active and interesting concrete experiences to use with children. These are in two forms: activities and investigations. The *activities* offer first-hand experiences through which children may learn concepts and procedures. The *investigations* offer chances for you and your students to inquire, as co-investigators if you wish, into open-ended problems and topics. Both kinds of learning experiences use everyday, easy-to-get materials and can also enrich school science programs.

The third purpose of Part II is to provide explanations of subject matter that can help you where you may feel lacking in background. These are tied to the learning experiences and give useful, everyday examples of science concepts and principles at work. Of course, you can build a good subject-matter background as you investigate with children. The explanations are provided in an effort to assist you in guiding children confidently and creatively.

Acknowledgments

I personally wish to thank all of the many people who helped with this edition of *Science in Elementary Education* and the *How to Teach Elementary School Science* and *Concepts and Experiences in Elementary School Science* versions. I especially wish to thank Carol Briscoe, The University of West Florida; George O'Brien, Florida International University; and Cynthia Ledbetter, University of Texas—Dallas, who reviewed the manuscripts and provided suggestions for the eighth edition. I would also like to extend my gratitude to other colleagues at The University of West Florida who reviewed applicable sections of the text, including Lisbeth Dixon-Krauss, Russell Lee, and Keith Whinnery. Additionally, I am grateful to Brad Potthoff from Merrill/Prentice Hall for his encouragement and constructive comments.

This edition of *Science in Elementary Education* and the corollary *How to Teach Elementary School Science* include seven vignettes. I extend my sincere thanks to Norman Lederman, Oregon State University; Ken Tobin, Florida State University; George O'Brien, Florida International University and Angela Alexander, Pine Villa Montessori, Dade County School District, Florida; Jerry Mayernik, North Hills School District, Pennsylvania; Carol Parker, Escambia County School District, Florida; Sue Dale Tunnicliffe, International Council of Associations for Science Education Primary Projects and Cambridge University; and Christine Peters, Harborcreek School District, Pennsylvania, for sharing their experiences with us and reviewing the respective chapters.

I would also like to acknowledge the reviewers of this text: S. Wali Abdi, The University of Memphis; Leonard J. Garigliano, Salisbury State; Marlene Nachbar Hapai, University of Hawaii at Hilo; Charlotte Iiams, Moorhead State University; Robert J. Miller, Eastern Kentucky University; Michael Odell, University of Idaho; and David Pepi, University of Wisconsin–River Falls.

Most importantly, I would like to show my heartfelt appreciation to my wife, Darlene, for her daily editorial assistance and to my children, Joe and Brenda, for their patience during the revision.

—*Joseph M. Peters*

BRIEF CONTENTS

CONTENTS

Summary of Investigations

SUMMARY OF ACTIVITIES

PART

I

HOW TO
TEACH ELEMENTARY
SCHOOL SCIENCE

CHAPTER 1

SCIENCE IN ELEMENTARY EDUCATION

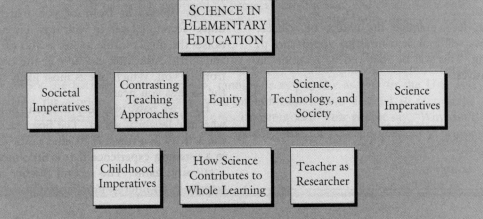

SCIENCE IN ELEMENTARY EDUCATION

Societal Imperatives

Contrasting Teaching Approaches

Equity

Science, Technology, and Society

Science Imperatives

Childhood Imperatives

How Science Contributes to Whole Learning

Teacher as Researcher

Vignette 1-1 (continued)

that it causes cancer. It seems that everything causes cancer. I'm not going to do anything different until they decide once and for all."

The case of U.V. rays is not unique. "Flip-flops" in the opinion of scientists and doctors have occurred with respect to aspirin, alcohol, cold fusion, and Vitamin C. Indeed, such changes have become the object of jokes.

What does this have to do with teaching elementary-level students about the nature of science? These flip-flops we so often see are really not weaknesses of science. They are *not* reasons for the general public to disregard scientific knowledge or lose faith in the scientific way of thinking. These "flip-flops" constitute one of the most important strengths of science—in fact, they *are* science. That is, scientific knowledge is self-correcting based upon new empirical evidence or new ways of interpreting data. The knowledge, although tentative, is based upon volumes of data and should not be disregarded. Disregarding scientific knowledge severely limits the quality of decisions that we each make about our lives.

WHAT IS THE NATURE OF SCIENCE?

There are as many answers to this question as there are books, However, at the level of generality that will be useful to you as an elementary teacher there is a strong consensus. Strictly speaking, science can be defined as a body of knowledge, a process, and a way of knowing or constructing reality. The *nature of science* refers to those characteristics of scientific knowledge that derive directly from how the knowledge is developed. Of importance to you as an elementary science teacher are the following characteristics:

1. There is no single set or sequence of steps in a scientific investigation (i.e., there is no such thing as *the* scientific method).

2. Scientific knowledge (both theories and laws) is subject to change (i.e., all scientific knowledge is tentative).

3. Scientific knowledge must be at least partially supported by empirical evidence (i.e., scientific knowledge must involve the collection of data and must be consistent with what we "know" about the world and be testable).

4. Scientific knowledge is partially the product of the creative imagination of the scientist (i.e., all scientific knowledge combines both empirical evidence and the creative interpretation of data by scientists).

5. Given the importance of scientists' individual creativity, scientific knowledge is necessarily subjective to some degree (i.e., scientific knowledge is not totally objective as is commonly believed).

6. Scientific knowledge is a product of both observation and inference.

By carefully addressing these characteristics of scientific knowledge and keeping in mind the developmental level of your students, you can help your students develop understandings that will help them in making decisions for the rest of their lives. In particular, your students will begin to develop a more balanced view of the "truth" of scientific knowledge. They will take "the truth" of science with an informed "grain of salt." This means that your students will heed the notion that the sun's rays can cause cancer and it also means that they will not disregard all future knowledge about the effects of the sun's rays if the scientific community alters its current position.

How Can You Teach the Nature of Science?

Although the current reforms in science education place a strong emphasis on students' understandings of the nature of science, you will find very few resources containing classroom-tested teaching ideas. The following is an idea that I have found to be successful for teaching elementary students about each of the six characteristics of scientific knowledge. This activity requires virtually no scientific background on the part of the students. Consequently, it is relatively risk-free.

1. Recreate the tube pictured in Figure 1-1. I suggest that you obtain a mailing tube from either the post office, the map room at a local library, or a store that sells posters. You may also use a piece of PVC pipe. Clothesline, twine, or rope from the local hardware store will do for the rope. The ring holding the ropes together is plastic; you can buy one at a crafts store. If a ring is not available, the lower rope can simply be looped over the upper rope. The ends of the tube can be sealed with rubber stoppers or taped.

2. Make an overhead (and class set of handouts) of what is pictured in Figure 1-2.

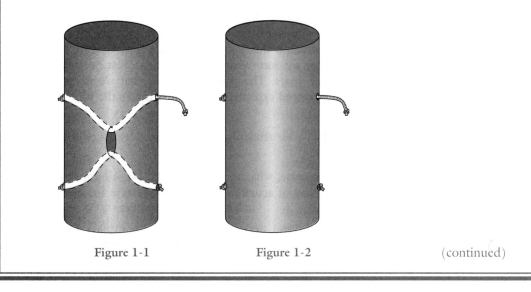

Figure 1-1   Figure 1-2   (continued)

would happen if you cut the nail in half? Would it be only half as strong? The teacher can invite students to write questions on the chalkboard. Most can be answered by experimenting with the materials on hand. A few questions may call for locating and carefully reading reference materials, or conferring with people who are most likely to have deeper knowledge about magnetism.

The first teacher in this example provides a concrete experience for students, but leaves students to learn more about magnetism through routine and unfocused reading. What is missing is an understanding of the nature of science and how to get children to think in scientific ways.

The second teacher uses the activity to provoke curiosity, generate various experiments, and examine procedures and assumptions. This gives students some direction as to exactly what to read or whom to confer with for answers *to their own questions.* The children conduct an investigation similar to that of scientists.

In two separate upper-level classrooms, two teachers are scheduled to teach the same three lessons. Here's how each begins each lesson:

Teacher 1:   Does cold air hold less moisture than warm air?

Teacher 2:   Why do our lips and skin seem so dry today?

Teacher 1:   Does air have weight? What is air pressure?

Teacher 2:   When you drink pop through a straw, what makes the liquid go up the straw?

Teacher 1:   Can sunlight cause a chemical change in things?

Teacher 2:   How many of you have seen colored clothing that has faded?

In each case, the first teacher has simply stated the science principle that will be taught in the form of a question. So in the first lesson,

for example, the children will learn that *cold air holds less moisture than warm air.*

The second teacher begins with an *application* of the principle. The lessons begin and end by referring to children's everyday experiences. This teacher—in agreement with what current reform efforts call for—wants science to be based on what students can apply in their everyday lives. Science principles, or *generalizations,* as we'll refer to them in this book, typically have many real-life applications. When we begin and end lessons with applications, it enables children to reflect on their experiences.

You have probably observed by now that the second way of teaching is likely to be more interesting and productive to you and the students. Yet, if you're like most persons who select elementary teaching as a profession, science is not likely to be your strongest subject. You may not feel confident about teaching science. Do not worry about this; you and the children can explore and learn together. What is important is that you begin to develop an awareness of the nature of science and how you can develop scientific skills and understandings with the students. One way to begin this development is to look at the essential ideas and processes that give a subject its value—its imperatives.

There are three sources of imperatives in science education: those that come from science as a discipline, those that reflect society's needs, and those that reveal how children develop and learn. Understanding these can help you to put into perspective the specific teaching methods of the following chapters and gain confidence from seeing the big picture.

SCIENCE IMPERATIVES

The imperatives from science as a discipline are found in *how* scientists go about finding out—

process; and *what* scientists have found out—*knowledge.* Although the two, in practice, are inseparable, it is convenient to look at them separately. Let's consider knowledge first.

Knowledge

You and I try to explain, predict, and control our experiences by generalizing about the patterns or regularities we observe:

Muscles get sore when overworked.

Quality and price go together.

Actions speak louder than words.

Knowing the generalization about sore muscles may cause you to say, "I overworked yesterday, that's why I'm sore!" (explain), or "I'm probably going to be sore tomorrow" (predict), or "I'm not going to overwork today" (control). Can you see how you might also use the other two generalizations for these three purposes?

Scientists, too, observe patterns and generalize about them. But they usually do so with far more precision and reliability. This is a big reason nonscientists can profit from the study of science and its methods.

Scientists use an ingenious array of tools and organized ways to search for patterns in objects and events. The generalizations they invent to explain what they observe may look like these:

Plants have adaptations that enable them to survive changing conditions.

Fossil remains show that some life forms have become extinct.

Eclipses happen when the earth, sun, and moon are aligned.

However, few scientists pretend to fully *explain* or understand natural events. What they do is to *describe* natural events and, when they can, to predict or control them. What they may call "explanations" (concepts, generalizations, principles, laws, theories) are really descriptions—often brilliantly conceived and useful, but

descriptions after all. How well a description enables them to "explain," predict, or control events becomes the chief measure of its worth.

Consider the concept of *mammal,* for example. Like other concepts, this one stands for a class of things with similar properties. Suppose a small whale gets tangled in a fishnet below the ocean's surface. Can you predict what will soon happen to the whale? You might think: "Whale—that's a mammal. Mammals are lung breathers. It will probably drown." Notice how the concept of whale as mammal brings up a property (lung breathing) associated with all mammals. This enables you to make a reasonably certain prediction. Or if a friend asks, "A whale *drown?* How?" you can explain by using the same property. Your understanding of the concept might also prompt you to influence or control the event, by swiftly cutting the net, for instance.

The generalizations of science help us in a similar way. The statement "Most matter expands when heated and contracts when cooled" interrelates several concepts. This generalization enables us to relate and explain a number of apparently different phenomena: a sidewalk that buckles and cracks in hot weather; telephone wires that sag in summer but not in winter; a tightly screwed jar lid that can be loosened by running hot water over it; rocks around a campfire that break apart when we douse the fire and rocks with water.

Learning key concepts and generalizations is an essential component of science education, because it increases our ability to solve problems and use scientific skills. Notice that Figure 1-3 shows that a large variety of animals can be classified as mammals, but only a handful need be studied to get a handle on the concept. Once we understand the physical properties of mammals, it's easy to classify even unfamiliar animals. Even if we don't know their names, we already know a great deal about them.

A similar transfer of learning happens with properly learned generalizations. Although few events may be studied to learn the generaliza-

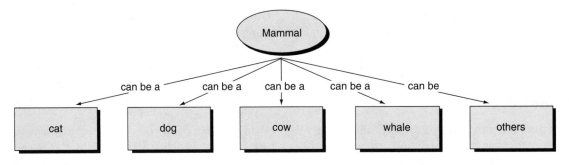

Figure 1-3
Concepts stand for a class of things with similar properties.

tion (Figure 1-4), many more may be applied. Organizing thoughts into concepts, generalizations, sequences, and other patterns broadens and deepens understanding. In contrast, facts which are studied without relating them to prior knowledge can be quickly forgotten. Learning the patterns of nature allows us to continually apply, or transfer, these concepts to new objects and events. The new facts collected are connected to existing mental structures, which aids in the future retrieval of the information.

Incidentally, have you already inferred how you might test to see if concepts and generalizations can be applied by students? You'll want to ask questions that contain examples of objects or events that have *not* been studied. If

the child can link *unstudied* examples of a studied concept or generalization, chances are that transferable learning has occurred.

Scientists search for patterns, but they also look for inconsistencies in the patterns. Under certain conditions, for example, plants may *not* adapt and survive. The occasional deviation from the usual allows scientists to sharpen their generalizations and theories. In the same vein, we may find that, when shopping, quality does not always accompany higher prices. Figuring out under what conditions this happens improves our previous notion and makes us better shoppers.

Children, too, can learn to refine their generalizations. A second-grade class placed various

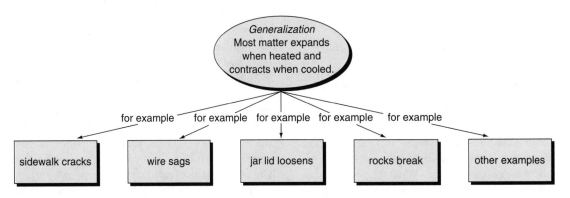

Figure 1-4
Generalizations enable us to relate and explain apparently different events.

small objects in water-filled pans to see which would sink or float. Some children summed up what they had learned by saying, "Light things float and heavy things sink." On hearing this, the teacher had them compare on a balance the weights of some things that had floated and sunk. A few objects that floated were heavier than some that had sunk. This made everyone look at the objects more carefully. Still, no one seemed to know what to say. When the teacher drew attention to the objects' sizes, the children soon concluded, "Things that are light for their size float. They sink when they are heavy for their size." Not bad, considering that the children had to think about two variables together, size and weight.

It is hard when dealing with natural events to foresee all the conditions that might cause them to change. This is why scientists see their generalizations and theories as *tentative,* always subject to change with new data. It also explains why generalizations may be stated in *probabilities,* a frequent practice when dealing with living things: "Persons who eat fatty foods run a greater risk of heart attacks than those who do not."

PARSIMONY.   Scientists may offer competing explanations or theories to account for a natural phenomenon. This is likely when the phenomenon can only be observed indirectly (the makeup of the earth's core, for instance), or has happened in the distant past (extinction of the dinosaurs, for example), and so cannot be fully tested. When competing theories account for the data equally well, scientists prefer on principle the simplest one. This principle of *parsimony,* which literally means the quality of being stingy or miserly, helps to keep the scientific enterprise more manageable and economical than it would be without it.

SPIRAL APPROACH.   If you switch to a higher grade after several years of teaching, don't be surprised if a previously taught gener-

alization shows up again in your curriculum guide. Because a science generalization consists of several concepts and accounts for many facts, it usually takes more than one exposure for students to learn it well. So curriculum developers may plan for children to study the generalization several times, at increasing levels of complexity and abstraction, and in different contexts, during grade levels K–2, 3–5, or 6–8. Consider an understanding of the nature of scientific investigation. This is studied from the early grades onward. Figure 1–5 shows how the *Benchmarks for Science Literacy* (American Association for the Advancement of Science [AAAS], 1993, pp. 6-7) are based on the spiral approach. We will refer to the *Benchmarks* throughout the activities in Section II of this text.

Notice the increased complexity as the students move from kindergarten to eighth grade. In curriculum development, this is known as an *interrupted spiral approach* to teaching concepts and generalizations. The approach embodies the need to restudy ideas at higher levels of complexity while it avoids needless repetition.

Process

Although the basic concepts and generalizations of science are tentative in nature, their high quality generally makes them last a long time. The quality is no accident. The processes and attitudes scientists use in seeking regularities have been screened over many years to get the best results. Scientists realize the futility of trying to construct immutable laws or truths. But they also understand that the quality of their knowledge is linked to the quality of the processes used to produce it. So scientists continually try to sharpen their observations and how they think about them.

Such an approach breeds a continuing curiosity, the willingness to listen to others' ideas, the caution to suspend judgment until enough facts are known, the readiness to try know who is receiving the drug or who is being given the placebo.

Objectivity may be difficult for children. Primary-level students view nonhuman objects in a subjective way. The child's environment often promotes fantasy over reality. Children commonly read stories or see TV cartoons in which animals talk, the sun smiles, and steam locomotives suffer pitiably as they huff and puff up a steep mountainside. Giving human characteristics to nonhuman objects is called *anthropomorphism*. Children usually have no trouble deciding whether such events are true or fictional. But sometimes they make anthropomorphic inferences without realizing it. These can take several forms.

Children may be quick to imbue some animals with human personality traits. But is a lion truly "braver" than a mouse? a fox "sly"? a wolf "nastier" than a dog? This is *personification*. Movies contribute to this form of anthropomorphism.

Sometimes children ascribe a conscious purpose to nonhuman things. Do plant roots really "seek" water? Do female birds find food for their young because "they don't want them to die"? This is *teleology*.

A third form of anthropomorphism, especially common in young children, is to endow almost any object with life and human feelings. I've had several primary-level students tell me it rains because "the clouds get sad and cry." Others, responding to the question, "Where is the sun at night?" have said, "It's tired and goes to sleep." This is *animism*.

Science educators today view anthropomorphic statements in the context of children's early attempts to explain their world. As children grow, these statements decrease and become more easily correctable. Anthropomorphism in all its forms can be overcome when students learn how to make proper inferences from their observations.

THE IMPORTANCE OF WORKING WITH DATA.   Children can learn scientific *knowledge* from books or other sources. But science *processes* must be learned by *working with data*. For instance, students may be told how the period of a pendulum is determined, and some may understand and remember it. But students who are given a few materials and guided to figure this out for themselves will soon be counting the number of swings per minute (measuring), trying various possibilities to change the swing rate (experimenting), taking notes of what they did (communicating), making graphs (more communicating), and drawing conclusions from their findings (inferring). These children are more likely to remember and apply the principle of pendulums throughout their lives, to clocks, playground swings, and metronomes.

Perhaps what makes processing data so effective in improving children's thinking is that they can actually observe the consequences of good and bad thinking. The objects they work with will usually "tell" them if they are on the right track: snails will eat only what they are adapted to eat and toy boats will sink like real boats when they are not buoyant. Science is a good subject in which to demonstrate observable consequences, because it presents so many opportunities to test ideas with concrete materials.

INTERACTIVE NATURE OF PROCESS AND KNOWLEDGE.   Process thinking is typically neglected in science education. One reason is that many teachers are unsure about how to teach it. In response, some curriculum writers press process teaching so hard they neglect subject-matter content. This approach runs against the inseparable nature of process and knowledge.

The science processes are not like computational skills in arithmetic. Nor are they like decoding skills in reading, which, once learned, may be applied in any subject-matter context. Cognitive psychologists say that the quality of the science processes we use is "domain specific." That is, *our ability to apply a process in a situation is strongly linked to our understanding of the organized field of subject matter that pertains to the situation* (Beyer, 1987, p. 164;

Gagné, 1985, pp. 145–150). A physician's observations of subtle weather signs are likely to be no more useful than a meteorologist's observations of subtle disease symptoms, if each tries to do the other's work. Their subject-matter background of concepts and generalizations is what gives purpose, meaning, and significance to what they observe in their chosen fields. Background knowledge is inseparably mixed with the process of observation. The same can be said of the other processes they use in their work.

This means that a curriculum must give children continual opportunities to learn thinking processes within a wide variety of subject-matter areas and conditions if the processes are to be generally useful. So the trend today is to guide children to apply thinking processes in all the school subjects. Because process and subject-matter concepts are open-ended, students can get better at processing data and learning concepts throughout their lives. An effective science curriculum gives chances to teach process thinking within all topics at all grade levels. Enabling you to identify and maximize these opportunities is an important objective of this book.

The imperatives of science, as an organized discipline, can set the foundation and tone for a quality science program, although there is more to science than just experimentation. The authors of *Project 2061* (AAAS, 1989) discuss things such as the designed world, human society, and their interrelations with science. Therefore, it is important to consider some societal imperatives in addition to science imperatives.

SOCIETAL IMPERATIVES

As you saw on page 10, you are likely to teach better and stimulate more interest and appreciation in lessons when you apply science learning to everyday life. It's fun for students to learn

how eyeglasses work when they study light energy and the eye. And it's interesting for them to make their own flashlights from simple materials when studying electrical energy. A well-planned curriculum usually contains many of these everyday applications.

It is important to educate people and change people's attitudes in order to cope with today's challenges. Naturally, the education system plays an major role in this process. For example, science education is focusing on such things as AIDS, endangered species, wetlands, environmentally safe food, uncontaminated drinking water, multicultural career opportunity, and gender equity in science-related careers.

Every society wants its contributing members to be literate; that is, to have enough background knowledge and ability to communicate, produce, and improve the general welfare. In a society as advanced and dynamic as the one we live in today, information increases at an accelerating rate. Under such conditions, people need a common core of knowledge. A common ground allows us to communicate more efficiently with one another and facilitates public policy.

Literacy serves as the common ground for discussing and understanding diverse and complex issues. In our everyday encounters with the media, such issues as toxic waste dumps, test-tube babies, AIDS, nuclear accidents, ozone, the greenhouse effect, and artificial body parts are examined. When making purchases, knowledge of specific technical information may be considered. For example, when buying a car, it is helpful to have some knowledge of horsepower, fuel economy, and anti-lock brakes. In order to secure a job, we are expected to know something. Our functioning and survival in our society are linked to literacy.

Science literacy is imperative in a society that leans heavily on science and technology. AAAS (1993) views literacy in the following way:

Project 2061 promotes literacy in science, mathematics, and technology in order to help people live interesting, responsible, and productive lives. In a culture increasingly pervaded by science, mathematics, and technology, science literacy requires understandings and habits of mind that enable citizens to grasp what those enterprises are up to, to make some sense of how the natural and designed worlds work, to think critically and independently, to recognize and weigh alternative explanations of events and design trade offs, and to deal sensibly with problems that involve evidence, numbers, patterns, logical arguments, and uncertainties (p. XI).

All children need a rich array of firsthand experiences to grow toward a full measure of science literacy. Quality science programs make it possible for advanced study, which can lead to many occupational choices and benefits to all society. An important area related to societal imperatives is equity.

EQUITY

Think for a moment about what the world would be like if half of the technological developments were cultivated by women? What advances would be made? What current problems would be minimized? What if an equivalent proportion of scientific discoveries were developed by people of color? How might the world be different?

Current science education reforms promote scientific literacy for all students as their central theme. The belief is that science should be comprehensible, accessible, and exciting for *all* students from kindergarten through twelfth grade. In reality, these goals are rarely achieved, *especially for underrepresented populations.* In a recent document from the National Science Foundation (NSF, 1996), we see a typical pattern of males scoring higher than females and white students scoring higher than blacks or Hispanics on national assessments.

Science has long been studied in the traditions of the white, Anglo male. This makes it difficult for females or minorities to place it in an understandable social context. Think about a living scientist. Is this person male or female? a person of color or white? What does this person look like? Stop for a moment and consider your image of a scientist. Do you have a stereotypical image?

Children often view a scientist as a white male, with a lab coat, pocket protector full of pencils, and long unkempt hair; a nerd with glasses. This furthers the problem of equity. Not only do most boys not want to be this "scientist", what woman or minority would want to be seen like this? As a teacher, your views of a scientist will probably be passed onto the students. Remediation of these images by bringing local minority and female scientists into the classroom is essential.

Equity and the Language of Science

Another way to help correct the imbalance is to think about how science is taught at the elementary level. If science is just rote learning of disjointed facts, it becomes especially hard for minorities who do not have a strong command of the language. Little wonder that these students do not elect to take more than the required minimum of science courses as they go on to high school. It's surprising that *every* student is not eventually turned off by this language-intensive, fact-only approach.

In an attempt to help students understand the "language" of the scientist, the National Science Teachers Association published *The Language of Science* (Mandell, 1974, p. 1). This book equated the language of science to a foreign language and stressed the importance of knowing the language to be a participant in the science classroom. Along these lines, Karen Gallas (1995) discusses why "science talk" is so important for children and why teachers need to help them develop the language of science. As Jay Lemke puts it,

> It is not surprising that those who succeed in science tend to be like those who define the "appropriate" way to talk science: male rather than female, white rather than black, middle- and upper-middle class, native English speakers, standard dialect speakers, committed to the values of Northern European middle-class culture (1990, p. 138).

What these three authors, and many others, are saying is that teachers need to understand that the language of science is often a barrier to equity in the classroom.

In summary, a major consideration in the development of a quality elementary science program will be the matter of gender equity. As an educator, it will be your responsibility to select science textbooks, teaching materials, and methodologies which present realistic role models for men and women in all walks of life. The current science literacy problem which exists in many minority populations may really just be a forewarning of an increasing science literacy problem with all students. Your contribution in the classroom will have a major impact on the types of career decisions students make.

One way to begin to involve all students in "real" science and increase their opportunity to learn is the science, technology, and society, or STS, approach.

SCIENCE, TECHNOLOGY, AND SOCIETY

The growing awareness of how science, technology, and society interrelate has generated an STS movement in science education. The National Science Teachers Association adopted the *Science–Technology–Society: Science Educa-* *tion for the 1980s* position statement in 1982. Their view is that several of the problems we face today can be solved only by persons educated in the ideas and processes of science and technology, and that scientific literacy is essential for living, working, and decision making in the 1980s and beyond (National Science Teachers Association [NSTA], 1982). They see STS as the teaching and learning of science in the *context of human experiences* and advocate that science should be real to students. Scientific problems which are provided for students to solve should be based on issues which are of genuine interest to students.

STS supplies a context whereby the students can begin to weigh issues such as the need for burning coal to produce electricity against the resulting acid rain, thermal pollution, and greenhouse effect. Elementary students work with these questions, follow up by testing their answers to the questions, and take action based on their findings. The *STS Issue Investigation and Action Instruction* model is a good example of this teaching strategy, since there are four critical factors: "(a) foundations, (b) awareness, (c) investigations, and (d) action phases" (Rubba, Wiesenmayer, Rye, & Ditty, 1996, p. 25). The model begins when the teacher assists students in understanding the nature of science and technology and their interactions. The instructor then helps the students understand the concepts and issues related to the topic during the awareness phase. They study the STS issue from every aspect, including the scientific and social science points of view. Students then experiment and investigate the STS issue. Finally, they develop ways to take action on the issue. Notice how this approach is in keeping with the balance of the science imperatives of knowledge and process. Students learn about the issue (knowledge) and then investigate the problem (process). It extends beyond the basic imperatives, however, and includes a societal focus that requires students to take action on issues.

In keeping with current reform efforts, science educators who advocate STS agree that the overall goal for science education was to develop scientifically literate graduates who could apply science to everyday life. These citizens would be able to understand the issues, take responsibility for the issues, and make informed decisions on these issues.

Energy and Environmental Education

One of the most important STS issues is energy. Most people now realize that we must continue to move from a position of exploiting the environment to conserving or using it wisely. Not only are resources of the planet limited, but almost every year we see a greater demand on these resources from other nations. The immensity of the changes needed in the United States is revealed in our annual consumption of energy. With only 5 percent of the world's population, the United States uses more than 25 percent of the world's energy.

The history of material progress everywhere closely parallels a rise in energy use. As fuels disappear, however, more attention will be turned to tapping into relatively inexhaustible sources such as solar, wind, tidal, and geothermal energy. Material progress and swelling populations have also increased air, water, and land pollution, along with the growing problem of managing solid waste.

Environmental awareness is critical for massive changes to happen. A society which has been educated about environmental concerns is more likely to be supportive of essential research and development, to consume less, recycle materials, and alter habits than harm the environment. What is needed is an understanding that the earth is a closed system with natural self-renewing cycles.

It is important that society as a whole continues to solve, or resolve, energy and environmental problems while working harmoniously with nature. Cooperation and common objectives are key aspects in developing solutions. Introducing these types of concerns in the early years of education provides society with the foundation for major changes.

Technology and Career Awareness

Solutions to energy and environmental problems will flow from applied science or technology. So will advances in health care, business, communications, agriculture, and many other areas.

As you saw earlier, scientists invent ideas to explain, predict, and *control* phenomena. Technology is that branch of science that is mainly concerned with controlling—or managing—objects and events in improved ways.

With the prevalence of technology in today's society, it is vital to prepare the future workforce for these occupations. Research scientists, professional engineers, skilled technicians, and computer operators are required to have the scientific knowledge to plan and design useful inventions and creative solutions. Demand will continue to grow for workers qualified in the areas of computer programming, service of electronic devices, operation of advanced medical equipment, and treatment of wastewater and solid waste.

Technology and the Curriculum

The following notions about teaching science still exist today.

> *"Even a new science textbook is dated by the time it's distributed."*

> *"I can't teach science. Who has time to keep up with it?"*

Contrary to these views, the basic ideas and processes taught in the science curriculum last a long time. Scientific information and vocabulary may change, but many basic concepts remain unchanged or are only slightly altered.

Technology is one facet of science that is dynamic, not only in itself but in specific facts. Consider the shift from copper telephone wires to fiber optics, the change in the precise measurement of the speed of light from 186,198 miles per second to 186,282 miles per second, or the discovery of new subatomic particles.

Basic concepts and generalizations in effective science programs are often linked to technological applications: aeronautics, telecommunications, electric circuitry, soil conservation, and food processing. Learning about these applications can change the way children view many of the useful gadgets around us. Understanding how systems operate develops a realistic perspective toward the mechanisms of everyday life. Yet a worthwhile *elementary* curriculum will probably always be rooted in the basic ideas and processes of science because it yields a bigger payoff: students understand more basic science and so more applications, including technology.

CHILDHOOD IMPERATIVES

The application of concepts and processes of science to society's problems is the reason why science education is such an important subject in school. However, since we are dealing with elementary-level students, we need to match what is to be taught with the student's interest and developmental level.

Perhaps you have heard the expression, "To a child who's discovered the hammer, all the world is a nail." It captures nicely the broad curiosity and inner need of children to try things out for themselves whenever they are free to do so. Science education is of great value to children because it richly enhances these and other attributes that loom so large in their development. But the nature of childhood also makes us recognize several other realities.

For example, because broad generalizations and skills are so useful in science study, it is tempting to increase their scope so they apply to more and more phenomena. When we deal with children, though, there is always the question of when to stop. Explanations become continually more abstract and remote from common experience. As a generalization or process approaches the most advanced scientific model, it is less likely that children can learn it or will even want to. To persist is simply to have them bite off more than they can chew. So teaching generalizations about molecules in the primary years, for example, or insisting that *all* variables be controlled in experiments is likely to be self-defeating.

It is important for children to understand and see the purpose of what they are doing. Also, they need to reach short-range goals as they head toward those farther away. Children usually learn best when working with concrete or semiconcrete materials and limited generalizations. This is most necessary with younger students.

It is unlikely that any publisher or curriculum office can develop a program that suits every child or class. It will be your responsibility to create a suitable match between students and the curriculum. This will require understanding, in some detail, the imperatives of childhood, particularly how children learn science.

HOW SCIENCE CONTRIBUTES TO WHOLE LEARNING

So far you've examined some imperatives to help you judge the good and bad in science teaching. But your work as an elementary-school teacher goes far beyond the teaching of science. No subject in the curriculum stands alone. After all, we want to provide a basic *gen-*

metaphors would be the teacher as a "grand-mother," a "ship's captain," a "military officer," a "policewoman," a "psychologist," or a "resource manager" (see Lorsbach [1995] for an example of metaphors as applied to elementary science education or Briscoe [1991] for a study of a specific teacher who used metaphors to assist in teacher change).

No matter which metaphor you choose, reflective teaching through the use of teacher research is important to your ongoing professional development and the success of your students. Thinking about metaphors can help you explore your role as a teacher. For instance, thinking about changes to your current teaching practices in light of a "new metaphor" can help a teacher develop new teaching methodologies consistent with the desired changes. If you change from being a "dictator" to a "speaker of the house," this would have some obvious affects on your teaching routines. Students would be able to have a say in their education instead of you deciding everything for them.

The important aspect of metaphors is to consider them as a means to conceptualize your teaching and beliefs. If you find that your metaphor is like the "teacher as comic" or "teacher as drill sergeant" metaphor, then careful selection of a new metaphor (or multiple metaphors) may be warranted.

SUMMARY

1. Science is an organized search for regularities or patterns and inconsistencies that may occur in them. Scientists and nonscientists alike generalize about the regularities they observe.

2. Scientists invent concepts and generalizations to explain the patterns they observe and, when possible, predict and control objects or events that fit the patterns. Learning science concepts and generalizations increases intellectual power because we can apply this knowledge.

3. Varying conditions may produce inconsistencies in the patterns scientists observe. The generalizations they invent may be stated as probabilities and change with new data.

4. The learning of concepts and generalizations is ongoing and integrative so science curricula present them at least several times, with increasing refinement and complexity, within the elementary grades.

5. Science is a search for publicly observable and verifiable evidence. This evidence must describe interacting objects to establish cause-and-effect relations. Correlation is not the same as evidence of causation. Acceptable evidence is always subject to change with new data and nothing is proved.

6. Knowledge and the science processes are interactive, so effective curricula present opportunities to teach the processes within all topics and grade levels.

7. When problems and changes emerge in a society, coping with them raises the need to educate people and change attitudes.

8. Your view of science teaching makes a big difference in what students actually experience. As a teacher, you need to be sensitive to equity and multicultural issues.

9. Science should be comprehensible, accessible, and even exciting for *all* students.

10. STS is an approach to teaching where the students learn through phases such as foundations, awareness, investigations, and action.

REFLECTION

1. One way to begin exploring how you will teach elementary science is to investigate your attitudes toward science. Fill in the information on Figure 1–6 and be ready to share it with your classmates. If you have time, compare your attitudes with those of your parents, friends, or study partner.

2. Write down your memory of elementary sci-

Positive	Better	Average	Poor	Negative
Inclusive				Exclusive
Popular				Weird
Invigorating				Exhausting
Safe				Dangerous
Fun				Boring
Beneficial				Harmful
Rewarding				Punishment
Involving				Lethargic
Important				Trivial
Innovative				Ancestral
Enjoyable				Mundane
Influential				Worthless
Powerful				Ineffective
Exciting				Monotonous

Figure 1-6
Attitudes toward science and science teaching. Place a check in the box which best describes your attitude.

ence experiences. Which of these experiences are hands-on activities and which are memorization activities? Be ready to share with others the implications of why you would remember one more than the other.

3. Observe an elementary science class at your practicum site and note how the teacher provides equity in terms of gender. Does the teacher call on boys more than girls? Are the boys dominating the experiments? Are the girls afraid to answer questions or provide explanations? Think of ways to promote equity in your classroom and share these with the class.

4. What is your metaphor for teaching science? Write down some possible metaphors and explain the advantages and disadvantages of each. What are some metaphors that your past teachers have used? Did you agree or disagree with this approach? Why? Be ready to share this information with your classmates.

REFERENCES

American Association for the Advancement of Science. (1989). *Science for all Americans, Project 2061.* Washington, DC: Author.

American Association for the Advancement of Science. (1993). *Benchmarks for science literacy.* New York: Oxford University Press.

Beyer, B. K. (1987). *Practical strategies for the teaching of thinking.* Boston: Allyn and Bacon.

Briscoe, C. (1991). The dynamic interactions among beliefs, role metaphors, and teaching practices: A case study of teacher change. *Science Education, 75,* 186–199.

Chall, J. S. (1986). *Stages of reading development.* New York: McGraw–Hill.

Gagné, E. D. (1985). *The cognitive psychology of school learning.* Boston: Little, Brown.

Gallas, K. (1995). *Talking their way into science: hearing children's questions and theories, responding with curricula.* New York: Teachers College Press.

Kren, S. R. (1979). Science and mathematics: Interactions at the elementary level. In M. B. Rowe (Ed.), *What research says to the science teacher* (Vol. 2). Washington, DC: National Science Teachers Association.

Lemke, J. L. (1990). *Talking science: language learning and values.* Norwood, NJ: Ablex Publishing.

Lorsbach, A. W. (1995). The use of metaphor by prospective elementary teachers to understand learning environments. *Journal of Elementary Science Education, 7*(2), 1–26.

Mandell, A. (1974). *The language of science.* Arlington, VA: National Science Teachers Association.

National Science Foundation. (1996). *The learning curve.* Washington, DC: Author.

National Science Teachers Association. (1982). *Science–technology–society: Science education for the 1980s.* A position statement. Washington, DC: Author.

Rubba, P. A., Wiesenmayer, R. L., Rye, J. A., & Ditty, T. (1996). The leadership institute in STS education: A collaborative teacher enhancement, curriculum development, and research project of Penn State and West Virginia University with rural middle/junior high school science teachers. *Journal of Science Teacher Education, 7*(1), 23–40.

U.S. Department of Education. (1986). *What works. Research about teaching and learning* (2nd ed.). Washington, DC: Author.

Wellman, R. T. (1978). Science: A basic for language development. In M. B. Rowe (Ed.), *What research says to the science teacher* (Vol. 1). Washington, DC: National Science Teachers Association.

SUGGESTED READINGS

Hopkins, D. (1985). *A teacher's guide to classroom research.* Bristol, PA: Open Court Press. (An easy-to-follow guide on what action research is, how to research, and why classroom research is important).

Lakoff, G., & Johnson, M. (1980). *Metaphors we live by.* Chicago: University of Chicago Press. (A look at how metaphors shape our thinking).

Penick, J. E. (Ed.). (1988). *Focus on excellence: Elementary science revisited.* Washington, DC: National Science Teachers Association. (Thirteen of the best school science programs in the country and how they developed.)

Rhoton, J., & Bowers, P. (1996). *Issues in science education.* Arlington, VA: National Science Teachers Association. (This book contains sections on science education reform, change, professional development and research in the classroom.)

Thirunarayanan, M. O. (Ed.). (1992). *Think and act. Make an impact. Handbook of science, technology, and society* (Vol. 2, STS in action in the classroom.). Tempe, AZ: Arizona State University. (Volume two of this series was written by classroom teachers and contains many STS-related activities.)

Waks, L. J. (1992, Winter). The responsibility spiral: A curriculum framework for STS education. *Theory Into Practice, 31*(1), 12–18. (How educators can identify, select, organize, and sequence learning activities to promote effective science/technology/society education.)

Yager, R. E. (Ed.). (1993). *The science, technology, society movement. What research says to the science teacher* (Vol. 7). Arlington, VA: National Science Teachers Association. (This is the seventh in a series of books designed to present research from a classroom teacher's perspective.)

HOW CHILDREN LEARN SCIENCE

HOW
CHILDREN
LEARN
SCIENCE

Behaviorism in
the Classroom

Constructivist
Theories

B. F. Skinner

Cognitive
Theories of
Learning

Radical
Constructivism

Social
Constructivism

David Ausubel

Piaget

Why is it important to study how children learn science? Why not just teach science as a amalgamation of vocabulary and facts, using the "foreign language" approach that many of us experienced in elementary school science? Consider the following:

During our lifetime, more was learned about science and nature than in the 5,000 years which preceded our birth. Coupled with this is a revolution in how we can observe our surroundings. For example, compare the first telescope with the Hubble space telescope currently in use.

All of the information in the world doubles every 18 months. Despite this, we need to have an understanding of the natural world and the technological advances which will be integral to everyday life and the workplace of the future. Scientific literacy is the key to solving environmental problems and remaining globally competitive.

Technological and scientific advances in biotechnology, computer processing speeds, worldwide Internet connectivity, and new areas of science such as chaos theory are changing the nature and study of traditional science.

What does all of this mean in terms of the elementary school child and how he *learns* science? We, as teachers, will have to prepare students to function in this changing society—to make informed decisions, solve problems, engage in public discourse, and debate issues which will face us in the future. As the American Association for the Advancement of Science and others have indicated, science needs to be for *all* (American Association for the Advancement of Science [AAAS], 1993).

Teachers must provide the proper learning environment to meet our nation's educational challenges. Educators must employ the new strategies of cooperative learning, problem-centered learning, and authentic assessment. *In order to do this, we have to first understand how the child builds her knowledge base. We must ask ourselves, What causes the child to learn something? Why do some students understand a scientific concept and others do not?* Vignette 2-1 examines one view toward children's learning. The rest of the chapter looks at some of the theories which are associated with how a child learns.

SKINNER'S BEHAVIORISM IN THE CLASSROOM

In preparation for a class play about the nine planets and their characteristics, you are helping a group of students remember the planet names for a song which they will sing at the end of the play. You have promised individual children that, if they can recite the song correctly, they will be rewarded. The students will receive "teacher dollars," your class reward system by which students can earn money and buy things during monthly class auctions. The students are eagerly reciting the song and some are now able to name all nine planets. Even as some attention spans dwindle and students become disinterested, your small words of encouragement continue to re-engage them in this activity.

Why is it that children will respond in this way when they are complimented? The answer is in the components of behavioral psychology, of which B. F. Skinner is one of the best known advocates. This approach to understanding the child has as its core the ability to build knowledge from small, reinforced components into more sophisticated levels of learning. Skinner's extensive work with laboratory animals led him to develop theories about how humans form operant responses to conditions provided to them from others or the environment. The responses to conditions manifest themselves in the form of operant behaviors, such as reading

VIGNETTE

2-1

CHILDREN'S LEARNING

Dr. Ken Tobin

Florida State University

"Hold it! Hold it! Oh no! Ana, you've got to hold it while I connect the roof on." Michael is agitated with Ana. They have been working on building a castle for three days now and still the walls will not stay up. They planned a good castle and the drawings looked very good, but the materials Ms. Roberts had given them to build with were not working.

Ana is feeling grumpy about this whole activity. It is not her fault that the stupid walls will not stay up. Every time she holds it up the pins come loose. Why can't they use glue anyway? "Castles are not made out of pins and straws!" she retorts.

Ms. Roberts is pleased with the activities. The students are busy and they are doing science. Furthermore, the activities in which they are engaged involve manipulatives, oral language, drawing, writing, social studies, and literature. The idea of building castles arose from their studies of Germany. It's neat that students are problem solving. She perceives her role to be that of a facilitator: closely observing her students, learning from listening to them, and helping them to meet their goal of building a castle.

Teachers have long accepted a hands-on approach for science. Recently the term hands-on/minds-on has become a popular way to describe school science. Ms. Roberts's Grade 3 science lesson is typical of what can be observed in many elementary classrooms. The activity is consistent with a hands-on/minds-on metaphor and the teacher's role is conceptualized as a facilitator. However, even though there is extensive hands-on activity, communication, and problem solving, the development of scientific ideas is absent. Scientific knowledge does not reside in the materials, ready to be mysteriously released during hands-on activities. On the contrary, scientific knowledge needs to be co-constructed in interactions in which students and the teacher interact verbally using a shared language. For example, the realization that a structure can be made rigid through the use of triangular braces is a reasonable goal for the activity described. But in this case it is unlikely that students could construct that understanding. If they do include triangular braces in their structure, will they associate that with increased rigidity of the structure? Manipulations of materials are a context for rich conversations in which those who know science can facilitate the learning of those who do not know. It is essential that the teacher mediate between the languages of the child and of science. This does not imply a return to the days when teachers transmitted facts in lectures or the principal learning resource was a textbook. But it does require students to *talk science*—in ways that connect to their experiences in other subject areas and to their lives outside of school.

and writing. In other words, this theory of learning focuses on the human response to a condition provided by another individual or the environment, such as reacting to praise in the above example. Educators refer to this approach as S–R, or stimulus–response, theory since there is an initial stimulus and then a response to the stimulus. For teachers, the implication is that the correct stimulus can be used to change student behaviors.

Since behaviorism is a very mechanical approach to learning that deals with external control over the learner, it cannot completely explain the complexities of the individual learning process. Additionally, it is very difficult for the classroom teacher to break down each component of the material to be learned into a reinforceable segment which can be rewarded in some way. For these reasons behaviorism has been replaced by learning theories that focus on the development of knowledge by the learner rather than development of stimulus which would cause students to behave in a certain way.

Classroom Applications of Behaviorism

The reward and reinforcement elements of behaviorism, although limited in their ability to provide a deeper understanding of content, are very useful in classroom discipline systems which involve reward and punishment. Behavioristic approaches can also be useful in memorizing facts or very basic information since rewards, such as praise by the teacher, can be given when a correct response is achieved. When direct instruction is used, immediate feedback and reinforcement can often help facilitate the learning process. As an elementary science teacher, you should note that behaviorism is an ineffective way to teach science processes and problem solving, since it does not generally promote learning with understanding—*a theme of the educational reform movements throughout America.*

Cognitive Theories of Learning

Cognitive theories of learning are centered on the nature and organization of knowledge as well as how it is acquired. Existing knowledge, therefore, influences how new knowledge is built. Whereas behaviorists view the child's mind as a blank slate, cognitive theorists accept that the child has many genetically "prewired" neural connections in place to build on. As the child interacts with the world, she reorganizes these connections in a meaningful way.

Contributions of Piaget

You are in your classroom during a planning period, trying to decide whether to provide a unit on gravity and struggling with whether or not the children will be able to understand the theory of gravity. Questions run through your mind, such as:

> *What can children learn in science at this particular level of development? How does their ability to reason grow throughout elementary school?*

Jean Piaget, a developmental psychologist, has provided important contributions to the understanding of children's thinking. His books and research suggest that the ability to think develops in several noticeable stages. The three stages which elementary teachers are most concerned with are the preoperational stage, from about 2 to 7 years old; concrete operational stage, from about 7 to 12 years old; and formal operational stage, from about 12 years old on.

Preoperational children are not yet able to do certain kinds of thinking Piaget calls operations, or mental tasks. The latter part of the stage, which lasts from about four to seven years, is known as the intuitive thought substage. Since this is the time when most children begin school, we'll start our study of children's thinking at the intuitive period of their mental development.

"Intuitive thought" captures well how four- to seven-year-olds think. They typically use their sense impressions or intuition rather than logic in forming judgments. They also tend to remember only one thing at a time.

Concrete operational children, on the other hand, can do much logical thinking, but the ideas they consider must be tied to concrete materials they can manipulate. They must have some firsthand experience with the materials to think about them.

In the stage of *formal operations,* children are able to think much more abstractly; there is far less need to refer to concrete objects. With experience, they can handle formal logic.

As an elementary school teacher, you will work mainly with children at the intuitive and concrete operational stages of mental growth. It is interesting to observe how children develop from intuitive thought, to concrete thought, to the beginnings of formal logical thought. Learning how children think can give you a fascinating filter for reflecting on what they do or say. Best of all, it can help you guide each child in learning science. The next sections will describe typical behaviors of intuitive thinkers, concrete thinkers, and formal thinkers.

Intuitive Period Behaviors

What can you expect of children ages four to seven? We will consider their thinking in four related areas. (The same four areas will also be examined later in describing the concrete thinker and formal thinker.) We begin with intuitive children's notions about causes of events.

CAUSE-AND-EFFECT THINKING.   The logic of intuitive children with regard to causes can be unpredictable. They may think nothing of contradicting themselves when explaining some event. If you ask them why an object sinks in water, they may say it is "too small" to float. Another time, it is "too large." If you point out this inconsistency, the typical child may shrug and say, "Well, it is."

Four- to seven-year-olds often give magical explanations for events: "The sky is held up by angels." Or they may suppose that lifeless objects have conscious awareness and other human qualities. Clouds move because they "want to." There is thunder because "the sky is angry." Natural events may happen to serve a human need or purpose: "It rained because the farmers needed it."

RELATIVE THINKING.   Of special interest is the self-centered view of intuitive children. This affects how they relate to other people. Ask them to point to *your* right arm when they are face-to-face with you and they point to your left arm. It is difficult for them to put themselves in another's position. The same problem with orientation may come up when they put on clothing.

This egocentric quality also surfaces in their language. They take for granted that everyone understands, and is interested in, what they are saying. They assume that words mean the same to others as they do to them. If the listener gets confused, intuitive children may simply repeat the original message more loudly. The idea has not yet developed that we need to say things in certain ways to communicate clearly.

Their egocentrism may also affect their perception of objects. So the moon and sun follow *them* as they walk. It doesn't occur to them that others also see the same apparent motion.

Four- to seven-year-olds have difficulty interrelating several ideas at one time. Take time, distance, and speed. If two model wind-up cars start together on a path, the faster one will travel farther in the same time. But intuitive children cannot properly interrelate the time/speed/distance variables. Unless they have seen one car overtake and pass the other, they focus on the stopping points. When asked to explain the different end points, they typically say that one car must have traveled longer than the other.

In this stage, there are misconceptions about the relative nature of other physical properties. Some objects are always "heavy," others are always "light." Some are always "large," others are always "small." It is only gradually that properties such as size, texture, hardness, volume, thickness, and the like can be viewed in relative terms.

CLASSIFYING AND ORDERING.   The abilities to classify and arrange objects or ideas in some logical order are basic to thinking in both science and mathematics. Analyzing likenesses and differences helps us to better understand our environment.

Intuitive thinkers usually learn to sort objects well. But they are limited to considering only one property at a time. They can put all the objects of one color in a pile and those of another color in a second pile. They can also go on to subdivide these objects using another descriptive property.

In Figure 2-1, for example, the objects shown have two different colors and two different shapes. An intuitive child has sorted the objects by color: blues and nonblues (reds). The child can also go on to subdivide the blues by shape. This means he or she might sort out the blue circles from the larger group of blue shapes. You will find such skill is fairly common even at the lower primary level.

Is this true classification? Piaget would not think so, because the intuitive child cannot keep the part–whole relationship in mind. If you ask, "Are all the blue objects squares?" the child will say, "No." This, of course, is true. There are blue circles as well as blue squares. But if you ask, "Are all the squares blue?" the intuitive child is likely to say "No" again, which is wrong. The notion of class inclusion is too abstract to grasp at this stage. Try this with some children at your practicum site or in your neighborhood.

Intuitive children don't see that the blue squares are included as a part of a larger class of blue objects. How can all of a smaller group be only a part of a larger group? This is too abstract to grasp. Similarly, it's hard for them to realize that they can live at the same time on a street *and* in a town *and* in a county *and* in a state *and* in a country. The ability to order or arrange objects in a series, small to large or thick to thin, grows fast during the intuitive stage.

Let's consider how these children might seriate different-sized sticks from smallest to largest. Four- or five-year olds may only be able to order a few sticks in some consistent sequence. Six-year-olds usually do better, but they rely on trial and error. They will continually size up each stick with the next, then replace each as needed, perhaps several times. Only during the last part of the intuitive stage—around age seven for many children— is trial and error replaced by a more systematic attack. These children may look first for the largest and smallest pieces, then arrange

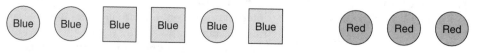

Figure 2-1
An intuitive child can sort objects by color (blues and nonblues).

the others with the end objects always in mind. Again, the key to success is the ability to hold two or more things in mind at the same time.

CONSERVATIVE THINKING. Perhaps the most widely known findings of Piaget are the intuitive child's abilities of conservation. By conserve Piaget means the ability to realize that certain properties of an object remain unchanged or can be restored even though the object's appearance is changed. Take a paper bag, for instance. Even if you flatten the bag, it still weighs the same and can be opened again to its original capacity. Intuitive children, though, may fail to conserve number, length, amount, area, weight, and volume—an important ability for science and mathematics understandings.

Conservation of number is easily tested. If you put a dozen checkers in two matched rows, intuitive children are quite sure each row contains the same number of checkers. That is because they see a one-to-one correspondence between the checkers. But spread out one row or bunch it together and the intuitive child becomes confused. Now it will seem that there are comparatively more (spread-out row) or fewer (bunched row) checkers in the altered group.

The ability to conserve length is necessary before you can ask children to measure meaningfully. Intuitive thinkers will agree that two identical strings are the same length when laid out together. But move one ahead of the other, and they may now say it is longer. This is not simply a misunderstanding of the term longer. It literally seems longer to them.

Their thinking shows the same limits when they are tested for the conservation of liquid substance. If you show intuitive children two identical glasses filled with water, they will probably say each contains the same volume of water. But suppose you pour the contents of

one glass into a taller, narrower glass. They are likely to say that the taller glass contains more water.

These students show the same perception with conservation of solid substance. Suppose you show them two identical balls of clay. They will agree each is made up of the same amount of clay. Now flatten out one into a large disk, and they probably will say the clay disk has more clay than the clay ball. It seems larger to them.

The same happens when they are asked to conserve area. Two toy buildings side by side on a paper lot seem to take up less space than when the buildings are placed far apart.

Similarly, they cannot conserve weight. They believe a solid object weighs more after it is cut up in the form of several smaller pieces. Or if a soft plastic ball is compressed into a smaller ball, they feel that it weighs less.

Intuitive children also believe that changing an object's form affects its overall size or volume. A clay object submerged in a half glass of water causes the water to rise to a level that equals the volume of the clay object. They do not realize that no matter how the object is reshaped in solid form, it will displace the same volume of water.

Do you see the common thread in these ways to check on the child's conservation of number, length, substance, area, weight, and volume? All give the learner a choice between a perceptual impression and logic. Intuitive children usually choose their perception.

Intuitive children cannot reverse their thinking. For older children, there is an ability to undo, at least mentally, what has been done. We can easily change directions in our thinking and imagine a reversed or restored condition. Intuitive children lack this flexibility: Focusing on the object's present appearance, they are tied to their perception.

The inabilities of preoperational children to compensate when an object's appearance changes and to reverse their thinking are the chief reasons they cannot perform operations in the Piagetian sense. Let's next look at some mental operations that are possible in the next stage of development.

Concrete Operational Behaviors

The concrete operational stage is representative of the thinking you can expect of many children ages 7 to 12 years old. A comparison of the child in the stage of concrete operations with the intuitive thinker reveals many differences. We will examine the four areas mentioned before: cause-and-effect thinking, relative thinking, classifying and ordering, and conservative thinking.

CAUSE-AND-EFFECT THINKING. Unlike intuitive children, concrete operational students usually avoid contradictory explanations for events. If a contradiction is pointed out to them, they try to straighten it out. They don't ignore it or otherwise show unconcern as younger children may.

Natural events are no longer seen to happen through magic or to fit some human convenience or purpose. The concrete thinker sees the need to make a physical connection between an effect and its cause. So natural objects or events are influenced by other natural objects or events.

The development in thinking is only slight at first. For example, they may now say "the wind comes from the sky" rather than "the wind comes to keep us cool." And a bicycle goes "because the pedals go around" rather than "because a bicycle can go." Notice the linking of physical objects in the first of each of these paired statements. This is a key difference in logical growth that first appears at the early part of the concrete stage.

In the last part of the concrete stage, the child uses logical thought processes even though scientific evidence may be lacking. For example, a 10-year-old may say to you, "It's colder in winter because the earth is farther away from the sun." This is entirely logical, even though it is wrong. (The earth–sun distance is actually less when the United States has winter. It is the earth's tilted axis that is responsible for seasons.)

RELATIVE THINKING. The egocentric quality found in intuitive students also changes in the concrete stage. Children become aware of viewpoints that differ from their own and they are able to consider what others think. Therefore, they may try to get evidence to support their ideas or attempt to convince their peers.

Concrete thinkers can mentally put themselves in another's place. For instance, they realize the someone opposite them will see direction in an opposite way. Also, the relationship between time and distance as a ratio that determines speed will begin to form at this stage.

When performing experiments, they can be aware of a few of the changeable conditions (variables) that might affect the results. To assist them in their thought process, the relationships they consider should be linked to concrete or pictorial objects. Take this problem, for example:

> *Bill is shorter than Jane.*
>
> *Bill is taller than Mary.*
>
> *Who is the tallest of them all?*

The concrete operational thinker will proceed to draw stick figures to assist in arriving at an answer.

CLASSIFYING AND ORDERING. The first true classification appears during the concrete stage. These children recognize the class-inclusion principle. They understand that if all *robins* disappear, there still would be other *birds* left. But if all birds disappear, there would be no *robins* left.

However, it may be impossible for them to make classifications that require increasingly abstract organizations. If shown objects that have several properties and asked to classify them, they can easily organize them into four groups according to four different properties. Yet it is more difficult for them if they are asked to classify the four groups into three groups and logically justify the new groupings, and even more difficult if they are asked to form the three groups into two groups.

The concrete child's ability to order (seriate) objects is fairly systematic, but continues to improve. It is not until about age nine or later before one can consistently place objects of different weights in series. The ability to seriate objects by the volume of water each displaces, or to seriate by viewing solid objects, is not consistent until the formal operations stage.

The concrete thinker's improved ability to seriate objects means he can better follow a succession of steps or changes in some process. The intuitive child tends to see each step as a separate entity, but the concrete thinker is aware of and understands the connection between the steps.

CONSERVATIVE THINKING. Perhaps the most obvious and dramatic difference that appears in concrete thinkers is their ability to conserve number and length. Unlike intuitive children, they can consider more than one thing at a time. They can reverse their thinking and hold in mind a sequence of changes. But the ability to conserve develops gradually.

Table 2-1 shows the usual sequence of children's concept development. However, the ages shown may vary somewhat when the same children are tested by different testers, since test procedures, children's responses, and interpretations of responses may not be wholly uniform. Notice that the displaced volume concept is not conserved until the stage of formal operations. This is probably because, of the concepts shown, it is the most abstract. It incorporates something from most of the others.

Formal Operations Behaviors

Some children begin to show evidence of formal operations at about age 12 or even earlier. But they are not likely to be classifiable as formal operational until they are 15 or 16. Even then, few students can operate consistently at the formal level, particularly when the material to be learned is new to them. This is also true of adults. Probably most adults and adolescents think at the concrete operational level most of the time. What the schools can do about this is a matter for further research.

Table 2-1
Usual Sequence of Concept Development

Conservation Concept	Age of Conserve (Years)
Number	6–7
Length	7–8
Substance (solid and liquid)	7–8
Area	8–10
Weight	9½–10½
Displaced volume	12–15

The chief difference between the concrete operational child and the formal operational child is the latter's ability to understand or comprehend basic principles which are more abstract. Like a skillful checkers player, the formal thinker can think through several moves ahead without touching a checker. A concrete thinker, on the other hand, is limited to considering one move at a time.

CAUSE-AND-EFFECT THINKING.   The beginning formal thinker thoroughly enjoys developing theories or hypotheses to explain almost any event. At the same time, the child is developing the skill to separate the logic of a statement from its content. Consider, for example:

The moon is made of green cheese.

Green cheese is good to eat.

Therefore, the moon is good to eat.

The logic of this proposition is sound. However, we cannot say the same for its factual assumption! The concrete thinker would reject this proposition outright because of its content. ("That's silly!")

Another critical difference between the concrete and the formal thinker is the way each considers the various conditions (variables) that may affect an experiment. Suppose a child is presented with five jars, the liquid contents of which may be mixed in any combination (Piaget & Inhelder, 1969). Only one combination of three jars produces the desired yellow color. The concrete thinker tends to combine two liquids at a time. But then the child may stop or just dump together at random three or more liquids. The formal thinker, however, typically thinks through all the combinations in a systematic way before starting. First come the pairs, then the triple combinations, $1 + 2 + 3$, $1 + 2 + 4$, $1 + 2 + 5$, and so on.

It is during the formal operations stage that children can control variables by holding them constant in mind. This enables them to do quick "thought" experiments. "If all things are equal except . . . , then . . ." becomes a convenient way to appraise hypotheses. This is not typical of concrete thinkers.

RELATIVE THINKING.   Children in the formal operational stage begin to understand relative position and motion. At this point, predictions become possible. Higher-order abstractions are possible at this stage. Children can define concepts with other abstract concepts such as "Light energy is the visible part of the electromagnetic spectrum." Concepts can also be explained with analogies and similes like "An orbiting satellite is like a ball on a string that you whirl around your head."

Interestingly, the beginning formal thinkers' vigorous habit of using logic to organize and explain everything in the physical world brings out an egocentric equality in their relations to others. They cannot understand at first why everyone is not as logical as they are. "If pollution is ruining the cities, then why isn't the gasoline engine outlawed?

CLASSIFICATION AND CONSERVATION.   Formal thinkers are able to reclassify grouped objects in a way not available to concrete thinkers. They can recombine groups into fewer but broader categories with more abstract labels. Also, they can classify things in a hierarchical way.

The following is an example of the ability to classify. Suppose some formal thinkers have tested six white powders to learn more about their properties. They might arrange their data as in Figure 2-2.

Besides the ability to conserve the displacement of volume mentioned before, formal thinkers can also conserve solid volume. They realize that a building twice as high as another needs only half the base to equal the overall size of the other building.

Notice that this concept is like the conservation of solid substance concept usually achieved

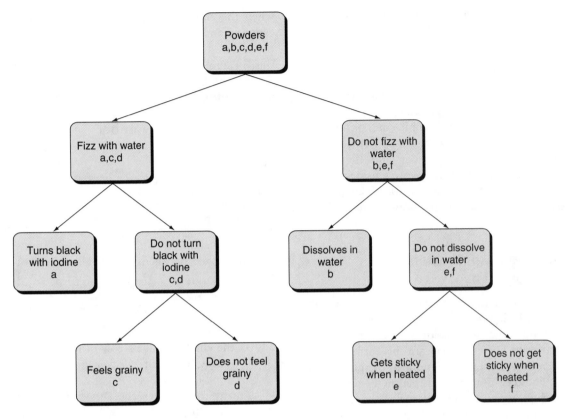

Figure 2-2
Formal thinkers are able to classify things into subgroups and keep the interrelations in mind.

at age seven or eight. Yet, the conservation of volume comes unexpectedly late. This shows the value of finding out what is really going on rather than simply following what others assume.

Assimilation and Accommodation

How do we organize our memory? What was Piaget's perception of how we learn? Will your students' prior knowledge affect subsequent learning?

The answers to these questions can be found in the notion of schemas. A *schema* is a concept, model, or pattern of thought. When we are confronted with new knowledge, we try to make sense of it by fitting it into appropriate, existing schema. In this instance, we are trying to fit the new concept or experience into an existing pattern of action, image, model, theory, or concept. Piaget called this *assimilation.* In other words, if a child sees a cardinal for the first time, she could fit this into a *bird* schema. This schema may contain mental images of robins, pigeons, and sparrows. Since this new object has the same basic size, shape, and other characteristics such as flight, the child can assimilate it into existing knowledge structures. If the child sees an ostrich, however, this may not easily fit into the existing structure. A completely new structure is then formed which is a combination of the earlier *bird* schema and this new example of a bird which is much larger and does not fly. Piaget called this an *accommodation*. These two processes of assimilation and accommodation are never completely independent, but operate in a dynamic equilibrium. We are constantly seeking what Piaget termed *equilibration* as we try to understand the world around us. Equilibration involves using assimilation and accommodation to form new mental structures which are more useful in future experiences.

Classroom Applications of Piaget's Theory

Your understanding of children's thinking can be greatly improved if you try your hand at assessing some of their ideas. You can start by discovering where they are in forming the important concepts of number, length, solid and liquid substance, area, perimeter–area relationship, weight, and volume. Your growing skill in interpreting how children think will be far more useful than merely labeling their general stages of mental growth.

The methods suggested here will be like those developed by Piaget and associates. If your time with and access to children are limited, and you are interested in primary-level teaching, try at least two younger children of different ages (9 and 12, for example) and any three of these tests: conservation of perimeter–area relationship, weight, displaced Volume A, and displaced Volume B.

You will need to work with each child separately. Everything in each task should be done directly by the child or, when necessary, by you in full view of the child.

The usual sequence of development in conserving a concept is this: First, the child depends almost completely on perceptions in forming judgments. Then there is a transition period,

when the child shifts uncertainly between perceptions and logic. Finally, the child is sure of her logic—thinking controls perceptions. With this in mind, after administering each task, decide whether the child is a nonconserver (N), in a transitional state (T), or a conserver (C).

Conservation of Number

MATERIALS

Eight red and eight black checkers (or paper disks or buttons).

PROCEDURE

1. Arrange eight black checkers in a row. Leave some space between each (Figure 2-3).

Figure 2-3

2. Ask the child to make a row of red checkers by putting one red checker next to each black one (Figure 2-4). Ask if now there are as many red as black checkers or fewer and why the child thinks so. If the child establishes equivalence, continue. Otherwise, stop at this point.

Figure 2-4

3. Next, move the red checkers farther apart from each other. Ask if there are now more black or red checkers, or if there is the same number (Figure 2-5). Then, ask why the child thinks so.

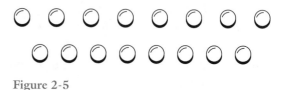

Figure 2-5

4. Finally, bunch the red checkers close together and repeat the same questions (Figure 2-6).

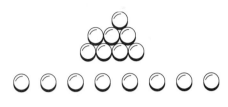

Figure 2-6

Note: The child who answers consistently that the number of checkers remains the same and satisfactorily tells why each time is a conserver (C) as to this concept. The child who says that the total number changes with each shift is a nonconserver (N). The child whose answers are inconsistent or who fails to give a satisfactory reason for each statement is in a transitional (T) stage. A similar appraisal can be made for each of the following tasks as well.

Conservation of Length

MATERIALS

Two identical soda straws (or strings or pipe cleaners).

PROCEDURE

1. Place the two straws together as in Figure 2-7. Ask the child if they are the same or different in length, then why the child thinks so. If the child says they are the same, continue. If not, stop the activity here.

Figure 2-7

2. Move one straw ahead about one-half length, as in Figure 2-8. Repeat your questions.

Figure 2-8

3. Bend one straw into a Z shape (Figure 2-9) and repeat the question again. To clarify, you might ask whether an insect would have to crawl the same or a different distance on each straw.

Figure 2-9

Conservation of Solid Substance

MATERIALS

Two ball-shaped identical pieces of clay; knife.

PROCEDURE

1. Ask the child if the two clay pieces have the same amount of clay (Figure 2-10). If the child doesn't think so, have him remove some clay from one until they seem equivalent. If equivalence cannot be established, discontinue the activity.

Figure 2-10

2. Let the child flatten one ball. Ask if both clay pieces contain the same or different amounts of clay, then ask why he thinks so (Figure 2-11).

Figure 2-11

3. Have the child shape the flattened clay back into a ball and reestablish equivalence.

4. Tell the child to roll one clay ball into an elongated "snake" form (Figure 2-12). Ask the same questions as in Step 2 above.

5. Again, have the child shape the distorted clay back into a ball shape. Reestablish equivalence.

6. Now cut one of the clay balls in half. Point to the ball, then to the two pieces. Ask if the ball is made up of more, less, or the same amount of clay as the two pieces. Find out why the child thinks so.

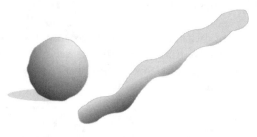

Figure 2-12

7. You may want to continue cutting one clay ball into smaller and smaller pieces. Ask the same questions as in Step 6, but be sure you reestablish equivalence before each cutting.

Conservation of Liquid Substance

MATERIALS

Two identical drinking glasses; one tall narrow glass; one glass of greater diameter than the others; pitcher of water; food coloring; medicine dropper.

PROCEDURE

1. Put a drop of food coloring in one of the paired drinking glasses. Pour water into both glasses exactly to the same level, about three-fourths full (Figure 2-13). Ask the child if both glasses contain the same volume of water, then why she thinks so. If the child does not think they are equivalent, she may add water with the medicine dropper until satisfied. Continue only after equivalence is established.

Figure 2-13

2. Let the child pour the colored liquid into the tall, narrow glass. Ask if this glass contains the same or a different volume of water as the glass of clear water, then why she thinks so (Figure 2-14).

Figure 2-14

3. Have the child pour the colored water back into the original glass and observe the paired glasses. Reestablish that the volumes of colored water and clear water are equivalent.

4. Now let the child pour the colored water into the wide-diameter glass (Figure 2-15). Ask the same questions you posed in Step 2.

Figure 2-15

Conservation of Area

MATERIALS

Two identical sheets of green construction paper; eight small, identical wood blocks or white paper squares.

PROCEDURE

1. Place the two green sheets side by side. Tell the child to pretend that these are two fields of grass on which cows feed. Ask if there are the same or different amounts of grass on the two fields for the cows to eat. Be sure the child believes the fields are equal before continuing.

2. Put a wood block or paper square on the lower left-hand corner of each "field." Explain that each block represents a farm building. Ask the same questions as in Step 1. Establish equivalence again before continuing.

3. Place a second block next to the first block on one sheet, but on the other sheet place another block far from the first block (Figure 2-16). Ask the same questions as in Step 1.

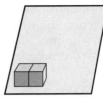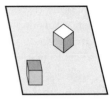

Figure 2-16

4. If the child establishes equivalence, add one block at a time to each green sheet. On one sheet, place each block to form a row. On the other sheet, the blocks should be scattered. Ask the same questions as in Step 1. Be sure the child establishes equivalence each time before you add blocks and ask the questions.

Conservation of Perimeter– Area Relationship

MATERIALS

Two identical 12-inch strings whose ends are tied to form two separate, identical loops.

PROCEDURE

1. Put one loop on top of the other, so the child sees that the loops are identical.

2. Have the child arrange the loops into two identical circles, side by side. Be sure equivalence is established: Is the first circle as big around as the other? Is there just as much space inside?

3. Now pull the second loop into a narrow, oval shape. Ask: Are the two circles still as big around, or is one smaller than the other? Why do you say that? Is the space inside still the same or does one have less space? Why do you say that? The perimeter stays the same in each case, but the area changes in the second case. The oval shape has less area inside. This can be checked by placing the loop over graph paper and roughly checking the number of blocks enclosed by the loop

in both cases. Interestingly, intuitive thinkers often do better on detecting the larger area than concrete thinkers, who may allow their logic to overcome their perception.

Conservation of Weight (Mass)

MATERIALS

Two identical balls of clay; knife; equal-arm balance.

PROCEDURE

1. Place the two clay balls before the child. Ask him if the balls are equal in weight. The child may use the balance as needed until agreeing that the balls weigh the same.

2. Let the child flatten one ball into a pancake shape. Ask if the weights are now the same or different, then why he thinks so. Afterward, the child may use the balance as desired to discover the equivalence. If equivalence can be established, continue.

3. Cut the pancake-shaped piece into two pieces. Ask if the weight of the two pieces together is the same or different from the weight of the unchanged clay ball. Then, ask why he thinks so. Afterward, the child may use the balance as needed to discover the equivalence. Listen for any comments as this is done.

Conservation of Displaced Volume

Note: This concept may be tested in two ways. In Example A, two clay objects of the same weight but apparently different volumes are used. In Example B, two film cans of the same volume but different weights are used.

EXAMPLE A

MATERIALS

Small clay ball; knife; tall, narrow drinking glass half-filled with water; rubber band; spoon.

PROCEDURE

1. Place the glass of water before the child. Have her gently submerge the ball in the water and notice that the water level rises. The glass can be encircled with the rubber band exactly at the water line to mark the level (Figure 2-17).

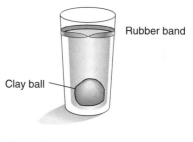

Rubber band

Clay ball

Figure 2-17

2. Remove the clay ball with a spoon. Hold the wet ball briefly over the glass, so if it drips, the water will go into the glass. Now let the child flatten the ball. Be sure, however, that it is still small enough to be submerged again in the water. Ask the child to what level the water will rise when the object is placed again in the water. Then ask why she thinks so.

3. If equivalence is established, cut the flattened ball into two pieces. Ask to what level the water will rise when the two pieces are placed in the water. Then ask why she thinks so.

EXAMPLE B

MATERIALS

Two identical plastic film cans (fill one with pebbles, the other with pennies; both cans must be sinkable); tall, narrow drinking glass half-filled with water and encircled with a rubber band; spoon.

PROCEDURE

1. Have the child inspect and then test the weight of the two film cans to note comparable sizes and weights. She should conclude that the cans are identical except for weight.
2. Let the child fully submerge the lighter can. Have her adjust the rubber band so it marks the water line. Then remove the can with a spoon.
3. Ask the child how high the water will rise compared to the rubber band if the heavier can is submerged and why she thinks that is the case.
4. Now let the child fully submerge the heavier can. How can she explain this finding? A conserver will say that the volume or size of the can, not weight, affects the rise in water level.

How to Evaluate Your Task Administration

It's very possible for two persons to get very different results when administering the tasks to the same child. Please keep in mind that the tasks are not like a standardized test. They are best suited to a clinical interview setting. The interviewer may use similar questions with different children to begin a task, but follow-up questions must be varied to best get at what each child seems to be thinking at any time.

The language used in an interview must be understandable to the child for worthwhile results. It helps to keep all directions and words at that child's developmental level. If you are not sure the child will understand some terms or directions, try to clarify these before you begin. Do not elaborate on words or procedures since this often adds to the child's confusion and makes it more difficult for him to respond naturally.

In most of the conservation tasks two sets of materials are compared, both before and after a change is made to one set. It's necessary that the children you test believe by themselves that the paired sets are equivalent before a change is made.

The tasks are best done in a relaxed setting by someone with an accepting, uncritical manner. Avoid saying "Good," or "That's right." Natural, unguided responses are the best clues to a child's understanding.

David Ausubel

Ausubel, like Piaget, is considered a cognitive psychologist. He is noted for his advocacy of expository, or direct, teaching. In his theory, there are three stages to the successful teaching of a concept. First, the teacher needs to supply an advance organizer. Second, the teacher must present the information. Finally, the teacher needs to reinforce the connection which was established.

The advance organizer provides a background from which the new concept is developed. In other words, it bridges the gap between the known and the unknown. Advance organizers can be mental outlines which are based on what the student already knows and can be used to provide a basis for incorporating new knowledge. To be successful, new concepts should relate to the child's prior experiences. The advance organizer, then, serves as a starting point from which new concepts are developed.

The second teaching step is to present the information. Here, the material is provided to the students in a well-organized format that helps the students understand and retain the new information. Generally, the teacher would begin with generalized ideas about the concept to be taught and then move into specifics.

The third part of Ausubel's strategy is to strengthen the cognitive organization. New information is integrated into the child's existing knowledge base. Connections between the old and new information are developed and strengthened. Ausubel points out that if these three steps are followed, meaningful learning occurs.

CLASSROOM APPLICATIONS OF AUSU-BEL'S THEORY. Although Ausubel was not directly opposed to the discovery learning advocated by most of his contemporaries, he felt that expository learning was important in the classroom. This especially held true when relatively large amounts of new information were taught. His focus was on the logical organization of information, the relationship between the new material and existing knowledge, and the learner's intent. Ausubel's focus provided the difference between what he considered *meaningful learning* and *rote learning*. Meaningful learning occurs when the child has intent, or wants to learn the material (Ausubel & Robinson, 1969).

CONSTRUCTIVIST THEORIES

What does it mean to know? What does it mean to be a knower? Is there a relationship between the knower and the known?

Although these questions appear to be philosophical in nature, they are at the heart of the current *paradigm* of how students learn. The knower–known relationship is the basis for the current reform movement in education, which emphasizes the active role of the learner and the facilitator role of the teacher.

Epistemology refers to the nature of knowledge and how it is developed. Constructivist epistemologies are those in which the learner, or knower, constructs his own knowledge. The types of constructivism presented here are social constructivism and radical constructivism.

Vygotsky

Lev Vygotsky was born in the same year as Piaget, but died unexpectedly at the age of 38, leaving behind more than 180 works. Vygotsky was not well known in our country until recently, when English translations of his work became more widespread. Like Piaget, he believed that learners construct their own knowledge and that there is a deeper meaning that goes beyond perception. Whereas Piaget placed an emphasis on the child's internal processes, Vygotsky was more concerned with the social interaction in the development of what he termed *scientific concepts.*

COGNITIVE AND CONCEPT DEVELOP-MENT. Cognitive development is a matter of an individual's social interaction within the environment. The mechanism of social behavior and the mechanism of consciousness are the same (Vygotsky, 1978). In other words, we know ourselves because of our interactions with others. Consciousness can only be explained in terms of socially meaningful activity. *Psychological tools,* similar to the tools which a carpenter would use to help control the building process, help us to control mental behavior.

Signs were also incorporated into this theory. His term *semantic mediation* referred to how we, as humans, take notes in class or keep an appointment book or any other activity which helps us to remember important dates or information. These signs that assist us in remembering are representative of our culture and are unique to humans. All animals share mental behaviors such as attention and perception (lower or biological forms); however, semantic mediation provides a level of understanding that separates human thoughts from those of other animals. This higher-order thought process is known as *cultural mental behavior,* as opposed to the natural mental behavior common to all animals (Vygotsky, 1981).

The main difference between the lower biological forms and higher social forms is the shift that occurs from outside control (teacher and peer-supported activity) to self-directed (autonomous) control. Social collaboration is gradually lessened as the child takes on more responsibility for her own learning. To put it

Heaps	Child groups objects into random categories
Complexes	Traits of objects are analyzed and concrete factual relationships among diverse objects are established.
Potential Concepts	Transition from the concrete and spontaneous to the abstract and scientific concept.
Genuine Concepts	Abstract and systematic concepts that are common to a culture.

Figure 2-18
Vygotsky's stages of concept development.
SOURCE: Adapted with permission from *Vygotsky in the Classroom* by Lizbeth Dixon-Kraus.
Copyright © 1996 by Longman Publishers.

another way, the development of higher forms of mental processes occurs through the child's enculturation into society as a result of the educational process. Instruction is one of the principle sources of the child's concepts. For Vygotsky, as for Piaget, the stages of concept development reflect a maturation process.

Figure 2-18 illustrates the stages of concept development from simple labeling of objects to abstract and systemized knowledge of scientific concepts (Dixon-Krauss, 1996).

The Zone of Proximal Development and Scaffolding

Vygotsky noted that when children were placed in groups that were under the guidance of an adult or collaborated with a more experienced peer, they could perform at levels higher than were possible when working on their own. Furthermore, what was possible in the group situation would be possible later on an individual basis. What the child can do in cooperation today, he can do alone tomorrow. For instance, if a child was able to complete a classification of leaves based on common properties with the assistance of a more knowledgeable classmate,

this same child could later complete this classification task independently.

Social constructivists would argue that the only good kind of instruction is that which marches ahead of, and leads, development. Instruction must be aimed not so much at the *ripe* as at the *ripening* functions (Vygotsky, 1962). So with group or teacher assistance, a child's instruction should always be slightly ahead of what was possible for her on her own. If the student can already complete a classification based on two properties, but not on three, instruction should be directed at classifying with three properties under the guidance of the teacher or learning group.

The term *zone of proximal development* is used to indicate the difference between what a child can do with the help of a more knowledgeable other and what the child could do independently. The goal of instruction is to actively engage the student in solving problems within the zone of proximal development. The teacher's role is that of a facilitator or mediator, one who provides an environment where learning in the zone of proximal development is maximized. The teacher acts as a *scaffold* and provides just the right amount of support to accomplish the developmental goal. This is analogous to painters who use a scaffold. They may reach many areas independently, but when they cannot reach an area on their own, they require a scaffold to assist them in performing the task. Correspondingly, painters would not use a high scaffolding to paint a baseboard. The implication here is that the teacher should not provide more guidance than is needed for developmental support, since too much support will not promote the development of independent thought in children.

CLASSROOM APPLICATIONS OF SOCIAL CONSTRUCTIVIST THEORY. Think about how scientists, engineers, doctors, computer technicians, and other professionals carry on activities within the workplace. Do they work independently or as a team?

Collaborative learning and thinking is the foundation of Vygotsky's theory. It is the very means by which the child learns the fundamentals of society. It is the method of moving from lower learning to higher learning, and the system by which activities within the child's zone of proximal development are successful. Scientific experimentation and problem-centered activities, or those that have multiple solution paths, provide the framework for successful science experiences, much like the scientists and engineers engaged in collaborative research. Your role as a teacher will be to facilitate this type of activity and adapt the curriculum to meet the students' needs.

Finally, it is important for students to understand the language of science. It is a foreign language for them—one with more new terms than a foreign language text. Social constructivist theory suggests that the child constructs an understanding of language from the whole to its parts. If this is the case, then the elementary classroom should surround children with stories and trade books on science topics, so that students are exposed to the content of science through a whole language or integrated approach to learning. Vocabulary should remain in the context of what is read, not encountered as a separate, out-of-context, memorization drill. Science instruction should be a model of how science is performed by scientists.

Radical Constructivism

Drawing on the work of Piaget, researchers in the late 1970s began to refocus their investigations from looking at the Piagetian stages of development to looking at the actual content of the individual child's thinking. A new emphasis was placed on the child's *active construction of knowledge*. Constructivist theories began to be adopted by numerous theorists. Radical constructivism represented an entirely new way of looking at things. The social constructivists, like Vygotsky, acknowledged social interaction as playing an important role in the construction of knowledge. Radical constructivists, however, felt that *society itself must also be analyzed*, since it is constructed by the individual. Let's put it another way. For the social constructivists, society played a role in knowledge construction. For the radical constructivists, knowledge also *constructs society*.

This radical change in epistemological orientation led to the term *radical constructivism*, where the knowledge itself was as much a subject of study as the knower and method of knowing. A good working definition for constructivism as a theory is that it assumes *knowledge cannot exist outside of the minds and bodies of cognizing beings*. There is a reality which exists, but we can never truly know that reality. We can only know about it in a personal and very subjective way. When negotiation occurs between people, agreement can be reached within our societal system and a generally agreed-to construct is formed, such as scientific theories. For example, we do not really know "gravity"; we just have basically agreed upon what we experienced about its effects. Thus, gravity becomes a construct for us within our society. Not everyone would agree with this, however. In fact, some would argue that gravity does not work the way we think it does. They have constructed new ideas such as "string theories."

The radical constructivist model has important implications for the classroom teacher, since knowledge as a truth, or one correct answer, is no longer the focus. The focus is shifted to how the person constructs knowledge that enables her to think. The teacher's responsibility in this model is to structure the learning environment in such a way as to facilitate learning that society regards as the most viable in helping the individual make sense of the world and deal with everyday life. As one researcher put it:

> From that perspective (radical constructivism) there is no way of transferring knowledge—every knower has to build it up for himself. The cognitive organism is first and foremost an organizer who interprets experience and, by interpretation, shapes it into a structured world. That goes for experiencing what we call sensory objects and events, experiencing language and others; and it goes no less for experiencing oneself. "Intelligence organizes the world while organizing itself." (von Glasersfeld 1982, 613)

A constructivist model describes the learning process in terms of the *student,* not the teacher. We cannot prescribe a curriculum for everyone. Notwithstanding, when students are actively engaged, they are constructing knowledge. Learning is taking place, not as a result of the teacher transferring the knowledge from a text or his or her personal knowledge base, but as the students interpret and make sense of their surroundings.

As the students interpret their surroundings, the new interpretation is influenced by their prior knowledge. It is, therefore, the teacher's role to facilitate activities which will guide the learner into developing meaningful concepts. Constructivists generally agree that discourse is especially important in order to *negotiate meaning* and *develop socially agreeable constructs.* Therefore, open-ended questioning is important before, during, and after activity periods.

CLASSROOM APPLICATIONS OF RADICAL CONSTRUCTIVISM. If knowledge is the result of constructive activity, then it cannot effectively be transferred to a passive receiver. The construction of knowledge has to be an active process by the individual learner. The role of the teacher is to orient the learner in a general direction and then attempt to prevent the learner from going in directions that would be inappropriate.

In order to accomplish this, teaching must be changed from the rote learning proposed by behaviorists, such as Skinner, to a well-thought-out series of logical steps. Since all knowledge is individually constructed, the teacher must take the student into account in all learning situations. The curriculum shouldn't be viewed as a set of right answers to be learned. It needs to be considered as a culturally developed set of ideals which are generally agreed upon as important to that society.

The teacher's role as a facilitator of the curriculum is to provide the resources for learning, engage students actively, and refocus children's activity when appropriate so that they remain productive in the learning process. Often this is done by posing a problem to solve or inviting students to make an observation. The teacher then steps aside and allows the students to interact with the environment and each other. The teacher would only intervene when necessary to refocus student discussion in a more productive way, initiate a new pattern of activity, or begin an assessment activity for the students to express their personal understanding.

Robert Yager (1991) described the constructivist learning model (CLM) as a promising new model in learning. It focuses on the learner instead of the teacher. Building on the work of the researchers at the National Center for Improving Science Education, Yager introduced a set of constructivist strategies for teaching, which are provided in Figure 2-19.

As you can see, the CLM is an ongoing four-part process. First, you get the students to think about a phenomena in a new way. Then they explore the phenomena and develop explanations or solutions (constructs). Finally, they

---

Invitation

Observe surroundings for points of curiosity

Ask questions

Consider possible responses to questions

Note unexpected phenomena

Identify situations where student perceptions vary

Exploration

Engage in focused play

Brainstorm possible alternatives

Look for information

Experiment with materials

Observe specific phenomena

Design a model

Collect and organize data

Employ problem-solving strategies

Select appropriate resources

Discuss solutions with others

Design and conduct experiments

Evaluate choices

Engage in debate

Identify risks and consequences

Develop parameters of an investigation

Analyze data

Proposing Explanations and Solutions

Communicate information and ideas

Construct and explain a model

Construct a new explanation

Review and critique solutions

Utilize peer evaluation

Assemble multiple answers/solutions

Determine appropriate closure

Integrate a solution with existing knowledge and experiences

Taking Action

Make decisions

Apply knowledge and skills

Transfer knowledge and skills

Share information and ideas

Ask new questions

Develop products and promote ideas

Use models and ideas to elicit discussions and acceptance by others

---

Figure 2-19
Constructivist strategies for teaching.
SOURCE: R. Yager, "The Constructivist Learning Model." Reprinted with permission from NSTA Publications, September 1991, from *The Science Teacher*, National Science Teachers Association, 1840 Wilson Blvd., Arlington, VA 22201-3000.

share their new ideas with others or re-explore the phenomena in a new way.

The new constructivist theories focus on the learner and the learning environment. This makes your job as a teacher–facilitator different from what you may have experienced from your teachers in elementary school. As you read through the remaining chapters, think about how you can use the tenets of constructivism to enhance the learning environment of your students.

SUMMARY

1. Piaget provided insight into how children grow intellectually. He defined the stages children go through as they develop and the characteristics of these stages. He also explained the learning process as a dynamic balance between assimilation and accommodation and a result of seeking equilibration as new experiences were presented by the teacher.

2. Constructivist research augments Piaget's work and redefines the teacher's role as facilitator of active construction of an individual, subjective, self-constructed knowledge. There is social constructivist theory (in which society plays a major role in the child's development) and there are radical constructivist theories (where the child independently constructs knowledge). Either way, the constructivist curriculum is not a set of right answers and truths to be taught, but a set of culturally accepted ideals used to guide learning. The elementary science teacher must understand the goal of the curriculum, the individual child, and how to structure the learning environment to meet his needs in the elementary science classroom.

REFLECTION

1. Try some of the Piagetian tests on children at your practicum site. What observations can you make? Compare these with the students in your methods class. What do you note?

2. Discuss constructivism with a teacher at your practicum site. What is her viewpoint? Discuss it with your educational psychology professor. What is her viewpoint? The current science education research trend is toward a constructivist perspective. Why do you think this is so? What are some views of your methods instructors?

3. Observe students in a classroom working together to solve a problem. Does it become clear that there are students who could not have completed the problem on their own? What is the teacher's role as students engage in the collaborative activity? How can you, as an outside observer, tell if the children are learning? How will the teacher know if learning has occurred? Share your findings with classmates.

REFERENCES

American Association for the Advancement of Science. (1993). *Benchmarks for science literacy.* New York: Oxford University Press.

Ausubel, D., & Robinson, F. (1969). *School learning.* New York: Holt, Rinehart, and Winston.

Dixon-Krauss, L. (1996). Vygotsky's sociohistorical perspective on learning and its application to western literacy instruction. In L. Dixon-Krauss (Ed.), *Vygotsky in the classroom: Mediated literacy instruction and assessment* (pp. 7–24). White Plains, NY: Longman.

Piaget, J., & Inhelder, B. (1969). *The psychology of the child.* New York: Basic Books.

vonGlasersfeld, E. (1982). An interpretation of Piaget's constructivism. *Revue Internationale de Philosophie, 36* (4), 612–635.

Vygotsky, L. (1962). *Thought and language* (p. 104). E. Hanfmann & G. Vakar (Eds.). Cambridge, MA: MIT Press.

Vygotsky, L. (1978). *Mind in society: The development of higher psychological processes.* M. Cole, V. John-Steiner, S. Scribner & E. Souberman (Eds.). Cambridge, MA: Harvard University Press.

Vygotsky, L. (1981). The genesis of higher mental functions. In J. V. Wertsch (Ed.), *The concept of activity in soviet psychology* (pp. 144–188). Armonk, NY: Sharpe.

Yager, R. (1991). The constructivist learning model. *The Science Teacher, 58*(6), 52–57.

SUGGESTED READINGS

Bodrova, E., & Leong, D. J. (1996). *Tools of the mind. The Vygotskian approach to early childhood education.* Upper Saddle River, NJ: Merrill/Prentice Hall. (A guide to incorporating Vygotsky's ideas into teaching.)

Bybee, R. W., & Sund, R. (1982). *Piaget for educators* (2nd ed.). Prospect Heights, IL: Waveland Press. (An overview of Piaget's theory.)

Chaille, C., & Britain, L. (1991). *The young child as scientist: A constructivist approach to early childhood education.* New York: HarperCollins. (How children construct knowledge.)

Dixon-Krauss, L. (Ed.). (1996). *Vygotsky in the classroom: Mediated literacy instruction and assessment.* White Plains, NY: Longman Publishers. (An overview of Vygotsy's theory including the zone of proximal development and scaffolding.)

Duckworth, E. (1987). *"The having of wonderful ideas" and other essays on teaching and learning.* New York: Teachers College Press. (A Piagetian view of education.)

Tobin, K. (Ed.). (1993). *The practice of constructivism in science education.* Washington, DC: AAAS Press. (An edited compilation of the nature of constructivism and what it means for teachers.)

CHAPTER

3

PLANNING AND FACILITATING ACTIVITIES

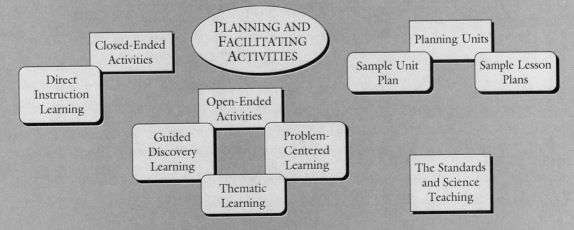

Direct Instruction Learning

Closed-Ended Activities

PLANNING AND FACILITATING ACTIVITIES

Planning Units

Sample Unit Plan

Sample Lesson Plans

Open-Ended Activities

Guided Discovery Learning

Problem-Centered Learning

Thematic Learning

The Standards and Science Teaching

Can you envision working for a company where talking to other employees throughout the day was discouraged or completely prohibited? where each work assignment lasted exactly 45 minutes, regardless of completion? and where you went home each day only to repeat exactly what you did at work earlier? This may be representative of our experiences in elementary school. We were *products of education* instead of participants in the learning process. Most of us did not solve problems, engage in meaningful conversation, or go home in pursuit of a better product. Instead, we were passed from teacher to teacher and were provided a systematic quality control (report card) until receiving the terminal approval slip (diploma). Our education was much like the assembly-line approach to building cars: Students came through the system and were molded by teachers. Teachers contributed to the finished product, but seldom reflected on how the product would be used, or how it could be made better. This inflexible process did not encourage any of the skills needed for the 21st century. A dynamic process is needed to develop the ability to solve problems, continue lifelong learning, and transform information into meaningful knowledge.

You, as an elementary teacher, can transform your classroom into a better learning environment through meaningful science activities. There are two basic kinds of activities you can use to meet the wide variety of individual differences and objectives faced in classrooms today—*closed-ended* and *open-ended activities.* For a quick view of what each is like, see these two problems:

$$3 + 3 = ?$$
$$? + ? = 6$$

The first problem has only one correct answer; the second has many. Closed-ended problems and activities lead to a single response. They foster *convergent* thinking. Open-ended activities and problems lead to a wide variety of responses. They produce *divergent* thinking.

Both types of activities and thinking are needed in learning and solving problems.

Closed-ended activities tend to be short and tightly focused. Open-ended activities are usually longer, and branch out into many related questions. In the concepts and experiences chapters, we have labelled the closed-ended experiences *activities* and open-ended experiences *investigations.*

Closed- and open-ended activities also differ in other ways. To see how, let's consider each type. We begin with some common closed-ended examples involving children 5 to 12 years old. In each case the children are active— they do things.

CLOSED-ENDED ACTIVITIES

In a primary class, children are learning that vibrations are needed to make sounds. It is obvious that a guitar string moves to and fro when plucked. But what vibrates when a drum is struck? A child is directed by the teacher to sprinkle some sand lightly on the drumhead of a toy drum. The child strikes the drumhead with a stick. The sand is observed to be bouncing up and down as the drumhead vibrates. The harder the drumhead is struck, the higher the sand bounces and the louder the drum sounds.

In a middle-level class, some children are learning that limestone is a rock that can be identified by putting acid on it. The acid bubbles when it touches the rock. Several children put these rocks into small cups of vinegar, which is a weak acid. Nothing happens at first, but moments later they see streams of tiny bubbles rising from the submerged rocks.

In an upper-level class, some children are learning about air pressure. One child reads how to use unequal air pressure to crush a metal container. To demonstrate this, the teacher heats one inch of water in an empty aluminum soft drink can to boiling on a hot plate. As the can and water heat up, the air inside warms and expands. Some of this heated air, as well as steam, escapes through the uncapped opening. The can is then removed from the hot plate with tongs and quickly turned upside down in cold water. As the gasses inside the can cool, they require less space than before, because some air and steam have escaped. Therefore, they exert less pressure inside the can. The children are surprised to watch the can quickly cave in as the stronger outside air pressure exerts its force.

Notice that each of these closed-ended activities illustrates some idea or procedure with concrete materials. Working with concrete materials helps the children to form realistic concepts or learn useful techniques. Once a closed-ended activity has made its point, there is no need to continue. Closed-ended activities, when taught well, help children construct a solid subject-matter background that is rooted in experience.

Direct Instruction

A common way to demonstrate closed-ended activities is through direct instruction. Direct instruction is a teacher-centered, structured approach to teaching. The teacher employs lectures, worksheets, recitations, demonstrations, or specific-answer questions in a prearranged sequence that is generally based on a lesson plan. The teacher is very much in control of the lesson.

The advantages to direct instruction are that the teacher can arrange the sequence of activities ahead of time. This reduces the number of teaching decisions during a lesson. This is especially helpful for inexperienced teachers who are preoccupied with management issues or want to be sure they cover a certain curriculum. It is also helpful when introducing a new skill (such as classification or learning to use a new piece of equipment) or when safety issues prevent student exploration. A more important advantage

is that direct instruction can be used to build the knowledge base for future learning. Teachers can spend as much time as needed to think through which analogies, metaphors, activities, and questions will best support the concept they want to develop *before* the lesson. Instruction continues systematically until the teacher feels comfortable that the students, overall, have grasped the concept.

A disadvantage to direct instruction is that since students construct knowledge at their own pace, the teacher's pace may not match the students'. Students are not free to further explore topics on their own when they are interested. They are subject to what the teacher selects as themes or important concepts. Problem-solving and higher-order thinking skills are better developed through a more independent learning situation.

Another disadvantage of direct, or teacher-centered, instruction is that the teacher may have gender, cultural, or other biases which will limit learning for some students. In other words, the students are subject to everything from the teacher's point of view—not their own. For example, if the teacher unconsciously believes that boys are better suited for science than girls, she may call on boys more often to answer a question or to assist in a demonstration. This reinforces the cultural disadvantage girls have in the sciences.

Planning a Direct Instruction Lesson

Teacher education students are exposed to lesson planning early in their professional preparation, and planning is an important component of science education which is reflected in the Standards (see page 77). There are many models for planning a lesson. The *objectives, materials, procedure, and evaluation of students format* is an example of a general lesson plan format. Figure 3–1 presents an enhanced format, designed to help you think about the science lesson in a new way. It challenges the

Contextual Framework

Overview of the Lesson

Science Themes (From AAAS Project 2061)

Scientific Skills

Curricular Integrations

Materials

Supplies

Equipment

Procedure

Steps to Follow or Problem to Solve

Closed-Ended or Open-Ended Questions

Assessment

Student Assessment

Teacher Assessment

Bibliography

Sources for Content Information and Children's Literature

Figure 3–1

Lesson plan format.

SOURCE: *Excellence in Educating Teachers of Science,* Peter A. Rubba, Lois M. Campbell and Thomas M. Dana, eds. Copyright 1993 by ERIC Clearinghouse, Columbus, OH.

teacher to look at the activities from multiple perspectives.

The first section is the *contextual framework.* This is an overview of the lesson in your own words. A lesson topic, a specific grade level, any curricular objectives, and applicable performance objectives can be included here. Next in

the contextual framework are the science themes. These originate in the *Benchmarks* (American Association for the Advancement of Science [AAAS], 1993). Science themes are needed to see the "big picture" of science and how this lesson fits into that. Specifically, your lesson should support the development of one or more common themes. These include *systems, models, consistency, patterns of change, evolution,* and *scale.* For each lesson, consider how you address one or more of these themes. Scientific skills—such as classification, observation, measurement, inference or prediction, communicating, and experimentation—should also be addressed as part of the contextual framework. If you are unsure about these skills, refer to the section on skills found on pages 80–96. The last thing to consider as part of the contextual framework is curricular integrations. In other words, in what ways can social studies, language arts, reading, mathematics, art, music, or physical education be incorporated into the lesson?

Next in the lesson plan is a listing of materials. Both consumable and nonconsumable things should be listed here. Remember to list materials for the teacher demonstration and student participation.

The procedure section of a direct instruction lesson plan is *very specific.* It has numbered steps which are logically arranged to meet time and curricular requirements. Every step is written out so that the teacher does not forget anything. Careful thought is given to what the teacher wants to say and do during the class period. These thoughts are written down in an expanded outline form. Specific teacher questions can also be placed here. This ensures that you will not forget to ask something important. A direct instruction procedure plan would look like the one in Figure 3–2.

Next, a lesson plan must address assessment. How will you assess the students? Chapter 7 provides an in-depth view on student assessment. Teacher self-assessment should also be

Contextual Framework

Overview of the Lesson

This lesson centers on the names of the nine planets and their relationship to the sun. The students will be asked to name the planets in order, give an approximation of their size, and be able to understand the concept of a satellite of a planet.

Science Themes

Systems—The solar system is a common example of a system. It is a group of planets; their satellites; and solid, liquid, and gaseous material in an interrelated organization.

Models—The idea of a model is established as students create models of the solar system.

Consistency—The planets rotate in consistent patterns in the solar system.

Patterns of Change—Patterns of change are modeled as stars are formed and the visibility of planets changes throughout the year.

Evolution—There is a lot of verified data on the evolution of the solar system. The launching of new spacecraft to study the solar system and beyond brings relevancy to this topic.

Scale—Scale is established as the various sizes of the planets are compared.

Scientific Skills

Classification—Classification activities are promoted as students develop classification systems for the planets (by composition, temperature, and size).

Observation—The students will observe the night sky and record data.

Measurement—The students will measure and recreate a scale model of the solar system.

Inference/Prediction—The students will infer why the temperature of Venus is high, based on that planet's characteristics.

Curricular Integrations

Measurement activities integrate *mathematics* into this lesson.

Art is incorporated into this lesson as students draw planet and star models.

Social studies are integrated into this lesson as students discuss ancient theories of an earth-centered solar system.

Materials

Supplies

Large sheets of paper; crayons, markers, or paints.

Equipment

Inflatable planetarium (two large sheets of black painter's plastic with both sides taped together lengthwise to form a large dome. A box fan is taped to one end and turned on to inflate the dome.

Figure 3-2
Direct teaching lesson plan for planets.

(continued)

Procedure

Steps to Follow

1. Introduce the vocabulary:
   Mercury, Venus, Earth, Mars, Jupiter, Saturn, Uranus, Neptune, Pluto, moon, satellite, orbit, asteroid, rotation, revolution (Use definitions from end of the chapter and have students repeat the words. Write the definitions on the overhead for them to copy.)
2. Read the chapter on the planets from the student's text. Discuss origins of the solar system.
3. Demonstrate the relative distances between planets by creating a model with students acting as the sun, planets, and satellites (see specific measurements in the text).
4. Demonstrate the rotation of the earth and moon and their revolution around the sun using students to represent the sun, earth, and moon (see picture in supplemental materials).

Closed-Ended Questions

A. What is the center of the solar system?
   Describe its characteristics.
B. What is the first planet from the sun?
   Describe its characteristics. (Repeat for the rest of the planets. Note: Neptune will remain the ninth planet until Pluto's eccentric orbit causes it to be further away from the sun in 1998.)
   What is the difference between the moon and a satellite? (Note: The moon is earth's satellite. All other "moons" are called "satellites" by astronomers.)
C. Define an orbit.

Open-Ended Questions

A. Which planets are colder? What is a possible cause for their low temperature?
B. Give some possible reasons for Venus being so hot. (Discuss greenhouse effect.)

Steps to Follow (continued)

6. Develop three planet classifications (Monday).
7. Redraw the scale model of the planets from the text, measuring exactly from the book. (Tuesday).

Figure 3-2 (continued)

considered in this section of the lesson plan, especially for beginning teachers who need to practice reflecting on their instruction. You may want to videotape or audiotape the lesson, have a peer teacher or administrator observe the les-

son, seek student feedback in some way, write personal observations in a journal, or use a school-based assessment form.

The lesson plan concludes with a bibliography. All sources used in planning should be

8. Draw a picture of the night sky with fluorescent crayons (Wednesday).

9. Find pictures of the winter and summer night sky from other books and magazines (Thursday).

10. Take students into the planetarium and demonstrate the position of the stars and planets using the portable star projector. Have students display their fluorescent pictures (Friday).

Additional Activities (select one)

11. Research what causes eclipses of the sun or moon.

12. If you started today and traveled 1,000 miles per hour to the planet Jupiter, determine how old you would be when you reached your destination.

13. Most people incorrectly believe that the distance from the northern or southern hemisphere of the earth from the sun causes the seasons. Research the real cause of the seasons.

14. Research the planets on the NASA Internet sites.

Assessment

Student Assessment

1. Design a mnemonic sentence to remember the planets.

2. Describe in your journal what life would be like on the planet Jupiter. How would it compare to life on the moon?

3. Write to NASA for more information on space exploration and present it to the class.

Teacher Assessment

Videotape lesson and review it at home.

Bibliography

Branley, F. M. (1987). *The planets in our solar system.* New York: Thomas Crowell.

Cole, J. (1990). *The magic school bus lost in the solar system.* New York: Scholastic.

Lauber, P. (1982). *Journey to the planets.* New York: Crown Publishers, Inc.

National Geographic Society (Producer). (1987). *The planets* [laserdisc]. Washington, DC: National Geographic Society.

Scholastic. (1994). *The magic school bus explores the solar system* [CD-ROM]. Microsoft Corporation.

listed here, including audiovisual, computer-based, and Internet links. Also include any fiction or nonfiction books which will be made available to students.

In summary, closed-ended activities tend to be limited. Outcomes are predictable and specific. Children follow someone else's ideas or procedures. To boost children's thinking processes, independence, and creativity, you need to offer open-ended experiences.

OPEN-ENDED ACTIVITIES

Most good teachers encourage children to try their own ideas about how to investigate and organize objects or events, as seen in Vignette 3–1. This allows children to discover things for themselves. When students are given some autonomy, some suggestions lead to others—there is almost no end to what may be investigated.

Open-ended activities allow students to study objects and events in two very useful ways. Students can (1) observe similarities and differences in the *properties* of things, and (2) discover *conditions* that can produce or change properties (thus the name *discovery learning*).

Note the contrast in this pair of questions:

1. What materials will rust?
2. In what ways can you get some objects to rust?

When children examine the present properties of comparable things, they learn that properties usually exist in varying degrees. As students inspect these variable degrees of properties, they will observe, describe, contrast, measure, and classify them. This is why open-ended investigations of things with comparable properties are so well-suited for intuitive-level students and others who lack experience with the materials being examined. A common way to facilitate open-ended activities is through the guided discovery approach.

Guided Discovery Lesson Plan

Guided discovery learning is a less teacher-oriented and more student-oriented instructional method. Students are guided in exploration of materials. They observe a phenomena, gather data on their own, make comparisons, draw inferences, and arrive at conclusions. Teachers

follow up on what has been discovered and point out any misconceptions. Students are then free to explore once again. This method is especially valuable in making connections between science vocabulary and scientific concepts.

Remember the lesson plan components from Figure 3–1. The same general procedures are used here, too, and students are provided time to *discover* concepts based on initial information.

In guided discovery, follow-up discussion and questioning is critical. The direct instruction approach spells out exactly what is to be learned. Guided discovery, on the other hand, allows students to explore on their own. Sometimes students form *misconceptions*. Misconceptions are when you think something is one way but it is really another. For example, if you ask a child what would happen if an astronaut "dropped" something like a pen on the moon, he may reply that it would float away. In guided discovery, you may next ask why the *astronaut* does not "float away." Students may answer that the astronaut's heavy boots weigh him down and keep him from floating away. Of course, the moon does have gravity and this is what keeps the astronaut from floating away. The pen actually does fall toward the moon as it would on earth. However, since the moon has less mass, the pen falls with less force than here on earth. In synopsis, everything on the moon is attracted to it or the rocks and dust would also float away. In guided discovery activities, it is critical to follow up after student exploration and determine whether students have made correct assumptions. Figure 3–3 presents a guided discovery lesson for electricity.

Problem-Centered Learning

As you progress from the teacher-control to the student-control position of the teaching/learning continuum, students become more involved in the planning and implementation of lessons.

OPEN-ENDED DIVERGENT THINKING UNIT
Mr. Jerry Mayernik
Northway School District, Pennsylvania

A thin strip of yellow tape in the school hallway marks the starting line for the test track. In a few minutes, colorful cans of many sizes will clink, clank, and thump their way down the long, narrow test course, with students whispering encouragement to their carefully constructed devices as the cans slow down, wiggle, and begin the trip back to the starting line. At no time are science terminology, textbook pages, or vocabulary words referred to as the children test, refine, and retest their "Comeback Cans."

In my sixth-grade science class, the school year begins with a demonstration of "Herbie, the Wonder Can", a three-pound coffee can, rigged with a rubber band and a large fishing sinker inside. When Herbie is carefully rolled across the classroom, it magically slows, stops, and returns to its starting point. After students are shown how to construct a similar device, they are challenged to build their own Comeback Can and test it against the best efforts of Herbie. The next day, cans of all sizes and construction litter the windowsill, ready to challenge Herbie in a test of endurance. Which can will roll the longest distance and return to the yellow stripe? After several cans traverse the track, students begin to realize that variations exist in their methods of construction. Some cans have thicker rubber bands, some thinner. Some devices are larger, some fatter, some longer. The masses inside are small, huge, and everywhere in between. Which of these variables are critical to can performance? What are the optimal can size, rubber band width, and mass? Students are encouraged to study the construction of the leading cans and modify or refine their cans as they like. Finally, after weeks of testing and retesting, trial and error, and elation and frustration, the top cans compete in the Comeback Can Derby. The five winning can-builders are awarded small trophies in honor of their efforts.

This activity promotes divergent thinking. Although the Comeback Cans have a common construction, the task encourages a wide variety of responses. The winning cans have never been constructed in quite the same way. This activity allows students to explore, analyze, and adapt. It encourages children to attempt a novel approach (like a "Bigfoot" can, with plexiglass "wheels" twice the diameter of the other competitors). The experience provides the "mental hooks" upon which learners will hang physics concepts in high school.

Contextual Framework

Overview of the Lesson

Electricity has become very important to modern man. The commonplace nature of electricity makes it an excellent topic of discovery in the elementary classroom.

Science Themes

Systems—This activity requires the investigator to create a system that includes a power source, a power transmission, and a power consumer.

Models—This activity is done on a small scale but is representative of a much larger system. Through the creation of series and parallel circuits, students will be better able to understand how/where electricity is generated, transported, and used.

Consistency—Electrical systems require consistency. Dry/wet cells are designed to provide a constant voltage, so that a device is not damaged by surges or suppressions in current. Likewise, the power derived at power stations requires a feedback system of substations, switching devices, transformers, and monitors to ensure that constant voltage is maintained.

Patterns of Change—Power generation undergoes many changes as new technologies are created to maximize the amount of energy produced from fossil fuels, while limiting harmful effects to the environment. Nuclear and solar technologies are changing the way electricity is generated. Batteries are also changing, as new materials are being tried to create longer-lasting, more powerful, rechargeable, less expensive batteries.

Evolution—The production and use of electricity may have important evolutionary significance. Animals, including man, may need to undergo evolutionary change in response to electromagnetic fields, or may have already changed in response to the availability of light and heat from electricity.

Scale—Scale is inherent to a study of electricity. Large-scale generators and transformers produce high-voltage electricity at the power stations. Next, the power is transmitted through high-tension lines to substations. From the substations, electricity is scaled down and sent to neighborhoods where it is again stepped down into a usable voltage for home use. Generally, a house has three wires coming into it. One is a common ground and two are hot wires, at 110 volts each. From there, electricity may go to electronic appliances, where it is further scaled, or transformed, into a much lower voltage, such as 9 volts.

Scientific Skills

Classification—Students will be able to classify various types of circuits into series or parallel.

Observation—Students will observe the various ways that light (or do not light) the bulb.

Measurement—Students check individual batteries to ensure that they are producing a current.

Inference/Prediction—Students will predict various ways to light the bulbs and then test the predictions. Students will infer that their house circuit is a parallel circuit as they discover the differences between the two circuits.

Figure 3–3
Guided discovery lesson plan for electricity.

Communication—Communication skills will be developed as students interact in small groups to solve the problem. Communication of the results will also occur as groups share their findings.

Experimenting—Students will have to *identify the variables* which cause the bulb to light up. They will also *explore relationships* between the batteries, wires, and bulbs. Students will *construct hypotheses* of the differences between series and parallel circuits. They will have to *design* a solution to the batteries and bulbs problem.

Curricular Integrations

In language arts, there are numerous stories and poems based on electricity themes. Most children have experienced the lack of electricity in their homes at one time or another, opening up possibilities for creating short stories.

In mathematics, there can be experiences related to meter readings/billing and electrical usage, comparisons of electrical usage among appliances, and measuring voltages.

Art can be incorporated into an electrical activity in a variety of ways. Students can draw a picture of their experiences during an electrical blackout.

Music could become part of the lesson, as a discussion of how instruments have evolved through the use of electricity.

Social studies is important to the study of electricity. American communities all depend on electricity. A comparison between cultures based on the availability of electricity is important.

Safety is vital to any discussion of electricity. Local power companies are excellent sources for safety topics.

Materials

Supplies

Light-bulb-shaped paper for student stories. Pamphlets on safety precautions around electricity.

Equipment

Class set of batteries, wires, and bulbs.

Procedure

Steps to Follow

1. The introductory activity/advance organizer includes stories and poems based on electrical themes as a way to introduce the topic. A brief discussion of power outages will also be done as appropriate.
2. The first activity is to "light the bulb". Students are provided one battery, one wire, and one light bulb, and instructed to individually design an investigation which would result in lighting the bulb. Guide them as to what a complete circuit is and explain the path of electricity through the bulb, if necessary. Remind them that the electrons have to go in *and* out of the light bulb and battery.

(continued)

Closed-Ended Questions

A. What do you notice about the light bulb? (It has a base, filament, and glass enclosure.)

B. What makes the bulb light? (Electron flow through the filament.)

Open-Ended Questions

A. What were some probable ways that the light bulb was invented?

B. What are some creative ways to light a bulb?

Steps to Follow (continued)

3. The second activity is to create a circuit with two dimly lit bulbs and another circuit with two brightly lit bulbs. Students are provided two light bulbs, one battery, and four or more wires to produce a series and parallel circuit. Note that the materials only provide for one circuit to be produced at a time. Once the first one is designed, students will have to diagram the finding and then continue with the other circuit. Provide this diagram if necessary.

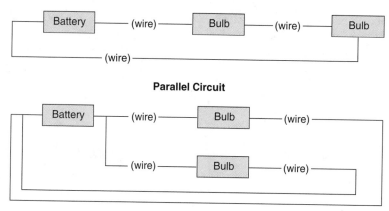

Closed-Ended Questions

A. How are the lights in this room wired? (parallel)

B. What happens to the old-style Christmas tree twinkle lights when a bulb is removed? (They all go out, because it is a series circuit.)

Open-Ended Questions

A. Why do you think buildings are wired in parallel instead of series circuits?

B. What are some ways to create a parallel circuit?

Figure 3–3 (continued)

Steps to Follow (continued)

4. Science/Technology/Society extension activity on determining appliance power consumption and reading a power meter from power company handout. Discuss how cultures rely on energy.

5. Discuss how electricity is produced and various types of fuel. Discuss the impact on the environment (thermal pollution from steam cooling; greenhouse effect from giving off carbon dioxide; acid rain from burning sulphur; electromagnetic fields from electricity transmission.)

Closed-Ended Questions

A. What form of fuel does our local power company use?

Open-Ended Questions

A. If we were to close down all of the electrical generation plants which use fossil fuels, what impact would that have on society?

B. What are some ways people could conserve energy?

C. How did you feel when the power was out last time? How did it change your life?

Assessment

Student Assessment

1. Students will complete a written story based on experiences they have had dealing with electricity.

2. Students will go to a hardware store and check types of wire and fuseboxes to determine which would be most appropriate for their house.

3. Students will actually make a series and parallel circuit (light the bulbs).

4. Students will interview family and friends to see which type of fuel (fossil, solar, nuclear) they prefer when generating electricity and why.

5. Students will record in their science notebooks the various ways they lit the bulbs.

Teacher Assessment

Invite a peer teacher to come into the room and observe questioning technique, particularly with regard to teacher dominance of questions versus students' independent inquiry.

Bibliography

Bains, R. (1982). *Discovering electricity.* Mahwah, NJ: Troll Associates.

Berger, M. (1989). *Switch on, switch off.* New York: Franklin Watts.

Johnston, T. (1988). *Energy: Making it work.* Milwaukee, WI: Gareth Stevens Inc.

Markle, S. (1989). *Power up: experiments, puzzles, and games exploring electricity.* New York: Antheneum.

Mayes, S. (1989). *Where does electricity come from?* Tulsa, OK: EDC Publishing.

Siegel, B. M., & Stone, A. H. (1970). *Turned on: A look at electricity.* Englewood Cliffs, NJ: Prentice Hall Inc.

Silverstein, S. (1981). *A light in the attic.* New York: HarperCollins Publishers. (Poems and drawings, including some about electricity.)

Once provided an initial question, students continue an investigation until a problem is solved.

In *Science for All Americans* (AAAS, 1989), there is a message to all science teachers that good teaching starts with questions about nature or explorations of phenomenon which are interesting to students and at their level. The authors go on to say that, as students become familiar with the things around them, they will begin to question and find answers to these questions. This idea is at the very heart of problem solving in elementary science. Children are very inquisitive during the elementary years. Promoting and developing this inherent trait will provide life-long skills in solving everyday problems. One way to increase problem-solving ability is through *problem-centered learning.*

Problem-centered learning is a method of teaching and learning which focuses on children's ability to construct their own meaning for concepts. Through problem-centered activities, children learn to view science as a meaningful, dynamic activity. They see science as a human endeavor in which they can participate.

You will notice that the guided discovery lesson plan is very similar to the other lesson plans, except that its procedure section contains a problem for the students to solve, as opposed to a specific procedure. Generally, a problem-centered lesson will also have more open-ended questions, because the teacher is not presenting specific concepts or definitions which are repeated by the students.

Learning with an Integrated Approach

It may not come as a surprise to you that, overall, elementary teachers see a value in their students learning science. What you may not understand is why they do not *teach* science more throughout the week. One reason commonly given is that there is more pressure from parents and administrators to have the students score high on standardized reading and math tests. One way to satisfy both worlds is to teach more science without detracting from reading and mathematics. This can be done by integrating other content areas with science.

Children's books are captivating to youngsters and are useful in developing emerging concepts. They place new vocabulary in a context which makes it easier to construct meaning. For example, if a student looks at a selection of dinosaur books, she will begin to develop the concept of *dinosaurness*. She will relate the pictures she sees to the story she is reading to determine what characteristics belong to the dinosaur. Books allow children to learn from a *whole language approach*. The notion of the whole language movement is to use real books to teach reading literacy in a natural context. It is a method in which meaning is constructed from an entire passage (top down) instead of individual words (bottom up).

Educators have taken whole language a step further and developed the concept of *whole learning,* in which all content areas are integrated and often based on story themes. Obviously, rote memorization of science facts does not lead to an understanding of science any more than learning disjointed words in language class would lead to an understanding of poetry or literature. Whole learning as applied to science can be thought of as a synergy of scientific knowledge, process skills, and attitudes. Children begin to value science because they enjoy reading about it in an interesting context. Math, language, social studies, and science activities based on literature build on familiar contexts and further reinforce a positive attitude toward science and other subjects (see Tchudi & Lafer, 1996, for examples). In summary, the advantages of whole learning are that it allows the child to:

■ *Learn in a social environment that fosters rich language activities.*

- *Science concepts are put into a meaningful context by connecting them with children's literature and other content areas.*

- *The time spent on science learning is increased, since it becomes a part of the normal reading and mathematics curriculum.*

Planning a Lesson with Children's Literature

When choosing books to use in a whole language lesson, keep the following points in mind:

- *Is the book appropriate for your students' developmental level?* Do not use a book just because it has the same title as the unit which you are currently studying. Check to see if it is written at an appropriate reading level. If you are not going to read it to the class, make sure that your advanced readers can read it to other students.

- *Is the content appropriate?* Before placing a book out to be read by the students, be sure that the content will not develop further misconceptions about the topic under study. Students have many false notions about scientific phenomena and you do not want to reinforce these or add to them. Pre-read each book and note any inconsistencies, eliminating nonsupportive books.

- *Will the book be interesting to your students?* Select a wide variety of books if possible. This will ensure that you meet the individual needs of the students. Consider gender and cultural diversity when selecting books. Look for colorful illustrations and a good story line.

- *Does the book encourage scientific investigation?* Your purpose for starting with children's literature is to provide a baseline for further knowledge and process skill development. Select books which are good springboards to further learning.

For teaching ideas using children's literature see:

Bosma, B., & DeVries Guth, N. (1995). *Children's literature in an integrated curriculum: the authentic voice.* New York: International Reading Association & Teachers College Press.

Butzow, C. M., & Butzow, J. W. (1989). *Science Through Children's Literature. An Integrated Approach.* Englewood, CO: Teacher Ideas Press.

Butzow, C. M., & Butzow, J. W. (1994). *Intermediate Science Through Children's Literature. Over Land and Sea.* Englewood, CO: Teacher Ideas Press.

Fredericks, A. D., Meinbach, A. M., & Rothlein, L. (1993). *Thematic Units: An Integrated Approach to Teaching Science and Social Studies.* New York: HarperCollins.

LeCroy, B., & Holder, B. (1994). *Bookwebs. A Brainstorm of Ideas for the Primary Classroom.* Englewood, CO: Teacher Ideas Press.

Shaw, D. G., & Dybdahl, C. S. (1996). *Integrating Science and Language Arts. A Sourcebook for K-6 Teachers.* Boston: Allyn and Bacon.

A good example of an integrated, problem-centered lesson is one on Oobleck. The teacher can begin by reading the story *Bartholomew and the Oobleck* (Geisel & Geisel, 1977). Once the story is read, a mixture of Oobleck (made beforehand) is passed out for student exploration. They interact with the Oobleck and determine its properties. Through this experience they are working on many scientific skills. They also explore content knowledge as they discuss new words and ideas in a small group social setting. Finally, the students are developing values and attitudes as they begin to use their natural curiosity to explore a scientific phenomena.

Mathematics can be integrated by measuring the amounts of water and cornstarch it takes to make "good" Oobleck. Social studies are integrated in a discussion of kingdoms, since the story is based on a king. Art can be integrated when students create mosaics with water-based paints and the Oobleck mixture. The sourcebook for arranging this experience is *Oobleck. What Do Scientists Do?* (Sneider, 1985). See Figure 3–4 for a sample lesson plan.

The assessment of this integrated experience should be in keeping with its constructivist nature. Students should be assessed on the product (knowledge), process (skill), and attitude (value) of the experience. Literature/language activities can become an assessment exercise as students write (or orally present) a creative story. Students could also write descriptive adjectives about Oobleck. These are used to create poetry, such as cinquains or diamantes.

Scientific attitudes can be assessed as students are asked how they feel about the fact that even scientists cannot agree on why Oobleck acts the way it does. Students should also be challenged to come up with their own explanation as to why the material behaves the way it does.

Concept maps (see page 172) would be an appropriate way to determine content knowledge in this case. Students can be provided a key word such as *Oobleck* and asked to develop links based on what they know.

PLANNING UNITS

Making and teaching a unit is a surer way to become competent than merely reading about it. When you begin a unit, keep the following in mind.

1. Is the unit based on a small number of concepts?

2. Do the lessons relate to students' experiences, provide feedback about their present knowledge, and move smoothly into the first activity of each sequence?

3. Are some open-ended activities included?

4. Can a variety of science processes be used in the activities?

5. Are the activities appropriate for the students' abilities?

6. Are useful activities from other subject areas integrated into learning sequences?

7. Do students *apply* their knowledge in assessments or simply recall it?

8. Does the unit plan allow enough time for children to learn what is proposed?

In deciding how to make your own textbook-based units, there are three main things you need to know:

How to determine which *generalizations* to use.

How to gather more *activities*, if needed, to teach each generalization.

How to introduce, or *bridge* into, each generalization's sequence of activities.

Determining Generalizations

The chapters or units of most textbooks are organized around three to ten main generalizations or concepts. Make a tentative list of such generalizations. Then go through the chapter to see if your list reflects the main parts of the chapter. Change the generalizations as needed to match what you find, if you want to stick closely to the textbook's contents. Your task is to wind up with as few big ideas as possible without combining unrelated ideas. When making a unit, you need to know the generalizations in order to compile extra activities.

Whether you use one or several text chapters as a base for a unit, it is important to think through their basic organization. This sort of analysis boosts your confidence by providing a sense of direction. It leads to the feeling that, if

Contextual Framework

Overview of the Lesson

Children can become scientists as they explore the world around them. When they encounter a new situation, they can observe, classify, measure, infer, predict, communicate, and experiment to solve problems and gain new information or ideas. Children's curiosity is stimulated as they complete activities. This activity is designed to acquaint children with a substance which does not behave as other substances do. Specifically, the Oobleck mixture gets harder as it is manipulated and softer when it is left alone. This is in direct opposition to materials such as playdough or clay.

Science Themes

Systems—Oobleck is a physical/chemical system made up of molecules that interact with each other and the environment. To understand the nature of Oobleck, we must consider its behavior as an integrated system comprising interacting parts and energy.

Models—In considering the manner in which molecules or atoms are arranged in Oobleck, students will create pictorial or mental models of the structure of this particular type of matter.

Consistency—Although we can cause temporary changes in Oobleck by inputting energy in one form or another, students will notice the system tends to maintain its properties and reorganize itself into the same physical consistency and structure as before the system was disturbed.

Patterns of Change—Oobleck seems to be both solid and liquid at the same time. Oobleck can be compared to other substances and the patterns of change which are represented as liquid and solid states are interchanged.

Scale—The behavior of Oobleck may be caused by scale. The sizes of the molecules allow them to interact in ways that a larger substance cannot interact.

Scientific Skills

Classification—Students will compare and contrast Oobleck and other materials in an attempt to classify it according to its properties.

Observation—Students will use all of their senses to observe the substance (provide a caution on tasting the material).

Inference/Prediction—The students will infer from the data collected such nonobservable properties of Oobleck as what it is made of or how the atoms might be arranged.

Communication—Students will communicate their findings to the group. They will also communicate with each other when developing theories of why Oobleck behaves the way it does.

Experimenting—The students will design and carry out experiments to alter Oobleck, to find its properties, and to explain its behavior.

Curricular Integrations

For language arts, the teacher can record the words used to describe Oobleck and discuss descriptive adjectives. Descriptive poetry, such as cinquains or diamantes, can be developed.

Mathematics activities can be developed as students compare densities of other substances to that of Oobleck.

Figure 3–4
Thematic lesson plan for Oobleck.

(continued)

Art can be integrated into this lesson as children experiment with water-based paints and the Oobleck mixture.

Physical education is promoted as students act out the behavior of Oobleck molecules.

Social studies is a natural integration as kingdoms are discussed. Also, the interaction between science and society can be stressed.

Safety during the Oobleck activity is stressed when using heating devices. Also, caution on eating the substance or getting it on clothing should be noted.

Materials

Supplies

Two or three boxes of cornstarch; green food coloring; water; small objects such as marbles, coins, rubber stoppers; other common substances or materials which can be used to explore. (*Note:* Prepare Oobleck by placing one or two boxes of cornstarch in a mixing bowl and mixing in small amounts of green-colored water. Continue until the consistency is like a thick plaster.)

Equipment

Thermometers, heat source (microwave), balance, graduated cylinders.

Procedure

Problem to Solve

1. The problem to be solved is to use the materials provided to find out as much about Oobleck as possible. While students explore, walk around the room questioning students as to what they are doing, why they are doing it, and what else they can do to gain information about Oobleck.

Closed-Ended Question

A. What happens to the Oobleck as you continue to squeeze it in your hands? (It hardens.)

Open-Ended Question

A. What did you find out about Oobleck?

Problem to Solve (continued)

2. Continue exploration with Oobleck and develop a theory as to why Oobleck behaves the way it does.

Open-Ended Questions

A. What do you think causes Oobleck to behave this way? Have students explain why it behaves as it does and suggest what materials it might be made from.
B. What possible explanations do you think scientists give for the behavior of Oobleck? Discuss scientific theory and why scientists cannot completely agree on why it behaves as it does. Discuss the tentative nature of science, theoretical models and their use, and the scientific search for explanations.

Figure 3–4 (continued)

Problem to Solve (continued)

3. Experiment with other materials, looking for ones that behave the same way as Oobleck.

Open-Ended Questions

A. What other substances do you think behave like Oobleck?

B. How could the king have eliminated Oobleck from the kingdom?

Problem to Solve (continued)

4. Record the words used to describe Oobleck and discuss descriptive adjectives.
5. Art/PE extensions from above.

Closed-Ended Question

A. What is a kingdom?

Open-Ended Question

A. Why do you think America is a democracy and not a kingdom?

Assessment

Student Assessment

1. Assign group reports that explain why the mixture behaves as it does. Require such items as a hypothesis, data collected, a summary of the data, and conclusions.
2. Write a story about your own day in the kingdom as the Oobleck fell. What did you find out about the Oobleck in the kingdom?
3. Take a small amount home and ask a parent or friend to provide their thoughts on Oobleck.
4. Find out more about Newtonian and non-Newtonian fluids.
5. Leave Oobleck out for one week. What effect does this have on the substance? Explain why this happens.
6. Use descriptive adjectives to develop poetry, such as cinquains or diamantes.

Teacher Assessment

Audiotape the lesson and review the tape with the following questions in mind. How did the students react to the investigation? What percentage of the time was I dominating the discussion and how often were students actively discussing Oobleck?

Bibliography

Geisel, T. S., & Geisel, A. S. (1977). *Bartholomew and the Oobleck.* New York: Random House. (Original work published 1949 by Dr. Suess.)

Kerr, D. A. (1983). Quick clay. *Scientific American, 209* (5), 132–142.

Sneider, C. I. (1985). *Oobleck. What do scientists do?* Berkeley, CA: Lawrence Hall of Science.

Walker, J. (1978). The amateur scientist. *Scientific American, 239* (5), 186–198.

Walker, J. (1982). The amateur scientist. *Scientific American, 246* (1), 174–180.

needed, you can make a few changes and add some ideas. It helps you to decide what is important and what is not.

Finding Activities

Activities can come from a wide variety of sources, including trade books and the teacher's guide to the students' science text. The following resource books contain hundreds of experiments, demonstrations, and other things to do in class:

> Bosak, S. (1992). *Science Is* . . . .New York: Scholastic.
>
> Lowery, L. F. (1985). *The Everyday Science Sourcebook: Ideas for Teaching in the Elementary and Middle School.* Palo Alto, CA: Dale Seymour.
>
> Sewall, S. B. (1990). *Hooked on Science: Ready to Use Discovery Activities for Grades 4–8.* West Nyack, NY: The Center for Applied Research in Education.
>
> Strongin, H. (1991). *Science on a Shoestring.* Reading, MA: Addison-Wesley.

These and many other activity books are available from the National Science Teachers Association, 1840 Wilson Blvd., Arlington, VA 22201.

There is also a series of books available from the Activities Integrating Math and Science Foundation, P.O. Box 8120, Fresno, CA 93747-8120. Some of the titles are *The Sky's the Limit, Floaters and Sinkers,* and *From Head to Toe.*

How many open-ended investigations should you plan for? That depends a lot on how diverse your class is. Cultural diversity and disadvantaged populations in the classroom may require more experiences to make connections.

After you have researched the topic and grouped some good learning activities under each generalization, arrange them in some log-

ical teaching order. The sequence of content in the class textbook can provide the overall direction here. Remember to cluster concrete activities ahead of reading and other secondhand activities when possible.

Determining Bridges (Introductions)

Now that you have located some activities for each generalization, you will need some way to introduce each of these main parts of the unit to students and move smoothly into each accompanying set of activities. Teachers call this phase "bridging" because it takes the children from where they are to the beginnings of where they need to go.

A useful introduction, or bridge, relates to students' experiences and present understandings. It stimulates them to use their present constructions as you interact with them. Pupil responses and questions give you some insight into what they already know about the generalization or topic to be studied, including their misconceptions. The last part of the bridge also leads into the first activity in each sequence.

You may want to introduce the children to the entire unit at one time by asking questions based on all the generalizations. However, many teachers believe it is easier and more meaningful to the children to introduce only one section at a time. Of course, a brief statement about the overall unit topic should be made in any case.

Ideas for bridging into each set of activities usually can be found in the textbook or its teacher's edition. Most modern programs reflect the constructivist view. They are likely to begin a unit or lesson with an opportunity for the teacher to find out what children already know and relate this to what they will learn. For many more examples of bridges, see the investigations in Part II of this book. Notice how each bridge ends with an "Exploratory Problem," which leads into the first activity of the investigation.

When supplementing a textbook unit, consider these suggestions:

1. Thoroughly read the unit to grasp what it is about.

2. Look for places where you can use local resources.

3. Look for opportunities to integrate reading, math, language, and other subjects into lessons.

4. Look for chances to use some concrete activities.

5. Estimate the total time needed to teach the unit, then fit the text's lessons into the block of available time.

Some teachers feel restricted by the book format, even an improved one. Without the publisher's full array of multimedia resources to draw from, they see mostly closed-ended activities that illustrate ideas in the book rather than broad chances for real inquiry. They see relatively short, tightly controlled lessons when they want students to ask more questions and pursue strong interests over longer periods of time. These teachers are aware of some ways to augment the book unit, but for them these measures don't go far enough. They want the book to be one tool among several, rather than the main event. What they *really* want is a practical way to design their own multimedia unit, and a format that allows them to work flexibly with their students.

A Sample Unit

For a sample unit developed in this way, see Figure 3–5. Notice that the unit is written on index cards. This is a convenient way to keep track of generalizations, activities, and bridges. Suggestions for using the format follow.

Write one broad generalization at the top of each 5-inch-by-8-inch card. *This is for your reference only,* not for teaching to the children.

Sections of the book may be headed by problems, topics, or themes. If one seems useful, you might prefer to first write this heading, then the generalization. Next, write your sequentially arranged activities under each generalization, leaving a space for the bridge. Then write the bridge. Be sure to relate the last part of the bridge to the first activity, so you can move smoothly into it.

The use of cards has advantages. They can be shuffled in any desired sequence. It is easy to add and take away generalizations and activities. Special sections can be fitted in: bulletin board ideas, news clippings, notes, or whatever else is desired to make the unit complete and easier to teach.

Also, notice the marginal notes for science processes written next to some activities. These can remind you of what to stress in such activities. Several "open-ended" notes serve the same function. Open-ended activities are often the easiest and best way to meet students' individual differences in unit teaching.

Finally, note that there is a specific assessment section for each of the four main parts of this unit. For Generalizations I and II, assessments are stated as questions. For Generalizations III and IV, they are stated as pupil behaviors to observe. Which method do you prefer? Some teachers use both.

THE STANDARDS AND SCIENCE TEACHING

The National Science Education *Standards* (National Research Council [NRC], 1996) include principles of teaching. In conjunction with content, program, and assessment standards, they are a holistic approach to bring about needed changes in the classroom. As you can see from the following two standards, the

EARTH'S CHANGING SURFACE

This is a fourth-grade unit on the forces that tear down and build up the earth's surface. Children also learn how rocks are formed and several ways soil is conserved. Fifteen periods of about 50 minutes each are planned for the unit. (See block plan on back of this card.)

(Front of card)

	April 6–10	**April 13–17**	**April 20–24**
Monday	Generalization I, Activity 1 (Ask class for materials for Act. 2.)	Gen. II, Act. 1	III, Act. 3 (Ask for rocks and jars Gen. IV, Act. 2, 4.)
Tuesday	I, Act. 2 (See custodian for materials for Act. 3.)	II, Act. 2	III, Act. 6, assess. (Ask for rocks and jars, IV, Act. 2, 4.)
Wednesday	I, Act. 3 (Ask class for materials for Act. 6.)	II, Act. 3 or 5	Gen. IV, Act. 1, 2
Thursday	I, Act. 4 or 5	II, Act. 4, assess.	IV, Act. 2, 3
Friday	I, Act. 5 or 6, assess. (Ask for materials for Gen. II, Act. 1, and milk cartons from cafeteria.)	Gen. III, Act. 1, 2 (Ask volunteers for Act. 3 to bring materials.)	IV, Act. 4, 5 assess. (Follow up on crystal growth next week.)

Order library books. Also AV materials by March 6 for I (4), II (3), III (1, 2). Phone II (5), III (4).

(Back of card)

Figure 3–5
Sample unit.

Gen. I. Weathering and erosion constantly wear down the earth's surface. (Class text pages 61–68.)

Bridge

How far down do you think the soil goes? What is beneath the soil? What are some ways rock may get broken up? How might broken up rocks and soil be removed? What does *weathering* mean? *erosion?*

Activities

(obs.)	**1.**	Define weathering and erosion. Tour school grounds for examples. (Open-ended.)
(exp.)	**2.**	Plants break rocks experiment, text p. 63. (Open-ended.)
(infer.)	**3.**	Dirt mountain erosion demonstration, Schmidt p. 56.
	4.	Films: Face of Earth (15 min.), Work of Rivers (10 min.).
	5.	Read text pp. 61–68 and library books. SUMMARIZE weathering and erosion forces.
(class.)	**6.**	Kids find and sort picture examples of forces that bring change. Display. (Open-ended.)
	7.	Haiku poetry on forces that change the earth's surface.

(Front of card)

Materials

2. Plaster of paris; bean seeds; paper cups.

3. Shovel; hose. (See custodian.)

4. MP204; MP206 (AV center).

6. *Nat'l Geographic, Arizona Highways* back issues; scissors; construction paper; paste.

Assessment

How many examples of weathering and erosion can you find on the school grounds? Find some examples we did not observe on our first tour. Make a record.

Also use end-of-section questions, p. 68.

(Back of card)

Figure 3–5 (continued)

Gen. II. Topsoil is composed of mineral, vegetable, and animal matter; topsoil is conserved in several ways. (Pages 69–77.)

Bridge

What are some reasons farmers might be interested in erosion? How might they guard against soil erosion? What makes up soil? Let's see for ourselves.

Activities

(class.)	**1.**	Small-group analysis of soil samples. Sort objects found. (Open-ended.)
(exp.)	**2.**	Plant seeds in poor and good soil samples, text p. 72. (Open-ended.)
	3.	Introduce six study prints on soil erosion. See "Conserving Our Soil" videotape.
	4.	Read text, pages 69–77, and library books. SUMMARIZE ways to conserve soil.
	5.	Possible visit by agent, Soil Conservation Service. (Practice interview and listening skills.)

(Front of card)

Materials

1. Magnifiers; old spoons; sack of good topsoil; newspapers; clean pint milk cartons.
2. Bean seeds; sack each of good and bad soil; milk cartons.
3. SP (set of 6) 117; Vid. 440.1 (AV center).
5. Bill Johnson, Soil Cons. Service, 555-6600.

Assessment

What are some ways you might prevent erosion on our school grounds? Think about the examples you found before. Discuss these ways with two partners. Then give a report.

We don't live on farms. What difference would it make to us if most farm soil erodes?

Also use end-of-section questions, p. 77.

Figure 3–5 (continued)

(Back of card)

Gen. III. Lava flows and crustal movements continually build up the earth's surface. (Pages 77–84.)

Bridge

Does anyone know what a volcano is? What do you think makes a volcano happen? What is an earthquake? Has anyone been where there was an earthquake? Let's find out some surprising ways the earth's surface changes.

Activities

1. Film: Earthquakes and volcanoes (30 min.).
2. Explore Internet for related information (25 min.).

(meas.)

3. Make clay models of volcanoes, p. 79. Also "seismograph," special project Hone, p. 28. (Art and construction.)
4. Guest speaker with northern California earthquake slides. (Or locate earthquake pictures.)
5. Use maps to locate active volcanoes.
6. Read text, pages 77–84, and library books. SUMMARIZE how mountains are formed.

(Front of card)

Materials

1. MP 254 (AV center).
2. Internet-connected computer.
3. Two colors of clay; newspapers; rulers; scissors. (Seismograph volunteers, check Hone book for materials.)
4. Orville McCreedy, 286–6147. (Or, past *Nat'l Geographics,* 1989 issues.)

Assessment

Children will construct cutaway models of volcanoes and, using the models, explain how volcanoes may happen.

Also use end-of-section questions, p. 84.

(Back of card)

Figure 3–5 (continued)

Gen. IV. Three kinds of rocks are formed as the earth's surface wears down and builds up.

Bridge

Thank you for bringing so many different rocks. What makes them look different? Which of these might have come from volcanoes? How else might some have been made? Before we find out, let's see how many different properties of these rocks you can observe.

Activities

(commun.)	**1.** Partners do rock description game. (20 questions—lang. develop.)
(exper.)	**2.** Crystal growing activity, p. 91. (Open-ended.)
	3. Read text, pages 85–93, and library books.
(class.)	**4.** Sort rocks as to basic type, p. 90. (Open-ended.)
	5. SUMMARIZE Gen. IV and whole unit.

(Front of card)

Materials

2. Baby food jars; string; paper clips; sugar; hot plate; teakettle; newspaper.

4. Children's rock samples—stress variety; heavy paper sacks; several hammers.

Assessment

Children will be able to control the size of "rock" crystals by varying the cooling rates of hot sugar solutions.

Children will be able to identify some properties of rocks and explain how these are clues to the rocks' formation.

Also use unit test questions, p. 93.

Figure 3–5 (continued)

(Back of card)

emphasis is on how the teachers can best support the needs of the students as they learn.

Teaching Standard A (National Research Council, 1996, p. 30). Teachers of science plan an inquiry-based science program for their students. In doing this, teachers:

■ Develop a framework of yearlong and short-term goals for students.

■ Select science content and adapt and design curricula to meet the interests, knowledge, understandings, abilities, and experiences of students.

■ Select teaching and assessment strategies that support the development of a student understanding and nurture a community of science learners.

■ Work together as colleagues within and across disciplines and grade levels.

Teachers should be able to effectively plan short-term and long-term instruction. They do this by selecting activities which will meet the needs of their students. Collaborative planning with other teachers is emphasized, since this promotes integrated learning.

Teaching Standard B (National Research Council, 1996, p. 32). Teachers of science guide and facilitate learning. In doing this, teachers:

■ Focus and support inquiries while interacting with students.

■ Orchestrate discourse among students about scientific ideas.

■ Challenge students to accept and share responsibility for their own learning.

■ Recognize and respond to student diversity and encourage all students to participate fully in science learning.

■ Encourage and model the skills of science inquiry, as well as the curiosity, openness to new ideas and data, and skepticism that characterize science.

Teaching and learning in science is about questioning and exploring the world around us.

Teachers need to be able to facilitate the learning process through an awareness of the students and good questioning techniques. Teachers also must model appropriate behavior. A natural desire to investigate modeled by a teacher will become a part of the students' repertoire as well.

Teaching Standard C (National Research Council, 1996, pp. 37–38). Teachers of science engage in ongoing assessment of their teaching and of student learning. In doing this, teachers:

■ Use multiple methods and systematically gather data about student understandings and ability.

■ Analyze assessment data to guide teaching.

■ Guide students in self-assessment.

■ Use student data, observations of teaching, and interactions with colleagues to report student achievement and opportunities to learn to students, teachers, parents, policy makers, and the general public.

This teaching standard demonstrates a concern for assessment. Individual, group, and self-assessment are all necessary components of an effective science program. It is also important to adequately convey your expectations to others, including parents, administrators, and especially the students.

Teaching Standard F (National Research Council, 1996, p. 51). Teachers of science actively participate in the ongoing planning and development of the school science program. In doing this, teachers:

■ Plan and develop the school science program.

■ Participate in decisions concerning the allocation of time and other resources to the science program.

■ Participate fully in planning and implementing professional growth and development strategies for themselves and their colleagues.

This teaching standard emphasizes the importance of planning and professional development.

SUMMARY

1. Closed-ended problems and activities lead to a single response. They foster *convergent* thinking. Open-ended activities and problems lead to a wide variety of responses. They produce *divergent* thinking.
2. Lessons can be taught in a direct teaching, guided discovery, or problem-centered learning fashion. As you reduce teacher control and increase student autonomy, students are required to take charge of their learning. More meaningful relationships are formed with problem-centered learning.
3. When planning a unit, there are three main things you need to know: (1) how to determine which *generalizations* to use, (2) how to gather more *activities* to teach each generalization, and (3) how to introduce, or *bridge* into, each generalization's sequence of activities.

REFLECTION

1. Take a lesson plan which you have recently completed and rewrite it in the form of a problem-centered lesson to share with the class.
2. Search the Internet for some lesson plan data bases. A good starting point is to use the key words *lesson, +plan, +science.*
3. Observe the next five science lessons while at your practicum site. Note the use of open-ended and closed-ended activities. How could more open-ended activities be incorporated?
4. Ask several adults one of the misconceptions questions. Do you notice any pattern in their answers? Did your classmates have similar experiences?

REFERENCES

American Association for the Advancement of Science. (1989). *Science for all Americans.* Washington, DC: Author.

American Association for the Advancement of Science. (1993). *Benchmarks for science literacy.* New York: Oxford University Press.

Briscoe, C., Peters, J., & O'Brien, G. E. (1993). An elementary program emphasizing teacher's pedagogical content knowledge within a constructivist epistemologic rubric. In P. A. Rubba, L. M. Campbell & T. M. Dana (Eds.), *Excellence in educating teachers of science* (pp. 1–20). Columbus, OH: ERIC Clearinghouse.

Geisel, T. S., & Geisel, A. S. (1977). *Bartholomew and the Oobleck.* New York: Random House. (Original work published 1949 by Dr. Suess).

National Research Council. (1996). *National science education standards.* Washington, DC: National Academy Press.

Sneider, C. I. (1985). *Oobleck. What do scientists do?* Berkeley, CA: Lawrence Hall of Science.

Tchudi, S., & Lafer, S. (1996). *The interdisciplinary teacher's handbook. Integrating teaching across the curriculum.* Portsmouth, NH: Heinemann.

SUGGESTED READINGS

American Association for the Advancement of Science. (1993). *Benchmarks for science literacy.* New York: Oxford University Press. (Provides a tool for designing a curriculum based on what students should know in science at specific developmental levels.)

Eby, J. W. (1992). *Reflective planning, teaching, and evaluation for the elementary school.* Upper Saddle River, NJ: Merrill/Prentice Hall.

National Science Teachers Association. (1996). *Pathways to the science standards: Guidelines for moving the vision into practice.* Arlington, VA: Author. (A practical guide to help put the national standards into practice during teaching and assessment.)

Shymansky, J. A. (1996). Transforming science education in ways that work: Science reform in the elementary school. In J. Rhoton & P. Bowers (Eds.), *Issues in science education* (pp. 185–191). Arlington, VA: National Science Teachers Association. (This chapter discusses curriculum and instruction in light of science education reform.)

CHAPTER 4

SCIENTIFIC SKILL DEVELOPMENT

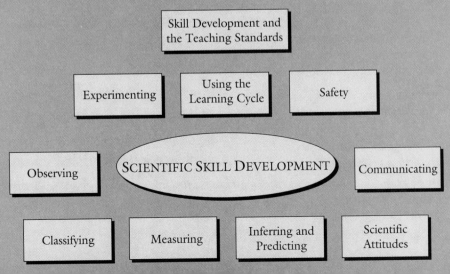

Skill Development and the Teaching Standards

Experimenting

Using the Learning Cycle

Safety

Observing

SCIENTIFIC SKILL DEVELOPMENT

Communicating

Classifying

Measuring

Inferring and Predicting

Scientific Attitudes

In 1929, John Dewey noted that education emphasized the learning of *fixed conclusions* rather than the advancement of intelligence as a *method of action*. He went on to say that schools separate knowledge from the *very activities which would give the knowledge meaning*. By this, he meant that teachers concentrated on teaching facts and conclusions, rather than teaching experimentation that would develop the skills necessary to investigate facts or develop new knowledge.

The educators of the 1990s and beyond must heed Dewey and focus on the skills or "activities" to which he referred. The goal of science *should be* problem solving and developing the skills necessary to remain competitive in the global marketplace. Scientific ventures —such as genetic engineering, drug research, telecommunications, nuclear fusion, and environmental monitoring—are increasingly done as cooperative ventures between many nations. In order for Americans to remain competitive, educators must start today to prepare a diverse workforce capable of scientific research and investigation. To paraphrase Dewey, *intelligent action* is the lone definitive resource of mankind (1929). This *action* of education refers to such entities as the science process skills. These are what scientists, adults, *and children* use to *do science*. Vignette 4-1 discusses—from a classroom teacher's and professor's point of view—how the use of scientific skills makes science meaningful and *active*.

As you study the skills of observing, classifying, measuring, communicating, inferring, predicting, and experimenting, ask yourself the following questions:

How will this skill fit into my elementary curriculum?

Do I fully understand this skill and am I prepared to teach it to children?

What are some examples of activities I can do to promote this specific skill?

OBSERVING

The process of observing is the taking in of sense perceptions. It is our job to help children use all of their senses when they observe similarities, differences, and changes in objects or events. Students can learn that each of the senses is a gateway to observing different properties of objects. *Seeing* allows them to notice properties such as size, shape, and color of objects and how the objects may interact. *Hearing* makes knowable properties of sounds such as loudness, pitch, and rhythm. *Touching* teaches the meaning of texture, and is another way to discover sizes and shapes of objects. *Tasting* shows how labels such as bitter, salty, sour, and sweet can be used to describe foods. *Smelling* calls for associating objects with odors, such as smells "like perfume" or "like cigar smoke."

Properties enable children to compare and describe likenesses and differences among objects. This leads to explorations that require several of the other processes, such as classifying and communicating.

You can ask broad and narrow questions to guide learning in observing or any of the other science processes. For example, in a primary-level class, children are examining bean seeds that have been soaked to make them easy to open. The teacher invites everyone to observe by saying:

What do you notice about your seed?

Later, some narrower questions are posed:

How many parts did you find?
How does the seed feel to you without its cover?
What does it smell like?

In a middle-level class, students are raising tadpoles in a large jar. On Monday morning,

VIGNETTE

4-1

SCIENTIFIC SKILL DEVELOPMENT
Dr. George E. O'Brien
Florida International University
and
Angela M. Alexander
Pine Villa Montessori School, Dade County Public Schools, Florida.

STUDENTS WORKING WITH MYSTERY OBJECTS

Picture a small community school just 30 miles from downtown Miami, but in a rural, farm region of South Florida. The students in the school typically do not venture outside the neighborhood and trips to the local supermarket and department stores are rare. Frequently, when teachers bring hands-on, minds-on activities (Flick, 1993) to class, children anticipate the fun that is coming next. This particular day, the fourth-grade teacher has arranged her children in cooperative learning groups, and the children are excited, curious, and anxious about what is going to happen in the science lesson.

Each group receives plastic gloves, dissecting needles, hand lenses, and an oval-shaped object wrapped in aluminum foil. Can the children predict and/or infer what the objects are? Students are told to unwrap the foil from the objects carefully and to inspect the objects. An initial reaction from many students is "Wow, I don't know if I really want to touch this." These reactions fade fast. Using dissecting needles, students are asked to separate parts that make up the whole of the oval-shaped objects, record observations, and make inferences concerning what the objects or their contents might be and why they think so. Quickly some of the students discover or infer that they are working with bones. Some students say they are working with wishbones, and one child says these are hog bones (because hogs have a lot of bones). Some students think they can make out a bird's head, while one student thinks she can see parts of a hamster. Some students guess that they are working with dinosaur teeth, human teeth, or some kind of fossil.

Students from each group sort the bones. The task of sorting and organizing the bones into recognizable entities is a problem-solving challenge. The challenge of discovering the mystery objects piques the students' curiosity. Although on this day, no one infers the objects to be owl pellets, the pieces of bones lead to more discoveries about the animals that are consumed by barn owls.

(continued)

Vignette 4-1 (continued)

Up the road from the elementary school, a professor of elementary science methods at the University has set up the activity the same way as the fourth-grade teacher. He leads his students through the same challenge of identifying the contents of owl pellets. As bones are uncovered and carefully removed and placed to the side on plain white sheets of paper, university students use dichotomous keys (classification) to identify skulls removed from the barn owl pellets. There is much debate and negotiation (communication) in the cooperating groups concerning the identity of the skulls. As skulls of small mammals, including moles and shrews (Order Insectivora), and rats, voles, and mice (Order Rodentia) are identified, students take pride in their individual and group accomplishments. As a follow-up activity, students are asked to diagram food webs with a barn owl at the highest trophic level and grass seeds at the lowest level. The sequence of activities helps students to construct knowledge of diets of barn owls and other birds of prey, food webs showing that energy passes from one organism to another on a higher level through consumption of that lower organism, and other ecological concepts.

In the fourth-grade classroom, the teacher brought books for students to research owls. Could the children identify the contents of the owl pellets? Yes. In much the same ways that university students had identified prey, children were able to identify skulls of different animals. All of the students—at the elementary school and university—solved the mystery of finding out the contents of the pellets. The students, by collecting information from the evidence (in this case, produced by barn owls about 12 hours after consuming a meal by casting, or regurgitating, undigestible hair and bones as a pellet) and using science process skills (in this activity: analyzing, communicating, observing, inferring, classifying, predicting, extrapolating, synthesizing, evaluating, measuring, interpreting information, and making conclusions) enjoyed participation in the active, intellectual process of science. Science surveys and interviews conducted by the instructors after these lessons emphasized hands-on, inquiry-based science, revealed positive attitudes toward science (in both groups) and positive attitudes toward science teaching (in the university group).

Learning Science Is an Active Process

Teachers of science—whether at the elementary school or the university—should believe that learning science must be an active process. Learning science is something students do, not something that is done to them. When an instructor focuses on actively engaging students in doing science, then a natural connection of learning concepts, scientific skills, and attitudes follows. In these classrooms, a focal question in planning science lessons is, What will the students be doing? Will the students be observing, classifying, measuring, predicting, inferring, collecting data, graphing, experimenting, and/or communicating? The better the teacher understands the level of skill development that the students have, the better he can choose activities to match the needs of the students. Primary and lower elementary teachers should seek to construct activities which engage students in observing, classifying, measuring, using numbers, making inferences, predicting, indicating time and space relations, graphing, collecting data, and communicating. Teachers of the lower elementary grades should not hesitate to construct many lessons that engage children heavily in making careful observations (using each of the five senses of sight, hearing, smell, touch, and taste), recording observations in numerous ways (e.g., drawings, pictures, poems, rhymes, songs, graphics, essays, field journals, etc.), measuring objects with numerous tools in the English and metric systems, and communicating results of activities in many modalities (written, pictorial, graphic, and oral). Upper elementary teachers should plan activities which engage students in the basic process skills as listed above, along with more integrated science process skills including formulating hypotheses, identifying, manipulating and controlling variables, designing experiments, interpreting data from experiments, making operational definitions, and constructing models. Teachers should periodically assess the process skills of the children to better match activities to the children's development. Teachers need to indicate to the children the importance of concurrently developing process skills and scientific attitudes. This advocacy of science education serves the greater goal of promoting scientific literacy for all students.

MAKING CONNECTIONS TO OTHER IMPORTANT ELEMENTS OF SCIENCE INSTRUCTION/LEARNING

Just as it is important for students to be active in their learning, it is equally important for the teacher to be an active inquirer and visible partner to the students during the instructional process. What follows are some comments from the fourth-grade teacher who taught the lesson on owl pellets.

"I approach teaching science in a way that empowers the students. The students will be given the power to create their own learning environment. The exploration chosen often comes from the students' needs. For example, if my students asked whether fire would go out if it were covered, that would be the area of discovery in a future lesson. These ideas on what to teach come from discussions I have with my students many times a day.

"When the children are working on activities that require an experimental design, I go to each group to discuss how they will set up the experiment. While the students are working on this task, I go from group to group and question the groups on why they chose to set up their experiment this way. The questions are not prepared questions, but are asked so that I have a full understanding of the experimental set-up, including the materials the students will need. I hope these questions will lead the groups to identify the variables that can be considered, but if they do not consider the variables, it is OK. Some experimental set-ups will be better than others, but all proj-

(continued)

Vignette 4-1 (continued)

ects will be acceptable. Each group of students will be working from what their group knows. They will be exposed to all the other groups' experiments, which will encourage them to consider other variables in their next exploration. I feel it is also important for the students in the group to self-evaluate their group's experiment. This includes what they think was best about their experiment and what they think they need to improve upon. This helps me to know where the group is in the learning process and what they will be focusing on in the next experiment.

"Before they begin the experiment, the groups need to predict what they think will happen. They may also predict why they think it will happen. When the children start the experiment, I go from group to group asking each group questions about their experiment so I can understand their thinking and/or explanations. I keep notes on each group and record their responses to questions and any misconceptions which I detect. The group devises a plan and collects data according to the plan. Then the students explain what they think happened in the experiment and share any data collected and recorded by the group with other groups.

"In my class, I feel the students are in charge of their own learning. The teacher sets up situations in which the students are in charge of their learning. The teacher manages situations in which the students can discover and invent on their own to reach understanding. Science process skills are important in my classroom, as is development of critical thinking. The students are encouraged to reach understandings which allow them to be better able to explain their theories. I encourage students to reconsider any misconceptions which they might have, and I have students discuss different opinions to see if a consensus can be reached."

The classroom setting described above includes the following characteristics:

1. Students are engaged in a motivating classroom environment that provides encouragement and frequent student–teacher interaction.

2. Students can integrate science processes and problem-solving skills.

3. Students are encouraged to actively construct knowledge and explanations.

4. Students can use familiar objects in real-life settings.

5. Students are given the opportunity to encounter natural phenomena through first-hand experiences.

6. Students are involved in varied classroom settings, including individualized instruction, cooperative learning, whole-class demonstrations, and interest centers.

7. Students employ risk taking, divergent thinking, and self-initiated questioning.

8. Student activities are developmentally appropriate and capitalize on student interests.

9. Students are encouraged to create a learning community where everyone's opinions, questions, and conceptions are valued.

Obviously, an elementary classroom teacher preparing a science lesson has to focus on the question, "What will the students be doing?" But just as importantly, the teacher needs to be cognizant of how other important factors—selection of instructional materials, physical limitations of children (e.g., in using manipulatives), choice of management strategy, selection of overall instructional strategy (e.g., Learning Cycle, Generative Learning Model, Constructivist Learning Model, and Search-Solve-Create-Share Problem Solving Model), assessment techniques, cognitive developmental levels of the children, decisions on prerequisite and hierarchy of tasks, and relevant or related science misconceptions—relate to inquiry-based hands-on science.

REFERENCES

Council for Environmental Education. (1992). "Owl Pellets." In *Project WILD K–12 Activity Guide* (144–145). Bethesda, MD: Author.

Flick, L. B. (1993). The meaning of hands-on science. *The Journal of Science Teacher Education, 4* (1), 1–8.

they rush to the jar as soon as the classroom opens. They see a small sign that reads:

What changes do you observe since Friday?

During sharing time, everyone learns what the students have noticed. Then the teacher asks a narrow question to zero in on an interesting change that has been missed:

How has the water level changed since Friday?

In an upper-level class, children are comparing plastic but real-looking cat bones and rabbit bones from a kit. The teacher says:

In what ways are the two sets of bones alike?

The need for a few narrower questions comes up later during a discussion:

How do their back leg bones compare?

How do their skulls compare?

For some examples of *observing* applied in investigations, see:

Your Side Vision and Color (p. 219),

A Way to Generate Electricity (p. 347),

Mealworms and What They Do (p. 452), and

The Filtering of Polluted Water (p. 569).

CLASSIFYING

Most intuitive thinkers can select and group real objects by some common property, such as color, shape, or size, selecting a different property each time they make a new group. In a primary-level class, some of the children remove small objects from bags they have brought from home. The teacher says:

Think of one property, such as a certain shape. Sort all the objects that have that property into one pile. Leave what's left in another pile.

Later, to open up the activity, the teacher says:

What other properties can you use to sort your objects?

Other children in the primary classroom are grouping pictures according to whether they show living or nonliving things. Later, they will be asked to take the pictures of living things and group them into animal and plant categories.

Many middle-level children can classify an object into more than one category at the same time and hold this in mind. In a middle-level class some children have classified animal pictures into three groups with two subgroups each: mammals, birds, and fishes have been divided into meat eaters and plant eaters. They have done this in response to their teacher's question:

How can you group these animals by kind and by what they eat?

Some upper-level students can also reclassify according to other properties that fit their purposes. In an upper-level class, several students have a large collection of animal pictures. They start off by dividing them into groups such as mammals, birds, and fishes, but then decide that this will not further their purpose. They want to alert people to animals of different locations that are threatened with extinction. How to do this?

After talking with the teacher, they decide to classify their pictures according to the animals' natural homes or habitats: woodlands, grasslands, and marshlands. These pictures are then subgrouped into endangered and nonendangered animal categories. Later, they subdivide further for in-state and out-of-state animals. Their classmates request more pictures:

Can you bring in ones that show animals that are dying out in different environments in our state or other states?

We're really short on grassland reptiles.

This example demonstrates a major point about classification: that it is done to fit a purpose. What works to fulfill the intent of the classifier is what counts. Objects can be classified in many different ways.

For some examples of *classifying* applied in investigations, see:

A Bottle Xylophone (p. 286),
How to Measure Bulb Brightness (p. 340),
Some Common Levers (p. 363), and
The Properties of Rocks (p. 540).

MEASURING

Thinking about properties in a quantitative way naturally leads to measuring them. To measure is to compare things. At first, at the primary level, children may be unable to compare an object with a standard measuring tool, such as a meter stick or yardstick. Instead, they find out who is taller by standing back to back. They find out which of two objects is heavier by holding each object in their hands. Eventually, they begin to use nonstandard measuring devices, such as paper clips or lengths of string to measure their desks.

There is good reason to start off measuring in this way. Remember that intuitive thinkers *do not conserve* several concepts that deal with quantity. Changing the appearance of an object still fools them. Children who think that merely spreading out some material gives them more, for example, have to be taught differently than children who conserve quantity. Most young children find it difficult to work meaningfully with standard units of measurement, such as centimeters and inches, until about age seven.

Intuitive thinkers can build readiness for working with standard units by using parts of their bodies or familiar objects as arbitrary units to measure things. A primary child may say that "The classroom is 28 of *my* feet wide."

Concrete Referents and Improvised Tools

One way to improve the ability of children to measure and estimate accurately is to have numerous concrete objects in your classroom for them to refer to as needed. Meter sticks, yardsticks, and trundle wheels are useful for thinking about length. Containers marked with metric and English units are good for measuring liquid volumes.

Similar references are needed for other concepts involving quantity. A kilometer may be a round trip from the school to the police station; a mile, from the school to the post office. Meanings associated with time can be developed by many references to water or sand clocks (containers with holes punched in the bottom) and real clocks. Temperature differences become meaningful through using several kinds of thermometers.

By the time they leave elementary school, most children will have had some experience with a variety of measuring instruments such as the ruler, meter stick, yardstick, balance, clock, thermometer, graduated cylinder, protractor, and wind gauge. When possible, children themselves should choose the right measuring tool for the activity under way. Sometimes they can make their own tools when they need them. Inventing and making a measuring instrument can be challenging and interesting.

Measurement and the Metric System

Scientists everywhere have long used the metric system because it is simpler and faster, since all of its units are defined in multiples of ten.

The three basic units most commonly used in the metric system are the *meter, liter,* and

Table 4-1
Comparison of Length, Volume, Mass, and Temperature

Length	
1 millimeter (mm)	= The diameter of paper-clip wire
1 centimeter (cm)	= The width of a formed paper clip
1 meter (m)	= 1,000 millimeters (mm)
1 meter (m)	= 100 centimeters (cm)
1 kilometer (km)	= 1,000 meters (m)
1 kilometer (km)	= About the length of nine football fields
1 kilometer (km)	= About six-tenths of a mile
Volume	
1 milliliter (ml)	= About one-fifth of a teaspoon
1 liter (l)	= 1,000 milliliters (ml)
1 liter (l)	= 100 centiliters (cl)
1 liter (l)	= Slightly over a quart
1 kiloliter (kl)	= 1,000 liters (l)
Weight (Mass)	
1 milligram (mg)	= About 1/1000 of a paper clip
1 gram (g)	= 1,000 milligrams (mg)
1 gram (g)	= 100 centigrams (cg)
1 kilogram (kg)	= 1,000 grams (g)
1 kilogram (kg)	= About 2.2 pounds
Temperature	
0 degrees Celsius	= Freezing point of water
100 degrees Celsius	= Boiling point of water

gram. A meter is used to measure length, a liter is used to measure liquid volume, and a gram is used to measure weight or mass. Strictly speaking, the terms *mass* and *weight* mean different things in science. Mass is the amount of material or matter that makes up an object. Weight is the gravitational force that pulls the mass. On the moon, for example, an astronaut's weight is only about one-sixth of what it is on earth. But the astronaut's mass stays unchanged.

Temperature in the metric system is commonly measured by the *Celsius* (C) thermometer, named after its inventor, Anders Celsius. It has a scale marked into one hundred evenly spaced subdivisions.

Prefixes are used in the metric system to show larger or smaller quantities. The three most common prefixes and their meanings are

- *milli* one-thousandth (0.001),
- *centi* one-hundredth (0.01), and
- *kilo* one-thousand (1,000).

Take a closer look at Table 4-1 to see how the prefixes are used in combination with the basic units.

Before your students use different metric standards, have them consider the right standard for the job. Children will usually discover that the metric system is easier to use than the English system.

Conversions from, or to, the English system should be avoided since they are confusing. If your curriculum calls for work with both metric and English measures, give students a lot of practice with concrete materials for both systems. Treat each system separately, instead of shifting back and forth. For some examples of *measuring* applied in investigations, see:

Echoes (p. 277),

The Volume of Air You Breathe (p. 499),

How Water Sinks into Different Soils (p. 537), and

An Earth–Moon Model (p. 617).

COMMUNICATING

Communicating means putting the information or data obtained from our observations into some form another person can understand, or some form that we can understand at a later date. Children learn to communicate in many ways. They learn to draw accurate pictures, diagrams, and maps; make proper charts and graphs; construct accurate models and exhibits; and use clear language when describing objects or events. The last of these activities is usually stressed in elementary science.

It is important to say things or to show data in the clearest way possible. We can help children learn this by giving them many chances to communicate, and by helping them to evaluate what they have said or done.

In a primary-level class, some students are seated on a rug. They face a bulletin board on which many pictures of vehicles are pinned. Each picture has a number, so the pictures can be quickly located. The teacher has suggested a game: A child describes the properties of a vehicle ("I'm thinking of a green object. It has four wheels and fits in my garage.") and the others try to identify the object. The child who identifies the object first gets to be the new describer. The original describer is rewarded by getting the picture. Wild guessing is discouraged by reminding the children to consider the data. After each identification, the teacher asks questions, such as

What did Maria say that helped you to find the picture? What else would be helpful to say? Did anyone get mixed up? How do you think that happened?

In a middle-level class, two children are working with a simple balance that has a peg-board-type (perforated) beam. They hang iron washers from opened paper clips hooked to different parts of the beam. They are working out problems written on problem cards. After a while, the teacher says:

What problem cards of your own can you make? Will your partner understand your directions? If not, try to figure out why.

In an upper-level class, students want to find out the warmest time of the day. Temperature readings are made on the hour from 10 A.M. until 3 P.M. for five days in a row and then averaged. They decide to record their results on a line graph, but don't know whether to put the temperature along the side (vertical axis) or along the bottom (horizontal axis) of the graph. Is there a "regular" way?

The teacher helps them to see how graphs are arranged in their mathematics text. The change being tested is called the *manipulated variable* by scientists. In this case, time is usually placed along the bottom axis. The change that results from the test is called the *responding variable*. In this situation, temperature is the responding variable and is placed along the vertical axis.

Defining Operationally

Defining operationally is a subprocess of communicating, usually introduced after the primary grades. To define a word operationally is to describe it by an action (operation) rather than just by other words. For example, suppose you invite some students to hold an evaporation contest: Who can dry water-soaked paper towels fastest? They begin to speculate excitedly. But there is just one thing they will have to agree on before the fun begins. How will everyone know when a towel is "dry"? This stumps them, so you pose another open question that hints at *actions* they could take: What are some things they could *do to the towel* to tell if it is dry? Now, they start coming up with operations (actions) to try:

Squeeze the towel into a ball and see if water comes out.

Rub it on the chalkboard; see if it makes a wet mark.

Tear it and compare the sound to a dry towel you tear.

Hold it up to the light and compare its color to an unsoaked towel. See if it can be set on fire as fast as an unsoaked towel.

Put an unsoaked towel on one end of a balance beam; see if the other towel balances it.

The children agree that the last operation is easiest to observe and least arguable. It is stated as an operational definition: "A towel is dry if it balances an unsoaked towel from the same package." Now the activity can begin.

Had the open question not worked, one or two narrow questions such as "How would squeezing the towel show if it is dry?" could have been posed, followed later with a broad question, like "What else could you do to the towel to tell if it is dry besides squeezing it?"

When operational definitions are not used, it is easy to fall into the trap of circular reasoning: What is the condition of a *dry* towel? It contains no moisture. What is the condition of a towel that *contains no moisture*? It is dry. Or, to borrow from children's humor, consider this example:

He is the best scientist we've ever had.

Who is?

He is.

Who is "He"?

The best scientist we've ever had.

There are some predictable times when the need for operational definitions will come up. Watch children's use of relative terms such as *tall, short* (How tall? short?), *light, heavy, fast, slow, good,* and *bad* (What is "bad" luck?).

Recording Activities

Recording is another subprocess of communicating. When activities require time to gather data (e.g., growing plants over many weeks), or when there are many data to consider (e.g., discovering how much Vitamin C many juices contain), it is often sensible to make a record of what is happening. Without a record, it is harder to remember what has happened and to draw conclusions. In a way, recording can be considered communicating with oneself. Many teachers ask their students to make records in a notebook or *data log*. Records can be in picture or graph form as well as in writing. But however the data is recorded, it should be clear.

In a primary-level class, some children are recording the growth of their plants with strips of colored paper. Every other day, they hold a new strip of paper next to their plant and tear off a bit to match the plant's height. They date the strips and paste them in order on large paper sheets. A growth record of the plants is clearly visible to all of the students.

Other children in the class have drawn pictures of their plants at different stages, from seed to mature plant. These they make into record booklets at the teacher's suggestion. They describe each picture for the teacher, who swiftly writes their short statements on paper slips. The children paste these beneath their pictures. The result is a "My Plant Storybook" for each child, who can proudly read it before impressed parents.

In a middle-level class, there are five groups at work with narrow strips of litmus paper. (This chemically treated paper changes color when dipped into acidic or basic liquids.) The children want to find out whether five mystery liquids in numbered jars are acidic, basic, or neutral. Each group has a recorder who notes the findings on a data sheet. At the end of the work session, the teacher asks how the results of all the groups should be recorded on the chalkboard. It is decided as outlined in Table 4-2. Notice that by having a code, (A: Acid, B: Base, N: Neutral), written to one side, the teacher cuts down on the time needed to record the findings. The data are now compared, differences noted, and possible reasons discussed. Careful retesting is planned to straighten out the differences.

In an upper-level class, some children want to find out whether there is a pattern to the clouds passing over the city in the spring. They have made a chart that has three columns: one each for March, April, and May. In each column is a numbered space for each day of that month. Next to about half of the days the children have drawn the weather bureau cloud symbols for the cloud cover, if any, on those days. Even though the record chart is only partly completed, a sequential pattern is taking shape. After the chart is completed, the children will compare it to data gathered by the local weather bureau office for the same months in previous years.

For some examples of *communicating* applied in investigations, see:

Table 4-2
Acidity of Mystery Liquids

Group	1	2	3	4	5	
Miranda	A	B	N	B	A	
Tasha	A	B	N	B	A	A: Acid
Evan	A	A	N	A	A	B: Base
Britton	A	B	N	A	A	N: Neutral
Brenda	B	B	N	B	B	

INFERRING AND PREDICTING

The usual meaning of *inferring* is to interpret or explain what we observe. If Carol smiles when she greets us (observation), we may infer that she is pleased to see us (explanation). The accuracy of our inferences usually improves with more chances to observe. Several like observations may also lead us to *predict* that the next time we see her she will smile (observation), because she will be pleased to see us (explanation). For convenience, then, view the process of inferring as having two parts: We may make an *inference* from what we observe, and we may predict an *observation* from what we infer. Let's now look at children *explaining* observations, then later, in another section, *predicting* them.

Inferring as Explaining

There are at least three common ways we can help children infer properly from observations. However, intuitive-level students may have a very limited overall understanding of this process.

First, we can get them to distinguish between their observation and inference. In a middle-level class, two children are looking at a picture of shoeprints in the snow. One set of prints is much smaller than the other (observation). One child says, "One of these sets of shoeprints must have been made by a man and the other by a boy" (an inference). The other child says, "That's true" (another inference).

Hearing this, the teacher asks an open question to make them aware of other possibilities:

In what other ways could these prints have been made?

They think for a moment and come up with other inferences: Perhaps two children made the prints—one wore his father's shoes; or maybe it was a girl and her mother; or it could have been a girl and her older brother.

The teacher points out that what they have observed is still the same; but there is more than one way to explain the observation. If the children look at the tracks closely, they may *conclude* that one of their inferences is likelier than the others. A *conclusion* is simply the inference in which one has the most confidence after considering all the evidence.

A second way children infer is to interpret data they have observed or recorded. Remember the students who were using litmus paper to identify mystery liquids? When several groups recorded their data, they noticed that some data were inconsistent. Some liquids were labeled both acidic and basic. The children inferred, from this, that the litmus test was done incorrectly by one of the groups. After the tests were redone, all the data became consistent. So the children inferred that their final labeling of the mystery liquids was probably correct.

Recall the cloud data study. The sequential pattern the children saw when they examined their data was an inferred pattern. Later, when they compare their pattern with the weather bureau's, they will be able to evaluate the quality of their inference.

A third way to help children infer is to let them observe and interpret only indirect evidence or clues. Scientists must often depend on clues rather than clear evidence in forming possible inferences. For example, no scientist has visited the middle of the earth, yet earth scientists have inferred much about its properties.

Children can learn to make inferences from incomplete or indirect evidence, and they can also learn to become wary of hasty conclusions. In a primary-level class, some students are working with two closed shoe boxes. One box contains a round (cylindrical) pencil. In the other box is a six-sided pencil. The children's problem is, which box has which kind of pencil?

They tip the boxes back and forth and listen intently, inferring correctly the contents of the two boxes. When the teacher asks them what made them decide as they did, one child says, "You could feel which one was the bumpy pencil when it rolled." The other child says, "The bumpy one made more noise."

Later, the teacher puts into the boxes two pencils that are identical except for length. The students now find that correct inferring is harder, so they become more cautious. What observations must they rely on now?

In the middle and upper grades, children can do an excellent job of inferring the identity or interactions of hidden objects from indirect observational clues. In science, this way of inferring is called *model building*. (The second of the following four investigations is mainly devoted to model building.)

For some examples of *inferring* in which children make explanations, see these investigations:

How to Keep Heat In or Out (p. 250),

Hidden Parts of Electric Circuits (p. 333),

Making Casts of Animal Tracks (p. 450), and

Why We Have Seasons (p. 613).

Predicting

To *predict* is to forecast a future observation by inferring from data. The more data that are available, the more confidence we can have in the prediction; the reverse is also true. We can be very confident that spring will follow winter, but not at all confident that spring fashions this year will be exactly like those of a year ago. Without some data, we can only guess about future observations; to predict is impossible.

When students put their data in graph form, there are usually many chances to predict.

Upper-level children measure and record on a graph the time candles burn under inverted glass jars. After they have recorded the times for 100-, 200-, and 300-milliliter jars, the teacher says, "How long do you think the candle will burn under a 250-milliliter jar?"

Notice that predicting the time for a 250-milliliter jar would require students to read the graph between the present data—they have the times for a 200- and a 300-milliliter jar. This is called *interpolating*. If the teacher asked students to predict the candle-burning time of a 400-milliliter jar, the children would need to go beyond the present data. This is called *extrapolating* from data. Using these processes to predict is more accurate than guessing.

Children often need assistance when predicting. Simple diagrams can help them to reason through data. If they cannot calculate precise predictions, just asking them to predict the direction of change is useful. Primary-level students might be asked, "Will *more* or *less* water evaporate when the wind blows?" Middle-level children might be asked, "Will a *higher, lower,* or the *same* temperature result when these two water samples of different temperatures are mixed?" For some examples of *predicting* applied in investigations, see:

The Mixing of Hot and Cold Water (p. 242),

Inclined Planes (p. 361),

Wheel-Belt Systems (p. 370), and

Evaporation (p. 585).

EXPERIMENTING

To a child, experimenting means "doing something to see what happens." While this is overly simple, it does capture the difference between experimenting and the other six science processes. In experimenting, we change objects or events to learn how nature changes them. This section is about how children can discover the various conditions of change. Experimentation builds on the concept of open-ended investigations.

Experimenting is often called an *integrated* process skill, because it may require us to use some or all of the other process skills: observing, classifying, inferring and predicting, measuring, and communicating. That is one reason some curriculum writers may reserve experimentation for upper-grade activities. But experimental investigations can vary in difficulty. With guidance, even intuitive thinkers can benefit from experimentation. This does not mean any hands-on activity can properly be called experimenting. Some generally accepted criteria which separate hands-on activities from experimentation are:

1. Children should have an idea they want to test (hypothesizing).
2. Children should vary only one condition at a time (controlling variables).

To many educators, almost any investigation is experimenting, as long as the child changes an object for a purpose and can compare its changed state to the original one. This is the position taken in this book.

Hypothesizing

How do we get students to form ideas they want to test before they manipulate objects? There are several ways of getting children to state operations that they want to try. For elementary students, stating operations as questions such as "Will dropping a magnet make it weaker?" or "Does adding salt to water make things float higher?" is a clear and easy way for them to state hypotheses. It makes them focus on what they want to do to produce some effect, or on what effect to observe and connect to a cause.

In science, a hypothesis is often stated in an if–then manner: *If* I do this, *then* I believe this will happen. *If* a magnet is dropped, *then* it will get weaker. You may want to use the if–then form with upper-level students. But for most children, stating a hypothesis as an operational question is easier and more understandable.

Allowing students to explore the properties of real objects stimulates them to suggest their own ideas for changing them. Their curiosity usually prompts them to state operations they want to try, or to be receptive to broad and narrow questions you ask. For example, in a primary-level class, some children have been making and playing with toy parachutes. They tie the four corners of a handkerchief with strings and attach these to a sewing spool. Some release their parachutes while standing on top of the play slide and watch them fall slowly to the ground. Others simply wad the cloth around the spool and throw their parachutes up into the air.

A few children have made their parachutes from *different* materials. They are quick to notice that some parachutes stay in the air longer than others. After they go back to the classroom, they discuss their experiences. Then, the teacher says:

> We have plenty of materials to make more parachutes on the science table. How can you make a parachute that will fall slower than the one you have now?

The children respond in different ways: "Make it bigger," "Make it smaller," "Use a lighter spool," or "Make it like Martha's." These are the children's hypotheses. Some children may say nothing, but peer intently at the materials. They are hypothesizing, too, only nonverbally. The children's ideas need testing so they can find out what works. Now the children have purposes for doing further work with parachutes.

Where did the children's hypotheses come from? When the children first observed their parachutes in action, they did much inferring ("Jimmy's parachute is bigger than mine. It stays up longer." "Corinne has a big spool. Her chute falls fast.") It is natural for people to be curious about the quality of their inferences. *Hypotheses are simply inferences that people want to test.*

Exploring the properties of concrete materials provides the background that most children need to think. They cannot offer broad explanatory hypotheses to test concepts or theories. This calls for the deeper background and concept-seeking mind of the formal operational thinker. This is the reason some *what* questions, such as "What makes a ship float?," are hard for children to handle. Instead of broad, generalizable hypotheses, concrete thinkers are likely to offer limited hypotheses, best phrased as operational questions, that are tied to the objects they have observed or manipulated.

Intuitive thinkers also do this, as you saw in the foregoing example. But they are far more limited in this ability than concrete thinkers. Their teacher provided more real materials to think about during their discussion, instead of relying on talk alone. Even so, many children will need the teacher's personal attention to follow through in a meaningful way. Most intuitive thinkers can only think about one variable at a time. This limits the experimenting they can do, because they are unlikely to control other variables that might affect the outcome. So primary-level investigations usually lean more heavily on the other six science processes.

Controlling Variables

To find out exactly what condition makes a difference in an experiment, we must change or vary that condition alone. Other conditions must not vary. In other words, they must be *controlled* during the experiment.

Suppose you think that varying the size of a parachute will affect its falling rate. A good way to test the variable would be to build two para-

chutes that are identical in every way except size. These could then be released at the same time from the same height. After repeated trials, you could infer whether size made a difference in your test.

Don't expect intuitive thinkers or early concrete thinkers to reason in this way. They will not think of the many variables or conditions that can influence their experiment. They may unwittingly change several variables at the same time. Their intent is simply to make a parachute that will fall slower than another, not to isolate variable conditions. On the other hand, young children will grasp the need to control some variables. Typically, they will insist on releasing their parachutes from the same height and at the same time. Otherwise, "it won't be fair," they will tell you.

The parachute experiment is more than just a trial-and-error activity. The children have observed parachutes and have done some inferring about their observations. The changes they try will reflect thinking we can call hypothesizing. And although they may not think of controlling *all* the possible variables, they are conscious of *some*. This is the nature of children. How well they do and how fast they progress are influenced by how we scaffold their experiences. Here are more examples of teachers helping their students construct the idea of experimentation.

In a middle-level class, the children have worked with seeds and plants for about two weeks. The teacher says:

We've done well in getting our plants started. But suppose we didn't want our seeds to sprout and grow. Sometimes in nature seeds get damaged, or conditions are not right for seeds to grow. What could you do to keep seeds from sprouting and growing?

The children begin suggesting operations to try, as shown in Table 4-3. These are their hypotheses; at this point, they need not be framed as operational questions. The teacher

Table 4-3
Things That May Keep a Seed from Growing

Squashing it	Cutting it in half
Chewing it	Not watering it
Freezing it	Watering it with salt water
Boiling it	Microwaving it

writes all of these on the chalkboard, regardless of content. The teacher then gets them to screen the hypotheses for those that may have possibilities:

With which conditions might the seed have some chance to live? Suppose Jimmy squashed his seed just a little. Would the seed sprout? Would the plant look squashed? Would this happen with any kind of a seed? How about some of the rest of these conditions?

This mixture of broad and narrow questions is posed slowly, to give the children time to think. The students discuss a number of possibilities. After a while, the teacher says:

How can we test our ideas?

It soon becomes obvious that some children are going to do several things at one time to their seeds, so the teacher says:

Suppose Beth squashes her seed and also freezes it. How will she know which one stopped the seed from growing?

The children decide to change just one condition at a time. Pairs of students quickly form operational questions from hypotheses they want to test: Will squashing a bean seed keep it from sprouting? Will cutting a bean seed in half keep it from sprouting? Interest is high as experimenting begins.

In an upper-level class, the children are working in pairs. They are testing their reaction time by catching dropped rulers. In each pair, one child holds the ruler just above his partner's hand. When he releases the ruler, the partner catches the ruler between her thumb and forefinger. The ruler number closest to the top of his pinched fingers is recorded. This is her "reaction time." After a few minutes, the teacher asks the students to give their reaction times. He writes these on the board in the form of a histogram, as shown in Table 4-4. Histograms are used to classify data in a way that encourages thinking about the differences in the data.

After a few moments, in a discussion with the children on how the scores are distributed, the teacher says:

Suppose everything and everyone were the same in our experiment. How would the histogram

Table 4-4
Reaction Time Numbers

						X					
						X					
						X					
				X		X					
				X	X	X	X				
		X		X	X	X	X				
		X		X	X	X	X	X	X		
X		X		X	X	X	X	X	X		X
1	2	3	4	5	6	7	8	9	10	11	12

look? Well, what differences were there that may have given us these results? What conditions might affect reaction time?

The children start forming hypotheses: "Not everybody did it the same way," "Some people have faster reaction times," "Some kids have more practice," "I was tired today." After a discussion to narrow down and clarify different ideas, the teacher says:

How are you going to test your ideas?

The children state their ideas as operational questions. Will people have the same reaction time if they do the experiment in exactly the same way? Does practice give you a faster reaction time? Do people who feel "tired" (defined as having less than 8 hours of sleep) have slower times than when they don't feel tired? Everybody agrees that they must do the experiment in the same way each time to control the test variables. Then each question is tested separately under the controlled conditions.

For some opportunities for *experimenting* in investigations, see:

The Melting of Ice Cubes (p. 237),

A String Telephone (p. 272),

How Salt Water and Other Liquids Affect Plants (p. 405), and

How to Train Goldfish (p. 447).

USING THE LEARNING CYCLE

The learning cycle is an inquiry approach to learning scientific skills. It is a methodology that can translate the skills and vocabulary used by scientists into a more meaningful learning experience for students. The learning cycle began several years ago as part of the *Science Curriculum Improvement Study* (SCIS) and is gaining in popularity in recent years (Odom &

Settlage, 1996). It is now found in programs such as the *Full Option Science System* (FOSS) by the Lawrence Hall of Science and some of the *Biological Sciences Curriculum Study* projects. The assumption behind the learning cycle is that it is consistent with the way students learn.

Charles Barman (1989) has modified the original terminology of the learning cycle to make it more understandable for elementary teachers. He suggests three phases as follows:

1. *Exploration Phase.* The first phase of the cycle is student-centered; the teacher plays the role of a facilitator, observing, questioning, and assisting students as needed. The students interact with materials and each other during this phase.

2. *Concept Introduction Phase.* This teacher-centered phase is characterized by naming things and events. The teacher's function is to gather information for students pertaining to their explorations in the first phase. The teacher works with students to develop vocabulary and introduce pertinent information.

3. *Concept Application Phase.* This activity-oriented phase is, again, student-centered and allows students to apply freshly learned information to new situations. The teacher presents a new problem to solve, allowing students time to apply what they have learned.

As you can see in Figure 4-1, there is also an evaluation and discussion aspect to this cycle. This is an interactive component throughout each phase. In the concept introduction phase, the teacher may rely on traditional assessments such as paper-and-pencil tests (see Chapter 7 on assessment). In the exploration or application phase, the teacher may rely on alternative means of assessment. In either case, the cycle is supported by a continuous evaluation. This prevents students from constructing misconcep-

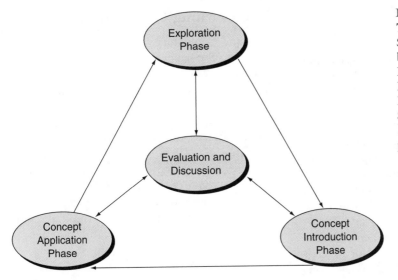

Figure 4-1
The learning cycle.
SOURCE: Adapted from a figure by Charles Barman in "A Procedure for Helping Prospective Elementary Teachers Integrate the Learning Cycle into Science Textbooks." *Journal of Science Teacher Education, 1* (2), p. 22.

tions. The ongoing assessment allows for a holistic approach to evaluation that includes activity-based evaluation. Consider possible evaluation strategies as we further explore the three phases.

Exploration Phase

As we discussed earlier, this is a student-oriented phase. Remember the constructivist model presented in Figure 2–19 (page 48). It begins with an *invitation* to students to observe surroundings and look for interesting phenomena. The teacher's function is to scaffold the learning environment based on the concepts she feels are important for the students to learn at that time. Students can be involved in classifying what they have observed as part of the invitation. They can also be involved in measuring or making informal inferences based on their observations. Once the students have completed the invitation phase of the constructivist model, they begin the exploration phase: conducting experiments, collecting and organizing data, and communicating their findings to their peers.

For example, if you would like to develop an understanding of floating and sinking, you could have students observe pictures of various objects either floating or sinking. Next, you could ask a series of questions designed to engage students in a discussion of the phenomena. Here they would begin to make inferences as to why objects floated or sank. It would be important for you to identify the various students' explanations as to why some objects float or sink, noting similarities and differences in their perceptions or explanations. Students could even test several objects during this phase and make a chart of which ones float or sink. Assessment during this phase could be as informal as open-ended questions or as structured as individual student interviews.

Concept Introduction Phase

During this phase, the teacher begins to focus the questioning, organize the information, and guide the class into an agreed-upon concept: a process termed *concept invention*. He assists students in naming the objects and concepts (vocabulary development) and experimenting with the newly formed concepts, relating them to the experiences from the exploration phase. In terms of the constructivist model, students are now in the "proposing explanations and solutions" phase, and are looking for ways to construct new explanations.

In the floating and sinking example, the teacher would introduce terminology and concepts such as *weight, surface tension,* and *density.* Specific definitions would accompany these terms, related to the students' explorations. Questioning about why the students think some objects float and some sink would be based on both the new vocabulary and definitions and the explorations. Students would measure various densities in support of concept development. Finally, the students would construct the notion that objects that are denser than water will sink and those that are less dense will float.

Concept Application Phase

Now it is time for the students to apply their new knowledge and skills. Students are provided with similar situations and challenged to implement their new concepts. In terms of the constructivist model, the students are now taking action on what they have learned. They make decisions about the new explorations and apply newly learned knowledge and skills.

In terms of the floating and sinking example, the teacher may provide new items for students to hypothesize about and test. The teacher may also complete a performance-based evaluation (see page 165) at this point, checking how many objects the student can correctly identify as "floaters" and "sinkers." Different experiments may test the new knowledge or lead back to the exploration phase of the cycle. For example, the teacher may ask students to float a paper clip in a cup of water. The students know that the paper clip is denser than water, so now they have to experiment with surface tension, bringing them back to the exploration phase.

The Learning Cycle and Textbooks

In many elementary schools, a textbook series makes up the science program. Such books contain many activities. Their purpose is to illustrate in concrete ways ideas presented in the books. Teachers sometimes call the worst of these activities "cookbook experiments," because the problems, materials, directions, and even conclusions are furnished. There is little chance for children to construct meaningful knowledge. All that children are required to do is follow the recipe. Although more authors now use activities that require thinking, there are ways to modify "cookbook" activities into meaningful experiences. One way is to employ the learning cycle.

Start not with reading the text, but with related explorations designed to invite students to want to explore more. Try an experiment out of the book as a discovery activity, not as a set of directions to follow. Then use the text to develop the vocabulary and concepts. Finally, try some related experiments from the text or supplemental materials.

If you are involved in selecting the textbook for your science program, pay attention to the ways authors lead into the activities and the comments following them. Look for questions that are posed *before* the experiment, with extending information *following the experiment.* This enables you to use the author's questions to explore beforehand, then introduce the experiment, and finally, use the book's information to extend the children's learning after the experiment is completed.

SAFETY

Experimentation and process skill development is at the heart of science instruction at the elementary level. Teachers should take every opportunity to develop these skills *in a safe way.* Before you begin the school year, develop a short list of basic safety rules to post in your classroom for students to read (you can read the list to them if necessary). Consider the following as you develop your rules.

■ Walking versus running

■ Respect for the teacher, others, and property

■ Touching or tasting with permission only

■ Dressing safely for activities

■ Knowing location of fire exits and safety equipment

■ Following directions

■ Using an agreed-upon signal to stop an activity quickly and quietly (in case of an emergency).

Remind students of the rules periodically. Some other general considerations before doing an experiment include:

■ Will the activity involve chemicals? If so, check material safety data sheets and, if needed, carefully try the experiment out before involving students.

■ Supervise all students at all times. Do not allow independent activity in separate unsupervised rooms or during lunch periods. This invites trouble.

■ Remember, as class size increases, safety considerations also increase. It is much harder to watch 40 students than 20.

■ Field trips pose special concerns. Check with the principal before going on trips, and invite parents to assist in the supervision. Have students use the buddy system. Remember, even with parents along, you are solely responsible.

■ Do not store hazardous materials or dangerous items in your classroom. Seek the help of the custodial staff in arranging for safe environments.

■ Check your room for unsafe equipment such as old thermometers that contain mercury or formaldehyde, which is carcinogenic.

■ Make sure fire extinguishers, first aid kits, eyewash stations, and related items are in working order, and consider taking a first aid course before you start teaching.

■ Remember safety goggles (almost every state requires these) and review safe procedures before activities. Have students tie back long hair and loose clothing before beginning activities.

■ Check for potential electrocutions and ensure all outlets are properly grounded. Outlets near water should be the ground-fault type.

■ Check for allergies before completing any activity with food or drinks.

In the upper elementary grades, consider a *safety contract* in addition to posting the rules. Remember, you are the role model. You cannot expect students to wear safety glasses if you never wear them. Additionally, check with your school, school district, and the state before the school year begins. They may have safety guides and special rules to follow. The National Science Teachers Association has a position statement on safety. Write to them or check their web site (http://www.nsta.org/) to find out more information. Finally, remember that, as a classroom teacher, you are liable for the welfare of your students. You do not want to undergo tort proceedings and jeopardize your career over negligent acts.

SCIENTIFIC ATTITUDES

Part of developing scientifically is acquiring positive scientific attitudes. Experimentation and other skills are not fully developed if they are completed in a negative framework or only finished to "get it over with." Science is different from activities such as learning to spell, where the task is simple and there is only one correct answer. Science includes developing attitudes and questioning those attitudes. The development of these attitudes is part of the job for elementary teachers. We will consider five categories related to attitudes.

Curiosity

"To be a child is to touch, smell, taste, and hear everything you can between the time you get up and when your parents make you go to bed. I don't have to *teach* curiosity. It's there already." The kindergarten teacher who said that echoes many of her elementary school colleagues. Yet in some classes, there are children who lack interest in science.

Walk into two adjoining classrooms: one with a hands-on science program and another where students just read and do worksheets during science time. Handing concrete materials to children is like rowing downstream or cycling with the wind at your back. Making children sit still and be quiet for long periods is like rowing upstream or riding into the wind: you can do it, but it's best avoided. Children lose a lot of their curiosity unless they are allowed to do what comes naturally.

Teachers who maintain or spark students' curiosity apply science to everyday life. These teachers also use several open-ended investigations during a teaching unit.

Inventiveness

To be inventive is to solve problems in creative or novel ways. This contrasts with simply taking a known solution and applying it to a problem at hand: It's good to apply what you know about a car jack to change a flat tire, but what do you do when there's no jack? Inventive people may apply their knowledge to solve problems much as other persons do. But they are more likely to show fluency, flexibility, and originality in their thinking.

Fluency refers to the number of ideas a child gives when challenged with a problem. We can promote fluency by asking open-ended questions.

Flexibility is the inclination to shift one's focus from the usual.

Originality is shown when students generate ideas that are new to them. We can promote originality by encouraging children to use their imagination and combine others' ideas in new ways, and by withholding evaluative comments until all ideas are in.

Critical Thinking

To think critically is to evaluate or judge whether something is adequate, correct, useful, or desirable. A judge does this when she decides whether there is adequate evidence of guilt. In this case the judge has a standard in mind against which a judgment is made. This is key to critical thinking: Know the accepted standard and decide whether or to what degree it is being met.

A problem we face as teachers of elementary-age children is that there are numerous standards of behavior in science. Many are highly sophisticated. Let's see if we can reduce them to a manageable few and restate them on a level that makes sense to young minds.

There are three overall standards for critical thinking in science that most children can gradually understand and learn to make decisions about: open-mindedness, objectivity, and willingness to suspend judgment until enough facts are known.

The open-minded person listens to others and is willing to change his mind if warranted. An objective person tries to be free of bias, considers both sides in arguments, and realizes that strong personal preferences may interfere with the proper collecting and processing of data. Someone who suspends judgment understands that additional data may confirm or deny what first appears. Looking for further data improves the chances for drawing proper conclusions.

Try having several groups work on the same activity, then report and compare findings. It soon becomes obvious when people refuse to listen to others, push their own ideas, and jump to conclusions before all groups have their say.

Critical and creative thinking go hand in hand. It's artificial to separate them. When problem solving or experimenting, for example, children should be encouraged to generate a number of possibilities, rather than just consider the first idea suggested. You also want them to critically appraise all the ideas, so they can tackle what looks most promising. Controlling variables in experimenting gives students another chance to generate suggestions, but they must also think: "Will these controls do the job?" Later, if groups come up with different findings, critical thinking is again needed to answer why. Perhaps one or more variables were not controlled after all. You can see that creative and critical thinking are different sides of the same coin.

When students seek information, there are a number of sources available to them, including themselves, printed matter, audiovisual materials, electronic information, and knowledgeable persons. Certainly, children can be cautioned to check copyright dates and agreement with what is known, to consult more than one source, and to note conflicts in fact. This is especially important when exploring the Internet, where information is posted from everyone who has access to it. Children often do not critically appraise information. As educators, we can help children learn ways to consult these sources efficiently and to understand what the sources say.

Persistence

Most elementary science activities can be completed within a short time. But some require a sustained and vigorous effort. To do our best work often takes persistence. Children sometimes lack the persistence to stick with a worthwhile goal. Primary-level students often want

instant results. Their short attention span and need for physical activity can easily convert into impatience. You can combat this impatience by arousing children's interests.

Uncertainty

Another important attitude to develop is the ability to understand or accept uncertainty. Much of this centers on students understanding the nature of elementary statistics. There are some events which can be predicted well and some which cannot. We do not always know all of the variables in a given situation, nor do we always have representative data of a population. For instance, the weatherperson on television can only predict rain tomorrow based on the percentage of times it rained with similar weather conditions (such as air pressure, wind patterns, or cold/warm fronts).

Elementary students should be aware that evidence is not always complete and, therefore, predictions may not always be precise. Experiments are influenced by lack of accurate observation, lack of knowledge of compounding factors, or lack of a model to explain the variables effectively. Scientists do not always have all the answers, but must theorize on the observations and experimental results they do have.

Developing Attitudes

Early learning of attitudes begins with imitation and later comes from experiencing the consequences of having or not having the attitudes. The open-minded, accepting teacher who reflects positive attitudes is more likely to influence students in positive ways than one who lacks these qualities. In a science program where children use science processes, they can develop attitudes just as the scientists do. You simply help students compare the consequences of having or not having scientific attitudes.

Open-ended activities bring out the consequences at every turn. Success in science is bound up with curiosity, inventiveness, critical thinking, persistence, and tolerance for uncertainty. Children learn, in a more limited way, the same habits of mind as scientists and other reflective people. Successfully practicing these attitudes helps build self-esteem.

SKILL DEVELOPMENT AND THE TEACHING STANDARDS

The National Science Education *Teaching Standards* (National Research Council [NRC], 1996) discuss the importance of making investigations a part of the elementary science program.

Teaching Standard D (National Research Council, 1996, p. 43) Teachers of science design and manage learning environments that provide students with the time, space, and resources needed for learning science. In doing this, teachers:

- Structure the time available so that students are able to engage in extended investigations.
- Create a setting for student work that is flexible and supportive of science inquiry.
- Ensure a safe working environment.
- Make the available science tools, materials, media, and technological resources accessible to students.
- Identify and use resources outside the school.
- Engage students in designing the learning environment.

Making the time and materials available for inquiry are essential to a successful science experience for elementary students. Safety is also an important concern, since students at this level are developing lifelong safety habits.

Teaching Standard E (National Research Council, 1996, pp. 45–46) Teachers of science develop communities of science learners that reflect the intellectual rigor of scientific inquiry and the attitudes and social values conducive to science learning. In doing this, teachers:

- Display and demand respect for the diverse ideas, skills, and experiences of all students.
- Enable students to have a significant voice in decisions about the content and context of their work and require students to take responsibility for learning of all members of the community.
- Nurture collaboration among students.
- Structure and facilitate ongoing formal and informal discussion based on a shared understanding of rules of scientific discourse.
- Model and emphasize the skills, attitudes, and values of scientific inquiry.

Standard E underscores the importance of modeling scientific skills and attitudes as well as social values which are beneficial to science learning.

SUMMARY

1. In *observing*, students learn to use all of their senses, note similarities and differences in objects, and become aware of change.
2. In *classifying*, students group things by properties or functions; they may also arrange them in order of value.
3. *Measuring* teaches them to use nonstandard and standard units to find or estimate quantity. Measurement is often applied in combination with skills introduced in the mathematics program.
4. *Communicating* teaches students to put observed information into some clear form that another person can understand.
5. In *inferring*, children interpret or explain what they observe. When students infer from data that something will happen, usually the term *predicting* is used. When people state an inference they want to test, usually the term *hypothesizing* is used. So predicting and hypothesizing are special forms of inferring.

6. In *experimenting*, we often guide students to state their hypotheses as operational (testable) questions and help them control variables within their understanding.

REFLECTION

1. What other scientific skills can you think of to teach children? What approaches could you take to develop these skills in elementary students?
2. How well do you know the science processes? Try the activities from one of the books listed in the Suggested Readings. Try them out with students at your practicum site and compare their results with your classmates.
3. Interview an elementary student and compare her scientific attitudes to those in this chapter. Share these results with the class or your instructor.

REFERENCES

Barman, C. R. (1989). A procedure for helping prospective elementary teachers integrate the learning cycle into science textbooks. *Journal of Science Teacher Education, 1* (2), 21–26.

Dewey, J. (1929). *The quest for certainty: A study of the relation of knowledge and action.* New York: G. P. Putnam's Sons.

National Research Council. (1996). *National science education standards.* Washington, DC: National Academy Press.

Odom, A. L., & Settlage, J., Jr. (1996). Teachers' understandings of the learning cycle as assessed with a two-tier test. *Journal of Science Teacher Education, 7* (2), 123–142.

SUGGESTED READINGS

Bowers, P. S., & TeBockhorst, D. (1993). Science labs in the elementary school: One approach for improved concept and process skills attainment. In G. M. Madrazo Jr. & Motz (Eds.), *Sourcebook for science supervisors* (4th ed., pp. 109–112). Arlington, VA: National Science Teachers Association. (This chapter presents an argument for elementary science laboratories with science specialists.)

Gabel, D. L. (1993). *Introductory science skills* (2nd ed.). Prospect Heights, IL: Waveland Press Inc. (A comprehensive workbook of scientific skill development and assessment.)

Ostlund, K. L. (1992). *Science process skills.* Menlo Park, CA: Addison-Wesley. (Ways to assess each of the science processes, with material lists and reproducible worksheets.)

Rezba, R. J., Sprague, C., Fiel, R. L., Funk, H. J., Okey, J. R., & Jaus, H. H. (1995). *Learning and assessing science process skills* (3rd ed.). Dubuque, Iowa: Kendall/Hunt. (A workbook of scientific skill development and assessment.)

Roberts, R. M. (1989). *Serendipity: Accidental discoveries in science.* New York: John Wiley and Sons, Inc. (Provides examples of how scientists engaged in experimentation may often have unexpected results—much like what can happen in the elementary classroom.)

HOW TO USE DIFFERENT RESOURCES TO TEACH SCIENCE

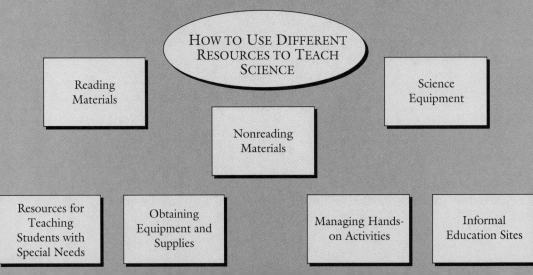

HOW TO USE DIFFERENT RESOURCES TO TEACH SCIENCE

Reading Materials

Science Equipment

Nonreading Materials

Resources for Teaching Students with Special Needs

Obtaining Equipment and Supplies

Managing Hands-on Activities

Informal Education Sites

Science teaching should not be confined to a specific time period in the elementary classroom. Rather, science learning should be a part of a child's everyday encounter with the world. Zoos, museums, aquariums, parks, science centers, and technology exhibits are examples of rich learning environments for the child.

Similarly, within your classroom, science should not be studied from a text, exclusive of other resources. *Science should involve **all** students exploring through any available resource.* The effectiveness of the science program you have in your classroom will largely depend on your attitude toward science learning, what materials you have to teach with, and how you use these materials. In some situations, all you will have available is a set of science texts. You will have to find creative ways to supplement the texts with other materials and experiences.

Will this be a big problem for you? Probably not if you are willing to learn more about your students and the resources available to you. This chapter should help you learn about many sources of materials commonly available and ways to use them.

Obtaining Equipment and Supplies

Despite inadequate funds for science supplies, some teachers seem to have no trouble getting many materials to teach science. Sometimes they achieve this by turning loose volunteers eager to help—students and their parents. They supplement these materials with a few others from commercial sources. Let's see how these methods can help you get supplies.

Children and Parents as Resources

Most of the materials used in elementary science programs are easy to find. The term *kitchen chemistry* suggests that many can be found right at home in the kitchen. Most of the time, students themselves can get what is needed for hands-on learning experiences.

When everyday materials are brought to school and used by children, they can continue the experience at home if necessary. That is common with open-ended investigations. Also, students are likely to have a hand in planning the experience. This usually makes its purpose clear and develops in them a commitment to follow through. And by having more materials, more children can participate.

The best materials to request are reusable or no-cost items. Children should clearly understand that they need their parents' permission before bringing any items to school. Parents can be especially helpful in acquiring materials if you contact them directly. One of the best times to request their help is at the beginning of the year during Parents' Night or some other introductory meeting. Consider passing out a photocopied list of inexpensive items which can be found in most text series.

Parents' Night is also a good time to ask for parent or grandparent volunteers who might give special help in one or more instructional units. Be specific about your needs. If you have other needs and do not know who to ask, check with your state's science teachers association or the National Science Teachers Association's Local Leaders. The Local Leaders program was developed to enhance science teaching in local communities. A listing of the state group or local leader closest to you can be found in each year's *NSTA Handbook* available from:

NSTA, 1840 Wilson Blvd.,
Arlington, VA 22201-3000.

Commercial Sources

It would be hard for us to rely on children or parents for everything needed in a science program. Commercial sources, including science supply houses, hardware stores, drugstores, and department stores, need to be used. Many school principals or Parent Teacher Organizations keep a petty cash fund for small purchases.

Science Kits

What kind of science kit should you have if given a choice? Some schools provide self-contained science kits. For example, the Delta Science Modules provide materials for an entire class, a teacher's guide, an assessment rubric, and storage modules on a number of topics such as butterflies and moths, the water cycle, and magnets. They also have a series of mini kits called "Science in a Nutshell." These are collections of hands-on materials and activity guides to use in small groups. Example topics include body basics, crystal creations, and electromagnetism.

Many publishers have also developed kits, sometimes called "science labs." These contain equipment and supplies to accompany their science text series or other program. Some labs contain basic materials for all the activities at a given grade level. Others may provide materials for a specific unit of instruction or module. Publishers' kits hold several advantages over the general variety. They contain multiple items for hands-on experiences, and so they allow most of your students to participate individually or in small groups. Appendixes B and C list other programs and suppliers.

READING MATERIALS

If you believe that children need to explore many materials firsthand to learn science, you have plenty of company. Most educators do. But some science topics and questions are hard or impossible to handle that way. For example, consider the following questions:

What makes a volcano erupt?
How do scientists know about the dinosaurs?

It can take far too much time to sample firsthand all the things students need to know. Time and financial considerations may also constrain children's firsthand exploration of some science topics, so educators see a need to teach some science through indirect sources, including books and other printed materials. At the same time, they want students to use reading to learn in the content areas and continuously become better all-around readers.

Let's look at some reading materials you are likely to find in your classroom. Science education offers four main sources for reading:

- Textbooks
- Trade books
- Reference materials
- Language experience charts

Textbooks

In many schools, a coordinated series of textbooks is the science program. Table 5-1 details some of the differences that exist between these science textbooks and reading textbooks.

Observe how the properties of science textbooks all point to reading as a thinking process. When perusing a reader, the child who does not recognize certain words can usually proceed with understanding after decoding and pronouncing them. But in a science textbook, the real problem with many words may be not knowing their meaning *after* they have been recognized. Consider the following example:

> The batsmen were merciless against the bowlers. The bowlers placed their men in slips and covers. But to no avail. The batsmen hit one four after another with an occasional six. Not once did a ball look like it would hit their stumps or be caught (Tierney & Pearson, 1981, p. 56).

Did you find the meaning of this paragraph hazy? If so, you have probably never experi-

Table 5-1

Differences Between Reading Books and Science Texts

Reading Textbooks	Science Textbooks
Purpose—learn to read	Purpose—read to learn
Stories in narrative form	Information in expository form
Mostly common words	Many technical words
Everyday references	More remote references
Simpler concepts	More complex concepts
Graphic aids simple	Graphics more complex
Readability at/below grade	Difficult readability

enced the British sport of cricket. But note that the lack of meaning does not come from the strangeness of the words. Nearly all the words are simple and quite recognizable when considered in isolation. Instead, the problem comes from the unfamiliarity of the context.

This is one reason you cannot depend on readability formulas when you check the difficulty level of a science or social studies textbook. Most formulas have you count the number of words and length of sentences, and sometimes the number of words that appear on word lists. These measures do not include familiarity of context, an important consideration in science texts.

A more valid estimate of readability requires judgments about things a reading formula might miss:

■ How abstract are the ideas for intuitive-level or concrete-level students?

■ How many abstractions are presented?

■ How familiar to children are the contexts in which the ideas are presented?

■ How clear is the syntax—the ways in which the words are put together?

Probably the best way to estimate clarity is to give a *cloze* (derived from "closure") test. Here, children typically read a typed 250-word pas-

sage from the beginning of a chapter. Beginning with the second sentence of the passage, every fifth word is deleted and its space left blank (leave last sentence intact). Students write a word in each blank that makes the most sense to them as they read the passage. A score above 55 percent correct usually indicates that the reading material is at an instructable level.

In primary grades, a modified cloze, with suggested answers, is best, because young children can not access their lexical background as well as older children can. Figure 5-1 illustrates part of a modified cloze test for primary children.

VOCABULARY AND MEANING. The simplicity of words can be misleading if the context is unfamiliar to students. Consider which is harder for a child to read: *tyrannosaurus rex* or *energy*? If you chose the first item, you probably think *read* merely implies being able to pronounce words.

If you chose the second word you realize that *read* means to comprehend. But most children know what a dinosaur is, and comprehend. You can easily supply the first term to a child, and enjoy learning a long, impressive name for one. *Energy,* on the other hand, is an elusive, difficult concept that builds slowly in the child's mind only after many firsthand expe-

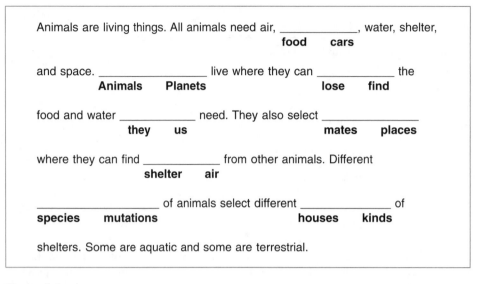

Figure 5-1
Example of a primary cloze passage.

riences. To read in the full sense of the term a child needs to decode *and* comprehend.

READING FOR MEANING.   Just as you may need help to understand the paragraph on cricket, children often need help to understand what they read in science textbooks. You can give such aid before, during, and after they read. Here's how.

Before Reading [about 5 minutes, excluding Item 1]

1. Furnish real or vicarious experiences before reading, if your students have little or no background with the concepts to be learned. Be sure to use appropriate vocabulary.

2. Relate what your students are about to read to what they have studied or otherwise experienced before.

3. State some clear purposes for reading.

4. Briefly introduce a few vocabulary words you have selected from the text, to help students recognize them in print.

During Reading [about 5 to 15 minutes]

1. Have students read silently and adjust their pace to suit their purposes.

2. Move around the room to help students as needed, but instruct them to use self-help first when they meet unknown words, as follows:

   a. Pass over the word and finish the sentence; use context clues and any accompanying graphics to grasp the meaning.

   b. Analyze the word for familiar roots, prefixes, and suffixes.

   c. Use the text's glossary or a dictionary, being careful to select the definition that makes the most sense.

   d. Ask for the teacher's help.

3. Have students who finish early switch to self-selected library books on the topic, or reference books, to gather additional information on the questions raised.

How can you help students who cannot read the textbook independently? You can read to them aloud as they follow in their books. Do this in an *interactive* way. That is, have them participate enough for you to check whether they can keep up with you and understand what is being read.

Check whether your pacing is all right by occasionally omitting an easy word and having a child supply it *without breaking your rhythm,* if possible. Move around as you read and signal who will supply the word by lightly tapping someone on the arm a second or so before you omit the word.

To monitor understanding, ask a low-level factual question and invite brief responses every paragraph or so. Some textbooks include questions to promote comprehension. Students will feel encouraged if you periodically remind them through appreciative comments that *they understand well what they are reading.* Interactive reading can change a frustrating failure experience into an encouraging success experience.

Above all, avoid round-robin reading. This is boring and ineffective. Children typically read much faster silently than orally. Few children read well orally unless they are familiar with the material. They are preoccupied with the mechanics of the reading and understand less when reading aloud.

After Reading [10 to 15 minutes, excluding item 2]

1. Have students respond to the main purposes or questions first posed.

2. Many text programs supply activity sheets at the ends of sections. Distribute these now.

MORE TEXTBOOK USES. Treating the text as an important tool within a unit of instruction will offer the most possibilities for a variety of worthwhile uses. Here are some extra ways you can profitably use a science text and its accompanying teacher's manual:

■ As a source of investigations, activities, problems, and basic science principles.

■ *As a check-up source for experiments and ideas.*

■ *As an information source.*

■ *As a source of additional examples to reinforce a previous activity.*

■ *As a summary of important ideas in units of instruction.*

Trade Books

Children's *trade books* are excellent sources for elementary science information. They are often developed around one topic, such as simple machines, weather, or electricity. Most schools now have instructional resource centers that contain collections of trade books. (For titles, see the end of each chapter in Part II of this book.)

Trade books are probably the best means we have of providing for individual differences in reading. With a variety of trade books, students with differing reading levels are given the chance for challenging and interesting reading material that is appropriate for their level.

Children's trade books are not just limited to interesting expository treatments of science topics. They also include biographies, autobiographies, diaries, reports of major scientific events, and science fiction. Children often find these books inspirational and exciting. They are also an excellent means to stimulate creative writing.

CHILDREN'S LITERATURE AND SCIENCE LEARNING. Children's literature is an excellent source for helping children experience, interpret, and personalize abstract concepts presented in science (Krauss, 1992). Learning science requires children to access prior world knowledge, elaborating and expanding this knowledge, then organizing and restructuring prior knowledge to include new concepts.

Literature helps children extend their awareness of scientific phenomena such as:

■ *Ecological awareness:* Nature, life cycle, and wildlife topics are common in children's literature.

■ *Scientific and technological awareness:* Science fiction highlights the human, moral, and ethical issues of advanced technological knowledge.

■ *Awareness of scientific inquiry:* Biographies of famous scientists illustrate use of the scientific method.

■ *Awareness of subjective scientific explanations:* Poetry provides subjective and imaginative interpretations of the world.

CREATIVE WRITING.   Here are some ideas for creative writing that you can use repeatedly with different trade books.

Diary.   Write an entry from an event in the life of George Washington Carver or Marie Curie. ("February 18, 1897. Is it impossible? I have now tried dozens of ways to . . . ")

Letter to a Famous Scientist from the Past or Present.   ("Dear Dr. Einstein:")

Interview with a Famous Person.   ("What was it like being an astronaut, Mr. Glenn?" "It had its up and downs, Sally," he said with a grin.)

Future Autobiography. ("An exciting page from your life in the field of _____ !")

TV or Radio Script.   A "You Are There!" reenactment and report of the first landing on Mars, first colony on the moon, development of the first human clone, first successful brain transplant, or a peaceful visit to earth by creatures from another planet.

FINDING THE BEST TRADE BOOKS. Thousands of trade books are printed every year. It's difficult to keep up with what is published and pick out quality material. Fortunately, there are several places to turn to for help. Among the more useful sources is the annotated bibliography "Outstanding Science Trade Books for Children," prepared annually by the National Science Teachers Association and the Children's Book Council. The list is published in the March issue of *Science and Children* (see Appendix A). Another resource is:

American Association for the Advancement of Science. *Science Books and Films.* Washington, DC: Author (1776 Massachusetts Avenue, N.W. 20036).

Reference Books and Other Reading Matter

How useful are *encyclopedias* for children? They do provide additional information. But most are hard for younger children to read without help. Discourage the practice of copying information out of the encyclopedia. When this happens, comprehension may reach the vanishing point. Help the children interpret information. If necessary, read short segments aloud so individual students can jot down in their own words facts they wish to report or know.

"What's this bug?" "Is that bird a robin?" Children like to name and find out more about what they observe. From time to time you might need to use *identification books* in the classroom. These references classify, name, and usually give interesting information about living and nonliving things. It is important to have books that are well illustrated. An excellent and inexpensive series of books with color illustrations is the *Golden Guides* series. It is available in inexpensive paperback editions at many bookstores and from the publisher:

Western Publishing Company, 1220 Mound Avenue, Racine, WI 53404. Some representative titles are *Birds, Weeds, Flowers, Stars, Reptiles and Amphibians, Rocks and Minerals, Spiders, Fossils, Pond Life,* and *Seashores.* There are also *Golden Science Guides* on topics such as the *Heart, Weather, Ecology, Geology, Light and Color,* and *Oceanography.*

Language Experience Charts

"How can children read *science* material if they can barely read at all?" This lament is a familiar one in some schools. But science material can readily be made to serve the needs of beginning readers.

It is natural for young children to learn new vocabulary words when they have firsthand experiences in science. They are more likely to organize and remember these experiences if they summarize and record what they have learned. The making of a language experience chart prompts them to describe their experiences in a form that can be written down. The technique is well suited to primary-level students or older children who read poorly or not at all.

In a first-grade room, the teacher suggests that the class make a chart to tell parents about a just-finished chick-hatching activity. A general discussion follows about the events and their sequence. The teacher lists some key words on the chalkboard as they come up: *incubator, turned over, hatched, shells, fluffy.*

Refer to the key words to establish a sequence: What happened first? next? Once the sequence is determined, individual students are invited to dictate what happened. Each child is called on to describe one event or respond to one narrow question about an event.

The teacher carefully writes what is said on a sheet of large lined paper but tries to keep each sentence short and clear, so everyone can read it. He says each word aloud as he writes, then reads the whole sentence aloud, has the dictating child do so, and then the whole class reads the sentence out loud. For example:

Mr. Simpson gave us six chicken eggs.

We put them in an incubator.

We turned them over every day.

Three chicks hatched after 21 days.

They broke the shells and got out.

They were wet.

Then they got dry and fluffy.

The class next reads aloud the entire chart in unison. Then individual volunteers each read a line in response to some questions. A title is agreed on and written above the first line.

Being aware of individual differences, the teacher asks the children to copy as few as four to as many as seven lines of the story on lined paper and circulates to help as needed. Students also copy several words of their own choosing onto their individual word lists for later use.

Children with sparse early reading backgrounds probably would find the preceding language experience chart too hard. To make it easier, ask narrow questions, keep the chart message limited to fewer lines at first, use shorter sentences and more word repetition, and furnish sentence patterns when you can, such as:

"How many eggs did we get?"

We got six eggs.

Regularly summarizing students' experiences on charts rapidly improves their sight vocabulary of commonly spoken words. It becomes easier for them to read longer sentences and focus on new science words as successive charts are read. This also makes them more able to write and read their own charts about their science experiences.

NONREADING MATERIALS

What nonreading resources can you expect to find in most schools today? They may include:

- still pictures,
- models,
- microscopes,

■ televisions,

■ videocassettes, and

■ microcomputers and related equipment.

Strictly speaking, even these materials may require some reading. Select and use each resource for a specific purpose, just as you would a book.

Pictorial Materials

You can use pictures and television in three general ways:

1. To introduce or overview lessons and raise problems.

2. To help answer questions or explain difficult ideas.

3. To summarize or extend with more examples what has been studied.

Illustrations, or pictures, are probably among the most common aids used in elementary science. There are many magazines in which suitable illustrations may be found. Books may also contain helpful photographs or drawings. Sometimes you can get valuable pictures from old or discarded books.

Growing numbers of teachers are using *videodiscs* (see page 145) in place of still pictures and slides. These can be imported into computers for multimedia projects. Publishers sometimes include discs with science series.

Television programs in science are now regularly scheduled in many school districts, on cable, closed circuit television, or a public broadcasting station. Schedules and teaching guides are generally distributed to teachers. The teacher typically presents an overview of the lesson, raises some questions or points to consider with the students, and acts as a discussion leader after the telecast. A *VCR* may be helpful for taping shows to replay at convenient times. Many elementary science specials and TV programs are also available on videocassettes.

The nation's largest disseminator of instructional television, the Corporation for Public Broadcasting, allows schools limited copying privileges for numerous shows. Some of its best programs for elementary science are *3-2-1 Contact, Square One Television, Newton's Apple,* and the *Magic School Bus Series.* It's likely that your local public television authority has these series and others. For a free comprehensive listing of CPB programs correlated with the most used elementary science programs, write to:

Corporation for Public Broadcasting, Office of Education, 1111 Sixteenth Street, N.W., Washington, DC 20036.

Bill Nye the Science Guy and *Beakman's World* are also popular with elementary students. These personalities have Internet sites (see page 143).

Science Equipment

When you begin teaching, you will need resources for science activities. What types of equipment will enhance your open-ended and closed-ended activities?

Microscopes and Dissecting Scopes

"Let's see what the grasshopper's mouth looks like!" Sometimes children want to see a small object more clearly than they can with the naked eye. For the most part, a hand lens or magnifier is sufficient, especially for primary-level children. From about Grade 3 on, a *microscope* may also be helpful. One example of a good elementary microscope is shown in Figure 5-2. This instrument uses a light source instead of a mirror to insure that students will be able to see images. Attachments can also be purchased to connect cameras to the lenses.

Figure 5-2
A suitable microscope for elementary schools.

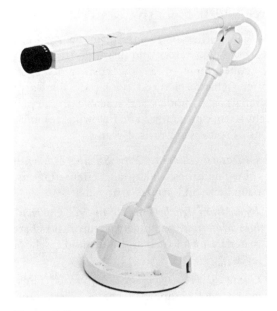

Figure 5-3
A video camera/microscope combination.
Courtesy of Cannon Visual Communications.

A dissecting microscope may also be effective for looking at small objects. These do not require slides and are generally more powerful than a hand lens.

Because it is difficult to be sure of what children are viewing, and since the number of microscopes will often be limited, many teachers prefer a *video camera/microscope* combination (see Figure 5-3). With this instrument, it is possible to project an enlarged image of the specimen onto a television screen—especially convenient when instructing a whole class, because everyone can view together what is taking place.

Models

School and district instructional media centers often have models you can borrow for instruction. These may range from the familiar globe model of the earth to a model skeleton that can be taken apart and assembled again.

In many classrooms, time is also given to constructing models and apparatus. The best kinds of constructions teach an idea or process or help to gather data. Working constructions such as telegraphs, weather instruments, and electric circuit boards encourage thoughtful planning on the part of children.

Less useful are constructions that might be called props. These are more decorative than functional. A model volcano that flows with colored baking soda and vinegar is an example. This is not to say that such materials are useless, since they have a purpose in dramatic play or art-centered activities.

Free and Inexpensive Materials

You can borrow or acquire many instructional aids from commercial and institutional sources, by request only or at low cost. Videotapes, posters, charts, pictures, booklets, samples of materials, and models are available to supplement science programs. The following compilations of sources are revised yearly.

Educators Guide to Free Science Materials (films, filmstrips, slides, tapes, transcriptions, pamphlets, and printed materials)

Elementary Teachers Guide to Free Curriculum Materials (pamphlet, picture, and chart materials for elementary and middle school levels)

Guide to Free Computer Materials (films, videotapes, pamphlets, charts, disks, and more)

These guides are often found in university and school district curriculum libraries. All are available at reasonable cost from:

Educators Progress Service, 214 Center Street, Randolph, WI 53956.

NSTA Reports, the newsletter of the National Science Teachers Association, contains a section on freebies. Be sure to use school stationery whenever you request free supplementary materials, since you will then be more likely to receive them.

INFORMAL EDUCATION SITES

It is possible to get so engrossed in acquiring materials for firsthand experiences, books, and other instructional aids that we forget there is an out-of-class environment for science exploration. Consider the zoo experience in Vignette 5-1. What could be considered a fun-only field trip can be turned into a real learning experience for your students. In fact, the school building itself is a good place to start.

School and Surroundings

Objects and events introduced in science programs become more understandable when they show up as real-life examples in familiar places: Why are there cracks in the masonry and plaster? How do the automatic fire sprinklers work? How many simple machines does the school custodian use?

Things are also happening on the school grounds. Why are they planting ground cover on the hill? What makes the hot asphalt on the playground "steam" after the cloudburst? What are the names of the birds around the schoolyard, and where do they nest?

Community Resources

Where can your students see science-related objects and events in their community? There might be many places to explore: a zoo, wooded area, garden, nursery, greenhouse, pond, brook, bird refuge, observatory, natural history museum, road cut, construction site, waterworks, sewage treatment plant, dairy, airport, and weather bureau. These are rewarding places for elementary school students to visit.

Before you take a trip, some preparation will help make it worthwhile. A school district catalog of suggested places to visit in the community may be available. This can furnish the necessary details for educational trips. In general, however, you will want to keep the following points in mind:

1. Be clear about the purpose for leaving the classroom.
2. Check with the principal about school policies.
3. Visit the site yourself.
4. Plan with the children what to look for on the trip.

VIGNETTE

5-1

USING THE ZOO AS A SCIENCE EDUCATION RESOURCE

Dr. Sue Dale Tunnicliffe

ICASE Primary Projects and Homerton College, University of Cambridge, England

Visits to live animal collections can provide excellent opportunities for science learning, if the teachers taking the students are familiar with the pedagogy of such visits and what opportunities are available. The knowledge that is needed by teachers for zoo visits (and those to other animal collections such as natural history museums) include:

1. the stages of a visit in terms of the attention of pupils during the visit to the animals;

2. the features of anatomy and behaviors of the animals that the students are likely to notice spontaneously;

3. the colloquial or everyday names the students will use and any scientific names you want to be used;

4. being able to identify and understand the concepts that you wish your students to acquire.

Otherwise the content of the conversations generated replicates that of family groups who visit the zoo for leisure purposes.

STAGES OF A VISIT

Students—and their accompanying adults—do not focus on exhibits in the same manner throughout their visit. It is important to be aware of the different phases within a school visit and plan activities for your students accordingly.

First of all, groups undergo an orientation phase, when they look around and find their way. The duration of this stage can be shortened if you provide orientation to the site at school. Such orientations can be achieved through showing slides or a video, providing the groups with a timetable, discussing opportunities for visits to the gift shop, when and where lunch is to be taken, and similar "housekeeping" arrangements.

(continued)

Vignette 5-1 (continued)

Following orientation, the group embarks upon a concentrated phase of focussing on the tasks you have set looking in a concentrated manner at exhibits, or participating in an educational activity provided by the zoo. It is unrealistic to expect the students to be involved in a focused task throughout the visit. After their concentration wanes, they move into the leisure-looking phase, during which their comments and observations are similar to those of "non-education" visitors. Finally, there is a leave-taking phase when the attention of the group is concerned with gathering together for the journey home.

SPONTANEOUS OBSERVATIONS OF PUPILS
(AND ACCOMPANYING ADULTS)

There is a fundamental pattern that elementary students, their accompanying adults, and family groups follow when looking at animal exhibits. It is important to be aware of this so that you can plan your activities for young students and the questions the accompanying adults or the activity sheets will ask of them, so that these topics are the starting points for science observations. Children spontaneously notice certain phenomena, so use these as the introduction to the topic you plan.

NAMES

Children spontaneously use everyday or colloquial names. Use these names when referring to the animals, but make it clear to everyone which additional name(s) you want them to use and where, so that zoological classification can be developed with the students during the visit or back in school.

These everyday or colloquial names include the use of the term *animal* to mean only mammals. Within the mammals, people talk about cats, horses, zebras, rhinos, elephants, lions, tigers, hippos, bats, and seals. Visitors rarely use the specific names unless the animal is particularly well known or has captured the public's imagination, e.g., snow leopard. The identifying term *bird* is provided for any bird other than very memorable ones such as ostrich, eagle, penguin, vulture, and parrot. Reptiles are never referred to as such, unless the term is used by the zoo to designate a building, such as Reptile House. Reptiles are generally referred to individually as snakes, crocodiles (usually including the other crocodilians), turtles (for any of the chelonia), and lizards. I have never heard the term *reptile* applied by school groups to animals displayed in zoos. Few zoos show amphibians, but the everyday terms *frog* and *toad* are used to refer to most of the specimens. Fish are called *fish* by the identifier except for sharks, piranhas, eels, and any particular species about which the visitor happens to have firsthand knowledge, such as chubb or perch. Young students, those under seven years, are unable to cope with two names for one animal; if they call a shark by that name, they deny that it is also a fish. Similarly, all insects and arachnids are "bugs" (in the everyday sense, not the zoological one) unless they know the name, such as ladybug. Spiders are just that unless they are a tarantula or black widow.

ANATOMICAL FEATURES AND BEHAVIOR SPONTANEOUSLY NOTICED

When looking at the structure of the animals, the student will spontaneously comment on the shape, size, color, any particularly unusual feature such as horns, and parts that disrupt the body outline and/or move, such as legs and tails. If the animal is performing some behavior, the students will notice it. The position of the animal within the enclosure or display case is important to the children and school. Groups also refer in about half of all conversations to other aspects of the exhibit such as rocks and trees or feeding bowls. Very often such nonanimal aspects are used in referring to the location of the animal.

If the animal is doing nothing, the children will query whether it is real, a common question posed about crocodilians in zoos. In the museums, the children will be interested in the authenticity of the specimens and how they were prepared for display. Thus, the meaning of the word *real* depends on the context in which it is used. Often, children use the word *real* to refer to whether the animal is alive or not.

SCIENCE LEARNING OPPORTUNITIES

The science learning opportunities in a zoo or museum for elementary students are: content (science facts), the process (science method and inquiry), and science language and communication skills.

The science content can be biological or physical. The biological content is either botanical (which highlights the role of plants in the food chain and forming the natural habitats of animals) or about the animals.

Zoological studies can focus on taxonomic studies or on adaptations to the environment, including adaptations for feeding. Animal behaviors are used to establish the taxonomy of a specimen as well as to study adaptation and forms. Behavior is thus another important area of study, in which students can make, record, and interpret their firsthand observations of the animals. Such studies require the students to observe salient features of animals, such as form, number of locomotory organs, and body covering.

Elementary students should be able to group animals into their major groups—mammals, reptiles, birds, fish, amphibians, arthropods, mollusks, and annelid worms and say why they make these categorizations. Students should be able to use branching keys and picture keys at Grade 4, and by Grade 6 they should be able to use and con-

(continued)

Vignette 5-1 (continued)

struct dichotomous keys. Students should develop an understanding of the needs of animals and the essential life processes—and be able to identify how individual specimens meet them.

However, zoos are often poor at providing realistic habitats, and visiting a zoo with the aim of learning about natural habitats is often unrealistic. Such studies may be more satisfactorily pursued in natural history museums with natural-looking dioramas.

Animal behavior studies can be frustrating if the students are looking for action. Inaction is just as important, and should be used constructively. Find out before your visit which animals are likely to be active and visible within their enclosures. Ask about the pattern of the day of inactive and inaccessible animals, so that the students can be given a time chart for these animals and can identify which part of their activity profile the animals are in when the students observe them. Ask the students to find the pattern of these animals' days so that the lack of activity is not a source of frustration, but an active learning experience.

Adaptation to the environment is a topic that is often well presented by zoo education programs. Decide which adaptations you wish your students to focus on. Very popular topics are birds' beaks (studying adaptations within this class of animals for different types of food and hence different habitats), feet in mammals and birds, color of body coverings, and camouflage.

Planning and delivering the opportunities for experiences that involve your students is essential. Instead of replying with a name when a student asks "What is that animal?", ask the student to work out what it could be as far as she is able. Should a student identify an animal, ask him what features enabled him to make that identification.

Science is about communicating. If scientists don't communicate, no one else knows of their work. Encourage your students to share their observations and findings in a variety of ways: a science report, drama, art, a journalist's report, or a spoken address.

It is very important to communicate to the chaperones who accompany your students the aims and objectives in terms of education outcomes, as well as the "housekeeping" details. If this is not done, the experience that students within the chaperoned groups receive is different from that experienced by the students with you. It is up to us as the teachers to ensure that each student has equal access to an effective experience.

5. Develop behavior and safety standards to be remembered.

6. At the site, make sure everyone can see and hear adequately.

7. Ask questions if desired.

8. After returning to the classroom, help students evaluate the trip.

When it is impossible to arrange visits away from the school, resource persons from the community may be able to visit your classroom.

Many districts compile lists of informed persons who are willing to volunteer. For an example of ideas concerning informal education, see:

Druger, M. (Ed.). (1988). *Science for the Fun of It: A Guide to Informal Science Education*. Arlington, VA: National Science Teachers Association.

Rennie, L. R., & McClafferty, T. (1995). Using visits to interactive science and technology centers, museums, aquaria, and zoos to promote learning in science. *Journal of Science Teacher Education, 6* (4), 175–185.

RESOURCES FOR TEACHING STUDENTS WITH SPECIAL NEEDS

Inclusion is a concept which is becoming the standard in most K–12 classrooms. An inclusive classroom is one where there is a mix of physical and mental developmental levels of students, accommodating those identified as disabled in some way. According to the Department of Education, nearly 12 percent of students were identified as disabled during the period 1991–1994 (U.S. Department of Education [DOE], 1994). This number represents an increase from earlier times, primarily due to the *Education of All Handicapped Children Act* (Public Law 94–142; now renamed the Individuals with Disabilities Education Act), which guarantees a free, appropriate education in the least restrictive environment for students with disabilities. Science instruction should be a part of this "appropriate education."

There are some problems with science instruction for students with disabilities, however. A recent study (Stefanich & Norman, 1996) includes information that:

- students with mild disabilities received only 1 minute of science instruction for every 200 minutes of reading instruction,

- elementary science teachers have little training or experience in teaching students with disabilities, and

- most teachers agree that disabled students benefit from hands-on instruction, yet the reality is that they are generally taught from the textbook.

Elementary teachers need to understand that the special educator will probably not take primary responsibility for science instruction, since students will be in regular classrooms. The elementary teacher will have to seek out opportunities during college and through in-service to gain a better understanding of disadvantaged children and how to teach them effectively. The following sections are designed as a first step in assisting you with this.

Assisting Students with Disabilities

Mainstreaming presents both opportunities and challenges to people in schools. Mainstreamed children learn to live and work in settings that are more likely to develop their potentials to the fullest. The other children profit from a heightened sensitivity and a greater capacity to live and work with individual differences.

The challenges largely come from the diversity of handicaps found in special education. Everyone who comes to your classroom has been identified as a teachable child. To help ensure this, you should share in the placement decision. The disabled students who require the most change in the science curriculum are the totally blind or deaf children. For most students with disabilities, a solid hands-on program gives the multisensory experiences they need to learn science well.

Also, realize that an Individualized Education Plan (IEP) is developed for each child by a *team* of persons. Included on the team is at least one person qualified in special education. With a team, you are able to draw on more skills, information, and ideas than by working alone. Responsibility for the child's progress is shared by the team. In many states, the IEP is also accompanied by whatever special instructional media and materials the team believes are essential to meet objectives.

What are some of the characteristics of students with disabilities you are likely to teach? How can you generally help them? What resources can you draw on that apply specifically to science? The following sections will review the visually impaired, hearing impaired, orthopedically impaired, and mentally disabled students.

VISUALLY IMPAIRED. The problems of visually impaired children may range from poor eyesight to total blindness. Most mainstreamed students will have at least some functional vision; however, these students frequently lack firsthand experience with many objects, which is reflected in their language. Vocabulary and descriptive capacity, therefore, need considerable strengthening. Keep in mind the following points with visually impaired students:

1. Use concrete, multisensory experiences to build a greater store of needed percepts.

2. Give plenty of time to explore and encourage the use of descriptive language during explorations.

3. Encourage communication with the student throughout activity periods.

4. Use tactile cues with materials, such as a knotted string for measuring.

5. Walk the child through spaces to demonstrate barriers and tactile clues.

6. Encourage the use of any remaining vision.

7. Encourage other students to be sensitive about their use of phrases such as "over there," "like that one," or any descriptions that require vision.

8. Be tolerant of, and prepared for, spilled or scattered material.

9. Use oral language or a recorder for instructions and information.

10. Pair the child with a tactful, sighted partner who can assist in the scaffolding process discussed on page 45.

The American Printing House for the Blind (see page 122 for address) produces several current elementary science series in large print and braille. Illustrations and graphs are often in the form of touchable raised-line drawings.

HEARING IMPAIRED. The hearing of these children may range from mildly impaired to totally deaf. Most wear a hearing aid and have partial hearing. Communication is easier when the child can read lips and certain facial movements, and when sign language is used. Delayed language development is common. When teaching science to the hearing impaired, remember to:

1. Use concrete objects—pictures, sketches, signs, and the like—to get across ideas.

2. Seat the child close to you or the sound source.

3. Give clear directions and face the child as you speak.

4. Speak with usual volume and speed.

5. Model, rather than correct, pronunciations for the partially deaf child.

6. Allow longer periods of wait-time.

7. Make sure you have the child's attention; use direct eye contact.

8. Use gestures and body language, but don't exaggerate these.

9. Avoid speaking for the child or having classmates speak for the child.

10. Talk with the child frequently about what she is doing.

11. Maintain good lighting in the classroom.

ORTHOPEDICALLY IMPAIRED. Orthopedically impaired children typically have gross or fine motor malfunctions that cause problems in locomotion, coordination, balance, and dexterity. One of the most common impairments is cerebral palsy. Orthopedically disabled students may use walkers, wheelchairs, crutches, braces, or other aids. Keep in mind the following when teaching the orthopedically impaired:

1. Encourage participation in all possible activities.
2. Modify activities as much as possible to avoid frustrations.
3. Encourage the use of limbs to the fullest ability.
4. Find alternative ways to manipulate things.
5. Allow alternative methods for the child to respond.
6. Keep traffic lanes clear in the classroom.
7. Acknowledge and deal openly with feelings of frustration.
8. Have another student assist the child in moving to the next activity if needed.
9. Promote the child's confidence and independence whenever possible.
10. Use activities that foster problem solving and growth in thinking skills.
11. Present materials and activities at a comfortable height for individuals in wheelchairs.

MENTALLY DISABLED STUDENTS. Mentally disabled students show significantly subaverage abilities in cognitive tasks and often in motor development. They are likely to have problems in learning, remembering, problem solving, and life skills. Other frequent characteristics are short attention span, poor selective attention, and limited ability to make choices. Children who are victims of alcohol- or drug-abusing parents may exhibit these conditions. Often, the mentally disabled child will require shorter work periods, more concrete tasks, more direct and structured instruction, and more frequent reinforcement, because of her short attention span. Keep in mind the following points when teaching science to mentally disabled students:

1. Use a variety of hands-on teaching methods and materials.
2. Be sure you have the child's attention before you give directions and frequently have them repeat directions.
3. Demonstrate and model as you give simple, clear directions.
4. Review new concepts and vocabulary.
5. Break tasks down to simple, step-by-step parts if necessary.
6. Use the least complex language possible when giving instructions.
7. Outline expectations clearly for the child before work begins.
8. Review and summarize ideas and procedures frequently. Have the child recapitulate experiences.
9. Give positive reinforcement immediately after each small success.
10. Give responsibility within the child's limits, and let the child observe and assist in a role before giving him responsibility.
11. Apply previously constructed concepts to everyday experiences.
12. Begin instruction with what the child knows and build on that.

DISABLED CHILDREN. Disabled students are much more likely to have a poor self-concept than other children. Many adults realize this, but overprotect the disabled in order to compensate. Unfortunately, this inhibits development and confidence. Disabled children, in turn, often learn and accept overdependence, so a cycle develops that feeds on itself. Keep the following in mind:

1. Consider whether help is *necessary*, rather than convenient.
2. Except for obvious needs, get consent from the child before giving help.
3. Don't persist if the child declines help; let the child discover whether help is needed.
4. Provide prompts instead of answers.
5. Allow peers to help or offer help matter-of-factly.

DISABLED AS INDIVIDUALS. There are many other kinds of disabilities found in mainstreaming, including the learning disabled, the speech/language impaired, the health impaired and those with multiple handicaps. Be aware that entire books are devoted to each one of these and the previously described handicaps. Fortunately, there is no need to become an expert in special education to help a specific mainstreamed child. Although it is nice to have some general knowledge about a handicap, *it is far more important to know how that handicap affects a particular child and what the child's individual instructional needs are.* You learn this by working with the child.

RESOURCES FOR SCIENCE TEACHING. There are several sources that offer programs and information to better teach the students with disabilities in the regular classroom. An excellent and well-tested program is *FOSS*, the *Full Option Science System.* Designed for *both* handicapped and nonhandicapped students in Grades K–6, it was developed at the Lawrence Hall of Science. FOSS is an outgrowth of earlier projects to improve science education for visually impaired and physically disabled students. Several modules at each grade level include lesson plans in the earth, life, and physical sciences. Extension activities include work in language, computer, and mathematics applications. The developers worked hard to match activities with students' ability to think at dif-

ferent ages. Further work was done to make the program easy to instruct and manage. The commercial distributor of FOSS is:

> Encyclopedia Britannica Educational Corporation, 310 South Michigan Avenue, Chicago, IL 60604.

Some further sources that can help you plan lessons for children with different disabilities are:

> Alexander Graham Bell Association for the Deaf, 3417 Volta Place, N.W., Washington, DC 20007.

> American Printing House for the Blind, P.O. Box 6085, Louisville, KY 40206.

> Center for Multisensory Learning, Lawrence Hall of Science, University of California, Berkeley, CA 94720.

> ERIC Clearinghouse on Handicapped and Gifted Children, 1920 Association Drive, Reston, VA 22091.

> National Center on Educational Media and Materials for the Handicapped, Ohio State University, 154 West 12th Avenue, Columbus, OH 43210.

Working with Limited English Proficiency Students

Not long ago, only a few cities in the United States contained significant numbers of schoolchildren whose native language was not English. Today they are present in nearly every school. Foreign-born students who do not speak English may be placed in bilingual classrooms and taught by someone who is proficient in both English and the foreign language. As the students acquire some English proficiency, they are mainstreamed for larger parts of the school day. In other schools, they are taught in all-English classrooms. As a regular classroom teacher, expect to have at least some students of limited English proficiency (LEP) from time to time.

Many LEP students experience some culture shock, since what they observe now may differ radically from their earlier environment. They may be reluctant to speak because they are afraid to make mistakes. Your warm acceptance and frequent praise will boost their confidence. Whatever you can do to reduce anxiety, to increase meaning of content studied, to model good English, and to increase chances to informally interact with English speakers will benefit them. Here are some things that can work for you.

1. Use a listening–speaking–reading–writing sequence in teaching whenever possible. Listening lays the foundation for the other language skills. It's easier to speak what we have first heard, read what we have spoken, and write what we have read.

2. Use multisensory, hands-on teaching methods whenever you can. Concrete materials, investigations, demonstrations, audiovisual media, graphs, and diagrams are more likely to foster meaningful learning. One great advantage of hands-on science over most other subjects is that the actual doing demands little verbal ability.

3. Pair LEP students with bilingual partners or in cooperative learning groups to increase the scaffolding effect.

4. Speak slowly, use short sentences, and rephrase what you say if a child seems unsure rather than just repeating what you have said. Use body language, props, pictures and sketches to clarify your words.

5. Check more specifically whether a child understands by asking questions answerable by *yes* or *no*, or by having the child do something you can observe, such as point to an object.

6. Avoid idiomatic expressions; they can be confusing when taken literally: "It's as easy as pie."

7. Make whatever you refer to as concrete as possible—what you know the children have done or observed in the past. Give observable examples in the present as well: "The handle of this pencil sharpener is also a lever."

8. To help students build schemata, write key concepts and vocabulary used during a lesson on the chalkboard. Often make a concept map to outline what is to come in a lesson or to summarize the content of a lesson.

9. Emphasize and repeat key words of the lesson as you teach. This cues the child about what to remember and how the words sound.

10. For the easiest and most meaningful reading, make language experience charts. Try interactive reading as well. (Pages 111, 109.)

Students who are becoming proficient in English require some extra time and attention, but they can also enrich the curriculum by bringing multicultural knowledge and perspectives to what is studied.

There are sixteen regional resource centers for bilingual education in the United States that offer training and technical support services to schools. For the center nearest you, call or write:

The National Clearinghouse for Bilingual Education, 1118 22nd Street, N.W., Washington, DC 20037 (Telephone: 800-321-6223).

These references from the National Clearinghouse can also further your work with LEP students:

Hamayan, E., & Perlman, R. (1990). *Helping Language Minority Students After They Exit From Bilingual/ESL Programs: A Handbook for Teachers.*

Short, D. J. (1991). *Integrating Language and Content Instruction: Strategies and Techniques.*

Working with Gifted Students

What can you expect from mainstreamed students classified as gifted by your district? Gifted children display many of the same developmental qualities as most children. What is different is the greater *degree* to which, and the *speed* with which, these qualities develop. In kindergarten, for example, gifted students may perform like second graders. By their senior year in high school, they typically outperform average college seniors on academic tests.

What are some of their attributes? Compared to other students, the gifted child is much more likely to:

1. Tolerate ambiguity and complexity.
2. Have a longer attention span.
3. Be a highly curious and sharp-eyed observer.
4. Be a top-notch reader who retains what is read.
5. Have a well-developed speaking and listening vocabulary.
6. Have learned the basic skills well.
7. Understand complex directions the first time around.
8. Be imaginative and receptive to new ideas.
9. Be interested in broad concepts and issues.
10. Have one or more hobbies that require thinking.

Gifted students who show all or most of these attributes are often placed in a full-time special class or a pull-out program for part of the school day. But many are totally mainstreamed. How can we challenge these children?

A common problem with having gifted children in regular classrooms is that the curriculum is restrictive and unchallenging for them. They soon become bored and often will seek attention in disruptive ways.

A way to handle this is to use many open-ended investigations and activities. This stimulates the kind of creative, divergent thinking gifted students need to grow toward their potential. Fortunately for us as teachers, these and other experiences described next also work well for most of the nongifted students.

A second important way to help mainstreamed gifted students is to encourage them to build a large knowledge base. This is usually easy because of their broad curiosity, strong ability to locate and understand information, and ability to remember what they find out. A wide variety of open-ended science investigations stimulates them to try multiple observations and experiments and to read for background. Gifted children readily sense how a broad array of knowledge feeds their creative and problem-solving abilities. This motivates them to learn even more.

A third way to help gifted students is to let them manage their own learning through individual and small group projects, including those done for school science fairs. The investigations in Part II of this book can be valuable here, as can the references at the end of this section. Independent study also is fostered when we show students how to locate and use references, trade books, and other instructional materials in the school library.

A fourth way to help gifted students is by exposing them to persons in science and other professions who can serve as information sources and future role models. This is particularly important for students who come from economically disadvantaged backgrounds. Gifted children have the interest and quickly develop the capacity to correspond with knowledgeable adults, interview them by phone or in person, and understand much of what they see and hear.

We can also help gifted students by attending to their social skills as they interact with other children. Some of these students may be advanced academically but be average in social and personal skills. Not only are these skills needed for success in many professions, but for personal happiness as well. A central objective for mainstreaming the gifted is to help them communicate and get along with persons of all ability levels.

Remember that gifted students may not necessarily be gifted in math and science. Monitor your expectations to make sure that you are not expecting too much from a child who may be gifted only in language, art, music, or another area.

The following references can help you work with the gifted and the nongifted:

Hege, P. MAP: *Student Counseling Guide.* Durham, NC: Duke University Talent Identification Program (1121 West Main Street, Suite 100, 27701; includes resource information).

De Vito, A., & Krockover, G. H. (1991). *Creative Sciencing.* Glenview, IL: Scott Foresman (Good Year Books). (A broad spectrum of creative activities to explore concepts.)

De Vito, A. (1989). *Creative Wellsprings for Science Teaching.* W. Lafayette, IN: Creative Ventures. (Imaginative projects and puzzlers.)

MANAGING HANDS-ON ACTIVITIES

Many new teachers feel overwhelmed at the thought of transitioning from student teaching a few students or an entire class—under another teacher's supervision—to independently teaching their own class. What are some strategies for coping with this situation?

Whole-Class Teaching

If you have a shortage of materials for an activity, one way to resolve this problem is to work with the entire class at one time. A well-thought-out seating arrangement and a mixture of broad and narrow questions addressed to individual children can be effective. It is important for individual children to have quick access to the materials when called on or when they want to do something to find out what happens.

Figure 5-4 shows how this can be done. A low table is placed near a chalkboard, and movable chairs are arranged before it in a semicircle. Half the children sit on chairs, and half sit cross-legged on the floor in front of the chairs. Everyone is close to the table and has a clear view. There is ready access to the table as individual children are called on to participate. An arrangement of this kind is very useful with younger children since it is easy for them to lose interest or become distracted when seated some distance away from the activity.

The semicircular pattern is also convenient at other times. If a candle flame, hot plate, or other potentially hazardous item is needed in an activity, you can demonstrate the activity in a safe setting (don't forget safety glasses). You can also set standards with students for small-group activities and assign areas of the room for working. After several groups have completed their work, you can reassemble them into the initial seating pattern for easier reporting or discussion.

With older children there is less need for this type of seating arrangement. The regular grouping of desks and chairs may serve for most occasions, but keep the materials table reasonably close to all the children when exper-

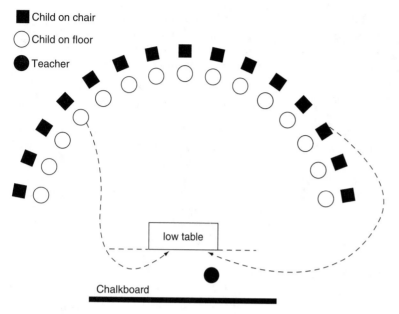

Legend:
■ Child on chair
○ Child on floor
● Teacher

low table

Chalkboard

Figure 5-4
This arrangement makes it easy to either view or participate in an activity before the whole class.

iments and demonstrations are done before the entire class. There is usually no trouble with class control when everyone can see what is happening. In some schools, you will find a remote-controlled mirror in combination with a demonstration table. This allows for all students to see demonstrations.

Group Teaching

When more materials are available, you can organize the class into smaller groups of two, three, or four students each. Many activities need two people, so even numbers usually work best. Suppose, for example, you have five sets of materials for one activity. You can divide the class into five groups, and have each work with one set.

You can do much the same thing with one set of materials for each of five activities. Here, the children rotate from one table or learning station to the next after a designated time (see Figure 5-5).

Cooperative Learning and Inquiry Task Groups

There are many models of cooperative learning appropriate for science education. There are distinct advantages and disadvantages to each model but, overall, the advantages to cooperative learning are that:

■ Each student has an opportunity to assume a leadership, recording, managerial, or communicative role on a rotating basis.

■ Scaffolding is maximized since each group will contain knowledgeable others who can contribute new insights and allow students to learn things which they could not have on their own.

■ There is less traffic throughout the classroom since only one student per group will gather materials, intermediate, or clean up afterwards.

■ It is easier to manage a small number of groups than to oversee every student completing each activity.

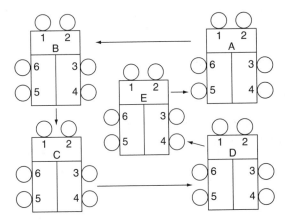

Figure 5-5
This arrangement shows how children might move from one learning station to the next after a designated time.

■ There may only be enough materials for a select number of groups, instead of each student.

Some disadvantages can be that:

■ Children construct knowledge on their own and therefore each child should perform, record, and communicate *each* activity. This way they can construct concepts for themselves as opposed to someone else completing the activity while they record information, gather materials, or clean up.

■ Heterogeneous groupings can lead to gender bias as the traditional male-dominant pattern appears and the boys "take over" activities.

■ Noise levels may go up in the classroom as groups communicate among themselves.

As you can see, the advantages and disadvantages are not so clear that one could make a quick decision either way. What you will have to do is weigh the pros and cons for the activity which you are considering. If you are contemplating the use of cooperative learning, the Inquiry Task Group Management System has proven to be effective for managing cooperative

activities (Jones, 1990). This model is based on small groups of three or more students who perform a specific task in support of a science activity. The assignment of roles allows for an orderly and productive learning situation. The system also indirectly teaches leadership, recording, and maintenance skills as students rotate to new roles with subsequent activities. Figure 5-6 illustrates the various roles which students perform.

ADVANCE PREPARATION. Select an interesting and worthwhile investigation. What materials are needed that you have on hand or must be brought in? Are there enough materials for two to four students? Sometime before the science period, select a group of students to prepare trays or shoe boxes of materials for each group.

BEGINNING/INTRODUCTION. Usually children are anxious to get started right away, so make the introduction as brief as possible. Review social skills (respect for others, listening) or safety rules and introduce the activity.

Ask someone to repeat the directions for the class *while* you have the responsible students pick up the materials. This prevents dead time. If one or two groups still have questions, their group will try to answer them first. Say *everything* you need to say *before* the whole class gets down to work! Interrupting the class with further directions and other afterthoughts distracts the children, wastes time, and often requires more effort than expected.

MIDDLE/WORK PERIOD. Walk around to different groups and observe how they are doing. Try to spend no more than a minute with one group so you can keep attentively circulating. Stand when possible where you can see all groups as you assist one group. Sometimes, simple eye contact with a child who starts to get off task quickly stops misbehavior. Encourage students to help themselves as much

Title	Role
Principal researcher	The person in charge of all procedures and personnel. They perform the activity.
Staff accountant	The child appointed to record, process, and verify the data and group activities.
Maintenance engineer	The person responsible for cleaning up after the activity and returning equipment.
Group ambassador	The only person allowed to communicate with the teacher or ambassadors from other groups.
Resource manager	The person charged with securing the materials needed to complete the activity.
Scientific consultant	The person who provides advice or assistance where needed.
Media specialist	The person who will prepare a presentation to the class.

Figure 5-6
Group job descriptions.
NOTE: When using three students, combine the role of Maintenance Engineer, Ambassador, and Resource Manager and use the title "Manager"). For four students, combine the roles of Maintenance Engineer and Resource Manager. When there are more than four children, add additional roles as needed.

as possible. Quietly praise helpful behavior as you notice it. If there is a problem, give the group time to work on it (unless it is a safety issue). Model what to do rather than criticize unhelpful behavior. Make a few brief notes about helpful behavior or any other matter you may want to bring up later with the whole class. A class reward system may be helpful if continual social problems occur (page 30).

When it is time, give the signal for cleanup. Wait until everyone stops and makes eye contact with you. Then tell the class to continue. Be sure that all groups begin and end cleanup at about the same time.

END/CLEANUP AND DISCUSSION. Students responsible for cleaning up should work quickly. Other students should stay in their seats and work quietly. The maintenance engineer makes sure everything is present, then quickly takes the tray back to the materials table. If some things need cleaning, this may be done at a later time.

You might also mention several helpful comments or courtesies on positive behaviors you observed in some groups. Recognize the group before the class, and its members will appreciate and welcome these contributions from their peers even more.

SUMMARY

1. The quality of your science program is strongly influenced by the teaching resources you select. Most elementary programs use common, everyday materials.

These are ordinarily easy to gather, especially if you ask others to help.

2. Both reading and nonreading classroom materials are needed to teach science. Reading materials include textbooks, trade books, reference materials, and language experience charts.

3. Nonreading materials include kits, free and inexpensive items, models, microscopes, and visual aids. The school yard, zoos, science centers, and museums also present concrete examples of objects and events introduced in the science program.

4. Some special resources and ways to use them are needed for mainstreamed exceptional students. A school advisory team is likely to meet with you to compose an Individualized Education Plan (IEP) for each disabled student. You can help students of limited English proficiency by reducing their anxiety, increasing content meaning, modeling good English, and giving them many chances to informally interact with English speakers. Gifted and talented children thrive on open-ended, divergent investigations and activities.

5. The Inquiry Task Group Management System is a good way to assist in hands-on activities. This model is based on small groups of three or more students who perform a specific task in support of a science activity.

REFLECTION

1. Write to several of the contact agencies listed in this chapter and start a resource collection for when you start teaching. Share some of the better items with the class.

2. Observe an elementary science class and focus on the students reading the text. Are they comfortable with the information or struggling to read it (either silently or orally)? Ask some specific questions to see whether the students understand what they are reading. If not, use the cloze method or

check with the language arts professor and determine other ways to evaluate the text.

3. Are there students with disabilities at your practicum site? Discuss the impact this has on the classroom teacher, both with the teacher and with your classmates.

REFERENCES

Jones, R. M. (1990). *Teaming up!* LaPorte, TX: ITGROUP.

Krauss, L. D. (1992). Whole language: Bridging the gap from spontaneous to scientific concepts. *Journal of Reading Education*, 18, 16–26

Stefanich, G. P., & Norman, K. I. (1996). *Teaching science to students with disabilities: Experiences and perceptions of classroom teachers and science educators.* A special publication of the Association for the Education of Teachers in Science. (Available from AETS, University of West Florida, 11000 University Parkway, Pensacola, FL 32514.)

Tierney, R. J., & Pearson, P. D. (1981). Learning to learn from text: A framework for improving practice. In E. K. Dishner (Ed.), *Reading in the content areas* (p. 56). Dubuque, IA: Kendall/Hunt.

United States Department of Education. (1994). *Mini-digest of educational statistics: 1994.* Washington, DC: Author.

SUGGESTED READINGS

Brandwein, P. F., & Passow, H. A. (Eds.). (1989). *Gifted young in science.* Washington, DC: National Science Teachers Association. (Advice from 34 scientists, teachers, and scholars on how to develop learning environments that encourage the precollege gifted at all levels to reach their potential.)

Cawley, J. F. (1994). Science for students with disabilities. *Remedial and Special Education, 15*(2), 67–71.

Johnson, D. W., & Johnson, R. T. (1994). *Learning together and alone: Cooperative, competitive and individualistic learning* (4th ed.). Boston: Allyn & Bacon.

Lewis, R. B., Doorlag, D. H. (1995). *Teaching special students in the mainstream* (4th ed.). Upper Saddle River, NJ: Merrill/Prentice Hall.

Russell, H. R. (1990). *Ten-minute field trips.* Washington, DC: National Teachers Association. (How to take advantage of the immediate environment with quick visits for specific purposes.)

Saul, W., & Jagusch, S. A. (Eds.). (1992). *Vital connections: children, science, and books.* Portsmouth, NH: Heinemann. (A comprehensive look at the place of science literature in the lives of children.)

Scarnati, J. T., & Weller, C. J. (1992). The Write Stuff. *Science and Children, 29*(4), 28–29. (Explains four purposes for writing assignments in science.)

Shulz, J. B., & Carpenter, C. D. (1995). *Mainstreaming exceptional students: A guide for classroom teachers* (4th ed.). Boston: Allyn & Bacon.

CHAPTER 6

HOW TO ARRANGE AND MANAGE COMPLEMENTARY EXPERIENCES

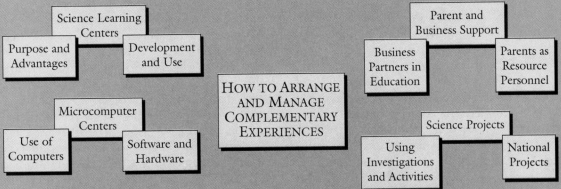

Science Learning Centers

Purpose and Advantages

Development and Use

Microcomputer Centers

Use of Computers

Software and Hardware

HOW TO ARRANGE AND MANAGE COMPLEMENTARY EXPERIENCES

Parent and Business Support

Business Partners in Education

Parents as Resource Personnel

Science Projects

Using Investigations and Activities

National Projects

Do you remember when you were in elementary school? Did your teacher have areas of the classroom set aside for investigations? What technologies were available in the classroom? What kind of ongoing projects did you work on to increase your scientific learning? Do you remember integrating science with other subject areas? How well did your science program prepare you for everyday life or for a career in science?

Now think about the classroom in which you plan to teach. How will it be arranged for learning? Will you use today's technologies? Do you envision students with a wide developmental range and varied interests actively engaging in scientific discovery?

If you were one of the many students to consider science class as "just the facts," then ask yourself the following question: Will you *teach as you were taught* in elementary school? Consider the subsequent statements as you contemplate the classroom in which you would like to teach.

In the Thirty-First Yearbook of the National Society for the Study of Education (1932), a recommendation for a continuous, integrated program for elementary science was advocated. In the Forty-Sixth Yearbook (NSSE, 1947), this challenge was repeated. In the Fifty-Ninth Yearbook (NSSE, 1960), the contest of the space race again prompted educational professionals to look at the inadequate elementary science program in light of needed changes. Each report recommended systematic, activity-based instruction in science that was to begin in kindergarten, or before. Yet most adults you talk to cannot remember learning anything but science facts or vocabulary.

In surveying teachers, the Department of Education found that 84 percent of American teachers consider the copy machine as the one "essential" information technology. Today, people in every sector of society—including healthcare providers, military personnel, and assembly line workers—are highly skilled individuals who

rely heavily on technology to perform their jobs. Training is an ongoing process for these individuals. Yet a teacher trained 20 years ago could walk into today's classroom and begin teaching without any difficulty. Retraining workers in basic skills (including scientific skills) costs industry and the military billions of dollars.

Fortunately, thoughtful teachers see a need to complement the basic science program and go beyond the vocabulary-only elementary science curriculum. They augment it with more supplementary and individualized activities. They find that all children learn differently, and that the best learning takes place through activities that boost the opportunity to learn and the quest for lifelong learning.

As you may note from the above statements, there is a gap between how elementary science instruction *should* be taught and the realities of many classrooms. This chapter shows three ways of using individual or small-group experiences to complement basic instruction—learning centers, microcomputer centers, and projects—then suggests ways to enlist parents' and business partners' aid in enriching what their children learn.

SCIENCE LEARNING CENTERS

A classroom learning center is a place where one or several students at a time can do activities independently through materials and directions found there. A learning center may be arranged so children may choose the activities they can do, or are interested in, and work at a pace that is right for each person. Some teachers also permit children to select the times they go to a center and partners to work with, if any.

An example of a science learning center on weather for an elementary class is shown in Figure 6-1. The center allows children to explore

Figure 6-1
A science learning center.

an area of high interest independently, and develop a background that they may use in a variety of ways. About four children can use this center satisfactorily at one time.

Notice the activity sheets on the bulletin board. Children use these to write down data or make drawings. Completed sheets are placed in a basket on the teacher's desk for later examination.

Observe some other features of this center. Children's literature is available for reading by students either individually or in a peer tutoring situation. A weather radio is available for listening to the weather service and noting data such as temperatures and rainfall, and a tape of pertinent weather information can be listened to by individual students.

Notice the materials for the students to interact with. There are alcohol-filled thermometers to record temperatures, a wind gauge, and a tornado simulation bottle. There is also a "weather book" that contains blank pages for students to use to draw and color the weather each day. To construct this center, the teacher considered these matters:

Purpose and objectives

Activity cards and worksheets

Materials and their resupply

Record keeping and evaluation

The physical setup

See now how each of these matters affects the making of a learning center.

Deciding the Purpose of a Learning Center

The first thing in making a science learning center is to decide its purpose. Do you want it for general enrichment? While this is the most common purpose, centers may also be used to complement an instructional unit or present an entire unit when materials are few. For instance, unit activities may require microscopes, but only several may be handy. The best way to teach the unit, or at least furnish some complementary activities, might be to schedule several children at a time into the science learning center.

As a rule, avoid activities whose outcomes take more time to happen than you assign students to be at the center. Children generally want things to happen *now*. There are, though, occasional exceptions to the rule. In the activity shown in Figure 6-2, taken from a "Things That Change" learning center, students start a "changes" jar. They put in materials they believe will deteriorate and will view these slow changes (away from the center) over the course of a month or longer. But the other change activities at this center happen much faster: Ice cubes melt, liquids evaporate, and mixtures fizz.

Developing Activity Cards and Record Sheets

How can you communicate activities in the most understandable and appealing ways? The directions on activity cards must be simple, so independent work is possible. Use short sentences and easy words. Draw pictures beside key words if the cards are intended for less able readers (see Figure 6-2).

Despite your best efforts, some children may not be able to read your directions. Keeping in mind the scaffolding approach from page 45, you may want to pair the child with a good reader who will help. In some schools, the policy is to have multi-age grouping for classes.

Figure 6-2

A "changes" jar begun at a center allows children to continually observe, away from the center, slow changes.

Other schools have parents, a teacher aid, or a cross-age tutoring program to assist students.

A few teachers find that recording directions on a tape recorder works satisfactorily. Teachers of primary-level children usually find that they must briefly introduce each new activity to the entire class before most children can do the activity by themselves.

Try to make the design of your activity cards appealing and different for each topic. To do this, you might design the cards to go with the topic. For example, with the topic "The Melting of Ice Cubes" make each card look like an ice cube. For "five senses" make nose-, eye-, finger-, tongue-, and ear-shaped cards. Above all, make the cards as childproof as possible. Cut them from heavy paper or tagboard. Avoid having thin, easily bendable parts. For future use, cover them with transparent contact paper or laminate them with your school's laminating machine.

Include as many open-ended activities as you can that have possibilities for process-skill development. These make it possible for children to suggest additional activities, which they enjoy doing.

Record sheets are a convenient way to know what the child has done, if you cannot directly observe the child at work. A record sheet may be simply a plain sheet of paper on which the child has made a drawing or recorded some data after an activity-card suggestion.

Some teachers like to have a record sheet for every activity. Other teachers reserve record sheets only for activities in which data recording is necessary for the activity to make sense—graphing temperature or other changes, keeping track of results from testing different materials, or drawing a conclusion from a number of facts. Sometimes record sheets are also called "skill sheets," "laboratory sheets," or "data sheets." See Figure 6-3 for an example of an activity card and its accompanying record sheet.

Materials

Kitchen science activities that can be done with common materials are perfect for science centers. The children themselves may be able to bring in most of what is needed.

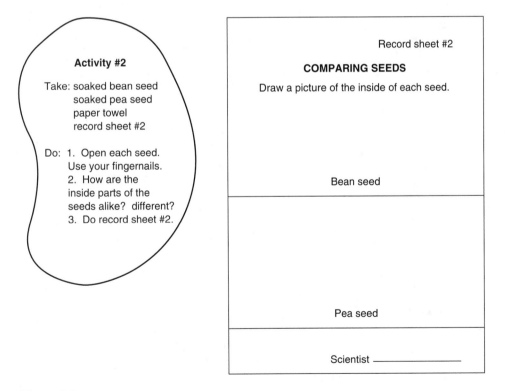

Figure 6-3
An activity card and its accompanying record sheet.

This is a good way to dispel the idea that science is a strange enterprise conducted with expensive and mysterious objects. You can also use printed and audiovisual materials or items loaned by local colleges or museums in your center.

Record Keeping and Evaluation

Observing children in action is the best way to learn what they need help with and what they can do. Yet if many activities are going on, it's hard to keep track of everything each person has tried.

One way to record progress is to have a master list of all the center's activities or objectives with the children's names written to one side. If each activity has a record sheet, these can be filed by the child in a folder at the center. Check the record sheet against your master list. The record sheet will show what activity was performed. Develop your own code system for recording the quality of the work, indicating what is incomplete, and what should be done over.

Sometimes it may be better to have a record system in which the child refers only to his own work. To do this, some teachers give each child who uses a center a record sheet containing only activity numbers. (See Figure 6-4) A space is left at the top for any center title to be written in. A line is drawn under the last number that equals the center's total activities. On completing an activity, the child circles the activity number on her sheet. This record sheet is kept handy for the teacher to review during informal or scheduled conferences. To save time, only the more important objectives may be sampled. The record sheet is filed in the child's science folder, along with worksheets and other work products.

Keep an eye on how successful your center is in meeting your objectives and holding the children's interest. What is there about the activities that appeals to the children and gets the job done? Why are students avoiding or doing poorly with other activities? Ask the children to give their views as well. Together you can continually improve the quality of your center's learning opportunities.

Record Sheet
Science Learning Center

on Magnets

Circle activity finished:

(1)	8	15
2	9	16
3	(10) LM	17
(4) LM	11	18
(5)	(12)	19
6	13	20
7	14	21

Scientist Melinda

Figure 6-4
A record system in which each child refers only to his own work prevents children from making critical comparisons of each other.

Schedule individual conferences periodically to learn more about each child's accomplishments. Can the child profit from further study in the form of an independent project? (See page 149 for details.) Such a project can be particularly valuable with the able and older child. This may be the time to set up a "contract" between you and the child. Or, the child may make a preliminary study before deciding with you on the exact topic, time, and goals for the contract.

Arranging the Physical Setup

Where is the best place to put a science learning center? How should it look? What are some ways to cut down the work in setting up new centers? These are some things worth thinking about.

Can children work inside the classroom without interfering with others? Do activity outcomes happen at the center during the allotted times? Locate the center where it will not interfere with other activities and where it is visible to you at all times. Will wall space be needed? Take this into account, too.

You can draw enlarged background pictures by making a transparency of a picture and then projecting the transparency with an overhead projector. With it, you can enliven your center's background with familiar characters for child appeal: Barney, Power Rangers, or Ninja Turtles. It's also interesting to use mystery, surprise, oddities, contrast, and drama in captions or pictures. You can purchase a preconstructed backboard for your center or make one with available wood or heavy cardboard.

Timesaving Shortcuts: Converting Investigations into Centers

Probably the easiest way to make a learning center is to derive it from one or more of the open-ended learning experiences described in this book. Most of the investigations in the activity section can be readily changed into centers. Examples of investigations that meet the criteria for a good center are:

The Makeup of Colored Liquids, 215.

Wheel-Belt Systems, 370.

The Properties of Leaves, 410.

Snails and What They Do, 458.

Figure 6-5 shows a center made by a teacher from the investigation on page 488. Table 6-1 details how the various steps in the investigation evolved into the different parts of the learning center.

Figure 6-5
Many science investigations can be readily made into learning centers.

Table 6-1
Parts of a Center May Be Derived From an Investigation

Center ⟷ Comes from ⟷ Investigation	
Leading question	Exploratory problem
Try this	Try this section
Picture	Traced from page 528
Activity-card problems	Discovery problems

Managing the Science Learning Center

How can you schedule, introduce the center to children, and keep things running smoothly? It's hard to say precisely what will be useful in every situation, since schools and individual classrooms vary so much.

If you have never worked with learning centers, start out with a familiar topic. Always use clear directions and check to see that the students understand the procedure. Demonstrate an activity to get their interest and model appropriate behavior with materials. Finally, keep in mind that the noise level in the classroom may increase slightly. Use a prearranged signal if things get too noisy. Allow yourself plenty of time at first to ensure a successful learning experience.

Chances are your experience with science learning centers will be rewarding. If so, consider increasing the use of centers through a more flexible arrangement involving several subjects. Some teachers reserve mornings for the three Rs and unit teaching. Afternoons are for individualized enrichment and skill-building activities at different learning centers, such as the following:

- Science
- Social studies/multicultural center
- Fine arts center
- Hobby center
- Literature center
- Writing center
- Speaking and listening center
- Math center

Work at the centers may be either assigned or optional. This allows you freedom to vary time and other considerations, and to assist and confer with individuals. You and each child can cooperatively decide on ways to pursue interests, knowledge, and skills. The best learning usually happens when children themselves take an active part in planning their learning.

Live Animal Centers

The use of living creatures such as mealworms, hermit crabs, lizards, fish, mice, hamsters, and rabbits is an excellent way to develop observational skills and responsibility with your students. When using animals, first refer to the school or district policy to determine which animals are acceptable, if any. The best policy is to have a veterinarian become your "partner in education" and ensure that the animals in your classroom are safe for the students to interact with.

Care for the animals should be primarily the students' responsibility; however, you should monitor the cleaning, feeding, and exercise. Help out only in cases when the students can-

6-1

MICROCOMPUTERS IN THE CLASSROOM
Carol Parker
Escambia County School District, Florida

Over the years, the microcomputer has evolved from just another additional tool in my classroom, similar to the overhead projector, to the most indispensable component in my instructional repertoire. One reason for this transformation has been the development of software programs that match elementary curriculum needs and allow for hands-on activities at the same time. For example, probeware such as *Science Toolkit* allowed my students to take accurate measurements of temperature and light when they were doing scientific experiments. The computer enabled them to record and analyze data with minute differences just as professional scientists would do.

Another hands-on experience was made possible with *Lego Dacta* kits. The students were able to test theories involving motion, distance, and rate by constructing cars from Lego blocks and small motors, and attaching them to a special interface connected to the computer. They used the Logo language to program their cars to travel a certain distance in a given amount of time. They could make predictions about how many seconds it would take to traverse the distance and then test their ideas.

The computer also became an essential means to simulate activities that would be too dangerous to conduct in real life. For example, during a study of chemical and physical change, I hooked up a laserdisc player to my computer and used the *Windows on Science* laserdisc program from Optical Data to search for examples of chemical change. The students were amazed to watch two poisonous substances (sodium and chlorine) combining to form the harmless table salt we use daily. With the computer, we could observe an earthquake as it was happening in Japan and the effects of a tornado as it swirled over a town.

The introduction of a modem allowed my students to connect with other classrooms. We participated in a the Long Distance Learning Network sponsored by AT&T. One of our projects involved researching local inventors and sharing the information online with classes in Australia, Russia, Germany, Oklahoma, and New Jersey. In a project closer to home, we requested samples of sand from schools located along Florida's coastline, then analyzed the samples for mineral content and transmitted the results online.

Word processing was a crucial aspect of our computer use, for reports as well as creative writing assignments. With only one computer in the classroom, it was difficult to

(continued)

Vignette 6-1 (continued)

allow enough time for everyone to key in their writing. This was solved by using the computer lab in the school one period a week for keyboarding. Each student had his own data disk and would spend the 45-minute period inputting the material already composed and then saving to disk. Many students as young as first grade became proficient at composing at the keyboard from their notes. The introduction of the Alpha Smart Keyboard and the DreamWriter has improved the input problem, as these diskless laptops can be taken to a student's desk for keyboarding, and the compositions can be uploaded to a desktop computer later for editing and printing.

The microcomputer has the potential to become an even more integral component of the elementary classroom. Presentation programs such as *HyperStudio, Digital Chisel,* and *PowerPoint* give students the opportunity to design exactly how they wish to demonstrate what they have learned in a unit of study, and access to the Internet will provide them with the chance to publish their presentations for viewing by a worldwide audience.

not provide effective care. Refer to Appendix D for care of animals.

Possible ideas for animal centers are to have students observe life cycles, compare growth rates, or observe eating patterns. It is a good idea to provide a daily observation log to be completed by the students if they are observing animals.

MICROCOMPUTER CENTERS

Most historians agree that a revolution occurred in education soon after the printing press was invented. The printed book became the "tool" of its time. Today, technology, especially computer technology, is the high-tech educational tool of the twenty-first century. Historians tell us that there was a resistance to books in the fifteenth century. However, as people relied on the printed word for educational opportunity, this technological advancement became common-

place. Similarly, resistance to using computers in science is changing today.

A recent study (Weiss, 1994) indicated that 77 percent of elementary science teachers felt that computer use should be a part of science instruction. Future professional educators must understand and make full use of tools like the Internet, CDs, laserdiscs, distance education tools, and other technologies.

Just a decade ago, a single microcomputer for a school was rare. Now, there is a ratio of at least one computer for every twelve students and the short-term goal is to have a one-to-five ratio (Riley, 1996). Computing power is now to the point where the average home video game will soon have the computing power of the largest supercomputer manufactured. What does this mean for you as a teacher? You will be challenged to use *technology as a learning tool,* instead of *learning about the tools of technology.* Elementary students will access scientific information as well as collect, store, analyze, and display data as seen in Figure 6-6.

Figure 6-6
Students are enthusiastic about computer-assisted instruction.

The Uses of Computers

At first, school microcomputers served mostly for drill and practice in math and language. But now they are also being used to teach broader applications through simulations, microcomputer-based laboratories, multimedia, spreadsheets, databases, and the Internet. With more machines, there are improved chances for us to apply them in complementary science activities and for occasional whole-class teaching.

Setting up a microcomputer center for science study, whether in your classroom or school instructional materials center, raises some of the same questions as other learning centers:

What do you want to accomplish?

Are other means of instruction better?

What kinds of hardware and software are available?

Who will use the center and when?

What will they need to know?

Consider now the kinds of programs you are likely to see in your school.

Types of Software

Software can be purchased on 3½-inch disks or compact disks. Many programs can be downloaded directly from the Internet or networked machines in your school. Software is available to assist in learning science processes and concepts in categories such as:

- Tutorials and games
- Multimedia
- Simulations
- Internet access tools
- Spreadsheets
- Databases
- Word processing
- Research tools

TUTORIALS AND GAMES. These programs are used to teach vocabulary, facts, topical information, or skills—usually in small, bite sizes. Questions follow each chunk of presented information, and pupil responses trigger what appears next. The computer may also record responses for evaluation. Topics include simple machines and their applications, why the oceans are important for survival, how the human heart works, how to classify animals, common constellations, and properties of rocks, to name just a few. If you have older computers, lots of tutorials and game software may be available at your school.

MULTIMEDIA. Programs in which students look up information or further explore science topics in multiple media forms, such as pictures and sounds, are called *multimedia*. They are arranged so that a student can jump from one topic to another and view text, sounds, movie clips, or laserdisc sequences. Random access controls the media, unlike movies or audiotapes, which must be reviewed sequentially.

Examples of this category of software include the *Explorapedia* (Microsoft) and *Eyewitness Encyclopedia of Science* (Dorling Kindersley), which are children's interactive encyclopedias about the world of science and nature. *Grolier's Multimedia Encyclopedia* (Grolier) and *Encarta* (Microsoft) also provide information on a wide range of topics and include color pictures and sounds. *Animals in Our World* (Sunburst/Edunetics) provides information on characteristics of many animals through text and videos.

Multimedia software is useful when students are investigating a specific science topic or preparing a class report. Additionally, programs now take advantage of the newer computers' ability to play movie clips and sounds. These programs are especially useful for students who cannot read well on their own.

Do you want your students to try to create their own programs? *HyperCard* (Apple Computer) and *HyperStudio* (Roger Wagner Publishing) are examples of software that allow students to make their own multimedia presentations. The book *HyperCard Projects for Kids* (Ventura, 1992) lists ways to create science projects about such topics as the planets, parts of a volcano, and the continents/oceans.

With multimedia, each screen image is considered a *card* and a collection of these cards is a *stack*. When making stacks, students can type in text, import clip art pictures from other disks, scan their own pictures in, record sounds, control a laserdisc player, or link their cards to other programs. The advantages to using hypermedia are:

■ Students can research topics and make their own information stacks to share with others.

■ Classroom or school collections of hypermedia stacks provide information on a variety of topics from multiple perspectives.

■ The students feel good about themselves when they are able to create a simple stack and share it with others.

SIMULATION PROGRAMS. This software is generally available in IBM or Macintosh format and on floppy disks or CD–ROM. In simulations, students play roles in situations where they can explore scientific phenomena or approximate real events. For example, the *Magic School Bus* series (Scholastic/Microsoft) allows students to explore the human body, the solar system, and the ocean. *Dangerous Creatures* (Microsoft) allows students to explore the world of wildlife. Other programs develop early science skills through the help of an on-line friend such as *Sammy's Science House* (Edmark) or the "Science Dome" in *Gus Goes to Cyberopolis* (Modern Media Ventures). *The Voyage of the Mimi* (Sunburst) is a comprehensive collection of simulations and activities on science topics such as the whale.

Other simulations allow players to decide what to do when given certain data, and the computer instantly feeds back information. In *SimAnt* (Broderbund/Maxis), students take on roles of ants. They learn ant behaviors, including how to communicate with one another and how to avoid being done in by fierce red ants, ravenous spiders, and heavy human feet. Using scientific information, students develop strategies to survive, increase the size of their colony, and finally reach the ultimate reward—a safe home with a lavish food supply.

Simulations are an excellent way to present science phenomena that otherwise are too remote, dangerous, complex, costly, or time consuming. They teach the consequences of real-life decisions, yet allow students to escape from actually bearing them. Who could ask for anything more?

INTERNET ACCESS TOOLS. Connecting to the Internet requires either a network link (cable) between your school's system and your classroom computer or a dial-in Internet connection from your computer through a modem and a phone line to an Internet provider. Once connected, however, students can send *elec-*

tronic mail (e-mail) throughout the world, download files and software through a system called FTP or *file transfer protocol,* access online databases, view World Wide Web (WWW) sites, or communicate through on-line discussions called *newsgroups.* A common program for doing these tasks is Netscape (Mozilla). Netscape is available for the Macintosh™, Power Macintosh™, Windows™, and Windows 95™ operating systems. It is free to educators and can be downloaded directly from the Internet address ftp://ftp.mcom.com/navigator/. It is also available from most software distributors. The advantage of using Netscape for Internet communications is that it can navigate the various *protocols,* or connection types, of the Internet including e-mail, FTP, newsgroups, and the WWW. Netscape also has a search feature, so that you can supply key words and it will find all of the sites that relate to that key word.

What is out there in cyberspace? A steadily growing number of people, including most scientists and college professors, have an electronic mail address on the Internet. These are in the *user@location* format. Your students can send e-mail to people asking for specific information related to the science topics your class is investigating. There are also millions of WWW sites on the Internet to connect to, including zoos, science centers, museums, schools, research centers, and government agencies. These sites begin with a *http://* in the address. This stands for HyperText Transfer Protocol, the Internet's multimedia system. Your students can find information or explore these global sites for free, once a local Internet connection to your classroom is established. Science celebrities such as Mr Wizard (http://mrwizard.org/), Bill Nye the Science Guy (http://nyelabs.kcts.org/), and Beakman of *Beakman's World* (http://www.nbn.com/ you can/) have Internet addresses. Perhaps your school already has a *home page* or a globally accessible file of information on the Internet. Chances are that the college you are attending

is on the Web. Check with a computer support person to find out the address and how you could access the site.

What about the World Wide Web? Not only can your students access the Web, but they can become a part of the information superhighway by developing Web pages based on science topics. These can be placed on a *Web server* (a machine which is always connected to the Internet—check with a computer support person) and shared between classes within your building or across the ocean. *Intranet* is the name given to groups of computers which are not connected to the Internet, but are connected to each other within a school or company. The computers in an intranet use the same software and hardware as Internet-capable machines, but they cannot be accessed by others outside of the school. Likewise, students could not access the Internet from these machines, but could only look at locally stored Web pages.

The easiest way to develop a Web page is to use a new version of a word processing program such as ClarisWorks 4.0 (Claris) and save the file in a format called *WWW* for World Wide Web or *HTML,* which is HyperText Markup Language. HTML is the computer standard necessary for machines throughout the world to decode your finished work. It imposes standard codes to indicate paragraphs, different fonts, etc., so that a file written in HTML can be accessed by any computer on the Internet. HTML files generally work and look the same on any type of machine.

Science activities are abundant on the Internet. An example is the *Space Educators Guide* available at http://tommy.jsc.nasa.gov/~woodfill/SPACEED/SEHHTML/seh.html. A good printed resource for Internet activities is the book *Internet Activities Using Scientific Data* (Froseth & Poppe, 1995) available from the NOAA. The chapter on "Science and Social Studies" in *Integrating Telecommunications into Education* (Roberts, Blakeslee, Brown, &

Lenk, 1990) includes some exemplary pro-grams, such as the *National Geographic Kids Network*. This is a project that allows students to share their information with others through the Internet. Children in various schools gather data, transmit the data to a central computer, and share findings with other schools.

In one unit of the *Kids Network,* children in schools scattered around the nation measure the acidity of rain in their local area and send the data to a scientist collaborating with the program. The data are then pooled through a central computer, organized on charts and maps, and sent back to the students.

SPREADSHEETS. The use of spreadsheets will allow you to arrange and automatically compute data. A *cell* is an individual data point. It is the juncture of a row and column. Cells can contain text, numbers, or formulas which can compute values based on input or numbers in other cells and display the result. A change in one cell can cause changes in other cells. The use of a spreadsheet for a gradebook is a typical example. As new grades are entered, the stu-dent's final grade changes automatically based on the input. ClarisWorks (Claris) is a common tool for developing spreadsheets. The book *ClarisWorks 2.0 in the Classroom* (Claris, 1993), provides examples on how to use spreadsheets to determine the best factors for racing cars, compare body measurements, or find the best formula for bubble mixtures. Spreadsheets can also be used to predict data. If information on plant growth is collected for a period of time, a spreadsheet can determine future trends. A spreadsheet can be used to determine how long it would take a student to travel to another planet, given the speed of the spacecraft and distance of the planets.

DATABASES. A database is a way to create, categorize, sort, and view specific records. For example, a collection of records on *Animals A–Z* (Claris, 1993) can contain information like the type of animal, size, number of legs, skin type, and habitats. A database could be used to sort the information and display only records which match a certain criteria. For instance, by selecting number of legs as a criterion, the com-puter can automatically sort the records and list those animals with two legs. Other examples of the use of databases include categorizing infor-mation on rocks and minerals, weather, and volcano records.

WORD PROCESSING. Probably the most-used type of program is the word processing program, which can format text and check for spelling errors. This software is an excellent tool for science journals, writing science poetry, or creating science pal files to share over the Inter-net.

RESEARCH TOOLS. How do scientists use microcomputers? Can children use microcom-puters in similar ways? Science educators and computer specialists are digging deeply into both questions. The software and other materi-als coming from their efforts get children into the heart of science: gathering, organizing, and sharing real data.

Several software programs for students have accompanying hardware called *probes.* These are sensing devices that are connected through a cable to the computer. When used with the proper software, probes can measure tempera-ture, light, sound, heart rate, acidity of sub-stances, motion, force, pressure, and other properties of objects.

Several probe-type lab programs, called *microcomputer-based labs,* have had much use in elementary schools from about Grade 3 on. The *Bank Street Laboratory* (Sunburst) gives students chances to record and analyze graphs of temperature, light, and sound data. *Science Toolkit* (Broderbund) has rugged, easy-to-use probes for measuring light, temperature, time, and distance. Data can be organized into tables, charts, and graphs. Probe labs make it easy to gather a lot of data over short or long periods and then instantly convert the data into analyzable forms.

Computer Accessories

The *videodisc* or *laserdisc* is a thin aluminum plate, usually about the size of an old record, sandwiched between two layers of plastic (Figure 6-7). Each side may contain thousands of recorded still pictures and numerous film clips with sounds and narration—often in both English and Spanish.

A computer linked to a videodisc player can access the recorded material in any order within a few seconds and display it on the computer monitor. You can also display the material *without* a computer by connecting the player to a separate video monitor. In this case, you control the material through the player, with either a hand-held remote control or a bar-code reader.

A teacher's guide usually comes with a laserdisc. Each photo frame or sequence is given a number and bar code for identification. With the remote control, you punch in the numbers of your selection. Using the bar code reader is even easier: Lightly rub one end of the reader across the code, pointing the other end at the player, and push a button.

Most nationally published science programs today use videodiscs to some degree. Teacher guides may include whole-class lessons or suggestions for an individual or small group setting. With your microcomputer center, for example, you might select frames and animated sequences to follow up a lesson on earthquakes, then arrange bar code stickers or numbers in a sequence to guide students. Some science programs provide pupil worksheets with bar codes printed on them. In either case, students can interact with the material in the way they prefer. Students might also search out material themselves to integrate into small group or individual reports to the class.

Examples of laserdiscs for use in elementary science include *Voyage of the Mimi* by Sunburst, *The Planets* from the National Geographic Society, and *Dinosaurs, Gems and Minerals,* and *National Zoo* by the Smithsonian Institution. Some elementary science text series now include an accompanying laserdisc. These correspond to the material in the text and are accessed through barcodes (using a barcode reader) printed in the teacher's edition. *Science Horizons* (Silver Burdett Ginn) is an example of a videodisc series.

The *CD–ROM* (compact disc, read-only memory) is another way to bring a vast amount of computer-controlled audiovisual material into your classroom. About half the size of a videodisc, you insert it into a CD–ROM drive connected to a computer. The material is accessed through the keyboard and viewed on the computer screen. The CD–ROM is simply a

Figure 6-7
Videodiscs store audio and visual information that can be displayed on a computer screen or video monitor.

variation of the familiar audio compact disc. It's been used mostly for storing reference information, like encyclopedias and dictionaries, but its functions are expanding.

Today almost every computer is sold with a CD–ROM drive. A CD can currently hold about 5 billion bits of information (about 100 books) and technological advances will increase the amount to more than 50 billion bits. As of 1996, there are more than 10,000 CD titles available. One multimedia version of *Compton's Encyclopedia* (Jostens) includes on a single CD–ROM many thousands of photos and other illustrations, sixty minutes of speech, music, and sound, an interactive world atlas, and many other features besides the entire printed text.

If you want your students to use your classroom computer center for word-processing science reports and the like, consider attaching a *scanner* to your microcomputer. Like a photocopier, it allows the user to incorporate photos or drawings directly into a written report, multimedia presentation, or Internet WWW page.

A *digital camera* works like a regular camera but saves the image on computer memory instead of film. These pictures can be transferred to a computer and used in other programs, like scanned pictures. The disadvantage of these cameras is that they can only store a limited number of pictures at one time before they need to be downloaded to a computer.

Should you or a pupil want to deliver a presentation on the computer screen, it may be hard for the entire class to see what's displayed. A color or black-and-white *LCD* (liquid crystal display) *projection pad* on the overhead projector will project what's on the computer monitor. You can also use this system whenever you want to introduce new software or otherwise instruct the whole class on how to work with the computer.

Computer *videoprojectors* are now affordable for elementary schools. These connect to classroom computers and project the image on a screen. Their advantage over an LCD panel is that the picture is of a much better quality. Newer models will even work in normal lighting so students can take notes while viewing. Figure 6-8 shows some of the microcomputer equipment used in schools.

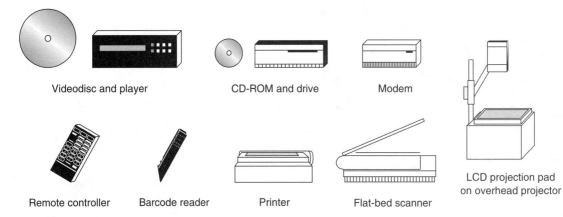

Videodisc and player　　　CD-ROM and drive　　　Modem

Remote controller　Barcode reader　Printer　Flat-bed scanner　LCD projection pad on overhead projector

Figure 6-8
Some equipment used with microcomputers in schools.

Microcomputer Advantages, Disadvantages, and Resources

You've already seen some ways computer-assisted instruction can benefit you and your students in both learning centers and larger settings. Let's look at several more advantages and then address a few concerns.

It takes only a brief experience with computers to see how much children delight in this medium. The immediate feedback to their responses prompts them to learn more quickly and surely. Slow or fast learners can go at their own pace with an infinitely patient teacher. When they respond incorrectly, a good program branches them into a remedial sequence that reteaches the material in simpler steps. When they respond correctly, a good program moves them quickly into harder material. Computers can truly individualize instruction.

Perhaps the greatest promise for computer-based instruction lies in simulations. The computer-controlled videodisc, CD–ROM, and other resources offer all kinds of opportunities for making decisions and solving problems in realistic settings. Any airline pilot can tell you that what's seen through the cockpit windshield of a flight simulator just after a right or wrong move comes uncannily close to the real thing. Now there are increasing chances for *children* to experience simulated experiences.

One problem with computers is that software made for one machine may not work in another. Expense is another concern. What can the school budget afford for the extensive hardware and software now available and soon to be developed? Fortunately, there is a growing supply of software available on the Internet, and much of it is available to teachers for free or for a minimal registration fee.

Another drawback of some elementary science software is a lack of accompanying hands-on experiences. This is more likely with older and stand-alone materials. The software integrated into today's comprehensive multimedia science programs usually provides for concrete activity.

Nearly everyone needs some extra guidance and practice to creatively apply this remarkable tool. If you're new to computing, it's easy to feel overwhelmed by the sheer quantity of unfamiliar technology and methods employed. But the good news is, there's plenty of help around to get you up to speed.

If you are new to a school, ask colleagues and the principal what machines and help are available at the school and district levels. Both in-service workshops and informal, person-to-person arrangements are common. Don't be surprised to meet students with considerable expertise at microcomputing. By the sixth grade, some children have had several *thousand* hours of experience with these machines at home and school. They can be invaluable aides to other students and you. Employ them in cooperative situations as much as possible. Consider joining a computer-user group for your school's brand of machine.

Software Sources and Reviews

How can you learn what is currently available and worthwhile? The supply of usable science software continues to grow. Software publishers are producing more materials that reflect the best thinking in constructivist psychology and science education. Science textbook publishers (today they are more accurately called multimedia science program publishers) are integrating software titles into text units and chapters. Some also develop their own software for that purpose.

There are numerous publishers of software. An easy way to find what's accessible is to inspect the catalog of a distributor of products from many companies. Two large distributors are:

Educational Resources
1550 Executive Drive
Elgin, IL 60123
1-800-624-2926

Cambridge Development Laboratory, Inc.
The Science Shop
214 Third Avenue
Waltham, MA 02154
1-800-637-0047

Comprehensive education software catalogs and application guides may also be obtained from the two main manufacturers of school microcomputers:

Apple Computer, Inc.
20525 Mariani Avenue
Cupertino, CA 95014
1-800-800-APPL
www address: http://www.info.apple.com/education

IBM Corporation
Education Software, Dept. 779
1 Culver Road
Dayton, NJ 08810
www address: http://www.ibm.com/IBM/IBMGives/k12ed/k12init.htm

You can find in-depth evaluations of educational microcomputer products in *PRO/FILES*, published by:

EPIE Institute
P.O. Box 839
Water Mill, NY 11976.

Another comprehensive guide to current software is *Microsoft Courseware Evaluation*, published by:

Northwest Regional Educational Laboratory
300 S.W. 6th Avenue
Portland, OR 97204.

Find further reviews and many suggestions for using classroom computers and related materials in these magazines:

Classroom Connect
Wentworth Worldwide Media, Inc.
1866 Colonial Village Lane
P.O. Box 10488
Lancaster, PA 17605-0488
http://www.wentworth.com

The Computing Teacher
University of Oregon
1787 Agate Street
Eugene, OR 97403

Electronic Learning
P.O. Box 3021
Southeastern, PA 19398

Media & Methods
1429 Walnut Street
Philadelphia, PA 19102

Science and Children
National Science Teachers Association
1840 Wilson Blvd.
Arlington, VA 22201-3000
(703) 243-7100
e-mail: s&c@nsta.org

Technology & Learning
2451 East River Road
Dayton, OH 45439

Online, *Children's Software Review* at the Internet address http://www.microweb.com/pepsite/Revue/Softnews/ will provide software news and ongoing reviews.

If you are unsure about a software program, keep in mind that the National Science Teachers Association [NSTA] (1992) presents the following guidelines on the use of computers in science education.

Computers should enhance, not replace, hands-on activities.

Tutorial software should engage students in meaningful interactive dialogue.

Simulation software should provide opportunities to explore concepts and models not readily available.

Microcomputer-based labs should permit students to collect and analyze data like scientists.

Networking should permit students to emulate the way scientists work and reduce classroom isolation.

SCIENCE PROJECTS

As professional educators, we have seen withdrawn or listless girls and boys who did not come to life until they began to create science projects. A *project* is an organized search, construction, or task directed toward a specific purpose. It's ordinarily done by one person, or a small team of two or three persons, with minimal guidance from the teacher. A project may clarify, extend, or apply a concept—and cause children to use science processes along the way. Most projects require a lot of independent effort so they are less appropriate for primary-level children who usually lack the skills and perseverance needed to operate independently.

The need for projects most often arises during a regular instructional unit. But projects may also begin with interests expressed by students or from a desire to have a science or engineering fair. The teacher's job is to provide some realistic project choices, give deadlines for completing the projects, tell how they will be presented, and check at times for progress. If you decide to focus on projects as a primary instructional activity, a tool for assisting in project-based science is PIViT or *Project Integration and Visualization Tool*. This tool helps teachers visualize and plan an integrated cur-

riculum. It is available at the Internet address http://www.umich.edu/~pbsgroup/ or by contacting:

Project-Based Science Group
1323 SEB, 610 E. University
Ann Arbor, MI 48109

Another tool is the *Curriculum Orchestrator*, which helps to plan the curriculum and activities and correlate them to national and state standards. To find out more about this tool, contact MediaSeek Technologies (1-800-372-3277) (http://www.mediaseek.com).

Using Investigations and Activities for Projects

Investigations that you might use with the whole class or in learning centers often present one or two extra open-ended opportunities to go beyond the basic investigation. For example, in "Wheel-Belt Systems," page 370, a follow-up question says, "What wheel-belt systems can you invent?" In "Mealworms and What They Do," page 452, a final question is, "What are some questions about mealworms you'd like to investigate?" In "The Filtering of Polluted Water," page 569, the last two questions asked are, "Would more or other materials work better?" and "How else could you improve your filter?" Exploration of these questions can be an enriching activity. You can also use investigations that the class is not familiar with. They can originate from questions such as "What causes the tides?" or "What makes the moon move through phases?"

Some activities are short-range, straight-forward demonstrations of concepts or procedures. These are closed-ended and give exact guidance to students. Some examples are:

What happens to water [pressure] with depth? (p. 568–569)

How high can water flow compared to where it comes from? (p. 569)

How can you show that air takes up space? (p. 578–579)

How can you tell if air in a balloon weighs anything? (p. 579–580)

Some activities give longer-range and more open-ended experiences. They may call for changing some variables or keeping records of observations for a time. Some examples are:

How can you make a "nerve tester" game? (p. 335–336)

In what places are seeds in the soil? (p. 400)

How can you measure changes in air pressure? (p. 590–591)

Some concrete activities may be extended and enriched afterward by consulting an outside source.

How are the colors made in comic strips? (p. 214)

What happens when your eyes tire from seeing one color? (p. 221)

How can you raise crickets? (p. 455–456)

Which foods have starch? (p. 505)

A local newspaper office, an eye doctor, a local pet shop owner, and a nutritionist might be suitable authorities in these cases. Projects like these allow children to extend their interest by applying interviewing and reference skills to answer real needs. If students have poor skills, try pairing them to promote scaffolding.

Using Curriculum Projects

Project WILD (Western Regional Environmental Education Council) is a national program which promotes interdisciplinary, supplementary environmental and conservation activities for all grade levels. Teachers who attend Project WILD workshops are trained to facilitate numerous projects and activities which can be found in the guide provided to participating teachers. The activities are grouped to take the elementary students from awareness of environ-mental concerns to the action of conservation and remediation.

Project Aquatic WILD (Western Regional Environmental Education Council) is the companion series to Project WILD and is based on water environments. It contains many aquatic-based activities and extensions to terrestrial WILD activities.

Project Learning Tree (American Forest Foundation), similar to WILD, is an environmental education project that has trees as its theme. Teachers who attend these certification workshops are shown how to facilitate integrated projects and activities based on diversity, interrelationships, systems, scale, and patterns of change.

Science Fairs and Invention Conventions

Consider having a *science fair* to display successful projects. This is exciting for students and excellent for public relations. It is wise to keep it modest at first—perhaps for only your class or parents' open house. At another time, you may want to work with a fellow teacher for a combined operation, or even organize a schoolwide fair. For details on organizing schoolwide and other science fairs, see:

Fredericks, A. D., & Asimov, I. (1990). *The Complete Science Fair Handbook*. Glenview, IL: Good Year Books.

National Science Teachers Association. (1990). *Science and Math Events*. Arlington, VA: Author.

National Science Teachers Association. (1988). *Science Fairs and Projects. Grades K–8*. Washington, DC: Author.

Tocci, S. (1986). *How to Do a Science Fair Project*. New York: Franklin Watts.

A "Certificate of Completion" or multiple prizes can formally recognize everyone's efforts, but downplay invidious comparisons, which elementary school students find hard to handle.

As part of the trend to teach science that children can apply to their lives, some science programs today recommend "invention conventions" as well as typical science fairs. Since technology is science applied to solve practical problems, the idea is to give girls and boys chances to develop solutions to their everyday problems and interests:

How can I tell how fast the wind is blowing? (A homemade wind gauge, fashioned from cardboard and wood, could fill the bill.)

I'd like to make a weird toy that rolls uphill by itself. (A hidden, twisted rubber band inside a coffee can may do the job.)

I've heard you can make a stool from newspaper that's so strong you can sit on it. (Rolled-up newspaper makes surprisingly sturdy columns.)

For a wealth of fun-filled ideas and ways to stimulate inventiveness in your students, see:

Caney, S. (1985). *Steven Caney's Invention Book*. New York: Workman Publishing.

Eichelberger, B., & Larson, C. (1993). *Constructions for Children: Projects in Design Technology*. Menlo Park, CA: Dale Seymour.

McCormack, A. J. (1981). *Inventor's Workshop*. Belmont, CA: David S. Lake Publishers.

If you are interested in a competitive awards program for projects, consider checking the National Science Teachers Association's Web site, which lists current national and regional science competitions at the address http://www.nsta.org/programs.

PARENT AND BUSINESS SUPPORT

Common sense and research tell us that students do better in school when their parents take an active interest in their studies. While parents want to help their children succeed, they may not know how to go about it, especially when the subject is science. How can you help parents nurture their children's efforts, and how can they support your science teaching? Your school's science program might include copy masters of letters to parents, concept summaries, and activities that parents and children could do together. Many newer programs include such materials. The letters periodically announce a new unit of instruction, briefly describe it, and state some things parents might do to complement lessons. The concept summaries, often in several languages, inform parents about ideas they might discuss with their children and how they might reinforce the science lesson with experiences outside of school. The activities usually relate to the unit being studied and feature everyday materials.

How Parents Can Help

Doing and discussing concrete activities with their children is a good way for parents to cultivate science interests and achievement. To further these objectives, some teachers keep fifteen to thirty shoe box kits containing activities that students can check out and take home. Kits are easy to prepare when you get parents to help. Here's a way to do so.

Inspect Part II of this book or other science source books for activities and investigations that might enrich your regular science program. Select any number of these and make one copy of each. During Parents' Night or similar meetings early in the school year, briefly introduce your science program—what topics students will study and some materials they'll work with—then show your shoe box kit and give its purpose. Pass out the duplicated activity sheets, have parents examine them, and then ask for volunteers to make the kits. Encourage the volunteers to do the activities with their children, discuss the results together, and return the completed kits.

Some teachers like to have parents experience firsthand a few children's activities across the curriculum. This puts them in better touch with their children's work. For a science activity that is a good icebreaker, try "How Useful Are Your Thumbs?" on page 483 in this text.

As mentioned earlier, remember that parents are also typically willing to supplement your science supplies with discardable items from around the home. Some will volunteer to assist at science learning centers or share their expertise in science or technology. But for these things to happen, parents need to hear details from you about what's needed.

Parents are usually more concerned about their children's progress in reading than in any other subject. Point out to them that research consistently underscores the value of parents reading aloud with their children, sharing books, and discussing concepts that come up in the reading (U.S. Department of Education [DOE], 1986). Show them several kinds of science trade books available that correlate with upcoming units. Students may check out these books from several sources, including the school or district or public library. If your school has a newer multimedia science program, check out the science-related literature books that typically accompany these programs.

Show parents examples of useful articles from a newspaper, news magazine, *National Geographic,* or other sources they might share with their children who, in turn, might share the information at school. Explain that this material is easier to understand and remember when it relates to topics and concepts being studied at school. Stress the need to discuss the articles with the children, since they are seldom written in an age-appropriate style. Mention, too, some titles of science periodicals for children. (See listing on page 631.) They contain excellent current material, are more age-appropriate, and will help students learn what to look for when scanning newspapers and other publications.

The National Science Teachers Association has a position paper on parental involvement. It notes that parents should encourage concepts and skills by:

seeing science everywhere,

doing science together,

developing a variety of skills, and

finding the appropriate developmental level.

The position paper has some good suggestions and is available through the Internet at http://www.nsta.org/handbook/parent.htm or by contacting NSTA directly at 1840 Wilson Blvd., Arlington, VA 22201-3000.

Probably some parents and children already will have visited a local natural history museum, zoo, observatory, bird refuge, or botanical garden. Ask parents about these experiences and suggest additional places recommended by seasoned colleagues and school district publications. A school catalog may describe and list places for families to visit at different grade levels or for certain units of instruction. And if *you* intend to take your class on study trips to these places, a parents' meeting is a good time to drum up volunteers to accompany the class.

You probably realize that we have mentioned more things to inform parents about than you will have time for in one introductory meeting, especially if you discuss other subjects. Periodic newsletters, a classroom newspaper, individual conferences, and further parent–teacher meetings all present more chances to reach them. The content of your message is far more important than its forum. When you give parents specific ways to help their children study science and support your efforts, everyone gains.

Business Partners

Businesses generally have not been very active in education in the past. This is changing as businesses are becoming more aware of the need to become active players in the classrooms of their future employees. The National Science Education *Standards* note that it will take a combined effort to achieve high standards in science education.

To get a better perspective on what businesses are supporting education in your area, contact the Triangle Coalition for Science and Technology Education, 5112 Berwyn Road, College Park, MD 20740-4129. A recent document entitled *A Look at Community Commitment to Educational Systematic Reform* lists 125 national and regional programs as examples of involvement. This organization also provides information on the Scientific Work Experiences for Teachers, or *SWEPT,* program.

Scientists are also good partners in education, especially from a "real" science or equity standpoint. The book *Science Education Partnerships* is a good resource in developing a partnership program in your school (Sussman, 1993).

SUMMARY

1. Teachers often complement their whole-class teaching with individual and small-group experiences, to meet the wide range of abilities and interests in their classes. Three common ways to do this are to use learning centers, microcomputer centers, and projects.

2. A classroom learning center is a place where one or several students at a time can do activities independently using materials and directions found at the center. The center may be organized so students can choose at least some of the activities and work at their own pace and learning level. Open-ended experiences usually serve best for these purposes. Many of the investigations in this book can be directly converted into learning centers.

3. A microcomputer center can be set up and run much like a regular learning center. Microcomputer software can include pro-

grams such as tutorials and games, multimedia, simulations, Internet access tools, spreadsheets, databases, word processing, and research tools.

4. A science project is an organized search, construction, or task directed toward a specific purpose, ordinarily carried out by one to three students. The need for projects often arises in instructional units through interests expressed by students. Both investigations and activities in this book may be converted into science projects.

5. Parents can complement what their children learn about science at school by participating with them in various out-of-school experiences. These might include doing science activities at home, reading and discussing trade books, and visiting museums or other community resources. Parents are also frequently willing to volunteer their assistance at learning centers, to make shoe box kits, to provide some low-cost materials, and to share science-related expertise.

REFLECTION

1. The policy in some schools is to not allow any type of live animal. In this case, you can search the Internet for sites which have permanently mounted cameras for your students to make "live" observations of such things as ant farms. What other types of environments can you find on the Internet? What other ways can you replace the use of classroom pets? Be ready to share your ideas with classmates.

2. With computers, you can *learn from computers, learn with computers, learn about computers, learn to think with computers, use computers to manage learning or complete science projects.* List examples of how computers and software can be used for each of these categories.

3. If you were to arrange a science competition in your classroom, what local community

resources or industries could help out? Try contacting one or two and see what types of resources are available to you as a classroom teacher.

4. Make a list of science-related television programs that are appropriate for children and parents to share. Review this list with students during your practicum visits. Share your list with classmates and decide on the top ten programs. Keep this list to share with parents in your classroom.

REFERENCES

Claris. (1993). *ClarisWorks 2.0 in the classroom.* Santa Clara, CA: Author.

Froseth, S., & Poppe, B. (1995). *Internet activities using scientific data.* (National Oceanic and Atmospheric Administration). Washington, DC: U.S. Government Printing Office.

National Science Teachers Association. (1992). *The use of computers in science education. An NSTA position statement* [On-Line]. Available: http://www.nsta.org/handbook/computer.htm.

National Society for the Study of Education. (1932). *A program for teaching science.* Chicago: University of Chicago Press.

National Society for the Study of Education. (1947). *Science education in American schools.* Chicago: University of Chicago Press.

National Society for the Study of Education. (1960). *Rethinking science education.* Chicago: University of Chicago Press.

Riley, R. (1996). *The national plan for educational technology* [On-Line]. Available: http://www.ed.gov/Technology/Plan/.

Roberts, N., Blakeslee, G., Brown, M., & Lenk, C. (1990). *Integrating telecommunications into education.* Upper Saddle River, NJ: Prentice Hall Inc.

Sussman, A. (Ed.). (1993). *Science education partnerships: Manual for scientists and K–12 teachers.* San Francisco, CA: University of California, San Francisco.

U.S. Department of Education. (1986). *What works—Research about teaching and learning.* Washington, DC: Author.

Ventura, F. (1992). *Hypercard projects for kids.* Grover Beach, CA: Ventura Educational Systems.

Weiss, I. R. (1994). *A profile of science and mathematics education in the United States: 1993.* Chapel Hill, NC: Horizon Research Inc.

SUGGESTED READINGS

Davis, S., & Botkin, J. (1994). *The monster under the bed.* New York: Simon & Schuster. (Discussion of the relationship between emerging technology and education.)

DeBruin, J. (1991). *Science fairs with style.* Carthage, IL: Good Apple. (A comprehensive guide for upper-grade projects.)

Dockterman, D. (1990). *Teaching in the one-computer classroom.* Cambridge, MA: Tom Snyder. (Describes a variety of ways one to several microcomputers can be effectively used in a classroom.)

Forcier, R. C. (1996). *The computer as a productivity tool.* Upper Saddle River, NJ: Merrill/Prentice Hall. (A good book on the applications of computers in education).

Hampton, C. H., Hampton, C. D., & Kramer, D. C. (1994). *Classroom creature culture: Algae to anoles.* (Revised ed.). Arlington, VA: National Science Teachers Association. (Guidelines for setting up live animal centers in the classroom. Also available as an ERIC microfiche, ERIC Document Reproduction Service No. ED 370 797.)

Harris, J. (1992). Mining the Internet (series). *The Computing Teacher, 20,* (1–8). (This series of articles presents features of the Internet from a teacher's perspective.)

Paulu, N., & Martin, M. (1991). *Helping your child learn science.* Washington, DC: U.S. Department of Education, Office of Educational Research and Improvement, 1991. (How parents can whet their children's science interests through home activities. One of a series on different school subjects. Available at $3.25 from OERI Outreach Office, 555 New Jersey Ave., N.W., Washington, DC 20208-5570.)

Pearlman, S., & Pericak-Spector, K. (1992, April). Helping hands from home. *Science and Children, 29* (7), 12–14. (Parent volunteers make active science more manageable.)

Poppe, C. A., & VanMatre, N. A. (1985). *Science learning centers for the primary grades.* West Nyack, NY: The Center for Applied Research in

Education, Inc. (A comprehensive book for those interested in setting up centers.)

Reynolds, K. E., & Barba, R. H. (1996). *Technology for the teaching and learning of science*. Needham Heights, MA: Allyn & Bacon.

Stone, G. K. (1981). *More science projects you can do*. Upper Saddle River, NJ: Prentice Hall. (A paperback book of many interesting projects for upper elementary students.)

CHAPTER 7

HOW TO ASSESS SCIENCE EDUCATION

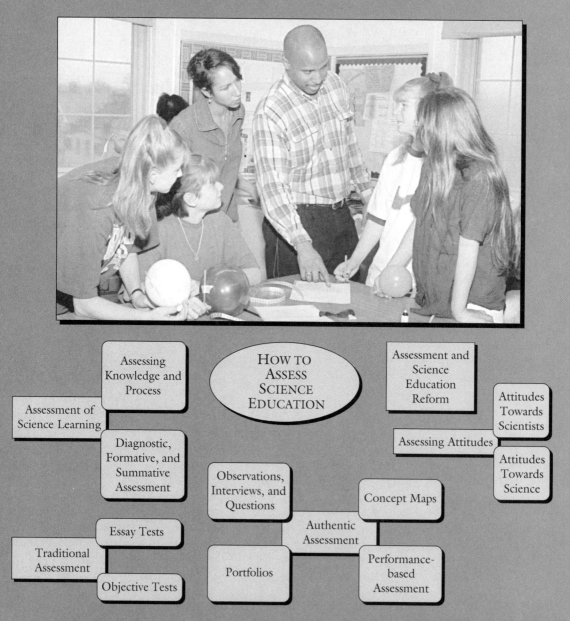

Assessing Knowledge and Process

HOW TO ASSESS SCIENCE EDUCATION

Assessment and Science Education Reform

Assessment of Science Learning

Attitudes Towards Scientists

Diagnostic, Formative, and Summative Assessment

Assessing Attitudes

Attitudes Towards Science

Observations, Interviews, and Questions

Concept Maps

Essay Tests

Authentic Assessment

Traditional Assessment

Portfolios

Performance-based Assessment

Objective Tests

How will you know if your students have learned a scientific concept? Is your method for assessing their learning in accord with the method you use when teaching? Will your current forms of evaluation support positive changes in your classroom, school, or district? The answers to these questions center on examining current practices in student assessment and exploring the new possibilities of what is called *authentic assessment.*

Although testing has been around for a long time, it was not until recently that it has come under scrutiny by science education professionals. Think about the following facts:

As early as 2000 B.C. the Chinese conducted civil service examinations and by the early 1900s, the civil service examinations were used as an equivalent to B.A., M.A., and Ph.D. degrees.

The Greeks used testing to assess physical and intellectual skills. Socrates used questioning mixed with teaching in much the same way as B. F. Skinner did with programmed learning.

As far back as the Middle Ages, European universities relied on formal examinations to award degrees.

In the early 1900s, the first standardized tests for measuring school instruction began to appear and by 1923, the Stanford Achievement test appeared.

In the U.S., as in most modern countries, college entrance, civil service, and professional accreditation has generally been equated to competitive examinations. Even selection and classification of military personnel is based on examination.

With these points in mind, you can begin to appreciate the long history of testing and evaluation. *High-stakes* testing, the kind which is referred to above, is done to indicate your ranking in reference to your peers. This type of testing is especially important in determining placements or comparing students, classrooms, schools, districts, states, or nations. In most instances, this type of evaluation is done *after* instruction has occurred.

So why the sudden focus on authentic assessment? It started with the report *A Nation at Risk* (National Commission on Excellence in Education, 1983), which provided a dismal view of American education. Shortly after this report, reform efforts were undertaken to raise test scores. Educators were concerned with raising scores on the minimal competency tests used in comparisons of students nationwide. Within a few years, though, educators realized that it was not teaching to the test that was the problem, *but the test itself.* The tests did not measure the higher-level thinking that was the desired outcome of education. Furthermore, the concentration was on after-the-fact comparisons, not on what would improve the ongoing learning process.

Science educators, in response to increasing emphasis on students' process skills and higher-order thinking skills, began to use a variety of approaches during science instruction. Teaching methods like integrated or thematic science units, cooperative learning during science explorations, and hands-on/minds-on activities replaced chapter reading, outlines, and vocabulary sheets. This necessitated a fresh look at how classroom teachers determined whether students were understanding the concepts or not.

Teachers began to ask themselves "Why teach one way and test another?" If we are concerned with students' conceptual understandings of science, skills, and problem-solving abilities, should we continue to use tests that only indicate knowledge of basic facts? Additionally, why limit the assessments to one form, such as a multiple choice test, when there are many alternative ways to evaluate student progress and teacher effectiveness?

Naturally, changes began to appear in the assessment strategies. Teachers shifted from a *testing and examination culture,* where students engaged in learning solely for testing purposes, to an *assessment culture,* where the distinctions between testing and learning were reduced. In the following sections, we will take a closer look at objectives and assessment, traditional assessment, authentic assessment, assessing attitudes, and the role of assessment in reform of science education.

OBJECTIVES AND THE ASSESSMENT OF SCIENCE LEARNING

Monitoring the status of students, accountability of students, accountability of teachers, improvement of instruction, and improvement of the learning environment, determining the best science program, and communicating your expectations to students are all reasons for using assessment in your classroom. You will find that assessment techniques can check students' process skill development, factual knowledge, conceptual knowledge, problem-solving ability, and higher-level understanding. For many beginning teachers, it is easier to concentrate on two areas at first: knowledge and skills of the students.

Scientific Knowledge

As you recall from Chapter 3, when you design and teach units and lessons, it is important to keep objectives in mind. In most units, you will want children to achieve knowledge and process skill objectives and gain positive attitudes. Usually, the science curriculum guide or textbook manual contains statements of objectives. From these sources, you can select those that seem to suit your students. Sometimes, though, the stated objectives are not much help. They may be vague or stated in such detail that you lose your sense of direction. You

are more likely to get better results if your mind is organized than if the organization is only on paper.

One good way to ease the load of coping with many objectives is to reduce the number of objectives. You can cut down on *knowledge* objectives by working toward concepts and generalizations rather than isolated facts. Some teachers recognize this, but then wrongly conclude that they can bypass the facts and directly teach these abstractions. This is unfortunate, because what children know about concepts and generalizations depends much on what they construct from hands-on study.

Take, for example, the primary-level generalization "Magnets attract things made of iron or steel." Children begin their study with concrete materials that bring out a fairly large number of facts. The children learn that a magnet attracts nails and metal coat hangers, and that these are made of iron. They find that scissors and some pins are attracted and that these are made of steel. They test other metal and nonmetal objects and discover that these are not attracted.

As students work together to learn these facts, the vocabulary needed to label emerging concepts is introduced by the teacher or more knowledgeable peer. Words such as *steel, iron,* and *rubber* are used by children as they mentally combine objects made of similar materials. Gradually, they combine these concepts, and so a hazy approximation of the generalization develops in their minds.

Stating these generalizations properly often requires a higher degree of internalization. Instead, ask children to demonstrate their knowledge by *applying* it in observable ways. This means they should do more than simply recall some facts. A higher level of understanding is revealed if they can use their knowledge of a generalization to *explain, predict,* or *control* objects and events, preferably those that are new to them. You may recall that this is also how scientists use these abstractions.

To "explain" is to tell how objects may have interacted to cause or prevent change. Children also explain when they give and justify new examples of a concept.

To "predict" means to forecast, using present information, a future observation of an object or event.

To "control" means to show how an object or event can be changed, or how a change can be slowed, speeded up, or prevented.

In a scientific view, to explain, predict, or control objects and events is *the* performance objective of all knowledge objectives. Consider it a constant objective, since it does not change, while individual generalizations do. If you keep this in mind, it becomes easier both to state and keep track of objectives. Notice next how this works.

Suppose your school requires statements of observable performance objectives in lesson plans. Here is how you might do so with magnet activities as an example. Students will:

Explain why some objects are not attracted.

Predict some objects that will and will not be attracted.

Show how to prevent a magnet from picking up an attractable object.

Suppose a middle-grade unit generalization is "Weathering and erosion constantly wear down the earth's surface." Your stated objectives might be as follows: Students will:

Explain why some rocks weather more than others.

Predict places where gullies may form.

Draw a sketch that shows two ways to slow erosion on a bare hillside.

Suppose, in an upper-grade unit on the human body, a generalization is "Automatic reflex actions (blinking, reaction to sudden pain, etc.) have survival value." Your stated objectives might be as follows: Students will:

Explain why automatic blinking has greater survival value than conscious blinking.

Predict two situations that will trigger an automatic reflex.

Make a sketch that shows how an injury might prevent a reflex action.

Notice that in the preceding sample objectives, no mention was made of how well a child should do, or under what conditions evaluation should take place. Because of the many differences in students, we must rely on our judgment in these matters. This is true whether we are concerned with knowledge or process objectives.

Science Processes

You can also reduce to a manageable size the number of process objectives you work with. Remember, there are only about seven broad processes in most elementary programs: classifying, observing, measuring, inferring and predicting, communicating, and experimenting. These, too, are constant objectives, in that we want children to constantly apply them in activities and so become ever more competent in their use. Each of these broad categories of processes can help you recall a cluster of related subprocesses, if these have been learned reasonably well. To do this, you will want to refer to the processes starting on page 80. The Part II of this book can also furnish many opportunities to practice the teaching of these processes. Notice that in both places they are stated as observable pupil actions. You can easily convert these statements into performance objectives for your own units.

Process objectives are assessed by providing a situation that requires the child to use the process. Most teachers appraise these objectives by observing children in action during activity time. But don't expect dramatic changes in a pupil's general ability to apply a broad process from one lesson to the next. This kind of growth requires practice in a variety of subject-matter contexts.

Whenever you plan a science activity, try to think of the broad thinking process involved. Then decide which specific subprocess can be used in the activity (see page 80). As you work with children, ask questions from time to time that generate these actions in the children.

Putting Assessment into Perspective

Some test experts see a difference between *assessment* and *evaluation,* even though the two terms now generally mean the same thing. To them, *assessment* is finding out *what* students have achieved. *Evaluation* is placing a *value* or grade on what is achieved.

There are only two basic ways to grade. We can compare a child's achievement to that of others in a defined population and place a value on it. ("Jim got more right than two-thirds of the class on this test—that ought to be an A. But this class didn't do as well as last year's—I'd better make it a high B.") Or we can define and pose some objectives for students and place a value on how many objectives were achieved. ("Ann met 7 out of 10 objectives—that deserves an A. But maybe only 9 or more should count as an A.")

The point is that placing a value on achievement (A, B, C or Superior, Good, Fair, etc.) is arbitrary. It depends on who makes the rules and how consistently they are followed. We typically are required to do some type of grading, of course, but this is best done within school district guidelines. Decisions on pupil promotion, retention, remedial instruction, and the like are strongly linked to grades. The lack of a common policy among and within schools in a district only invites trouble. Does teacher consistency in grading mean that grades awarded will be perceived by everyone as fair? Fairness, to borrow from a favorite cliché, is in the eye of the beholder.

This chapter reflects the view that the primary purpose of assessment is to improve the learning situation and pupil achievement. By finding out what and how well students achieve, we can improve our teaching.

Is assessment something you do *to* children or *with* them? Each emphasis reflects a different outlook. Have you ever been asked to do something important without knowing exactly how your performance was going to be appraised? Did you like the feeling? When we work out standards or expectations *with* students, they usually achieve more and see the assessment process in a different light. It puts their intelligence to work, so they can better guide their own learning within the limits of their maturity and experience. If you want to maximize your teaching effectiveness, make clear to children what makes up success in *everything* they do in your science program. Assess together a broad array of their work, not simply tests.

Even the noblest of intentions must heed the limits of time. Zero in on objectives that are most likely to yield a rich payoff. Let's look at some times when chances for assessment generally arise.

We have three main opportunities to appraise students' abilities: before, during, and after teaching the activities in each lesson. The introduction or bridge of a lesson is a good place to assess students' present knowledge, including misconceptions. This is called *diagnostic assessment.* It can be done in a written pretest, but usually the open-ended questions you put to the children serve better, because you can follow up what they say.

Appraising students' work behaviors during activities is *formative assessment.* This is an apt word, since what we observe helps to shape or form our immediate, responsive teaching behaviors. This quick feedback to students, in turn, helps them to form improved learning behaviors.

Finally, when we assess pupil achievement after activities, we practice *summative assess-*

ment. To do so, we can ask questions when we summarize and review previous activities. We can also appraise children's projects or other completed work, and use tests. Let's now examine ways to assess science achievement through traditional and authentic assessment.

TRADITIONAL ASSESSMENT

When we think of traditional assessment, we think of tests. Paper-and-pencil tests were the predominate assessment tool for many generations of students. So you may be thinking, if they were good enough for me, why shouldn't I continue to rely on them for my students? The answer to that question is in two parts. The first is in the origins of this type of assessment and the second is in the usefulness of traditional tests. The beginning of traditional testing protocols was in the behaviorist theory (see page 28), which predominated education during the 1920s and beyond. It was thought that any complex skill or understanding could be broken down into simpler, easily tested parts. Once these building blocks were mastered, an individual would be able to master the complex understandings. Stated another way: If a teacher wanted students to master a complex scientific skill, he would need to break it down into parts that could be individually learned and tested.

Unfortunately, the behaviorists could never effectively determine how the individual parts led to the complex skills. This became the biggest drawback to the behaviorist theory, since it could not account for the complexity of higher-level learning; that is, learning that involves the basic skills, the interaction among them, and the technique for identifying which basic skill to use at any given time.

The usefulness of traditional testing is generally hampered because tests are employed as an after-the-fact measure to check basic recall of facts. For many years, educators were in the

"we teach what we test" mode and tests of this nature were "fundamentally incompatible" to reform efforts (Resnick & Resnick, 1989). Vocabulary and definitions of scientific concepts were more important than the applications of the concepts, especially since that was what was tested most often. It was like learning all of the vocabulary of a foreign language without ever taking time to actually speak the language or converse with others using the language. We now know that immediate, corrective feedback is necessary for effective teaching of scientific concepts. This feedback can be gained through a combination of procedures, including traditional and authentic assessments.

WRITTEN TESTS

Written tests are typically found at ends of lessons, chapters, or units. They are designed to assess pupil understanding of science words, concepts, and generalizations; the ability to apply them; and the ability to do some critical thinking. A big drawback of most traditional tests is that the results come too late to affect the way the unit or lessons are taught. The immediate, corrective feedback necessary for effective teaching is absent if we rely on tests alone. Since only limited time is available, it's not always possible to go back and effectively take care of incompletely understood or misconceived material.

Another drawback of written tests is that it is hard to test science processes in that format. The processes are used most often in a context where children manipulate science materials. In other words, they perform some observable actions that demonstrate their ability to apply one or more processes, usually with their knowledge of a concept. What are some features of traditional assessment tools and how can some of them be better used in your classroom? Let's look at some of the possibilities.

Multiple Choice Tests

Multiple choice tests were at the very heart of the "drill and kill" curriculum that was pervasive in education for many years. They are not generally considered a tool in assessing meaningful learning. They are useful, however, in providing one piece of a complex assessment picture. When used correctly, they can be beneficial instruments in determining content knowledge and the vocabulary of science. In other words, multiple choice items may still provide a baseline measurement for your planning.

When using these types of tests, remember that they do not have to always occur after a chapter or unit. Try giving them beforehand to see if you need to focus on the language of science before application of the language. Keep in mind, though, that students will better learn the science vocabulary within the context of an activity. Learning the word *paramecium* while looking at pond water under a microscope is more effective than learning the book definition of a *paramecium*—"a larger protozoan than an amoeba."

When using multiple choice tests, remember to adjust the stems, or introductory portions of the question, as well as the distractors, or alternatives, to better suit your needs. For example:

Animals

a. reproduce

b. breathe oxygen

c. require food

d. all of the above

Plants

a. breathe only carbon dioxide

b. cannot reproduce

c. only make food, but do not use food

d. none of the above

One of the general differences between plants and animals is that

a. Animals live longer than plants.

b. Plants can only take in carbon dioxide and give off oxygen whereas animals only use the oxygen provided by plants.

c. Plants have roots so therefore they can never be found in other locations. Animals can move freely so they are able to relocate to different environments.

d. Plants use sunlight to make their own food and animals rely on the food produced by plants.

In each case, the answer is "d", but the third example requires the student to think beyond basic recall of facts and consider in more detail the characteristics of plants and animals. Another example would be to replace a basic recall question with illustrations such as:

In which circuit will the light bulb glow?

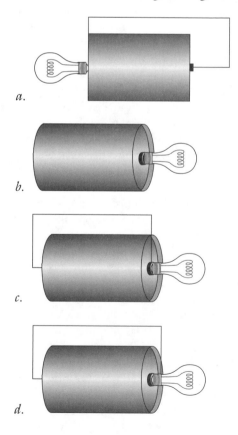

a.

b.

c.

d.

Instead of:

What is needed to light a flashlight bulb?

a. a battery

b. a wire

c. a light bulb

d. all of the above

Again, keep in mind that multiple choice tests are from the teacher's perspective and generally do not indicate deeper understandings by the student. Asking a student to identify a particular insect will not effectively show whether the student understands the characteristics of that insect or how it is related to other insects in its family, genus, or species.

True–False Tests

True–false items are basically 50–50 chance items. Try to eliminate guesswork in your true–false questions by using them to gauge attitudes or application of ideas rather than retention of fact or vocabulary. For example, compare the following two questions.

True or False: I like to test for pollutants in water samples of the stream that flows past the school.

True or False: Water testing is one way to determine whether a stream has pollutants.

The first question will reveal an attitude as well as reinforce the link between water testing and pollution identification.

Another good way to use true–false questions is to examine an application of the formula, rather than merely testing its recall.

True or False: If you were pushing a friend on a swing and moved her a total of 5 meters with a force of 2 newtons, you would have done 10 joules of work.

True or False: Work = force used × distance moved.

Matching Tests

These tests include a list of items in one column and a list of responses in another. For a good matching test, remember to keep the listed items and responses brief so as not to confuse the student. Also, it is good to allow for more responses than list items and to allow the student to use some responses twice or not at all. This promotes more critical thinking and reduces the likelihood of correct response based on guesswork.

Completion and Short Answer Items

Completion or short answer items require the student to respond to an item with a word or short phrase. The chances of guessing at an answer are greatly reduced, unless clues to the answers are inadvertently provided in the questions.

Short answer questions are often difficult to construct. In the following question, there are a number of possibilities.

Temperature is measured _____.

Possible answers may include by a thermometer, in degrees, in Celsius, in Fahrenheit, in Kelvin, by scientists, by nurses, or a number of other possibilities. Construction of these types of items will require careful planning as the test is constructed. An example of a more carefully worded question would be as follows.

The scale on a Fahrenheit or Celsius thermometer is divided into many equal lines or divisions called _____.

The desired answer to both questions is *degrees,* but the second question leaves little room for misinterpretation by the student. Short answer items require an objective interpretation when correcting them. Again, careful wording helps eliminate any problems as can be found in the following example.

Fuel can be _____.

Possible answers include something burned; something that can produce heat; in the form of a solid, liquid, or gas; gasoline; oil; natural gas; wood; coal; garbage; or a number of other possibilities. By rewording the question you could get at a more specific answer such as solid, liquid, or gas.

Fuel can be in one of three classes, _____, _____, or _____.

Essay Items

Essay items provide a bridge between traditional assessment procedures and authentic assessment practices. Essay questions are useful in evaluating whether students are able to clearly express personal ideas. This type of question can be designed to assess higher-order thinking, the ability to solve problems, or the capability to reason about the interrelationships between concepts.

Essay questions can be very subjective, because there is not one right or wrong answer. Questions can be too vague for students to understand exactly what answer the teacher wants. They may also be too obvious, in which case they are not effective in measuring achievement.

Language differences between students will affect useful ability to answer questions. Students with poor language skills will often do poorly on these items, regardless of content knowledge. Likewise, students with good language skills may be able to bluff through answers which they do not fully understand. As with other tests, careful construction of items will help make the test more meaningful. Compare the following two questions.

1. *What are the phases of the moon?*
2. *Explain what we would observe here on earth as the moon goes through its phases and why it appears this way.*

The first question is wide open for your students to interpret. They could respond by just listing new, first quarter, full, last quarter. The second question requires the student to provide an explanation for why the phases occur and what they would look like, as well as the names of the phases. Essay tests that are well constructed match what was learned in class; ask well-defined, explicit questions that are understandable to all students; and indicate, either in writing or through discourse, exactly what the teacher is looking for as an acceptable response. The teacher should set and communicate to the students her expectations for length, detail, and spelling prior to the test. A grading rubric should also be developed that lists the specifics of what is expected. Use of a checklist will eliminate most subjectivity.

AUTHENTIC ASSESSMENT

There is no doubt that assessment is in the forefront of the current educational reform efforts. Authentic assessment is an important way to ensure that national, state, and district reform efforts are effective. An authentic assessment procedure, like a portfolio or classroom observation, can be useful in determining the opportunity to learn science or the ability to perform process skills, but it does not generally provide an easy comparison of a standardized test score for a group of children. It does allow the observer to better evaluate conceptual development and problem-solving ability.

Your students should know how to *apply* what they have learned. They need to be able to solve real problems, make informed decisions based on sound scientific observations or experimentation, and understand the science–technology–society interactions that occur in everyday life.

Authentic assessment provides a close match between the learning activity and the evaluation activity. In fact, a good example of an authentic assessment is one in which the students do not even consider they are being evaluated.

Performance-based Assessment

A performance-based assessment will not only generate an answer by the students, but will indicate the process used by the students to arrive at that answer. There are valuable ways to assess the procedure the student uses to arrive at an answer. This is often more important than the answer itself. In fact, many times there will be more than one correct answer.

Examples of the products developed through this type of assessment include models based on scientific concepts, written material, decisions, and applications of process skills such as experiments with definite or undetermined conclusions. These activities are evaluated by teacher observation, interviewing the students, providing a written outline for the student to fill in, or a student's daily journal entry. Journals should be written in daily and checked often, so that a dialogue can occur between the student and the teacher. This will indicate if the student has misconceptions or if you need to adjust your instructional practice in any way.

For a quick reminder of a wide range of operations students may demonstrate in performance tests, look at the summary of science processes on pages 80–96. Assessing these operations requires students to be placed in contexts that allow them to gather and process data. To help yourself better track the achievement of process skills, develop a recording chart similar to the one in Figure 7-1.

In its purest form, a performance test has the child demonstrate operations with concrete materials. For instance, the test may ask a child to *measure* several irregularly shaped rocks to find the one with the greatest volume. Besides the rocks, materials might include a wide-mouth, clear plastic cup, spoon, marking pen, and container of water. To demonstrate this process, the child might partly fill the cup and mark the water level with the pen. Next, he might slowly submerge and remove each rock with the spoon, taking care each time to mark the water level and not spill water. If the process is performed properly, the child identifies the rock with the highest water level as having the most volume and the test item is scored correct.

Another performance test might ask a pupil to *infer* the identity of three unknown leaves by consulting a chart with descriptions of leaves. A variation might ask the pupil to *classify* a half-

Name	Classify	Observe	Measure	Infer	Communicate	Experiment
ROSE	(A-C-T)	(A-C-T)	(A-C-T)	(A-C-T)	(A-C-T)	(A-C-T)
DAVE	(A-C-T)	(A-C-T)	(A-C-T)	(A-C-T)	(A-C-T)	(A-C-T)
NINA	(A-C-T)	(A-C-T)	(A-C-T)	(A-C-T)	(A-C-T)	(A-C-T)
ALAN	(A-C-T)	(A-C-T)	(A-C-T)	(A-C-T)	(A-C-T)	(A-C-T)

NOTE: A = Achieved skill, C = Continuing to improve, T = Trouble applying

Figure 7-1
Process skill checklist.

dozen leaves by putting them into two or more groups and stating the observable property or properties she used to do so. If the groupings are consistent with the stated properties, the answer is scored correct.

Working with concrete materials is not always necessary. Performance tests could include students classifying pictures of leaves or animals, for instance. Another test would be to supply a chart that shows data from an investigation and ask the child to interpret the data and draw a conclusion.

When children are capable writers, some performance tests may be completed entirely with words. For *experimenting*, this problem might appear:

> *Suppose you want to find out whether bean plants will grow faster with Fertilizer A or Fertilizer B. How could you set up an experiment to find out?*

Or the problem could address a specific part of the experiment:

> *What variables do you need to control in the plant experiment?*

Some teachers with active, hands-on/minds-on science programs bypass performance tests. They believe that they get all the assessment data they need by observing children at work and interacting with them during regular activity times and follow-up discussions. This may be possible with a wide array of process-rich activities and systematic observing. But mandated performance tests are becoming more prevalent at school district, state, and national levels. Avoiding them entirely in the regular science program may cause students to do poorly on such tests. Reliability may also be affected, since your observations of certain students may be biased. One way to complete this type of assessment is through an instrument such as the example in Figure 7-2.

You will note from Figure 7-2 that this particular checklist is for a small group assignment.

You will have to modify the checklist to use individually or with different learning situations. Also, if you are working with early grades, you will find that teacher observation is the primary means of gathering assessment data. In these situations, it is important that you track progress over longer periods of time and record progress as students develop new skills.

Projects

It's a good idea to view science projects as normal and regular extensions of concepts and generalizations studied by the whole class. This view offers many chances for students to take on projects, and they are more likely to do their own work. It also makes assessment simpler, less formal, and more frequent than when projects are reserved for science fairs.

A good project usually requires self-assessment from start to finish. If guidelines are simple, and your comments regarding success are consistent, students will develop judgment in assessing their efforts during projects and when reporting them.

Projects also give many chances for students to display the scientific attitudes of *critical thinking* (Are the parts of the report logical and consistent?), *persistence* (Is there evidence that the child overcame difficulties?), *inventiveness* (Was the child resourceful in substituting materials?), and *curiosity* (Does the child ask further questions?). When you notice behaviors like these and give positive comments, you reinforce them.

Peer- or Self-designed Instruments

Try experimenting with allowing your students to design an assessment instrument or procedure. Often they will become more involved in the learning process if they are included in the decision making.

Completed by the Student

Student Names

List the names of the students in your group.

Problem to Be Solved

State the problem you are investigating in your own words.

Method or Strategy

How will you go about solving the problem?

Skills

Identify how you used the following skills while investigating this problem:

    classifying
    observing
    measuring
    inferring/predicting
    communicating
    experimenting

Results

Written Response
What did you find from your investigation?

Pictures
Can you illustrate your findings?

Verification and Communication

Did you compare your answer with other groups? Did you verify it with the teacher or some other source?

Teacher Checklist

_____ Students understood the problem.
          (0—no; 1—somewhat; 2—completely)
_____ Students developed a method/strategy to solve the problem.
          (0—no; 1—somewhat; 2—completely)
_____ Students used scientific skills in solving the problem.
          (0—no; 1—somewhat; 2—completely)
_____ Students were able to come to a conclusion.
          (0—no; 1—somewhat; 2—completely)
_____ Students communicated and verified their results.
          (0—no; 1—somewhat; 2—completely)
_____ Total (possible 10)

Figure 7-2
Performance-based assessment checklist (upper elementary).

Interviews

Interviews are an effective way to get information directly. They can be especially useful with early elementary students who cannot express their thoughts in writing. Keep in mind that the specific answers provided by the children are less important than the reasons why they responded as they did. Try to look for trends in thinking patterns and identify misconceptions.

When using interviews as an assessment tool, keep in mind that you should be accepting of all answers and value the child's thoughts and opinions. Put yourself in the child's perspective and ease the sometimes uncomfortable situation by:

selecting non-conflicting times to interview

sitting at floor level

talking in a cheerful tone, and

informing the child before the interview as to what you are doing.

Intervene only as necessary to keep the discussion focused on the topic. Word questions carefully to promote further discussion. Begin with questions such as:

Tell me about . . .

What do you think about . . .

How do you feel about . . .

Can you explain why . . .

Describe how you would . . .

How did you discover . . .

Maintain the discussion with questions such as:

What else can you say about . . .

What if you were to . . .

How is this related to . . .

Is there another way to explain . . .

How could we change . . .

What question should I ask the next student about . . .

Finally, allow students to create illustrations or use models as needed. Some students may even want to "speak" through a teddy bear or other object if they are too shy to speak directly to you. Do not mistake the child's being afraid to speak as a sign that they are unfamiliar with the concept discussed.

Journals

You saw earlier (pages 89–90) that recording data in a notebook or log is usually necessary when observations occur over time. Doing so makes it likelier that students will keep track of changes, observe more carefully, and think about what they are doing. Teachers may also ask children to respond in writing to questions in activities, for similar reasons. Notice how often questions appear in the investigations and activities section. This practice is typical of elementary school science. Students can appraise their recordings by comparing them with those of other group members. When data conflict, it's only natural for them to pursue reasons.

Today the concept of *writing to learn* is applied in all subjects. It holds much value for science. Many teachers have their students keep a science journal, which also may serve for recording data. A journal offers opportunities to improve science learning and practice important writing skills at the same time. Writing requires thinking, which changes with different purposes.

Descriptive writing can be used, among other possibilities, to identify things: "Can you describe an animal (plant, habitat, etc.) so well, without naming it, that your partner can tell what it is?"; or, "Make a chart that shows the properties of these rocks. Can your partner match the rocks to your descriptions?" Assessing these writings is straightforward. If there is a problem with a conflicting answer, both partners can work to figure out why.

Defining concepts in writing, before and after instruction, enables children to assess for themselves what they have gained from their studies. The questions, "What is soil and what is it made of?" may yield quite different results before versus after lessons.

Creative writing also can and should be linked to concepts being studied. If your students are writing a story about an imaginary visit to an outer planet, you might ask them to correctly use recently learned words, such as *orbit, acceleration,* and *zero gravity.* Cooperative learning groups can judge whether concepts are used correctly and consult with you as needed.

You can also ask students at different developmental levels to write summaries of what they have learned in a lesson, give an opinion and defend it, write a persuasive letter, compose interview questions, and do much other writing. Each form can be assessed for clarity, logic, and completeness.

It is important to have your students assess their own writing as much as possible, through clear directions and standards. You'll probably want to *sample* their work from time to time, but don't end up *doing* their work. Try providing some guidance for them to self-evaluate their work, such as:

> *How would you describe your level of participation in the activity?*
>
> *What contributions did you make to the solution of the problem?*
>
> *What best describes your role in the group (leader, recorder, materials manager, maintenance crew, liaison, or bystander)?*
>
> *How effectively do you manage time while completing tasks? What are you learning in science?*

Portfolios

Would you like to cultivate more self-assessment abilities like those described in Vignette 7-1? motivate increased effort in learning? show parents tangible and understandable evidence of what their children are learning? If so, con-

sider a *portfolio* for each child. This is a sampling of work over time, collected and stored in a folder. It gives observable evidence of knowledge, processes, and attitudes gained by the child over one or more science units. The work record may appear in any or all of these forms:

■ Tests—end of lesson, unit, performance
■ Activity log pages
■ Project or book reports
■ Concept maps, other graphic organizers
■ Charts
■ Graphs
■ Science journal pages
■ Creative stories
■ Science words learned
■ Artwork
■ Out-of-class assignments
■ Computer resources or data
■ Videotaped resources or data
■ Cartoons and analysis or explanation

These materials may be stored in a standard expandable folder, or a larger folder cut from poster board. Should you have a separate science portfolio? Or is it better to reserve a section for science in a more comprehensive portfolio? Primary-level teachers lean more toward comprehensive portfolios. Either type gets overstuffed and hard to store or manage, unless some material is sent home periodically or discarded. Storage considerations may prompt you to consider electronic portfolios. The advantage to electronic portfolios is that they can be easily stored on disk, reducing the amount of paper in the classroom. The disadvantage is that keyboarding skills of students may be inadequate or computer access may be limited in the elementary classroom.

Both the child and you should select items for the portfolio. When the child selects artifacts to demonstrate his learning, he can also jot down why he selected the item. This will

PORTFOLIO ASSESSMENT
Mrs. Christine Peters
Harborcreek School District, Pennsylvania

Over the last several years, I've been using portfolio assessment more and more. At first I felt somewhat uncomfortable with the notion. I worried about when I'd find the time in our hectic day to collect, sort, choose, meet, and interview. Now that I've been using this form of individualized assessment, I see that my first graders are the ones who are responsible for the selection process. This is actually the most important aspect of using portfolios. By involving the children in the decision-making process, they achieve a deeper sense of pride, a feeling of ownership about their work, and a desire for excellence.

In building portfolios, I am concentrating on the *process* of the child's learning as well as the *product*. My students are better able to focus on a specific goal rather than on a letter grade. I am also promoting a closer relationship with my students, because my assessment focuses on the development of a student's work over time. Not only do my students feel a great sense of pride, but I feel like the world's best teacher when I compare one of their spelling assessments from September to one from May. Or when I listen to one of my student's oral reading cassettes from the first week of school—when she knew very few words and didn't have enough skills to sound them out—and compare it to the middle or end of the tape when she is able to read anything she picks up.

The toughest part of using portfolio assessment is deciding when to fit the interviewing and selection process into your day. I have tried many different approaches and what I like the best is what I call "Free Choice Time." Every other Friday afternoon, the boys and girls in my classroom are free to do what they would like to do. Of course, I give them some guidance in what they are choosing from, and if there is any unfinished work for the day or week, that must be completed first. I will often invite one or two other adults into our room to help with the interviewing and selection process. Administrators, instructional and learning support teachers, and parents have all been involved in this process in my classroom in the past. It is valuable to use the same volunteers so that little time will be re-spent on "training," however, sometimes this is not possible.

A typical Free Choice Time in my first-grade classroom will look like this: A small group working in the science center on a food pyramid with pictures they've cut out of magazines; several children playing pictionary using the sand trays and shaving cream boards in the corner; a group of children making numbers out of clay to take to the kindergarten room; two children taping themselves reading one of the big books our class wrote entitled *Ten Black Dots* (also to take to the kindergarten classroom); and several children are reading books from our classroom library which they will then present to their classmates using puppets or posters they've made. At the same time, I (along with my adult volunteers) will be meeting individually with each of my 22 students. Before the students are individually interviewed, they are instructed as to what materials are required for their meeting. They have an idea of which (products) works they will want to place into their portfolio and they've thought about why they've chosen such pieces. During their interview, I go over the selected pieces and together (later in the year the students fill this out independently), we write out a Portfolio and Goals Survey. This survey states the data, the title of piece, why the piece was chosen, the favorite part of piece, what the piece shows, what the child has learned so far, what he wants to learn next, and things that will help him learn better.

If I have several adult helpers, and time permits, I also find it very valuable to go over one of my checklists with each child. One week I may share each child's oral reading checklist with them and the next week I'll share their writing or cooperative learning checklist. These are forms that I keep in their portfolios to record learning skills and behaviors that I observe in their daily work and in how they work with each other.

I love using portfolios in my primary classroom! The students enjoy having a collection of their work that progresses throughout the year. Even my students with learning difficulties can't help but see the progression of skill in their work. They all feel successful, and are always trying to do their best, hoping that what they are presently working on will be added to their portfolio. Parents are even excited about the portfolio assessment going on in my classroom. They can see their child's learning in concrete terms and become partners in the learning process. Parents are invited in often to view their child's works, and a few times a year, the portfolio is sent home along with a letter in which the parents are encouraged to give feedback.

It doesn't take much preparation to begin using portfolios in your classroom. All you need are some file and pocket folders, composition books, cassette and/or video tapes, large manila envelopes, and lots of stick-on notes. To store the portfolios I use a large plastic crate. A cardboard box would even fit the purpose. Some of the items that go into my students' portfolios are: my observations, their writing samples, journals, reading, writing, math, and cooperative learning inventories, art work, parent surveys, rubrics, book evaluations, and child-selected samples of day-to-day work.

Portfolio assessment teaches students how to learn and teaches teachers how to slow down, get to know each student and her strengths and needs, and develop a curriculum that appeals to each student's multiple talents. It encourages students—and teachers—to strive for excellence in all they do.

make the learning and assessment more relevant. You will also find that in order to have diverse student portfolios, you must have diverse learning opportunities in the classroom. Otherwise, the portfolio becomes a collection of the standard science tests and vocabulary sheets.

Everything should be dated, so items in a category can be put in order by time, and progress observed. Guide children to look for improvements in their work, and to discuss examples they have selected with their groups. Encourage them to pair an original effort with an improved version whenever possible. This can make them more conscious of their progress and help develop pride in work done well. It can also provide incentive for producing more work of good quality.

To help children set goals for themselves, periodically have them review and think carefully about their work samples. This might be done monthly or at the end of a unit. Some teachers ask their students to write thoughtful responses to these two questions:

What do I feel good about?

What do I want to improve?

Responses to the second question can make it easy to set goals with children. At the next periodic review, they can examine their portfolios for evidence that the goals were met.

Scoring the portfolio is a final consideration. Figure 7-3 shows a typical scoring method for elementary science portfolios.

Concept Maps

One message from researchers in human learning is especially clear: Organization and meaning go together. The better we are able to relate

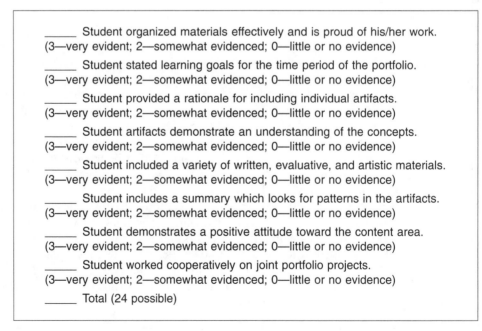

_____ Student organized materials effectively and is proud of his/her work.
(3—very evident; 2—somewhat evidenced; 0—little or no evidence)

_____ Student stated learning goals for the time period of the portfolio.
(3—very evident; 2—somewhat evidenced; 0—little or no evidence)

_____ Student provided a rationale for including individual artifacts.
(3—very evident; 2—somewhat evidenced; 0—little or no evidence)

_____ Student artifacts demonstrate an understanding of the concepts.
(3—very evident; 2—somewhat evidenced; 0—little or no evidence)

_____ Student included a variety of written, evaluative, and artistic materials.
(3—very evident; 2—somewhat evidenced; 0—little or no evidence)

_____ Student includes a summary which looks for patterns in the artifacts.
(3—very evident; 2—somewhat evidenced; 0—little or no evidence)

_____ Student demonstrates a positive attitude toward the content area.
(3—very evident; 2—somewhat evidenced; 0—little or no evidence)

_____ Student worked cooperatively on joint portfolio projects.
(3—very evident; 2—somewhat evidenced; 0—little or no evidence)

_____ Total (24 possible)

Figure 7-3
Portfolio assessment scoring rubric.

new information to what we already know, the easier it is to remember and use it. Science programs now commonly employ several different graphic organizers to help children construct meaningful relationships among the facts and concepts they learn. The *concept map* is probably the most used organizer. It's also an excellent means to assess conceptual knowledge.

Figure 7-4 shows a concept map that was developed by a student independently studying chameleons. It was generated with a computerized concept map program. As you can see from the map, it contains *nodes* representing the individual concepts and *links* connecting the concepts in a meaningful way. This type of assessment provides a richer view of the student's knowledge than typical objective tests.

A concept map, according to Novak and Gowin (1984), is a "schematic device for representing a set of concept meanings embedded in

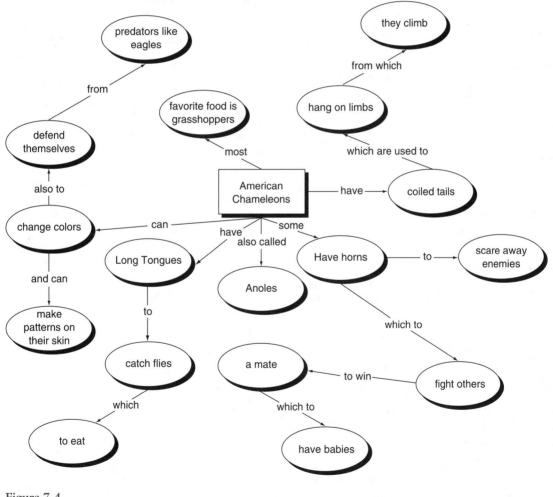

Figure 7-4
Concept map.

a framework of propositions" (p. 15). The propositions are used to link the concepts, and the map in its entirety is like a snapshot of the person's conceptual understandings. Concept maps can be used before, during, or after a learning activity to assess development of understandings. They are also an effective small group project. When done in groups, communication and negotiation among members help to identify student misconceptions.

Vee maps, similar to concept maps, are also useful in developing and conducting investigations. They are a "road map showing the route from prior knowledge to new and future knowledge" (Roth & Verechaka, 1993, p. 25).

Note that students often make different concept maps after receiving the same instruction. This happens even when they understand all the concepts in the way you intend. They may simply view relationships among the concepts differently. It is important for them to regularly compare their maps with partners and interact with you to more fully assess what they have learned.

Teacher Observations

The job of teaching is inexact at best. We might view it as a series of consecutively developed hypotheses. That is, each thing we do or say is a kind of hypothesis that we are uncertain will be accepted (learned) by the children. If much teaching takes place before feedback shows that learning has occurred, we may make many unwarranted assumptions.

We can observe, and often help students stay on track, in whole-class settings, but the most productive times are likely to be in individual and small-group situations. There are many chances for informal teacher–child contacts during the activity times in lessons. Notice what your students say and do when they interact with you, a partner, or other members of a small group. What you observe gives you data

for fast self-correction or for assisting individual students, if needed.

The quickest way to find out if students grasp concepts and processes is to ask questions and listen carefully to responses. By fashioning further questions to follow up responses, you can detect misconceptions and may be able to quickly address them. You can also discover much more about what students are learning.

Open-Ended Questions

An open-ended question is one where there is more than one correct response. The response may be an answer to a question, a procedure to arrive at a solution to a problem, or an opinion about something. The value of this type of question is that it can be answered differently by each student. This type of question is also useful in identifying misconceptions or promoting divergent thinking.

Evaluation of open-ended questions often lies in the completeness of the response. A clear, complete response that includes accurate information and/or the student's opinions is desirable. A rubric for scoring this type of question could simply be a six-point scale based on information provided by the student, such as the one in Figure 7-5.

Some guidelines for writing open-ended questions include:

Make sure that the question is understandable to the student.

Do not lead students to an answer; let them construct one on their own.

Make the questions interesting whenever possible.

Match the question with the content or process being studied.

Allow sufficient wait time for students to respond.

Student understands the question, provides a complete response, provides accurate information, justifies the response as needed, and provides additional information as requested.

5—all five areas complete

4—one of the above five is missing

3—two of the above five are missing

2—three of the above five are missing

1—four of the above five are missing

0—five out of five missing or no response

Name Types	Water Cycle	Hurricane Formation	Tornado Cause	Cloud
Bonnie	_____	_____	_____	_____
Chris	_____	_____	_____	_____
Shirley	_____	_____	_____	_____
Jonathan	_____	_____	_____	_____
Christine	_____	_____	_____	_____

Figure 7-5
Open-ended question scoring rubric.

Allow multiple students time to answer and ask further questions before going on to another question.

Attempt to get at deeper levels of understanding through increasingly complex questions.

Maintain students' interest through meaningful, thought-provoking questions.

ASSESSING ATTITUDES

Recall that scientific attitudes of children are often shown by their behaviors in four broad categories: curiosity, inventiveness, critical thinking, and persistence (see page 100). The sample behaviors listed under these categories are the kinds of actions you look for when you appraise growth in attitudes. Good times to do so are during hands-on activities and discussions. Remember, though, that broad attitudes cannot be developed quickly. They are a long-range by-product of the quality of learning activities and general atmosphere of your classroom.

Take time to sample attitudes periodically. If necessary develop an informal attitude inventory. It should include items such as:

Are you curious about nature or scientific phenomena?

Do you enjoy science as much as other subjects?

Do you complete science activities outside of class time?

Do you watch science-related shows at home on videotapes or television?

Have you read any science-related books lately?

Do you know a scientist in your neighborhood or community?

Do you like to answer questions during science class?

Have you considered a career in a science field?

In instances where the students cannot read, try using smiling, neutral, and frowning faces on a scoring sheet. They can respond to items as you read them.

Another good way to assess attitudes is with the Draw-A-Scientist Test (Mason, Kahle, & Gardner, 1991). In this test, children are provided a blank piece of paper and asked to "draw a scientist." The test is scored by counting the number of stereotypical indicators such as lab coats, pencils and pens in a shirt pocket, male gender, facial hair, and glasses. A high score on this test indicates that the student has a very stereotypical image of a scientist. Try this out with your students to see what their image of a scientist is like.

THE ROLE OF ASSESSMENT IN SCIENCE EDUCATION REFORM

President Bush, in response to numerous reports on education, announced national testing for fourth, eighth, and twelfth graders in science, English, mathematics, history, and geography. He was concerned that America would no longer be competitive in the global marketplace, and he wanted the U.S. to be first in the world in science and mathematics. His contention included a very important challenge that we improve "not only the methods and means that we have used in the past" for education, "but also the yardsticks we've used to measure our progress" (Bush, 1991, p. 2). Bush wanted the country to move from the usual easy-to-administer, cost-efficient multiple choice testing program to one that aligned with the new methods of teaching.

Many projects, either national or at the state level, set out to provide high standards for students in terms of content and also performance standards based on application of the content. The most comprehensive and widely accepted of these is the National Science Education *Assessment Standards* developed by the National Research Council (1996). They are available online at http://www.nap.edu/readingroom/books/nses/html/contents.html.

National Science Education *Standards*

The *Standards* were developed to make *scientific literacy for all* a reality. The *Standards* call for dramatic changes in how students are assessed nationwide. Below are the five assessment standards and a brief commentary on each.

1. *Assessment Standard A (National Research Council, 1996, p. 78): Assessments must be consistent with the decisions they are designed to inform.*

   ■ Assessments are deliberately designed.

   ■ Assessments have explicitly stated purposes.

   ■ The relationships between decisions and data are clear.

   ■ Assessment procedures are internally consistent.

Before using an assessment procedure in your classroom, ask yourself some basic questions. Why you are using one procedure or another? What questions do you hope to answer through the data collected? How will you analyze all of the data collected? Is your scoring rubric fair and consistent? Will this approach be helpful to the students and lead to good instructional decisions? These are important guidelines. Do not begin using portfolios just because the teacher next door started using them. Rather, begin using them because you see the value in an ongoing communication between yourself and the students.

2. *Assessment Standard B (National Research Council, 1996, p. 79): Achievement and opportunity to learn science must be assessed.*

   ■ Achievement data collected focus on the science content that is most important for students to learn.

   ■ Opportunity-to-learn data collected focus on the most powerful indicators.

   ■ Equal attention must be given to the assessment of opportunity to learn and to the assessment of student achievement.

The American Association for the Advancement of Science *Benchmarks* (1993) call for reducing the amount of material being covered. The goal of *teaching less but teaching it better* does not mean to teach science less often, but to teach fewer unrelated facts and spend more time making connections and refining skills. Similarly, assessment should focus on what is the most important. Standard B makes an interesting point that assessment of the opportunity to learn is as important as assessing the learning itself. Assessment is an ongoing process. Spend time before, during, and after instruction on assessment.

3. *Assessment Standard C (National Research Council, 1996, p. 83): The technical quality of the data collected is well matched to the decisions and actions taken on the basis of their interpretation.*

   ■ The feature that is claimed to be measured is actually measured.

   ■ Assessment tasks are authentic.

■ An individual student's performance is similar on two or more tasks that claim to measure the same aspect of student achievement.

■ Students have adequate opportunity to demonstrate their achievements.

■ Assessment tasks and methods of presenting them provide data that are sufficiently stable to lead to the same decisions if used at different times.

Validity is a term which is used to represent the ability of a test or other assessment tool to measure what it is supposed to measure. Given the objective to measure students' knowledge related to the names of the systems of the human body, a fill-in-the-blank or short answer test might be selected. If you want them to compare the digestive system of a human to an earthworm, then it would be more appropriate for them to have the ability to draw pictures and provide an open-ended response. A good assessment will indicate performance regardless of content. In other words, if students can classify leaves with a dichotomous key, then they should also be able to complete a similar classification of minerals. Also, the assessment must be appropriate for their developmental level and language/cultural diversity. If the assessment is out of context, then the student is not really being measured appropriately. For example, you cannot expect a student from the inner city to have the same understandings of soil erosion and farming practices as a student whose parents are actively farming.

Authentic assessment means that students are not being assessed to see how many famous scientists they can name, but to see how well they can perform the same tasks those scientists employ. Authentic assessment forms—like the performance test, teacher observation, and students writing in journals—are best for evaluating this type of hands-on/minds-on performance.

4. *Assessment Standard D (National Research Council, 1996, p. 85): Assessment practices must be fair.*

■ Assessment tasks must be reviewed for the use of stereotypes, for assumptions that reflect the perspectives or experiences of a particular group, for language that might be offensive to a particular group, and for other features that might distract students from the intended task.

■ Large-scale assessments must use statistical techniques to identify potential bias among subgroups.

■ Assessment tasks must be appropriately modified to accommodate the needs of students with physical disabilities, learning disabilities, or limited English proficiency.

■ Assessment tasks must be set in a variety of contexts, be engaging to students with different interests and experiences, and must not assume the perspective or experience of a particular gender, racial, or ethnic group.

Inherent to the Science Education *Standards* is the notion of science for *all* students. Gender, race, and cultural differences should not be evident in the results of assessments. Think about a performance-based assessment where students are asked to predict the distance a basketball will bounce depending on the height from which it is dropped. The students' experience levels with a basketball will vary depending on gender, national origin, and a variety of other factors. Providing a number of similar prediction opportunities with golf balls, tennis balls, soccer balls, and ping-pong balls will round out the assessment of prediction and create more meaningful data. In any case, the teacher should be sensitive to gender, race, cultural origin, language proficiency, disabilities, and religious differences, providing numerous ways for

students to demonstrate skills or conceptual understandings.

5. *Assessment Standard E (National Research Council, 1996, p. 86): The inferences made from assessments about student achievement and opportunity to learn must be sound.*

■ When making inferences from assessment data about student achievement and opportunity to learn science, explicit reference needs to be made to the assumptions on which the inferences are based.

Do not allow out-of-context assessments to guide decision making. The assessment decisions you make for your students are not necessarily generalizable school- or district-wide. Someone looking at the results of a performance-based classification of animals assessment you recently gave may interpret the results as a failure. You may view it otherwise, since you did this activity before instruction to see what transference there was from the recent activity on classifying candy. As you begin your selection of activities and assessment procedures, you may want to review the chapter on assessment in the National Science Education *Standards* or select other readings from the list at the end of this chapter.

SUMMARY

1. Effective teaching and assessment are more likely to occur when we have a few objectives in mind.

2. Assessment of objectives occurs mainly at three times: before activities (diagnostic assessment), during activities (formative assessment), and after activities (summative assessment).

3. There needs to be a match between the assessment instrument and the methodology used to facilitate learning. Performance measures work better than paper-and-pencil tests when you are facilitating process skill

development. Portfolios or journals are more appropriate when you want to assess individual achievement during activity or laboratory periods.

4. It is advantageous to evaluate students with more than one assessment tool and over longer periods of time. A combination of content (paper-and-pencil tests), attitudinal (surveys/interviews), and opportunity-to-learn instruments (teacher observations/portfolios/journals) will be more effective than a single essay question or multiple choice test.

5. Concentrate on assessment in your classroom. Many states are still debating the issue of assessment. Politics should not drive instruction in your classroom. Teaching to a state or national test will often be more detrimental to your students than just focusing on process skill development, higher-order thinking, and problem-solving abilities. Discuss your intentions with parents as well. Parents are accustomed to a grade as an only comparison. Take time to explain what a portfolio, or other assessment procedure, is and how it is used.

6. The focus in education has generally been on the curriculum and teaching methodology. The current attention to assessment completes the cycle. Teachers have a better understanding of what to teach and how to teach it if they use assessment effectively.

7. Changes in assessment procedures will not magically change instructional procedures. You need to look closely at both instructional and assessment practices.

8. Remember, you are not alone. Do not try to make sweeping changes over a very short period of time and without collaboration with peer teachers. Trying to change everything overnight soon leads to the feeling that "this is not working." Develop long-term plans and discuss your strategies with sympathetic teachers and administrators in your school or district. Seek out and provide ongoing feedback and support.

REFLECTION

1. Next time you are at your practicum site, interview a teacher and see what tools he uses for assessing students. Ask why he selected the particular methods for assessment and if he feels the procedures are effective in identifying misconceptions or skill development. Compare his views to your own.

2. Place yourself in the role of the instructor for this course. If you were going to assess college students on knowledge of assessment, what form or forms of assessment would you use? Indicate sample test items or authentic procedures. Compare these to other students in the class.

3. Find out what technological resources are available to assist you in developing portfolios. A program called SCRAPS can assist you in documenting a student's achievements into a database. This resource is available through an Internet search.

4. The rapid expansion of the Internet has brought with it the idea of electronic portfolios. Using a World Wide Web search protocol, find one or two sites which include assessment information. How are they designed? How could you adapt what you found to your classroom? Try the following sites:

Office of Educational Research and Improvement:

http://www.ed.gov/pubs/OR/Consumer-Guides/classuse.html (includes information on student portfolios.)

North Central Regional Educational Laboratory:

http://www.ncrel.org/ncrel/sdrs/areas/issues/content/cntareas/science/eric/eric-

6.htm (includes how to evaluate hands-on learning.)

ERIC Clearinghouse on Assessment and Evaluation

http://ericae.educ.cua.edu/ (a site devoted to assessment issues.)

REFERENCES

American Association for the Advancement of Science. (1993). *Benchmarks for science literacy.* New York: Oxford University Press.

Bush, G. W. (1991). *America 2000: An educational strategy.* Washington, DC: U.S. Department of Education.

Mason, C. L., Kahle, J. B., & Gardner, A. L. (1991). Draw-a-scientist test: Future implications. *School Science and Mathematics, 91* (5), 193–198.

National Commission on Excellence in Education. (1983). *A nation at risk.* Washington, DC: U.S. Department of Education.

National Research Council. (1996). *National science education standards.* Washington, DC: National Academy Press.

Novak, J. D., & Gowin, D. B. (1984). *Learning how to learn.* New York: Cambridge University Press.

Resnick, L. B., & Resnick, D. P. (1989). Tests as standards of achievement in schools. In *Proceedings of the 1989 ETS Invitational Conference,* 63–80. Princeton, NJ: Educational Testing Service.

Roth, W.M., & Verechaka, G. (1993). Plotting a course with vee maps. *Science and Children, 30* (4), 24–27.

SUGGESTED READINGS

Anderson, R. D., & Pratt, H. (1995). *Local leadership for science education reform.* Dubuque, IA: Kendall/Hunt Publishing Company. (How changing teaching and assessment practices will assist in the reform process.)

Brandt, R. S. (Ed.). (1992). Using performance assessment. *Educational Leadership, 49* (8). (Special issue on performance assessment.)

Brandt, R. S. (Ed.). (1994). Reporting what students are learning. *Educational Leadership, 52* (2). (Special issue on assessment practices.)

Hein, G. (Ed.). (1990). *The assessment of hands-on elementary science programs.* Washington, DC: National Science Teachers Association. (New assessment approaches for grades K–8 that focus on thinking processes.)

Herman, J. L., Aschbacher, P. R., & Winters, L. (1992). *A practical guide to alternative assessment.* Alexandria, VA: Association for Supervision and Curriculum Development. (Creation and use of alternative assessment procedures.)

Kulm, G., Malcom, S. M. (Eds.). (1991). *Science assessment in the service of reform.* Washington, DC: American Association for the Advancement of Science. (A look at assessment and reform, including policy, curricular, instructional issues, including an appendix of examples from the field.)

McShane, J. B. (Ed.). (1994). Assessment issue. *Science and Children, 32* (2), 13–51. (A collection of relevant articles on assessment.)

Raizen, S. A., Baron, J. B., Champagne, A. B., Mullis, I. V. S., & Oakes, J. (1989). *Assessment in elementary school science.* Washington, DC: National Center for Improving Science Education. (A synthesis of reports and recommendations on assessment).

Rhoton, J., & Bowers, P. (Eds.). (1996). *Issues in science education.* Arlington, VA: National Science Teachers Association and the National Science Education Leadership Association. (Anthology of current science education topics includes a section on assessment and evaluation.)

SUBJECT MATTER, INVESTIGATIONS, AND ACTIVITIES

How Part II Can Help You

Part II can help you to apply and learn more deeply the teaching strategies developed in Part I. It reflects the typical subject matter areas found in children's textbooks, school district science guides, the National Research Council's National Science Education *Standards,* and the American Association for the Advancement of Science's *Benchmarks.* To help bolster your science background, concepts are developed within several major topics in the first section of each chapter. These are followed by sample *Standards* and *Benchmarks* and then *investigations* and *activities* clustered according to the same topics. The investigations offer opportunities to inquire into a broad topic in open-ended ways.

INVESTIGATIONS

Each investigation is organized as follows:

Title. The learning topic is stated briefly for quick reference.

Introduction. Several questions or statements are given to arouse children's interest, tie in their former experiences, and sometimes introduce a needed term. This sets the stage for exploring a problem.

Exploratory Problem. A broad problem is posed to follow up the introduction. It is stated in a way that requires children to explore concrete materials. Think of the introduction and exploratory problem as a transition into your bridge.

Needed. Materials needed are listed next. These are the kind easily available at school and home.

Try This. Suggestions are made about how to explore the materials or learn some procedure. This is to help students build readiness for discoveries. If it is not needed, move directly to the discovery problems.

Discovery Problems. Both broad and narrow questions guide discoveries within several related activities. Marginal notes identify the science processes used in the activities.

Each investigation has a *Teaching Comments* section with these parts:

Preparation and Background. Comments tell how to get or prepare needed materials. Some additional information about the topic also is given.

Generalization. This is a statement of the science principle that explains the activities.

Sample Performance Objectives. Examples of a possible process objective and a knowledge objective are given to help you assess student performance. The investigations are mostly wide-ranging and open-ended, allowing for additional state, school district, or other objectives to fit your exact situation.

For Younger Children or *For Older Children.* One of these headings is found in most of the investigations. Suggestions are made about which activities are developmentally appropriate for the children.

Some Ways to Use the Investigations

What teaching style best suits your needs and those of your students?

Some teachers say they succeed with a loose, relatively unstructured way of working with their students. They pose mainly broad questions with their students; narrow questions or helpful hints are supplied only as a last resort. Frequent side excursions by students into newly aroused problems or interests are commonplace and welcome. Other teachers believe they have more success with a tightly structured, planned progression of activities. They believe their students learn more when specific objectives are pursued and carefully appraised. They do not ignore new problems and interests, but they view them as less important than helping students achieve main concepts.

The investigations of Part II have been planned to suit either teaching style. Here are a few suggestions about how you might use them.

When planning *units,* choose investigations that fit the unit topic or generalizations. Besides giving students suitable hands-on experiences, the open-ended nature of the investigations can help you provide for individual differences.

When using *learning centers,* remember to verbally preview the activities which will take place. List on the first activity card the remaining material to be learned, including the discovery problems. Then write each discovery problem on a separate activity card, or photocopy the problems and tape them to a card.

For *individual projects* or *small group work,* you might furnish the entire investigation without the "Teaching Comments" section. Children can decide which activities to stress after consulting with you.

For *whole class* work, it is easy to present each investigation as written, or to select parts that seem suited to your situation.

Grade Placement

Since all the investigations have open-ended opportunities, they are suitable for a broad range of learning levels. The activities within each typically range from simple or observational at the beginning to more complex toward the end.

Most of the investigations include some activities appropriate for children of varying abilities and ages, usually 5 to 12 years. You'll find suggestions for working with students at either extreme of the age-ability range in the Teaching Comments. In the simpler investigations, suggestions for older children are added. In the more complex ones, suggestions are added for younger children.

Some of the investigations do not include such suggestions. These investigations will probably be too abstract or otherwise unsuitable for primary-age children.

ACTIVITIES

The activities are usually narrower in scope than the investigations. They are mainly to help children learn concepts and procedures through direct experiences. They may be used independently or they may complement investigations and contribute to additional projects.

Each activity begins with a question to focus children's attention on some interesting event or procedure. Directions are then given to help students observe the event or develop the procedure. Occasionally, some information is given within the directions to help clarify the students' experience. Narrow questions are used to focus observations or help children think about what is happening. Broad questions may also be used to help extend the experience or stimulate thinking. A parenthetical Teaching Comment in many of the activities presents needed information for you, the teacher.

LIGHT ENERGY AND COLOR

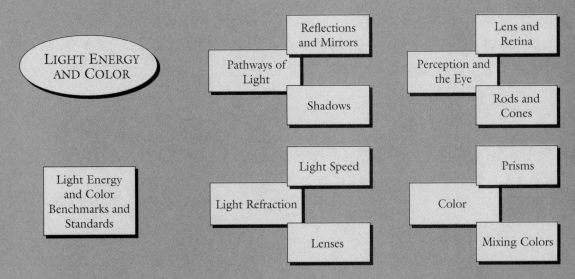

LIGHT ENERGY AND COLOR

Pathways of Light

Reflections and Mirrors

Shadows

Perception and the Eye

Lens and Retina

Rods and Cones

Light Energy and Color Benchmarks and Standards

Light Refraction

Light Speed

Lenses

Color

Prisms

Mixing Colors

Why does something look larger under a magnifying glass? What makes a rainbow? Why does writing appear backwards in a mirror? Children want to know many things about the behavior of light. These and other phenomena become understandable when we learn how light travels; how it can be "bent," or refracted; the nature of color; and how we see.

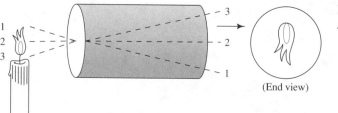

PATHWAYS OF LIGHT CONCEPTS
(Experiences begin p. 196)

Imagine reaching for something that is visible in front of you and not finding it there, or shining a flashlight in the darkness and having it illuminate only something in *back* of you. This, of course, is not likely to happen because light travels in straight lines.

It is true that a beam of light can "bend" under certain conditions, such as when going from air into water or glass, or the reverse (we will explore this more deeply in the next section). Scientists also know that light passing through space is attracted and curved by the gravitational fields of massive objects in space. Other than these exceptions, though, light does appear to travel in straight lines.

This property makes many interesting things take place. For example, look at the pinhole "camera" in Figure 8-1. Light from the candle flame shines through a narrow pinhole in the cereal box end. At the other end, an *inverted* image appears on waxed paper taped over the opening. Why? The numerals in the figure suggest an answer. If light travels in straight lines, the light going from spot one on the left can only go to spot one on the right, and vice versa.

Shadows

Because light travels in straight lines, it is easy to block it with objects. This is why we can identify an object from its shadow.

Only objects we cannot see through, such as metal and wood, cast true shadows. These are called *opaque* objects. *Transparent* objects, such as clear glass and cellophane, do not cast a shadow because very little light is blocked by them. *Translucent* objects, such as frosted glass and waxed paper, allow only some light to pass through; not enough light is blocked to produce a true shadow.

Children can learn to make large or small shadows and clear or fuzzy shadows. They can do this by varying the distance from the light source to the opaque object and the place where the shadow falls. Shadow exploration is interesting to children of all ages. It can lay the foundation for understanding some important principles of physics in later grades.

Reflections

There are several ways in which we can alter the pathways of light, and some are surprising. For instance, why do people powder their noses?

Figure 8-1
A pinhole "camera."

(End view)

Psychological reasons aside, they do it to scatter light reflections.

You know that a ball thrown straight down on smooth, level pavement bounces back up. Try it on rough gravel, however, and its return path is unpredictable. A smooth, shiny surface reflects light rays with very little scattering. But a rough or uneven surface may scatter the rays so thoroughly that reflections may be scarcely visible. What makes makeup powder so effective? Put some under a microscope. Greatly magnified, it resembles gravel!

Of course, even better reflections are possible with mirrors than with noses. Try sprinkling some powder or chalk dust over half of a mirror, leaving the remainder clear. Shine a flashlight on both sections of the mirror. Does the powder help to reduce glare? Scattered light rays are called *diffused reflections.* Light rays that are not scattered are *regular reflections.*

The only time we can see something that doesn't glow by itself is when light reflects off it and travels to our eyes, such as light reflecting off of the moon. Children generally do not think of light as reflecting off objects. Rather, there is the misconception that all objects are seen directly instead of the reflection of light which is cast from an object.

Mirrors

When you deal with flat, or *plane* reflectors, a special kind of regular reflection becomes possible. If you stand by a mirror and can see the eyes of another person, that person can also see your eyes. No matter from what position or angle you try it, the same results happen if you are close enough to the mirror to see a reflection. The angle at which light strikes a plane reflector (called the angle of incidence) always equals the angle at which it is reflected.

Some explanations of convex and concave mirrors can be discussed at the elementary level. Convex mirrors are those with a bulging center that reduces a wide field to a small area. This is

why they are used for rearview mirrors on some automobiles. Concave mirrors are those with a scooped-out center enabling them to magnify images. They are useful for cosmetic work or shaving. Observing images with flexible plastic mirrors is a way to demonstrate how bending a mirror to change its plane will change an image.

If we could not look at our photographs, or double reflections in two mirrors, we would never know how we appear to others. A mirror always produces a reversed image of the observer.

To learn why this is so, study Figure 8-2. In a sense, a mirror image is an optical illusion. Light rays reflect off the mirror into the boy's eyes. He stares outward along the lines of the incoming rays. To him, his image appears to be just as far in back of the mirror as he is in front of it.

Symmetry

Working with mirrors will enable you to introduce the concept of symmetry or the idea of balanced proportions in objects and geometric

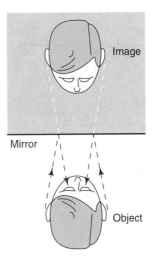

Figure 8-2
Why a mirror image is reversed.

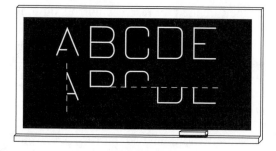

Figure 8-3
Symmetry in letters of the alphabet. Dotted lines show how to hold a mirror to reconstruct the original letters.

forms. The concept is of value in many fields, including biology, mathematics, and the arts.

A butterfly, for example, has symmetry. If you draw an imaginary line down the middle of its body, the left half is a near duplicate of its right half. A starfish has another kind of symmetry. If you turn its body around on an imaginary axis, a rotational balance is evident.

Children will be surprised at the ways a mirror can reveal balanced proportions. They can learn to predict which letter shapes will reveal the property of symmetry. Notice that each of the letters in Figure 8-3 is symmetrical. The left and right sides of A are opposite, but alike. The remaining letters are different in that the symmetry is vertical—that is, found in the tops and bottoms, but not laterally. A few letters like X, O, I, and H have both lateral and vertical balance. Some, such as L, F, and J, have none at all.

LIGHT REFRACTION CONCEPTS
(Experiences p. 209)

Have you ever jumped into the shallow part of a swimming pool only to discover it was deeper than it seemed? Light travels slower in water than it does in air. This results in an optical illusion, even though we may be looking straight down into the water.

The topic of reflection and refraction lends itself to misconceptions. Illustrations in textbooks are often inadequate and explanations are sometimes poor (Iona & Beaty, 1988). What is important is to allow children plenty of time to discuss their constructions regarding these concepts.

Density and Light Speeds

The speed of light changes when it travels into or out of media of different densities. The event is especially curious if the light beam enters or leaves a different medium at a slant. A change in speed may cause the beam to change direction of travel, or to *refract*.

Examples of refraction are all around us. A pencil placed partway into water looks bent. Distant images shimmer through unevenly heated air as we drive along a hot road. The scenery looks distorted through a cheap glass window because its thickness is uneven. Interestingly, the function of an automobile windshield wiper is to restore the rainy outside surface of a windshield to a plane surface. As water is wiped away, the light rays enter the glass at a uniform angle, rather than unevenly.

What happens when light enters or leaves water? Why does it bend? Let's look for a moment into the concept of *density* as it relates to this event. You know that anything in motion will slow down or stop when something is in the way. It is easy to dash across an empty room at top speed. Scatter some people around the room and the runner will slow down, bumping head-on into some people and deflecting off others.

A similar thing happens with light as it travels through air, water, and glass. Water is denser than air. It has more matter in the same space. Therefore glass is denser than water. When light enters a denser medium, it slows down. The reverse is also true. What makes light "bend" can be understood through an analogy.

Notice Figure 8-4. Sketch A explains why the coin in Sketch B appears to be in front of its true location. In the first sketch, the two wheels are rolling freely in the direction shown. But what happens when the leading wheel strikes the sand? The device moves on, but at a slightly different angle. To reverse this, if the device travels upward from the sand along the broken line, one wheel will hit the paved portion sooner. The direction will again change, but in an opposite way.

In Sketch B, light bends in a similar direction. As it leaves the water, the light bends slightly toward the horizontal. The observer sights along a stick toward where the coin seems to be. The line of sight seems to be a straight line from eye to coin, but it is not. If the stick is pushed into the water at the same angle at which it is poised (sliding it in the groove formed by a closed book cover may ensure this) it will overshoot the target.

Lenses

People have learned to control light refractions with lenses. Eyeglasses can correct certain vision problems. Magnifying glasses and optical instruments extend the power of sight far beyond that available to the naked eye.

Figure 8-5 shows how light refracts when passing through a convex lens. In Drawing A, the light rays enter the eye from two opposite slants. (It may help to think of the wheels–axle analogy again.) As the eye follows these slanted rays to the lens, they seem to continue outward, and so they form an enlarged image of the object.

How can we make the object appear even larger? Compare Drawings B and C. Notice that the two lenses differ in thickness, although their diameters are the same. Each will bring the sun's rays to a point or focus at a different distance. The distance from the point of focus to the lens is the *focal length*. Notice that the thicker lens has the shorter focal length. By extending the slanted rays outward, you can see why it magnifies more than the lens in Drawing C.

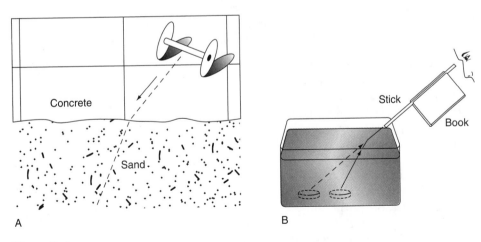

A   B

Figure 8-4
Light "bends" and changes direction (B) in the same way the wheels change direction (A) when they hit a different surface.

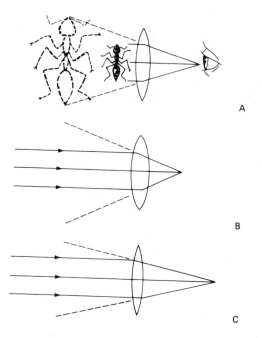

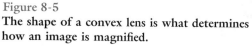

Figure 8-5
The shape of a convex lens is what determines how an image is magnified.

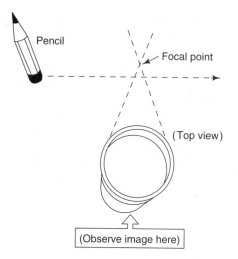

Figure 8-6
When an object that is inside the focal length of a convex lens is moved right, its image also moves right. But if the object is *outside* the focal length when moved right, its image moves left.

A curious thing may happen when we observe a moving object through a convex lens. Figure 8-6 shows the focal point of a small jar of water as light passes through it. (Though the jar is really a cylindrical lens, it acts as a convex lens in this example.) If a pencil is moved to the right *inside* the focal length of the lens, its image will also move to the right. But if it is moved to the right *outside* the focal length, its image will move to the left. The reason is apparent if we notice what happens beyond the focal point. The light rays cross and go to opposite sides.

Convex lenses *converge* light rays, or bring them together, as you have seen. Concave lenses cause light rays to *diverge*, or spread out. This causes objects viewed through them to appear smaller. You can see why in Figure 8-7. The light from the object slants outward toward X and Y as it goes through the lens

(remember the wheels–axle analogy). As the eye follows these slanted rays back to the lens, the rays seem to continue inward at a slant and form a smaller image of the object.

Thick drinking glasses and glass eye cups often have concave-shaped bases. Students can check if images are smaller by looking through them. Perhaps the easiest concave lens to make is simply to leave an air bubble in a small, capped jar of water. An object viewed through

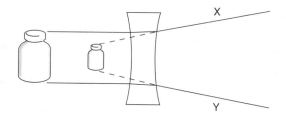

Figure 8-7
A concave lens makes objects appear smaller because the light rays diverge.

the bubble will look smaller, but if viewed through the convex part of the jar, it will appear larger.

Commercial lenses can teach a great deal. Children may learn even more, though, by fashioning their own lenses from a variety of transparent objects, containers, and fluids. A plastic soda bottle works well to "bend" light (Wilson, 1990). A clear glass marble will also magnify objects. So does a water drop or drops of other fluids. A small drinking glass with vertical sides (not tapered) magnifies things well when it is filled with water or other fluids. Narrow olive jars make especially powerful magnifiers. However, the best possibilities for controlled study of homemade lenses will happen if you use clear, small plastic pill vials.

COLOR CONCEPTS
(Experiences p. 212)

When our ancestors saw a rainbow, they were probably inclined to give a magical or supernatural explanation to account for it. Later, people thought that the colors came from the rain droplets through which sunlight passes. It was not until Isaac Newton (1642–1727) performed experiments with prisms that it was realized these colors were the parts of visible sunlight itself.

There are six universally recognized colors in the visible spectrum of sunlight: red, orange, yellow, green, blue, and violet.

A prism separates light because each color has a different wavelength and rate of vibration. Red light has the longest wavelength, with about 1,200 waves per millimeter, or 30,000 waves to 1 inch. Violet light has the shortest wavelength, with about twice that number of waves per unit. As a light beam passes through a prism, the longer waves are refracted least and the shorter waves most (Figure 8-8).

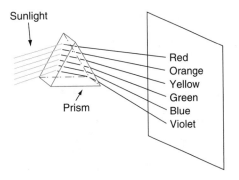

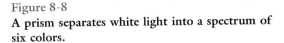

Figure 8-8

A prism separates white light into a spectrum of six colors.

Differences in colors are often compared with pitch differences in sound. A low sound is a result of relatively slow vibrations. Its visual counterpart is the color red. A high sound results from fast vibrations. Its counterpart is violet.

Mixing Colors

There are two basic ways we can mix colors: one with colored beams of light and the other with paints or dyes. When light beams of only three primary colors (red, blue, and green) are added together in the right proportions on a white screen, different color combinations occur. These are shown in the overlapping sections of Figure 8-9. When red, blue, and green are used as colored light beams, they are called the additive colors.

Scientists have found that three certain colored pigments can *absorb* these additive colors. That is, if you shine a red or blue or green light on the right pigment, there is almost no color reflection at all. The pigment looks black. Blue light is absorbed by a yellow pigment, and red light by a blue–green pigment called cyan. Green light is absorbed by a purple–red pigment called magenta.

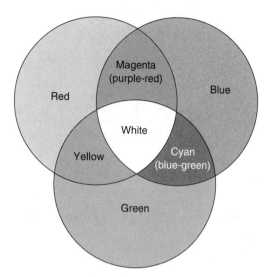

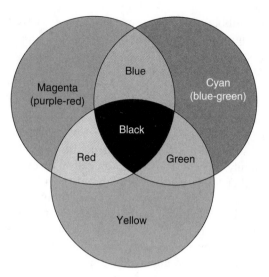

Figure 8-9
The additive colors. When beams of red, blue, and green light are added together in the right proportions, the overlapping colors result. Color television is produced by an additive process.

Figure 8-10
The subtractive colors. Paints and dyes absorb, or "subtract," some colors from white light and reflect what is left. Note the overlapping colors when the three primary pigments are mixed in the right proportions.

If a *white* light beam shines on these colored pigments, each will absorb, or "subtract," the specific color mentioned above and reflect to our eyes what is not absorbed. We can mix these pigments to get various colors, but the results we get from mixing all three are the *opposite* from mixing the three light beams. This is shown in Figure 8-10. In summary, when viewing an object, the color we see depends on (1) the color of light shining on the object and (2) the color reflected by the object to our eyes. Children can do some experiments with colored construction paper and colored light beams to help them understand these ideas and their practical effects. With ordinary materials, it is hard to predict the exact hues that will result from the many possible combinations. Another interesting activity is to use colored slides, a prism, and a slide projector to experiment with color (Dalby, 1991).

Don't be surprised if you find several boys in your class who are at least partly color blind.

One male in 12 has the deficiency, contrasted with only 1 in 200 females. Most commonly, reds and greens are seen in shades of gray; other colors are perceived normally. Rarely do color blind people see all colors in black and white and shades of gray.

PERCEPTION AND THE EYE CONCEPTS
(Experiences p. 217)

In this section, we will examine how the eye works and apply some ideas discussed previously. Although the eye has many parts, we'll concentrate on three parts directly involved in sight: the *iris, retina,* and *lens* (see Figure 8-11).

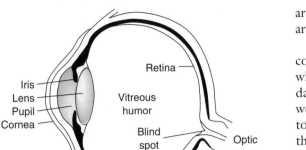

Figure 8-11
An eye illustration.

Iris

The iris contains pigment that absorbs some colors and reflects others. It is because the kind and amount of this coloring matter varies in individuals that eyes appear to be brown, hazel, or blue. Two sets of tiny muscles control the size of a small hole (pupil) in the iris. This regulates the amount of light entering the eye.

Cats' pupils can dilate far more than ours. This is one reason they see better than humans in near darkness. A dramatic example of this capacity appears when the headlights of an automobile suddenly shine into the eyes of a cat on a dark night. The two shiny round spots we see are the headlight reflections from *inside* the cat's eyes.

Retina

Why is it hard to see when we first walk into a darkened movie theater? Our eyes make a second important adjustment when light varies in brightness. The retina contains two kinds of light-sensitive cells: *rods* and *cones*. Cones are less sensitive than rods and are clustered near the back of the eyeball. They work best in strong light and enable us to see color. Rods

are distributed in other parts of the retina and are sensitive to dim light.

Chemical changes sensitize either rods or cones under certain conditions. For example, when we walk into a dark theater on a sunny day, it takes several minutes before the rods work well. To achieve optimum sensitivity, up to a half hour may be required. It is thought that cones are most sensitive to three basic colors: red, green, and blue. According to this idea, we see many colors because the basic colors are seen in various combinations.

Lens

An eye lens is convex in shape and works like any other convex lens, with one important difference. A muscle permits it to change shape. If a large, close object appears before you, the lens thickens. This refracts light rays entering the eye sharply enough for a focus to occur on the retina. However, light rays from a small or distant object enter the lens in a near parallel fashion. Only a small refraction is needed to bring the rays to a focus on the retina.

To experience this action, look at a distant object, then suddenly look at something a foot away. Do you feel the tug of your lens muscles pulling the lens? Do you find the near object is fuzzy for the brief instant it takes for the muscles to adjust lens thickness? In a camera, of course, focusing is achieved by moving the lens back and forth.

Eyeglasses

Two of the main vision problems corrected by eyeglasses concern image focus. In *near-sightedness,* the cornea or the lens may be thicker, or the eyeball longer, than normal. This causes an image to focus in front of the retina rather than on it. Notice in Figure 8-12 how the problem is corrected. Sketch A shows a normal eyeball. Sketch B shows a longer-than-normal eyeball and a focal point in front of, rather than on, the

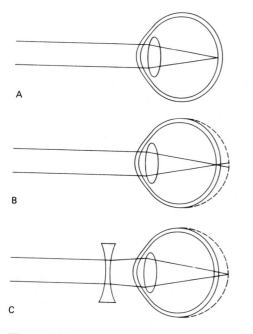

A

B

C

Figure 8-12
In near-sightedness an abnormally shaped cornea or eyeball causes an image to focus in front of the retina rather than on it. A concave lens can correct the problem.

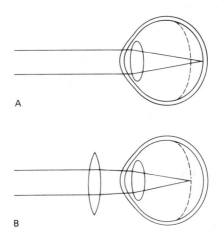

A

B

Figure 8-13
In farsightedness, the image focuses at some imaginary point beyond the retina. A convex lens corrects this.

retina. In C, a concave eyeglass lens spreads out the incoming light rays. This lengthens the focal point just enough to fall on the retina.

In *farsightedness,* the cornea or the lens may be thinner, or the eyeball shorter, than normal. So the focal point is at some imaginary distance beyond the retina. Sketch A of Figure 8-13 shows this happening with a shorter-than-normal eyeball. In Sketch B, a convex eyeglass lens corrects the defect by forcing the light rays to converge at a shorter focal point, which is on the retina.

Perception

An excellent example of how the brain and eyes work together takes place when we judge distance. Each eye sees an object from a different angle. The closer the object, the greater the difference between what the two eyes perceive. We actually see a tiny bit *around* the object. At the same time, we feel our eyes turn inward. With greater distances, the angle gets smaller. The brain interprets this accordingly.

Beyond about 50 yards, we rely mainly on size to judge distance. A small telegraph pole looks far away mostly because we know that telephone poles are large. We also use other clues such as increased haze and the surrounding scene.

A movie film flashes only *still* pictures on a screen. The apparent motion of a motion-picture projection results from *persistence of vision.* It takes about one-sixteenth of a second for an image to fade from our vision after it is withdrawn. By flashing 24 images a second on a screen, a projector creates the illusion of motion.

It took some experience before the present speed of projecting individual motion-picture frames was adopted. Early motion pictures were photographed and projected at much slower speeds. The short, unlighted pause between frames was noticeable. This is how the term *flickers* came about.

It is easy to experience the persistence-of-vision effect with a pencil and a small pad of paper. For example, children can be guided to draw a pole that falls over. First, an upright pole is drawn on the bottom and center of the first page. On succeeding pages, in the same spot, they draw the pole at successively lower angles, until it is horizontal. A total of about 20 pages is more than adequate. When the pad pages are rapidly flipped over, an animated sequence of a falling pole appears. Children enjoy making flip books.

LIGHT ENERGY AND COLOR BENCHMARKS AND STANDARDS

Examples of standards in the area of light energy and color are guidelines related to: how sunlight is made up of many colors; how light reflecting off objects allows us to see; and how light travels. Specific examples are as follows:

SAMPLE BENCHMARKS (AAAS, 1993).

- Light from the sun is made up of a mixture of many different colors of light, even though to the eye the light looks almost white. Other things that give off or reflect light have a different mix of colors (By grades 6–8, p. 90).

- Something can be "seen" when light waves emitted or reflected by it enter the eye (By grades 6–8, p. 90).

SAMPLE STANDARDS (NRC, 1996).

- Light travels in a straight line until it strikes an object. Light can be reflected by a mirror, refracted by a lens, or absorbed by an object (by Grades K–4, p. 127).

- Light interacts with matter by transmission (including refraction), absorption, or scattering (including reflection). To see an object, light from that object—emitted by or scattered from it—must enter the eye (by Grades 5–8, p. 155).

INVESTIGATIONS AND ACTIVITIES

PATHWAYS OF LIGHT EXPERIENCES
(Concepts p. 186)

INVESTIGATION: *A PINHOLE CAMERA*

Have you ever used a pinhole camera (Figure 8-14)? Light from an object shines through a tiny pinhole at one end. It travels to a waxed-paper screen at the other end. What you see is called an *image* of the object. What you see may surprise you.

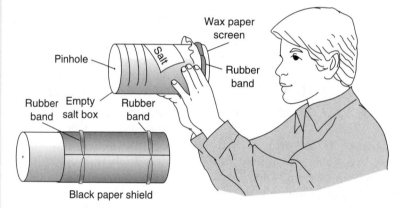

Figure 8-14

EXPLORATORY PROBLEM

How can you make and use a pinhole camera?

NEEDED

salt or cereal box   sticky tape   pin   black paper
three rubber bands   waxed paper   scissors

TRY THIS

1. Punch a hole in the center of the box bottom. Use a pin.
2. Remove the box top. Put waxed paper over the box's open end to make the screen. Use a rubber band to hold it.
3. Point the camera at brightly lit objects in or outside a *dark* room. What do you see on the waxed paper screen?

To use the camera in a *lighted* place, you must shield the screen from the light. Roll black paper into a large tube and fit it around the screen end of the box. Secure with two rubber bands. Press your face against the paper shield's open end to see images on the screen.

DISCOVERY PROBLEMS

experimenting   **A.** How must you move the camera to do these things? To make the image move right? left? up? down? To make the image get smaller? larger? What happens if the camera is still and the image moves? (For example, have person walk from right to left.)

experimenting   **B.** How can you make a brighter, sharper image appear on the screen? What will happen to the image if you change the pinhole size? line the inside of the box with black paper? white paper? use a longer or larger box or a shoe box? use paper other than waxed paper for the screen?

experimenting   **C.** How can you make a pinhole camera with a larger paper cup? How can a second cup be used as a light shield?

hypothesizing   **D.** What other ideas can you think of to try?

TEACHING COMMENT

PREPARATION AND BACKGROUND

Several kinds of boxes will serve for this activity, including milk cartons. If a black paper shield is used, it should be large. The observer's eyes will need to be about 30 centimeters (1 foot) away from the screen to see a sharp image.

Most children will be surprised to find that an upside-down image appears on the screen. You might sketch Figure 8-1 on the chalkboard and invite students to think through what happens.

GENERALIZATION

Light travels in straight lines.

SAMPLE PERFORMANCE OBJECTIVES

Process: The child can construct a pinhole camera and show how it works.

Knowledge: The child can explain how the flame image becomes inverted in Figure 8-1.

FOR YOUNGER CHILDREN

With teacher guidance, many primary children will be able to do the exploratory problem and discovery Problem A.

INVESTIGATION: *SHADOWS*

What is a shadow? How can you make a shadow?

EXPLORATORY PROBLEM A

How can you change the length and direction of a shadow?

NEEDED

white sheet of paper   flashlight
pencil   small nail
partner

TRY THIS

1. Put a nail, head down, on some white paper (Figure 8-15).
2. Shine the flashlight on the nail. What kind of a shadow do you see?

Figure 8-15

DISCOVERY PROBLEMS

experimenting **A.** How can you make a long shadow? a short shadow?

experimenting **B.** How can you shine the light on the nail so there is no shadow?

experimenting **C.** How can you make a shadow that points left? right?

predicting **D.** Let your partner turn off the flashlight and point it at the nail. Where will the shadow be when your partner turns on the flashlight again? (The flashlight must be held still.) Draw a line on the paper where you think the shadow will be.

predicting **E.** Can you tell how long a shadow will be?

EXPLORATORY PROBLEM B

What kinds of shadows can you make and see outdoors?

NEEDED

outdoor area   sunshine   partner

TRY THIS

1. Go outdoors into the sunshine.
2. Make some shadows on the ground (Figure 8-16).

Figure 8-16

DISCOVERY PROBLEMS

experimenting **A.** Can you and a partner make your shadows shake hands without really touching each other's hands?

experimenting **B.** How can you make your shadow seem to stand on your partner's shadow's shoulders?

experimenting **C.** How can you make a pale, fuzzy shadow darker and sharper?

experimenting **D.** How should you stand so your shadow is in front of you? in back of you? to your left? to your right?

predicting **E.** Draw a line where the shadow of some object is now. Where do you think the shadow will be in an hour? Draw a second line, then check to see later.

hypothesizing **F.** What are some other things you can try with shadows?

TEACHING COMMENT

PREPARATION AND BACKGROUND

In this investigation, children discover how to predict the lengths and directions of shadows. They learn how to make shadows dark and sharp and pale or fuzzy by changing the distance between an object and the light source. They also learn that this affects the shadow's size.

GENERALIZATION

A shadow may be made when an object blocks some light; a shadow may be changed by moving the object or the light source in different ways.

SAMPLE PERFORMANCE OBJECTIVES

Process: The child can manipulate a light source and object to vary a shadow's length and direction.

Knowledge: The child can state how a shadow's darkness and sharpness may be changed.

FOR OLDER CHILDREN

Try determining the sizes of objects by their shadows.

ACTIVITY: *HOW MANY PENNIES CAN YOU "MAKE" WITH TWO MIRRORS?*

NEEDED

two small mirrors   penny

TRY THIS

1. Fit two mirrors together like two walls joined to make a corner.
2. Place the penny between the mirrors. How many pennies do you see?
3. Change the mirror angle. Move the mirrors in other ways. Move the penny, too. What is the largest number of pennies you can make? the fewest number?

INVESTIGATION: *MIRROR REFLECTIONS*

What are some of the things you can do with a mirror?

EXPLORATORY PROBLEM A

Can you see someone's eyes in a mirror without the other person seeing your eyes in the mirror? (Say the other person is also looking into the mirror.) How can you find out?

NEEDED

small mirror   sticky tape   partner

TRY THIS

1. Tape a mirror flat against a wall at your eye level.
2. Have your partner stand in back and to the right of the mirror.
3. Now you stand in back and to the left of the mirror (Figure 8-17).

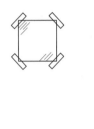

Figure 8-17

4. Move around slowly until you see your partner's eyes in the mirror. Can your partner now see your eyes in the mirror?

DISCOVERY PROBLEMS

predicting **A.** What will happen if you or your partner move farther to the side?

predicting **B.** What will happen if you or your partner move farther back?

inferring **C.** Is there any spot where you can see your partner's eyes without him seeing your eyes?

EXPLORATORY PROBLEM B

How can you use two mirrors to see over objects taller than you?

NEEDED

two small mirrors   soft clay   meter stick or yardstick

TRY THIS

1. Push a piece of clay into the meter stick near each end.
2. Push a mirror sideways into each lump of clay. Have the mirror surfaces face each other.
3. Fix the mirrors so they look like those in Figure 8-18. When done, you will have a *periscope*.
4. Hold the periscope upright. Look in the bottom mirror. What can you see? You may have to move the mirrors a little to see clearly.
5. Over what tall objects can you see with your periscope?

Figure 8-18

DISCOVERY PROBLEMS

experimenting **A.** How can you use your periscope to see around a corner?

experimenting **B.** How can you see around a corner with just one mirror on the stick?

EXPLORATORY PROBLEM C

What is the shortest mirror in which you can see your feet and head at the same time?

NEEDED

two small mirrors   meter stick or yardstick
sticky tape   partner

TRY THIS

1. You can use two small mirrors instead of a large, full-length mirror. Have your partner stand at arm's length from the wall.

2. Tape one mirror flat against the wall at your partner's eye level.

3. Hold the second mirror flat against the wall below the first mirror.

4. Move it slowly down the wall. Have your partner say stop when she can see her shoes in the bottom mirror.

5. Tape the bottom mirror flat against the wall.

6. Now your partner should be able to see her head and feet. The top and bottom mirrors are like the top and bottom of a large, full-length mirror (Figure 8-19).

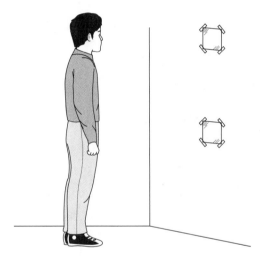

Figure 8-19

DISCOVERY PROBLEMS

measuring **A.** How long is it from the top of one mirror to the bottom of the other mirror compared to your partner's height? Half as long? three-fourths as long? just as long as your partner is tall? Measure and find out.

observing **B.** Does moving back from the mirror make a difference in the size needed?

experimenting **C.** Does the mirror size needed depend on a person's height? How could you find out?

predicting **D.** Can you predict the size of the shortest full-length mirror you'll need to see yourself? Switch with your partner and find out.

TEACHING COMMENT

PREPARATION AND BACKGROUND

When light strikes a mirror at an angle, it is reflected at the same angle in a different direction. That is why if you see someone's image in a mirror, it is possible for that person to see yours. This also explains how periscopes work. Notice in Figure 8-18 that the two mirror angles are identical. For the same reason, a full-length mirror needs to be only about half as long as you are tall.

Check that the mirror is taped *flat* against the wall in the last investigations. If it is not, an error in measurement is likely.

GENERALIZATION

When light travels to a mirror at a slant, it is reflected at the same slant in another direction.

SAMPLE PERFORMANCE OBJECTIVES

Process: The child can construct a workable periscope.

Knowledge: The child can demonstrate positions where two persons should be able to see, at one time, each other's image in a mirror.

FOR YOUNGER CHILDREN

Most primary children should be able to do the exploratory sections of Investigations A and B.

ACTIVITY: *How Can Two Mirrors Show What You Really Look Like?*

NEEDED

two mirrors

TRY THIS

1. Look into one mirror. Think of your image as another person facing you.
2. Wink your left eye, then your right. Which eye does the image blink each time?
3. Get two mirrors. Fit them together in the way that two walls are joined. Move them slightly so half of your face is seen in each mirror (Figure 8-20).
4. Wink each eye. Touch your left ear. Tilt your head to the right. What happens each time? Study Figure 8-20. How can you explain why your right eye appears on the left, like that of a real person facing you?

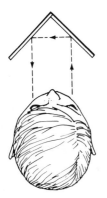

Figure 8-20

TEACHING COMMENT

Each mirror reflects half of the image onto the adjoining mirror. This puts it back to normal. A single mirror can only reflect an object backwards. This is why our one-mirror image is not how we look to others.

ACTIVITY: *HOW CAN YOU RELAY LIGHT WITH MIRRORS?*

NEEDED

three to four small mirrors
sunshine or bright flashlight

TRY THIS

1. Hold a mirror in the light. Reflect the light onto a wall.
2. Pick a target on the wall. Reflect the light so it shines on the target.
3. Reflect your light onto another mirror held by a partner. Have your partner try to hit the target.

   a. With how many mirrors can you and some partners relay the light and hit a target? How will you tell if light is being passed from every mirror? Make a drawing that shows how the mirrors were held to hit the target (Figure 8-21).

   b. Have a contest between two or more teams. Which team can hit a target fastest with light passed along from several mirrors? How can you make the contest fair?

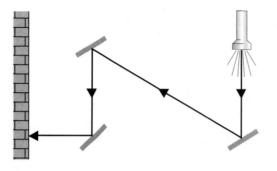

Figure 8-21

TEACHING COMMENT

Caution: If using a laser, caution children *not* to look directly into the laser. A fair contest will prevent one team from observing and profiting from the mistakes of the other. You can tell if every mirror in a relay is being used by shading each mirror in turn with your hand. The light shining on the target in each instance will disappear. Strong light is needed if more than two mirrors are used.

INVESTIGATION: *MIRROR BALANCE*

Suppose you made a small, simple drawing. Then you erased half of it. Could you hold a mirror on the drawing so it would seem whole again? Would it depend on the drawing? In what way? Drawings that allow you to do this are said to have *mirror* balance, or symmetry.

EXPLORATORY PROBLEM

How can you find out which things have mirror balance?

NEEDED

paper   pencil
small mirror   ruler

TRY THIS

1. Put the edge of your mirror on Line 1 of the butterfly in Figure 8-22. Can you see what seems like the whole butterfly? You can, because the butterfly has side-by-side balance.

2. Now put the mirror on Line 2. Can you see a whole butterfly now? You cannot, because a butterfly's body is balanced only one way.

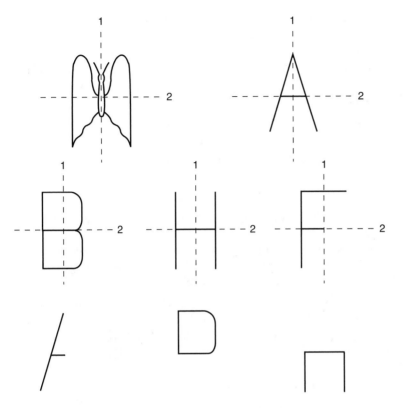

Figure 8-22

3. Some letters of the alphabet have balance, too. Put your mirror on Line 1 of the capital letter *A*. Can you see what seems like a whole letter *A*? You can, because capital letter *A* has side-by-side balance.

4. Now, put the mirror on Line 2. Can you see a whole letter *A*? You cannot, because this capital letter is balanced only one way.

5. Try your mirror both ways on capital *B*. Notice that you cannot see a whole letter on Line 1. But you can on Line 2. That is because a capital *B* only has up-and-down balance.

6. Try your mirror both ways on capital *H*. Notice that you see a whole letter both ways. A capital *H* has both side-by-side and up-and-down balance.

7. Try your mirror both ways on capital *F*. Notice that you cannot see a whole letter either way. A capital *F* has no balance.

DISCOVERY PROBLEMS

classifying   **A.** Which capital letters of the alphabet do you think have side-by-side balance? up-and-down balance? both kinds? no balance? Arrange the letters into four groups. Then check each letter with your mirror to see if you put it into the right group.

inferring   **B.** Some words may be made up of only letters from one group. How many words can you think of whose letters have only side-by-side balance? only up-and-down balance? only letters with both kinds of balance?

experimenting   **C.** Use what you know to write secret code words.

TEACHING COMMENT

PREPARATION AND BACKGROUND

This is an introduction to mirror symmetry. Symmetry is the idea of balanced proportions in the shapes of objects.

Try to have available small rectangular mirrors with the trim removed from the edges. The trim may obscure part of the reflected drawing or letter. ***Caution:*** If the mirror edges are sharp, cover them with a strip of cellophane tape.

GENERALIZATION

Some objects have evenly balanced or symmetrical shapes; a mirror may be used to explore an object's symmetry.

SAMPLE PERFORMANCE OBJECTIVES

Process: The child can classify the letters of the alphabet by their symmetry.

Knowledge: The child can draw or identify an object that is symmetrical.

FOR YOUNGER CHILDREN

Find and mount mirror-sized magazine pictures of objects and patterns. Some should, and some should not, be symmetrical. On what place or places in each picture can children put a small mirror to see the whole object?

Have them classify the pictures into two groups such as those they can make whole again and those they cannot. Challenge children to use their mirrors to change each picture or pattern. Colored pictures, particularly, are fascinating for young children to explore.

LIGHT REFRACTION EXPERIENCES

(Concepts p. 188)

INVESTIGATION: *SOME EVERYDAY MAGNIFIERS*

How can you make something seem larger? That is, how can you magnify it?

EXPLORATORY PROBLEM

What everyday objects can you use to magnify things?

NEEDED

two pencils
two jars of water (two sizes)
two clear-glass marbles (two sizes)
book
waxed paper
newspaper

TRY THIS

1. Place a piece of waxed paper on a printed page.
2. Dip a pencil tip into some water. Let a drop run off onto the waxed paper.
3. How does the print look through the water drop?

DISCOVERY PROBLEMS

observing   **A.** Make water drops of different sizes. Which drops magnify the print more?

observing   **B.** Put the waxed paper on a book. Make a row of drops, each drop bigger than the next. Hold up the book and paper to eye level. Look at the outline of the drops. Which are smaller and rounder? Which are larger and flatter? Which will magnify more?

predicting   **C.** Get two different-sized clear marbles. Which one do you think will magnify more? How much more? How will you find out?

observing   **D.** Get a narrow jar of water. Put your pencil inside. Does your pencil look larger? Move your pencil to different places, inside and outside the jar. Where does it look the thickest (Figure 8-23)?

observing   **E.** Get another, wider jar of water. Will it magnify more or less than the first jar?

inferring   **F.** What other everyday things can you use as magnifiers?

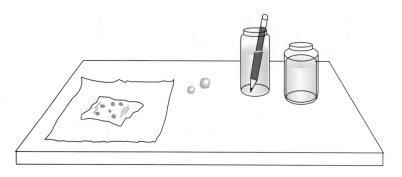

Figure 8-23

TEACHING COMMENT

PREPARATION AND BACKGROUND

Any clear, curved, transparent material acts like a lens. That is, light rays that pass through the material are bent. This may cause objects viewed through the lens to appear magnified. Children will enjoy and learn from trials with additional examples of clear glass and plastic materials. Clear, narrow plastic pill vials become especially good magnifiers when filled with water and capped.

The magnifying power of a glass marble may be measured by placing it on narrow-lined paper. The student counts the number of lines seen inside the clear marble. The marble with the fewest visible lines has the greatest magnification.

GENERALIZATION

A clear, curved object may appear to magnify things; a narrow, curved object magnifies more than one of greater diameter.

SAMPLE PERFORMANCE OBJECTIVES

Process: The student can measure the difference in magnifying power of two different improvised lenses.

Knowledge: When shown two water-filled containers of different diameters, the student can predict which will have the greater magnifying power.

FOR YOUNGER CHILDREN

Most young students should be able to do all but Discovery Problems C and E.

ACTIVITY: HOW CAN YOU MEASURE THE MAGNIFYING POWER OF A HAND LENS?

NEEDED

hand magnifying lens   sheet of lined paper   ruler   pencil

TRY THIS

1. Draw two or three evenly spaced lines between the printed lines on your paper. A half sheet of extra lines should be enough.
2. Pencil a small **x** in the middle of the paper where you have drawn lines.
3. Center the **x** in the lens. Move the lens up and down until the **x** looks most clear.
4. Count all the lines you see inside the lens (Figure 8-24).

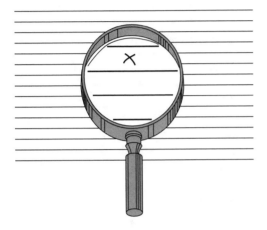

Figure 8-24

5. Count all the lines *outside* the lens that are between the first and last lines seen inside the lens.
6. Divide the larger figure by the smaller one. This gives the power of the lens. For example, if the answer is two, your lens makes things appear about twice as large as they are.
   a. What is the power of your lens?
   b. What is the power of other lenses you can try?
   c. How does the power of thicker lenses compare with thinner lenses?
   d. How far above the **x** must you hold different lenses to see it clearly?

TEACHING COMMENT

Thicker lenses usually magnify more than thinner lenses of the same diameter. The distance from the point of focus to the lens is the focal length. Because they have shorter focal lengths, thicker or curvier lenses must be held closer to the **x** to see it clearly.

COLOR EXPERIENCES

(Concepts p. 191)

INVESTIGATION: *HOW TO MIX COLORS*

Suppose you have two different-colored crayons. How can you use the crayons to make *three* different colors?

EXPLORATORY PROBLEM A

How can you make more than three colors with three different crayons?

NEEDED

white paper   crayons (red, yellow, and blue)   crayons of other colors

TRY THIS

1. Rub three short, thick lines *lightly* across the white paper. Make one red, one yellow, and one blue.

2. Rub three thick up-and-down lines *lightly* on the white paper, so they cross the first three. Use the same three colors (Figure 8-25).

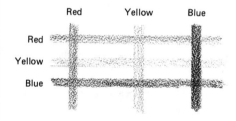

Figure 8-25

3. What colors do you see where the lines cross?

DISCOVERY PROBLEMS

observing   **A.** How many colors did you make?

experimenting   **B.** How many new colors can you make with crayons of other colors? Draw pictures and color them.

EXPLORATORY PROBLEM B

How can you make many colors by mixing water samples of several colors?

NEEDED

four baby food jars   paper towel
water   three drinking straws
food coloring (red, yellow, and blue)

TRY THIS

1. Fill three small jars half full with water.
2. Put two drops of different food coloring in each jar.
3. Put a different straw in each jar and stir the colored water.
4. Mix a little colored water from two jars into a fourth jar. Use a straw to lift out the liquid from each jar. (See Figure 8-26.)

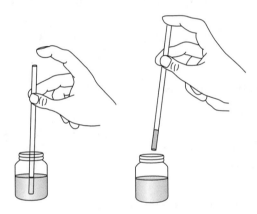

Figure 8-26

DISCOVERY PROBLEMS

experimenting and measuring **A.** How many new colors can you make by mixing two different colors each time? Use the same volume of each color when mixing colors. Keep a record.

observing **B.** What happens when you mix more of one color than another?

inferring **C.** Mix a mystery color made from two colors. Use more of one color than another. Can someone else figure out how to match exactly your mystery color? Can you match someone else's mystery color? Try many different colors.

TEACHING COMMENT

PREPARATION AND BACKGROUND

Children will get the best results when combining crayon colors if they rub lightly. When red, yellow, and blue paints or dyes are paired and mixed in the right proportions, we see green, orange, and purple.

GENERALIZATION

When red, yellow, and blue dyes are paired and mixed, they produce green, orange, and purple. Different shades are produced by mixing different proportions of the colors.

SAMPLE PERFORMANCE OBJECTIVES

Process: The child can infer what combinations of colored liquids produced a new color and the general proportions used.

Knowledge: The child can state how to produce varying shades of mixed colors.

FOR OLDER CHILDREN

You might begin with Discovery Problem B and move quickly to C.

ACTIVITY: *HOW ARE THE COLORS MADE IN COMIC STRIPS?*

NEEDED

colored comic strips from different newspapers   strong hand lens

TRY THIS

1. Study different comic strip pictures with a hand lens.
2. Notice how many colors are made from only a few colors.
3. Notice that some dots may be printed side by side. Or one colored dot may be printed partly over a dot of another color.
4. Observe how different shades are made by changing the distance between dots.
   a. What side-by-side colored dots do you see? What colors do they make?
   b. What overprinted colors do you see? What colors do they make?
   c. In what ways are cartoon colors from different newspapers alike? different?

TEACHING COMMENT

A dissecting microscope is ideal for analyzing colored comics.

INVESTIGATION: *THE MAKEUP OF COLORED LIQUIDS*

You know that a colored liquid can be made by mixing two or more colors. Most inks and dyes are made in that way. Some of the colors mixed to make another color are surprising.

EXPLORATORY PROBLEM

How can you find out the colors that make up a colored dye or ink?

NEEDED

food coloring (red, blue, green, yellow)   baby food jar half full of water
scissors   waxed paper
four toothpicks   white paper towel or coffee filters

TRY THIS

1. Cut some strips from a white paper towel. Make them about 10 by 2 centimeters (4 by ¾ inches).

2. Put one drop of red food coloring and one of blue on waxed paper. Mix them.

3. Touch the toothpick to the coloring. Make a sizable dot on the middle of one strip.

4. Hold the strip in a small jar that is about half full of water. The colored dot should be just above the water level (Figure 8-27).

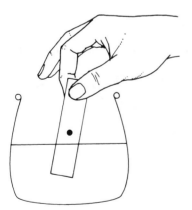

Figure 8-27

5. What happens to the coloring as water is soaked up past the colored dot? (This may take a minute or longer.) How many colors appear as the colored dot spreads out?

DISCOVERY PROBLEMS

observing **A.** What colors are in other food coloring samples? How are different brands of the same colors alike or different?

inferring **B.** Try a game with a partner. Mix drops from several food colors, then test them on strips. Keep a record. Remove the tested strips from the jar and let them dry. Can your partner tell which food colors were mixed for each strip? Switch places with your partner. Can you tell what mixed colors were used for your partner's strips?

observing **C.** What colors make up some inks?

observing **D.** What other paper or filters can be used? How do they change the color separation?

TEACHING COMMENT

PREPARATION AND BACKGROUND

The basic process of this investigation is called paper chromatography. The separate pigments that make up the color of a dye are absorbed at slightly different rates by the paper. This has the effect of spreading out the pigments, which makes them visible. Only washable (nonpermanent) dyes will work.

GENERALIZATION

The colors that make up a dye may be discovered through paper chromatography. Most dyes contain several blended colors.

SAMPLE PERFORMANCE OBJECTIVES

Process: Given the materials, the child can demonstrate how to use paper chromatography to analyze the colored pigments in a dye.

Knowledge: The child can predict the colors blended in several common dyes.

ACTIVITY: *WHAT COLORS MAKE UP SUNLIGHT?*

NEEDED

cake pan about half-filled with water   mirror
sunshine   white paper

TRY THIS

1. Place the pan in the sun. Have the mirror face the sun.

2. Hold the mirror upright against the pan's inside rim.

3. Slowly tip back the mirror. Light must strike the mirror below the water's surface.

4. Point the mirror toward a white wall or large sheet of white paper (Figure 8-28).

    a. What colors do you see on the wall?

    b. What happens to the colors if you stir the water lightly?

    c. Try using the light from a filmstrip projector inside the classroom. How will these colors compare with those of sunlight?

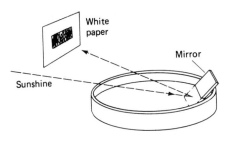

Figure 8-28

TEACHING COMMENT

This crude prism does an excellent job of refracting sunlight into its full spectrum of colors. Stirring the water mildly mixes the colors into white light again. The projector light's spectrum will be similar but not identical to that of sunlight.

PERCEPTION AND EYE EXPERIENCES
(Concepts p. 192)

INVESTIGATION: *How You See Distance*

Suppose you had to see for a while with just one eye. How might this make a difference in telling how far something is from you?

EXPLORATORY PROBLEM

How can you test if two eyes let you tell distance better than one eye?

NEEDED

two pencils	ball
empty soda bottle	partner

TRY THIS

1. Have a partner hold up a thumb at your eye level.
2. Hold a pencil upright, eraser end down, about 6 inches above the thumb. Using both eyes, try to touch the top of your partner's thumb with the eraser. Move the pencil down fairly quickly but gently (Figure 8-29).

Figure 8-29

3. Have your partner slightly change the distance his or her thumb is from you.
4. Using one eye, try again to touch your partner's thumb. Move the pencil down fairly quickly but gently.

DISCOVERY PROBLEMS

observing   **A.** In which trial was it easier to touch your partner's thumb?

observing   **B.** Does which eye you close make any difference? How does using two eyes compare with using one? (Be sure your partner slightly changes his thumb position for each trial.)

observing   **C.** Does which hand you use make any difference?

experimenting   **D.** How else can you test if two eyes are better than one for telling distance?

TEACHING COMMENT

PREPARATION AND BACKGROUND

When we see an object with two eyes, each eye views it from a slightly different angle. So our perception of the object's distance is usually more accurate than if only one eye is used. With distant objects, the advantage decreases. We tend to use size, background, and other clues to estimate distance.

In this investigation, it is important for an object's position to be moved for each trial. Otherwise, muscle memory alone from a preceding trial may allow the child to touch the object. For the test to be valid, the child should not benefit from experience. Also, the pencil should be moved down with some speed, although gently. If done slowly, self-correction becomes too easy.

GENERALIZATION

Two eyes are usually better than one for judging distance.

SAMPLE PERFORMANCE OBJECTIVES

Process: The child can demonstrate a test for distance perception with two eyes and one eye.

Knowledge: The child can predict situations in which distance perception is more difficult with one eye than with two eyes.

FOR YOUNGER CHILDREN

Younger students should be able to do most of the investigation with some teacher guidance.

INVESTIGATION: *YOUR SIDE VISION AND COLOR*

Suppose you notice an object from the corner of your eye while staring straight ahead. Can you notice it is there *before* you can tell its color? Or can you also tell the color at the same time?

EXPLORATORY PROBLEM

How far to the side can you tell different colors?

NEEDED

four small (5-centimeter, or 2-inch) paper squares of different colors
four larger (10-centimeter, or 4-inch) paper squares of different colors
partner

TRY THIS

1. Keep your eyes on some object across the room during this experiment.
2. Have a partner stand at your right side, about a step away.
3. Ask your partner to hold up a small colored square opposite your ear. (You should not know the color.)
4. Have your partner slowly move the square forward in a big circle (Figure 8-30).

Figure 8-30

5. Say "stop" when you first notice the square at your side.

6. Then tell your partner the square's color if you can.

7. If you cannot, have your partner move the square forward until you can tell.

DISCOVERY PROBLEMS

observing   **A.** Was it as easy to notice the color as the object itself?

observing   **B.** Will it make any difference if you try the test from your left side?

observing   **C.** Will it make any difference if you try different colors? Can you identify some colors farther to the side than others?

observing   **D.** Will it make any difference if you try the larger squares?

experimenting **E.** What results will you get if you test other people?

TEACHING COMMENT

PREPARATION AND BACKGROUND

The eye's inside lining, or retina, contains millions of cells sensitive to light intensity and color. Most of the eye's color-sensitive cells are clustered at the back of the eyeball near the optic nerve. To see color, some colored light must reach there. When light enters the eye at an angle, this area may not be stimulated. So we can usually detect the presence of an object at our side before we can distinguish its color.

Be sure the children keep their eyes fixed on some far object as they do this investigation, so they can properly test their side (peripheral) vision.

GENERALIZATION

An object at one's side can be noticed before its color can be identified.

SAMPLE PERFORMANCE OBJECTIVES

Process: The child can test different colors to determine the limits of side vision in identifying each.

Knowledge: The child can demonstrate that a colored object will be detected from the side before its color can be identified.

ACTIVITY: *WHAT HAPPENS WHEN YOUR EYES TIRE FROM SEEING ONE COLOR?*

NEEDED

construction paper (blue, yellow, red)
scissors
white paper

watch with second hand
pencil

TRY THIS

1. Pencil an **x** in the center of the white paper.
2. Cut out one small (5-centimeter, or 2-inch) square each of blue, yellow, and red paper.
3. Put the blue square on the **x**. Look at it steadily for 30 seconds.
4. Remove the square and look at the **x**.
   a. What color appears at the **x**?
5. Rest your eyes for a minute or so. Then try the yellow and red squares in the same way.
   b. What color appears after the yellow square? red square?

REFERENCES

American Association for the Advancement of Science. (1993). *Benchmarks for science literacy.* New York: Oxford University Press.

Dalby, D. K. (1991). Fine tune your sense of color. *Science and Children, 29* (3), 24–26.

Iona, M., & Beaty, W. (1988). Reflections on refraction. *Science and Children, 25* (8), 18–20.

National Research Council. (1996). *National science education standards.* Washington, DC: National Academy Press.

Wilson, J. E. (1990). Bent on teaching refraction. *Science and Children, 28* (3), 28–30.

SELECTED TRADE BOOKS: LIGHT ENERGY AND COLOR

For Younger Children

Baines, R. (1985). *Light.* Troll Associates.

Brockel, R. (1986). *Experiments with light.* Children's Press.

Carle, E. (1991). *My very first book of colors.* Harper Collins.

Carroll, J. (1991). *The complete color book.* Good Apple.

Collins, D. (1983). *My big fun thinker book of colors and shapes.* Education Insights.

Crews, D. (1981). *Light.* Greenwillow.

Goor, R., & Goor, N. (1981). *Shadows: Here, there, everywhere.* Crowell.

Livingston, M. (1992). *Light and shadow.* Holiday House.

Smith, K. B., & Crenson, V. (1987). *Seeing.* Troll Associates.

Suess, Dr. (1996). *My many colored days.* Alfred Knopf.

Taylor, B. (1990). *Bouncing and bending light.* Watts.

Taylor, B. (1991). *Color and light.* Watts.

Taylor, K. (1992). *Flying start science series: Water; light; action; structure.* Wiley.

For Older Children

Ardley, N. (1991a). *Science book of color.* HarBrace.

Ardley, N. (1991b). *Science book of light.* HarBrace.

Asimov, I. (1986). *How did we find out about the speed of light?* Walker, 1986.

Berger, M. (1987). *Lights, lenses, and lasers.* G. P. Putnam's Sons.

Catherall, E. (1982). *Sight.* Silver Burdett.

Cooper, M. (1981). *Snap! Photography.* Messner.

De Bruin, J. (1986). *Light and color.* Good Apple.

Dunham, M. (1987). *Colors: How do you say it?* Lothrop.

Hecht, J. (1987). *Optics: Light for a new age.* Macmillan.

Hill, J., & Hill, J. (1986). *Looking at light and color.* David & Charles.

Jennings, T. (1992). *Sound and light.* Smithmark.

Murata, M. (1993). *Science is all around you: water and light.* Lerner.

Simon, H. (1981). *The magic of color.* Lothrop.

Simon, S. (1985). *Shadow magic.* Lothrop.

Simon, S. (1991). *Mirror magic.* Lothrop.

Walpole, B. (1987). *Light.* Garrard.

Ward, A. (1991). *Experimenting with light and illusions.* Chelsea House.

Wilkins, M.J. (1991). *Air, light, and water.* Random House.

Whyman, K. (1986). *Light and lasers.* Watts.

Whyman, K. (1989). *Rainbows to lasers.* Watts.

Resource Books

Butzow, C. M., & Butzow, J. W. (1989). *Science through children's literature: An integrated approach* (eye, vision, optics topics pp. 169–173; shadows and light topics pp. 174–177). Teacher Ideas Press.

Shaw, D. G., & Dybdahl, C. S. (1996). *Integrating science and language arts* (color topics pp. 1–52). Allyn and Bacon.

HEAT ENERGY

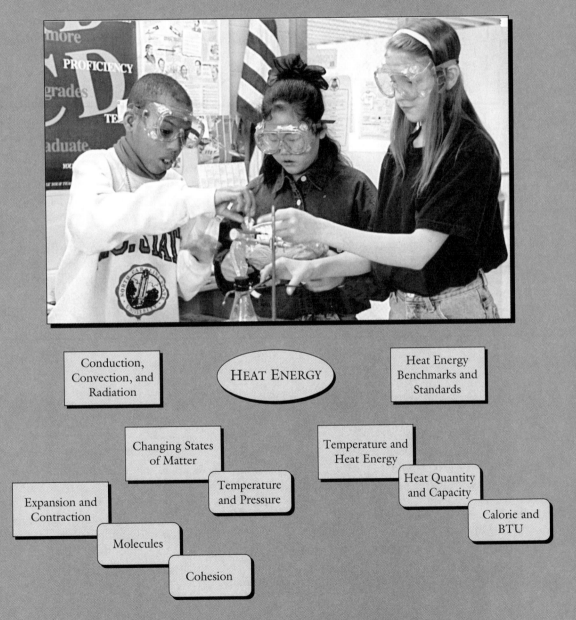

Conduction, Convection, and Radiation

HEAT ENERGY

Heat Energy Benchmarks and Standards

Changing States of Matter

Temperature and Pressure

Temperature and Heat Energy

Heat Quantity and Capacity

Expansion and Contraction

Calorie and BTU

Molecules

Cohesion

The rising cost of fuels has made more people realize that knowing about heat energy has economic as well as scientific value. Energy affects many aspects of our lives. This chapter considers what happens when materials are heated and cooled, how materials change state, the difference between heat and temperature, and how heat travels.

EXPANSION AND CONTRACTION CONCEPTS
(Experiences p. 233)

Question: How tall is the tallest building in the United States?

Answer: I don't know; it keeps changing.

Although answers like this seldom come up in normal conversation, it is a good one. The height of a tall structure may vary a half foot or more, depending on temperature differences when the measurements are taken. Likewise, a steel bridge may change more than a foot in length, and a ship captain may stride a slightly longer deck in southern waters than in northern waters.

Molecules

The molecular theory of matter offers an interesting explanation for these and many other events. To understand molecules, let's look for a moment at a drop of water. If we could subdivide it with an imaginary eyedropper for years on end, eventually we would get to a point where one more subdivision would produce two atoms of hydrogen and one of oxygen. Both are gases and, of course, look nothing like water. From this, we can say that a molecule is the smallest particle of a substance that can exist by itself and have the properties of that substance when interacting with other molecules.

Strictly speaking, only some gases are exclusively made up of molecules. Some liquids and many solids are composed of electrically charged atoms or groups of atoms called *ions*. But as nearly all ionic particles have physical properties very similar to molecules, it is convenient to treat them as such.

Is there any direct proof that molecules exist? Recently, yes. Pictures of some large molecules have been taken through powerful electron microscopes. But for the most part, scientists have had to rely on indirect evidence. It is a remarkable tribute to the brainpower of earlier scientists that they were able to forge so powerful a theory from their secondhand observations.

Many early experiments may be duplicated today. A unit of alcohol added to a unit of water results in slightly less than two units of liquid. When gold and lead bars are clamped together for a long period, there is a slight intermingling of these elements. Solid sugar crystals disappear when stirred into a liquid.

Matter is composed of tiny particles that have an attractive force (cohesion) between them. There is space between molecules. In a solid material, molecules are very close together and are relatively fixed in place because their cohesion is greater than that of gases or liquids. Molecules of most liquids are slightly farther apart; their weaker cohesion permits them to slide about and take the shape of a container. Gas molecules are widest apart and have almost no cohesive attraction. Therefore, they can conform to a container's shape or escape from an uncovered container.

Molecules are always in motion, but they come almost to a standstill at absolute zero (−460°F or −273°C). Above this temperature, molecules of solids vibrate in place, whereas liquid and gas molecules move faster and more freely. With increased temperature, motion increases and the molecules move farther apart. The reverse happens when temperature is decreased. This is why most matter expands when heated and contracts when cooled.

Water

If liquids *contract* when cooled, why do some water pipes burst in freezing weather? Although molecular theory states that liquids contract when cooled, we note an interesting exception when water temperature drops toward freezing. Water does contract in volume with decreased temperature until about 39°F (4°C). Then its molecules begin to assemble into a crystalline form that becomes ice at 32°F (0°C). The latticelike arrangement of these crystals takes up more space, about 4 percent more, than an equal number of free-moving water molecules. This is why water pipes and engine blocks of water-cooled automobiles may burst in winter.

It also explains why a lake freezes from the top down, rather than the reverse. At 39°F (4°C), water is densest and sinks to the bottom of the lake. Colder water, being less dense, floats to the surface. It freezes into surface ice and traps the heat energy in the slightly warmer water below. Unless the air temperature is extremely cold, this trapped energy is enough to keep the pond from freezing completely.

The importance of this phenomenon to living things can hardly be overestimated. Though it is clear that aquatic life is saved, consider what would happen to the world's climate if bodies of water froze from the bottom up. Because the heat trapped by ice would escape, ice formation would increase. Gradually, the earth's climate would become colder and would eventually become fatal to most life forms.

Differences in Cohesion

Different materials vary in their rates of expansion and contraction because their cohesive forces vary. It is easier to tear a paper sheet apart than an equally thin steel sheet because steel molecules attract one another with much greater force. A cohesive disparity is likewise true of alcohol and water. Notice in Figure 9-1 how water bulges above the glass rim when it is overfilled.

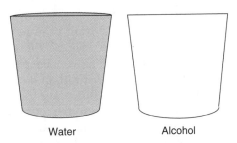

Water   Alcohol

Figure 9-1
Surface tension in alcohol and water.

The cohesive force of water molecules is greater than that of alcohol. This explains why equal amounts of heat energy cause alcohol to expand more than water. It is easier to overcome the weaker cohesive force. It also tells us why alcohol evaporates faster than water.

Expansion, contraction, and changes of state from solids to liquids and gases are the results of a constant tug of war between heat energy and cohesive force. Which side wins depends on which force is more powerful.

Safety

Some experiences will require use of a lighted candle. *Caution:* Supervise these occasions closely. Probably it will be advisable to handle any burning candle yourself. Never allow a child with long hair or loose, trailing apparel to work by an open flame. Always use a metal tray or other fireproof material to contain a burning or hot substance. Develop standards about not touching a hot plate or other materials at random.

CHANGING STATES OF MATTER CONCEPTS
(Experiences p. 237)

Sometimes we get so used to our environment it is hard to think of the things around us in new ways. Most everyone knows that air is a mixture of gases. Yet a favorite stunt of science demonstrators at high school assemblies is to grandly pour liquid air from one container to another. Many persons know that carbon dioxide is a gas. Yet it is possible to trip over some or drop it on your toe when it is in the form of dry ice. Steel is certainly a durable solid. But high-temperature tests for possible spaceship uses turn it into vapor.

Temperature

The state of matter at any given moment depends on its temperature. Temperature is a measure of the average speed of molecular movements. When increased heat energy is applied to a solid, its molecules vibrate faster. If the motion is powerful enough to overcome the molecules' cohesive forces, the molecules move farther away, and the solid becomes a liquid. If further energy is applied, the molecules move even faster and farther apart to become a gas. With loss of heat energy, the opposite occurs. The decreased speed of molecules enables cohesive force to be reasserted, thus forming a liquid, then a solid when enough heat is lost.

Does a solid become a liquid before it becomes a gas? Or a gas, liquid before it becomes a solid? Usually, but a mothball changes to a gas directly, as does dry ice. Frost is an example of vapor freezing directly into a solid state. These phenomena are examples of *sublimation.*

Different substances change state at different temperatures. Adding salt to fresh water lowers its freezing point. Sea water, for example, freezes at 28.5°F (−2°C) instead of 32°F (0°C). Unless the temperature is very low, sprinkling rock salt on an icy sidewalk melts the ice. We add an antifreeze liquid (ethylene glycol) to our automobile radiators to prevent freezing. A heavy salt solution would be even more effective, except for its unfortunate tendency to corrode metal.

What Pressure Does

Pressure also has an interesting effect on changes of state. As a liquid warms, some of its molecules move so fast they bounce off into the air. We recognize this as evaporation. The same thing happens with boiling, except the process is faster. To leave the surface of a liquid, though, molecules must overcome not only the cohesive pull of nearby molecules but also the pressure of air molecules immediately above.

At sea level, a square-inch column of air extending to outer space weighs 14.7 pounds (6.6 kilograms). At the top of a tall mountain there is much less air, therefore, less weight pressing down. With less pressure, it is easier for liquid molecules to escape into vapor form. So at 90,000 feet (27,000 meters), water boils at room temperature. Astronauts or pilots of high-altitude airplanes wear pressure suits, or are enclosed in a pressurized cabin, to keep their blood from boiling.

Since we normally associate boiling with a temperature of about 212°F, it is important to realize another practical effect of decreased pressure. Boiling-point temperature decreases about 1°F for each 550-foot increase in altitude. At a high location, it is hard to cook foods satisfactorily in an open container because of the low temperature at which boiling happens. A pressure cooker is almost a necessity.

The effect of a different kind of pressure is readily observable with ice. Why is it possible to skate on ice, when we cannot on other smooth surfaces? The answer is that we do not skate directly on the ice. Our body weight exerts enough pressure through the ice skate blades to liquefy the ice. This furnishes a water-lubricated surface on which we slide. As the temperature drops, however, it takes increasing pressure to melt the ice. It may be difficult to skate at all.

Heat Loss and Gain

Does an iced drink start warming up after the ice has half melted? A change of state always results in the absorption or release of heat energy. It requires energy for the fixed, jiggling molecules of a solid, like ice, to acquire a more freely moving liquid state. Interestingly, until an ice cube melts completely in a container of water, there is no appreciable increase in water temperature. The heat energy absorbed first changes the state of the frozen water, then raises the water temperature once the cube has melted. The next time you have an iced drink, try stirring the liquid until the last bit of ice has melted. You should sense no rise in temperature until after the frozen cubes have completely changed state.

Additional energy is required for liquid molecules to move fast enough and far enough apart to become a gas. Heat is absorbed from whatever accessible substance is warmer than the changing material.

So if you hold an ice cube in your hand, it removes heat from your body. More heat is required as the liquid evaporates. This is why evaporation has a cooling effect. As the speed of evaporation increases, so does cooling. This is why rubbing alcohol cools your skin more effectively than water. Ethyl chloride evaporates so quickly that it is used by physicians to numb flesh for painless surgery.

Conversely, heat energy is released when a gas condenses to a liquid or a liquid freezes to a solid state. That is because molecular motion continually decreases with each event. It used to be common in rural homes to place tubs of water near vegetable bins in the basement. As the water freezes, enough heat is given off to prevent the vegetables from freezing.

Heat is absorbed in evaporation and released through condensation. This principle applied in electric refrigeration. A liquid refrigerant moves at low pressure into the freezing unit. There it flashes into a vaporous state, cools rapidly, and absorbs heat. As the now slightly warmed vapor leaves the unit, a motor-driven pump compresses the vapor until it has changed to a hot liquid under high pressure. The liquid next circulates in tubes attached to the back of the refrigerator that radiate the heat into the air. The cycle then repeats itself.

TEMPERATURE AND HEAT ENERGY CONCEPTS
(Experiences p. 240)

You have seen before that the temperature of a material depends on the speed of its molecules. So molecules of a cold substance move slower than those of a hotter substance.

Heat Quantity

Although the concept of temperature is understood by many children, quantity of heat is a subtler idea. Consider a white-hot horseshoe just removed from a blacksmith's forge and a large bathtub of warm water. Which contains more heat? Very probably the water. The amount of heat a material contains depends on *how many* molecules it has, as well as how fast they are moving. This is why the owner of a large house pays larger winter heating bills than someone who owns a small house, although the same air temperature may be maintained. It also explains why it takes about half as long to bring one liter of water to a boil as two. There are half as many molecules to move.

Heat Capacity

Different materials have different capacities for heat energy. For example, it takes more heat for iron to reach a given temperature than an equal weight of lead. More energy is required to heat water to a given temperature than any other common material, liquid or solid, and water retains this heat longer.

The most important effect of water's high heat capacity is found in weather and climate. Because the earth's oceans and lakes gain and lose heat more slowly than the land, they moderate changes in air temperature throughout the world. The most noticeable effects are found in coastal regions. Summers are cooler and winters warmer there than they are inland.

The Calorie and the BTU

Two measures are commonly used to tell heat capacity: the calorie and the British Thermal Unit (BTU). A calorie is the quantity of heat needed to raise the temperature of a gram (about ounce) of water 1° Celsius. The caloric value of a food is found simply by burning a dry sample of known weight in a special chamber of a carefully insulated container of pure water. The temperature rise is multiplied by the weight of water in the container. For example, assume 50 grams of water rises 20°C. 50 × 20 = 1,000 calories.

To make calculations less cumbersome, a "large calorie" is used in finding heat value of foods. Equivalent to 1,000 small calories, the large calorie is what you see published in diet lists.

The British Thermal Unit, or the quantity of heat needed to raise 1 pound of water 1° Fahrenheit, is used widely by engineers. It is found by multiplying the mass of water by the temperature increase. So to raise the temperature of 5 pounds of water 30°F requires 150 BTU.

Of course, this information is more for you than for the students at this level. Yet it is not too early for many children to grasp the general idea of heat quantity. For this reason, we have included an activity in which children heat different-sized nails, put them in water, and measure the increases in water temperature.

Heat Conservation

Heat energy is *conserved* when liquids are mixed, that is, not lost but transferred in proportion to the original amount. One liter of warm water has half the heat energy of two

liters at the same temperature. Also, if two equal volumes of water at different temperatures are mixed, the resulting temperature is halfway between that of the two samples.

Thermal Equilibrium

In some elementary science curricula, the concept of *equilibrium* is introduced. For example, when water is brought to a boil, its temperature stays at 212°F or 100°C (at sea level) until all the water has evaporated. Because it loses heat energy as fast as it gains the energy, we see a state of dynamic equilibrium or a stable condition that remains until the water disappears.

A second example is seen when something cools. You know that when a jar of hot water is left standing long enough, it loses heat energy to the surrounding air and surface on which it rests. Eventually, the water temperature becomes stable when it reaches *thermal equilibrium* with these interacting objects. The air, of course, is the chief interacting object that influences the water's final temperature.

CONDUCTION, CONVECTION, AND RADIATION CONCEPTS
(Experiences p. 244)

Until the nineteenth century, it was generally thought that heat was a fluidlike substance (caloric) that could be poured from one material to another. Scientists now realize that heat is a form of energy, with *energy* being defined as the capacity to do work.

Changing Forms of Energy

Many experiments have shown that energy can be changed from one form to another. Our practical experience also shows that this is so. Electrical energy changes to heat in toasters and hot plates; chemical energy yields heat through fires and explosives; mechanical energy (motion) provides the force needed to overcome friction and, in the process, heat is released.

Heat, in turn, changes to other forms of energy. Hot fuel turns a generator to produce electricity, or gasoline is burned in automobile engines to produce mechanical energy.

If you put a pan of hot water in a cool room, after a while the water cools to room temperature. But place a pan of cool water in a hot oven, and the water warms to oven temperature. In moving toward thermal equilibrium, as we saw before, heat energy always travels from a place of higher temperature to one of lower temperature.

A misconception of what heat is may interfere with understanding how it travels. Instead of viewing cold as a lesser degree of heat, many students think that cold is distinctly different and the opposite of heat. So it's logical for them to think that "cold" leaves the ice cube in a drink and goes into the liquid, rather than that heat goes from the liquid into the cube, making it melt (Erickson, 1979).

Since heat is felt rather than seen, it may also affect children's understanding of how it travels. By about age eight, they begin to think of heat as something that travels from a source to another place. But before then, for example, they are more likely to view a hot stove or fire as something that instantly makes them warm (Albert, 1978).

In moving from one location to another, heat energy may travel in one or more of three ways: by *conduction, convection,* and *radiation.* Let's consider these ways one at a time.

Conduction

If you grasp the metal handle of a hot frying pan, you quickly let go. How is it possible for the heat energy to go from the hot stove grid to the handle? Molecular conduction is responsible. As heat energy enters the pan bottom, its molecules begin to vibrate faster. This motion is passed along, molecule by molecule, up the pan's sides to its handle. Eventually, all the particles are vibrating faster, and you feel the heat.

Of all solids, metals are the best conductors. Their molecules are very close together and transmit heat energy quickly. But each type of metal varies somewhat in conductivity. Copper is the best common conductor, followed by aluminum, steel, and iron. Other solids are comparatively poor conductors, including ceramic materials. This is one reason we use ceramic cups to hold hot coffee and microwave food.

Because molecules of liquids are farther apart than solids, it is reasonable to expect that they conduct heat less efficiently than solids. Our ordinary experiences with bathwater help confirm this thought. When hot water is added to cooler water, it takes a long time for the heat to reach all portions of the tub. For this reason, we stir the water a bit to hasten the process.

Gases are the poorest conductors of all. Their molecules are spread so far apart they do not collide often and regularly enough to pass on increased energy to any appreciable extent. This is why it is possible for frozen-food sections in supermarkets to have open counters. Very little heat energy is conducted downward from the warmer air above the counter.

Convection

Although liquids and gases conduct poorly, it is easy to heat a pan of water quickly to boiling temperature or quickly roast a frankfurter in the hot air over a fire. This means that there must be another, more efficient method of heat transfer in liquids and gases than conduction. To identify it, examine what happens when air is warmed.

Watch the smoke from burning material. Why does it rise? Is it unaffected by gravity? A clue to its behavior is found when smoke is pumped into an airless vacuum chamber. The smoke particles fall like lead weights. Therefore, smoke does not just "rise"; something must push it up.

When the glowing part of burning material warms the adjacent air, the increased energy agitates air molecules to increased speeds and they spread farther apart. Because fewer molecules take up a given volume of space, they are lighter than an equal volume of the surrounding air. The lighter air is pushed up with the smoke particles as it is replaced by heavier, colder air. As the mass of lighter air rises, it carries increased energy with it. This is why air near the ceiling is warmer than air near the floor.

When there is an opening for warm air to escape and cool air to flow into a room, a *convection current* is set up. This is what happens when we open a window at top and bottom to freshen the air in a room. It is also the primary cause of winds in the atmosphere.

Similar convection currents are set up in heated liquids. Warmed, expanded water in a pan rises as it is continually replaced by cooler, heavier water until the same temperature is reached in the entire container. Adding color to the liquid will help children to see this effect (Rubino & Duerling).

Because of the way convective currents move, a heating unit is usually located at the bottom of a hot-water tank and a cooling unit at the top of a refrigerator. Convection also helps to set up ocean currents. Warm water at the equator is continually being replaced by cold water flowing from the polar regions. Air convection currents form winds that contribute to the distribution of these giant water currents. A third important factor is the earth's rotation. Because water has a high heat capacity, ocean currents are responsible for altering the climates of many countries.

Radiation

A common example of the third method of heat transfer, radiation, is found in the fireplace of a house. This is especially noticeable when the air temperature is low. As you warm yourself in front of the fire, only the portion of your body that faces the fire feels warm. Conduction is poor, because air is the conducting medium. Convection is negligible, because most of the hot air escapes up the chimney. Heat reaches you primarily by radiation.

All vibrating molecules release a certain amount of energy through invisible heat rays called *infrared waves.* These waves largely pass through transparent materials like air and glass but are absorbed by opaque objects, which become warmer as a result. We are aware of radiant energy only when the emitting source is warmer than body temperature. The sun is by far our most important source of radiant energy. In its rays are found visible light, invisible infrared waves, and other forms of radiant energy.

From Solar to Heat Energy

An air traveler who goes from a cold to a tropical climate quickly notices many differences in the new surroundings. Among the most impressive are house colors, which are largely light pastels and dazzling white. Similar differences can be noted in clothing colors. Dark-colored materials absorb more sunlight than light-colored materials.

Figure 9-2 reveals why persons in tropical countries find a greater need for lighter colors than those who live farther away from the equator. Light is most intense when it is received from directly overhead. If the same amount of light is spread out over a larger area, any part of that area receives less light and so less heat.

The changing of solar energy to heat energy is most noticeable when there is an effective way of preventing the heat from escaping. A common example is the temperature rise within a tightly closed automobile parked in sunlight. The rapidly vibrating short waves of sunlight can pass through the windows. When they strike the upholstery they are absorbed, then

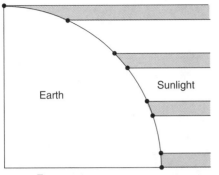

Figure 9-2
Light is most intense when received from exactly overhead. This explains why people in tropical climates find a greater need for light-colored clothing and buildings than others do.

reradiated as longer, slower-vibrating heat waves. The longer waves are largely unable to penetrate glass, so most of the heat stays inside, building up in intensity as sunlight continues to stream in. Because the same thing happens in greenhouses, this phenomenon is aptly called the *greenhouse effect.*

Our atmosphere is also warmed largely by reradiated heat waves. The atmosphere is like a giant glass cover that traps the longer, reradiated heat waves. However, this analogy is not perfect. Fortunately for us, the atmosphere is far less efficient than glass. A substantial amount of reradiated heat escapes into space. Were this not so, the earth's air temperature would become so hot it would be intolerable to life.

Because of the greenhouse effect, air temperatures get warmest in the afternoon rather than at midday. Although the sun is most nearly overhead at midday, the buildup of heat continues for several hours afterward.

Solar Heating for Homes

Solar energy is becoming a popular way to heat water and even entire homes, especially in the sunbelt regions of the south and southwest. Let's examine one way this is done.

A *flat-plate collector* is attached to, or built into, the house roof. Its purpose is to collect as much solar energy as possible. The collector, made of metal and glass, is positioned to face the sun. The glass is mounted just over a blackened metal plate. Water pipes, also painted black, are attached to the plate. Sunlight is absorbed by the plate and pipes. Water inside the pipes is heated by conduction. The glass cover contributes to the buildup of heat by trapping the absorbed light energy (Figure 9-3).

The heated water is stored in a large tank. Pipes circulate it throughout the house as needed. Other pipes are connected to hot water faucets in the house.

Notice the three conditions that affect the efficiency of the solar collector. The collector plate and pipes are painted black to absorb sunlight. A clear glass cover admits sunlight but prevents most of the absorbed energy from escaping. Finally, the collector is mounted on a slope that faces the sun.

Controlling Heat Loss

Knowing how heat travels permits us to control it. We use *insulation* to prevent or retard heat energy transfer. For example, to retard conduction we use poor conductors. Since air is a poor conductor, materials with air spaces, such as wood and wool, make excellent insulators.

In homes, convection and conduction are reduced by using hollow walls designed to trap the air. Because some convection takes place anyway, many homeowners fill the walls with a light, fluffy material, such as fiberglass or cellulose insulation.

An excellent way to insulate for radiation is to reflect it away, because it behaves like light as it travels. This is why insulating materials in the home may use a shiny foil exterior, particularly in the attic. It also explains why silver-colored paint is used on large gasoline storage tanks.

Figure 9-3
A flat-plate solar energy collector.

HEAT ENERGY BENCHMARKS AND STANDARDS

Students in early grades should develop an understanding that materials can exist in liquid, gas, or solid form. Experimentation with water can be effective in introducing them to the states of matter and how heat affects the movement of molecules and the state of a substance. Specific Benchmarks and Standards are as follows:

SAMPLE BENCHMARKS (AAAS, 1993).

■ Heating and cooling cause changes in the properties of materials. Many kinds of changes occur faster under hotter conditions (by Grades 3–5, p. 77).

■ Some materials conduct heat much better than others. Poor conductors can reduce heat loss (by Grades 3–5, p. 84).

SAMPLE STANDARDS (NRC, 1996).

■ Materials can exist in different states—solid, liquid, and gas. Some common materials, such as water, can be changed from one state to another by heating and cooling (by Grades K–4, p. 127).

■ Heat moves in predictable ways, flowing from warmer objects to cooler ones, until both reach the same temperature (by Grades 5–8, p. 155).

INVESTIGATIONS AND ACTIVITIES

EXPANSION AND CONTRACTION EXPERIENCES
(Concepts p. 224)

ACTIVITY: *HOW DOES HEAT AFFECT A SOLID?*

NEEDED

brass screw and screw eye (each screwed into the eraser end of a separate pencil, see Figure 9-4),
small dish and candle
matches

TRY THIS

1. Light the candle and fix it to the dish.
2. Try to pass the screw through the screw eye as in Figure 9-4. This should not be possible.

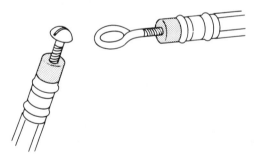

Figure 9-4

3. Heat the screw eye in the flame for a minute or so.
4. Try Step 2 again.
   a. Does the screw head pass through the heated screw eye? If so, keep passing the screw head through the eye. How many seconds go by before you cannot do it?
   b. What will happen if you heat the screw but not the screw eye? If you heat both screw and screw eye? How can you explain what happened in a and b?

TEACHING COMMENT

The screw eye should be slightly smaller than the screw head. Pliers can be used to slightly close or open the screw eye as needed. *Caution:* Supervise burning the candle closely.

INVESTIGATION: MEASURING TEMPERATURE WITH A WATER THERMOMETER

Many thermometers use red-colored alcohol or mercury in a closed tube. What happens to these liquids when they get warmer? cooler? You can make a water thermometer that works in much the same way.

EXPLORATORY PROBLEM

How can you make a water thermometer?

NEEDED

small soda bottle
soft clay
small card
plastic straw
sticky tape
crayon
red food coloring
pencil
thermometer
ruler

TRY THIS

1. Fill the bottle almost full with water.
2. Add some food coloring to the water so it is easy to see.
3. Dry the bottle opening with a paper towel. Then put the straw about halfway into the bottle opening.
4. Use clay to stop up the bottle opening and around the straw. Try to get a tight fit without getting the clay wet.
5. The water should rise about halfway up the straw beyond the clay. If not, move the straw up or down. Then press the clay down tightly again.

6. Put the bottle in the sun. After an hour, lightly mark the water level on the straw with crayon. Then put the bottle in a refrigerator for an hour and mark the level.

7. Measure the distance between the two marks. On a card, mark two dots the same distance and draw evenly spaced lines between. Give each line a number, with the highest on top. Put the column of numbers on the right side of the card.

8. Tape the card to the straw so the top and bottom numbers are even with the two marks on the straw (Figure 9-5).

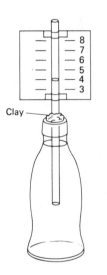

Figure 9-5

9. Use your water thermometer to record daily temperatures for a week. You might use a table like this:

Table 9-1
Daily Temperature Record

	Water Thermometer Readings				
Time	**M**	**T**	**W**	**TH**	**F**
9:30 A.M.	4	5			
Noon	6	7			
2:30 P.M.	7	7			

DISCOVERY PROBLEMS

measuring

A. At what time of day is it coolest? warmest?

inferring

B. During the week, what was the coolest morning? noon? afternoon?

predicting

C. How closely can you predict the noon temperature from the 9:30 a.m. temperature? the 2:30 p.m. temperature from the noon temperature? Try this for a few days.

communicating

D. Ask a partner to make another water thermometer. Keep two separate records. How closely do your readings agree with your partner's? If they do not agree, can you figure out why?

measuring

E. Get a regular thermometer. Measure the temperature with it and your water thermometer. Write the actual temperatures on the left side of the straw card. After a few days, use only your water thermometer to predict the real temperature. Then check the regular thermometer each time. How accurate is your water thermometer? How could you make it more accurate?

TEACHING COMMENT

PREPARATION AND BACKGROUND

A one-hole rubber stopper and glass tube are more reliable than clay and a straw. Wet the tube and stopper before inserting the tube. Hold the tube with a thickly folded paper towel to guard against breakage and use a twisting motion.

Water, especially with this large volume, takes considerable time to gain and lose heat, so readings should be hours apart. Rubbing alcohol responds more quickly to heat and may be substituted.

GENERALIZATION

Liquids expand when heated and contract when cooled.

SAMPLE PERFORMANCE OBJECTIVE

Process: The child can construct, calibrate, and read a water thermometer.
Knowledge: The child can explain how a liquid thermometer works.

ACTIVITY: *HOW DOES HEAT AFFECT AIR?*

NEEDED

empty soda bottle (cool)
round balloon
partner

TRY THIS

1. Snap the balloon opening over the bottle opening.
2. Wrap both hands around the bottle to warm it. Let a partner help, also.
   a. What happens to the balloon? What seems to be happening to the air inside the bottle?
   b. What will happen to the balloon when the bottle cools? Why?
   c. How else can you warm the bottle air? cool the bottle air?
   d. How could you find out if heated air expands by using only a balloon and string?

Teaching Comment

A partly filled balloon may be placed in sunlight. A string may be wrapped around it to compare before and after sizes. A round, moderately sized balloon inflates more easily than the small tubular kind.

Changing States of Matter Experiences
(Concepts p. 225)

Investigation: *The Melting of Ice Cubes*

Suppose you have a glass of water. It has the same temperature as the air. Would an ice cube melt faster in the water or air?

EXPLORATORY PROBLEM

How can you find out if water or air will melt an ice cube faster?

NEEDED

thermometer
small plastic bag
water
salt
ice cubes
spoon
two glasses (same)

TRY THIS

1. Measure the air temperature inside one glass with a thermometer.

2. Also measure the temperature inside a glass of water. It should be about the same as the air temperature. If not, let the water stand a while.

3. Find two ice cubes that are the same size.

4. Put one ice cube into the empty glass. Put the other into the glass of water.

5. Compare how fast the ice cubes melt (Figure 9-6).

Figure 9-6

DISCOVERY PROBLEMS

experimenting   **A.** How can you make an ice cube melt faster in water? Will stirring the water make a difference? Will an ice cube melt faster in warmer water? Does breaking or crushing the cube make a difference? Does changing the volume of water make a difference?

experimenting   **B.** How fast will ice cubes melt in other liquids? Will an ice cube melt faster in salt water? Does the amount of salt make a difference? What other liquids can you try? Can you predict the melting order of ice cubes in them?

TEACHING COMMENT

PREPARATION AND BACKGROUND

The first activity of this investigation requires water of room temperature. Blend warm and cold tap water. Or simply let a glass of water stand for a while.

   If you believe your students are capable, try asking only the leading, broad question in Discovery Problems A and B. Probably the students will suggest testing most of the variables posed in the narrow questions that follow.

GENERALIZATION

The melting time of an ice cube changes with different conditions.

PERFORMANCE OBJECTIVES

Process: When asked to test a specific variable, the child can set up an experiment in which other variables are controlled.

Knowledge: The child can predict several conditions that will affect the melting times of ice cubes.

FOR YOUNGER CHILDREN

Younger students can do the exploratory problem, if they are given water that is at room temperature, and respond to the narrow questions in A and B. But they typically will not control variables unless shown how.

ACTIVITY: *WHAT HAPPENS TO THE TEMPERATURE OF AN ICED DRINK AS THE ICE MELTS?*

NEEDED

two ice cubes
cup of water
thermometer

TRY THIS

1. Put the ice cubes in the water.
2. Take the water temperature once a minute throughout this activity. Stir the water a bit each time.
3. Repeat Step 2 until you get the same reading twice. Then answer these questions:
   a. What will happen to the temperature as the ice keeps melting?
   b. When does the water temperature rise again? (A graph can help you keep track.)

TEACHING COMMENT

The ice melting process can be speeded up by heating a metal cup on a hot plate turned to low. Similar results should happen.

TEMPERATURE AND HEAT ENERGY EXPERIENCES

(Concepts p. 227)

INVESTIGATION: *HEAT ENERGY*

Suppose you have two iron nails, one large and one small. Both are heated to the same temperature over a candle flame. Which nail do you think would have more heat energy in it? Or, would both nails have the same heat energy?

EXPLORATORY PROBLEM

How can you compare the amount of heat energy in heated nails?

NEEDED

pie pan
soft clay
candle and match
large and small nail
two small empty juice cans
water
pliers or tongs
clock
two small thermometers

Try This

1. Stick the candle upright in the middle of the pan with clay (Figure 9-7).
2. Fill both cans with enough water to cover the nails when they are dropped in later. Check to be sure the water level and temperature are the same in the cans.
3. Light the candle. Use pliers to hold both nails in the flame for three minutes.
4. Drop one nail into each can. Wait one minute. Then stir the water in each can lightly with a thermometer and check the temperatures.

Discovery Problems

measuring
A. Which can of water is warmer? Which nail had more heat energy in it?

observing
B. Maybe one nail was just cooler than the other. Suppose you heated both nails longer to be sure they are the same temperature. Would you still get uneven results?

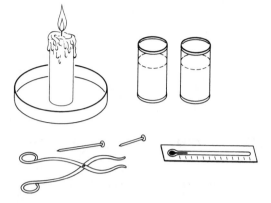

Figure 9-7

experimenting **C.** How can you give the *small* nail more heat energy than the larger one?

predicting **D.** Suppose you heated together a large aluminum nail and a large iron nail. Which, if either, do you think would have more energy?

communicating **E.** How can you see what happens to the water temperature for each minute you heat a nail? Make a graph to help.

Table 9-2
Minutes Nail Is Heated Versus Water Temperature

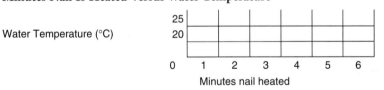

Water Temperature (°C)

Minutes nail heated

TEACHING COMMENT

PREPARATION AND BACKGROUND

Be sure to supervise this investigation closely for safety. *Caution:* Children should handle heated material only with tongs or pliers. Also, you might prefer to light and extinguish the candle. A hot plate can be used to heat more objects at a time than is possible with a candle.

GENERALIZATION

The amount of heat energy in the same materials depends on their mass as well as temperature.

SAMPLE PERFORMANCE OBJECTIVES

Process: The child can graph and interpret data.

Knowledge: The child can predict that the larger of two heated identical materials will contain more heat energy.

INVESTIGATION: *THE MIXING OF HOT AND COLD WATER*

Have you ever added cold water to cool down hot bath water? Have you added hot water to heat up cool bath water? You can learn to predict the temperatures of a water mixture.

EXPLORATORY PROBLEM

How can you predict the temperature of two mixed samples of water?

NEEDED

large container of hot water
large container of cold water
two small styrofoam cups
half-gallon milk carton with top cut off
two thermometers
paper and pencil

TRY THIS

1. Fill one small cup with hot water. Take the temperature of the water and record it.

2. Fill another small cup with cold water. Take the temperature and record it (Figure 9-8).

3. Pour both cups of water into the large carton. Take the temperature of the mixed water and record it.

4. Study your records. Let's say your recorded temperatures are like the ones in Table 9-3:

   Notice that the temperature of the mixture is halfway between the hot and cold temperatures (60 + 20 = 80, 40 is half of 80). Look at the temperature of your mixture. Is it about halfway between the hot and cold temperatures?

DISCOVERY PROBLEMS

predicting   **A.** Suppose you mix *two* cups of hot and *two* cups of cold water. How hot do you predict the mixture will be?

predicting   **B.** Suppose you mix two cups of only hot water. How hot do you predict the mixture will be?

Figure 9-8

Table 9-3
Temperature Recordings

Hot Water	Cold Water	Mixture
60°C	20°C	40°C

predicting **C.** Suppose you mix two cups of cold water with one of hot water. Will the mixture be hotter or colder than halfway between the two temperatures? How closely can you predict the temperature of the mixture?

TEACHING COMMENT

PREPARATION AND BACKGROUND

The temperature of mixed water depends on the temperature and the volume of each water sample mixed. When the volumes of water samples are equal, the mixture temperature is the average of the sample temperatures. But if the volumes are different, this has to be considered when figuring the average. For example, if one water sample is twice the volume of another, it will have twice the influence on the mixture temperature. *Caution:* Never heat the water beyond the point that someone can comfortably touch it.

GENERALIZATION

The temperature of mixed water samples depends on the temperature and volume of each sample. The mixture temperature is always somewhere between the high and low sample temperatures.

SAMPLE PERFORMANCE OBJECTIVES

Process: The child can measure water sample temperatures and calculate the average of several samples.

Knowledge: The child can purposefully vary the direction of temperature change (cold or hot) in a mixture by controlling the volume or temperature of added water.

CONDUCTION, CONVECTION, AND RADIATION EXPERIENCES
(Concepts p. 228)

ACTIVITY: *WHAT MAKES SOME THINGS FEEL COLDER EVEN WHEN THEY HAVE THE SAME TEMPERATURE?*

NEEDED

metal object
newspaper
piece of wood
thermometer

Try This

1. Hold the bulb of a thermometer against any metal object, such as scissors. Find its temperature. Do the same with a piece of wood and a folded newspaper. They should all be the same temperature. If not, keep them together and wait an hour or so.

2. Touch a metal object with one hand and some wood with the other. Compare the metal and newspaper, also.

   a. Which one felt coolest? warmest? Some materials conduct heat well and some poorly. Good conductors take away heat quickly from our warm skin, so they feel cool. Poor conductors take away heat slowly. This makes them seem warm because less heat is lost from our skin.

   b. What other materials can you compare at school and home? Make a record of what you find. Share your record with others who test heat conductors.

TEACHING COMMENT

It is assumed in this activity that the temperature of tested materials will be lower than body temperature. If your students seem capable, you might invite them to attempt an explanation after Problem 2a and withhold, for a time, the explanation given.

ACTIVITY: *HOW DO WARM AND COLD WATER FORM A CURRENT?*

NEEDED

two matched clear soda bottles
red food coloring
small card
white paper
cake pan or tray
hot and cold tap water

TRY THIS

1. Fill one bottle with cold and the other with hot tap water.
2. Add red coloring to the hot water bottle. Put this bottle on the pan.

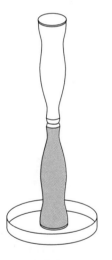

Figure 9-9

3. Hold a card tightly over the opening of the cold water bottle. Turn the bottle upside down and place it carefully on top of the hot water bottle (Figure 9-9).

   a. What do you think will happen if you remove the card? Try it and see. Be careful not to tip over the bottle. Hold white paper behind the bottle to see better.

4. Empty the bottles and do Steps 1 and 2 again, but now put the hot water bottle on top.

   b. What do you think will happen now when you remove the card? How can you explain the results?

ACTIVITY: *WHERE DOES WARMED AIR GO?*

NEEDED

yardstick or substitute
string
two thumbtacks
two matched paper bags
bit of clay
sticky tape
hot plate

TRY THIS

1. Stick a thumbtack into the middle of the stick near the edge. Tie string to the tack.

2. Hang the stick from the top of a wide table. Use another tack to fasten the loose string end there.

3. Fasten a string to each bag bottom with sticky tape.

4. Hang the bags upside down from the stick ends. Use a tiny bit of clay to balance the stick if needed (Figure 9-10).

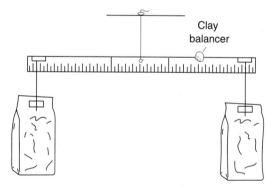

Figure 9-10

5. Place a cold, unplugged hot plate under a bag. (***Caution:*** The bag should be at least 30 centimeters or 1 foot above the hot plate since it is flammable.)

6. Plug in the hot plate.

   a. What do you think will happen to the bag when you turn on the hot plate?

   b. What will happen to the bag when you turn off the hot plate?

TEACHING COMMENT

For safety, it's best for you to demonstrate this activity, and to turn off the hot plate as soon as the bag rises.

INVESTIGATION: *SOLAR ENERGY AND COLORS*

Have you ever felt extra warm when wearing a colored shirt in sunlight? When a colored shirt soaks up sunlight, it does get warmer. But how does the kind of color affect how warm it gets?

EXPLORATORY PROBLEM

How can you compare how warm different colors get in sunlight?

NEEDED

sheets of different-colored construction paper (such as blue, red, green, white)
four thermometers
four paper clips
sunshine
partner

TRY THIS

1. Fold the four colored sheets in half. Clip together the open side.
2. Push a thermometer all the way into each folded, clipped sheet (Figure 9-11).
3. Place the sheets in a row where it is sunny.
4. Wait five minutes. Then check the thermometer temperatures.

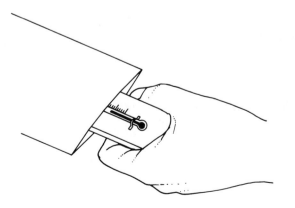

Figure 9-11

DISCOVERY PROBLEMS

predicting **A.** Before you check, what do you think the warmest to coolest colors will be?

classifying **B.** Suppose you also tried colored sheets such as orange, yellow, and black. Where would they fit in the order found in A?

observing **C.** How well can you feel the difference in heat among the colors? Close your eyes. Let a partner help you place your hands on the sheets. Can you feel the hottest and coolest sheets?

measuring **D.** Will a large colored sheet get warmer than a small one?

measuring **E.** Suppose you placed *all* the colored sheets in the shade. Would some colors still get warmer than others?

TEACHING COMMENT

PREPARATION AND BACKGROUND

It is possible on extra-bright, hot days for the temperature inside the paper folders to rise quickly. On such days, leave the thermometer tops exposed. Have someone observe and remove any thermometer before it rises near the breaking point.

GENERALIZATION

Absorbed sunlight changes to heat energy; darker colors get warmer than lighter colors.

SAMPLE PERFORMANCE OBJECTIVES

Process: The child can read a thermometer accurately to within one degree.

Knowledge: The child can select which colors are likely to be relatively warmer or cooler in sunlight.

FOR YOUNGER CHILDREN

With some help, younger students can detect by touch alone which colors become warmest or stay coolest in sunshine (Problem C).

ACTIVITY: *HOW DO GREENHOUSES AND CLOSED AUTOMOBILES GET WARM?*

NEEDED

two matched glass jars and cap
two thermometers

two pieces of dark cloth
sunshine

TRY THIS

1. Place each jar on its side. Put a piece of cloth into each. Place a thermometer on each cloth. Cap only one jar.

2. Turn the jars so their tops face away from the sun.

3. Watch the thermometers. Keep a record of any changes each minute. Remove a thermometer before it gets close to its highest temperature, because it can break.

   a. In which jar does the temperature climb faster? How much faster? A graph will help to answer these questions.

   b. How much, if any, difference in jar temperature will there be on a cloudy day?

ACTIVITY: *WHERE IS IT HOTTEST AROUND A LIGHTED LAMP?*

NEEDED

table or gooseneck lamp (shade removed)
ruler
small pane of glass
thermometer
watch

TRY THIS

1. Check the room temperature with your thermometer. Then switch on the lamp.

2. Hold the bulb end of the thermometer toward the lamp light. Try the three places shown in the picture (Figure 9-12). Keep the thermometer the same distance from the light each time. Wait for the thermometer to reach room temperature before trying a new place.

   a. How hot does the thermometer get in each place?

3. Turn the lamp upside down. Again, hold the thermometer bulb toward the light.

   b. How hot does the thermometer get? How can you explain your results?

4. Set the lamp upright again. Hold a piece of glass between the light and the thermometer. Hold the thermometer in all four places again.

   c. What are your findings now? How can you explain them?

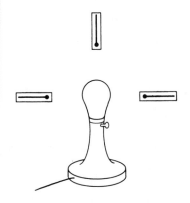

Figure 9-12

TEACHING COMMENT

Tape the edges of the glass shield with masking tape to avoid a nicked finger. A transparent shield of plastic kitchen wrap will also work. The temperature above an unshielded bulb should be highest because both convection and radiation occur. But convected heat is blocked by a transparent shield, so the temperature above a shielded bulb should be like that found in other positions around the bulb.

INVESTIGATION: *HOW TO KEEP HEAT IN OR OUT*

Most houses have an inside and outside wall. Packed between the double walls of many houses is *insulation*. This is a light, fluffy material that helps to keep heat in or out. You can work with cans of water and different materials to learn about insulation.

EXPLORATORY PROBLEM

What can you do to see how insulation works?

NEEDED

two small tin cans
hot water
two large tin cans with lids
piece of cloth
kitchen foil
different insulation materials
rubber band
ice cubes
thermometer

TRY THIS

1. Pour the same amount of hot water into each small can.

2. Cover each small can with the same size of foil. Use a rubber band to hold each cover tight (Figure 9-13).

Figure 9-13

3. Wrap one small can with cloth.

4. Put this can into one large can and cap it.

5. Put the other small can into a second large can and cap it.

6. After 20 minutes, remove the four can covers. Dip a finger into each small can of water. Which is warmer?

DISCOVERY PROBLEMS

measuring **A.** How much warmer is one can of water than the other? How can you use a thermometer to find out?

experimenting **B.** How hot can you keep a small can of water? Have a contest with a friend. Try different materials, such as sawdust, cotton, wool, puffed rice, or torn paper. Or try your own secret mix of materials. Put the materials between the larger and smaller can walls. Whoever has the warmer can of water after 30 minutes (or longer) wins.

inferring **C.** Can you figure out which single material is the best insulator? worst insulator? Does how tightly it is packed make a difference?

experimenting **D.** In summer, you want your house to stay cool. Does insulation keep heat out as well as in? Find out. How cool can you keep a small can with an ice cube inside? Have a contest with a friend. Whoever has the larger ice cube after one hour (or longer) wins.

inferring   **E.** Are the best materials for keeping the can warm also best for keeping the can cold? If not, which are best?

TEACHING COMMENT

PREPARATION AND BACKGROUND

Use matched one-pound coffee cans with lids for the larger cans. Small, identical juice cans will fit nicely into the coffee cans. Identical pieces of foil may be used to cap the small cans, so insulating materials do not fall inside. Either hot or warm water from the tap will do for this activity.

GENERALIZATION

Insulating materials may be used to slow the movement of heat energy

PERFORMANCE OBJECTIVES

Process: The child can test which of several heat insulating materials is most efficient.

Knowledge: The child can describe (explain) the contrasting properties of efficient and inefficient heat insulating materials.

REFERENCES

Albert, E. (1978). Development of the concept of heat in children. *Science Education, 62*(3), 389–399.

American Association for the Advancement of Science. (1993). *Benchmarks for science literacy.* New York: Oxford University Press.

Erickson, G. L. (1979). Children's conceptions of heat and temperature. *Science Education, 63*(1), 83–93.

National Research Council. (1996). *National science education standards.* Washington, DC: National Academy Press.

Rubino, A. M., & Duerling, C. K. (1991). Around the world in science class. *Science and Children, 28*(7), 37–39.

SELECTED TRADE BOOKS: HEAT ENERGY

For Younger Children

Ardley, N. (1983). *Hot and cold.* Watts.

Hillerman, A. (1983). *Done in the sun.* Sunstone Press.

Llewellyn, C. (1991). *First look at keeping warm.* Gareth Stevens.

Maestro, B., & Maestro, G. (1990). *Temperature and you.* Lodestar Books.

Oleksy, W. (1986). *Experiments with heat.* Children's Press.

Petersen, D. (1985). *Solar energy at work.* Children's Press.

Santrey, L. (1985). *Heat.* Troll Associates.

Stille, D. R. (1990). *The greenhouse effect.* Children's Press.

Wade, H. (1979). *Heat.* Raintree.

For Older Children

Adler, I., & Adler, R. (1973). *Heat and its uses.* John Day.

Bendick, J. (1974). *Heat and temperature.* Watts.

Cobb, V. (1973). *Heat.* Watts.

George, J. C. (1983). *One day in the desert.* Thomas Crowell.

Kaplan, S. (1983). *Solar energy.* Raintree.

Knapp, B. (1990). *Fire.* Steck-Vaughn.

Langley, A. (1986). *Energy.* Watts.

Mebane, R. C., & Rybolt, T. R. (1987). *Adventures with atoms and molecules.* Enslow.

Scott, J. M. (1973). *Heat and fire.* Enslow.

Whyman, K. (1987). *Heat and energy.* Watts.

Yount, L. (1981). *Too hot, too cold, or just right.* Walker.

Resource Book

Butzow, C. M., & Butzow, J. W. (1989). *Science through children's literature: an integrated approach* (states of matter topics pp. 200–205). Teacher Ideas Press.

SOUND ENERGY

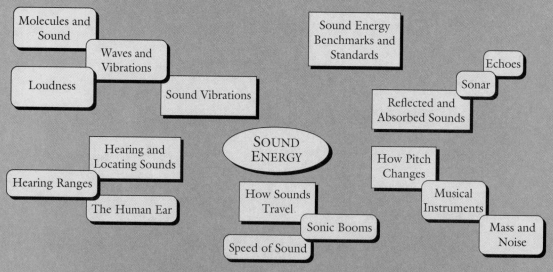

Molecules and Sound

Waves and Vibrations

Loudness

Sound Vibrations

Sound Energy Benchmarks and Standards

Echoes

Sonar

Reflected and Absorbed Sounds

Hearing and Locating Sounds

SOUND ENERGY

How Pitch Changes

Hearing Ranges

The Human Ear

How Sounds Travel

Musical Instruments

Sonic Booms

Mass and Noise

Speed of Sound

Play a radio loudly and the windows rattle. Watch a parade at a distance and the marchers seem to be out of time with the music. Sing in the shower and suddenly your voice takes on new dimensions. There are few topics that present so many accessible materials and interesting things to explore as sound energy.

In this chapter, we'll consider how sound vibrations are made; how sounds travel in air, water, and solids; how sounds are reflected and absorbed; how the pitch of sounds may change; and how we hear.

SOUND VIBRATIONS CONCEPTS
(Experiences p. 265)

Every so often in science fiction a sinister scientist invents a machine that can collect and play back all the sounds that have ever been made. At first the scientist uses the machine to help historians find out what King John *really* said at Runnymede, but soon after he offers the enemy military secrets discussed at the Pentagon.

Molecules and Sounds

Of course, all signs show that such a machine could never be invented. Sounds are simply waves of compressed molecules pulsating outward in all directions and planes from a vibrating source.

Consider the air around you. It is composed of tiny, individual molecules of different gases mixed similarly throughout the lower atmosphere. These molecules are rapidly and randomly moving about. A fast-vibrating source like the hummingbird's wings, a bell, a guitar string, and a "twanged" ruler held on the edge of a desk compress billions of these molecules with each back-and-forth movement because the molecules are in the way. Since air molecules are elastic, they quickly assume their original

shape after moving out of the vibrating object's path. But before this happens, they transfer energy to other molecules over a distance.

Please note that it is the *wave of energy* rather than the molecules that may travel a great distance. Each molecule may move less than a millionth of a hair's width, but this is enough to bump the next randomly moving molecule and pass on the outward movement. Figure 10-1 shows a wave motion resulting from a compression and rarefaction effect on molecules pushed by a vibrating ruler.

A sound fades away when energy behind the original vibrations is used in the transmitting process. As one molecule bumps another, it

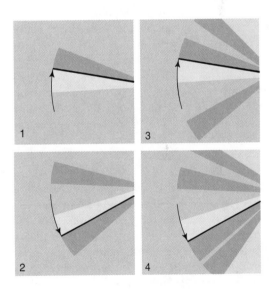

Figure 10-1

A vibrating ruler producing sound waves. In 1, the ruler is pushing the air molecules together (compression). Notice the thinned-out space below it (rarefaction). Picture 2 shows the opposite happening, with the first part of the sound wave now moving away. Picture 3 and 4 show another sound wave being produced. The wave moves outward as the molecules push others in the way, which in turn squeeze other molecules.

uses a tiny amount of energy. As more molecules are bumped, there is less energy available. The sound stops when energy of the randomly moving molecules exceeds the wave's energy. The molecules simply resume their normal helter-skelter movements.

Loudness

How is loudness explained? First, for the moment, let's call it *intensity;* "loudness" is what we actually hear. If our ears are working poorly, a very intense sound may be barely heard. So loudness is a matter of individual perception. Intensity, on the other hand, can be consistently and accurately recorded by a sensitive sound detector in terms of the *decibel,* a unit of measurement in sound. The distinction between loudness and intensity may be too subtle for most children.

You know that shouting requires more energy than whispering. A boost in energy forces any vibrating medium to vibrate to and fro more widely than usual, but in the same amount of time. This compresses molecules more forcefully, so the greater energy is able to move more molecules.

Of course, distance is also a factor in sound intensity. The farther away we are from the source, the weaker the sound. Molecules are pushed less because there is progressively less energy available.

Interestingly, the same mathematical relationship is found in sound loss as in other forms of energy such as light, magnetism, and electricity. Intensity fades with the square of the distance between any sound source and listener. At 20 feet (6 meters), a sound has only one-fourth the intensity it exhibits at 10 feet (3 meters) from the source.

Waves

Sometimes the analogy of a water wave is used to teach how sound travels. A pebble is dropped into water, and a circular series of ripples spreads out on the water's surface. This example may be useful to show to your class, but it contains two main defects. Water waves are up-and-down motions that travel at right angles to the line of the waves. These are called *transverse waves.* Sound waves come from back-and-forth motions that make longitudinal waves. This is the kind of wave you see when a row of dominoes falls, each one striking the next in order. Also, water waves move only horizontally, while sound waves travel outward in all planes. Many science teachers ask students to imagine sound waves as they would a series of rapidly blown soap bubbles, each enveloped within another that is slightly larger, all quickly expanding.

The wave idea is useful to distinguish between sounds and noises. A sound consists of regularly pulsating vibrations; the time interval between each compression and rarefaction is the same. Noise is heard when irregular vibrations are passed on.

Forced Vibrations

If you place the handle of a vibrating tuning fork against a table top, the sound suddenly gets louder. The vibrating fork forces the table top to vibrate with equal speed. This sets in motion many more air molecules than would the fork alone. Try putting a vibrating tuning fork against other objects. Almost any hard object can be forced to vibrate at the fork's natural frequency.

A peculiar example of forced vibrations can occur when a group of soldiers marches over a bridge. If there are enough persons marching in step, the entire structure can be forced to vibrate in time to the step, and the bridge may weaken or collapse. For this reason, soldiers do not stay in step when crossing a bridge.

Thomas Edison used his knowledge of forced vibrations when inventing the phonograph. He attached a sharp needle to a thin diaphragm that vibrated when sound waves struck it. The needle was placed against a cylinder wrapped with soft tinfoil. As he spoke, he slowly cranked the cylinder around and around. The vibrating needle cut a series of impressions into the metal. To play back his sounds, he placed the needle in the impression first scratched and cranked the cylinder. As it followed the impressions, the needle was forced to vibrate, thus causing the diaphragm to vibrate. Edison could hear his recorded voice!

Sympathetic Vibrations

Have you ever heard windows vibrate in their frames as a low-flying airplane passes overhead? Or noticed dishes faintly rattle occasionally as a loud radio is played? To see why this happens, consider two identical tuning forks. If one vibrates and is held near the other, the second one also begins to vibrate. But with two tuning forks of different pitches, only the struck one vibrates.

When forks are of identical pitch, sound waves arrive at the proper time to set the still fork in motion. Each additional air compression pushes a prong as it starts to bend in from a previous one. Each rarefaction arrives as the prong starts to bend back out. The steady, timed, push-pause-push-pause rhythm sets the fork vibrating in almost the same way as you would push someone on a swing.

When forks are of different pitch, the timing is wrong for this to happen. For example, a prong may bend inward properly with a compression, but as it starts to bend back, another air compression may strike it prematurely and slow or stop it. The same thing would happen with a moving swing that is pushed while only partway back on a downswing.

Every solid object has a natural frequency of vibration. If sound waves of that frequency push against an object, it may start resonating—vibrating sympathetically.

Remember that objects vibrate sympathetically only when they have the same natural pitch as the initial sound maker. On the other hand, objects *forced* to vibrate always do so at the frequency of the vibrating object placed against them, regardless of their own natural frequency.

You may have learned that a very loud note sung or played into a thin drinking glass can shatter it through violent sympathetic vibrations; such vibrations have the natural pitch of the glass. However, it is not true that seashore sounds may be detected in shell souvenirs unless someone is listening at the beach. What is heard are only sympathetic reflections of nearby sounds.

Properties of Objects and Vibrations

Suppose someone hands you two closed shoe boxes. Inside one is a marble. The other contains a small ruler. Could you tell which box contains which object by tipping them back and forth and listening to the sounds? Of course, you may say. But what allows you to do this?

Every object has certain physical properties that produce "appropriate" vibrations. We expect a round (cylindrical) pencil to roll smoothly and a six-sided pencil to roll roughly. We assume that a short pencil lying crosswise in a box takes longer to slide and bump against the side than a longer pencil, if the box is tipped from side to side.

How Sounds Travel
Concepts
(Experiences p. 268)

Watch a parade from afar and band members seem to be out of step with the music they are playing. See a carpenter hammering a nail on a distant rooftop, and you hear the sound as the hammer is lifted instead of when the nail is struck. Note the increasing speed of aircraft, and be assured that protests to the Federal Aviation Administration about sonic booms continue to mount.

Speeds of Sound

The speeds at which sound waves travel lie behind each of the events mentioned. Light travels so fast (about 186,000 miles or 297,000 kilometers per second) that it seems instantaneous to our eyes. But sound is another matter. At sea level and 42°F (6.5°C), sound waves move about 1,100 feet (330 meters) per second in the air, only as fast as a low-powered rifle bullet. Sound also travels in liquids and solids. It moves about 5 times faster in water than it does in air; in steel, sound may travel 15 times faster than it does in air. Three conditions affect the speed of sound: temperature, density, and the elasticity, or "springiness," of the molecules conducting the sound.

Density by itself does not increase the speed of sound. In fact, the speed of sound may decrease with density. But often associated with density is greatly increased elasticity of molecules. When highly elastic, close-together molecules of a solid transmit sound, it travels much faster than in either air or water.

Sounds travel faster when the temperature goes up. In fact, it is about one foot per second faster in air for every one degree Fahrenheit. Have you ever wondered why sounds carry such large distances on certain days? On a cold winter day with snow on the ground, for example, air next to the ground is often colder than the air far above the ground. Instead of a sound wave spreading out uniformly and rapidly dying out, the temperature difference causes parts of the wave to travel at different speeds.

Given the same medium and temperature, all sounds travel at the same speed. If this were not so, it would be hard or impossible to conduct concerts in large auditoriums. The reedy sound of an oboe and the brassy timbre of a trombone always reach your ears at the same time, if they are begun at the same time.

Sonic Booms

When children live where sonic booms often occur, someone may ask what happens when an airplane "breaks the sound barrier." We know that a sound-producing object sends out sound waves in all directions. When the object is set in motion, it continues to send out waves in all directions. But let's continue to increase this object's velocity. As it goes faster, it is harder for waves to travel outward in front of it. When an airplane reaches a certain speed (about 750 miles, or 1,200 kilometers, per hour; this varies greatly with altitude and temperature), air compressions of these sound waves pile up into a dense area of compressed air. This can subject the airplane to severe stresses.

A powerful engine and proper design enable an airplane to wedge through the dense air. But what happens to the compressed air? The tremendous energy is passed on, molecule to molecule, until it hits the earth as a booming shock wave. The shock wave continues on the ground in a wide strip that traces the airplane's flight path. It stops only when the pilot slows the aircraft to less than the speed of sound. Sonic booms that cause the least damage start at very high altitudes. By the time energy in the original area of compressed air is passed on to the ground, much of it has dissipated.

Similar shock waves are formed by an explosion, except they may move out equidistantly in all directions. Very rapid expansion of gases in an explosion compresses the surrounding air. As the shock wave of compressed air moves outward, it may flatten almost anything in its path until the pressure finally dissipates over a distance.

REFLECTED AND ABSORBED SOUNDS CONCEPTS
(Experiences p. 275)

Sound Reflection

One reason why singing in the shower is so popular has to do with the nature of sound reflections. As a sound hits the smooth walls, it bounces back and forth, seeming louder and prolonging the notes a little. This is pleasing to the ear. The smoother the reflecting surface, the better sound reflects. On a very smooth wall, sound reflections bounce off like light reflections from a mirror. The angle of reflection equals the angle of incidence.

Because sound can be reflected, we can direct or channel it in certain directions by using different devices. Open-air theaters often have a large shell-like structure surrounding the stage. (See Figure 10-2.) This enables sounds to be directed toward an audience with reduced energy loss. The same principle is used with cheerleaders' megaphones.

An even more efficient way to conserve sound energy is to enclose it in a tube. Because the sound is kept from spreading out by continual reflections within the encircling wall, such concentrated sound loses energy slowly

Figure 10-2
Open-air theaters often have a shell-like structure to reflect sounds to the audience.

and may travel a long way. Sometimes children use garden hoses as speaking tubes because these work well at surprising distances.

A reverse application of this reflection principle is found in the old-fashioned ear trumpet and in the ears of animals such as rabbits and donkeys. In these cases, sounds are "gathered," or reflected inward. Besides large ears, many animals have the additional advantage of being able to cock them separately in different directions.

Echoes

Since sound takes time to travel and can be reflected, it stands to reason that at a certain distance you should be able to hear a distinctly separate reflection of an original sound, an echo. Most persons need an interval of at least one-tenth of a second to distinguish between two sounds. If the interval is shorter than this, you hear one sound, much like the way your brain interprets separate frames of a motion picture as continuous motion.

If we assume that a sound wave travels at a speed of 1,100 feet (330 meters) per second, in one-tenth of a second it travels 110 feet (33 meters). To hear an echo, or a distinguishable, separate sound, we must stand far enough away from a reflecting surface for the sound wave to travel a total distance of 110 feet (33 meters). Since the sound travels *to* the reflecting surface and *back* to our ears, a distance of 55 feet (16.5 meters) from the surface is adequate to hear an echo. Remember, this distance varies a bit with temperature variations.

Sometimes the combination of a loud sound and many distant reflecting surfaces produces multiple echoes, or *reverberations*. A common example is thunder, which may reverberate back and forth from cloud to earth and among air layers of varying densities.

An interesting application of echo detection is found in a United States Navy device called *sonar*. (The term is coined from the words *SO*und *NA*vigation and *R*anging.) This appa-

ratus sends a sound wave through the water and detects reflections from any direction. The time between an initial sound and its received echo enables a sonar operator to know the distance of a reflector, whether it is a submarine or an underwater obstruction. Similar devices are used on fishing vessels to detect schools of fish.

A strange use of sound reflections is found in the bat. By listening to reflections of its cries, a bat flying in total darkness avoids collisions and may even catch insects in midair. (See Figure 10-3.)

Absorbed Sounds

Have you ever noticed how different sounds seem in a room before and after furnishings are installed? Rugs, drapes, and cloth-covered furniture absorb more sound waves than we commonly realize. But even a furnished room may have a "hollow" sound if the walls and ceilings are hard and smooth.

Porous acoustical tile on ceilings cuts down sound reflections. So does the use of rough, porous plaster blown on with a compressed-air applicator. Besides absorbing some sound

Figure 10-3

A bat's ears are well suited for echo ranging.

waves, a rough surface interferes with the wave reflection, just as light is diffused when it hits an irregular surface.

Sometimes older children ask, "What happens to a sound when it goes into a porous material?" It appears that sound energy is changed to heat energy. The regular pulsating movements of a wave are broken up into the normal, irregular motions of individual molecules. As this happens, any energy passed into the porous substance is transmitted to other air molecules, slightly raising the temperature.

HOW PITCH CHANGES CONCEPTS
(Experiences p. 281)

Many pilots of crop-dusting airplanes actually rely on sound to gauge the safeness of their air speed. While flying low, it is hard to watch both an air-speed indicator in the cockpit and ground obstructions. Flying speed is therefore estimated by listening to the pitch of sound made by the vibration of the airplane's struts and wires as the wind rushes past. Some seasoned pilots can judge their margin of safety to within narrow limits by this method.

Sometimes children fasten small cards against the spokes of their bicycle wheels to simulate a motor sound while riding. As the spokes go around and hit the card, it vibrates and makes a sound. The pitch rises with increased speed of vibrations and lowers with decreased speed of vibrations.

Stringed Instruments

In a stringed instrument, pitch depends on the length, tightness, and thickness of the strings. Shortening a string causes faster vibrations, raising pitch. Lengthening it has an opposite effect.

Tightening a string also increases pitch, whereas lessening tension decreases it. A thick string vibrates more slowly than a thin one, and so produces a lower sound.

Why do different instruments, a violin and a cello, for instance, play a note at the same pitch and yet sound different? This is because of the *quality* of tone (timbre) produced by these instruments. Most vibrations include more than just simple, back-and-forth movements along a string's entire length. Although there is a fundamental vibration that governs the basic pitch, other parts of the string vibrate at faster frequencies. The combinations of vibrations are different with each string and with various stringed instruments. Together they produce tones of distinctly recognizable qualities.

Wind Instruments

In wind instruments, sound is made by a vibrating column of air. The vibrations may be started by a player's lips, as with trumpets and tubas, or by blowing past a reed, as with the saxophone and clarinet.

Pitch is regulated by changing the length of the air column vibrating within the instrument. In a wind instrument, such as the saxophone, air-column length is changed by opening and closing valves with the fingers. In a trombone, air-column length is regulated by pulling or pushing a long, closed double tube, called the slide.

The property of timbre is also present in wind instruments. In this case, it is caused by the combinations of additional air vibrations set up within each instrument. Quality of voices is produced in much the same way. This is regulated by the size and shape of air cavities in the mouth and nose.

Homemade Instruments

An interesting way for children to learn about pitch and tonal quality is for them to make their own stringed and wind instruments. Rubber bands of different sizes make pleasant sounds when placed around topless cigar boxes or sturdy shoe box lids. Strong nylon fishing line, fastened on pieces of wood with nails and screw eyes, also works well (see Figure 10-4). When the line is fastened to a screw eye, its tension is adjusted by turning the eye in the appropriate direction. Tuned properly, nylon fishing line sounds somewhat like the string on a regular instrument. Simple tunes can be composed and played on the stringed instruments that children fashion.

Soda straws and bottles make acceptable wind instruments. Interestingly, opposite results in pitch occur with partly filled soda bottles, depending on whether they are used as wind or percussion instruments. That is, if you blow over the tops of soda bottles containing varying volumes of water, the scale may go from low to high, left to right. However, if you *strike* the bottles sharply with a pencil, the opposite happens. The scale will go from high to low, left to right. With blowing, the bottle's *air* mainly vibrates; when striking the bottle, the *water* and glass mainly vibrate.

Mass and Noise

When a noise is made, the amount of mass in the vibrating object usually determines its pitch. A large, dropped wood block sounds lower than a smaller one. When thick paper is torn, it sounds lower than thin paper. A dropped nickel sounds lower than a dime. Both young and older children show interest in this phenomenon.

HEARING AND LOCATING SOUNDS CONCEPTS
(Experiences p. 287)

The ear must be ranked among the body's most remarkable organs. In our hearing, sound waves are channeled into the ear canal by the outer ear, which acts as a megaphone in reverse. As sound waves collide with the eardrum, this thin membrane of stretched skin begins vibrating at the same frequency as the waves.

Just inside the eardrum are three tiny, connected bones: the hammer, anvil, and stirrup

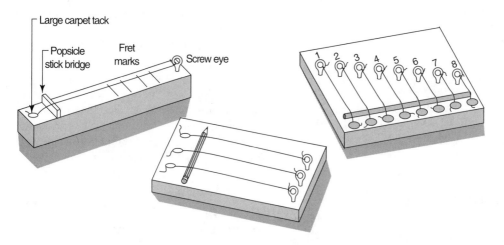

Figure 10-4
Children can experiment with pitch and tone by making their own instruments.

(see Figure 10-5). A vibrating eardrum starts the attached hammer shaking, and this movement is transmitted through the connected bones to the cochlea, or inner ear. This snail-shaped apparatus is filled with a watery fluid and lined with sensitive nerve endings that trail off to the auditory nerve and brain. The transmitted vibrations pass through the fluid and excite the nerve endings. These excitations are converted into electrical impulses that zip to the brain.

Children should learn some reasonable rules for ear care and safety. A sharp object jabbed into the ear may cause a punctured eardrum. This greatly impairs or prevents eardrum vibrations and results in hearing loss in the affected ear. They should also beware of a sharp blow against the outer ear. This compresses air within the air canal and may cause a ruptured eardrum. Blowing the nose forces air up through the eustachian tube. If a person is suffering from a cold, hard blowing may force germs up the tube and infect the middle ear.

Hearing Ranges

Although our ears are sensitive to a wide range of pitches, there are limits to what we can hear. Almost no one can detect a sound that vibrates less than about 16 times per second, or more than 20,000 times per second. As we grow older, this range is gradually narrowed.

Hearing ranges in animals often exceed those of humans. A bat may detect sounds that vary between 10 vibrations to 100,000 vibrations per second. A dog's hearing begins at only several vibrations and goes to 40,000 vibrations per second. This is why it is possible to use a "silent" whistle for calling a dog: The sound is simply too high for humans to hear. A cat's hearing is even more remarkable; it can detect sounds up to 50,000 cycles. Sounds that are inaudible to us are called *infrasonic* when they vibrate too slowly and *ultrasonic* when they vibrate too fast.

Locating Sounds

Most people can tell the direction from which a sound comes, even when blindfolded. With two ears, a sound usually reaches one ear just before the other. The slight difference is enough to let the brain interpret the information.

Persons with only one functioning ear can receive similar signals by quickly turning the head slightly on hearing the first sound. When the sound is very short, this may not be possible.

Sound Energy Benchmarks and Standards

Children in the early grades have trouble associating the characteristics of sounds with the properties of the sound's source. Experiences with activities involving the making and hearing of sounds will allow students opportunities to make these associations. Additionally, children will begin to understand that sounds are vibrations and travel in waves.

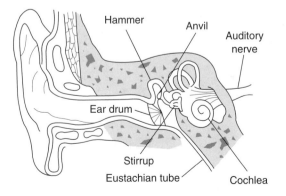

Figure 10-5
The human ear.

Some specific Benchmarks and Standards are as follows:

SAMPLE BENCHMARKS (AAAS, 1993).

■ Things that make sound vibrate (By Grades K–2, p. 89).
■ Vibrations in materials set up wavelike disturbances that spread away from the source. Sound and earthquake waves are examples. These and other waves move at different speeds in different materials (By Grades 6–8, p. 90).

SAMPLE STANDARDS (NRC, 1996).

■ Sound is produced by vibrating objects. The pitch of the sound can be varied by changing the rate of vibration (By Grades K–4, p. 127).

INVESTIGATIONS AND ACTIVITIES

SOUND VIBRATIONS EXPERIENCES
(Concepts p. 255)

ACTIVITY: *WHAT MAKES YOUR VOCAL CORDS WORK?*

NEEDED

vocal cords

TRY THIS

1. Hum softly and feel your throat. Feel your voice box vibrate.
2. Hum with tightly closed lips. Then pinch your nose.
   a. What happens? Why?
3. Breathe out as much air as you can from your lungs. Try to say something *without* taking in air.
   b. What happens? Why?
4. Try to say your name the way a cat or cow makes sounds—while breathing air *in*.
   c. What happens? Why is this hard to do?

TEACHING COMMENT

Air is needed in all these cases to make the vocal cords vibrate. It is hard to speak while breathing in because the normal way humans make sounds is by breathing out.

ACTIVITY: *HOW CAN ONE VIBRATING OBJECT MAKE ANOTHER VIBRATE?*

A. NEEDED

tuning fork

TRY THIS

1. Strike a tuning fork against a rubber heel. (Never against something hard.)
2. As the sound dies, place the handle end against a table top. Notice how the sound gets louder as the table top is also made to vibrate.

3. Try holding the vibrating tuning fork against many different objects.

   a. From which object can you get the loudest sound?

   b. Which object allows you to hear the tuning fork when it has almost stopped vibrating?

B. NEEDED

two matched large soda bottles
one small soda bottle

TRY THIS

1. Blow over the top of one large bottle to make a sound. Blow short, strong tones.

2. Hold the opening of a second large bottle close to your ear, but not touching. Blow short sounds again with the first large bottle.

   a. Do you hear the same note from the second bottle? If you are not sure, have someone else blow short notes on one bottle while you listen with the second bottle.

3. Do Steps 1 and 2 again, but this time listen with the small bottle.

   b. Do you hear the same note from the small bottle? Any note?

TEACHING COMMENT

Activity A is an example of forced vibrations. If a tuning fork is unavailable, a sturdy, stiff rubber comb may be used instead. Run a finger down the teeth ends while holding the comb against a surface. B is an example of sympathetic vibrations. If you vibrate one object, a second object may also vibrate if it has the same natural rate of vibrations as the first. No actual touching is necessary. The transfer of energy occurs in the air.

INVESTIGATION: *MYSTERY SOUNDS*

Can you hear something make a sound and tell what it is without looking?

EXPLORATORY PROBLEM

How can you find out if you can identify something by sound?

NEEDED

pairs of small objects that roll (crayons, ping-pong balls, marbles, pencils, BBs, small pill vials)
pairs of small objects that slide (buttons, paper clips, checkers, dominoes, bottle

caps, safety pins)
shoe box with lid
partner

TRY THIS

1. Place one object from each pair of rolling objects on your desk.
2. Give the other rolling objects to your partner. He should put these where you cannot see them.
3. Have your partner put one of his objects in the shoe box. You should not know which one it is.
4. Slowly tip the shoe box back and forth. Listen to the sound (Figure 10-6).

Figure 10-6

5. Look at the objects on your desk. Which one may be the same as the one in the box? Point to a desk object so your partner knows which one you picked.
6. Look inside the shoe box. Does the object inside match the desk object you picked?

DISCOVERY PROBLEMS

inferring **A.** How many of the *rolling* objects can you identify? Which object is easiest to tell? hardest to tell?

inferring **B.** Suppose your partner holds and tips the box. Can you tell each rolling object just as easily?

inferring **C.** How many of the *sliding* objects can you identify? Which object is easiest to tell? hardest to tell?

TEACHING COMMENT

PREPARATION AND BACKGROUND

This investigation mainly calls for children to make inferences by interpreting data. Try to use objects of about the same weight. This will eliminate weight as a clue. Children will focus on the sounds they hear or vibrations they feel in their fingers as they handle the shoe box.

GENERALIZATION

An object may be identified by the sounds it makes when interacting with another object.

SAMPLE PERFORMANCE OBJECTIVES

Process: After some practice, the child can infer the identity of several objects from the sounds they make.

Knowledge: The child can describe how the properties of an object are related to the sounds it makes.

FOR OLDER CHILDREN

Older students can be challenged by increasing the number and similarity of paired objects to select from.

HOW SOUNDS TRAVEL EXPERIENCES
(Concepts p. 257)

ACTIVITY: HOW FAST DOES SOUND TRAVEL?

NEEDED

large outdoor space   partner
hammer   piece of wood

TRY THIS

1. Go outdoors to a large, open space.
2. Place a thick piece of wood on the ground. Walk a few steps away.
3. Watch a partner sharply hit the wood once with a hammer.
   a. Do you hear the sound at about the same time the hammer hits?
4. Move farther away. Have your partner hit the wood again. Repeat this pattern several times until you are far away.

b. When do you hear each sound now? At the same time the hammer hits? Or does each sound appear later and later, *after* each hit?

TEACHING COMMENT

To ensure enough space for this activity, you might suggest two widely separated, familiar reference points at least the length of a football field.

ACTIVITY: *DOES SOUND TRAVEL FARTHER IN AIR OR IN WOOD?*

NEEDED

meter stick or yardstick
partner
wristwatch (one that ticks)

TRY THIS

1. Hold a wristwatch tightly against the end of a meter stick.
2. Touch the other end of the stick to a partner's ear. Only you should hold the stick (Figure 10-7).

Figure 10-7

    a. Can your partner hear the ticking through the wood? If not, move the watch forward on the stick until the ticking is heard.

3. Measure the distance between watch and ear when the ticking is heard.
4. Next, do not use the stick. Hold the watch in the air at ear level the same distance you found in Step 3.

    b. Can your partner hear the ticking now? (If you think your partner is just guessing, remove and then return the watch a few times. Each time, ask if the watch can be heard.)

    c. From how far away can you hear a ticking watch through wood? Try a broomstick, window pole, long narrow board, and other wood things around you.

INVESTIGATION: *THE VIBRATIONS OF METAL OBJECTS*

Many everyday objects made of metal make beautiful sounds when they vibrate. A metal coat hanger is one example. These things sound much better when you hear them through a solid material than through the air. String is one such solid material.

EXPLORATORY PROBLEM

How can you hear the sounds of a metal hanger through a string?

NEEDED

two matched metal hangers	scissors
yarn	different metal objects
several kinds of string	partner

TRY THIS

1. Cut a piece of string about 60 centimeters (2 feet) long.

2. Loop the middle of the string once around the hanger hook.

3. Wrap several turns of string end around the tip of each forefinger.

4. Gently put the tip of each wrapped finger into an ear (Figure 10-8).

5. Bend from the waist so the hanger hangs free. Ask your partner to strike a pencil and other objects gently against the metal. You can also make the hanger vibrate by yourself. Sway back and forth until the hanger swings. Then have it hit something that is hard.

DISCOVERY PROBLEMS

communicating   **A.** How can you describe the sounds you hear?

observing   **B.** What happens to the sound if your partner holds one of the strings? both strings?

experimenting   **C.** What kind of string will give the clearest, loudest sound? Cut off equal lengths of different kinds of string and yarn. Test them in pairs. Tie one string end to the hook of one hanger. Tie another

Figure 10-8

to a second matched hanger. Put one string end into each ear. Have a partner first strike one hanger, then the other. When you find the best string, try it with both ears.

inferring   **D.** Does the length of a string affect the loudness? If so, in which kind of string do you notice it most? (You can test pairs of strings as in C.)

observing   **E.** What sounds do other metal objects make? Test things such as old spoons, forks, cooling racks, oven racks, and different-sized cans.

TEACHING COMMENT

PREPARATION AND BACKGROUND

Oven cooling racks, barbecue griddles, and other gridlike objects of metal make particularly strange, even eerie, sounds. These sounds come from the overtones produced when the many parts of the object vibrate differently.

GENERALIZATION

The sounds of a vibrating object may be heard more loudly and clearly through a solid than through air.

SAMPLE PERFORMANCE OBJECTIVES

Process: The child can describe a sound an object makes well enough for another person to recognize the sound when it is made.

Knowledge: The child can select a string, from several different strings, that conducts sounds most efficiently.

FOR YOUNGER CHILDREN

Use the "Try This" sequence and Problem E as general experience activities.

INVESTIGATION: *A String Telephone*

Have you ever used a "string telephone"? It's a handy way to talk to someone far across a large room without shouting.

EXPLORATORY PROBLEM

How can you make a string telephone?

NEEDED

two sturdy paper cups
two paper clips
strong string (about 8 meters or 26 feet long)
partner
nail

TRY THIS

1. Punch a hole into the bottom center of each cup using a nail.
2. Put a string end into each hole.
3. Tie each string end to a paper clip. This will keep the string from slipping out of each hole.
4. Stretch the string tightly between you and your partner.
5. Speak into one cup while your partner listens with the other cup (Figure 10-9).

DISCOVERY PROBLEMS

observing **A.** Can you hear better through the string telephone than through the air? Whisper softly through the phone. Do it a little louder until your partner hears you. Then whisper to her at the same loudness without the telephone.

experimenting **B.** How can you stop a sound from reaching you on the string telephone?

experimenting **C.** Suppose two other children have a string telephone. How can you make a party line?

experimenting **D.** What can you do to make your phone work better? Try containers of different sizes and materials. Try different kinds of string and waxing the string with candle wax.

Figure 10-9

TEACHING COMMENT

PREPARATION AND BACKGROUND

Holding the string or letting it sag will dampen or stop sounds. So will touching the vibrating cup bottom. For a party line, cross and loop around once the lines of two sets of phones.

Cylindrical cereal boxes (for example, oatmeal boxes) and salt boxes work well for string telephones. Metal can bottoms are too thick and rigid to vibrate well. Hard string or waxed string is superior to softly woven string.

GENERALIZATION

Sound vibrations can travel through string and other solid materials.

SAMPLE PERFORMANCE OBJECTIVES

Process: The child can discover through experimenting at least one way to improve the performance of a string telephone.

Knowledge: The child can explain how sound travels from one string telephone to another.

FOR YOUNGER CHILDREN

Younger students can construct and explore how to operate a string telephone but may not be able to find ways to improve the telephone's performance.

ACTIVITY: *WHAT ARE UNDERWATER SOUNDS LIKE?*

NEEDED

half-filled aquarium tank or large glass bowl
partner
two spoons

TRY THIS

1. Press an ear against the tank *above* the water level. Listen.
2. Have someone repeatedly hit two spoons together inside the tank, but *above* the water.
3. Again, press your ear against the tank but *below* the water level. Listen.
4. Now have the spoons hit together *below* the water level (Figure 10-10).

   a. How can you describe the difference between the two sets of sounds?

   b. Does sound seem to travel better in water or in air?

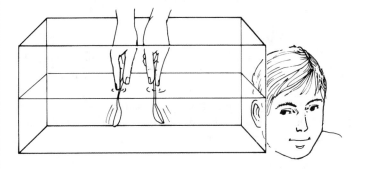

Figure 10-10

REFLECTED AND ABSORBED SOUNDS EXPERIENCES

(Concepts p. 259)

INVESTIGATION: *SOUNDS AND MEGAPHONES*

What do you do when you want your voice to go far? Do you cup your hands to your mouth? This helps to keep the sound from spreading out, so it travels farther. There's another way to do this. You can make a megaphone.

EXPLORATORY PROBLEM A

How can you make and use a megaphone?

NEEDED

sheet of heavy paper   sticky tape   two partners

TRY THIS

1. Roll up the paper from one corner to make a cone. The small opening should be large enough to speak into.
2. Fasten the two ends and middle with sticky tape (Figure 10-11).

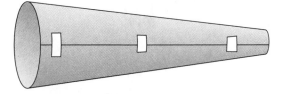

Figure 10-11

3. Have a partner stand across the room from you.
4. Point the megaphone toward your partner. Whisper some numbers.
5. Have your partner walk toward you until he hears you, then stop walking.

DISCOVERY PROBLEMS

inferring   **A.** Can your partner hear you without the megaphone? Have him stay where he stopped. Whisper numbers just as before. How can you tell if your partner hears you?

inferring   **B.** Can you send a message to someone without another person hearing? Have a second partner stand to one side of you. She should be as far from you as your first partner. Point the megaphone toward your first partner and whisper numbers. How can you tell if only your first partner hears you?

observing   **C.** How close must someone be to your first partner to hear you whisper?

EXPLORATORY PROBLEM B

How can a megaphone help us to hear better?

NEEDED

two megaphones   windup clock
sticky tape   meter stick or yardstick

TRY THIS

1. Put the clock on a table.

2. Stand where you cannot hear the clock.

3. Put the megaphone to your ear. Point it toward the clock (Figure 10-12).

Figure 10-12

4. Slowly move toward the clock until you hear it. Then stop.

DISCOVERY PROBLEMS

observing   **A.** Can you hear the clock without the megaphone at that distance?

predicting   **B.** How much closer will you need to be to hear it?

experimenting   **C.** Will different-sized megaphones make a difference in how far the sound travels? How can you find out?

TEACHING COMMENT

PREPARATION AND BACKGROUND

A megaphone tends to conserve sound energy by reflecting it in a specific direction. This allows sound to travel farther than when it spreads out in all directions. The effect also happens in reverse. The large end of a megaphone can gather sound and reflect it inward. If we listen at the small end, the sound is louder than without the megaphone. More sound energy reaches the ear.

GENERALIZATION

A megaphone reflects sounds in one direction. It may be used to increase our speaking or hearing range.

SAMPLE PERFORMANCE OBJECTIVES

Process: The child can test how a megaphone's size affects its efficiency.

Knowledge: The child can explain in everyday terms how a megaphone works.

INVESTIGATION: ECHOES

You probably know that smooth, hard walls reflect sounds well. A reflected sound that you hear is called an echo. Sound vibrations take time to travel to a wall and then back to you. When you are at the right distance, you hear the returning sound as a separate sound.

EXPLORATORY PROBLEM

How can you make an echo happen?

NEEDED

meter stick or yardstick   scissors
string   piece of wood
large outside wall   hammer

TRY THIS

1. Find a big wall outdoors in a large area. Try to locate a wall that has no buildings opposite it.

2. Measure a distance of about 25 meters (82 feet) from the wall. (You might cut a 5-meter string to speed up measuring.)

3. Hit a piece of wood once sharply with a hammer. Listen for an echo. If you hear more than one echo, try to find another place (Figure 10-13).

Figure 10-13

DISCOVERY PROBLEMS

measuring   **A.** How close can you be to the wall and still hear an echo?

measuring   **B.** How far away from the wall can you hear an echo? As you move farther away, does it take less or more time to hear the echo?

observing   **C.** Try another wall. How do the results compare with A and B?

observing   **D.** How many echoes will there be with two reflecting walls? Try to find two facing, widely separated walls. Stand at different distances between them and bang the hammer. How do these results compare with those from a single wall?

TEACHING COMMENT

PREPARATION AND BACKGROUND

A trundle wheel is even more efficient than a 5-meter string for quick measurements. This device is a wheel with an attached, broomlike handle. The wheel's size is such that when rolled once around on a surface, it travels one meter (or yard, as the case may be).

In B, students will probably run out of space before they can fully answer the question. However, they should become aware that increasing the distance also increases the time it takes to hear an echo.

In D, the clearest results should occur with two widely separated, opposing walls.

GENERALIZATION

Echoes may be heard when sounds are reflected over a distance.

SAMPLE PERFORMANCE OBJECTIVES

Knowledge: The child can predict that an echo will be heard later if the distance between the reflecting wall and the observer is increased.

Process: The child can reliably measure the shortest distance at which an echo may usually be heard.

FOR YOUNGER CHILDREN

Use the "Try This" suggestion and Problems A through C as large-group experiences without the measurements.

INVESTIGATION: *MATERIALS THAT QUIET SOUND*

Many people today are trying to cut down unwanted noise. They are putting materials around them that soak up sounds. These materials are called sound insulators. Some materials are better insulators than others.

EXPLORATORY PROBLEM

How can you find out which materials are good sound insulators?

NEEDED

shoe box   newspaper
pencil and paper   aluminum foil
windup alarm clock   different kinds of cloth
meter stick or yardstick   insulation materials of your choice

TRY THIS

1. Wind up an alarm clock. Set the clock to ring within a few minutes.
2. Put the clock inside a shoe box and put on the lid.
3. Wait until the alarm rings. Measure how far away you can hear the ringing (Figure 10-14).
4. Record the distance

Figure 10-14

DISCOVERY PROBLEMS

observing and measuring   **A.** Suppose you wrap a sheet of newspaper around the clock. From how far away can you hear the sound now? Record and compare this distance with the first one.

predicting and measuring   **B.** What will happen if you wrap the clock in cloth? Record and compare this distance with the other distances.

experimenting   **C.** What insulation materials will work best? Is it possible not to hear any ringing at all? Arrange your materials any way you want. All should fit inside the shoe box. How will you know whether the alarm has gone off?

TEACHING COMMENT

PREPARATION AND BACKGROUND

Loosely woven, soft, fluffy materials absorb sounds well. Hard surfaces reflect sounds. This is why a formerly empty room seems quieter after carpeting, drapes, and upholstered furniture are put in.

GENERALIZATION

Loosely woven, fluffy materials are good sound insulators.

PERFORMANCE OBJECTIVES

Process: The child can measure and compare the relative effectiveness of several sound insulating materials.

Knowledge: When shown several new materials, the child can predict which will be a more effective sound insulator.

FOR YOUNGER CHILDREN

Many younger students will be unable to measure the hearing distance with a meter stick. Let them measure with different lengths of string or the number of footsteps between them and the clock.

HOW PITCH CHANGES EXPERIENCES
(Concepts p. 261)

ACTIVITY: *WHAT HAPPENS TO PITCH AS SPEED OF VIBRATIONS CHANGES?*

A. NEEDED

comb
small card

TRY THIS

1. Hold a comb in one hand and a card in the other.
2. Pull the card tip across the teeth of the comb slowly and steadily. Listen to the pitch of the sound (how high or low it is).
3. Do Step 2 again, but faster this time. Listen again.
4. Try many different speeds. Listen each time.
   a. What is the pitch like when the vibrations are slow?
   b. What happens to the pitch as the vibrations move faster?

B. NEEDED

bicycle
small card

TRY THIS

1. Turn a bicycle upside down.
2. Crank a pedal around slowly to move the rear wheel.
3. Hold the tip of a card against the spokes as the wheel slowly turns. Listen to the pitch as the card vibrates.
4. Crank the wheel faster and faster. Listen again to the pitch as the card vibrates faster and faster.
   a. What is the pitch like when the vibrations are slow?
   b. What happens to the pitch as the vibrations move faster?

TEACHING COMMENT

Caution: For safety, be sure that fingers holding the card are well away from the spinning wheel.

INVESTIGATION: *HOW TO MAKE A RUBBER-BAND BANJO*

What kinds of stringed instruments have you seen? How are they played?

EXPLORATORY PROBLEM

How can you make a rubber-band banjo?

NEEDED

topless cigar box or stiff shoe box lid
ruler
eight rubber bands (four thick, four thinner)
pencil and paper

TRY THIS

1. Write the numbers *1* through *8* on the inside of the lid. Use a ruler to space them evenly across the whole lid.
2. Put four thick rubber bands around half of the lid. Space them from numbers *1* through *4*.
3. Put four thinner bands around the other half of the lid. Space them from numbers *5* through *8* (Figure 10-15).

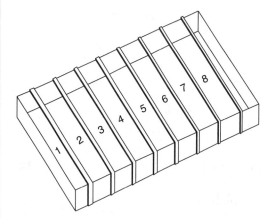

Figure 10-15

DISCOVERY PROBLEMS

observing   A. Pluck one of the rubber bands. How can you make a soft sound? A louder sound?

observing   **B.** Which bands—thick or thin—make the higher sounds? (The highness or lowness of a sound is its *pitch*.)

observing   **C.** What happens to the pitch when a band is shortened? Press down a rubber band halfway across the lid. Pluck the band half nearest you.

observing   **D.** How does tightening a band on the lid affect the pitch? loosening the band? (Pull the band up or down at the side of the lid.)

classifying   **E.** Can you make an eight-note scale? Tighten or loosen each band in order as needed. Pluck the bands *lightly* so each stays tuned.

observing   **F.** What songs can you play on your banjo? Try some simple songs first: "Mary Had a Little Lamb," "Merrily We Roll Along," "Three Blind Mice," and "Twinkle, Twinkle, Little Star."

communicating   **G.** Can you write songs well enough for other people to play?

TEACHING COMMENT

PREPARATION AND BACKGROUND

The tightness, thickness, and length of a rubber band (or string) all affect its pitch. Sounds are higher with taut, thin, short strings; they are lower with looser, thicker, or longer strings on any stringed instrument.

The tension of each rubber band may be adjusted by pulling up or down at the side of the lid. Friction between the band and lid will hold the band in place for a while. However, the band will need to be strummed or plucked gently. A sturdy lid is preferable to a flimsy one that bows in the middle.

GENERALIZATION

Length, tension, and thickness affect the pitch of a vibrating string.

SAMPLE PERFORMANCE OBJECTIVES

Process: The child can communicate to another child a familiar song by using written symbols, such as numbers.

Knowledge: When shown a stringed instrument, the child can predict the relative pitches of sounds the strings make.

FOR YOUNGER CHILDREN.

Many younger students can discover the factors that affect the pitch of a string. But they will do so less systematically and completely than older children. Many will be able to do Problems A–D.

INVESTIGATION: *A Soda-Straw Oboe*

Have you ever seen an oboe? It is a reed instrument. When the player blows on the mouthpiece, two flat, thin reeds vibrate. This makes the air inside the oboe vibrate. By opening and closing holes, the player makes different amounts of air vibrate. This changes the pitch of the notes played. You can make an instrument like this from a soda straw.

EXPLORATORY PROBLEM

How can you make a soda-straw oboe?

NEEDED

paper or plastic straws (one smaller to fit inside the larger one)
straight pin
cellophane tape
scissors
small paper cup

TRY THIS

1. Pinch the straw end between your thumb and forefinger to flatten it.
2. Snip off the flattened corners with scissors, as in the picture (Figure 10-16). If you have a plastic straw, cut to make a point.

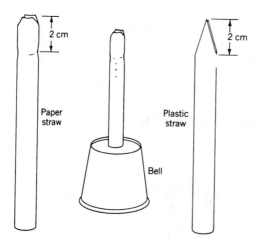

Figure 10-16

3. Put about 3 centimeters (1 inch) of the cut straw end into your mouth. Keep your lips closed but a little loose. Blow hard into the straw. If there is no sound, blow less hard until a sound is made.

DISCOVERY PROBLEMS

observing   **A.** What happens if you change the length of the straw? Join another straw of the same size to the first straw. To do so, slightly pinch the end of the second straw. Then gently push the pinched end into the first straw. Try adding a third straw in the same way.

observing   **B.** What happens if you change the length another way? Try to fit a smaller straw into the larger one. If it is too loose, wrap some cellophane tape around the end of the smaller straw. Slide the second straw up and down as you blow.

predicting   **C.** What do you think will happen if you snip off pieces of a single straw while blowing? Try it and see.

experimenting   **D.** How can eight people with different-sized straws play a song?

Teaching Comment

PREPARATION AND BACKGROUND

Paper straws typically work more easily than plastic straws in this activity. If students find it hard or impossible to produce a sound, often the cut "reed" is to blame. It may help to press down gently with the lips on the straw just below the flattened part. This will open up the reed slightly and let it vibrate more easily when blown. A plastic-straw reed should be pointed for best results.

A "bell" for the instrument can be made by punching a small hole in the bottom of a paper cup and inserting the straw end into it. It should noticeably increase the loudness of the instrument.

GENERALIZATION

The pitch of a wind instrument is changed by changing the length of the vibrating air column inside.

SAMPLE PERFORMANCE OBJECTIVES

Knowledge: The child can show at least two ways to change the pitch of a soda-straw oboe.

Process: The child can improve the performance of a soda-straw oboe by testing, observing results, and making changes.

INVESTIGATION: *A Bottle Xylophone*

Do you know what a xylophone looks like? This instrument has a row of different-sized blocks of wood. The player makes sounds by striking the blocks with two special sticks. You can easily make an instrument that works like a xylophone. But instead of wood, you can use bottles of water.

EXPLORATORY PROBLEM

How can you make a bottle xylophone?

NEEDED

eight matched soda bottles   pencil and paper   water

TRY THIS

1. Put different levels of water in each bottle.
2. Line the bottles in a row (Figure 10-17), in any order.

Figure 10-17

3. Tap each of the bottles lightly with a pencil. Notice how high or low each sound is. This is called *pitch*.

DISCOVERY PROBLEMS

observing   **A.** How much water is there in the bottle of highest pitch? lowest pitch?

classifying   **B.** Can you put the bottles in order from lowest to highest pitch?

experimenting   **C.** What must you do with the bottles to make an eight-note scale?

observing   **D.** Can you play a simple song? Put paper slips in front of the bottles. Number them from 1 to 8, for an eight-note scale. Notice the numbers of the notes you play.

communicating **E.** Can you write a song so someone else can play it correctly? Write on paper the numbers of the notes to be played. Use your own made-up song or a known song. Observe how well the song is played.

hypothesizing **F.** How can you improve the way you wrote your song?

predicting **G.** Suppose you blew over each bottle top. Now the air inside would vibrate rather than the water. How do you think that would affect each pitch? Try it and see.

Teaching Comment

PREPARATION AND BACKGROUND

Bottles made of plain glass make clearer, purer sounds than those made of rippled glass. If you or a child can play the piano, children may enjoy playing this eight-note xylophone either as an accompanying or as a leading instrument. Children may also enjoy singing with the instrument.

GENERALIZATION

An instrument's pitch depends on how much mass vibrates. As mass increases, pitch lowers. With less mass, the pitch gets higher.

SAMPLE PERFORMANCE OBJECTIVES

Knowledge: The child can predict which of two unevenly filled bottles will sound lower when struck.

Process: The child can correctly order an eight-note scale with proportionately filled bottles of water.

HEARING AND LOCATING SOUNDS EXPERIENCES
(Concepts p. 262)

ACTIVITY: *How Do You Locate Sounds with Your Ears?*

NEEDED

eight partners
quiet room
16 pencils

TRY THIS

1. Have your partners sit in a large circle about half the width of the classroom.

2. Sit in the center of the circle. Keep your eyes tightly closed. Listen with both ears.

3. Let each partner, in some mixed order, lightly tap two pencils together once.

    a. Can you tell from which direction the sound comes? Point to the spot each time. Have someone record how often you are right or wrong.

4. Now try Step 3 again, but this time listen with only one ear. Hold a hand tightly over the other ear.

    b. Can you locate the sounds as well as before?

    c. Will you get the same results with your other ear?

REFERENCES

American Association for the Advancement of Science. (1993). *Benchmarks for science literacy.* New York: Oxford University Press.

National Research Council. (1996). *National science education standards.* Washington, DC: National Academy Press.

Richardson, J. (1986). *What happens when we listen?* Gareth Stevens.

Spier, P. (1990). *Crash! Bang! Boom!* Doubleday, 1990.

Wade, H. (1979). *Sound.* Raintree.

Webb, A. (1988). *Sound.* Watts.

Wyler, R. (1987). *Science fun with drums, bells and whistles.* Messner.

SELECTED TRADE BOOKS: SOUND ENERGY

For Younger Children

Allington, R. L., & Cowles, K. (1980). *Hearing.* Raintree.

Barrett, S. (1980). *The sound of the week.* Good Apple.

Broekel, R. (1983). *Sound experiments.* Children's Press.

Friedman, J. T. (1981). *Sounds all around.* Putnam.

Hughes, Anne, E. (1979). *A book of sounds.* Raintree.

Jennings, T. (1990). *Making sounds.* Watts.

Lee, J. D. (1985). *Sounds!* Stevens.

Moncure, J. B. (1982). *Sounds all around.* Children's Press.

Oliver, S. (1991). *Noises.* Random House.

For Older Children

Ardley, N. (1991). *Sound waves to music: Projects with sound.* Watts.

Brandt, K. (1985). *Sounds.* Troll Associates.

Catherall, E. (1982). *Hearing.* Silver Burdett.

Kettlekamp, L. (1982). *The magic of sound.* Morrow.

Knight, D. C. (1983). *All about sound.* Troll Associates.

Knight, D. C. (1980). *Silent sound: the world of ultrasonics.* Morrow.

Kohn, B. (1979). *Echoes.* Dandelion.

Newman, F. R. (1983). *Zounds! The kid's guide to sound making.* Random House.

Pettigrew, M. (1987). *Music and sound.* Watts.

Riley, P. (1987). *Light and sound.* David & Charles.

Taylor, B. (1991). *Sound and music.* Watts.

Ward, A. (1991). *Experimenting with sound.* Chelsea House.

Ward, B. (1981). *The ear and hearing.* Watts.

Resource Books

Butzow, C. M., & Butzow, J. W. (1989). *Science through children's literature: an integrated approach* (sound and hearing topics, pp. 112–118). Teacher Ideas Press.

LeCroy, B., & Holder, B. (1994). *Bookwebs: a brainstorm of ideas for the primary classroom* (sound activities, pp. 57–63). Teacher Ideas Press.

Sullivan, E. P. (1990). *Starting with books: an activities approach to children's literature* (hearing impairment, pp. 23–25). Teacher Ideas Press.

MAGNETIC INTERACTIONS

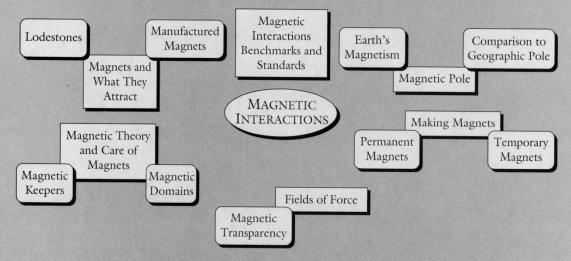

Lodestones

Manufactured Magnets

Magnetic Interactions Benchmarks and Standards

Earth's Magnetism

Comparison to Geographic Pole

Magnets and What They Attract

Magnetic Pole

MAGNETIC INTERACTIONS

Making Magnets

Magnetic Theory and Care of Magnets

Permanent Magnets

Temporary Magnets

Magnetic Keepers

Magnetic Domains

Fields of Force

Magnetic Transparency

At the primary level, magnets may be studied more than any other science topic. It is common for young children to have their own magnets and magnetic toys. This chapter considers several kinds of magnets and what they attract, how to make magnets, the field of force that surrounds a magnet, magnetic poles, and the theory and care of magnets.

MAGNETS AND WHAT THEY ATTRACT CONCEPTS
(Experiences p. 297)

There are many magnets around the home and classroom for us to use as examples in teaching. In kitchens, cloth pot holders containing magnets are placed on the sides of stoves. Automatic can openers have magnets to hold opened can lids. Cabinet doors remain closed because of magnets. Some people wear magnetic earrings. Toy stores have many toys that in some way use magnetism. At school, speakers, magnetic paper holders, and some games also have magnetics.

What Magnets Attract

In nearly all these cases, *the metals attracted to a magnet are iron and steel.* Less well known magnetic metals are cobalt and nickel. Among the more common metals *not* attracted by magnets are brass, aluminum, tin, silver, stainless steel, copper, bronze, and gold.

It will help you to know several facts that can clear up some common misunderstandings. For example, a question may arise about the attractable property of so-called tin cans. These are made of thin sheet steel and coated lightly with tin. Although tin is not attractable, steel is. Confusion may also result if some straight pins are attracted by a magnet and other identical-appearing pins are not because they are made of brass. Also, the U.S. five-cent piece is largely composed of copper and so should not be used as an example.

Lodestones

Natural magnets are sometimes called "lodestones," or "leading stones," because ancient mariners used them as crude compasses. Lodestones are made of magnetite, an iron ore found in different locations on the earth's crust.

Only some of these deposits are magnetized and theories have been developed to explain this phenomenon. One such theory holds that lightning may have been responsible. It is thought that electricity discharged into the ore may have arranged many atoms within the ore in a manner like that found in magnets.

Traces of magnetite are common in soils. A magnet dragged along the ground or in a playground sandbox may attract many particles. These particles can be an effective substitute in activities in which iron filings are used.

Manufactured Magnets

Artificial magnets are often made of steel and magnetized by electricity. Named for their shape, there are bar, V, U, horseshoe, and cylindrical magnets, to name the more familiar varieties (Figure 11-1). Each of these magnets attracts substances most strongly at the ends, or poles. The U, V, and horseshoe magnets are more powerful than the others when all factors are equal; they are bent so two poles attract instead of one.

Powerful alnico magnets are available at scientific supply houses and in commercial kits. These are made from aluminum, cobalt, nickel, and iron. Alnico magnets are used for home and commercial purposes.

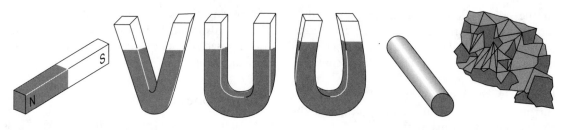

Figure 11-1
Magnets (A) bar; (B) V; (C) U-shaped; (D) horseshoe; (E) cylindrical; and (F) lodestone.

MAKING MAGNETS CONCEPTS
(Experiences p. 301)

Magnets made from a relatively soft material, such as iron, usually hold their magnetism only a short time. So they are called *temporary* magnets. Those made from a harder material, such as steel, retain their magnetism far longer. They are called *permanent* magnets. You can make either kind from common materials. Let's see how.

Temporary Magnets

A magnet can be made from an iron nail by stroking it in one direction with one pole of a permanent magnet. Its power increases with the number of strokes you apply. Be sure to lift the magnet clear at the end of each stroke before beginning another. Merely rubbing it back and forth will usually bring poor results. Within a few minutes after making this magnet, you will notice a marked loss in its power, regardless of how many strokes it has received.

A second way to make a temporary magnet is by holding a magnet very close to any attractable object. For example, if you hold a magnet near the head of a small nail, you may be able to pick up a few tacks or a paper clip with the nail. Move the magnet farther away from the nail head, and the objects typically will fall off the nail. This is called *induced* magnetism.

You can also make a temporary magnet by wrapping an insulated wire around a nail and connecting the two wire ends to a battery. This is an *electromagnet*. Any wire that carries an electric current generates a weak magnetic field around it. Wrapping the wire around the nail core concentrates the field into the core. Disconnect the wire from the battery and the nail is no longer an effective magnet.

Permanent Magnets

It takes longer to magnetize a steel object by stroking it with a magnet than it does an iron one. However, steel may hold its magnetism for years.

A more efficient way to make permanent magnets is by electricity. The steel object is placed into a tube wrapped in wire and attached to a battery or other electrical source. Current is applied for a few seconds to magnetize the object. An upcoming activity shows this method.

FIELDS OF FORCE CONCEPTS
(Experiences p. 304)

As children explore with magnets, they can observe that a magnet will attract from a distance. For example, a small nail or paper clip will "jump" to a nearby magnet. They will also see that the attractive force is strongest at the poles. This gives us the chance to introduce the field of force surrounding a magnet.

Inferring the Field

While we cannot see the field directly, its presence may be inferred. Sprinkle iron filings on a sheet of stiff white paper placed over a magnet, and you will see the filings distribute in an orderly way. Their greatest concentration will be at the poles. (See Figure 11-11.) Theoretically, a magnetic field extends outward to an indefinite distance. For practical purposes, the field ends when we can no longer detect it.

Magnetic Transparency

If you hold a powerful magnet against the *back* of your hand, it can attract and move a paper clip in the *palm* of your hand. A magnetic field can also go through many other materials without any apparent loss of power. It seems as if these materials are "transparent" to the field's lines of force. This makes it possible for people to wear magnetic earrings and plumbers to locate iron pipes in closed walls. *Caution:* Please note that computer disks and other media, televisions, and wristwatches may be affected by magnets. Materials of iron or steel are considered "opaque" to this force. When they are touched by a magnet, the force passes inside them and back into the magnet.

MAGNETIC POLE CONCEPTS
(Experiences p. 308)

Suspend a bar magnet from a string in North America and a curious thing happens: It points toward the north magnetic pole. Do the same in South America and it points toward the south magnetic pole. (This assumes no interfer-

ence from nearby metals.) A magnetized needle placed horizontally on a floating foam plastic chip or slice of cork also points toward a magnetic pole.

To see why this is so, consider the poles of a magnet. When another magnet or magnetized object is held near a suspended or floating magnet, the like poles (north–north or south–south) repel each other. The opposite poles attract each other.

Earth's Magnetism

The earth itself acts like a giant magnet. No one knows why, but there are some theories. One explanation holds that several parts of the earth's interior rotate at different speeds. The resulting friction strips electric particles from atoms. This causes an electric current to be generated that creates a magnetic field. Because the earth's core is supposedly made of nickel–iron, the effect is that of a huge electromagnet buried within the earth.

Recall the discussion before that dealt with magnetic fields of force. When iron filings are sprinkled on paper placed over a bar magnet, they reveal lines of force looping from one pole to another and concentrating at both poles. On a gigantic scale, a similar kind of magnetic field happens with the earth's magnetism. (See Figure 11-2.)

Lines of force from the earth's magnetism run roughly north and south far into space and then loop down to concentrate at the north and south magnetic poles. Therefore, a freely swinging magnet—bar, horseshoe, or any other type with dominant poles—aligns itself parallel to these lines of force. Since lines of force end at the magnetic poles, properly following a compass in the northern hemisphere eventually results in one's arrival at the north magnetic pole. This is located above the upper Hudson Bay region of Canada. If one follows a compass south, the trip ends near Wilkes Land, a part of Antarctica.

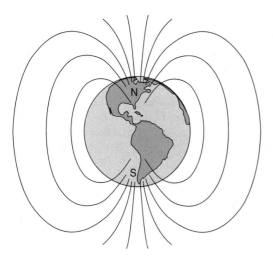

Figure 11-2
The earth has a magnetic field that is concentrated at both poles.

Geographic Poles

The north and south *magnetic* poles should not be confused with the north and south *geographic* poles. The geographic and magnetic poles are about 1,600 kilometers (1,000 miles) apart in the north and 2,400 kilometers (1,500 miles) apart in the south. In other words, when a compass points north it does *not* point true north, or toward the north star. Charts must be made for navigators that show the angular variation between true north and the direction toward which a compass points. These charts must be periodically changed, as the magnetic poles are slowly but continually shifting. (See Figure 11-3.)

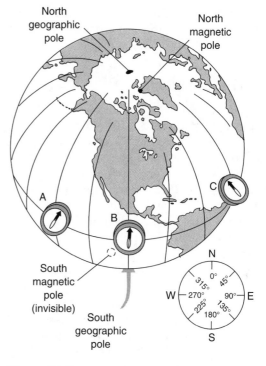

Figure 11-3
Note in A, B, and C an angle between the meridian on which the compass is located and the direction toward which the needle points. These differences must be added or subtracted from a compass heading to determine true north. For example, true headings for A, B, and C should all be 0°, or north. Actual readings are 35°, 5°, and 315°. A chart would show the need to subtract 35° from A, 5° from B, and the need to add 45° to C.

MAGNETIC THEORY AND CARE OF MAGNETS CONCEPTS
(Experiences p. 310)

Although magnetism has been known and used for many centuries, science cannot fully explain it. One theory, when simply explained, can be understood by children. It is based on observations they can make for themselves: Heating or repeatedly dropping a magnet will cause it to lose its magnetic properties. And, although a magnet may be broken into smaller and smaller pieces, each fragment continues to have a north and south pole. To find out why, you need to understand domains.

Magnetic Domains

Scientists believe that there are many tiny clusters of atoms, called *domains,* within potentially magnetic objects. The clusters are normally randomly arranged. But when an object is stroked in one direction, or otherwise magnetized, the domains line up in a single direction. See Figure 11-4. Notice that in Drawing A, the bar magnet could be broken into many pieces, yet each piece would continue to have opposite poles. Heating a magnet forces the domains into violent motion, and so they are likely to be disarranged, as in Drawing B. Repeatedly dropping a magnet jars the domains out of line, with the same result.

Caring for Magnets

Magnets can keep much of their power for years when properly cared for. Storing magnets improperly in the classroom is probably the chief reason why they quickly become weak. A small metal bar, called a *keeper,* should be placed across the poles of a magnet before it is stored. If the regular keeper has been lost, a nail can be substituted. Placing opposite poles of magnets together is another effective way to store them. Children can also learn not to drop magnets, which is another common reason why magnets become weaker.

Figure 11-5 shows two charts which provide guidance to help children remember some rules when handling magnets. The first chart is for primary children. The second is suitable for older children.

MAGNETIC INTERACTIONS BENCHMARKS AND STANDARDS

Magnets are commonly studied in the primary grades. Children should complete activities designed to observe and classify magnetic and nonmagnetic objects. Early activities will also lay the groundwork for future study of forces. Specific examples of Benchmarks and Standards are as follows:

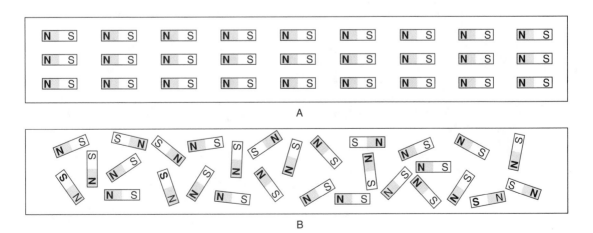

A

B

Figure 11-4
A magnetized (A) and unmagnetized (B) steel bar.

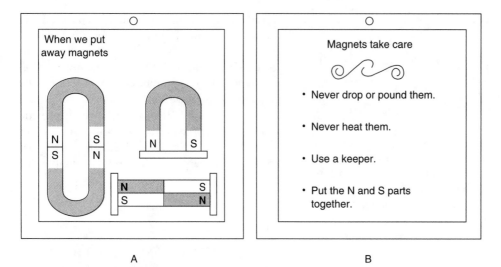

A   B

Figure 11-5
Sample charts to help children remember how to handle magnets.

SAMPLE BENCHMARKS (AAAS, 1993).

■ Magnets can be used to make some things move without being touched (by Grades K–2, p. 94).

■ Without touching them, a magnet pulls on all things made of iron and either pushes or pulls on other magnets (by Grades 3–5, p. 94).

SAMPLE STANDARD (NRC, 1996).

■ Magnets attract and repel each other and certain kinds of other materials (by Grades K–4, p. 127).

INVESTIGATIONS AND ACTIVITIES

MAGNETS AND WHAT THEY ATTRACT EXPERIENCES

(Concepts p. 291)

INVESTIGATION: *OBJECTS MAGNETS CAN PULL*

Have you ever played with a magnet? If so, what were you able to do with it?

EXPLORATORY PROBLEM

How can you find out which objects magnets can pull?

NEEDED

two bags of small objects   magnet

TRY THIS

1. Take out the objects from only *one* bag now.
2. Touch your magnet to each object.
3. Which objects are pulled by the magnet? Put these in a group.
4. Which objects are not pulled by the magnet? Put those in another group (Figure 11-6).

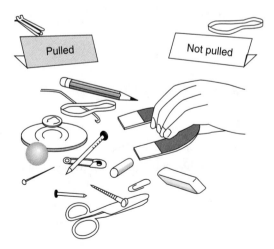

Figure 11-6

DISCOVERY PROBLEMS

observing

A. How are the objects in the pulled group alike?

inferring

B. Can you make a rule about which objects your magnet pulls? Put the objects back into the bag. Put the bag away.

predicting and classifying and inferring

C. Take out the objects from the *second* bag. Which do you think your magnet will pull? Will not pull? Put the objects into two groups. Now use your magnet on the objects in each group. Was every object in the right group?

predicting

D. Which objects around the room will your magnet pull? Record your prediction and verify.

observing

E. What other magnets can you try? Will they pull the same objects your first magnet pulled?

TEACHING COMMENT

Try to get a variety of attractable and nonattractable small objects for both bags of test materials. Here are some common objects and the chief metals or metal alloys that make them up:

nail ⟶ iron
wire ⟶ copper
pins ⟶ steel (or brass)
screws ⟶ brass (or iron or aluminum)
hair curler ⟶ aluminum
penny ⟶ bronze

Give children the names of metals as needed to help them generalize about their experience.

GENERALIZATION

A magnet pulls objects made of iron or steel.

SAMPLE PERFORMANCE OBJECTIVES

Process: The child can infer a rule about which objects magnets pick up.

Knowledge: The child can apply the rule to new objects by predicting which will be attracted to a magnet.

ACTIVITY: *HOW CAN A MAGNET SEPARATE MIXED MATERIALS?*

NEEDED

magnet	plastic spoon
salt	small jar with lid
kitchen plastic wrap	white paper with turned-up edges
iron filings	sandbox or loose soil

TRY THIS

1. Put two spoonfuls each of filings and salt into the jar.
2. Cap the jar and shake it to mix the two materials.
3. Pour the mixture onto a white paper "tray."
4. Try using the spoon to separate the filings and salt.
5. Now use the magnet, but first cover the poles with kitchen plastic wrap.
6. To remove the filings from the magnet, remove the kitchen wrap.

   a. Which was easier, Step 4 or 5?

   b. Many bits of iron may be found in sand and soils. Cover the magnet's poles again with wrap. Poke the magnet around in a sandbox or loose soil. How many iron bits do you find?

INVESTIGATION: *THE POWER OF MAGNETS*

Some people say you can tell how strong a magnet is just by looking at it. What do you think?

EXPLORATORY PROBLEM

How can you find out the power of a magnet?

NEEDED

several different magnets	two small pieces cut from a straw
pencil	sheet of lined paper
paper clips	

TRY THIS

1. Put a paper clip on two pieces of soda straw, placed on a sheet of lined paper.

2. Make a pencil mark at the front of the clip.

3. Line up an end (pole) of a magnet with the clip. (See Figure 11-7.)

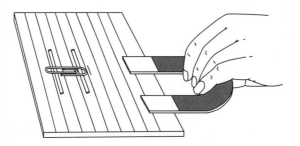

Figure 11-7

4. Slowly bring the magnet near the paper clip.

5. Stop moving the magnet when the clip moves.

6. Count the lines between the pencil mark and magnet.

DISCOVERY PROBLEMS

measuring and classifying **A.** Test several magnets. Which is the most powerful? Can you put them in order from weakest to strongest?

measuring **B.** Are both ends (poles) of magnets equally powerful? How can you find out?

observing **C.** Do all parts of a magnet pull the clip? Which part of a magnet is strongest? weakest?

experimenting **D.** What are some other ways to test a magnet's power? Do you get the same results?

TEACHING COMMENT

PREPARATION AND BACKGROUND

A magnet attracts objects most strongly at the ends or poles. The attractive power gradually weakens as you go toward the center of the magnet. The center has very little or no magnetic attraction.

GENERALIZATION

Magnets vary in power; magnets attract objects most strongly at their poles.

SAMPLE PERFORMANCE OBJECTIVES

Process: The child can measure the relative power of several magnets and arrange them in order from least to most powerful.

Knowledge: The child can describe the parts of a magnet that are likely to be most and least powerful.

MAKING MAGNETS EXPERIENCES
(Concepts p. 292)

INVESTIGATION: *HOW TO MAKE MAGNETS*

Suppose you have an iron nail and a magnet. With these materials, you can make another magnet.

EXPLORATORY PROBLEM

How can you make a magnet?

NEEDED

strong magnet
two matched iron nails
steel straight pins
two screwdrivers (large and small)

TRY THIS

1. Get a large iron nail. Touch it to some steel pins to see if it attracts them.
2. Put one end of the magnet on the nail near the head.
3. Stroke the whole nail with the magnet 20 times. Stroke in one direction only (Figure 11-8).
4. Touch the nail again to some pins. How many pins does the nail attract? Record this number.

DISCOVERY PROBLEMS

observing   **A.** How much stronger can you make your nail magnet? How many pins does it attract after 30 strokes? 40 strokes? Record how many pins are attracted each time.

observing   **B.** How strong is the nail magnet after 10 minutes? Compare.

observing   **C.** Test the other nail, to see if it attracts pins. If not, stroke this nail *back and forth,* instead of just one way. How strong is the magnet after 20 strokes? 30 strokes? 40 strokes?

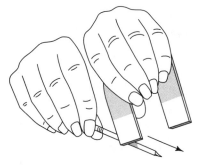

Figure 11-8

predicting   **D.** Suppose you stroke a *small* steel screwdriver one way with a magnet. How many pins will it attract after 20 strokes? 30 strokes? 40 strokes? Record and compare your findings with those for the nail.

predicting   **E.** Suppose you stroke a *large* steel screwdriver one way with a magnet. Will you get the same results?

predicting   **F.** How strong do you think both screwdrivers will be after 10 minutes?

hypothesizing   **G.** What other objects can you make into magnets? How strong can you make each one?

TEACHING COMMENT

PREPARATION AND BACKGROUND

An iron or steel object may be magnetized by stroking it with a magnet. A soft iron object that is magnetized, such as a nail, weakens after several minutes. A steel object, such as the shank of a screwdriver, retains its magnetism. However, steel is harder to magnetize. Only a strong magnet is likely to produce significant results. Stroking an object both ways with a magnet is less effective than stroking it in one direction. Use steel straight pins to test the strength of whatever magnets are made.

In Problems D and E, observe whether students test *each* screwdriver for magnetism *before* they proceed.

GENERALIZATION

Iron and steel may be magnetized by a magnet; steel holds its magnetism longer than iron.

SAMPLE PERFORMANCE OBJECTIVES

Process: The child can infer by comparing data that there is a connection between the number of strokes used to magnetize an object and the object's magnetic power.

Knowledge: The child will say that a steel object should be used if a permanent magnet is to be made.

ACTIVITY: *HOW CAN YOU MAKE LONG-LASTING MAGNETS WITH ELECTRICITY?*

NEEDED

thin (number 26 or 28) insulated copper wire
magnet
three D-size flashlight cells
pencil
3-by-5-inch file card
scissors
two steel bobby pins
tacks
sticky tape

TRY THIS

1. Tightly roll a small file card around a pencil. Fasten it with sticky tape.

2. Tightly wind about 80 turns of thin copper wire in one direction around the tube. Leave 30 centimeters (1 foot) of wire free at each end. Tape the coil ends so the wires stay tightly wound.

3. Strip the insulation from the wire ends with scissors.

4. Remove the pencil from the tube. Put a straightened bobby pin inside.

5. Put three flashlight batteries together as in the picture. (See Figure 11-9.)

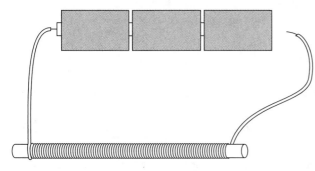

Figure 11-9

6. Touch the stripped ends of the wire to opposite ends of the batteries. Do this for no more than 5 seconds.

7. Remove the bobby pin and touch it to some tacks.

   a. How many tacks does the bobby pin pick up?

   b. Suppose you made a second bobby-pin magnet by stroking it with a regular magnet. Could you make it as strong as or stronger than the "electrocuted" bobby pin? If so, how many times would it need to be stroked? Find out.

   c. Magnetize with electricity other things that will fit into the tube. Which objects can be magnetized? Which will hold most of their magnetism over a week or more? Which will not?

FIELDS OF FORCE EXPERIENCES
(Concepts p. 292)

INVESTIGATION: *MAGNETIC FIELDS*

Have you found that some objects can be attracted to a magnet even when the magnet doesn't touch them? That's because around every magnet there is an invisible *field of force*. The magnet pulls on any attractable object within its field. Although the field is invisible, there are ways to tell where it is.

EXPLORATORY PROBLEM

How can you find out about a magnet's field of force?

NEEDED

container of iron filings
four matched bar magnets
four matched horseshoe or U magnets
two sheets of stiff white paper with turned-up edges
partner

TRY THIS

1. Place a bar magnet on a table. Lay a sheet of white paper with turned-up edges over it.

2. Sprinkle some iron filings on this paper tray. Do this over and around where you think the magnet is (Figure 11-10).

3. Observe closely how the filings line up and where they are thick and thin.

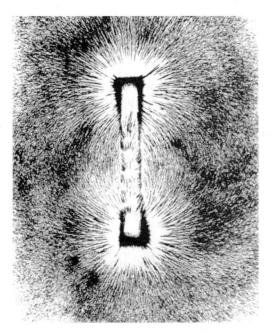

Figure 11-10

DISCOVERY PROBLEMS

inferring **A.** Ask your partner to observe your magnetic field, but don't tell how you arranged you magnet or what kind it is. Can your partner make one just like it?

inferring **B.** Have your partner make a magnetic field for you. Can you match it?

predicting **C.** Here are more fields for you and your partner to try: How will two bar magnets look with like poles close together? unlike poles close together? How will horseshoe or U magnets look with like and unlike poles close together? First, draw what you predict.

experimenting **D.** What fields can you make with different combinations of magnets, positions, and distances apart?

inferring **E.** What were the easiest fields of force for you and your partner to figure out? the hardest fields to figure out?

Teaching Comment

PREPARATION AND BACKGROUND

Students should learn that iron filings only crudely show a magnet's field of force. The field extends much beyond where the filings stop.

Permanent inference sheets of magnetic fields can be easily made. These will allow individual students to do the activity by trying to match the sheets. To make a permanent record of a field, use plastic spray to fix the filings on a stiff sheet of paper. Hold the spray can far enough away from the sheet that filings are not blown away. For best results, be sure to use fine, powderlike filings and sprinkle lightly. Let the spray dry before removing the sheet from the underlying magnets.

You may also use a magnetic field detector available from scientific supply companies. These show the lines of force more accurately and work very well with refrigerator magnets.

GENERALIZATION

A field of force surrounds a magnet; it is most powerful near the ends or poles.

SAMPLE PERFORMANCE OBJECTIVES

Knowledge: The child can point out the most and least powerful areas in a magnetic field.

Process: When shown a record of a magnetic field, the child can infer the positions and distances apart of several magnets.

INVESTIGATION: *DOES MAGNETISM GO THROUGH OBJECTS?*

Do you think magnetism can be blocked by some materials? If so, which ones? Do you think it can pass through other materials? If so, which ones?

EXPLORATORY PROBLEM

How can you find out if magnetism can go through materials?

NEEDED

ruler
strong magnet
books
small paper clip
thread
small thin materials to test

TRY THIS

1. Set up your objects as in Figure 11-11. Be sure that the clip does *not* touch the magnet.

2. Make the space between the clip and magnet as big as possible, but do not let the clip fall. Slowly pull the thread end to widen the space.

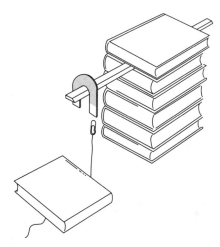

Figure 11-11

3. Test one of your thin, flat materials. Put it in the space between the clip and magnet without touching them.

4. Does the clip stay up? Then magnetism can go through the material. Does the clip fall? Then magnetism cannot go through the material.

DISCOVERY PROBLEMS

predicting **A.** Which of your materials do you think magnetism will go through? Which will magnetism not go through? Put the materials in two piles, then test them to find out.

predicting **B.** Will magnetism go through *two* materials put together? Test the materials to find out. (Be sure the two materials can fit between the magnet and clip.)

experimenting **C.** Do you think magnetism will go through water? How can you find out?

experimenting **D.** What are other ways to test if magnetism can go through your objects?

TEACHING COMMENT

PREPARATION AND BACKGROUND

In the Exploratory Problem, try to provide materials thin enough to pass between the paper clip and magnet.

GENERALIZATION

Magnetism goes through many objects, but not those made from iron or steel.

SAMPLE PERFORMANCE OBJECTIVES

Process: The child can infer the location of a hidden iron object by using a magnet.

Knowledge: Given a magnet and several objects, the child can show that magnetism passes through objects unless they are made of iron or steel.

FOR YOUNGER CHILDREN

Younger children should be able to do most of the activities in this investigation.

MAGNETIC POLE EXPERIENCES
(Concepts p. 293)

ACTIVITY: *HOW CAN YOU MAKE A NEEDLE COMPASS?*

NEEDED

two sewing needles
magnet
cork top (thin slice or styrofoam chip)
water
drinking glass
paper towel

TRY THIS

1. Place a glass on a paper towel. Fill it to the brim with water.
2. Magnetize a needle. Stroke it 10 times, from thick end to point, with the magnet's *S* pole.
3. Scratch a narrow groove in the sliced cork top. Lay the needle in the groove. (This will keep it from rolling off.)
4. Carefully place the cork and needle on the water surface (Figure 11-12).
   a. In which direction does the needle point?
   b. Move the needle gently so it points somewhere else. Wait a few seconds. What happens?
   c. Use your magnet. How can you *push* away either end of the needle with it?
   d. How can you *pull* either end of the needle with the magnet?
5. Replace the magnetized needle with one that has not been magnetized. Float the cork and needle on the water as before.
   e. What do you think will happen if you try steps 4a through 4d again? Find out.

Figure 11-12

TEACHING COMMENT

A glass filled to the brim with water keeps a floating cork centered. With less water, the cork will drift against the glass's sides.

ACTIVITY: HOW CAN YOU USE A COMPASS TO TELL DIRECTIONS?

NEEDED

topless cardboard box (large)
partner
large open area
magnetic compass

TRY THIS

1. Go to a large, open space outdoors. Study the compass. Notice how the needle points. Turn the compass so that the part marked "north" is under the pointing needle.
2. Walk 20 steps toward the north and observe the needle. While walking, try to keep the needle exactly on north.
3. Stop, then turn completely around. Look at the compass. Now "north" is behind you and "south" is straight ahead. The other end of the needle should point south. Walk 20 steps toward the south while watching the needle. Keep it exactly on south. If you do so, you should return to where you started.

a. Can you use only your compass well enough to walk somewhere and find your way back? How close will you get? Mark where you are. Put a box over your head so you cannot see around you. Looking at only your compass, walk 300 steps north and then 300 steps south. Have a partner watch out for you.

b. How well can you do Step 3a *without* a compass?

c. How can you use your compass to walk east or west? Practice these directions as in Steps 1 through 3, and then try the box test again.

TEACHING COMMENT

"North" as shown on a compass may vary slightly from true north because of regional magnetic variation. For the purpose of this activity, such variation may be ignored.

MAGNETIC THEORY AND CARE OF MAGNETS EXPERIENCES
(Concepts p. 294)

ACTIVITY: *WHAT ARE SOME WAYS A MAGNET CAN LOSE ITS MAGNETISM?*

A. NEEDED

magnet
concrete sidewalk
two large matched nails
tacks or paper clips

INTRODUCTION

Test to see how *dropping* a magnet affects its magnetism. (Use magnetized nails so that regular magnets will not be destroyed.)

TRY THIS

1. Magnetize two nails. Stroke each nail its whole length 30 times with one pole of a magnet.

2. Test to see if each nail magnet attracts the same number of tacks. If not, stroke the weaker magnet until it is equally strong.

3. Hold one nail high and drop it on a hard surface. Do this 20 times.

4. Test each nail again. You might record what you find in this way:

	Dropped Magnet	Other Magnet
Before	6 tacks	6 tacks
After	2 tacks	5 tacks

   a. How did dropping the nail magnet affect it?

   b. What will happen if you drop the second nail magnet?

B. NEEDED

magnet
candle and match
two large matched nails
cake pan (to hold candle)
tacks or paper clips
glass of water
pliers or tongs

INTRODUCTION

Test to see how *heating* affects magnetism.

TRY THIS

1. Again, do Steps 1 and 2 in Section A.

2. Use pliers to hold one magnetized nail upright in a candle flame for three minutes.

3. Before testing, dip the nail in water to cool it.

4. Test the two nails. Record your findings as in Section A.

   a. How did heating the nail magnet affect it?

   b. What will happen if you heat the second nail magnet?

TEACHING COMMENT

Iron nails do not retain magnetism very long. So it is possible that the second magnet, too, will be weaker during the post-test. But this change should be slight. *Caution:* Supervise the candle activity closely for safety.

REFERENCES

American Association for the Advancement of Science. (1993). *Benchmarks for science literacy.* New York: Oxford University Press.

National Research Council. (1996). *National science education standards.* Washington, DC: National Academy Press.

SELECTED TRADE BOOKS: MAGNETIC INTERACTIONS

For Younger Children

Freeman, M. (1980). *The real magnet books.* Scholastic.

Jennings, T. (1990). *Magnets.* Watts.

Kirkpatrick, R. K. (1985). *Look at magnets.* Raintree.

Knight, D. C. (1967). *Let's find out about magnets.* Watts.

Podendorf, I. (1971). *Magnets.* Children's Press.

Schneider, H., & Schneider, N. (1979). *Secret magnets.* Scholastic.

Wade, H. (1979). *The magnet.* Raintree.

For Older Children

Adler, D. (1983). *Amazing magnets.* Troll Associates.

Adler, I., & Adler, R. (1966). *Magnets.* Day.

Catherall, E. A., & Holt, P. N. (1969). *Working with Magnets.* Whitman.

Fitzpatrick, J. (1987). *Magnets.* Silver Burdett.

Freeman, M. B. (1968). *The book of magnets.* Four Winds.

Santrey, L. (1985). *Magnets.* Troll Associates.

Sootin, H. (1968). *Experiments with magnetism.* Norton.

Victor, E. (1967). *Exploring and understanding magnets and electromagnets.* Benefic.

Ward, A. (1991). *Experimenting with magnetism.* Chelsea House.

Resource Book

Shaw, D. G., & Dybdahl, C. S. (1996). *Integrating science and language arts: a sourcebook for K–6 teachers* (physical cycles including magnetism pp. 93–110). Allyn and Bacon.

ELECTRICAL ENERGY

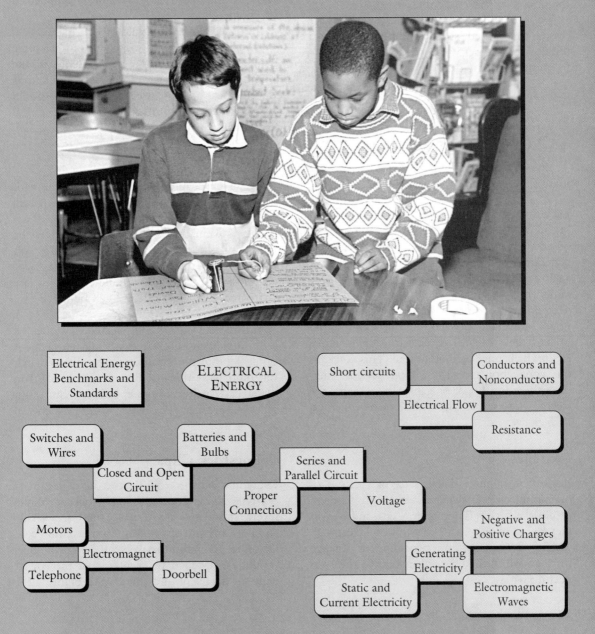

Electrical Energy Benchmarks and Standards

ELECTRICAL ENERGY

Short circuits

Conductors and Nonconductors

Electrical Flow

Resistance

Switches and Wires

Batteries and Bulbs

Closed and Open Circuit

Series and Parallel Circuit

Proper Connections

Voltage

Motors

Electromagnet

Telephone

Doorbell

Negative and Positive Charges

Generating Electricity

Static and Current Electricity

Electromagnetic Waves

Can children learn to appreciate the advantages of a ready source of electricity? One good beginning is for them to count the number of electrical devices we use and then try to devise nonelectrical substitutes for them. By doing activities like those in this chapter, children should also begin to appreciate some of the things that make electrical energy available and the principles that make them work.

We'll consider how electrical circuits are closed and opened, some conditions that affect the flow of electricity, electromagnets, and ways to produce electricity.

CLOSED AND OPEN CIRCUIT CONCEPTS
(Experiences page 326)

Each time we push a button or flip a switch that "turns on" electricity, there is a continuous flow of electrical energy in wires connected from the generating plant to our appliance and back again to the plant. On a smaller scale, much the same thing happens when a battery is connected to a miniature bulb. If there is a continuous connection between the source of electricity and the appliance or device using it, lights go on, bells ring, or motors spin. This continuous connection is called a *closed circuit.* Anytime there is a break or gap in the circuit, the electric flow stops. This condition is called an *open circuit.*

Switches

Regardless of their shape, size, or method of operation, electric switches serve only to open or close a circuit. They offer a safe and convenient way of supplying the flow of electricity when we want it by providing a linkage through which the energy can flow to the connecting wires.

Batteries

Much of the work in this chapter calls for the use of dry cells, copper wire, and flashlight bulbs. Size D flashlight cells or number 6 dry cells should be used because they are safe, fairly long lasting, and relatively inexpensive. When fresh, they deliver 1½ volts of electricity, as contrasted with 110 to 120 volts or so supplied in the home.

In other words, it would take as many as 80 of these cells connected together to have a force usually supplied by the current found in the home. *Caution:* House current is dangerous for electrical investigations and children should be reminded never to use household electrical currents for investigations.

Bulbs

Because the chapter calls for experiments with miniature bulbs (flashlight-type bulbs), it will be helpful to understand how to use them properly. Miniature bulbs are designed to be used with a loosely specified number of 1½ volt dry cells. Therefore, there are one-cell, two-cell, or multi-cell bulbs. One-cell bulbs are sometimes marked "1.2v," 2-cell bulbs "2.5v," and so forth.

If three dry cells are connected to a one-cell bulb, it is likely that the thin tungsten filament inside will burn out quickly. Be careful to match the bulb with the number of cells used. Too many cells will cause the bulb to burn out quickly; too few will cause it to glow feebly, if at all.

Fahnestock Clips

Many unit activities call for the use of commercial-type miniature bulbs and sockets. While several substitutes are possible, these are usually cumbersome and less useful. For maximum ease in using miniature sockets, Fahnestock clips should be fastened to each side of the socket with the screws found there. (See Figure 12-1

Figure 12-1
A number 6 dry cell and two D cells connected in complete circuits.

for an example.) To connect a wire, simply press down on the springy, open end of the clip and insert the wire end into the exposed half-loop. The wire stays in place when you release the pressure on the clip.

Wire

The wire you use should also be selected with an eye to convenience. Number 22 wire is excellent for almost every activity. Get plastic-covered solid copper wire, rather than cotton-covered wire consisting of many small, twisted strands. These strands become unraveled at the ends, and cotton insulation is harder to strip off than a plastic covering.

Insulation can quickly be removed with a wire-stripper (Figure 12-2); this device also cuts wires efficiently. With the wire suggested here, scissors may serve almost as well.

Connections

There are several easy ways to connect cells and bulbs, depending on the kinds of materials you have. Figure 12-1 shows how a D-size cell and a number 6 cell can be connected to form a closed or complete circuit. Tape or a wide rubber band will hold the stripped wire ends snugly against the D-cell terminals. The center terminal (positive), recognizable by the bump, corresponds to the center terminal on a large cell. The opposite terminal (negative) is equivalent

to the rim-mounted terminal on the large cell. The third arrangement needs only a single wire, with one end touching the negative terminal and the other wrapped around the bulb base. The base touches the positive terminal to complete the circuit. Notice that the wire end wrapped around the bulb base also serves as a bulb holder.

Series and Parallel Circuit Concepts
(Experiences page 329)

There are only two basic ways to connect electrical devices in a circuit: through series or parallel wiring (Figure 12-3).

Connecting Wires

In series wiring, all of the usable electricity flows through each bulb or appliance. A chief disadvantage of this circuit is obvious to anyone who has had a bulb burn out in an old-fashioned, series-type string of Christmas-tree lights. When one bulb burns out, the circuit is broken and all the lights go out. All the bulbs must then be tested to discover which one needs to be replaced.

To avoid the troubles of series circuits, most wiring for home and commercial use is parallel wiring. In this kind, electricity flows through a main wire and through branching wires connected to it as well, as shown in Figure 12-3(B). (In this figure, the Fahnestock clips represent the branching wires.) If a light or other fixture should burn out, no other light or fixture is affected. Bulbs receive electricity whether or not the others are in use. And when children make parallel circuits, they will notice no change in bulb brightness as bulbs are added.

Figure 12-2
A wire stripper.

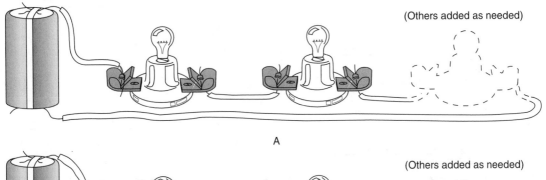

(Others added as needed)

A

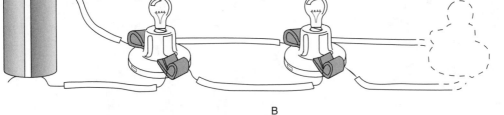

(Others added as needed)

B

Figure 12-3
Two contrasting circuits: (A) Lights in series, and (B) lights in parallel.

Connecting Cells

Cells can also be arranged in series and parallel as shown in Figure 12-4. A wide rubber band can serve to affix wires to flashlight cells, but the cells will buckle where they join unless they are enclosed. A sheet of rolled, stiff paper can be used for this purpose. If children work in pairs, these holders may not be required, as four hands should be able to hold everything together.

Note that in the series examples, negative terminals (–) are joined to positive (+) terminals. In the parallel examples, positives are joined to positives and negatives are joined to negatives.

Voltage

Hooking up cells in series increases the *voltage*, or pressure, behind the flow of electricity. In contrast, arranging several or more cells in par-

allel makes available a longer-lasting supply of current without increasing the voltage. For example, a bulb connected to two cells in series will burn about twice as brightly as when the cells are connected in parallel. However, the bulb will burn about two times longer with the parallel arrangement.

An analogy, as shown in Figure 12-5, can clarify why these differences take place. Cells in series are like connected tanks of water with one mounted higher than the other. The force of the flow is directly related to how many higher tanks are used. In contrast, cells in parallel are like water tanks mounted on the same level. The water flows at about the same rate as it would with one tank. So in this case, the water supply lasts about twice as long as in the other setup.

In studying circuits, children have many interesting chances to make predictions about which bulbs will light and to make inferences about hidden wires.

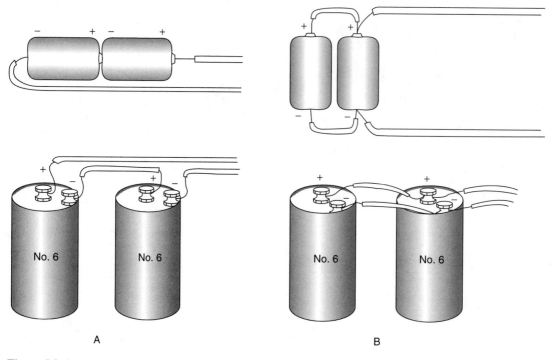

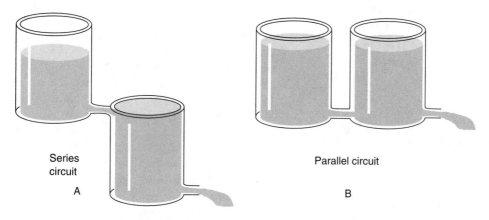

Figure 12-4
Batteries arranged in series (A) and parallel (B).

Figure 12-5
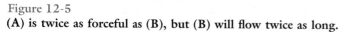
(A) is twice as forceful as (B), but (B) will flow twice as long.

ELECTRICAL FLOW CONCEPTS
(Experiences 338)

Conductors

The term *conductor* is usually given to any substance that permits an easy flow of electricity. Metals are by far the best conductors of electricity, and so they are commonly used for wires. Although several of the precious metals are better conductors, copper is most often used, as it is comparable in efficiency and yet cheap enough to produce in quantity.

We often hear the term *nonconductor* for materials such as rubber, glass, plastic, cloth, and other nonmetallic substances. This is misleading, as almost anything will conduct electricity if given enough voltage. These materials are better called poor conductors, or *insulators.*

This is why electricians may wear rubber gloves, and electric wires are covered with cloth, plastic, or rubber. It also explains why appliance plugs are covered with rubber or plastic, and glass separators are used on power line poles to keep apart high voltage lines.

Some poor conductors become good conductors when wet. Pure, or distilled, water is a poor conductor, but when dissolved minerals are added to it, it becomes a fairly good one. Wet human skin is a far better conductor than dry skin. For this reason, it is safer to turn appliances on and off with dry hands.

Resistance

Although metals conduct electricity much better than nonmetals, there is still some resistance in metal wire to the flow of electrons. Of course, the longer the wire, the greater will be the resistance.

You may have experienced the gradual dimming of lights in a theater or adjusted the brightness of dashboard lights in an automobile. The change in both cases may have been caused by a *rheostat,* or dimmer switch. One kind of rheostat increases or decreases the length of wire through which electric current flows, thereby increasing or decreasing the wire's resistance. A simple model is shown in Figure 12-6. Some metals have so much resistance to the flow of electricity that they glow brightly when there is enough electrical pressure or voltage to force relatively large quantities of electricity to flow in them. Unfortunately, most metals melt or evaporate within a short period of time when hot enough to give off light.

This necessitated a long search by Thomas Edison for materials to be used as bulb filaments before he was able to find reasonable success. Some of the materials he tried reveal the exhaustive character of the search. Bamboo slivers, sewing thread, even human hair, were carbonized and tested!

Tungsten, sometimes called wolfram, is the metal used in *incandescent bulbs* today. (Any bulb that gives light from a very hot filament is called an incandescent bulb.) With a melting point of almost 3,400°C (6,200°F), tungsten is well able to withstand the temperature caused by the movement of electricity through its highly resistant structure. An inactive gas, such as argon, is pumped into the bulbs to help pre-

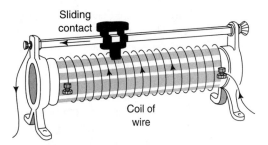

Figure 12-6

A simple rheostat, or dimmer switch.

vent the burning away of the filament. Still, some of the tungsten evaporates eventually, and the filament separates, breaking the circuit. The ever-darkening appearance of the portion of the bulb next to the filament shows the deposition of the evaporating tungsten. Electric heaters also have wires of highly resistant metal. Most heaters today use nichrome wire, a combination of nickel and chromium.

So far, you have seen that length and composition of wire affect resistance to the flow of electricity. Another factor is the diameter of the wire. An analogy here will help explain why size of wire affects resistance. Imagine part of a large crowd in a sports stadium converging into a narrow passageway. As some of the people begin to enter the passageway, the forward speed of the crowd slackens. At the end of the passageway, the forward pace again picks up.

A thick wire presents a broad pathway for the flow of electricity. A narrow wire constricts the flow. In the "effort" to crowd through the narrow pathway, much friction is created, and the wire grows hot. If the wire is thin enough and made of material like tungsten, it can also produce much light as it heats.

Circuit Hazards

You have seen that when bulbs or appliances are wired into a circuit, they show resistance to the flow of electrical energy. At the place where the energy enters these resistors, a change of energy takes place. Some of the electrical energy changes into heat (heater) or light (bulb) or sound (radio) or motion (motor). In other words, a significant amount of electrical energy is "used up," or changed.

Suppose, though, there is no resistor connected in the circuit. Because the copper wire has relatively low resistance, a great surge of electricity flows through the wire. The wire now heats up rapidly, even though it normally offers little resistance to a current.

Short Circuits

In residential and commercial circuits, intense heating of the wires may come from a "short circuit." This may happen when two bare wires touch each other, preventing the main supply of current from flowing through the resistor. Since the resistor is largely bypassed, a huge amount of electricity flows.

A common cause of short circuits happens when an appliance cord is placed under a heavily traveled rug. If the insulation between the two internal wires wears away, they may touch and a short may develop. A circuit is not necessarily shortened in length for a "short" circuit to occur. The essential thing is that the resistor is bypassed.

Overloaded Circuits

Overloading a circuit is perhaps an even more frequent cause of wires overheating. Many older houses, for example, were wired when only a few of today's common appliances were widely used. Small-diameter, lightly insulated wires were adequate then. But as more and more of today's appliances are added to circuits, intense heating occurs and poses a potential threat of fire.

Fuses and Circuit Breakers

Fuses and circuit breakers protect us from the fire hazard. In some older houses, a screw-in-type fuse contains a narrow metal strip that melts at a fairly low temperature. When a fuse is placed in a circuit, the electricity must travel through the strip. Should the wire heat up dangerously, the strip melts and the circuit opens, thereby shutting off the current.

A bimetallic strip circuit breaker is used instead of a fuse in many houses. This consists of two thin, metal ribbons fused together. The ribbons are made of two different metals. When placed in a circuit and heated, the bimetallic strip bends away from one of the contact points, opening the circuit. The bending is the result of different expansion rates of the metals.

Another modern type of circuit breaker works because any wire containing current electricity generates some magnetism. Increasing the supply of current has the effect of increasing the magnetism. When a movable steel rod is enclosed in a coil of wire placed in a circuit, it may be pulled upward as the current (and so magnetism) increases. If the rod is connected to a contact point, its upward movement will result in the circuit being opened. A spring catch that can be reset by hand prevents the rod from dropping down again. An electromagnetic device that operates this way is called a *solenoid*.

ELECTROMAGNET CONCEPTS
(Experiences page 343)

In 1820, a professor of physics at Copenhagen made a discovery that opened up for development one of the most useful devices ever conceived, the electromagnet. *Hans Christian Oersted* had believed for years that there was a relationship between magnetism and electricity. Despite much research, Oersted had not succeeded in discovering a useful connection between these two phenomena. One day, while lecturing to a class, he noticed that a wire carrying electric current was deflecting a nearby compass needle. Oersted realized immediately that the wire was generating a magnetic field. His later experiments, writings, and lectures helped spread the new concept of electromagnetism to the world.

The telephone, electric motor, and many other tools of modern living had their origin in Oersted's work and related discoveries. Consider some of these devices now.

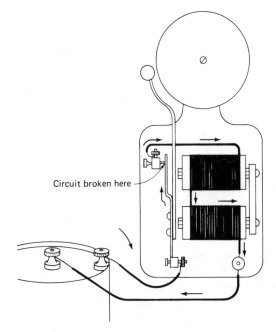

Circuit broken here

Figure 12-7
An electric bell or buzzer.

Electric Bell

An electric bell or a buzzer operates because its electric current is "interrupted," or continually turned off and on. Figure 12-7 shows how this happens. Follow the current as it moves from the battery into the bell. When the current flows around into the two electromagnets, they pull the metal clapper, which rings the bell. The act of moving the clapper breaks the circuit at the contact point, and the electricity stops flowing. The clapper then springs back into place and current flows again to repeat the cycle.

The Telephone

Figure 12-8 shows how the telephone works. Notice the complete, or closed, circuit between the transmitter and receiver. When we speak into the transmitter, a very thin metal

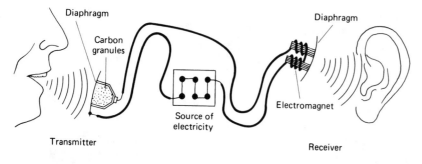

Figure 12-8
A telephone circuit.

diaphragm vibrates from sounds we make. The diaphragm variably squeezes the carbon granules behind it. Loud sounds, for example, squeeze the granules more tightly than soft sounds. This makes the granules conduct variable electrical pulses rather than a steady current.

The electrical impulses rather than the voice itself are transmitted in the wire. So they are able to travel to the other telephone's receiver almost instantly rather than at the much slower speed of sound. As the variable electric current reaches the receiver, it also causes the electromagnets to pull the diaphragm in a variable way. This sets the diaphragm vibrating in the same manner as the first one, and sounds are created.

To summarize, sound energy is used to vary electric energy at one end, which is then used to make sound energy at the other end. Students can experiment with old telephones and batteries to see how this works.

Electric Motor

You may know it is possible to rotate a suspended bar magnet with a second bar magnet. This is because unlike poles attract each other, and like poles repel each other. The suspended

magnet is rotated by alternately attracting and repelling each pole. To do this, you twist the bar magnet you are holding so the poles are attracted at first and then repelled. If timed properly, the suspended magnet will rotate smoothly.

You can demonstrate a similar technique with an electromagnet. However, you will not need to twist it to make the suspended magnet rotate.

Figure 12-9 shows how to proceed. First, find the pole on the electromagnet that is the opposite of the bar magnet's nearer pole. It will attract the bar magnet. Next, reverse the way you touch the terminals on the battery. This will also reverse the poles on the electromagnet. The nearer pole of the bar magnet will now be repelled. Rotate the suspended magnet smoothly by touching the battery terminals first one way, then the opposite way. A child can hold the electromagnet in one fixed position while you do this.

In an electric motor, the electromagnet spins. A device reverses the current automatically, which continually reverses the poles of the electromagnet. The electromagnet spins because it is first attracted to, and then repelled from, another magnet inside. An electric motor is really a spinning electromagnet.

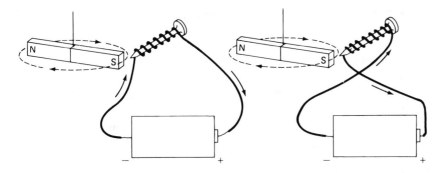

Figure 12-9
You can get a bar magnet to spin by alternately reversing the way you touch the wire ends of an electromagnet to a battery's terminals.

GENERATING ELECTRICITY CONCEPTS
(Experiences 345)

Electricity can be generated in several ways. First we will consider how to produce static electricity, then current electricity, and last, electromagnetic waves that can be sent to various places without wires.

Static Electricity

Not all electricity is useful. Almost everyone has experienced some form of *static electricity:* the crackling sound of hair when it is combed after having been washed and dried; the slight shock felt when a metal door knob is touched after scuffing across a rug; the flash of lightning that briefly illuminates a darkened sky. In each case, an electric charge appears to build up on an object and then stay there (hence, the name *static*) until a conductor provides a route through which the charge can escape. Although forms of static electricity vary considerably, their causes are similar. To understand these

causes, it will be helpful for us to peer briefly into the makeup of molecules and atoms.

We know that most matter is made up of *molecules.* A molecule is the smallest bit of any substance that retains the chemical properties of that substance. If we subdivide the molecule further, it no longer resembles the original substance; we have arrived at the atomic level.

Only two of the particles of which an atom is composed need concern us here: *electrons* and *protons.* Each of these particles has a tiny electric charge. The electron's charge is a *negative charge* and the proton's charge is a *positive charge.*

In their "normal" state, atoms have as many electrons as protons. Because these particles attract each other with equal force, they balance or neutralize each other. The atom is said to be *neutral,* or uncharged. But electrons are easily dislodged or torn away from atoms by rubbing and other means.

When neutral, unlike materials are rubbed together, one tends to lose electrons to the other. For example, when a hard rubber rod is rubbed with a wool cloth, the cloth loses some of its electrons to the rod. This gives the cloth a positive charge and the rod a negative charge. When a glass rod is rubbed with silk, however, some electrons leave the glass and go onto the silk cloth. This gives the silk a negative charge and the glass a positive charge.

The basic law of static electricity is *like charges repel and unlike charges attract each other.* Children may discover that identical objects rubbed with the same material will repel each other. If the objects are rubbed with different materials, they will usually attract each other.

What causes lightning? It is produced by friction. A cloud contains varying amounts of dust particles, rain drops, air (gas) molecules, and sometimes ice crystals. When violent currents occur in clouds, these substances rub together in various combinations. If a huge electric charge is built up, it may be attracted by an oppositely charged cloud or the ground. When this happens, we see lightning. (Thunder results when the air through which lightning passes quickly heats up and cools. The rapid expansion and contraction of the air forces air molecules to smash together, which causes loud sounds.)

Current Electricity

Static electricity is both unreliable and hard to manage, so we use current electricity to meet our needs. This generally comes from two sources: batteries and huge power plants.

Children are curious about how a battery can "make" electricity. Some think it is stored, like water is stored in a tank. What really happens is that chemical energy changes into electrical energy.

This is how an automobile battery works. When two different metal strips (zinc and copper, for example) are placed in an acid, both strips begin to slowly dissolve. However, the zinc dissolves faster than the copper. A surplus of electrons from the dissolving parts of the zinc strip builds up on the rest of the strip, giving it a strong negative charge. Some electrons are also released at the slower-dissolving copper

strip, but these go into the acid, leaving the copper strip with a positive charge. If we connect the end of the zinc strip to the end of the copper strip with a wire, a continuous circuit is set up. Electrons flow from the zinc strip through the wire to the copper strip. If we connect a bulb in this circuit, it lights; a connected starter starts an automobile engine.

Many pairs of dissimilar metal strips, or *electrodes,* can be used to get this effect, and other liquids besides acid can work to release and hold electrons. Such liquids are called *electrolytes.*

A "dry" cell or flashlight battery works in a way similar to the "wet" cell just described. A moist, paste-like electrolyte is used in place of a liquid. The electrodes are most commonly a carbon rod (found in the center of the cell), and a zinc cylinder (which surrounds the paste and rod).

Dry cells are convenient, but they are too weak and expensive for widespread residential or commercial use. *Mechanical energy,* the energy of motion, is by far the main method for generating electricity. Today, most electricity is produced by changing the energy in fuels and falling water.

In hydroelectric power plants, water falls on the blades of huge wheels, causing them to revolve. Other power plants may use oil, coal, natural gas, or atomic energy to heat water into steam. The steam forces giant turbines to whirl. Either large magnets are spun rapidly inside a wire coil, or a wire coil is spun inside of magnets. Both options cause electrons to flow into the wire.

Producing Electromagnetic Waves

You know that a steady electric current produces a weak magnetic field around a wire. This is why we can make an electromagnet. Long ago, scientists learned that by rapidly varying the electric current in a wire they could change the magnetic field. Instead of a steady field, rapidly vibrating energy waves were given off by the wire. These are called *radio waves*.

At a radio station, music or voice vibrations are changed into a variable electric current. The method is like that used in a telephone transmitter. The vibrating current is strengthened until strong radio waves are given off by the wire carrying the current. The waves are beamed off in all directions from a tall tower. Some of the waves strike a radio antenna. A weak current begins vibrating in the antenna, and the current is picked up and strengthened in the radio. A connected loudspeaker vibrates and produces sound energy much like a telephone receiver.

ELECTRICAL ENERGY BENCHMARKS AND STANDARDS

The idea of a complete circuit is complex for most students. They have difficulty conceptualizing that the electrons not only flow *from* the source, but that there must be a complete circuit back *to* the source. It is important to use hands-on activities to develop this understanding. Further recommendations for electrical principles include:

SAMPLE BENCHMARKS (AAAS, 1993)

■ Electric currents and magnets can exert a force on each other (by Grades 6–8, p. 95).

■ Make safe electrical connections with various plugs, sockets, and terminals (by Grades 3–5, p. 293).

SAMPLE STANDARDS (NRC, 1996)

■ Electricity in circuits can produce light, heat, sound, and magnetic effects. Electrical circuits require a complete loop through which an electrical current can pass (by Grades K–4, p. 127).

■ Electrical circuits provide a means of transferring electrical energy when heat, light, sound, and chemical changes are produced (by Grades 5–8, p. 155). ✐

INVESTIGATIONS AND ACTIVITIES

CLOSED AND OPEN CIRCUIT EXPERIENCES
(Concepts p. 314)

INVESTIGATION: *HOW TO MAKE A BULB LIGHT*[1]

Have you ever used a flashlight? The electricity to light the bulb comes from one or more batteries. You don't need a flashlight to make the bulb light. You can do it with a single wire and a battery.

EXPLORATORY PROBLEM

How can you light a flashlight bulb with a wire and a battery?

NEEDED

D-size battery
2 wires (6 inches or 15 centimeters long)
two flashlight bulbs
paper and pencil

TRY THIS

1. Remove the insulation from both ends of the wire.
2. Put the bulb bottom on the raised button end of the battery. (See Figure 12-10.)
3. Touch one wire end to the metal side of the bulb.
4. Touch the other wire end to the battery bottom.

Figure 12-10

---

[1] Also see the sample lesson plan in Chapter 3, page 60.

DISCOVERY PROBLEMS

experimenting **A.** How many other ways can you light the bulb? Keep a record of what you do. Make drawings of the circuits.

predicting **B.** Study each of the drawings in Figure 12-11. Which ways will light the bulb? Which will not? Record your predictions and then test them.

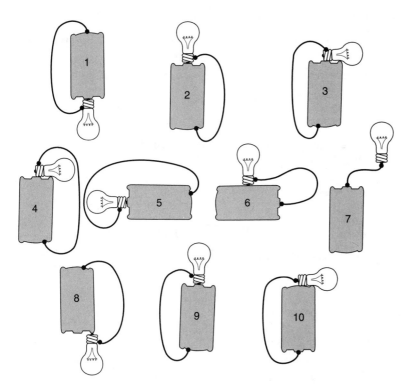

Figure 12-11

experimenting **C.** How many ways can you light a bulb with two wires? (Use one battery.) Record your observations.

experimenting **D.** How many ways can you light two bulbs with two wires? (Use one battery.) Record your observations.

TEACHING COMMENT

Use number 22 or 24 bell wire, available at most hardware or electrical supply stores. Be sure that the plastic covering is stripped from both ends of the wire to ensure good contact. *Caution:* Advise students to quickly notice, and discontinue trying a connection, if the wire they use to connect the bulb and battery begins to get warm. This happens when the bulb (resistor) is bypassed and the wire ends touch only the battery terminals—a type of short circuit.

GENERALIZATION

Electricity flows when there is a complete circuit; there are several ways to light a bulb.

SAMPLE PERFORMANCE OBJECTIVES

Process: The child can connect a battery and bulb with wire in several different ways to light the bulb.

Knowledge: The child can describe the bulb and battery parts that must be connected for a bulb to light.

FOR YOUNGER CHILDREN

Many younger students can do the exploratory activity, especially when plastic battery and bulb holders are used.

ACTIVITY: *How Can You Make Some Paper-Clip Switches?*

NEEDED

flashlight bulb
sticky tape
bulb holder
scissors
D-size battery

two paper clips
cardboard
six paper fasteners
five small wires

TRY THIS

1. Cut a small piece of cardboard. Punch two holes in it and put in two paper fasteners as in Figure 12-12.

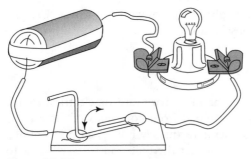

Figure 12-12

2. Strip bare the ends of the wires with scissors. Assemble the rest of the materials as shown. Bend a paper clip for the switch.

   a. What happens when you move the switch on and off the paper fastener? How does this switch work in the circuit?

3. Suppose you have a stairway light. You need to control it from both upstairs and downstairs. Make a pair of switches to control a single light. Do it as in Figure 12-13.

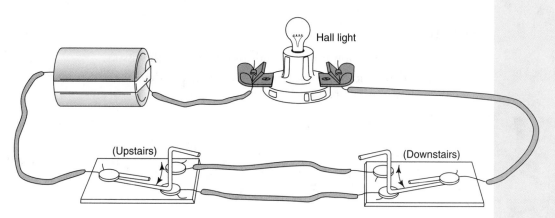

Figure 12-13

   b. What happens when you move each switch from one paper fastener head to another? What would happen if there was only a single wire between the two switches? How do these switches work?

TEACHING COMMENT

For the light to work properly, all connections need to be tight. Be sure the paper fasteners are securely seated and the wires are stripped of insulation where contact is made.

SERIES AND PARALLEL CIRCUIT EXPERIENCES

(Concepts p. 316)

INVESTIGATION: SERIES CIRCUITS

What does the word *series* mean to you? Here, it means placing electric bulbs in order, with one ahead or behind the next one.

EXPLORATORY PROBLEM

How can you set up a series circuit?

NEEDED

three flashlight bulbs
four wires
three bulb holders
two D-size batteries

TRY THIS

1. Remove the insulation from the ends of each wire with scissors.
2. Use two bulbs and bulb holders, two batteries, and three wires. Set up the circuit as shown in Figure 12-14.

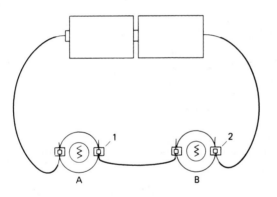

Figure 12-14

DISCOVERY PROBLEMS

predicting   **A.** Suppose you remove Light A. What will happen to Light B? If you remove Light B, what will happen to Light A?

predicting   **B.** Suppose you disconnect the wire at Place 1. What do you think will happen to Light A? Light B?

predicting   **C.** Suppose you disconnect the wire at Place 2. What will happen to Light A? Light B?

observing   **D.** Add another bulb to the series. Use one more wire, bulb, and bulb holder. What, if anything, happens to the lights?

inferring   **E.** How can you explain the results in A through D? That is, how does electricity seem to flow in a series circuit?

TEACHING COMMENT

PREPARATION AND BACKGROUND

If any wire or bulb is disconnected, all the bulbs go out. This is because all of the electricity flows through each connected part in a series circuit. For the same reason, adding more bulbs to the circuit causes all the lighted bulbs to get dimmer. Each resistor cuts down the available flow of electricity.

GENERALIZATION

In a series circuit, all the electricity flows through each connected part.

SAMPLE PERFORMANCE OBJECTIVES

Knowledge: The child can set up a working series circuit with two or more bulbs.

Process: The child can predict the effect on other parts of a series circuit when one or more parts are disconnected.

INVESTIGATION: *PARALLEL CIRCUITS*

What does the word *parallel* mean to you? Here, it means placing electric wires side by side in a parallel circuit.

EXPLORATORY PROBLEM

How can you set up a parallel circuit?

NEEDED

three flashlight bulbs
six wires
three bulb holders
two D-size batteries

TRY THIS

1. Remove the insulation from the ends of each wire with scissors.
2. Use two batteries, two bulbs and bulb holders, and four wires. Set up the circuit as shown in Figure 12-15.

DISCOVERY PROBLEMS

predicting   **A.** Suppose you remove Light A. What will happen to Light B? If you remove Light B, what will happen to Light A?

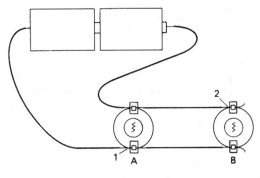

Figure 12-15

predicting   **B.** Suppose you disconnect the wire at Place 1. What do you think will happen to Light A? Light B?

predicting   **C.** Suppose you disconnect the wire at Place 2. What will happen to Light A? Light B?

observing   **D.** Add another bulb to the circuit. Use two more wires, a bulb, and bulb holder. What, if anything, happens to the brightness of the lights?

inferring   **E.** How can you explain the results in A through D? That is, how does electricity seem to flow in a parallel circuit?

TEACHING COMMENT

PREPARATION AND BACKGROUND

In a parallel circuit, the wires are arranged to bypass a burned-out or missing light. Therefore, adding more bulbs to the circuit does not noticeably affect bulb brightness. Each bulb beyond receives the same flow of electricity (but all bulbs must have the same resistance in order to burn equally bright).

GENERALIZATION

In a parallel circuit, the electricity flows both to and around each connected bulb.

SAMPLE PERFORMANCE OBJECTIVES

Knowledge: The child can set up a working parallel circuit with two or more bulbs.

Process: The child can predict the effect on other parts of a parallel circuit when one or more parts are disconnected.

INVESTIGATION: *HIDDEN PARTS OF ELECTRIC CIRCUITS*

Suppose you have a folder like that shown in Figure 12-16. Notice the four holes on the front cover. Each hole has aluminum foil underneath, so each looks the same. Now, look at the back of the front cover. A foil strip goes from Hole 1 to Hole 3. It conducts electricity like a wire. However, only small pieces cover Holes 2 and 4. Suppose you do not know where the strip is, and you cannot open the folder.

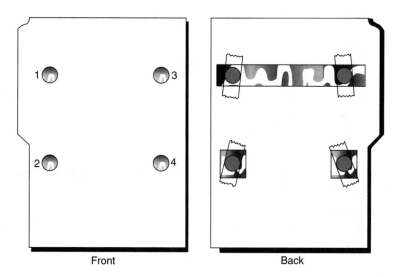

Front   Back

Figure 12-16

EXPLORATORY PROBLEM

How can you test for and find the hidden strip?

NEEDED

paper punch	ruler
D-size battery	pencil
manila folder	scissors
aluminum foil	two wires (30-centimeter or 12-inch)
sticky tape	flashlight bulb

TRY THIS

1. First prepare your own folder. Cut a regular-size folder in half, the shorter way. (Save half for later use.)

2. Punch four holes and cover them with foil as in Figure 12-16. Fasten the foil with sticky tape. Number the holes on the cover.

3. Now prepare your tester as in Figure 12-17. Bare the ends of two wires. Tape the ends to a battery. Bend one of the opposite wire ends into a loop. Wrap the other end around the bulb base and twist it to hold it fast.

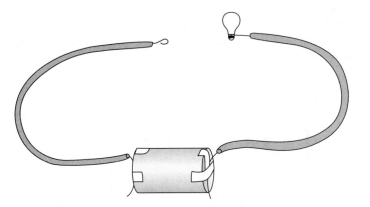

Figure 12-17

4. Touch the bulb bottom to the looped end of the other wire. If the bulb lights, you are ready to test your folder.

5. Press the bulb bottom into one hole. Press the wire loop into another hole. Test these pairs of holes; see which completes the circuit and lights the bulb:

1—2   2—3   3—4
1—3   2—4
1—4

DISCOVERY PROBLEMS

inferring and experimenting   **A.** Suppose you have tested another folder. Here are the results:

Paired Holes	Bulb Lights
1—2	yes
1—3	no
1—4	yes
2—3	no
2—4	yes
3—4	no

Let's say there are two strips connecting holes. How do you think they are arranged? Is more than one way possible? Make drawings of your ideas. Then prepare a folder and test your ideas.

inferring

B. Can you test and find out how different folders are "wired"? Have others prepare hidden circuits for you. (You can do the same for them.) Keep a record of your results and what you observe. Then open each folder to check your observations.

TEACHING COMMENT

PREPARATION AND BACKGROUND

In this case, the foil strip conductor is hidden and stretches between two holes. Touching the bulb bottom and the free wire end to the strip completes the circuit, allowing electricity to flow. The free wire end is bent into a loop to avoid gouging the foil.

GENERALIZATION

Parts of an electric circuit may be inferred from tests if the wires are hidden.

SAMPLE PERFORMANCE OBJECTIVES

Process: The child can use a circuit tester to connect hidden wires and infer the location of the wires.

Knowledge: The child can explain that a bulb lights when an electric circuit is completed in any of several combinations of connections.

ACTIVITY: *HOW CAN YOU MAKE AN ELECTRIC "NERVE TESTER" GAME?*

NEEDED

bare copper bell wire (60 centimeters or 2 feet)
number 22 or 24 insulated wire
clay
flashlight bulb

sticky tape
bulb holder
heavy cardboard
scissors

TRY THIS

1. Put two lumps of clay on some cardboard, as shown in Figure 12-18.
2. Bend the heavy bare copper wire as shown and stick each end into a clay lump.
3. Cut three pieces of the lighter, insulated wire as shown. Bare the ends.
4. Attach the three wires to the bulb holder and battery. Attach the free end of the battery wire to the end of the heavy wire. Twist it around and push the twisted wires slightly into the clay.

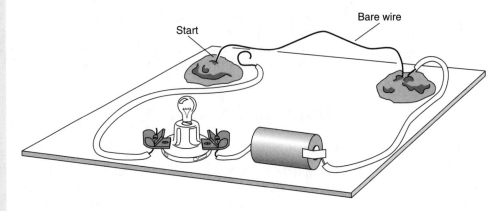

Figure 12-18

5. Bend the free end of the light bulb wire around a pencil to make a slightly open loop. Touch the loop end to the heavy wire. See if the light goes on.

6. To play the game, carefully place the open loop over the heavy wire so the wire is inside the loop. Move the loop from one end to the other and back without touching the heavy wire. If it touches, the light will go on. The person who lights the bulb least often wins. Predict and observe the following:

   a. Who has the steadiest nerves in the class?

   b. How does practice help?

   c. Is your left hand shakier than your right hand?

   d. Are people shakier before or after lunch? What other things might affect how shaky people are?

TEACHING COMMENT

Any single-strand, somewhat stiff wire will serve for the heavier wire. Even a piece cut from a wire coat hanger will work if the paint is sanded off. To make the bulb light more brightly when the wire is touched, use two batteries in series.

ACTIVITY: HOW CAN YOU MAKE A TWO-WAY BLINKER SYSTEM?

NEEDED

two flashlight bulbs and holders
four large tacks
two small wooden blocks
hammer
thin aluminum pie pan

scissors
sticky tape
wire (6 meters or 7 yards long)
D-size battery
partner

TRY THIS

1. Cut three short pieces of wire and two equally long wires, as shown in Figure 12-19. Bare the ends of all five wires.

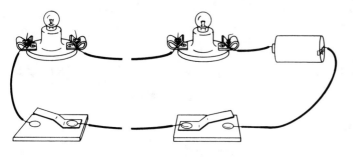

Figure 12-19

2. Cut 2 strips 10 centimeters (4 inches) long from the pie pan. Attach the strips, wires, and battery. Use tape to fasten wires to the battery. Use a hammer to pound in the tacks.

3. To send dot–dash signals, press the key a short or longer time. The second key must be held down by your partner while you are sending a message. Both lights will flash on and off as signals are sent.

4. Try using the International Morse Code to send signals:

A	B	C	D
.—	—...	—.—.	—..
E	F	G	H
.	..—.	——.	....
I	J	K	L
..	.———	—.—	.—..
M	N	O	P
——	—.	———	.——.
Q	R	S	T
——.—	.—.	...	—
U	V	W	X
..—	...—	.——	—..—
Y	Z		
—.——	——..		

a. What messages can you send and receive?

b. How can you send clearer messages?

TEACHING COMMENT

If both lights are dim, add a second battery in series; if only one bulb is dim, replace it with another that matches the bright bulb.

ELECTRIC FLOW EXPERIENCES
(Concepts page 319)

INVESTIGATION: *MATERIALS THAT CONDUCT ELECTRICITY*

You know electricity can travel through a wire, but how about other materials?

EXPLORATORY PROBLEM

How can you find out which materials conduct electricity?

NEEDED

small wooden objects	sticky tape
pencil	small plastic objects
small glass objects	flashlight bulb
flashlight (D-size) battery	small rubber objects
small metal objects	two wires (30 centimeters or 12 inches long)

TRY THIS

1. Arrange your materials as shown in Figure 12-20, except for the key. Bare both ends of each wire. Be sure the wire is wrapped tightly around the bulb base by twisting the end.

2. Touch the bulb bottom to the end of the other wire. If the bulb lights, you are ready to test materials.

Figure 12-20

3. Get some objects to test, such as a key. Touch the bulb bottom to one part. Touch the end of the other wire to another part. If the bulb lights, the object is a conductor of electricity. If it does not light, the object is a nonconductor.

DISCOVERY PROBLEMS

observing and communicating **A.** What, if any, rubber objects are conductors? plastic objects? metal objects? wooden objects? glass objects? Make a chart like this one to record your findings:

Object	Made From	Conductor	Nonconductor
Key	metal	X	
Others			

observing **B.** Some objects are made of several materials. With a pencil you can test wood, paint, metal, rubber, and graphite. Which of these will conduct electricity?

observing **C.** Look around the room. What other objects can you test that are made of several materials?

inferring **D.** Make your conductor tester more powerful. Use two batteries end to end. Test some materials again. How do these results compare with your first results?

TEACHING COMMENT

PREPARATION AND BACKGROUND

If the bulb is to operate properly, the wire wrapped around the bulb base should be twisted tightly for good contact.

GENERALIZATION

Metals are usually good conductors of electricity; most other solid materials are non-conductors or poor conductors.

SAMPLE PERFORMANCE OBJECTIVES

Process: The child can classify materials as electrical conductors or nonconductors after testing them with an electrical circuit.

Knowledge: Shown new materials, the child can predict which will, or will not, conduct electricity.

INVESTIGATION: *How to Measure Bulb Brightness*

Have you noticed that a bulb burns less brightly as a battery wears down? A bulb's brightness can help you know how fresh a battery is.

EXPLORATORY PROBLEM

How can you measure the brightness of a lit flashlight bulb?

NEEDED

two sheets of paper   partner
flashlight bulbs   several batteries of the same size (D)
wire (30 centimeters or 12 inches long)   pencil

TRY THIS

1. Have a partner light a bulb with one battery and wire.
2. Tear a small piece from a paper sheet.
3. Hold it tightly against the bulb. Can you see the glow through the paper? (See Figure 12-21.)
4. Tear off another piece of paper. Hold both pieces together tightly against the bulb. Can you still see the glow through the double thickness?

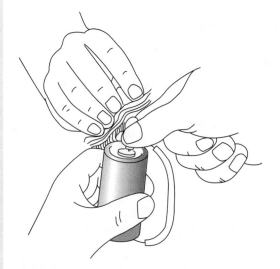

Figure 12-21

5. Keep adding pieces until you cannot see the bulb's glow.

6. Record the largest number of pieces through which you saw a glow.

DISCOVERY PROBLEMS

measuring and classifying

A. Get some batteries of the same size. How can you compare how strong each is? Can you put them in order from weakest to strongest? Record your findings.

predicting and communicating

B. How many times brighter will the bulb be with two batteries? three batteries? Add batteries end to end. The raised button end of each battery should face the same way. Record your findings.

measuring and classifying

C. Get different flashlight bulbs. How can you compare how brightly each burns? Can you put them in order from dimmest to brightest? Record findings. Will someone else get the same results?

TEACHING COMMENT

PREPARATION AND BACKGROUND

Most fresh D-size flashlight batteries can be interchanged and a given bulb will glow with no noticeable difference in brightness. However, as batteries wear down unevenly, the brightness is affected.

GENERALIZATION

The brightness of a flashlight bulb may vary because of its resistance to electricity and the power of the battery.

SAMPLE PERFORMANCE OBJECTIVES

Process: The child can measure the relative brightness of lighted flashlight bulbs.

Knowledge: When shown a lighted bulb that glows dimly, the child can explain that one reason for the dimness may be the weakness of the battery.

ACTIVITY: HOW CAN YOU MAKE A DIMMER SWITCH?

NEEDED

graphite (pencil "lead" about 7 centimeters or 3 inches)
circuit tester
sticky tape

TRY THIS

1. Tape each end of the graphite to a table top.
2. Touch the bulb base of the tester to the graphite. Touch the wire end just next to it. The bulb should light.
3. Slowly, move the wire end of the tester along the graphite. Move it first away from the bulb, then back again, as in Figure 12-22.

   a. What happens to the bulb brightness as the graphite connection gets longer? shorter?
   b. Where have you used dimmer switches at home or elsewhere?

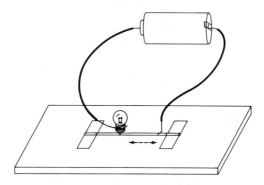

Figure 12-22

Teaching Comment

Graphite from either a mechanical or a cut-apart wooden pencil may be used. Graphite is resistant to electricity. If the tester bulb does not light, try adding one or two more batteries in series.

Activity: *How Does a Fuse Work?*

NEEDED

three D-size batteries
small piece of heavy cardboard
three short wires
two all-metal tacks
flashlight bulb and holder
foil from a gum wrapper
scissors

TRY THIS

1. Prepare the fuse. Cut a piece from the gum wrapper about 4 centimeters (1.6 inch) long and 0.5 centimeter (.2 inch) wide. Leave the paper attached to the foil. Cut a V-shaped nick in the middle of the piece, so there is barely any foil left.

2. Bare the ends of the wires. Also, bare a small section in the middle of two wires.

3. Set up the materials as shown in Figure 12-23.

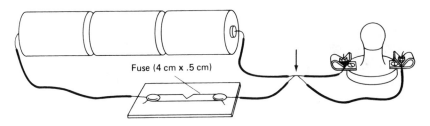

Fuse (4 cm x .5 cm)

Figure 12-23

4. Holding the insulated part of the wire, touch one bare wire part with the other. This makes a short circuit.

   a. What happens to the fuse? to the wires? to the light?

   b. Why do you think it is important to have a fuse in a house current?

ELECTROMAGNET EXPERIENCES
(Concepts page 321)

INVESTIGATION: ELECTROMAGNETS

Suppose you have some wire, a large nail, and a flashlight battery. With these materials you can make a magnet or an electromagnet.

EXPLORATORY PROBLEM

How can you make an electromagnet?

NEEDED

pencil	partner
box of paper clips	large iron nail
wire (2 meters or about 6 feet)	two flashlight batteries

TRY THIS

1. Get a large nail. Touch it to a paper clip to test the nail for magnetism. The nail should be free of magnetism to start.

2. Bare the wire ends. Wrap the wire tightly around the nail. Leave about ½ meter (1½ feet) of wire free at both ends.

3. Have your partner touch the bare wire ends to a battery. (See Figure 12-24.) Touch the nail end to some paper clips. How many paper clips does your electromagnet pick up?

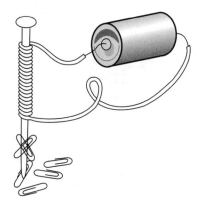

Figure 12-24

4. Have your partner move one wire away from the battery. What happens? *Note:* Do not leave the battery connected for more than 10 seconds each time.

DISCOVERY PROBLEMS

observing

A. Which end of your electromagnet will pick up more clips?

experimenting, communicating and predicting

B. How can you change the strength of your electromagnet? Make a record of what you try and the results. What will happen if you wrap more wire around the nail? What will happen if you take away the iron nail? What will happen if you switch a pencil for the nail? What will happen if you use an aluminum rod instead of the nail? What will happen if you use two batteries end to end?

observing

C. Can an electromagnet attract anything a regular magnet cannot attract?

TEACHING *COMMENT*

PREPARATION AND BACKGROUND

Use number 22 or 24 bell wire insulated with plastic. Strip off some insulation at both ends so good contact can be made with the battery. A regular D-size flashlight battery works well. Be sure to advise children that the wires should be held to the battery no more than about 10 seconds without interruption. Otherwise, its power will be drained quickly. A 3- to 4-inch iron nail should be adequate for the core of the electromagnet. If possible, get a similar-sized rod of aluminum. It will present an interesting contrast if used in place of the nail.

Most of the materials attracted to an electromagnet fall when the electromagnet is disconnected from the battery. One paper clip or other light item may remain. This shows that there is some magnetism left in the nail.

GENERALIZATION

Electricity flowing through a wire acts like a magnet; its magnetic power can be increased in several ways.

SAMPLE PERFORMANCE OBJECTIVES

Process: The child can state at least one hypothesis about how an electromagnet's strength may be increased.

Knowledge: The child can demonstrate how an electromagnet works.

FOR YOUNGER CHILDREN

Some primary students may have trouble manipulating the materials.

GENERATING ELECTRICITY EXPERIENCES
(Concepts page 323)

INVESTIGATION: *STATIC ELECTRICITY*

When you comb your hair on a dry day, does it crackle and stick to the comb? Have you felt a shock when you touched something after crossing a carpet? These are examples of static electricity. You can get static electricity by rubbing different objects together.

EXPLORATORY PROBLEM

What objects can you rub together to produce static electricity?

NEEDED

plastic spoon and fork	piece of wool and nylon
paper and pencil	sticky tape
heavy string	plastic bag
rubber comb	

TRY THIS

1. Attach string to the spoon with sticky tape. Attach it where the spoon balances. Hang the spoon from a table edge. Tape the string end to the table.

2. Hold the fork backward. Bring the fork handle near the hanging spoon handle, but don't touch it (Figure 12-25). Notice that probably nothing happens. So far, there is no static electricity.

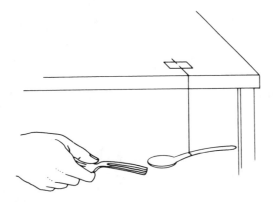

Figure 12-25

3. Rub each handle with some wool. Bring the fork handle near the spoon again. Watch what happens.

4. Rub one handle again with wool but the other with nylon. Watch what happens. (Static electricity may have either a positive [+] or a negative [−] charge. When two objects have the same charge, positive or negative, they *repel* or push each other away. When each has a different charge, they attract each other.)

DISCOVERY PROBLEMS

inferring

    A. Did each object in Step 3 have the same charge or did they have different charges? How about in Step 4?

observing and communicating

    B. What happens when you rub the handles with different materials? Which combinations make the handles repel? attract? Keep a careful record. To do so, you might set up a chart like this:

Fork Rubbed With	Spoon Rubbed With		
	Wool	Plastic	Nylon
Wool	Repel		
Plastic			
Nylon			

predicting

After you complete the first column, can you predict the remaining results?

experimenting

C. What results will you get if you substitute other objects for the plastic fork? For example, what happens if you rub a rubber comb with each material?

TEACHING COMMENT

BACKGROUND AND PREPARATION

Almost any plastic items may be substituted for the fork and spoon. The use of a heavy string will keep the suspended object from spinning too freely. Students will find that using an unlike material in Problem C will change their findings. Postpone this activity on rainy or especially humid days, as results will be less noticeable.

GENERALIZATION

Rubbing different materials together may produce static electricity. Like charges repel, and unlike charges attract each other.

SAMPLE PERFORMANCE OBJECTIVES

Knowledge: The child can demonstrate that identical objects rubbed with different materials will develop unlike static charges.

Process: The child can use data on a simple chart to predict new data.

INVESTIGATION: *A WAY TO GENERATE ELECTRICITY*

Have you ever seen an electric generator in a power plant? Usually, a huge magnet spins and produces an electric current in a coil of wire. You can even produce a current by moving a small magnet in and out of a small coil of wire. But the current will not be enough to light a bulb. To tell that there is a current, you need a current detector, or *galvanometer*.

EXPLORATORY PROBLEM

How can you generate electricity and tell it is being produced?

NEEDED

insulated wire (12 meters or 13 yards)
magnetic compass
two strong magnets (one stronger)
scissors
sticky tape

TRY THIS

1. Bare the wire ends with scissors.
2. Coil 50 turns of wire around your hand. Slip off the coil and fasten it in three places with sticky tape. This will keep the coil tight.
3. Wrap 20 turns of wire narrowly around the compass. This will be your galvanometer (Figure 12-26).
4. Twist the bare ends of the wire together to close the circuit.
5. Push a magnet end into the coil. See how the compass needle moves. Pull the magnet out of the coil. Watch again how the needle moves. This shows you have

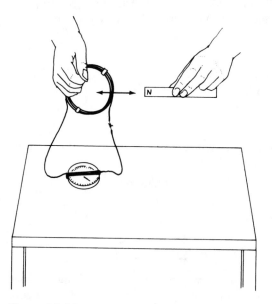

Figure 12-26

generated a current each time. The farther the needle moves, the stronger the current. (However, be sure the magnet is far enough from the compass so it does not *directly* affect it. You want the electricity in the *wires* to move the needle.)

DISCOVERY PROBLEMS

observing   **A.** Does it make any difference if the coil or magnet moves?

observing   **B.** What happens to the needle if you move the magnet faster? slower?

observing   **C.** What difference does it make if you move the magnet's other end?

observing   **D.** How does using a stronger or weaker magnet affect the compass needle?

observing   **E.** How does changing the number of turns in the coil affect the needle?

experimenting   **F.** What is the strongest current you can generate? That is, how far can you make the compass needle move?

TEACHING COMMENT

PREPARATION AND BACKGROUND

By moving the magnet alternately in two directions, the current that is produced also alternates directions. This is shown by the compass needle moving first one way, then the other. The mechanical energy used to move the magnet comes, in this case, from the students. The teaching strategy of the discovery sequence is to give enough experience for students to experiment on their own in F.

GENERALIZATION

An electric current may be generated when a magnet and a wire coil interact. A galvanometer may be used to detect the current.

SAMPLE PERFORMANCE OBJECTIVES

Knowledge: The child can construct a crude galvanometer and use it to detect small differences in electric currents.

Process: The child can generate a stronger electric current by experimenting with several variables.

REFERENCES

American Association for the Advancement of Science. (1993). *Benchmarks for science literacy*. New York: Oxford University Press.

National Research Council. (1996). *National science education standards*. Washington, DC: National Academy Press.

SELECTED TRADE BOOKS: ELECTRICAL ENERGY

For Younger Children

Bailey, M. W. (1978). *Electricity*. Raintree.

Berger, M. (1990). *Switch on, switch off.* Harper Collins.

Bains, R. (1981). *Discovering electricity*. Troll Associates.

Challand, H. (1986). *Experiments with electricity*. Children's Press.

Curren, P. (1977). *I know an electrician*. Putnam.

Lillegard, D., & Stoker, W. (1986). *I can be an electrician*. Children's Press.

Taylor, B. (1991). *Batteries and magnets*. Watts.

Wade, H. (1979). *Electricity*. Raintree.

For Older Children

Ardley, N. (1984). *Discovering electricity*. Watts.

Brandt, K. (1985). *Electricity*. Troll Associates.

Cobb, V. (1986). *More power to you!* Little, Brown.

De Bruin, J. (1985). *Young scientist explores electricity and magnetism*. Good Apple.

Gutnik, M. J. (1986). *Electricity: from Faraday to solar generators*. Watts.

Mackie, D. (1986). *Electricity*. Penworthy.

Math, I. (1981). *Wires and watts*. Scribners.

Provenzo, E. F., & Provenzo, A. B. (1982). *Rediscovering electricity*. Oak Tree.

Stanley, L. R. (1980). *Easy to make electric gadgets*. Harvey.

Taylor, B. (1990). *Electricity and magnets*. Watts.

Vogt, G. (1985). *Electricity and magnetism*. Watts.

Vogt, G. (1986). *Generating electricity*. Watts.

Ward, A. (1986). *Experimenting with batteries, bulbs, and wires*. David & Charles.

Whyman, K. (1986). *Electricity and magnetism*. Watts.

Zubrowski, B. (1991). *Blinkers and buzzers*. Morrow.

Resource Books

Butzow, C. M., & Butzow, J. W. (1989). *Science through children's literature. An integrated approach* (batteries and electric circuit topics, pp. 226–231). Teacher Ideas Press.

Shaw, D. G., & Dybdahl, C. S. (1996). *Integrating science and language arts. A sourcebook for K–6 teachers* (electric circuit topics, pp. 102–103). Allyn and Bacon.

SIMPLE MACHINES AND HOW THEY WORK

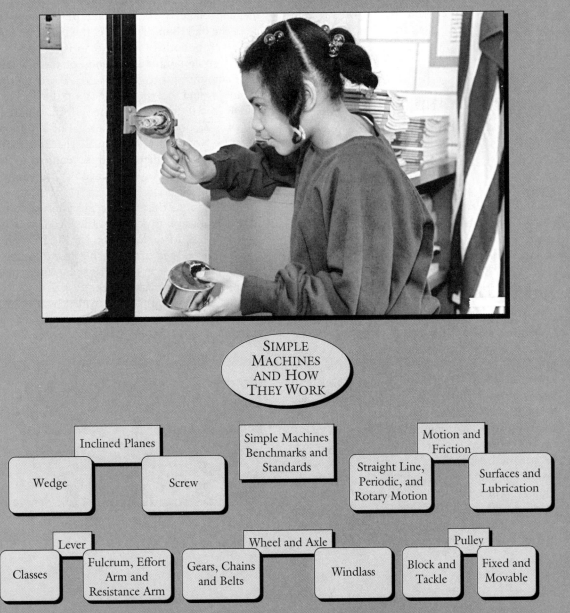

SIMPLE
MACHINES
AND HOW
THEY WORK

Inclined Planes

Simple Machines
Benchmarks and
Standards

Motion and
Friction

Wedge

Screw

Straight Line,
Periodic, and
Rotary Motion

Surfaces and
Lubrication

Lever

Wheel and Axle

Pulley

Classes

Fulcrum, Effort
Arm and
Resistance Arm

Gears, Chains
and Belts

Windlass

Block and
Tackle

Fixed and
Movable

Imagine a parade of the world's machines including airplanes, tweezers, bulldozers, baby carriages, computers, and egg beaters—almost endless line of inventions without which we would fare far less well. But perhaps the most remarkable thing about these inventions lies in their construction. All machines, no matter how complex, are variations of just six simple machines. These are the inclined plane (ramp), wedge, screw, lever, wheel and axle (windlass), and pulley. We'll consider these machines and the effects of motion and friction on them in this chapter.

SCREWS AND INCLINED PLANES CONCEPTS
(Experiences p. 361)

For any machine to do work, force must overcome gravity, inertia, molecular cohesion (the binding force that holds materials together), and friction. Machines may be used to reduce the force needed to do work, speed up work, or change the direction of a force.

Inclined Planes

Although they may not have thought about it, even small children have had experiences with inclined planes, such as climbing stairs, walking up a hill, or coasting down a slanted driveway on roller skates. They know from these experiences that it is harder to climb a steep hill than a gradual hill. Children may even unknowingly use the idea that distance may be increased to decrease force, as when a bicycle rider rides diagonally back and forth up a hill. This background of common experiences lets us focus on force/distance relationships fairly quickly when working with inclined planes.

Does an inclined plane or other simple machine make work "easier"? No, if we mean that some part of the total effort is saved. In terms of *work,* or force moving a resistance over a distance, it is impossible to get out of a machine any more than is put into a machine. Another way of saying this is:

Effort times distance equals resistance times distance, or ED = RD.

Let's apply this idea to the inclined plane in Figure 13-1. Suppose we want to push a 50-pound barrel to a height of 5 feet and the inclined plane is 10 feet long. If we were to push the barrel up the incline, it would take less force (25 pounds of force) than if we were to pick it straight up (50 pounds of force.) The total amount of force to move the barrel up the incline would be the distance of the incline, which is 10 feet, times the effort required, which is 25 pounds. This is a total of 250 foot-pounds. Notice that this equals the 250 foot-pounds of work which would be required to lift the barrel straight up a distance of 5 feet times an effort of 50 pounds.

This assumes that we are physically able to do the work in both cases. Yet it *is* easier for us to apply less force for a longer distance and time. Muscles get tired quickly from concentrated, heavy work. It is in that sense, then, that a simple machine makes work "easier."

The reduction of force provided by a simple machine is called its *mechanical advantage.* This is found by *dividing the force of the resistance by*

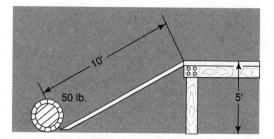

Figure 13-1
An inclined plane.

the force of the effort. In the foregoing example, the mechanical advantage is

$$\frac{R\,(50\;pounds)}{E\,(25\;pounds)} = 2$$

In other words, it is twice as easy to lift the barrel with the inclined plane as without it. Or we can say it takes half as much effort.

Students can make crude measurements to grasp the force/distance relationship. For instance, a string can be used to compare the length of an inclined plane with the height to which it rises. A rubber band attached to an object may have a ruler held beside it to measure different degrees of applied force in terms of "stretch." A spring scale, if available, will be even more effective than a rubber band.

Wedges

A wedge can be thought of as two inclined planes placed back to back. Although the classic use of this machine has waned along with professional rail-splitters and wood-choppers, the wedge principle is employed in many other ways. For example, "streamlining" is a way of better enabling objects to pierce air and water. More speed can be achieved with the same amount of applied force. Paper cutters, knives, pencil sharpeners, nails, and needles are all wedges we use every day for cutting or piercing functions.

Screws

"The screw is just an inclined plane wrapped around a nail." This is what one child said, and it is a fairly accurate description. We usually think of the screw as a nail-like object with a spiral thread that holds together pieces of wood or metal. But other applications of this machine are all around us.

There are spiral staircases, roads that wind around a steep hill or mountain, vises for workbenches, clamps to hold things together,

adjustable piano stools, and the adjustable parts of wrenches, to name just a few. Sometimes a screw is not so obvious, like propellers for ships and airplanes.

When used to lift things, the mechanical advantage of the screw is the greatest of any simple machine. It is relatively easy for a small person to lift up the front of an automobile with a screw-type jack, and jackscrews employed by house movers actually lift entire houses off their foundations. As with an inclined plane, though, the price paid for such a gain in force is increased distance.

Each time a screw is given a complete turn, it advances into a piece of wood or lifts an object only as far as the distance between its threads. This distance is called *pitch* and is illustrated in Figure 13-2. The paired drawings show that two screws of similar size, but different pitches, would vary in the number of times turned if screwed into some wood or used to lift something. We expect a steep spiral staircase to take more effort than a longer, gradual one when walking up to the same height. Likewise, the steeper the pitch of a screw, the more force is needed to make it rotate. However, it advances farther and faster than one with a narrower, more gradual pitch.

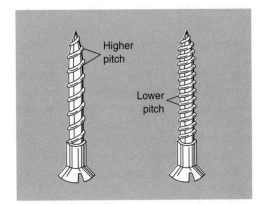

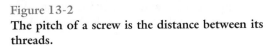

Figure 13-2
The pitch of a screw is the distance between its threads.

The mathematical relationships here are identical to those of other simple machines. Mechanical advantage is again found by dividing resistance by effort.

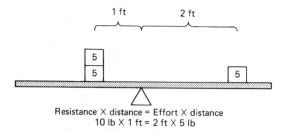

Figure 13-3
To find the mechanical advantage of a lever, divide the effort-arm length by the resistance-arm length.

LEVER CONCEPTS
(Experiences page 363)

No one knows who actually first contrived the lever, but it has been known and used for a very long time. The ancient Greek scientist Archimedes is supposed to have said he could move the world if given a long enough lever, a fulcrum, and place to stand. It is widely assumed that primitive people also had knowledge of levers, but probably only in a practical way.

The principles of this simple machine are used in so many ways that a moment's reflection produces surprising examples: The ancient Japanese sport of judo is based on knowledge that the human skeleton is comprised of lever systems. Also, a golfer with long arms may swing the club head faster than a golfer with shorter arms.

Three Parts

The seesaw is a lever familiar to most children. It has three parts: (1) *fulcrum,* or point on which it pivots; (2) *effort arm,* the part on which the force is exerted; and (3) *the resistance,* or load, arm, that part which bears the load to be raised. When the seesaw is perfectly balanced on the fulcrum, the resistance and effort arms will alternate if two equally heavy riders alternately push against the ground to make the seesaw go up and down.

As with other machines, effort times distance (from the fulcrum) equals resistance times distance (from the fulcrum). This is shown in Fig-

ure 13-3. The mechanical advantage in this example is 2. Another way to calculate the mechanical advantage is simply to divide the effort-arm length by the resistance-arm length. Friction is usually so minor in the lever that it does not need to be taken into account.

Primary children can arrive at an intuitive understanding of the "law of levers" if they are given experience with balancing objects.

Three Classes

Levers are found with parts arranged in three different combinations called *classes.* Children do not need to memorize these combinations or even their examples. But analyzing how everyday levers work can sharpen their observation and classification skills. Notice the three arrangements in Figure 13-4. Seesaws, crowbars, and can openers are first-class levers. Two levers of this kind are placed together in tools such as scissors and pliers. By varying the effort-arm length, you change the amount of required force or gain in speed and distance. This type also changes direction of movement. You exert force in a direction opposite to which the load moves. If both effort and resistance arms are equal, however, a first-class lever can change only the direction of a force. Neither

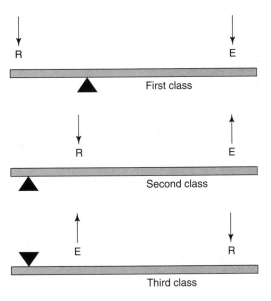

Figure 13-4
Three classes of levers; *R* is resistance, E effort.

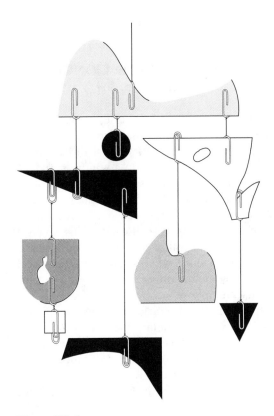

Figure 13-5
A tagboard and paper clip mobile.

reduced force nor gain in speed and distance takes place.

Second-class levers are illustrated by the wheelbarrow and post puller. A nutcracker illustrates joined, double levers of this type. Speed or distance are not as likely to be considerations when using a second-class lever as in the previous case.

Should you forget third-class levers, just think of your arm. Your elbow is the fulcrum, your bicep provides the effort at a point just below and opposite the elbow, and your fist represents the load or resistance. Other common applications are found in the broom, baseball bat, fly swatter, and fishing pole, to name just a few. Sugar or ice cube tongs represent double levers of the class. Analysis of this lever reveals that force is traded to get added speed or distance. With a fishing pole, for example, you want to increase the speed of your hands to hook a nibbling fish securely before it can react and get away.

Mobiles

A mobile is a combination of several suspended levers with attached figures. In some mobiles, even the figures may function as levers (Figure 13-5).

When children work on mobiles, they may have problems balancing the figures and keeping them from touching. For solutions, they need to think about variables such as figure size and shape, string length, best position for figures, and where to fasten them. This sharpens their thinking skills. Mobiles are also an interesting way to combine artwork with science.

WHEEL AND AXLE CONCEPTS
(Experiences p. 369)

The windlass, or wheel and axle, is a commonly misunderstood simple machine. Although a windlass looks like a wagon wheel and axle, it is different. We put wheels on a wagon to reduce friction by lessening the surface area that comes in contact with the road. Its axles are stationary. Greater "leverage" is indeed present in a large wheel compared to a small wheel. This is why a large wheel can roll over uneven ground more easily than a small wheel. Still, a wagon wheel and axle combination is not regarded as a simple machine.

In a windlass, the axle and wheel are firmly fixed together. Spinning the axle causes the wheel to rotate; force at the axle is traded off to gain an advantage in speed and distance on the outside of the wheel. By turning the wheel, though, an advantage in force can be gained; speed and distance are then reduced or sacrificed at the axle.

A windlass is really a continuous lever on a continuous fulcrum. Therefore, when a handle is placed anywhere on the wheel, it becomes the end of the force arm. The axle's radius is the load arm. Figure 13-6 illustrates this idea.

The theoretical mechanical advantage in a windlass is calculated like that of a lever. If the effort-arm length is 18 inches and resistance arm length is 2 inches, mechanical advantage equals 9. Because friction is so great with a windlass, however, actual mechanical advantage is found only through dividing resistance by effort.

Placing the windlass handle (effort) ever farther away from the axle (fulcrum) decreases needed effort, just as it did with the lever. At the same time, it increases the distance through which the effort is applied.

Understanding the force/distance relationship makes it easy for children to see why a meat grinder needs a longer crank than a pencil sharpener (Figure 13-7), for example, and why

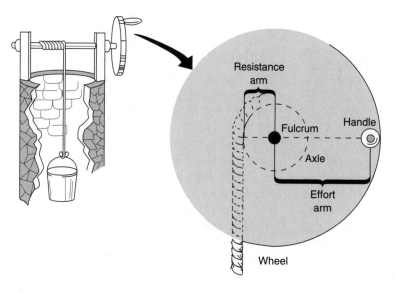

Figure 13-6
A windlass is a lever.

Figure 13-7
A pencil sharpener can be used as a wheel and axle.

a large steering wheel is easier to turn than a smaller one.

Gears, Chains, and Belts

Wheel and axle combinations may be modified to interact with one another by using belts, chains, and wheels with toothlike projections (gears). The bicycle is a common example of two modified wheels and axles joined by a chain. Because the front gear, or sprocket, is larger than the rear sprocket, one turn of the larger sprocket forces several or more turns of the smaller rear one. Older students can find the theoretical mechanical advantage of the larger sprocket by counting and comparing the number of teeth on each sprocket.

PULLEY CONCEPTS
(Experiences page 374)

Pulleys for teaching can be bought through science supply houses. Yet in elementary school activities, two clothesline pulleys or two smaller single pulleys, found in most hardware stores, should work just as well. "Single" pulleys have but one grooved wheel or sheave. Some pulleys have two or more sheaves for combined use with other pulleys in heavy lifting.

Fixed and Movable Pulleys

As its name implies, a *fixed pulley* is securely fastened to some object. A *movable pulley* moves vertically—or laterally, as the case may be—with the load (Figure 13-8).

The pulley's similarity to a lever and windlass is diagrammed in Figure 13-8. As with a windlass, the wheel-like arrangement is really a continuous lever.

Observe why a fixed pulley can do no more than change the direction of a force. Like a seesaw whose fulcrum is centered, the effort arm and resistance arm are of equal length. There is no useful mechanical advantage. If one foot of rope is pulled downward, the resistance moves upward one foot. This happens, for example, when a flag is raised on a flagpole.

Notice why a movable pulley offers a theoretical mechanical advantage of two. The resistance arm is only half the effort-arm length. Like a wheelbarrow, this is a variation of a second-class lever. Distance is traded for decreased effort. We must pull the rope two feet for each foot the load is lifted.

Block and Tackle

By placing a fixed and movable pulley in combination, we are able not only to change the direction of a force but also to decrease the force necessary to lift a load. Such an arrangement is called a *block and tackle* (Figure 13-9). By adding more movable pulleys (or pulleys with two or more sheaves), effort can be reduced even further.

Friction finally limits how far we can go in adding pulleys to reduce effort. It can be partly overcome by greasing or oiling the axle.

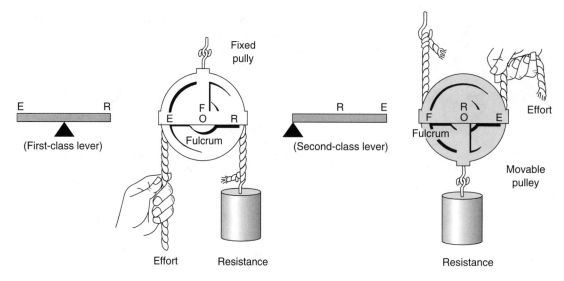

Figure 13-8
A fixed pulley offers no mechanical advantage because its effort and resistance arms are equally long. A movable pulley, however, does make work easier because its resistance arm is only half the length of the effort arm.

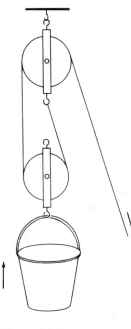

Figure 13-9
Block and tackle.

Since each rope in a block-and-tackle setup supports an equal fraction of a load, it is easy to know the theoretical mechanical advantage. Two supporting ropes have a mechanical advantage of two, three ropes three, and so on. Because of friction, though, actual mechanical advantage must be calculated through dividing resistance by effort, as with all simple machines.

Students may use a rubber band (or spring scale) in the activities to measure differences in the force needed to lift things with pulleys. To attach a rubber band, first fashion a paper-clip hook. Simply pierce or loop the pulley cord at the place where you wish to measure needed force, insert the hook, and then attach a rubber band to it. As before, a ruler can measure the amount of stretch.

MOTION AND FRICTION CONCEPTS
(Experiences p. 376)

Most machines we use are *complex;* that is, they are combinations of simple machines. It is interesting to see how these machines and their parts move and interact.

Three Basic Motions

Some machines have mainly a *straight-line motion*. A few examples are toy or real trains, bicycle (turning requires some leaning), roller skates, and steamrollers.

Some machines or their parts make a repeated forward and backward movement called *periodic motion*. The pendulum in a grandfather clock is one example. Others are a swing, a mechanical walking doll, a metronome, and some lawn sprinklers.

A number of machines or their parts make a continuous spinning motion in one direction as they work. This is *rotary motion*. A few examples are the merry-go-round, the turntable on a record player, a rotary lawn sprinkler, and clock hands.

It can be fascinating to examine mechanical toys and other machines. Their parts are designed to produce a particular motion and, in some cases, to change it.

Any moving machine or part continues to produce its designed motion unless another force is applied to alter, reverse, or stop it. When we rotate a telephone dial, for instance, a metal stop prevents us from going beyond one rotation. A spring then returns the dial to its original position. Also, the front wheel of a moving bicycle may be turned by applying a force to the handlebars. But what happens if the force is applied too strongly? Perhaps painful experience has taught you that bicycle

and rider will continue in a straight line until road friction finally stops both.

Friction

Accompanying all motion is *friction,* the resistance produced when two surfaces rub together. No surface is perfectly smooth. The tiny ridges in a "smooth" surface, or the larger bumps and hollows in a rough one, catch and resist when the surfaces rub together. The mutual attraction of molecules on the opposing surfaces also adds to the resistance we call friction. Surface pressure is another condition that affects friction. A heavy object has more friction than a lighter one.

Lubricating a surface is effective because the oil or grease fills in the spaces between ridges and bumps. Opposing surfaces mostly slide against the lubricant rather than rubbing against each other.

In many machines, ball bearings or roller bearings are used to change sliding friction to rolling friction. Rolling friction is less than sliding friction because a load-bearing rolling object rolls over tiny surface ridges or bumps rather than catching against them.

Friction reduces a machine's efficiency by robbing some of its power (and so its energy). It also creates heat as surfaces rub and wears out parts. But not all of its effects are bad. Friction also allows us to brake a car or bicycle, walk or run, or write on paper. A frictionless world would create far more problems than it would solve.

SIMPLE MACHINES BENCHMARKS AND STANDARDS

Practical examples of the uses of simple machines will help reinforce the types of simple machines and how they can be used in combination with each other. Forces and motion related to the use of simple machines are common themes, as evidenced in the following sample Benchmarks and Standards:

SAMPLE BENCHMARKS (AAAS, 1993).

■ The way to change how something is moving is to give it a push or a pull (by Grades K–2, p. 89).

■ Something that is moving may move steadily or change its direction. The greater the force is, the greater the change in motion will be. The more massive an object is, the less effect a given force will have (by Grades 3–5, p. 89).

SAMPLE STANDARDS (NRC, 1996).

■ The position and motion of objects can be changed by pushing or pulling. The size of the change is related to the strength of the push or pull (by Grades K–4, p. 127).

■ The motion of an object can be described by its position, direction of motion, and speed. That motion can be measured and represented on a graph (by Grades 5–8, p. 154).

INVESTIGATIONS AND ACTIVITIES

SCREWS AND INCLINED PLANES
EXPERIENCES

(Concepts p. 352)

INVESTIGATION: *INCLINED PLANES*

It is easier to walk up a steep hill or a low hill? Suppose both hills were the same height, but one was twice as long. Which would be easier then? A hill is a kind of *inclined plane*.

EXPLORATORY PROBLEM

How can you measure the force needed to use an inclined plane?

NEEDED

flat board (60 centimeters or 2 feet)   seven same-sized books
flat board (120 centimeters or 4 feet)   paper clip
rubber band (or spring scale)   roller skate
ruler

TRY THIS

1. Lay an end of the smaller board on one book (Figure 13-10).

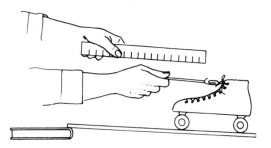

Figure 13-10

2. Place a roller skate on the board. Hook a bent paper clip around the tied shoelace. Attach a rubber band.

3. Pull the skate slowly up the board. Measure with a ruler how much the rubber band stretches. (Or measure the pull with a spring scale.)

4. Now make the inclined plane or "hill" three books high. Do Steps 2 and 3 again.

DISCOVERY PROBLEMS

measuring   **A.** What was the difference in rubber band stretch in the two trials?

measuring   **B.** How much stretch will there be with "hills" of different heights? Measure also a height of two books, then five and six books. (Do not measure four books now.) Record what you find on a graph such as this:

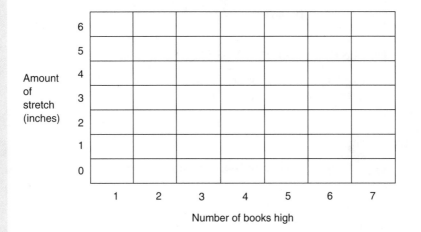

predicting   **C.** Examine your graph data for heights of one, two, three, five, and six books. Can you predict the stretch for four books? Write this down and then test your prediction.

predicting   **D.** Examine your data again. Can you predict the stretch for seven books?

predicting   **E.** Switch this board for one twice as long. Suppose you used one through seven books again. What do you think your results would be? Write down your ideas and then test them.

inferring   **F.** What pictures of different inclined planes can you bring to school?

TEACHING COMMENT

BACKGROUND AND PREPARATION

One long board, rather than two different-sized boards, can be used to demonstrate how changing board lengths affects the force needed to go up a given height. The books may first be placed under the midpoint of the board, and the board tilted. The tilted part beyond the books may be ignored. However, this can confuse some students, especially the younger ones. Pairs of boards of almost any lengths may be used, but the larger one should be twice as long as the smaller one.

A spring scale is likely to yield more accurate measurements than a rubber band. A rubber band may not stretch uniformly and, of course, does not indicate force in standard units. Try several rubber bands to select one that stretches easily for heights of one to seven books. If needed, snip and use a single strand.

Two kinds of predicting occur in this investigation. In Problem C, the child predicts *within* the data (interpolating); in D, the child predicts *beyond* the data (extrapolating).

GENERALIZATION

The force needed to go up an inclined plane increases with height and decreases with distance.

SAMPLE PERFORMANCE OBJECTIVES

Knowledge: The child can state that doubling the length of an inclined board halves the force needed to go up a given height.

Process: The child can accurately predict needed force within and beyond graphed data for an inclined plane.

FOR YOUNGER CHILDREN

Try the activity without the graphing of data. Younger students generally notice and understand why there are differences in rubber band stretch.

LEVER EXPERIENCES
(Concepts p. 354)

INVESTIGATION: *SOME COMMON LEVERS*

Have you used a baseball bat? a seesaw? a house broom? These and many other things we use are examples of *levers*. How levers work can be surprising. Some that look almost alike work differently. Some that look different work the same way.

EXPLORATORY PROBLEM

How can you tell in which ways levers are alike and different?

NEEDED

Real or picture examples of levers in everyday things (canoe paddle, crowbar, paper cutter, baseball bat, seesaw, post puller, house broom, can opener, wheelbarrow, tennis racket, golf club, boat oar)

TRY THIS

1. Figure 13-11 shows a fishing pole in action. Notice how this lever is used. The tip carries the load or resistance (R). The opposite end, which is held, moves very

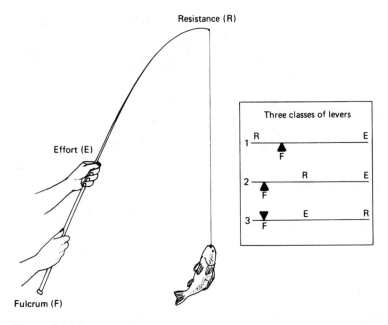

Figure 13-11

little. This is the fulcrum (F). To pull up the resistance takes effort (E). This happens *between* the fulcrum and resistance.

2. Study the three smaller drawings in Figure 13-11. Levers can be grouped into three classes, depending on how they are used. Each group has a place for the fulcrum, resistance, and effort. But notice that, in each group, the placement of these points is different. This is a good way to tell them apart.

DISCOVERY PROBLEMS

classifying   **A.** In which group does the fishing pole belong?

classifying   **B.** Examine real or picture examples of many levers. Use them, or think of how they are used. In which group does each belong? Here's a way to record what you find:

Lever	1. RFE	2. FRE	3. FER
Fishing pole			✓
Paper cutter			
Others			

inferring   **C.** Which of these levers are really alike?

classifying   **D.** Examine the bottom half of your arm. It is a lever, also. In which group does it belong?

inferring   **E.** Play a game with some friends. Think of a common lever. Can they find out what it is by asking questions? You can answer only yes or no. If they get stuck, act out the way it is used. (A good way for them to begin is to find out the load–fulcrum–effort order.)

classifying   **F.** What other real or picture examples can you find? In which group does each belong?

TEACHING COMMENT

BACKGROUND AND PREPARATION

It is the *internal* order of resistance–fulcrum–effort that counts in classifying levers. So there is no difference between R–F–E or E–F–R, for example (this may be a difficult concept for a few students).

    It is not important for children to memorize the internal order of each class. But it is worthwhile for them to develop skill in observing and classifying likenesses and differences in objects.

    In Problem D, the part played by the upper arm muscle (bicep) in moving the forearm may be confusing. The actual pull on the *forearm* is just below and opposite the elbow on the inside.

GENERALIZATION

Levers may be grouped by where places on each are used for the resistance, fulcrum, and effort.

SAMPLE PERFORMANCE OBJECTIVES

Knowledge: The child can demonstrate where to place a lever on a fulcrum to reduce effort.

Process: The child can classify examples of levers into three groups by how they work.

INVESTIGATION: *SOME COMMON DOUBLE LEVERS*

Scissors are an example of a double lever that has cutting parts. We use many tools that are double levers. How many can you name or describe? Some that look almost alike work differently. Some that look different work about the same way.

EXPLORATORY PROBLEM

How can you tell in which ways double levers are alike and different?

NEEDED

pliers	tweezers
lemon squeezer	nutcracker
sugar tongs	tin snips

TRY THIS

1. Figure 13-12 shows a pair of scissors. Notice how the parts are used, especially the cutting parts. When you cut something, it resists being cut. So each part that does this work is called the *resistance* (R).

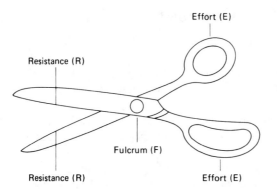

Figure 13-12

2. Notice where the two parts of the scissors join and pivot. This is the *fulcrum* (F).

3. Observe the handles in action. To cut something requires force or effort, so each of these parts is called the *effort* (E).

DISCOVERY PROBLEMS

observing **A.** All tools that are double levers have parts for the resistance (R), fulcrum (F), and effort (E). But they are not always in that order. Examine some real or picture examples of double-lever tools. Which tools are arranged differently? How many different arrangements do you find?

classifying **B.** You can classify these and other double levers by how the three parts are arranged. In which group will each fit? Here's a way to record what you find:

Double Lever	1. RFE	2. FRE	3. FER
Scissors	✓		
Pliers			
Others			

inferring   **C.** Can you name parts of your body that work like a double lever?

classifying   **D.** What other real or picture examples of double levers can you find? In which group does each belong?

TEACHING COMMENT

BACKGROUND AND PREPARATION

In classifying double levers, it is the *internal* order of the resistance–fulcrum–effort that counts, just as it did with single levers. There is no difference between R–F–E and E–F–R, for example.

GENERALIZATION

Double levers may be grouped by how places on each are used for the resistance, fulcrum, and effort.

SAMPLE PERFORMANCE OBJECTIVES

Knowledge: The child can explain where the places are on double levers for the resistance, fulcrum, and effort.

Process: The child can classify examples of double levers into three groups by how they work.

INVESTIGATION: *THE MAKING OF A MOBILE*

Notice the balanced group of objects in Figure 13-13. This is a *mobile*. The word means "something that moves." Even a tiny breeze can move the objects. They may almost seem to be alive!

What kind of mobile objects would you like to make? Fishes, birds, butterflies, balloons, and airplanes are all fun to do. You can even use cutout letters of your name.

EXPLORATORY PROBLEM

How can you make a mobile?

NEEDED

plastic soda straws
tagboard
thin knitting yarn
sticky tape
paper clips
ruler
scissors
crayons or paints and brushes

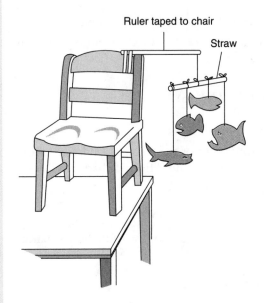

Ruler taped to chair

Straw

Figure 13-13

TRY THIS

1. Cut some strings of yarn 20 to 30 centimeters (8 to 12 inches) long.

2. Tie one end of each string to a paper clip.

3. Decide what kind of objects to hang. Then cut three or four objects from tagboard.

4. Set up a place to hang your mobile. Tape a ruler to a chair. Put the chair on a table.

5. Hang the objects from a straw with yarn. Loop the yarn once around the straw. Make half a knot. Then, pull the yarn tight. Clip the paper clip to each object in the usual way.

6. Try to balance the objects. Slide the yarn on the straw. Change where each object is clipped if necessary.

DISCOVERY PROBLEMS

experimenting and hypothesizing

A. How can you make a mobile with more straws and objects? It will help to draw your mobile on paper first. Start with a few materials. Add more later. Think about these things:

What can you do to balance your objects?

How can you keep the objects from touching?

How big should each object be? What shape? Where should each be placed?

How long should each string be? Where is it best to clip the string on each object?

hypothesizing **B.** How can you color your objects with crayons or paints?

TEACHING COMMENT

PREPARATION AND BACKGROUND

Making mobiles is an interesting way to combine artwork with valuable concepts about balance.

GENERALIZATION

For mobile objects to balance, we consider variables such as object size and shape, weight, string length, best positions for the objects, and where to fasten them.

SAMPLE PERFORMANCE OBJECTIVES

Process: When shown a simple unbalanced mobile, the child can infer which variable or variables need attention.

Knowledge: The child can explain how to make a mobile.

FOR OLDER CHILDREN

Invite older children to use common, but light, three-dimensional objects for mobiles (bottle caps, empty milk cartons, wire hangers) in multiple tiers.

WHEEL AND AXLE EXPERIENCES
(Concepts p. 356)

ACTIVITY: *HOW DOES A SCREWDRIVER HANDLE MAKE WORK EASIER?*

NEEDED

screwdriver with round handle
masking tape
piece of soft wood
screw
hammer

TRY THIS

1. Tap in the screw so it sticks into the wood.
2. Hold the screwdriver below the handle at the steel shank. Try to turn the screw.
3. Now hold the handle. Again, try to turn the screw.
   a. Which was easier?
   b. Maybe your hand slipped on the smooth steel shank. Probably it did not slip on the handle. What will happen if you wrap tape around both parts and try again?
   c. Which is easier this time?
4. Look at the screwdriver on end from the steel tip toward the handle. Notice the difference in width between the steel shank and the handle.
   d. Why do you think it is easier to turn a screw using the handle rather than using the shank?

INVESTIGATION: *WHEEL–BELT SYSTEMS*

Have you ever noticed how bicycle gears turn? The two gears are connected by a chain. When you push one gear around, the other moves too.

A gear is just a wheel with teeth. There are many ways to connect wheels. Often, they are connected with belts. Several connected wheels are called a *wheel–belt system*. You can make your own wheel–belt system with spools and rubber bands.

EXPLORATORY PROBLEM

How can you make a wheel–belt system?

NEEDED

four empty sewing spools	board (about the size of this page)
four finishing nails	our rubber bands
crayon	hammer

TRY THIS

1. Pound four nails into the board as shown in Figure 13-14.
2. Make one crayon dot on the rim of each spool.
3. Put a spool on each of two nails.
4. Place a rubber band around the two spools.
5. Turn one spool. Watch the other spool turn too.

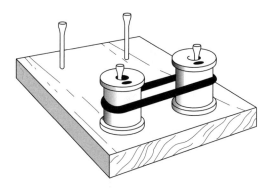

Figure 13-14

DISCOVERY PROBLEMS

predicting   **A.** How will the spools turn when connected in different ways? Notice the drawings in Figure 13-15. Each set of spools starts with the left spool. An arrow shows how each is turning. Another spool in the set has a question mark. It is next to a dot on the spool rim. See how the spools are connected.

Will the dot on the rim turn left or right? Make a record of what you think. Then use your wheel–belt board to find out.

predicting   **B.** Notice the Figure 13-16 drawings. How should the spools be connected to turn in these ways? How many different connections can you think of? Make drawings of what you think. Then, use your wheel–belt board to find out if they work.

experimenting   **C.** What wheel–belt systems can you invent? Make up and trade some problems with friends. Fix your board so you can use more spools.

TEACHING COMMENT

PREPARATION AND BACKGROUND

Part of an end piece from a discarded vegetable crate is ideal for the wheel–belt system base. Be sure that only finishing nails are pounded into the wood. These nails have small heads, allowing the spools to slip easily over them.

Note that this investigation deals only with the direction the spools turn. By using different-sized spools, children also can study how size governs the speed of turning. Because much slipping will happen with the rubber bands, the size–speed relationship cannot be determined accurately. Children can get the idea better by inverting a bicycle and studying the relative turnings of the large gear and the small gear.

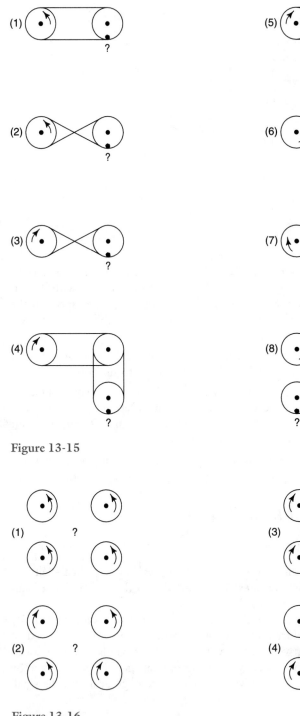

(1)

(5)

(2)

(6)

(3)

(7)

(4)

(8)

Figure 13-15

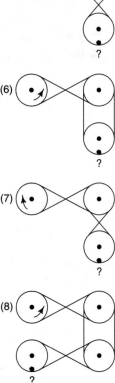

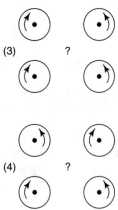

(1)   ?

(3)   ?

(2)   ?

(4)   ?

Figure 13-16

GENERALIZATION

A wheel–belt system can be used to change the direction of a force.

SAMPLE PERFORMANCE OBJECTIVES

Process: When shown a two-, three-, or four-wheel–belt system, the child can predict the direction each wheel will turn.

Knowledge: The child can point out some everyday examples of wheel–belt systems or their equivalents.

FOR YOUNGER CHILDREN

Many primary students work well with wheel–belt systems. But use fewer spools than with older children.

ACTIVITY: *HOW DO BICYCLE GEARS AFFECT SPEED?*

NEEDED

10-speed bicycle   chalk

TRY THIS

1. Observe the different-sized gears or sprockets on the rear wheel. Notice that all are smaller than the large pedal sprocket. See how a chain connects the large sprocket with a smaller one.
2. Adjust the chain so it is on the largest of the small gears.
3. Turn the bicycle upside down. Face the chain side.
4. Move the near pedal around. Notice how the rear wheel turns.
   a. How many times does the wheel turn compared to the pedal? Chalk a spot on the rear tire. Crank the pedal around one full turn. Count the turns made by the chalked wheel.
5. Adjust the chain so it is on the smallest rear gear. (You may have to set the bicycle upright to do so.)
   b. Crank the pedal one full turn. How many times does the rear wheel turn now?
   c. How does changing the rear gear size affect how fast you can go?

TEACHING COMMENT

Ten-speed bicycles have two different-sized front sprockets. When the smaller one is used, it causes the pedals to revolve faster. This decreases the forward speed, but allows less force to be used. For simplicity, use only one front sprocket in this activity.

PULLEY EXPERIENCES
(Concepts p. 357)

INVESTIGATION: *How Pulleys Work*

Many people use *pulleys* to help them work. Have you used a pulley to raise and lower a flag on a flagpole? Painters and roofers use pulleys to haul supplies up and down. Sometimes people work with only a single pulley, but often two or more are used together.

EXPLORATORY PROBLEM

How can you set up one or more pulleys to lift a load?

NEEDED

two single-wheel pulleys
sticky tape
rubber band or spring scale
book
strong cord
ruler
broom handle or stick
scissors
paper clip

TRY THIS

1. Make a place to hang the pulley. Lay a stick over the backs of two separated chairs. Use tape to keep it from sliding. Loop and tie cord around the stick. Hang a pulley from the loop.

2. Set up a single pulley as shown in Figure 13-17(A). This is a fixed pulley. Use a book for the load. Pull the cord *down* to lift the load. Practice a few times.

3. Now set up the pulley differently, as shown in Figure 13-17(B). This is a *movable* pulley. Pull the cord *up* to lift the load. Practice a few times.

DISCOVERY PROBLEMS

observing

A. What differences do you notice in using both pulleys?

measuring

B. Which takes less force to lift the load, the fixed or movable pulley? How much less? To measure, hook a rubber band to the pull cord with a paper clip. Measure the stretch with a ruler, or use a spring scale.

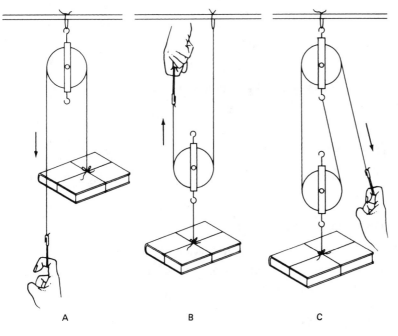

A   B   C

Figure 13-17

measuring

C. How far must you pull the cord to lift the load 1 meter (3 feet) with each pulley? Measure length of pull from where the cord leaves the pulley.

predicting

D. See Figure 13-17(C). It shows a fixed and a movable pulley working together. This is a *block and tackle*. Which do you think takes less force to lift a load: a single fixed pulley or a block and tackle? How far must you pull the cord with each to lift the book 1 meter (3 feet)? Predict and then measure to answer each question.

predicting and measuring

E. Compare the block and tackle with the single movable pulley. Which do you think takes less force to lift a load? How far must you pull the cord with each to lift the book 1 meter (3 feet)? Predict and then measure to answer each question.

observing

F. What examples of pulleys can you find in the classroom? school? How do they work?

observing

G. What other pulleys can you collect and try? How do they compare with the three pulleys of this investigation?

TEACHING COMMENT

BACKGROUND AND PREPARATION

If a spring scale is used, be sure the load does not exceed its capacity.

If you plan to do this investigation in a whole-group setting, consider placing the broomstick holder and supporting chairs on a table. This will help students to get a clearer view.

GENERALIZATION

A fixed pulley changes the direction of a force. A movable pulley reduces force needed to lift a load.

SAMPLE PERFORMANCE OBJECTIVES

Knowledge: The pupil can set up a block and tackle to lift a load.

Process: The child can measure the difference in force applied, and the distance a rope is pulled, with a single and fixed pulley.

FOR YOUNGER CHILDREN

Let younger students experience the basic activity and manipulate the block and tackle.

MOTION AND FRICTION EXPERIENCES

(Concepts page 359)

ACTIVITY: *HOW DO MACHINES AND THEIR PARTS MOVE?*

NEEDED

magazine pictures of different machines
toy machines

INTRODUCTION

Some machines move mostly in a straight line when they work, such as a locomotive and roller skates. Some machines or their parts go back and forth, such as a grandfather clock and swing. Some machines or their parts go around, such as a merry-go-round and bicycle wheel.

TRY THIS

1. Find pictures of machines and machine parts in magazines.
2. Cut out and group the pictures by how the machines or their parts seem to move.

   a. Which machines or parts move mostly in a straight line?

   b. Which go back and forth?

   c. Which spin or go around as they work?

   d. Which machines do all of these things? some of these things?

   e. How do some toy machines and their parts move?

3. Look for real examples of machines working. Watch how they and their parts move. Make a record of what you find out.

   f. What machine can you make up and draw? How will your machine or its parts move? What work will it do?

INVESTIGATION: *PENDULUMS*

Have you ever seen an old-fashioned grandfather clock? One kind has a long weighted rod underneath that swings back and forth. The swinging part is called a *pendulum.* You can keep time with your own pendulum made with a string.

EXPLORATORY PROBLEM

How can you make a string pendulum?

NEEDED

thin string (about 1 meter or 1 yard long)
meter stick or yardstick
pencil
three heavy washers
paper clip
clock or watch with second hand
sticky tape
graph paper

TRY THIS

1. Tape a pencil to a table edge so it sticks out.

2. Bend a paper clip into a hook shape. Tie one string end to the hook.

3. Loop the free end of the string once around the pencil. Tape the string end to the table top.

4. Put two washers on the hook (Figure 13-18).

5. Move the washers to one side and then let go. Each time the washers swing back to that side, count one swing. Be sure the string does not rub against the table edge.

DISCOVERY PROBLEMS

measuring

A. How many swings does the pendulum make in one minute? Have someone

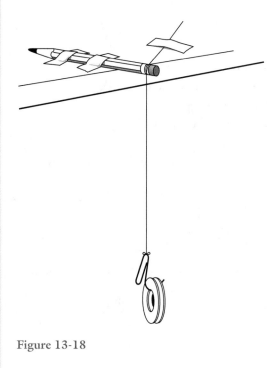

Figure 13-18

help by observing the second hand on a clock. Then you can count the swings.

hypothesizing

B. Do wide swings take more time than narrow swings? Suppose you let go of your pendulum far to one side. What difference might that make in the number of swings it takes in one minute?

hypothesizing

C. Does the amount of weight used change the swing time? What might happen if you use a one-washer weight? a three-washer weight?

hypothesizing

D. Does the length of string used make a difference in swing time? (Measure length from the pencil to the end of the washers.) What might happen if you use a short string? longer string?

experimenting

E. How can you get your pendulum to swing 60 times in 1 minute?

inferring

F. Suppose you had a grandfather clock that was running slow. What could you do to its pendulum to correct it? What if it was running fast?

communicating, predicting, and experimenting **G.** How well can you predict with your pendulum? Make a graph such as the one shown in Figure 13-19. Try several string lengths for your pendulum. Count the swings for each length. Let's say you find that a 20-centimeter string swings 65 times in 1 minute. Make a mark on your graph where lines running from these two numbers meet. (See Figure 13-19.) Make marks for three or four other string lengths and their swings. Then draw a straight line between the marks. Suppose you know the length of a pendulum, but you have not yet tried it. How can you use your graph to predict its number of swings? Suppose you know the number of swings of a pendulum, but you have not yet measured its length. How can you use your graph to predict the pendulum's length? How can you make your predictions more accurate?

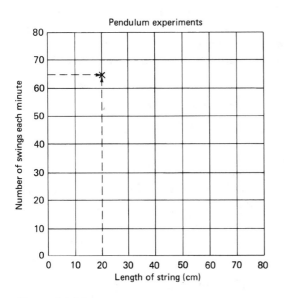

Figure 13-19

TEACHING COMMENT

PREPARATION AND BACKGROUND

The timing of events is possible with a pendulum because its to-and-fro motion recurs with near-perfect regularity. Through manipulating variables, children can discover that the *length* of the weighted string affects the swing rate, or period, of a pendulum. Be sure your students realize that one complete swing consists of the swing out *and* return movement.

GENERALIZATION

A pendulum is any object that swings regularly back and forth; its length affects its swing rate.

SAMPLE PERFORMANCE OBJECTIVES

Process: The child can accurately predict the swing rate of a pendulum for one minute by using graph data.

Knowledge: The child can state how to increase and decrease the swing rate of a pendulum.

FOR YOUNGER CHILDREN

An easy way for younger students to see the effect of manipulating a variable is to set up two identical pendulums. When both are set to swinging, they should perform in the same way. Thereafter, change only one variable at a time with one pendulum—weight or width of swing or length—so its performance may be contrasted with the unchanged pendulum. This strategy can keep the investigation concrete and understandable from the beginning through Problem D or E.

INVESTIGATION: FRICTION

Suppose someone asks you to slide a wooden box across the floor. On what kind of floor surface would it be easiest to start the box sliding? hardest? When an object catches or drags on a surface, we say much *friction* is present. If it slides or moves easily, little friction is present.

EXPLORATORY PROBLEM

How can you find out about the friction of different surfaces?

NEEDED

two same-sized wooden blocks	paper clip
ruler	two round pencils
thumb tack	sheets of sandpaper
sticky tape	waxed paper
thin rubber band	kitchen foil
three wide rubber bands	construction paper

TRY THIS

1. Place a wood block on a wood table. Fasten a rubber band to it with a thumb tack.

2. Hook the rubber band with an opened paper clip. Hold the rubber band end over the end of a ruler. (See Figure 13-20.)

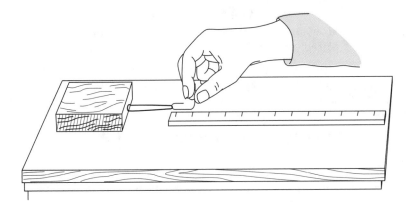

Figure 13-20

3. Pull the rubber band very slowly. Observe where the rubber band end is over the ruler. How far does the band stretch before the block moves? Read the ruler to the nearest whole number. Always make the reading *before* the block starts to slide.

DISCOVERY PROBLEMS

measuring

A. How much will the rubber band stretch if you pull the block a second time? a third time? Record the results and the average for the three trials as shown below:

Surface Tested	Stretch for Each Trial (cm)	Average Stretch (cm)	Predicted Stretch
Wood	11 15 13	13	
Others			

measuring and predicting   **B.** How much will the band stretch if the block is placed on other surfaces? Tape a small piece of kitchen foil to the table and place the block on it. Test this and other surfaces such as sandpaper, waxed paper, or construction paper. (To prepare a rubber surface, wrap three wide rubber bands around the block.) Try to predict first how far the band will stretch each time. Record the results.

measuring   **C.** How much will the band stretch if the block is placed on its side? if a second block is put on top?

measuring   **D.** How much will the band stretch if two round pencils are placed under the block?

experimenting   **E.** How can you make the most friction between the block and surface? least friction? (Use more materials if necessary.)

TEACHING COMMENT

Two identical wooden play blocks can be used for this investigation, or cut 2 4-inch squares from a 2-inch by 4-inch piece of wood. A *thin* rubber band works best to pull with. To make it even stretchier, cut and use it as a single strand. If available, a spring scale may be used to compare results. There should be little relative difference, although the spring scale may be calibrated in ounces or grams. *Caution:* Make sure the tack that holds the rubber band to the block is secure before the band is pulled.

GENERALIZATION

Friction between two surfaces depends on the force that presses the surfaces together and the materials that make up the surfaces; some surfaces have more friction than others.

SAMPLE PERFORMANCE OBJECTIVES

Process: The child can measure with a ruler how much a rubber band stretches to test the friction between a wooden block and the surface on which it rests.

Knowledge: The child can predict that a smooth surface will have less friction than a rougher one.

FOR YOUNGER CHILDREN

Younger students may not be ready to use a ruler for measurements. Instead, they may mark a piece of paper, in place of a ruler, to show the rubber band's relative amounts of stretch. Before this is done, allow time for them to play with and become familiar with the different materials.

REFERENCES

American Association for the Advancement of Science. (1993). *Benchmarks for science literacy.* New York: Oxford University Press.

National Research Council. (1996). *National science education standards.* Washington, DC: National Academy Press.

SELECTED TRADE BOOKS: SIMPLE MACHINES AND HOW THEY WORK

For Younger Children

Barton, B. (1987). *Machines at work.* Harper & Row.

Gibbons, G. (1982). *Tool book.* Holiday House.

Kiley, D. (1980). *Biggest machines.* Raintree.

Lampton, C. (1991). *Sailboats, flag poles, cranes: using pulleys as simple machines.* Millbrook Press.

Lauber, P. (1987). *Get ready for robots.* Scholastic.

Rockwell, A., & Rockwell, H. (1985). *Machines.* Harper & Row.

Robbins, K. (1983). *Tools.* Macmillan.

Wade, H. (1979a). *Gears.* Raintree.

Wade, H. (1979b). *The lever.* Raintree.

Weiss, H. (1983). *The world of machines.* Raintree.

Wilkin, F. (1986). *Machines.* Children's Press.

Wyler, R. (1988). *Science fun with toy cars and trucks.* Messner.

For Older Children

Adkins, J. (1980). *Moving heavy things.* Houghton.

Baines, R. (1985). *Simple machines.* Troll Associates.

Barrett, N. S. (1985). *Robots.* Watts.

Brown, W. F., & Brown, M. G. (1984). *Experiments with common wood and tools.* Macmillan.

Fleisher, P., & Keeler, P. (1991). *Looking inside: Machines and constructions.* Macmillan.

Gardner, R. (1980). *This is the way it works.* Doubleday.

Hellman, H. (1971). *The lever and the pulley.* Lippincott.

James, E., & Barkin, C. (1975). *The simple facts of simple machines.* Lothrop.

Jupo, F. (1972). *The story of things (tools).* Prentice-Hall.

Lefkowitz, R. J. (1975). *Push, pull, stop, go: A book about forces and motion.* Parents.

Taylor, B. (1990). *Force and movement.* Watts.

Weiss, H. (1983). *Machines and how they work.* Harper & Row.

Resource Books

Butzow, C. M., & Butzow, J. W. (1989). *Science through children's literature. An integrated approach* (force and movement topics, pp. 197–199). Teacher Ideas Press.

Shaw, D. G., & Dybdahl, C. S. (1996). *Integrating science and language arts. A sourcebook for K–6 teachers* (wheel and gear topics, pp. 96–100). Allyn and Bacon.

PLANT LIFE AND ENVIRONMENT

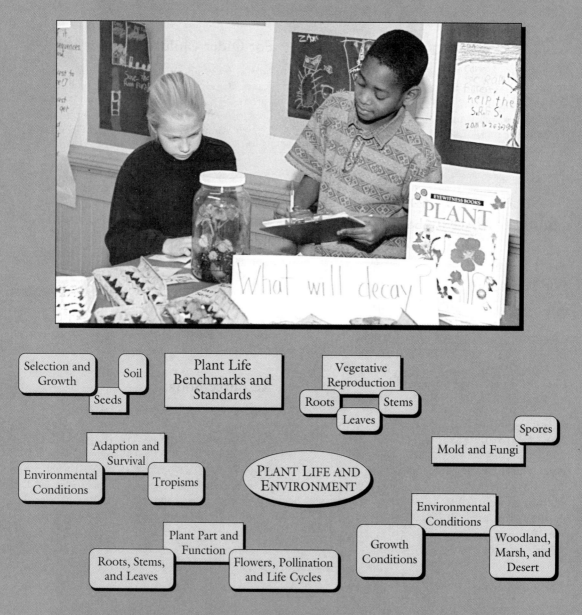

Selection and Growth

Soil

Seeds

Plant Life Benchmarks and Standards

Vegetative Reproduction

Roots

Stems

Leaves

Spores

Mold and Fungi

Adaption and Survival

Environmental Conditions

Tropisms

PLANT LIFE AND ENVIRONMENT

Environmental Conditions

Growth Conditions

Woodland, Marsh, and Desert

Plant Part and Function

Roots, Stems, and Leaves

Flowers, Pollination and Life Cycles

"Chances for open-ended experiments are greater with plants than with any other area of elementary school science." That is what one longtime teacher said, and we agree. At the same time, there is more need for planning ahead and keeping track of activities so that they may be interrelated. Living things take time to grow, and growth rates can seldom be exactly predicted.

The most complex and familiar plants we see are those that produce seeds, of which there are two basic groups. One group is the *gymnosperms*. These plants are flowerless; they develop seeds attached to open scales or cones. Evergreens such as pine, hemlock, spruce, juniper, fir, and redwood are examples of gymnosperms. There are about 600 species.

The second and far larger group (about 250,000 species) is the *angiosperms,* or flowering plants. These form their seeds in closed compartments or cases within the flower.

In this chapter, we'll consider seeds and ways they grow, how new plants can be started from plant parts, how environmental conditions affect plants, how plant parts work, and how plants respond to their environment. A brief, final section takes up the tiny plantlike organisms called *molds*.

SEED-RELATED CONCEPTS
(Experiences p. 396)

"Where do seeds come from?" is a question curious children may ask when they study flowering plants. Seeds are produced in a central part of the flower called the *ovary*. As the ovary ripens, its seeds become enveloped either by a fruity pulp, a pod, or a shell, depending on the kind of plant.

Pears and peaches are fruits whose pulp we eat. Beans, peas, and peanuts are examples of seeds enclosed in pods. When we "shell" string beans, lima beans, peas, or peanuts, we are removing these seeds from their pods. Walnuts, pecans, and coconuts have hard outer shells.

Seed Parts

Seeds come in many different shapes, colors, and sizes. Still, they have three things in common: a protective seed cover, a baby plant (embryo), and a food supply that nourishes the seed as it pushes up through the soil and grows into a young plant. In some plants, such as the bean and sweet pea, the food supply is in two seed "leaves," or cotyledons (Figure 14-1). In other seeds, such as corn and rice, there is only a single cotyledon.

Growth Stages

What happens when a seed grows into a young plant or seedling? For an example, look at Figure 14-2. In A, the seed swells from moisture in the soil. The coat softens and splits. A tiny root and stem emerge. In B, the upper part of the stem penetrates the soil surface and lifts the folded cotyledons out of the seed cover. In C, the cotyledons and tiny plant leaves unfold. Roots deepen and spread. In D, roots become more extensive. The cotyledons are smaller and shriveled. Nearly all the food supply is con-

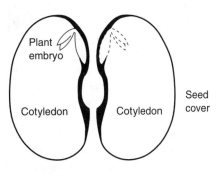

Figure 14-1
Parts of a bean seed.

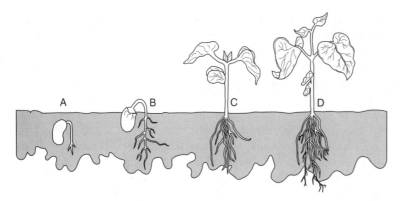

Figure 14-2
From seed to seedling.

sumed. The plant begins to make its own food through photosynthesis within its maturing leaves. In a short while, the shriveled cotyledons, now useless, will drop off the growing plant. This growth process, from seed to seedling, is called *germination*.

Survival Conditions

Some flowering plants produce thousands of seeds a year. If they all grew into plants, before long there would scarcely be room on earth for anything else. Fortunately, a variety of factors enable only a small percentage of wild seeds to grow. Seeds are destroyed by birds, insects, bacteria, and other organisms. And unless proper conditions of moisture, temperature, and oxygen are present, seeds remain dormant. After several years in a dormant state, all but a few kinds of seeds lose their potential ability to germinate. These few, however, may not lose this ability for hundreds or even thousands of years.

Weeds are everywhere about us. What makes them so prolific? Perhaps you have noticed that weeds appear at different times during a growing season. This is because growth requirements of moisture, temperature, and oxygen vary greatly among different kinds of seeds. Of course, this has great survival value.

How Seeds Travel

We know that people plant seeds in gardens. But they do not plant weeds in fields and vacant lots. Nor do they plant seeds in many other places where plants grow. Where do these seeds come from?

Students can learn that seeds travel in several ways. Some are scattered through the actions of animals and people. The sharp hooks or barbs on the cocklebur, burdock, and beggar tick cling to clothing or animal fur (Figure 14-3). Birds eat fleshy fruits but may not digest the hard seeds. The seeds pass out of their bodies some distance away. People throw away fruit pits or watermelon seeds. The wind blows many seeds. Some, such as the goldenrod, milkweed, and dandelion, have "parachutes." The maple tree seed has "wings." Water can carry seeds from place to place because many seeds float. The capacity of seeds to disperse widely and in different ways is another survival feature.

Sprouting Seeds

It is much cheaper to buy seeds (the kind you eat) at a grocery store than at a seed store, even though a smaller percentage will grow. Some easy-to-grow seeds are kidney beans, lima beans, pinto beans, whole green peas, and yellow peas.

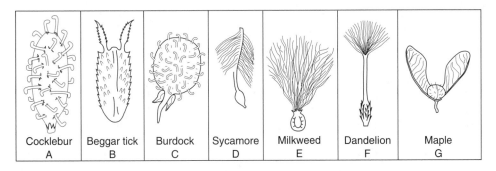

| Cocklebur A | Beggar tick B | Burdock C | Sycamore D | Milkweed E | Dandelion F | Maple G |

Figure 14-3
Some common seeds.

To ensure that only live, healthy seeds are planted, treat them as follows:

Soak the seeds in water for several hours to soften them.

Remove the seeds and drop them into a mixture of one part liquid bleach to eight parts water.

Take out the seeds immediately after immersing them.

To sprout the treated seeds, first soak several paper towels in water. Fold and place them in an aluminum pie pan or dish. Place the treated seeds on top of the wet towels. Then cover the pan with clear plastic wrap to prevent the water from evaporating.

Inspect the seeds every day. Within several days to a week, many bean or pea seeds will have parts sticking out of the seed cover. These sprouted seeds are alive. They are likely to grow into plants if planted while moist and cared for properly.

Soil

All containers may be filled with garden soil, sand, sawdust, or vermiculite, an inexpensive insulating material made up of fluffy bits of mica. Only the garden soil will have minerals needed for healthy growth of plants beyond the seedling stage.

The other "soil" materials let more air circulate around the seed cover and plant roots. They are also more porous and so they are harder to overwater. Plants rooted in these materials may be more easily removed, examined, and replanted without serious root damage.

Small holes punched in containers will aid good drainage. Any water runoff can be caught in a saucer placed below. If holes cannot easily be made, as with a glass jar, include an inch of gravel in the jar bottom before adding soil. Water only when the soil surface feels slightly dry.

Instruct students to plant seeds only slightly deeper than their length. But always follow instructions on the seed package for seed store varieties. Since it takes energy to push through the soil, a small seed planted too deeply runs out of food before it reaches the surface. Also, keep the soil somewhat loose so air can get to the roots.

VEGETATIVE
REPRODUCTION CONCEPTS
(Experiences p. 401)

Many people think that only seeds produce new flowering plants. Yet some of the most useful and interesting ways to grow new plants are through the propagation of roots, stems, and even leaves. This is called vegetative reproduction.

Roots

Consider the orange-colored tap root of the carrot plant (the part we eat). A carrot plant is usually grown from seed in the spring and harvested some months later. If left in the ground, however, all parts above the soil surface die as the weather becomes cold. No growth occurs during this time. As warmer weather approaches, tender shoots grow from the tap root and emerge into sunlight. These grow into stems and leaves. Some time thereafter, flowers and seeds are produced. Like a seed, a tap root provides the food energy needed for shoots to emerge and grow. Parsnips and beets are other examples of tap roots that grow in this way (Figure 14-4).

New plants may be grown from tap roots in the classroom by embedding them in moist

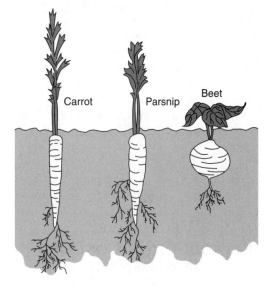

Figure 14-4
Carrots, parsnips, and beets have tap roots.

sand or garden soil. A favorite method of many teachers is to cut off all but the top quarter of a tap root and imbed it in a small bowl containing a layer of pebbles and some water. At least half of the root cutting is above water to assure a sufficient oxygen supply. When sufficient foliage and roots have emerged, cuttings are planted in garden soil for full growth.

Stems

Most ground-cover plants, such as grass, strawberry, and ivy, spread quickly after planting. These plants send out stems or runners that take root, push up shoots, and develop into new plants. These lateral stems may spread above ground, like the strawberry plant and Bermuda grass do, or below ground, like quack grass. The most persistent weed grasses are of the underground-stem variety, as frustrated lawn growers will testify.

New plants may be propagated from stem cuttings of the geranium and begonia. Other common plants whose stems grow independently are the coleus, oleander, philodendron, and English ivy. Dipping the ends of stem cuttings in a commercial hormone preparation may start root growth in half the usual time.

Sometimes on opening a bag of white potatoes, we find some of them beginning to sprout. Usually, this happens when the potatoes are left undisturbed for a time in a dark, warm place. White potatoes are swollen parts of underground stems, called *tubers*. The dark spots, or "eyes," are buds, from which shoots grow.

Farmers today seldom, if ever, use potato seeds in growing crops. Instead, they cut potatoes into several bud-bearing parts and plant these. Each bud grows into a new plant that produces more potatoes.

Occasionally, we see shoots growing from onion bulbs stored in the home pantry. Bulbs, too, are modified stems. All contain thick, fleshy leaves wrapped tightly around a small, immature stem. Tulips and gladioli are typical flowers that may be grown from both bulbs and seeds.

Leaves

Even some *leaves* may develop into whole plants. Suggestions follow for using an African violet, echeveria, and bryophyllum plant.

Use a fresh African violet leaf with attached petiole (leaf stalk). Put the stalk into an inch of water in a drinking glass. For better support of the leaf, use a card with a hole punched in it placed across the glass rim. Insert the leaf petiole through the hole and into the water. After roots begin to grow, plant the leaf in rich soil.

The bryophyllum leaf is sometimes sold in variety stores under the name "magic leaf." To propagate, pin it down flat on damp sand with several toothpicks or straight pins. Tiny plants should grow from several of the notches around the leaf rim.

Why Vegetative Reproduction?

Sometimes children ask, "If plants can grow from seeds, why are the other ways used?" There are several reasons. All of these methods result in whole plants in far less time. Also, some things cannot be grown from seed (such as seedless oranges). In this case, branches of seedless oranges are grafted onto an orange tree grown from seed.

But the most important reason is quality control. We can never be sure of the results when we plant seeds of some plants. Vegetative reproduction carries the assurance that the new plants will be very much like the parent plant. If large, healthy potatoes are cut up and planted, for instance, we probably can harvest near-identical specimens.

All the foregoing methods of vegetative reproduction are asexual. In other words, reproduction does not require involvement of plant sex organs. Certain lower animal-like forms also can reproduce themselves asexually. In another section, we will discuss sexual reproduction in flowering plants; that is, how fertile seeds are produced.

ENVIRONMENTAL CONDITIONS CONCEPTS
(Experiences p. 403)

Plants grow and flourish only when the environment provides proper amounts of minerals, water, light, temperature, and—more indirectly—space. Because the classroom is an artificial habitat, or home, for plants, students will need to furnish the conditions the plants need to survive.

Growth Conditions

Children will find that soil-watering requirements for plants are like those for germinating seeds. Overwatering causes the plant to die of oxygen deprivation or disease. Underwatering usually results in a droopy, malnourished plant. The absence of vital soil minerals and extremes in temperature also have a weakening, or even fatal, effect on plants.

Crowding of plants is harmful to growth largely because competition deprives individual plants of enough of what they need for good growth. Even the hardiest plants develop to less than normal size under crowded conditions.

Green plants need light energy to manufacture their own food, but not necessarily sunshine. Electric lights may be substituted.

Many commercial flower growers take advantage of this fact to regulate the growth rates or blooming times of their flowers to coincide with different holidays. Plants generally grow faster when exposed to light for increased time periods. But overexposure retards growth and delays normal blooming times.

Three Habitats

Even the casual observer can notice that different kinds of plants live in different habitats. Cacti are unlikely to be found in woodlands, and ferns do not ordinarily live in deserts. It may be hard for us to take students directly to different habitats. It is possible, though, to bring several habitats to the classroom in miniature form.

The *terrarium* is a managed habitat for small land plants and, if desired, small animals likely to be found with the plants. Three basic kinds are the woodland, marsh, and desert terrariums. Almost any large glass or plastic container will do for the basic structure. An old aquarium tank is usually best, but a large jar turned on its side will also do. The container should be thoroughly cleaned before use.

To make a *woodland terrarium,* cover the bottom of the container with a 2.5-centimeter (1-inch) layer of pebbles, sand, and bits of charcoal mixed together. This layer will allow drainage, and the charcoal will absorb gases and keep the soil from turning sour. Add to the bottom layer a second layer about twice as thick, consisting of equal parts of rich garden soil and sand mixed together with a bit of charcoal. Sprinkle the ground until moist, but do not leave it wet, as molds may develop.

Dwarf ivy, ferns, liverworts, and lichens are ideal plants. Partridge berry and mosses provide a nice ground cover, if desired.

After a week or so, the plants should take hold, and a few small animals can be introduced. A land snail, earthworms, a small land turtle, a salamander, or a small frog are suitable for a miniature woodland habitat. A little let-tuce will feed the snail or turtle; earthworms get nutrition from the soil. Food for frogs and salamanders might include small live insects, such as mealworms, flies, sow bugs, ants, and the like. A small, shallow dish pressed into the soil can serve as a water source.

Keep the terrarium covered and out of the sunlight to avoid the buildup of heat. A glass sheet loosely fitted to permit air circulation will help keep high humidity inside, reducing the need to water the soil. Here, too, water will evaporate from the soil, condense on the underside of the glass cover, and fall as "rain" in a miniature water cycle.

To make a *marsh terrarium,* the soil must be more acidic and damper than in the previous terrarium. Cover the container bottom with pebbles. Add to that a 6-centimeter (3-inch) layer of acid soil and peat moss mixed in about equal parts. These materials can be bought at a plant nursery.

Suitable plants are the Venus's-flytrap, sundew, pitcher plant, mosses, and sedges.

Some appropriate animals include frogs, toads, small turtles, and salamanders. Again, press a small, shallow dish of water flush with the soil surface for the animals. Keep this terrarium covered and in a cool part of the room.

To make a *desert terrarium,* cover the container bottom with about 3 centimeters (1 inch) of coarse sand. Sprinkle this lightly with water and an equally thick layer of fine sand on top. Get a few small potted cacti or other desert succulents. Bury these so the pot tops are flush with the sand surface. Sprinkle plants lightly with water about once a week.

Suitable animals are lizards, including the horned toad. Push a partly buried dish into the sand for their water source. Mealworms and live insects will do for food. Place a stick and a few stones in the sand on which the animals may climb or rest. This terrarium may be left uncovered and in the sun.

PLANT PART AND FUNCTION CONCEPTS
(Experiences p. 407)

Children are usually surprised to learn that, besides fruits and vegetables, all the meat they eat has originally been derived from green plants. Flesh-eating animals depend on plant-eating animals. This is true in the ocean as well as on land. Everything alive basically depends on food synthesized from raw materials in the leaves of green plants.

The plant itself depends on the proper working of its several parts to produce this food. In this section, we'll examine how these parts work. Let's begin with plant roots.

Roots

The experience of weeding a garden makes us very conscious of one function of roots: They anchor the plant. We also know that food storage in roots enables the plant to survive when food making cannot occur. Another function of roots is the absorption of soil water.

Plants that are transplanted sometimes grow poorly for a while, or even die. This is usually due to damage done to tiny, very delicate root hairs that grow from the older root tissue (Figure 14-5). It is the root hairs that absorb nearly all the water, rather than the older fibrous material.

There may be billions of root hairs on a single plant, enough to stretch hundreds of miles if laid end to end. If laid side by side in rows, they would take up the floor area of an average-sized home. Root hairs are so small they are able to grow in the tiny spaces between soil particles and make direct contact with water and air trapped therein.

Growth takes place largely at the tip of a root. A tough root cap protects the sensitive

Figure 14-5
A seedling has many root hairs.

growing portion as it punches through the soil. Because the soil is abrasive, the root cap tissue is continually worn off and replaced by new tissue.

Stems

Water absorbed by the roots goes into the stems, through which it is transported by narrow tubes to all parts of the plant. Dissolved minerals in the water are deposited within the cells of these parts. When water reaches the leaves, some of it evaporates into the air.

Exactly how does this continual movement of water happen in the plant? This has been a mystery until recent times. Modern molecular theory gives an answer.

As you know, molecules that are alike have an attractive force which binds them together (cohesion). These molecules may also be attracted to unlike molecules (adhesion). The thin tubes that transport water in a plant run from root to stem to leaf. Adhesion of water molecules to the tube walls helps to support the tiny water column. Cohesion causes the water molecules to stick together. As water molecules evaporate into the air, they "tug" slightly at the molecules below because of cohesive attraction. Because of cohesion, all the other molecules rise in a kind of chain reaction unless an air bubble separates some molecules to a distance beyond their effective cohesive attraction.

Leaves

A leaf seems thin and simple in structure from the outside. Yet the intricate mechanisms within it, which produce the world's food supply, have never been fully duplicated by scientists.

Inside the leaf cells is a green-pigmented chemical, *chlorophyll*. Chlorophyll enables a leaf to chemically combine carbon dioxide from air with water to form a simple sugar. The energy needed to power this chemical synthesis in the leaf comes from sunlight, which is absorbed by the chlorophyll. *Photosynthesis,* as the process is called, literally means "to put together with light."

From the sugar leaves manufacture, the plant cells make starch, which may be stored in all parts of the plant. With additional compounds received from the soil and through soil bacteria, plant cells can manufacture proteins and vitamins.

Carbon dioxide is taken up in photosynthesis and oxygen is released as a waste product. But when a plant consumes the food stored in its cells, it takes up oxygen and gives off carbon dioxide as a waste product. Fortunately for us, much more oxygen is released to the air through photosynthesis than is used by plants

in oxidizing their stored food. In fact, green plants are the chief source of the world's present oxygen supply.

How do these gases enter and leave the leaf? Thousands of microscopic openings, called *stomates,* may be found in a green leaf. In land plants, these are largely, but not exclusively, located in the leaf's underneath surface. Each *stomate* is surrounded by special cells that regulate the size of the opening (Figure 14-6). Water in the leaf evaporates into the air through the stomates, a process called *transpiration.* Regulation of these openings has great survival value. In dry spells and at night, the stomates stay closed, thereby preventing any appreciable loss of water.

Interestingly, most of the photosynthesis on earth happens in the ocean within uncountable numbers of microscopic algae that float on and near the water surface. We have not yet learned how to use the tremendous food supply this source potentially affords to a hungry world.

Flowers

Many people value flowers because of their beauty. But for flowering plants, flowers have a more vital function. They are the only means by

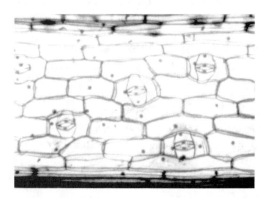

Figure 14-6
Guard cells (stomates) in a leaf.

which species can naturally survive. The flower is the reproductive system of a flowering plant. Its two principal organs are the *pistil,* which contains unfertilized egg cells, and *stamens,* which produce dustlike *pollen* cells. (See Figure 14-7.)

When a pollen grain lands on the sticky end of a pistil, a tube begins to grow that "eats" its way down to the pistil base, or *ovary.* There, it joins onto an egg cell, or *ovule.* A sperm cell released from the pollen grain travels down the tube and unites with the ovule. Other ovules in the ovary may be fertilized by additional pollen in the same way.

The ovules, now fertilized, begin growing into seeds. The entire ovary begins to swell as a fleshy fruit begins to grow around the seeds. As the ovary becomes larger, parts of the flower drop off. Finally, a whole fruit forms. In the apple, the ovary is enveloped by a stem part that swells up around it. The next time you eat an apple, look at the core end opposite the fruit stem. Quite likely the tiny dried-up remains of the pistil and stamens will be visible.

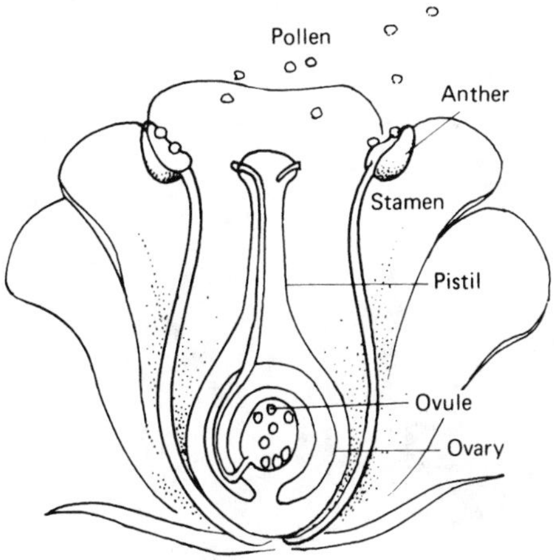

Figure 14-7
Parts of a flower.

When examining flowers with children, use single flowers, such as tulips and sweet peas, rather than composite flowers, such as daisies and sunflowers. The centers of these composite types consist of many tiny flowers, each complete with pistil and stamens. They are too small to be readily observed and may be confusing to the children.

Pollination

Self-pollination happens when pollen from a flower's own stamens fertilize the ovules. *Cross-pollination* occurs when pollen from another flower perform this function. However, pollen must be from the same type of flower for fertilization to take place.

Much pollination happens through gravity, as when pollen simply falls from tall stamens onto a shorter pistil. Or pollen may fall from a flower high up on a stem to one lower down. Insects are also primary distributors of pollen. As they sip nectar from flowers, pollen grains rub off onto their bodies. When the insects visit other flowers, these grains may become dislodged. It is interesting to note that bright colored and fragrant flowers are visited by the most insects. Wind is also an important distributor of pollen. In spring, the air contains billions of pollen grains, bringing pollination to plants and hay fever to many people.

Life Cycles

Many garden flowers and vegetables grow from seed, then blossom, produce seeds, and die in one growing season. These are known as *annuals.* Examples are petunias, zinnias, beans, and tomatoes. Those that live two seasons are *biennials.* Examples are hollyhocks, forget-me-nots, carrots, and turnips. Plants that live more than two growing seasons are *perennials.* Trees and most shrubs fit into this classification.

ADAPTION AND SURVIVAL CONCEPTS
(Experiences p. 416)

Adaptation

If you were asked to invent a plant, what adaptive properties would you want it to have for survival value? Whatever your design, it would be wise to have your plant regulate itself to some extent according to its needs.

Assume it has the same needs as other plants. Because it requires water, and water soaks down into the soil, you would want the plant roots to grow downward. But what if there were no water below the roots? You would want roots that could overcome the pull of gravity and grow toward a water source, even if the source were to one side or above the roots.

Because the plant needs light, you would want the stem to be able to grow toward a light source if light became blocked or dimmed. At the same time, it would be desirable to design the leaf stalk to give maximum exposure of the leaf to sunlight. An efficient stalk should be able to grow longer if another leaf blocks its light. It might also turn the leaf perpendicular to the sun's rays as the sun appears at different positions in the sky.

Most green plants respond to gravity, water, light, and touch. These responses to environmental stimuli are called plant *tropisms*. Let's see why they happen.

Tropisms

Figure 14-8 shows a radish seedling growing on wet blotting paper inside a water glass. The glass has been placed on its side for 24 hours. Notice that the seedling shoot, or stem, is beginning to curve upward, although the root

is starting to grow downward. *Both* reactions are responses to gravity.

Why the opposite directions? Check the magnified sections of the seedling. Gravity concentrates plant hormones *(auxins)* all along the bottom cells from the beginning of the stem to the root tip. The cells along the bottom of the stem are stimulated by the hormones to grow faster than cells above. Growth of these cells is fastest by the stem tip (left inset). As these bottom cells become elongated, the stem begins to curve upward. Root cells, however, are much more sensitive than stem cells. So the concentration of hormones along the bottom root cells has the opposite effect; it inhibits cell growth. Top cells are least affected and elongate faster, so that the root tip begins to curve downward. Cell growth is fastest by the tip (right inset).

Tropistic responses seem to be the result of plant hormones that concentrate in various parts of the plant. As we have seen, this causes some cells to grow faster than others. Such responses can happen only in growing tissue.

Survival and Environment

The survival of plant (and animal) species is more than a matter of properties the organism

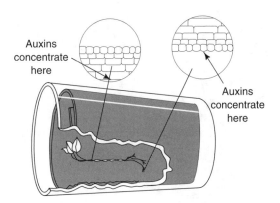

Auxins concentrate here

Auxins concentrate here

Figure 14-8
Seedling shoots curve upward and roots grow down almost as soon as sprouting occurs.

inherits by chance. The environment also plays a part because it is continually changing.

For example, a long dry spell will favor plants with small bad-tasting leaves and deep roots. Why? Large-leafed plants will lose too much water to survive. Shallow-rooted plants will not be able to tap moisture deep down. Plants with tasty leaves will be eaten first by hungry, thirsty animals.

MOLD AND FUNGI CONCEPTS
(Experiences p. 417)

In recent years, growing molds has become popular in elementary science programs. It offers students many chances to experiment with variables at several levels.

Molds are a subgroup of a broader group of organisms called fungi. Some common examples of other fungi are mushrooms, mildews, puffballs, and yeasts. Molds will grow on a wide variety of animal and plant materials and some synthetic materials.

Tiny, seedlike spores from molds are found in the air almost anywhere. When the spores settle on a substance, they may grow. Molds get the nutrients they need to live from the material they grow on. Unlike the green plants, molds and other fungi cannot manufacture their own food.

Molds may grow under a wide variety of conditions. But those found commonly in classrooms are most likely to thrive when it is dark, moist, and warm.

PLANT LIFE BENCHMARKS AND STANDARDS

Throughout the elementary years, it is important that children build an understanding of biological concepts through direct experiences with living things. Plants are excellent sources for observational activities, classification tasks, and experimentation. A sampling of Benchmarks and Standards related to the study of plants in the elementary classroom is as follows:

SAMPLE BENCHMARKS (AAAS, 1993).

- Plants and animals have features that help them live in different environments (by Grades K–2, p. 102).
- Plants and animals both need to take in water, and animals need to take in food. In addition, plants need light (by Grades K–2, p. 119).

SAMPLE STANDARDS (NRC, 1996).

- Each plant or animal has different structures that serve different functions in growth, survival, and reproduction (by Grades K–4, p. 129).
- Plants and some microorganisms are producers—they make their own food (by Grades 5–8, pp. 157–158).

INVESTIGATIONS AND ACTIVITIES

SEED-RELATED EXPERIENCES
(Concepts p. 385)

INVESTIGATION: SEED PARTS

What is inside a bean seed? Can you draw a picture of how it might look inside?

EXPLORATORY PROBLEM

How can you find out about the parts of seeds?

NEEDED

bean seeds
paper towel
corn seeds
glass of water

TRY THIS

1. Soak some bean and corn seeds in water overnight.
2. Open a soaked bean seed with your thumbnails (Figure 14-9).

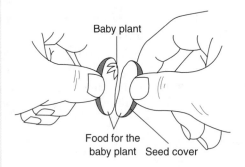

Figure 14-9

DISCOVERY PROBLEMS

observing   **A.** What do you notice about your seed?

How many different parts do you find?

How does the seed feel to you without its cover?

What does the seed smell like?

observing **B.** Open the corn seed. How is it like the bean seed? How is it different?

observing **C.** Soak and open other kinds of seeds. In what ways are they alike and different?

communicating **D.** How well can you describe a seed? Put a seed among three different kinds of seeds. Describe it. Will someone be able to pick it out?

TEACHING COMMENT

PREPARATION AND BACKGROUND

Seeds from flowering plants have three things in common: a protective seed cover, a baby plant (embryo), and a food supply. The food nourishes the sprouted embryo as it pushes up through the soil and grows into a young plant. When its food supply is gone, a green plant can make (photosynthesize) its own food from substances in air, water, and soil if light shines on it. In some plants, such as the bean and sweet pea, the food supply is located in two seed halves, or cotyledons. In other seeds, such as corn and rice, there is only a single cotyledon.

GENERALIZATION

Most seeds have a baby plant, food supply, and cover.

SAMPLE PERFORMANCE OBJECTIVES

Process: The child can state several likenesses and differences she has observed among different seeds.

Knowledge: When shown a seed he has not already examined, the child can predict that it consists of an embryo, food supply, and cover.

FOR OLDER CHILDREN

If possible, let older students gather and examine some seeds from evergreen plants such as the pine, hemlock, spruce, fir, juniper, and redwood. They may observe how the seeds are attached to open scales or cones. Have them look up information about the reproductive process of such plants.

INVESTIGATION: *THE GROWTH OF SEEDS*

Where do green plants come from? Have you planted seeds? What did you do?

EXPLORATORY PROBLEM

How can you plant seeds so they may grow?

NEEDED

soil
bean seeds soaked overnight in water
water
paper towel
pencil
topless milk carton or paper cup
pie pan

TRY THIS

1. Poke holes into the carton bottom with a pencil or nail.
2. Put the carton on a pie pan.
3. Fill the carton almost full with soil.
4. Water the soil slowly until water leaks into the pie pan.
5. Poke a hole in the soil. Make it about as deep as the seed you plant is long (Figure 14-10).

Figure 14-10

6. Put the seed into the hole. Cover it with wet soil. Tap the soil down lightly.
7. Water the soil when it feels dry to your touch, but not more than once a day.
8. Measure your growing plant three times a week. Put a strip of paper alongside. Tear off some to match the plant's height. Date the strips and paste them on a large sheet of paper. What can you tell from this plant record?

DISCOVERY PROBLEMS

experimenting **A.** Try some experiments with more materials. In what kind of soil will a seed grow best? Try sand, sawdust, or soil from different places. Or mix your own soil from some of these.

experimenting **B.** Will a seed live and grow if you water it with salt water? How much salt can you use? What else might you use to "water" a growing seed?

experimenting **C.** Will a broken or damaged seed grow? Will a seed that was frozen or boiled grow? Will a seed grow if the seed cover is taken off?

experimenting **D.** Does the position of a seed make a difference? For example, what will happen if you plant a seed upside down?

Teaching Comment

PREPARATION AND BACKGROUND

A seed that is soaked before it is planted will sprout faster than one planted dry. But don't leave a seed in water longer than overnight. It may die from insufficient air.

GENERALIZATION

Some plants grow from seeds; proper conditions are needed for seeds to sprout and grow.

SAMPLE PERFORMANCE OBJECTIVES

Process: The child sets up an experiment to test a condition that may affect seed growth.

Knowledge: The child describes how seeds may be properly grown into plants.

FOR YOUNGER CHILDREN

Be sure that these children learn right away how to properly plant and care for a growing seed.

Activity: *How Deep Can You Plant a Seed and Still Have It Grow?*

NEEDED

six sprouted bean seeds
sticky tape
tall, clear jar with straight sides
black paper

TRY THIS

1. Plant two seeds in soil at the bottom of the jar. Place the seeds next to the glass, so they can be seen.

2. Add more soil. Plant two seeds in the middle of the jar the same way.

3. Add more soil. Plant two seeds near the top of the jar.

4. Wrap black paper around the jar. Remove the paper for a short time to observe the seeds each day. Water the seeds as needed.

   a. Which seeds will have enough food energy to grow to the surface?

   b. What would happen if you planted smaller seeds, like radish seeds?

ACTIVITY: *IN WHAT PLACES ARE SEEDS IN THE SOIL?*

NEEDED

shoe boxes
outdoor places
clear kitchen wrap
small shovel
plastic bags

TRY THIS

1. Line some shoe boxes with plastic bags.

2. Half-fill each shoe box with bare soil from a different place. Record where each place is on the box. Try garden soil, soil where weeds grow, and other bare soils.

3. Water the soil so it is damp. Cover each box with clear kitchen wrap.

4. Leave each box in a warm, well-lighted place for several weeks or more.

   a. In which box do you expect seeds to grow?

   b. In which box, if any, did seeds grow?

   c. Will wild plants grow in the exact places from which you took soil? Observe these places from time to time.

VEGETATIVE REPRODUCTION EXPERIENCES
(Concepts p. 387)

ACTIVITY: *HOW CAN YOU GROW NEW PLANTS FROM CUT STEMS?*

NEEDED

three clear plastic drinking glasses
soil
sand
water
knife
healthy geranium plant

TRY THIS

1. Cut a strong stem about 13 centimeters (5 inches) long from the plant. Cut just below where leaves join the stem. Trim away all but two or three leaves on top.

2. Stick the cutting into a half-glass of water. Watch for roots to appear.

3. Some cuttings grow roots faster when placed in sand or soil. Make two more cuttings. Plant one at a slant in a glass containing sand. Plant the other the same way in soil. The stem end should be against the glass. In this way, you will be able to see roots start. Keep the soil or sand damp.

   a. In which container does the cutting grow roots fastest?

   b. Does the thickness of a cutting affect root growth? Does the length of a cutting? Plan ways to answer these questions.

TEACHING COMMENT

Caution: Handle the knife yourself or closely supervise its use.

ACTIVITY: *HOW CAN YOU GROW SWEET POTATO VINES?*

NEEDED

sweet potato
wide-mouth plastic drinking glass
three toothpicks
water

INTRODUCTION

Sweet potatoes are the swollen root ends of the sweet potato plant. You can grow beautiful, trailing vines from them indoors.

TRY THIS

1. Place the sweet potato in a glass of water, stem end up. (This end has a small scar where it was attached to the plant.) Stick toothpicks in the sides to support it, if needed. Only about one-third of the sweet potato should be in the water. Keep the water level the same during this activity (Figure 14-11).

Figure 14-11

2. Leave the glass in a warm, dark place until buds and roots grow. Then put it in a sunny or well-lighted place.

   a. How long does it take before you see the first growth?

   b. What changes do you notice as the buds and roots grow?

   c. What happens to the sweet potato as vines grow?

ACTIVITY: *HOW CAN YOU GET NEW GROWTH FROM TAP ROOTS?*

NEEDED

two fresh carrots (one small and one large)
knife
two low glass jars
gravel

TRY THIS

1. Cut off the top 5 centimeters (2 inches) of each carrot. (You can eat the rest.) Trim away any stems and leaves growing from the top.

2. Put gravel into each jar. Stick each carrot top about halfway into the gravel.

3. Fill each jar with just enough water to cover the bottom. Leave each jar in a warm, well-lighted place. Observe each day.

   a. How long does it take for stems and leaves to grow?

   b. What happens to the tap root part as stems and leaves grow?

   c. Which, if either, carrot top shows more growth?

   d. What will happen if you plant the carrot tops in soil?

   e. Can you get new growth from other tap roots? Try a beet, turnip, and parsnip.

TEACHING COMMENT

Caution: For safety you may wish to cut the carrots.

ENVIRONMENTAL CONDITIONS EXPERIENCES
(Concepts p. 389)

INVESTIGATION: *HOW COLORED LIGHT AFFECTS PLANT GROWTH*

Plants need light to grow. But must it be white sunlight? Perhaps plants will grow just as well or better in colored light.

EXPLORATORY PROBLEM

What can you do to find out how plants grow in colored light?

NEEDED

four cellophane or plastic sheets (red, green, blue, and clear)
four topless shoe boxes
scissors
lawn area
sticky tape

TRY THIS

1. Cut out the bottoms of four shoe boxes. Leave a 2.5-centimeter (1-inch) border on all sides.

2. Cover each cutout bottom with a different-colored cellophane sheet. Fasten the sheets with sticky tape.

3. Place the shoe boxes close together, with cellophane sheets facing up, on a healthy patch of lawn. Lift the boxes once each day for two weeks to observe the grass. Water the grass as needed but do not mow it (Figure 14-12).

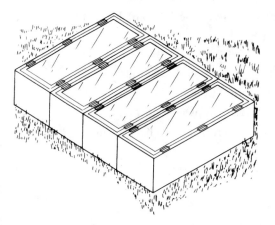

Figure 14-12

DISCOVERY PROBLEMS

observing   **A.** What differences, if any, do you notice each day in the grass under the boxes?

observing   **B.** How do the grass samples compare in height and color?

communicating   **C.** What kind of a record can you make to keep track of what happens?

inferring   **D.** What color seems best for grass growth? worst?

hypothesizing   **E.** What other colors can you test? How will the grass be affected?

experimenting   **F.** How can you test other plants? How will they be affected?

TEACHING COMMENT

PREPARATION AND BACKGROUND

Other kinds of plants may be tested with shoe boxes as shown in Figure 14-13. Punch holes in the sides of the box for adequate air circulation. Boxes may be slipped off quickly for observing, measuring, and watering the plants.

Some children may also like to try growing plants under artificial light. A gooseneck lamp with a 50-watt bulb works well as a light source. If the bulb is left on 24 hours a day, students may discover that plant growth slows down.

GENERALIZATION

Plants grow better in natural light than in colored light.

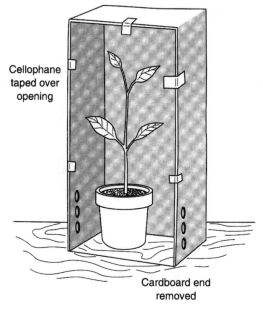

Cellophane
taped over
opening

Cardboard end
removed

Figure 14-13

SAMPLE PERFORMANCE OBJECTIVES

Knowledge: The child can name the light colors that are most likely and least likely to help plants grow.

Process: The child can make a record from daily observations of plants and correctly infer from it.

FOR YOUNGER CHILDREN

Try the basic activity and Problems A and B.

INVESTIGATION: *HOW SALT WATER AND OTHER LIQUIDS AFFECT PLANTS*

Many places have too little fresh water to grow plants. So some people want to use ocean water. How do you think salt water would affect land plants?

EXPLORATORY PROBLEM

How can you find out what salt water does to plants?

NEEDED

six containers of healthy young radish plants
measuring cup
iodine-free salt
other liquids
teaspoon

TRY THIS

1. Mix a teaspoonful of salt into a half liter (or pint) of water.
2. Water one container of plants with only this salt water. Water a matched container of plants with only fresh water. Observe both sets of plants each day (Figure 14-14).

Figure 14-14

DISCOVERY PROBLEMS

observing   **A.** What changes do you notice from day to day? Keep a record of what you observe.

experimenting   **B.** Will the plants live if *any* salt is in the water? How much can you use?

experimenting   **C.** How will other plants be affected by salt water?

experimenting   **D.** What other liquids can be used to water plants? How do you think the plants will be affected?

TEACHING COMMENT

PREPARATION AND BACKGROUND

If ocean water is available, it may be used in place of the salt water mixture. For Problem B, the ocean water may be diluted with fresh water.

GENERALIZATION

When watered with salt water, land plants die or grow poorly.

SAMPLE PERFORMANCE OBJECTIVES

Knowledge: The child predicts plant destruction or poor growth when certain land plants are watered with ocean water.

Process: The child finds through experimenting how much salt water, if any, sample radish plants can tolerate.

FOR YOUNGER CHILDREN

Most younger students will be able to do the activities if help is given in matching plants and otherwise controlling variables.

PLANT PART AND FUNCTION EXPERIENCES
(Concepts p. 391)

ACTIVITY: WHAT ARE PLANT ROOTS LIKE?

NEEDED

places where weeds grow
newspaper
small shovel
magnifying glass
pail of water
notebook

TRY THIS

1. Dig up some small weeds from both dry and wet places if possible. Try not to damage the roots. Dig deeply and loosen the soil around the weed. Then slip the shovel under it.
2. Soak the roots in water to remove the soil.
3. Carefully place each plant inside a folded newspaper. Observe the plant roots in class.

a. Which plants have a single, large tap root with smaller branching roots?

b. Which plants have branching roots?

c. Can you see tiny root hairs with a magnifying glass? On what parts of the roots do most appear?

d. What other differences among the roots do you notice?

INVESTIGATION: *How Water Rises in Plant Stems*

We usually water the *roots* of a plant. How, then, does water in the roots get to the leaves?

EXPLORATORY PROBLEM

How can you use a celery stalk to study how water travels in plant stems?

NEEDED

white celery stalk (fresh, with many leaves)
red food coloring or water-soluble ink
glass of water
knife
ruler

TRY THIS

1. Put a few drops of red coloring into the glass of water. This will help you to see how the water moves through the stalk.

2. Cut off the lower end of the stalk at a slant.

3. Put the stalk into the colored water right away (Figure 14-15).

4. Leave the stalk where it will get bright light.

DISCOVERY PROBLEMS

observing and communicating   **A.** Check the stalk every hour. How far does water rise in one hour? in more than one hour? Make a record of what you see each time.

observing   **B.** After a few hours, or the next day, remove the stalk. Cut it across near the bottom. What do you notice about this cutoff part?

observing   **C.** Cut the stalk the long way. What do you notice? Can you find any long colored tubes?

experimenting   **D.** Use other stalks for experiments. What can you do to change how fast the water rises? For example: Does

Figure 14-15

the number of leaves on the stalk make a difference? Does the amount of light make a difference? Does wind make a difference? Will using liquids other than water make a difference? Have a race with someone to see whose celery stalk wins.

experimenting

E. How can you *prevent* water from rising in the stalk if it stands in water?

experimenting

F. Get a white carnation with a long stem, or some other white flower. How can you make it a colored flower?

predicting

G. Suppose you split the flower stem partway up and stand each half in different-colored water. What do you think will happen to the flower?

TEACHING COMMENT

PREPARATION AND BACKGROUND

Sometimes the water-conducting tubes in a celery stalk or flower stem become clogged. To open the tubes, make a fresh diagonal cut across the stalk or stem base. Immerse *quickly* to keep air bubbles from forming in the tubes.

GENERALIZATION

Stems conduct liquids from one part of a plant to another; light, wind, and the condition and number of attached leaves affect the conduction rate.

SAMPLE PERFORMANCE OBJECTIVES

Process: The child can change the rate at which water rises in a stem by manipulating one variable.

Knowledge: The child can state how to color a carnation after experimenting with celery stalks.

FOR YOUNGER CHILDREN

Caution: You will want to do whatever cutting of stalks is necessary.

INVESTIGATION: *THE PROPERTIES OF LEAVES*

Have you ever collected different kinds of leaves? There are more than 300,000 different kinds! How can you tell one leaf from another? What do you look for?

EXPLORATORY PROBLEM

How can you describe the properties of leaves?

NEEDED

six or more different leaves
partner
pencil and paper

TRY THIS

1. *Size:* How large is the leaf? Compare their sizes with other things in the classroom.

2. *Shape:* What is the shape of the leaf? Some are oval; some are almost round. Others are shaped like a heart, star, or other figure.

3. *Color:* What is the color of the leaf? Most fresh leaves are green, but some are darker or lighter than others. Some leaves have other colors.

4. *Veins:* These are the small tubes that carry liquid throughout the leaf. How do the veins look? In some leaves, they are side by side. In others, the veins look like many Vs in a row with a main center vein. Some leaves have several long veins with Vs. In a few leaves, veins cannot be seen.

5. *Edges:* What do the leaf edges look like? Some are smooth. Some edges are wavy. Other leaf edges look like saw teeth (Figure 14-16).

6. *Feel:* How does the leaf feel to you? Is it rough? smooth? waxy? hairy? slippery? sticky?

7. *Smell:* What does the leaf smell like? Some leaves may not have a noticeable smell.

Figure 14-16

DISCOVERY PROBLEMS

classifying and inferring

A. Play a game with a partner. Sort your leaves into two groups according to one property (shape, veins, and so forth). Let your partner study your groups. Can he tell which property you used to sort your leaves? Try other properties. Take turns with your partner in this sorting game.

communicating

B. How well can you describe your leaves? Can you make a chart that someone else can use to identify them? Make a chart of all the properties you observe about your leaves. Label your leaves in A, B, C order. Try to remember which is which.

Leaf	Shape	Veins	Edges	Size	Feel
A					
B					
C					
D					

C. Give your completed chart and your leaves to your partner. They should be out of order, so your partner must study your chart to tell which leaf is A, B, C, and so on. Which chart descriptions were helpful? Which confused your partner? How could these be made clearer?

TEACHING COMMENT

PREPARATION AND BACKGROUND

Important: To further the processes of careful observing and communicating, use only leaves that are roughly similar in this investigation. You want different kinds of leaves, but if each is grossly and obviously different from others this will defeat the purpose of the investigation. It is best to do this investigation with fresh, unblemished leaves, such as weed leaves. Copy leaves on a copy machine and have students cut them out to use in class if needed.

GENERALIZATION

Leaves vary in size, shape, color, texture, vein pattern, and other properties; no two leaves are identical.

SAMPLE PERFORMANCE OBJECTIVES

Process: The child can communicate leaf descriptions that enable other persons to identify the leaves.

Knowledge: The child can state at least five of the general properties that can be used to describe leaves.

FOR YOUNGER CHILDREN

Most primary-level children should be able to do Discovery Problem A, and some should be able to do B.

INVESTIGATIONS: *How Leaves Lose Water*

A plant usually takes in more water than it can use. What do you think happens to the extra water?

EXPLORATORY PROBLEM

How can you find out if water is lost from leaves?

NEEDED

fresh leaf with stalk
water

plastic water glasses (four matched)
petroleum jelly
knife
paper towel
two cardboard squares
scissors

TRY THIS

1. Fill one glass almost full with water.
2. Make a small hole in the center of a piece of cardboard.
3. Cover the glass with the cardboard.
4. Take a fresh leaf. Cut off at a slant the tip of its stalk.
5. Quickly put the stalk into the hole in the cardboard.
6. Seal around the hole with petroleum jelly.
7. Put another glass upside down on top of the cardboard.
8. Leave the glass in sunlight for several hours (Figure 14-17).

DISCOVERY PROBLEMS

hypothesizing **A.** Do water drops form inside the top glass? Where do you think they come from?

experimenting **B.** Maybe water drops would appear in the glass without the leaf. How could you find out?

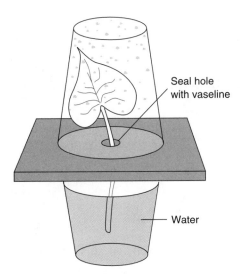

Seal hole
with vaseline

Water

Figure 14-17

experimenting   **C.** What affects how many water drops appear? Leaf size? the kind of leaf? the freshness of the leaf? Does the amount of light affect how many drops appear? How can you find out?

experimenting   **D.** From which side does the leaf give off water? Top? bottom? both sides? How can you use petroleum jelly to find out?

communicating   **E.** Keep a record of your results. Compare your record with others.

TEACHING COMMENT

PREPARATION AND BACKGROUND

Many tiny openings, called *stomates,* are found in a green leaf. Gases are taken in and released through them during the leaf's food-making process. Water, in the form of water vapor, is also released through the stomates. In this activity, the released water vapor is trapped by the plastic cover. It then condenses into visible water drops on the plastic. In land plants, stomates are usually found in the bottom leaf surface. Water loss varies with weather conditions and the size and kind of leaf.

GENERALIZATION

Plants lose water through tiny openings in their leaves; the amount of water lost depends on several conditions.

SAMPLE PERFORMANCE OBJECTIVES

Process: The child will arrange a second (control) setup when needed, as in B.

Knowledge: The child can state at least one condition that influences the rate of water loss in leaves.

ACTIVITY: *HOW CAN YOU MAKE LEAF RUBBINGS?*

NEEDED

different leaves with thick veins
tissue paper
crayons

TRY THIS

1. Place tissue paper over a fresh leaf.

2. Rub a crayon back and forth. A beautiful vein pattern will appear.

3. Try different colors and leaves.

4. Play a matching game with someone.
   a. Can your partner match each of your patterns with the right leaf? Can you match your partner's patterns and leaves?
   b. How can you use your patterns to make holiday or greeting cards?

ACTIVITY: *HOW CAN YOU LEARN ABOUT PLANT BUDS?*

NEEDED

small branches and twigs from plants
nail
pruning shears or knife
jar of water

TRY THIS

1. Find a low tree or bush with fallen leaves.
2. Look for small branches or twigs that have buds. Observe just above where each leaf was attached to the twig or stem.
3. Cut off a few twigs that have buds. (Ask permission first.)
   a. How are the buds arranged? What patterns, if any, do you notice?
4. Pick apart one or two buds with a thin nail.
   b. How can you describe the buds?
   c. Which of the remaining buds will grow leaves? To see, stick the twig into a jar of water. Change the water every two or three days.

TEACHING COMMENT

The beginning of spring is a good time to collect twigs for budding.

ACTIVITY: *WHAT IS INSIDE FLOWERS?*

NEEDED

several flowers
straight pin
newspaper
magnifying glass

TRY THIS

1. Bend back a few flower petals to see inside, as shown in Figure 14-7.
2. Remove one of the stamens. Pick apart the anther, the part on the end.
   a. Can you see any dustlike pollen? What color is it? How does the pollen look under a magnifying glass?
3. Examine the pistil end.
   b. What does it look like? Is it sticky when touched?
4. Use a pin to carefully slit open the pistil's thicker end.
   c. Can you see any baby seeds inside? What do they look like?
5. Examine other flowers in the same way.
   d. How are other flowers alike? different?

TEACHING COMMENT

Florists are usually willing to donate unsalable flowers to schools.

ADAPTION AND SURVIVAL EXPERIENCES
(Concepts p. 394)

ACTIVITY: HOW DOES GRAVITY AFFECT A GROWING PLANT?

NEEDED

paper towels
soaked radish seed
plastic drinking glass
plastic kitchen wrap

TRY THIS

1. Line the inside of a glass with a wet, folded paper towel.
2. Crumple and stuff some towels inside the lined glass. This will hold the first towel in place.
3. Put a soaked radish seed between the glass and the first towel. The seed should be in the middle of the glass.
4. Pour about 2.5 centimeters (1 inch) of water into the glass.
5. Wait until the seed sprouts, grows leaves, and roots.
6. Pour out what water is left. Cover the glass with kitchen wrap to keep the towel lining moist.

7. Tip over the glass onto one side.

   a. What happens to the upper stem of the plant over the next few days?

   b. What happens to the roots?

   c. What will happen if you tip over the glass onto the opposite side?

ACTIVITY: *HOW CAN YOU MAKE A PLANT GROW TOWARD THE LIGHT?*

NEEDED

small and large paper cups
bean seeds
soil

TRY THIS

1. Plant one or two bean seeds in a small paper cup of soil. Water as needed.
2. Wait until leaves appear.
3. Punch a hole into the side of the large paper cup with a pencil.
4. Cover the small cup with the large cup. Uncover briefly when you need to water.
5. Leave the cups in a well-lighted place. Be sure the cup hole faces the light.

   a. What do you notice after a few days?

   b. What do you think would happen if you turned the plant around? (Be sure the cup hole faces the light.)

MOLD AND FUNGI EXPERIENCES
(Concepts p. 395)

INVESTIGATION: *HOW MOLDS GROW*

On what things have you seen molds? How did the molds look?

EXPLORATORY PROBLEM

How can you make a mold garden?

NEEDED

aluminum foil
large pickle jar with lid

sand
baby food jars with lids
water
bread slice
magnifying glass
small pieces of different foods
tissue paper
clay
spoon
medicine dropper

TRY THIS

1. Fill a large glass jar about one-third full with sand.

2. Put the jar down on its side. Shake the jar so the sand settles evenly.

3. Sprinkle some water on the sand to make it damp. Use a spoon.

4. Put different objects that might mold on the sand.

5. Screw the lid on the jar (Figure 14-18). Do not remove it.

6. Leave the jar where you can observe it each day.

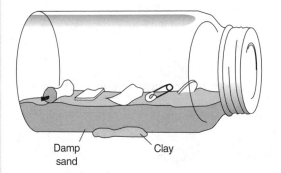

Damp
sand   Clay

Figure 14-18

DISCOVERY PROBLEMS

hypothesizing and communicating   **A.** On which objects do you think molds will grow? Which will not mold? Which do you think will be covered by molds first? last? Keep a record of your results.

experimenting   **B.** Try some experiments. How can you get a fresh piece of bread to mold? Keep the bread inside a baby food jar (or plastic bag). Keep the lid on each jar after starting each experiment, B through F.

experimenting

C. Is water needed for molds to grow on bread? If so, how much? Fresh bread may contain some moisture. How can you start with dry bread?

experimenting

D. Will bread molds grow better in the dark or light? How about dim light?

experimenting

E. How can you *prevent* mold from growing on a piece of bread?

experimenting

F. What other experiments would you like to try?

TEACHING COMMENT

PREPARATION AND BACKGROUND

For bread experiments, try to get the white home-baked kind or store bread without preservatives. Commercial bread often contains a mold-inhibiting chemical called sodium propionate. ***Caution:*** The molds or other organisms in this investigation are typically harmless. However, play it safe by having children (1) keep all moldy materials covered, (2) wash their hands if a mold is touched, (3) avoid sniffing molds, (4) avoid growing molds in soil samples, and (5) dispose of all used, still-closed containers in a tightly sealed bag.

GENERALIZATION

Some molds grow well under dark, moist, and warm conditions.

SAMPLE PERFORMANCE OBJECTIVES

Process: The child can set up an experiment to test one condition that may affect mold growth.

Knowledge: The child can state one or more conditions that influence the growth of molds.

FOR YOUNGER CHILDREN

Most primary children can profit from setting up the mold garden and observing and recording results.

REFERENCES

American Association for the Advancement of Science. (1993). *Benchmarks for science literacy.* New York: Oxford University Press.

National Research Council. (1996). *National science education standards.* Washington, DC: National Academy Press.

SELECTED TRADE BOOKS: PLANT LIFE AND ENVIRONMENT

For Younger Children

Busch, P. (1979). *Cactus in the desert.* Crowell.

Challand, H. (1986). *Plants without seeds.* Children's Press.

Gibbins, G. (1991). *From seed to plant.* Holiday.

Kirkpatrick, R. K. (1985). *Look at seeds and weeds.* Raintree.

Kuchalla, S. (1982). *All about seeds.* Troll Associates.

Lauber, P. (1981). *Seeds: pop, stick, glide.* Crown.

Miner, O. I. (1981). *Plants we know.* Children's Press.

Moncure, J. B. (1990). *What plants need.* Child's World.

Penn, L. (1986). *Wild plants and animals.* Good Apple.

Selsam, M. E., & Hunt, J. (1977). *A first look at flowers.* Walker.

Taylor, B. (1991). *Growing plants.* Watts.

Tresselt, A. (1992). *The gift of a tree.* Lothrop, Lee & Shepard.

Webster, V. (1982). *Plant experiments.* Children's Press.

For Older Children

Bates, J. (1991). *Seeds to plants: Projects with botany.* Watts.

Cochrane, J. (1987). *Plant ecology.* Watts.

Coldrey, J. (1987). *Discovering flowering plants.* Watts.

Conway, L. (1980). *Plants.* Good Apple.

Conway, L. (1986). *Plants and animals in nature.* Good Apple.

Gallant, R. A. (1991). *Earth's vanishing forests.* Macmillan.

Holley, B. (1986). *Plants and flowers.* Penworthy.

Hogner, D. C. (1977). *Endangered plants.* Crowell.

Lambert, M. (1983). *Plant life.* Watts.

Leutscher, A. (1984). *Flowering plants.* Watts.

Marcus, E. (1984). *Amazing world of plants.* Troll Associates.

Penn, L. (1987). *Plant ecology.* Watts.

Sabin, L. (1985). *Plants, seeds, and flowers.* Troll Associates.

Taylor, K., & Burton, J. (1993). *Forest Life.* Dorling Kindersley.

Resource Books

Butzow, C. M., & Butzow, J. W. (1989). *Science through children's literature. An integrated approach* (tree topics, pp. 49–54; seed topics, pp. 55–60). Teachers Ideas Press.

Fredericks, A. D., Meinbach, A. M., & Rothlein, L. (1993). *Thematic units: An integrated approach to teaching science and social studies* (plant topics, pp. 123–131). HarperCollins.

LeCroy, B., & Holder, B. (1994). *Bookwebs: a brainstorm of ideas for the primary classroom* (seed activity, p. 69). Teachers Ideas Press.

Shaw, D. G., & Dybdahl, C. S. (1996). *Integrating science and language arts. A sourcebook for K–6 teachers* (plant topics, pp. 60–62). Allyn and Bacon.

CHAPTER

15

ANIMAL LIFE AND ENVIRONMENT

Animal Life and Environment

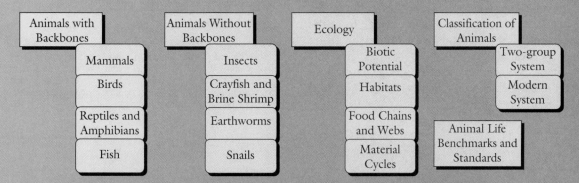

Animals with Backbones	Animals Without Backbones	Ecology	Classification of Animals
Mammals	Insects	Biotic Potential	Two-group System
Birds	Crayfish and Brine Shrimp	Habitats	Modern System
Reptiles and Amphibians	Earthworms	Food Chains and Webs	Animal Life Benchmarks and Standards
Fish	Snails	Material Cycles	

Can a gnat have *anything* in common with an elephant?

Despite their enormous diversity, all animals share certain common needs and physical properties. By carefully observing how animals are formed, we can place them into groups with common properties. These groups enable us to learn many of the interesting adaptations of animals without having to study each group member.

This chapter discusses animals with backbones, animals without backbones, and interactions of living things with each other and their environment, or ecology. But right now, let's briefly consider some ways to classify animals.

CLASSIFICATION
OF ANIMALS CONCEPTS
(Experiences p. 445)

Of some 1,250,000 different forms of living things, animals make up almost 1,000,000. They run, walk, crawl, fly, slither, and swim. They range in size from microscopic organisms to the blue whale, which may be up to about 30 meters (100 feet) long. Their colors embrace all shades of the spectrum. The diversity of animals is truly amazing.

How do scientists keep track of them? A system developed by the great Swedish naturalist Carolus Linnaeus (1707–78) provided the foundation for modern classification. Its basis is the physical structure of the living thing. Six main categories are used, which range from the general to the particular description of group properties.

For example, let's classify a dog. Parenthetical remarks refer to the general meaning of each category.

Kingdom Animalia (the subject belongs to the animal, not the plant, kingdom).[1]

Phylum Chordata (it has a backbone or a notochord).

Class Mammalia (it is a mammal).

Order Carnivora (it eats meat).

Family Canidae (it belongs to a group with doglike characteristics).

Genus Canis (it is a coyote, wolf, or dog).

Species Canis familiaris (it is a common dog).

Such a system has important advantages to biologists. It is possible to pinpoint most living things and to note relationships that otherwise might be easy to miss. Because the system is accepted by scientists the world over, accuracy of communication is realized.

For elementary school science, however, you will want to work with a simpler classification scheme. The following one should be useful and will fit nicely into any more formal structure the child may develop later in high school and college. Although in this chapter we will not study all the subgroups described, seeing the overall classification scheme should be helpful to you.

We can divide the entire animal kingdom into two huge groups, each with a manageably small number of subgroups.

ANIMALS WITH BACKBONES (VERTEBRATES)

Mammals (human, dog, etc.).

Birds (sparrow, penguin, etc.).

Reptiles (turtle, lizard, etc.).

---

[1] Some scientists have named a third kingdom called protists, which includes single-celled plant-like and animal-like organisms. Other scientists have classified living things into five kingdoms: monera (for example, bacteria), protists, fungi, plants, and animals.

Amphibians (frog, toad, etc.).

Fishes (carp, bass, etc.).

ANIMALS WITHOUT BACKBONES (INVERTEBRATES)

Echinoderms Animals with spiny skins (sand dollar, starfish, etc.).

Arthropods Animals with jointed legs: insects (fly, moth, etc.); arachnids (spider, scorpion, etc.); crustaceans (crab, lobster, etc.); myriapods (millipede and centipede).

Mollusks Animals with soft bodies (clam, snail, etc.).

Worms (flatworm, segmented worm, etc.).

Corals and relatives (sea anemone, coral, etc.).

Sponges (The natural sponges we use are the fibrous skeletons of these animals.)

When young children use the term *animal*, they are inclined to mean mammal, or at best, another animal with a backbone. Yet the five classes of vertebrates—mammals, birds, reptiles, amphibians, and fishes—make up a scant 5% of the animal species in existence.

Animals without backbones make up the rest. Insects, which make up 70% of all animals, represent by far the largest class of invertebrates. There are more than 800,000 species. (A species is a group whose members can generally reproduce only among themselves.)

ANIMALS WITH BACKBONES CONCEPTS
(Experiences page 445)

Despite their fewer numbers, the five classes of vertebrates represent the highest forms of life on this planet. We'll begin with the most advanced form, mammals.

Mammals

Look around long enough and you will find animals everywhere: below the ground (mole, gopher, woodchuck); on the ground (humans, giraffe, elephant); in trees above the ground (monkey, sloth, tree squirrel); in the air (bat); and in the water (whale, seal, dolphin). What can such a diverse collection of creatures have in common? All of them are mammals. That is, all have some fur or hair, and all have milk glands. To be sure, you will not find much hair on a whale, only a few bristles on the snout. And sometimes fur or hair is greatly modified, as with the porcupine's quills. But look closely enough, and if it is a mammal, it has hair.

Both male and female mammals have mammary, or milk, glands. (You can see how the term *mammals* originated.) Ordinarily, of course, only the female produces the milk used in suckling the young.

Another distinction of mammals is their intelligence, the highest of all animal groups. But other unique properties are few and subtle.

INTERNAL DEVELOPMENT. Mammals are usually born wholly formed, although growth continues to the adult stage of the life cycle. The embryo develops within the mother from a tiny egg fertilized by a sperm cell from a male of the same species.

During its development, the embryo is attached to the mother by a placenta, or membranous tissue. Water, oxygen, and food pass from mother to embryo through this tissue. In turn, liquefied waste materials flow the other way. These are absorbed into the mother's bloodstream, sent to the kidneys, and eliminated. The navel pit in the abdomen of humans, or "belly button," is a reminder of this early state of our development.

The two known exceptions to this developmental pattern are the spiny anteater and duck-billed platypus, both of Australia. Each lays eggs. The hatched young, though, are cared for and suckled by the mother just like other mammals.

WARM-BLOODED. Mammals are warm-blooded and have efficient hearts with four definite chambers. Their blood temperatures stay at relatively the same level, whether the air warms or cools. Animals of lesser complexity are cold-blooded. That is, their blood temperature changes as their environmental temperature changes.

It is both an advantage and a disadvantage to be warm-blooded. Vigorous activity is possible within most air temperature ranges. But the body heat of mammals must be conserved, or death occurs.

In cold climates, thick blubber or fur performs this function, as does hibernation, and, in some cases, migration. In warm climates, humans perspire. Some animals estivate, or become relatively inactive for a period in whatever suitably cool refuge can be found.

Some cold-blooded animals can withstand great cold or heat, but most depend on a narrow temperature range for normal activity or survival. We will go into more detail later with several specific animals.

Although the terms are still relative, it is more accurate to say, "constant-temperatured" and "variable-temperatured" rather than "warm-blooded" and "cold-blooded" when we refer to animals. In hot weather, for example, a "cold-blooded" animal might have a higher body temperature than a "warm-blooded" one.

TEETH. The teeth of mammals are particularly interesting to observe since they seem adapted to specific uses. We can see the four main kinds of teeth by examining our own in a mirror. In front are the chisel-like incisors. On both sides of these teeth are the cone-like canines. Farther back are the front molars, and last, the back molars. Now note how these teeth are used by several kinds of mammals.

Prominent, sharp incisors are characteristic of gnawing mammals such as rats, mice, gerbils, guinea pigs, hamsters, muskrats, beavers, and rabbits. The incisors of these rodents grow continuously at the root and are worn down at the opposite end by gnawing. When prevented from gnawing, incisors may grow so long that the animal cannot close its mouth, and so starves to death.

The flesh eaters have small incisors and prominent canines, sometimes called "fangs." Their molars have curved, sharp edges. The canines are useful for tearing meat. The molars are suited for chopping it into parts small enough to swallow.

Plant eaters have wide, closely spaced incisors and large, flat-surfaced molars. Canines do not appear. The incisors work well in clipping off grasses and plant stems. The molars grind this material before swallowing.

You and I are omnivores; in other words, we are capable of eating both plants and animals. Human teeth include all four types.

Classroom Mammals

The classroom is likely to be a restrictive place for mammals, so it is wise to select those that will fare reasonably well there. It is also important to get an animal that can be used to fulfill some lasting educational purposes. (Most school districts have policies as to what animals, if any, are permitted in classrooms.)

Experienced teachers often recommend use of white rats and gerbils (Figure 15-1) over common classroom animals such as white mice, hamsters, and guinea pigs.

Although simple cages for rodents can be homemade from strong screening material, a commercial cage is usually more secure and better suited to the animals' needs. A commercial cage, like that shown in Figure 15-2, should serve well and last indefinitely.

Following are some suggestions for housing and caring for a female and male white rat or gerbil.

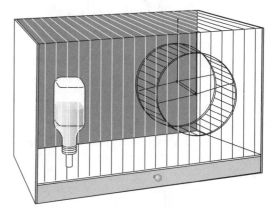

Figure 15-2
A commercially produced cage such as this is well suited for housing white rats.

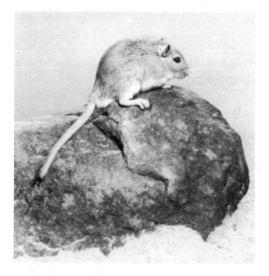

Figure 15-1
A gerbil.

CAGE. Use a commercially produced cage with exercise wheel and inverted water bottle as recommended. Cover the floor with a four-page thickness of newspaper. Scatter a generous covering of sawdust, wood shavings, peat moss, or shredded newspaper over the paper. Remove the floor covering and replace with fresh materials twice a week or more often if odor develops.

The cage should be in a draft-free location, as rodents are quite susceptible to colds. Ideally, the temperature should not fall below 15°C (60°F). However, a deep floor covering usually provides some insulation against the loss of heat energy, since the animals will burrow into it.

FOOD.[2] Dry pellets for small laboratory animals, including rats, are sold at most pet and feed stores. In addition, provide bits of carrots, lettuce, cheese, and bread for the animal to eat. A constant supply of pellets and other nonper-

ishable food may be left in a small, flat container in the cage. However, remove any perishable food within an hour after it has been offered. A fresh bottle of water and tray of pellets should last over weekends, but provisions for feeding will need to be made for longer periods.

HANDLING. White rats are typically very gentle, likable creatures. They should be handled daily for a short period. This tames them and accustoms them to being around children.

Caution: Although there is little chance that a white rat will bite if treated gently, remind children to keep their fingers away from the animal's mouth when handling it. Notify the school nurse immediately if *any* classroom animal bites a child. Although the bite itself is usually minor, germs the animal may harbor in its mouth may cause infection unless the wound is promptly treated.

BREEDING. Rats usually breed within a few days. Provide some loose cotton or shredded newspaper that the female can use in preparing a nest. Remove the male from the cage after it appears obvious that the female is pregnant.

---

[2] For food and other requirements of animals often kept in classrooms, please see Appendix D.

Return the male to the pet store, or give it to the Humane Society.

About three to four weeks after mating, the female will give birth to eight or more young in the nest. Do not disturb the female for ten days after this event. The newborn young will be blind and hairless. They may be weaned gradually to a regular diet after they are about two weeks old. Feed them milk that contains soft bread crumbs for a week and adult food thereafter.

All rats should be given to a responsible party after completion of this activity. Abandoned rodents become wild and add quickly to the local pest population.

During the eight weeks or so of working with these animals, try to have time for frequent, short class discussions about the behavior and habits of the caged rats. Emphasize the birth, appearance, care, feeding, and physical development of the young. You may note rapid day-to-day improvement in children's verbal reporting skills as they tell the latest news about their rats. It is also an excellent journal-writing activity.

Use a chart with rotating names for assigning tasks such as replacement of water, paper, and food. Most children are delighted to serve. This may be an excellent opportunity to motivate students and help them achieve a greater sense of responsibility.

Birds

"A bird is an animal with feathers." This is a primary child's definition, but it really cannot be much improved. Almost all other properties we see in birds may be found here and there among other animal groups, although not in the same combinations. The coloring and construction of birds' feathers vary tremendously, from the luxuriant plumage of a peacock to the scruffy covering of a New Zealand kiwi.

Although we ordinarily think of birds as fliers, chickens and road runners seldom fly, and some birds, like the ostrich, penguin, and kiwi, cannot fly at all.

FOOD AND HEAT LOSS. "He eats like a bird." How often we have heard a person who eats sparingly described this way. It is hardly fitting. Few other animals possess such voracious appetites for their size. Many birds must eat their weight in food each day just to stay alive.

To see why this is so, examine a small, flying bird closely. Notice that its body volume is relatively small when compared to the large surface area of its skin. As body volume decreases, the relative size of skin surface increases. If this seems unclear, inspect a pint and a quart milk carton. The small carton holds only half as much but clearly has more than one-half the surface area of the larger carton.

A large skin surface area causes heat energy to radiate rapidly away from the body. This is bad when the body volume is small, because the heat generating capacity is also small. To generate enough heat energy for normal functioning when heat energy is quickly being radiated away, a high metabolic rate (the rate at which food is oxidized and assimilated) must be maintained. The rapid burning of fuel causes body temperatures in birds of 39° to 43°C (102° to 110°F), the highest of any animal group.

The same principle of volume relative to surface area applies to mammals, too. Smaller mammals usually eat more for their size than larger ones. As we travel toward the earth's polar regions, we can observe a general increase in mammals' body size. As body volume increases, the relative size of skin surface decreases. Comparatively less heat energy is radiated away. This has great survival value.

FLIGHT ADAPTATIONS. The bodies of most birds are well suited for flight. Inside are several air sacs connected to the lungs. Many bones are hollow, or nearly so, and further reduce body weight. Even a chicken has relatively little marrow in its longer bones. It is said that the evolutionist Charles Darwin had a pipe stem made from a wing bone of an albatross.

The body of a bird is streamlined and closely fitted with three kinds of feathers. Next to the skin are fluffy, soft down feathers. These contain numerous "dead-air" pockets that help conserve body heat. Contour feathers hug the body closely, and large flight feathers help to propel and steer the bird as it flies.

Most birds continually preen their feathers. This is done by using the bill to press a drop of oil from a gland located just above the tail and then spreading the oil over the feathers. A shiny, waterproof coating results. It is so effective that a duck can float for many hours without becoming waterlogged. If the oil were suddenly removed, a swimming duck would disappear into the water like a slowly submerging submarine.

If you can locate a large, recently molted feather, dip it in water before and after washing it in soap or detergent. Notice how water soaks in after the washing.

The thick white meat or breast section on poultry is partly the result of selective breeding by humans. However, nearly all birds have their largest and strongest muscles in this section because these muscles control the major wing movements.

SENSES. The remarkably keen eyesight of birds has been well advertised. Less known is that they have three eyelids. Two shut the eye, and the third, which is transparent, sweeps back and forth, cleaning away dust or other foreign matter without need for blinking. Eyes of most birds are located on the sides of the head. So they must continually cock the head to one side to see directly forward. Their hearing is also acute despite the lack of outer ears. Two small earholes suffice. On the other hand, birds do not appear to discriminate well among various odors or tastes.

BEAKS AND FEET. Most birds have horny beaks; their various shapes show great diversity of function. Although all known modern birds are toothless, fossil records indicate that a variety of toothed birds lived in ancient times. The feet of birds are equally diverse in form. On the legs we find scales, which reveal their evolutionary connection to the reptiles.

Figure 15-3 shows some common structures and functions of birds' bills and feet. The duck's bill is useful for scooping up small fish and plants in water because it is shaped like a shovel. The scooped-up water spills out through the uneven sides of the bill, but the food remains inside. The duck's webbed feet are useful for paddling in water.

The woodpecker's bill is like a large, pointed nail, useful for digging insects out of tough tree bark. (The bills of most other insect catchers

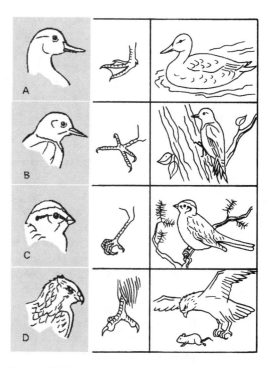

Figure 15-3
(A) Duck, (B) woodpecker, (C) sparrow, (D) hawk.

are more slender.) Its feet can dig securely into a vertical tree trunk.

The sparrow's bill is small, but strong enough to crack open seeds and some nuts, like a pet canary's does. Its feet are useful for perching because they automatically close around a tree limb. It requires no effort, and the bird may sleep in this position without danger of falling.

The hawk's bill is like a sharp hook, useful for tearing the flesh from bones of field mice and other small animals it preys on. Its feet are useful for grasping and holding its prey.

REPRODUCTION. As in mammals, sexual reproduction begins with an egg cell fertilized within the female by a sperm cell. However, fertilization is not necessary for an egg to be laid. Many chickens lay an egg every day. We eat these unfertilized eggs.

An egg acquires its hard shell in the lower part of the hen's oviduct, or egg-conducting tube. Glands produce a limy secretion that gradually hardens over a period of hours before the egg is laid. The shell is porous and permits both oxygen to enter and carbon dioxide to leave. In a fertilized egg, this is essential for life in the developing chick embryo.

CHICK HATCHING.   It is fairly easy to hatch chicks in the classroom. To do so, you will need fertilized eggs and an incubator. Get the eggs from a hatchery or farmer. Buy a small incubator from a pet shop or scientific supply house. It is essential to success that a near-constant temperature of 38° to 39°C (101° to 103°F) be maintained for the 21-day incubation period. Fertilized eggs should be turned over twice a day. This keeps the growing embryo from sticking to the shell. A mark placed on the egg will allow you to keep track of egg positions.

In 21 days, or sooner if the eggs have not been freshly laid, the hatching will take place. This process may take several or more hours. Since some hatching may happen at night, it is

good to have several eggs. This will increase the chance that a few chicks will hatch during school hours.

Children can observe how a chick breaks out of its shell using a tiny "egg tooth" on top of its beak. This drops off shortly after the chick emerges. (See Figure 15-4.) The chick will look wet and scraggly until its downy feathers dry. No food is necessary for at least 24 hours, as it will have digested the egg yolk and some egg white before breaking out of the shell. (It is a common misconception that an egg yolk *is* the undeveloped embryo, rather than the chick's principal food.)

CARING FOR CHICKS. Chicks need constant warmth. This is furnished by a brooder, or warm box. An incubator can be used temporarily if the lid is raised, but it may be too confining after a few days. If the chicks are to be kept for more than several days, use a cardboard box with a shielded, goose-neck lamp shining into it.

Chick feed may be bought at a pet store. Leave some feed and clean water in dishes within the brooder at all times. A fresh newspa-

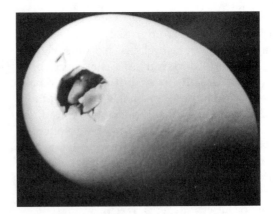

Figure 15-4
A chick starts to peck itself out of the egg. Note the egg tooth.

per floor cover each day will keep the brooder clean.

Reptiles

Many children know that snakes are reptiles but are unaware that the term also includes turtles, lizards, alligators, and crocodiles. What do these animals have in common? Typically they have dry, scaly skin. Those with feet have five toes which bear claws. All are lung breathers, which means that even an aquatic turtle will drown if placed underwater for an extended time period.

COLD-BLOODED. Reptiles have well developed hearts with three chambers (some have almost four). Unlike mammals and birds, reptiles are cold-blooded. In winter, reptiles in relatively cold climates hibernate below ground; they become unable to move when the temperature drops very low. It is no accident that reptiles are rare in regions beyond the temperate zones and proliferate in the tropics.

REPRODUCTION. In reptiles, reproduction begins with the internal fertilization of an egg, similar to mammals and birds. But the process thereafter is different enough to warrant our attention. All of the turtles and most of the lizards and snakes lay eggs in secluded areas on land. The eggs have tough, leathery covers, and for the most part depend on the sun's warmth for incubation.

Some snakes and lizards retain the egg internally until the incubation period is complete. The young are then born alive. However, the process differs from the development of mammalian young.

In mammals, as was noted, the embryo is attached to the female and nourished directly through a placental membrane. In reptiles, there is no internal attachment. The egg incubates until the growing embryo inside is sufficiently developed to hatch and so leave the female.

EYES. Turtles and most lizards have three eyelids, as do birds. Snakes have no eyelids. A transparent, horny cover over the eye protects it from injury as the animal moves among sticks and vegetation. Just before a snake sheds its skin, up to several times a year, the transparent eye cover becomes milky in color. Interestingly, the only easy way to tell the several species of legless lizards from snakes is to note whether the eyes blink.

COMMON LIZARDS. Children may bring lizards, often swifts, to class. (See Figure 15-5.) In the southwestern United States, it is common for children to bring the gentle and easily tamed horned toad. Nearly all lizards may be housed satisfactorily in a terrarium containing some sand and placed where it is sunny. The anole (American chameleon), the kind often bought at fairs and pet shops, is more suited to a woodland terrarium. (See page 390 for descriptions of terrariums.)

Chameleons are interesting for children to observe. Like many lizards, they change body

Figure 15-5
A typical small lizard, the Eastern Fence Swift.

color under different conditions of light, temperature, and excitation. However, the color change is greater in chameleons than in most other lizards. It is brought about by dilation and contraction of blood vessels in the skin.

Many lizards have fragile tails that break off easily when seized. In some species, the broken-off tail part wriggles about animatedly, thereby often distracting the attention of a would-be captor until the lizard escapes. Lizards can grow back (regenerate) new tails.

CLASSROOM SNAKE. If possible, try to get a small, tame snake for the children to examine. Let the children touch it and learn that it has dry, cool skin, rather than a slimy coating. Children can learn that nearly all snakes in this country are highly beneficial to humans, and that snakes consume many thousands of destructive rodent and insect pests each year.

At the same time, students should learn an intelligent respect for snakes. If poisonous snakes appear locally, show pictures of what they look like. *Caution:* Instruct children never to hunt for snakes unless accompanied by a responsible and informed older person. In the continental United States, the rattlesnake, copperhead, water moccasin, and coral snake are dangerous to humans.

Amphibians

These are animals that typically spend part of their lives in water and part on land. The main kinds are frogs, toads, and salamanders. Amphibians represent an interesting evolutionary link between fishes and reptiles and have many properties of both groups. If animal life originally began and evolved in the sea, as is generally supposed, it is probable that early amphibians were the first vertebrates to emerge from the water and live successfully on land.

COLD-BLOODED. Amphibians are cold-blooded and have hearts with three chambers.

Like other cold-blooded animals, they hibernate in cold weather, usually by burrowing in the ground or mud. The adults breathe through lungs, but are also able to absorb some oxygen through the skin. The latter method of breathing is especially useful in hibernation. Still, skin breathing is inadequate for sustained activity, and even a frog will drown eventually if forced to remain underwater.

Frogs and salamanders usually have moist, smooth skins that must remain moist if they are to survive. For this reason, a bowl of water is needed in a terrarium that houses these creatures.

FROGS AND TOADS. One day a child may show you a small amphibian and ask, "Is this a toad or a frog?" Although it is hard to distinguish between them all the time, a toad usually has dry, rough skin. Its body is broad and fat, and the eyelids are more prominent than those of frogs. Another indicator is where it was caught. Frogs are likelier to live by water, whereas toads are mostly land dwellers (Figure 15-6).

Can toads cause warts? Many children think they can. The toad's warty-looking tubercles are glands that secrete a fluid that can sicken attacking animals. But the substance cannot cause warts. It may irritate the eyes, though, if they are rubbed after handling a toad. Advise students to wash their hands after playing with a toad.

SALAMANDERS. Less common than frogs and toads are salamanders; chances are that few students will have these as pets. Most salamanders have four legs of the same size and long, tubular bodies with tails. Superficially, they resemble lizards and are often mistaken for them. They differ from lizards in several ways: The forelegs of salamanders have four toes instead of five; they have no claws; and typically the skin is smooth rather than rough. *Caution:* A salamander's skin may secrete a mild poison,

Figure 15-6
Toad (left) and frog. Notice the external eardrum, just behind and below the eye.

so hands should be thoroughly washed after handling it.

REPRODUCTION. Perhaps the most striking difference between amphibians and the other groups we have examined is in their means of reproduction. Female amphibians lay their eggs in water or in very moist places on land. Immediately after the eggs are laid, the males fertilize them by shedding sperm over them. Therefore, fertilization is external, unlike that in higher-order animals.

A single female frog or toad may lay several thousand eggs at one time. The eggs are coated with a thick, jellylike substance that quickly absorbs water and swells in size. This substance protects the developing embryo and serves as a first source of food. Eggs may often be found in ponds in spring. Look for gelatinous clumps (frog) or strings (toad) near grassy edges or where cattails grow.

After one or two weeks, the embryo hatches as a tadpole, or "polliwog," which looks completely unlike the adult. It is only after several months to several years, depending on the species, that tadpoles acquire the adult form. (See Figure 15-7.) This process of changing forms, called metamorphosis, is another distinct departure from the growth and development pattern of higher animals.

In their initial growth stages, tadpoles breathe like fishes; that is, they obtain oxygen from water through tiny gills. Be sure to "age" tap water for at least 24 hours to rid it of chlorine before adding it to the container in which

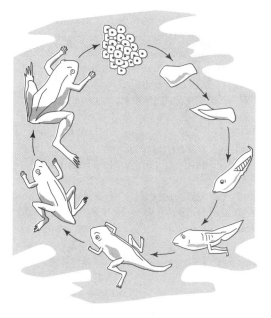

Figure 15-7
Metamorphosis of the frog.

the tadpoles are kept. Use tap water only if pond water is not available.

Fishes

Next to mammals, fishes are the vertebrates that present the greatest diversity in appearance, adaptations, and habits. Certainly, fishes are most numerous, both as individuals and in numbers of species. (When only one species is referred to, *fish* is both singular and plural. *Fishes* means those of several species.) Fossil records show that these creatures were the first animals with true backbones.

BREATHING. Fishes are cold-blooded and have hearts with only two chambers. They breathe through gills instead of lungs. Gills are composed of thousands of blood vessels contained in hair-like filaments located in back of the head on both sides. We cannot easily see these filaments on a live fish, as gill covers conceal them.

A fish breathes by opening and closing its mouth. In the process, water is taken in and then forced out of the gill openings. As water passes over the gills, oxygen dissolved in the water filters into the filaments and blood vessels and then circulates throughout the body. At the same time, carbon dioxide passes out of the filaments and is swept away.

One of the advantages in carefully classifying living things by structure is that it enables us to see relationships we might otherwise miss. In fishes, for example, an organ called the "air bladder" appears to be a forerunner of the lung. The bladder is an air-filled sac usually located in the middle of a fish between its kidney and stomach. By compressing and expanding its air bladder, a fish can rise and descend in the water.

In the lungfish, this organ has been modified into a crude lung, enabling it to breathe air directly in addition to breathing through the gills. A lungfish typically lives in a muddy pond or marsh, which may dry up in summer. It survives by burrowing into the mud and breathing air supplied through a hole in the mud cover. When its pond fills again with seasonal rainfall, the lungfish resumes the normal gill-breathing behavior of fishes. The lungfish appears to be a clear link between fishes and amphibians in the long evolutionary march of vertebrates from the sea.

BODY. The body of a fish is well suited for its environment. Its streamlined contours offer a minimum of resistance to the water. A slimy, mucous-like secretion that exudes between the overlapping body scales further reduces friction and insulates the skin from attack by microorganisms. A large tail fin, wagged from side to side, propels it through the water. Vertical fins on top and bottom keep the fish on an even keel while it is moving. Two pairs of side fins, one pair near the gills (pectoral fins), and the other pair farther back (pelvic fins), balance the fish when it is stationary. These fins are also used to assist turning, in the manner of oars, and for swimming backward. When held out laterally, they brake the swimming fish to a stop. Pectoral fins correspond to forelegs, and pelvic fins correlate to hind legs, in other animals.

SENSES. The eyes of a fish are always open, since it has no eyelids. Focusing is done by shifting the pupil forward and back, rather than by changing the lens shape, as in humans.

So-called flatfish, such as the flounder and halibut, lie on one side. Both eyes are arranged on one side of the head. Because these fish are typically bottom dwellers, this eye arrangement permits greater vision.

Although there are no external ears, fish hear with auditory capsules deep within the head. In many fishes, a lateral line of sensory scales extends along both sides of the body from head to tail. These scales are particularly sensitive to sounds of low pitch. Some expert anglers claim that a fish can hear heavy footsteps (always of other, inexpert anglers, of course) on a nearby bank.

The taste sense appears to be mostly lacking, but a fish is sensitive to smells. Nostril pits on the snout lead to organs of smell just below. The whole body, and especially the lips, seems to be sensitive to touch. In species like the catfish, extra touch organs are found in the form of "whiskers."

REPRODUCTION. In fishes, reproduction is accomplished by either external or internal fertilization of the egg, depending on the species. The female goldfish, for example, lays eggs on aquatic plants. The male fertilizes the eggs by shedding sperm cells over them. Goldfish usually reproduce only in large tanks or ponds.

Guppies and many other tropical varieties use internal fertilization. The male has a modified anal fin that carries sperm. The fin is inserted into a small opening below the female's abdomen, and sperm cells are released. Fertilized eggs remain in the female's body until the embryos hatch and are "born." Many of the young guppies are eaten by the adult fish, unless sufficient plant growth makes it difficult to detect them.

To raise as many guppies as possible, place the pregnant female (its underside will look swollen) and some plants in a separate container. After the young are born, remove the mother. The young may join the adult guppies safely in about one month.

Try not to be too efficient at breeding guppies, however. Someone good at arithmetic has calculated that a single pair will become three million guppies in a year, assuming all generations and offspring stay alive. A female guppy may produce several dozen young every 4 to 6 weeks at a water temperature of 21° to 27°C (70° to 80°F).

Male guppies differ from the females in several ways. They are about half the size (exclusive of the tails), much narrower in body, and more brilliantly colored (Figure 15-8).

Figure 15-8
Male (right) and female guppy.

Setting Up an Aquarium

An aquarium is an excellent source to observe ecological principles firsthand. In this watery habitat, plants and animals interact with each other and their environment, and reproduction takes place in several ways. It is possible to see a near balance of nature through the interactions, and the consequences when there is an imbalance.

CHILDREN'S AQUARIA. It is easy for children to set up a number of small aquaria for short-range observations of a week or two. For the containers, they may use large, wide-mouth jars or plastic shoe boxes. One or two goldfish and a few sprigs of water plants per container should do nicely. Tap water can be put into the containers and aged for at least 24 hours before the fish are introduced. A tiny amount of fish food, no more than the fish can eat in a few minutes, should be sprinkled on the water once a day. A more elaborate, long-range habitat for aquatic animals and plants is described next.

TANK. The materials needed are a tank, some clean sand (not the seashore variety), a few aquatic snails and plants, and several small fish. A rectangular tank of 19- to 23-liter (5- to 6-gallon) capacity serves best for a classroom aquarium. The rectangular shape has less viewing distortion than a bowl. It also permits more oxygen from the air to dissolve in the water because of the relatively greater surface area exposed at the top.

The tank must be clean. Dirt, grease, or caked lime can be removed by scrubbing thoroughly with salt and water. The salt is abrasive enough to have a scouring effect. Should detergent or soaps be needed, repeated rinsing of the tank is essential. Any residue may be harmful to future inhabitants. About two inches of clean sand may then be placed and spread evenly on the bottom of the tank.

PLANTS. A pet store can supply several varieties of inexpensive plants, any of which will serve well. *Sagittaria* and *vallisneria* will produce more oxygen than others and are rooted plants. Anchor the plants firmly in the sand. If necessary, also anchor with several clean stones. Placing the plants toward the back of the tank will permit easier viewing of the fish.

WATER. Put a large piece of paper or cardboard over the plants before pouring or siphoning water into the tank. This prevents the plants from becoming dislodged and helps to keep the sand in place. The paper should be removed immediately thereafter. Should tap water be used, it must stand for at least 24 hours to permit the chlorine to escape and the water to reach room temperature. The water level should be about an inch lower than the tank top.

Moving the tank after it is filled may warp the tank seams and start a leak. (If a leak does occur, apply epoxy glue to the inside joints and seams after thoroughly drying out the tank.)

ANIMALS. Goldfish and guppies are among the best fishes to use, as they can withstand a broad temperature change. But do not mix the two, because goldfish prey on guppies. Small catfish, sunfish, minnows, zebras, and bullheads are also easy to keep and interesting to observe.

If several water snails are bought at the pet store along with the plants and fish, they will add interest and value. Snails keep the aquarium clean by scavenging excess fish food and eating the green slime (algae) that may form on the glass. Only a few are needed, as they multiply rapidly and can become a problem. Children delight in examining snails' eggs, laid on the glass sides, and seeing the snails scrape off and eat the algae. A few hand lenses placed around the aquarium make the viewing easier.

A properly set-up aquarium needs little attention. Plants give off some of the oxygen needed by the animals and absorb some of their waste materials. The animals also provide carbon dioxide needed by the plants to photosynthesize. What if the aquarium is *not* properly set up? Here, we can look for clues that may indicate improper light, temperature, oxygen, and feeding.

LIGHT. If algae grow rapidly on the sides, there is too much light. A northeast corner location or other place of good but indirect light should work best. Adding more snails and wrapping black paper around the tank for a while can retard growth of algae. But it may also be necessary to clean the tank. Algae will not hurt the fish unless there is so much that some decays. However, visibility may be hampered.

TEMPERATURE. If the temperature is too low, reproduction will slow down noticeably or stop. Some fish may die. The best temperature range for fish recommended here is 10° to 21°C (50° to 70°F). An exception is the guppy, which requires 21° to 29.5°C (70° to 85°F) water if you want it to reproduce.

When most kinds of tropical fish are used, a heater is a necessity. This can be in the form of a light bulb mounted in the cover of the tank, although an immersible heater works better.

OXYGEN SUPPLY. Insufficient oxygen is indicated when fish stay very close to the surface of the water. This is where the greatest amount of oxygen dissolved directly from the air is located. Occasionally, some fish might be seen to break the surface and gulp air directly. Insufficient surface area or overcrowding can cause this condition.

About an inch of goldfish (not including the tail) per gallon is proper. If guppies are used, about six per gallon are satisfactory. Having too many snails will also add to an oxygen-poor condition. Increase the number of *sagittaria* and *vallisneria* for more oxygen.

CLOUDY WATER. A cloudy water condition occurs from overfeeding the fish or not removing dead plants and animals. Bacterial action on uneaten food and other organic matter poisons the water and promotes the growth of other microorganisms. The most practical solution is to discard everything but the fish, filter, and gravel, carefully clean the tank, and begin again.

FEEDING. Only a small sprinkling of packaged fish food every other day (enough to be completely eaten in five minutes) is required for feeding. Tiny bits of chopped beef and earthworm can also be used. Feeding is not needed over weekends, but some means for feeding during vacations is necessary.

COVER. A glass top or piece of kitchen plastic wrap may be used to cover the aquarium. For better air circulation, leave some space open or punch a few holes in the plastic-wrap cover.

A top helps to keep the water clean and cuts down on loss of water through evaporation or loss of an overly athletic fish. It also shows condensation and precipitation in a small water cycle, because water droplets form on the bottom surface and fall back into the tank.

ANIMALS WITHOUT BACKBONES CONCEPTS
(Experiences p. 452)

As mentioned at the beginning of this chapter, the invertebrates make up most of the animals on earth. Of these, insects are by far the largest group. We'll begin this section with insects and why they have done so well, and then consider four more animals you might have for many classroom activities: crayfish, brine shrimp, snails, and earthworms.

Insects and Life Cycles

If we were to eliminate all insects, some very undesirable consequences would take place. Here are only a few: Probably half of all the flowering plants on earth would disappear since bees, flies, moths, and butterflies help to pollinate them. Most of the land birds would vanish because their main source of food is insects. Biological research would be hampered because the short life cycles of insects are ideal for quick results in medical and hereditary studies.

As mentioned, insects make up an astounding 70% of all animal species. Hundreds of new species are discovered each year. They are found almost everywhere on earth. What makes them so successful?

LEGS AND SKELETON. The first thing we might note about insects is that they have jointed legs. Instead of an internal skeleton, such as we find in vertebrates, they have an external skeleton made of a crusty substance called *chitin*. Muscles and other body parts are attached inside to this semirigid exterior. To continue growing, an immature insect must *molt*, or shed its outside covering from time to time. We can see that the need for molting greatly limits insect size. A heavy body would collapse before the soft, new covering hardened. Jointed legs and an external skeleton are also typical of the several other classes that make up the arthropods.

THE ADULT INSECT. The easiest way to recognize an adult insect is to look for six legs and three body parts: head, thorax (chest), and abdomen (Figure 15-9). Notice that this leaves out spiders, which have eight legs, and many other arthropods such as sow bugs, centipedes, or scorpions.

The head contains a primitive "brain" and mouth parts that vary considerably among insect orders. Most insects have two compound eyes, which are aggregates of many lenses, and several simple eyes as well, each of which has only one lens. The eyes are always open since there are no eyelids. Two hairlike feelers or antennae, sensitive to touch and sometimes smell, are also found on most insect heads.

The middle section, or thorax, is where the six legs and wings are attached. Some insects have two wings, and others have four; a few have none.

The abdomen contains the organs of digestion, excretion, and reproduction. Tiny holes (spiracles) in the thorax and abdomen furnish

air for breathing. The air is piped into the internal organs by a network of connected tubes.

Crickets and katydids hear through a tiny eardrum located on each foreleg just below the "knee" joint. Look for an oval spot of slightly different color. Grasshoppers also have visible eardrums. These are located on each side of the abdomen's first section. Lift up the insect's wings and look for a disk-like membrane just above where the rear legs are attached.

SURVIVAL FEATURES. There are several reasons why insects have survived so successfully. Most can fly. This provides a great range for potential food. Insects typically have very sensitive nervous systems; they are particularly sensitive to odors related to their food. The thorax of an insect may be packed with striated muscles that can contract immediately on signal. This makes many insects difficult to catch. The compound eyes increase this advantage because they cover a wide-angle view.

Although insects are cold-blooded, as are all known invertebrates, their small size often permits them to secure adequate shelter when the weather becomes cold. Many pass through the winter months in a resting or inactive stage. Perhaps most important for their survival as a group is how quickly they produce new generations.

LIFE CYCLES. The life cycles of insects are most interesting. Eggs are fertilized internally and hatched externally. In most species, the insect goes through a complete metamorphosis of four stages as it matures: egg, larva, pupa, and adult. The hatched larva (caterpillar) eats continually and sheds its skin several times as it grows. Then it either spins a cocoon (moth larva, for example) or encases itself in a chrysalis (a butterfly larva, for example) and enters the pupa stage. The body tissues change during this "resting" period. Sometime later an adult insect emerges.

Some insects, such as the grasshopper, cricket, termite, and aphid, go through an incomplete

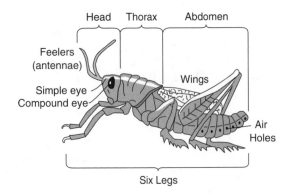

Head   Thorax   Abdomen

Feelers (antennae)

Simple eye
Compound eye

Wings

Air Holes

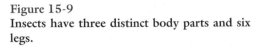

Six Legs

Figure 15-9
Insects have three distinct body parts and six legs.

metamorphosis of three stages: egg, nymph, and adult. The hatched young, or nymphs, resemble the adult except that they appear out of proportion and lack wings. As they grow, molting takes place at least several times. There is no pupa stage. (See Figure 15-10).

Students will relish observing some insects go through several stages of their life cycles, and they will learn from this procedure. Suggestions for doing so with crickets and mealworms are included in upcoming activities.

COMMON TYPES OF INSECTS. There are insects distributed throughout the world, from the polar regions to the tropics. They range in size from microscopic to more than 60 centimeters (24 inches). With 800,000 species already found, scientists believe more than 800,000 could be on the Earth. Some common insects are the butterfly, moth, and mealworm.

Butterflies and Moths. Some teachers like to show stages in the life cycles of butterflies and moths. Students will not be able to locate eggs, as these are usually too small to see. Even so, they should be able to find and bring

in caterpillars, cocoons, and chrysalises. Remind them to take several leaves from the plant on which the caterpillar was feeding when captured. A fresh supply may be needed every few days.

Use a glass jar or similar container to house each of these specimens (Figure 15-11). Place inside some soil and an upright twig from which the larva might suspend its chrysalis. Either a cheesecloth lid secured with an elastic band or a perforated jar top should provide enough air. Moisten the soil occasionally for cocoons and chrysalises, as they may dry up without sufficient humidity.

For a larger, more elaborate insect terrarium, see Figure 15-12. You will need two cake pans, a section of wire screen, paper fasteners, an upturned jar lid (for water), several twigs and leaves, and some soil. Roll the screen into a cylinder to fit inside the cake pans. Secure the screen seam with several paper fasteners. Put soil in the base. To make the base heavier and firmly implant a small branch, you may want to pour some mixed plaster of paris into the bottom cake pan before adding the soil.

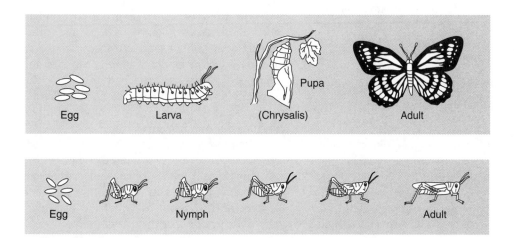

Figure 15-10
Grasshopper and butterfly metamorphoses.

Figure 15-11
A transparent jar may permit students to observe the life cycles of some insects.

Figure 15-12
A homemade terrarium for butterflies and moths.

To show the entire life cycle of an insect from egg to adult, raise some silkworm moths in class. Within about eight weeks, children will see larvae hatch from the eggs, feed busily for a time, spin cocoons and pupate, emerge from the cocoons as adult moths, mate, lay eggs, and die. Eggs and specific instructions can be purchased inexpensively from a biological supply house (Appendix C). The mulberry leaves on which the larvae feed are found in most parts of the continental United States.

Another insect with a short (six to eight weeks) life cycle is the greater wax moth. It also may be bought from several supply companies.

Mealworms. The grain beetle *(Tenebrio molitor)* is one of the easiest insects to keep and observe. It, too, undergoes a complete four-stage metamorphosis. This insect has a particularly interesting larval stage, during which time it is called a mealworm. Mealworms shed their skin from 10 to 20 times during the four or five months they remain in the larval stage. The entire metamorphosis takes six to nine months.

Cultures of this insect can be bought cheaply at pet stores.

Crayfish and Brine Shrimp

Crayfish, shrimp, lobsters, crabs, water fleas, and sow bugs make up a group of animals called *crustaceans*. Like the insects and other animals with jointed legs, crustaceans have an external skeleton made of chitin. Muscles and other body parts are attached inside to this semirigid exterior. Like insects, crustaceans need to shed their outside covering or molt several times in order to grow.

Unlike insects, which have three body parts, crustaceans have only two: a fused-together head and thorax, and an abdomen. All crustaceans but the sow bug and its relatives live in water. All breathe through gills and have two main pairs of feelers or antennae.

CRAYFISH. With its hard shell and five pairs of legs, the crayfish looks much like a lobster

(Figure 15-13). They are widely found in the United States, living in and along the banks of muddy freshwater streams, marshes, and ponds.

Crayfish are caught with minnow traps, scooped up with small nets, or simply pulled up when they grasp a chunk of fish dangling at the end of a string. Biological supply houses (see Appendix C) also furnish them.

Crayfish are found more easily at night, when they emerge from burrows or from between stones to prey on small fish and insects. During the day or night, they may also be caught by flipping over flat stones and quickly grasping them by hand from the rear. They can be safely brought back to the classroom in a plastic bucket loosely filled with wet grass and pond weeds and just enough water to cover the bucket bottom.

Crayfish need a roomy, shallow water habitat. A child's plastic wading pool is suitable for keeping them in a classroom. Their behaviors there give many chances for observing, reporting, and other language activities. Their interactions are particularly interesting to observe, as a recognizable "pecking order" soon emerges.

BRINE SHRIMP. Adult brine shrimp are no more than 12 millimeters (½ inch) long (Figure 15-14). However, these animals are crustaceans,

Figure 15-14
Brine shrimp.

just like their distant cousins, the shrimp, which we eat. Their tiny eggs are found around the shores of salt lakes and salt flats.

Brine shrimp eggs may be hatched in salt water within a wide range of salt concentrations. The eggs are produced in a curious way. The first group of eggs produced by the female hatch inside its body. What emerges are tiny, almost transparent brine shrimp. Any further eggs produced by the same female are released directly into the water. These eggs will hatch only if they are first dried. They may survive for years in a dry condition before being hatched.

Snails

Snails belong to one of the largest animal groups, the soft-bodied *mollusks*. Most live in the ocean; they include the squid, octopus, oyster, clam, and many other less familiar animals. Mollusks are divided into three subgroups according to how the foot is attached.

Snails are among the *belly-footed* mollusks (gastropods). They have a single shell and travel on what seems to be their abdomen, but what is really a soft, muscular foot. The foot secretes a mucus, or slime, that reduces friction and

Figure 15-13
A crayfish.

protects it from being irritated as the snail moves over different surfaces. The mucus is so effective that a snail may travel over a row of upturned razor blades without injury (although children should not try this).

Water, or pond, snails have two stalks, or tentacles, each with a tiny eye at the base. Most are smaller than the land snails, and many breathe through gills.

Land, or garden, snails are lung breathers and have four tentacles. The upper two have primitive eyes at the tips. The lower two carry organs of smell. When threatened, land snails retract their tentacles; water snails do not.

Like the water snail, the land snail has both male and female sex organs. It lays tiny, single eggs, up to about 100 at a time. These may be found in small depressions in the soil, often by the base of a plant. The tiny snails that hatch from the eggs eat leaves, as do the adults. The adults live for about five years.

Land snails need a humid environment to be active. When its habitat begins to dry out, a land snail usually attaches itself to some object. A mucous secretion forms and dries over its shell opening. This seal greatly reduces water loss. The snail may remain in this inactive state for months until its habitat becomes humid again.

Snails have file-like tongues that shred vegetation into bits small enough to be swallowed. In an aquarium, the tongue of a snail may be observed with a hand lens as it scrapes green algae off the sides of the tank.

Earthworms

The earthworm is a segmented worm, the most developed of three broad groups of worms. Its body may have more than 100 segments. The earthworm's peculiar way of eating is what makes it so valuable to farmers and gardeners: It literally eats its way through the soil. The decaying plant and animal matter in the soil is digested as it passes through the earthworm's body.

The eliminated soil is improved in fertility, but the side effects are even more important. The soil is loosened and aerated. Also, mineral-rich soil below the surface is brought up and mixed with mineral-depleted surface soil. The earthworm moves through and on the soil by alternately stretching and contracting its body.

Earthworms are skin breathers. That is, they take in oxygen and release carbon dioxide directly through the skin. For this to happen, the skin must be moist. Handling dries out their skin, so it is important to have wet hands or use a wet file card and spoon if much handling is necessary.

ECOLOGICAL CONCEPTS
(Experiences page 461)

In previous sections, you have seen some ways that animal bodies are adapted to the requirements of their physical environments. In this section, we take up some of the factors that influence the numbers and quality of animal populations. To do so, we will first need to examine some concepts from *ecology*, or the study of interactions of living things with each other and their physical environment.

Habitats and Their Dwellers

A *habitat* is the specific environment or place where an animal or plant lives. There are many different kinds of habitats. On land, we see desert, woodland, frozen tundra, farm, vacant lot, and garden habitats, to name just a few. Each contains animals and plants equipped to live in these locations. There are also many freshwater and saltwater habitats with their diverse living things. Some habitats fluctuate between a semidry and a watery condition, like seashores. Here, too, we see creatures equipped to live and continue their kind.

POPULATIONS. Within a habitat, we usually can find a number of organisms of the same kind that live and reproduce there. This is a *population.* A habitat is likely to have more than one population. For example, a "vacant" lot may contain a half-dozen different animal populations: worms, snails, spiders, or various insects. It most likely will contain different plant populations as well: dandelions, alfalfa, clover, various grasses, or various weeds.

COMMUNITIES. A human community is made up of people with different skills and needs. When groups of these persons interact properly, the community sustains itself. Likewise, a natural community is made up of interacting plant and animal populations. Plants grow when their needs for raw materials are met. Plant eaters eat some of the plants, and animal eaters eat some of the plant eaters.

FOOD CHAINS AND WEBS. The connection between plants, plant eaters, and animal eaters is called a *food chain.* For example, in a freshwater habitat, tiny fish called minnows eat water plants, and they in turn are eaten by frogs. We can diagram the relationship like this:

water plants → minnows → frogs

The arrows show the direction of food transfer.

Real-life food chains are seldom so simple. Usually more animals are involved, and they eat more than one kind of plant or other animals. For example, we may see something like Figure 15-15.

We can classify the organisms in this *food web* into three groups: producers (plants), consumers (animals), and decomposers (bacteria and molds). All three types are usually present in a food web. Consumers are further grouped as *predators* (animal eaters) and *prey* (those eaten by the animal eaters). Most preyed-upon animals are plant eaters.

A large percentage of plants and animals do not complete their life cycles because they are

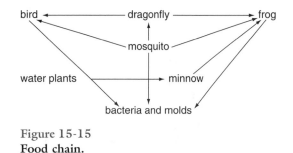

Figure 15-15
Food chain.

consumed. Those that do complete their cycle finally become food for the decomposers. These organisms are essential to new life because through decay they break down animal and plant matter into minerals, water, and gases. The minerals become part of the soil. The water and gases go back into the air. These elements are used again by growing plants.

AN ECOSYSTEM AND ITS ENERGY. To survive, animal and plant communities depend on interactions with the physical environment and with each other. Air, water, soil, temperature, and light all play a part in sustaining life. This web of relationships between a community and its physical environment is called an *ecosystem.* There is no strict agreement as to its size. Some scientists regard the whole earth as one ecosystem. To others, the term may refer to the interactions within a small habitat.

All life in any ecosystem depends on the transfer of energy. You saw how this happens with food webs. But there must be a source to start the energy transfer. That source is the sun. The process that makes the energy usable, of course, is photosynthesis. Even our fossil fuels hold the sun's energy, locked up millions of years ago in buried plant and animal forms.

Biotic Potential

A while back, we jokingly suggested that you not be too efficient at breeding guppies. A single pair might result in three million guppies in a year. A huge reproductive capacity is found in many other living things as well. The greatest increase possible in a population without deaths is called its *biotic potential*. For many reasons, no population achieves this potential. Let's look at some of these reasons.

LIMITING FACTORS. Every known organism needs certain environmental conditions to survive. Without certain supplies of air, chemicals, water, light, or proper temperature, for example, living things typically die. If only a certain amount of these factors is present, organisms may barely survive, but not reproduce. Every organism seems to have an optimum range of conditions in which it flourishes. Knowing these conditions is the key to successfully cultivating plants and raising animals.

Physical barriers, disease, and predators also limit populations. Sea plant growth stops at the shores, animals suffer from diseases just as humans do, and predators must eat to stay alive.

ADAPTATIONS. Both animals and plants (as we saw in the preceding chapter) have some adaptations that allow many to survive when limiting factors come into play. When winter comes, some birds migrate and some mammals hibernate or grow thicker coats of fur. At other times, many insects go undetected by predators because their body color blends into their surroundings. Grasshoppers may literally fly on to greener pastures when they run low on food. In a huge population sheer numbers allow some members to survive even with a combination of bad conditions.

With less prolific animals, such as birds and mammals, fewer offspring would seem to pose a greater risk to population survival. But the lack of numbers is compensated for by an increased capacity to care for their young.

For example, a bird may build a nest for its eggs and feed its young until they are ready to fly. It has the capacity to pick the proper materials from its environment and assemble them in a way that suits the function. The bird does not have to learn this task from older birds: It does the intricate job properly the first time.

So-called instinctive behavior is a common property of animals. A spider does not have to learn how to make its complex web. Nor does an ant have to learn to choose between a solution of high-energy sugar water and an artificial sweetener of little caloric value. There are many such examples in nature.

Such adaptations bring about a dynamic balance in population sizes. Limiting factors reduce populations, but adaptive behaviors counter these factors enough so that sizes stabilize.

The significant exception to the rule, of course, is the human animal. By eradicating most diseases and predators, the human population has grown at a fantastic pace. In the long run, however, limiting factors will exact their toll unless we, too, live in ways that make ecological sense.

POLLUTION. The problem of environmental pollution is that it introduces another limiting factor into ecosystems. Pollution usually happens faster than organisms can adapt to the changes introduced. The result is a decline in at least some of the populations subjected to the pollution. The populations most likely to decline are the more complex forms of plant and animal life, including humans. Those less likely to decline are the primitive plants and animals, the decomposers, and their kin.

Material Cycles

Scientists refer to the earth as a closed ecosystem. That is, almost no new raw materials enter or leave the system. Because an ecosystem ultimately depends on its raw materials, it is essential to life that these materials are never used up. Fortunately, they never are. The materials basic to life are used over and over in a kind of cycle. Next, we will consider three important cycles.

CARBON DIOXIDE–OXYGEN CYCLE. Living things need oxygen to convert stored food into energy. As a by-product, they give off carbon dioxide. This is true of plants as well as animals. Decomposers also release carbon dioxide as they work. Fortunately, plants need carbon dioxide to photosynthesize. During this process, the plants take in carbon dioxide and give off much oxygen.

Decomposers and animals give plants carbon dioxide, and plants give living things oxygen. The process is continual and may be diagrammed like Figure 15-16.

There is another side to this gas exchange that is important to realize. An essential part of living cells is the element carbon. Plants get the carbon they need from the food they make during photosynthesis. Animals get carbon from the plants they eat or from animals that eat plants.

NITROGEN CYCLE. Another cycle occurs with the element nitrogen. It, too, is an essential part of living cells. There is plenty of nitrogen in the air, but neither plants nor animals can use it in a gaseous form. How can it be converted into a form living things can use?

The basic way this is done in nature is through bacteria attached to the roots of plants such as clover, beans, alfalfa, and peas. The bacteria combine nitrogen with other elements to make chemical compounds called nitrates.

Plants absorb the nitrates as they grow. Animals eat the plants and therefore get the nitrogen they need. When the animals die, decomposers convert the nitrogen into a gaseous form again as part of the decay process.

This process is continual and may be diagrammed as illustrated in Figure 15-17.

WATER CYCLE. As you may know, water on the earth's surface continually evaporates, condenses at some altitude in the sky, and falls again as rain, hail, or snow. Living things need water to transport chemicals to cells and remove waste materials from cells. Plants release water through transpiration, a process whereby water vapor passes out mainly through leaves into the air. Animals release water through exhalation, perspiration, and in waste products. The released water goes into the air and becomes part of the water cycle.

Seen in this way, it is possible that a trace of the water that sustains you today may once have fallen on a dinosaur or on Julius Caesar's Rome.

ANIMAL LIFE BENCHMARKS AND STANDARDS

Elementary students place animals high on their list of topics which they are most curious about

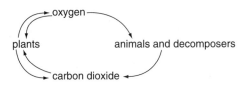

Figure 15-16
Carbon dioxide–oxygen cycle.

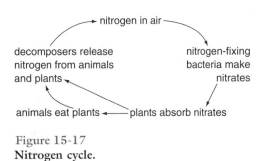

Figure 15-17
Nitrogen cycle.

and want to further explore. Animals provide basic understandings of interrelationships, habitat, cycles, structure, and function. There are many concepts related to animals, the following of which are provided as examples of basic Benchmarks and Standards:

SAMPLE BENCHMARKS (AAAS, 1993).

■ A lot can be learned about plants and animals by observing them closely, but care must be taken to know the needs of living things and how to provide for them in the classroom (by Grades K–2, p. 15).

■ All living things are composed of cells, from just one to many millions, whose details usually are visible only through a microscope. Different body tissues and organs are made up of different kinds of cells (by Grades 6–8, p. 112).

SAMPLE STANDARDS (NRC, 1996).

■ Organisms have basic needs. For example, animals need air, water, and food (by Grades K–4, p. 129).

■ Millions of species of animals, plants, and microorganisms are alive today (by Grades 5–8, p. 158).

INVESTIGATIONS AND ACTIVITIES

CLASSIFICATION OF ANIMALS EXPERIENCES
(Concepts p. 422)

ACTIVITY: *HOW CAN YOU CLASSIFY ANIMALS?*

NEEDED

Computer with Internet access
scissors
tape
newsprint end rolls (available from newspaper publishers)

TRY THIS

1. Search the Internet for pictures of animals and print pictures of various animals.
2. Cut out the pictures and arrange them on the newsprint according to your own classification system.
3. Compare your classification system with other students.
   a. How is your system the same or different?
   b. How do you think it would compare with the scientific system?

TEACHING COMMENT

Older children can look up scientific classifications of the animals and compare systems after they have developed their own classification system. Pictures from magazines can also be substituted for Internet pictures. As an extension activity, students can search the Internet for sites that show live animals, such as viewable ant farms.

ANIMALS WITH BACKBONES EXPERIENCES
(Concepts page 423)

ACTIVITY: *WHAT BONES MAKE UP A CHICKEN SKELETON?*

NEEDED

chicken bones (boiled and stripped clean)
tray or newspaper

TRY THIS

1. See the drawing of a chicken skeleton in Figure 15-18. Notice the different kinds of bones for each of its parts.

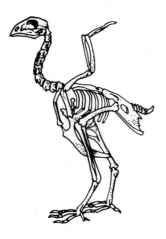

Figure 15-18

2. Examine the chicken bones brought from home.
   a. Can you find the leg bones?
   b. Which are the large back and breast bones?
   c. Which are the rib bones?
   d. Which are the wing bones?
3. What other bones can you find? Can you tell what they are?
   e. Which bones seem to be missing?

TEACHING COMMENT

The head bones and feet are usually not provided with store-bought chickens.

ACTIVITY: *HOW CAN YOU RAISE AND OBSERVE TADPOLES?*

NEEDED

pond water with some water plants and algae
plastic shoe box or aquarium tank

sloping rock for tank
hand lens
frog or toad eggs
fish food
small net

TRY THIS

1. Put the tadpole eggs and pond water into the tank. The water should have a few plants and algae for the tadpoles to eat.

2. Place a large, sloping rock into the tank. It should rise out of the water at one end. When the tadpoles grow legs, they can crawl onto the rock.

3. When the tadpoles grow legs, sprinkle some dry fish food into the tank twice a week.

4. Every two weeks replace the old pond water with fresh pond water. Use a small dip net to transfer the tadpoles.

   a. Use a hand lens to observe the tadpoles. When can you see these things happening:

   Tiny tadpoles with gills hatching from the eggs?

   Tiny tadpoles sticking closely to the water plants?

   Bodies and tails getting longer?

   Hind legs starting to grow?

   Gills disappearing?

   Front legs developing?

   Tails shrinking?

   b. What else can you notice about tadpoles?

TEACHING COMMENT

It is likely that the school semester will end before the tadpoles grow into adults. If so, let some children take the tadpoles home or release them where the eggs were found.

INVESTIGATION: *HOW TO TRAIN GOLDFISH*

Have you trained a dog or other pet to do something? Many animals can learn to respond to some signal. You can even train goldfish.

EXPLORATORY PROBLEM

How can you get goldfish to respond to a lit flashlight?

NEEDED

two goldfish in tank
fish food
flashlight

TRY THIS

1. Shine the flashlight into a corner of the tank. The fish should not swim toward the light.
2. Each day, sprinkle a little food near the same corner of the tank. At the same time, shine the flashlight on the food (Figure 15-19). Watch the fish swim toward the lighted food.

Figure 15-19

3. Do this for at least four days in a row.
4. At the next feeding time, just shine the light.

DISCOVERY PROBLEMS

observing   **A.** How do the fish act now when only the light is used?

observing   **B.** How many times will the fish respond if only the light is used? (Do not skip more than two feeding days.)

experimenting   **C.** How can you train the fish to respond to an *unlit* flashlight?

experimenting   **D.** How can you train the fish to respond to a sound?

observing   **E.** What differences, if any, are there in the behavior of the two fish?

experimenting   **F.** How will other fish, such as guppies, respond to training?

experimenting   **G.** Are some fish "smarter" (more quickly trained) than others? How could you find out?

TEACHING COMMENT

PREPARATION AND BACKGROUND

If the fish do not respond, try extending the training period. Also, make sure the fish are fed only sparingly. Should more fish and containers be available (plastic shoe boxes will serve), small groups can pursue different discovery problems.

Children enjoy telling others about training animals. Reporting their attempts and successes allows many chances for verbal and written language development (science journals).

GENERALIZATION

Animals can be conditioned to respond to signals.

SAMPLE PERFORMANCE OBJECTIVES

Knowledge: The child can describe how to condition a fish to respond to a signal.

Process: The child can determine through experimenting whether some fish learn more quickly than others.

FOR YOUNGER CHILDREN

Try the basic activity and Problems A and B.

ACTIVITY: *HOW DO TEMPERATURE CHANGES AFFECT A FISH?*

NEEDED

goldfish in small bowl of water
pitcher of ice water
watch with second hand
thermometer

TRY THIS

1. Notice how the fish's gills open and close. This is called a gill beat.

   a. How many gill beats does it make in one minute? Take the water temperature and record it.

2. Slowly pour ice water into the bowl. Do not lower the temperature more than about 10°C (15°F) below the starting temperature. Observe the gill beats again.

   b. How many beats does the fish make in one minute now?

3. Wait long enough for the water temperature to rise again to the first reading.

   c. About how many gill beats a minute do you think the fish will make? Watch and find out.

INVESTIGATION: *MAKING CASTS OF ANIMAL TRACKS*

When animals walk in mud or on damp ground, they leave tracks. By examining these tracks closely, we may be able to tell many things about an animal. A large, heavy animal may leave deep, large tracks. A track of a running animal may be pushed up a little at one end. Each kind of animal leaves a different track.

Animal tracks are interesting to study and keep, but rain can wash them away. There is a way you can save them. You can make a cast of an animal track.

EXPLORATORY PROBLEM

How can you make a cast of an animal track?

NEEDED

place with damp dirt
paper towel
thin cardboard
scissors
old plastic bowl
sticky tape
plaster of paris
newspaper
stick for mixing
water
petroleum jelly
flat-bladed, dull knife

TRY THIS

1. Have someone in your class make a shoe print in the damp ground. (It will be more fun if you don't know who that person is.)

2. Make a low wall around the shoe track with cardboard. Tape it closed.

3. Spread petroleum jelly thinly on the inside surface of the wall. This will keep the plaster from sticking to it.

4. Mix plaster of paris and water in a bowl. Go easy on the water. Make the mixture like a thick milkshake. Pour about 2.5 centimeters (1 inch) of the mixture into the wall (Figure 15-20).

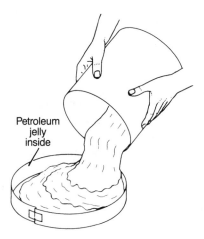

Petroleum
jelly
inside

Figure 15-20

5. Wait about an hour for it to harden. Remove the cast from the shoe print and take off the cardboard. Notice that the cast is an opposite or raised model of the shoe print. To make a model that looks like the real shoe print, you must make a second cast, or *mold*.

6. Spread petroleum jelly thinly over the top of the first cast. Place it on newspaper. Put a cardboard wall, also coated thinly with petroleum jelly, around the cast. Tape it closed.

7. Pour about 2.5 centimeters (1 inch) of plaster mix into the wall. Wait again an hour for it to set.

8. Remove the wall. Carefully slip a knife between the two casts to separate them. Clean off the petroleum jelly with a paper towel. The second cast should now look like the original shoe print.

DISCOVERY PROBLEMS

inferring **A.** What can you tell from the cast of the shoe print? Was it made by a girl or boy? How large or heavy might the person be? What kind of shoe was worn? Check by looking at different persons' shoes. Last, you can see if anyone's shoe fits the mold.

inferring   **B.** Make a cast of a track from an animal that does not wear shoes. What bird or other animal do you think it might be? How large or heavy might it be? Was it walking or running?

observing   **C.** Where can you find the most animal tracks around your school? home?

classifying   **D.** What kind of a collection of animal track casts can you make?

TEACHING COMMENT

PREPARATION AND BACKGROUND

If plaster of paris is in short supply, you might have students begin with a small animal track rather than a human footprint. Caution children not to spill plaster on their clothing. However, small spills may be brushed off after drying.

Almost any large discardable container will serve to mix the plaster and water. A plastic container can be bent to pour the mixture more neatly into a narrow form.

GENERALIZATION

We can infer some things about an animal from its tracks.

SAMPLE PERFORMANCE OBJECTIVES

Knowledge: The child can make a negative and positive cast of an animal track.

Process: The child can infer several properties of an animal from its tracks.

ANIMALS WITHOUT BACKBONES EXPERIENCES
(Concepts p. 435)

INVESTIGATION: *MEALWORMS AND WHAT THEY DO*

Have you ever seen a mealworm? You can buy them at a pet store to feed to lizards and fish. It's fun to observe mealworms and what they do.

EXPLORATORY PROBLEM

How can you find out about mealworms and what they do?

NEEDED

mealworms
spoon
three rulers
small card

shoe box lid
small jar of bran
magnifier
cotton swab
rough paper towel
ice cube
straw
black sheet of paper

TRY THIS

1. Put a mealworm in an upturned shoe box lid (Figure 15-21).

2. Use a spoon and card to move it to where you want.

3. Use a hand magnifier to see it more clearly.

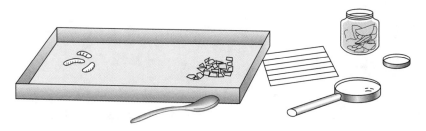

Figure 15-21

DISCOVERY PROBLEMS

observing   **A.** What do you notice about the mealworm? How many legs does it have? How many feelers on its head? What is on its tail end? How many body segments, or parts, does it have?

inferring   **B.** Put it on a rough paper towel, then on a smooth surface. On which does it seem to travel easier?

observing   **C.** Put a few more mealworms in the shoe box lid. Observe how they look and act. In what ways can you tell different mealworms apart?

experimenting   **D.** In what ways can you get a mealworm to back up? Which way is best?

observing   **E.** Suppose you place the mealworms on a slant. Will they go up or down? Does the amount of slant make a difference?

measuring   **F.** How far can a mealworm go in half a minute?

observing   **G.** Which food do they seem to like best? Try cornflakes, flour, bread, crackers, and other foods.

hypothesizing   **H.** Suppose you put two mealworms into a narrow straw, one at each end. What do you think will happen when they meet?

experimenting   **I.** Do mealworms like moisture? How could a cotton swab be used to find out? How else might you find out?

experimenting   **J.** Will a mealworm move to or away from a cold place? How could an ice cube be used to find out?

experimenting   **K.** Will a mealworm move to a dark or light place? How can black paper be used to find out?

predicting   **L.** Which way will a mealworm go each time (Figure 15-22)?

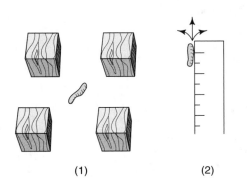

(1)   (2)

(3)   (4)

Figure 15-22

experimenting   **M.** How can you get a mealworm to go in a straight line for at least 10 centimeters (4 inches)? No fair touching it!

hypothesizing   **N.** What are some more questions about mealworms you would like to investigate?

observing   **O.** Watch the mealworm go through its life cycle. What do you notice at the different stages of life?

TEACHING COMMENT

PREPARATION AND BACKGROUND

Mealworms are the larval stage of the grain beetle, an insect often found in rotting grain or flour supplies. They may be bought cheaply at pet stores and are fed to a variety of small animals, including some fishes.

Mealworms can be kept in a closed glass jar containing bran or other cereal flakes. Punch small holes in the jar lid for air. A potato or apple slice can be added to provide extra moisture. When the old bran looks powdery, dump out everything, then wash and dry the jar. Put fresh bran and the live, healthy-looking mealworms back into the jar.

GENERALIZATION

Some behaviors of an animal are inborn, and some are influenced by its environment.

SAMPLE PERFORMANCE OBJECTIVES

Process: The child can test the preferences of mealworms as to temperature, light, food, and moisture.

Knowledge: The child can state the apparent preferences of mealworms as to temperature, light, food, and moisture.

FOR YOUNGER CHILDREN

Younger students should be able to do most of the activities in the investigation.

ACTIVITY: HOW CAN YOU RAISE CRICKETS?

NEEDED

several male and female crickets
plastic shoe box
custard cup or small dish
screen top for shoe box
paper towel
dry soil
dry oatmeal or bran
raisins
hand lens

TRY THIS

1. Put about 5 centimeters (2 inches) of dry soil into the container.

2. Fill the custard cup with soil. Sprinkle water on it until it is all damp. Bury it in the dry soil so the damp soil is even with the dry soil. (This is where the female can lay eggs.)

3. Scatter some pieces of torn paper towel around the container. (The crickets can hide underneath when they need to.)

4. Scatter some dry oatmeal and a few raisins at one end.

5. Put no more than three or four crickets inside the container. Cover it with a screen large enough to bend down at the sides.

   a. How do the crickets act? How do they use the pieces of toweling? How do the females lay eggs? How do the crickets eat? move about?

   b. What happens when cricket eggs hatch? What do the young (nymphs) look like? What do they look like as they get older? Use a hand lens to help you see.

   c. What else can you observe about the crickets?

TEACHING COMMENT

If children are unable to catch crickets in fields, they may often be bought at fish-bait stores. The female may be recognized by a long slender "tail," or *ovipositor*, through which it deposits eggs in damp soil. Note that from egg to adult takes about six months, with adults living about three months.

INVESTIGATION: *BRINE SHRIMP*

Have you ever visited a salt lake? If so, maybe you have seen *brine shrimp*. These small animals lay tiny eggs. You can find out many interesting things about brine shrimp, but first you will need to hatch the eggs.

EXPLORATORY PROBLEM

How can you hatch brine shrimp eggs?

NEEDED

vial of brine shrimp eggs
tap water
noniodized salt
magnifier
plastic teaspoon
small babyfood jars
measuring cup
small package of brewer's yeast

TRY THIS

1. Let a cup of tap water stand overnight. Then mix four teaspoons of salt into it.
2. Pour the water into several babyfood jars. Use one jar now (Figure 15-23). Cap and save the other jars for later use.
3. Take just a tiny pinch of eggs from the vial. Sprinkle them on top of the water.
4. Observe the eggs closely a few times each day. Use a magnifier to see better.

DISCOVERY PROBLEMS

observing	**A.**	When do you first notice changes in the eggs? What changes do you see?
observing	**B.**	When do you first notice tiny brine shrimp? How do they look to you? Can you describe what they are doing?
observing	**C.**	What changes do you notice as the brine shrimp grow? Observe them each day.
observing	**D.**	Do brine shrimp ever seem to rest or sleep? How can you find out?
observing	**E.**	How long does it take for a shrimp to start growing?
experimenting	**F.**	How long can you keep a brine shrimp alive?
experimenting	**G.**	Do newly hatched shrimp go where it is light or dark? How about month-old shrimp? How can you find out?
observing	**H.**	How can you tell which brine shrimp are female?
experimenting	**I.**	Will brine shrimp eggs hatch in fresh water? in water with twice as much or more salt than you first used?
hypothesizing	**J.**	Suppose you hatch many shrimp eggs in one jar and only a few in another. What do you think will happen as the shrimp grow?
hypothesizing	**K.**	What else would you like to investigate about brine shrimp?

Figure 15-23

TEACHING COMMENT

PREPARATION AND BACKGROUND

Brine shrimp are sold at pet stores for fish food. The eggs may be hatched in salt water. About four teaspoons of salt per cup of water work well for both hatching and growth. But the shrimp may hatch within a wide range of salt concentrations. Be sure to use either noniodized or marine salt.

About six weeks are needed for the shrimp to reach maturity under the best conditions. A water temperature of about 27°C (80°F) is ideal. Children will be able to distinguish female from male adults most easily by the females' egg pouches.

It is harder to keep brine shrimp alive for a lengthy period than it is to hatch them. Some precautions will help. Have students make a crayon mark on their jars at the beginning water level. Be sure any evaporated water is replaced by aged tap water containing the proper salt concentration. The water should stand for at least 24 hours to allow the chlorine to escape. Put a tiny pinch of baking soda in each shrimp container once a week to neutralize the acid that builds up. Above all, do not overfeed the shrimp. A tiny pinch of yeast once a week is adequate to grow the bacteria on which they feed.

As with other long-range observational activities, this one is ideal for motivating artwork and language experiences.

GENERALIZATION

Brine shrimp will hatch and grow from eggs, stay alive, and reproduce when conditions are like those of their natural habitat.

SAMPLE PERFORMANCE OBJECTIVES

Process: The child can observe and describe several developmental changes in newly hatched brine shrimp over a two-week period.

Knowledge: The child can state several environmental conditions that are favorable for maintaining live brine shrimp.

FOR YOUNGER CHILDREN

Younger students should be able to do this investigation through Problem C.

INVESTIGATION: *SNAILS AND WHAT THEY DO*

Have you ever seen a snail? If so, where? Many water snails live in and around the edges of ponds. Land snails can be found in gardens, lawns, and around damp soil. They are easiest to find early in the morning or at night. Land snails are usually larger than water snails, so they are easier to observe. What they do is surprising.

EXPLORATORY PROBLEM

How can you find out about land snails and what they do?

NEEDED

live land snail
small stiff card
wide-mouth glass jar containing some damp soil
magnifier
spoon
aluminum pie plate
ruler
sheet of black paper
piece of lettuce
paper towel
small paper cup of water

TRY THIS

1. Put a snail on a pie plate.
2. Use a spoon and card to move it where you want.
3. Use a magnifier to see it more clearly (Figure 15-24).

Figure 15-24

DISCOVERY PROBLEMS

observing   **A.** What do you notice about the snail? How does it move? How can you describe its head? shell? other parts?

observing   **B.** How many stalks (feelers) do you observe on its head? Which seem to have eyes? Which seem to be used for feeling?

observing   **C.** What happens when you gently touch the two longer stalks? the two shorter stalks? How close can you get before the stalks move?

experimenting   **D.** How can you get the two longer stalks to move in different directions?

observing   **E.** What happens when you tap the snail's shell gently?

observing   **F.** Try to put the snail upside down on its shell. Can the snail right itself? If so, how?

observing   **G.** Put the snail on a piece of black paper. Observe the silver trail it makes. How far does the snail go in one minute?

communicating   **H.** How well can you draw an animal? Make a drawing of your snail. Show it to someone who does not know you are studying snails. Can that person tell it is a snail?

communicating   **I.** How well can you describe an animal? Write a description of your snail without saying what it is. Show the description to someone who does not know you are studying snails. Can that person tell it is a snail?

observing   **J.** Give the snail some lettuce to eat. Observe its mouth parts with a magnifier. How does it eat?

experimenting   **K.** What foods does your snail seem to like best? Circle your snail with bits of different foods. Which does the snail go to first? What happens when you try this several times? How long should you wait between each trial? Why?

experimenting   **L.** Will a snail go to the dark or light? Put your snail in the pie pan. How can you use a sheet of black paper to find out?

experimenting   **M.** Will a snail go where it is dry or wet? How can you use a paper towel to find out?

hypothesizing   **N.** What other experiments would you like to try with snails? What other kinds of snails can you find to try?

TEACHING COMMENT

PREPARATION AND BACKGROUND

Land snails can be found where there is plenty of vegetation and moisture. They seem to prefer cool, shady places, especially under leaves, logs, and rocks. Early morning is probably the easiest time to collect snails, when leaves are heavy with dew. If collected in a dry "resting" condition, place them on a water-soaked paper towel to reactivate them.

Several collected snails may be kept in one glass jar. The jar top should have some holes punched into it for air. Place an inch or two of soil inside and keep it damp. For extra moisture, sink a bottle cap flush with the soil surface and fill it with water. Leave a small piece of lettuce inside for food. Keep the jar in a shady place. After several days, the jar will need to be cleaned.

Try to have a number of snails available for observation and experiments. Even when treated gently, this animal needs a rest period between activities.

GENERALIZATION

Some behaviors of an animal are inborn, and some are influenced by its environment.

SAMPLE PERFORMANCE OBJECTIVES

Process: The child can test the preferences of a snail as to light, food, and moisture.

Knowledge: The child can predict places where land snails are likely to be found.

FOR YOUNGER CHILDREN.

Younger children should be able to do most of the observational activities.

ECOLOGICAL EXPERIENCES
(Concepts p. 440)

ACTIVITY: *WHAT IS A FOOD CHAIN?*

NEEDED

six cards with one of these words or pictures on each (sun, plant, insect, toad, snake, hawk)
six persons
six pins

INTRODUCTION

Plants need the sun to grow. Many insects eat plants, many toads eat insects, many snakes eat toads, and many hawks eat snakes. This is one example of a food chain. See what happens when a food chain is broken.

TRY THIS

1. Each person should pin a card to his clothes.
2. Stand in line and hold hands in this order: sun, plant, insect, toad, snake, hawk.

a. What animal would die if there were no snakes to eat? (The snake person should drop hands now.)

b. What animals would die if there were no toads to eat? (The toad person drops hands.)

c. What animals would die if there were no insects to eat? (Insect person drops hands.)

d. What animals would die if there were no plants to eat? (Plant person drops hands.)

e. What would happen if there were no sun to let plants grow?

TEACHING COMMENT

Be sure to point out that these animals might eat a wider variety of food than is shown in this simple chain. However, the basic idea of interdependence is valid. This can be clarified further by making more food chains. Older children can connect two or more food chains to make a more complicated food web. Run strings between and among individuals in the web to show the intricate interrelationships involved.

INVESTIGATION: *HOW COLOR PROTECTS ANIMALS*

If you were an insect that lived in the grass, what enemies might you have? How might having the right color protect you from being eaten by birds and other animals?

EXPLORATORY PROBLEM

How can you test whether color affects the chances to survive?

NEEDED

brown and green construction paper
lawn area
scissors
bare dirt area
½ cup of bird seed
set of food colors
jar

TRY THIS

1. Cut out 100 same-sized pieces of green paper and 100 of brown paper. Make each piece about the size of your thumbnail.
2. Have someone scatter 50 pieces of each color on a lawn area.

3. Pretend the paper pieces are insects and you are a bird. Try to find as many pieces as you can in one minute. Let some partners help you (Figure 15-25).

Figure 15-25

DISCOVERY PROBLEMS

inferring **A.** How many pieces of each color paper did you find? Which color would be better if you were a lawn insect?

experimenting **B.** Suppose you were an insect that lived in a bare dirt area. Which color would be better? What could you do to find out?

experimenting **C.** How could colored seeds be tested with real birds? Mix a few drops of food coloring with water in a jar. Drop in the seeds to color them.

observing **D.** Observe closely insects on different plants. How are their colors like those of the plant? different?

observing **E.** How are other animals protected by their skin colors? Look in books and magazines for colored pictures of animals in their natural habitats.

TEACHING COMMENT

PREPARATION AND BACKGROUND

Try to have the colors of the construction paper match as closely as possible the lawn and bare dirt areas.

For the bird-seed activity, allow several hours between scattering the seeds and locating the surviving seeds. Make sure students realize that they may not be able to locate all the surviving seeds. How can they increase their chances of locating survivors? They may decide to enclose groups of seeds with string or to try other methods.

GENERALIZATION

Survival chances increase when an animal's color matches its surroundings.

SAMPLE PERFORMANCE OBJECTIVES

Process: The child can design a test of survival for colored seeds in different locations with real birds.

Knowledge: The child predicts smaller survival chances when an animal's color is unlike its surroundings and greater chances when its color is similar.

FOR YOUNGER CHILDREN

Try the basic activity. Be sure children understand the analogy of people representing birds and bits of colored paper representing insects.

INVESTIGATION: *ANT RESPONSES TO SWEETENERS*

Some people do not use regular sugar because it has high-energy value. Instead, they may use an artificial sweetener, which has very little energy value. Many people cannot tell the difference between the two. You probably know that ants and some other insects are attracted to sugar. But what attracts them? Is is the taste or something else?

EXPLORATORY PROBLEM

How can you test ant responses to real and artificial sugar?

NEEDED

one or more artificial sweeteners
sugar
two small matched bottle caps
water
two paper cups
teaspoon

TRY THIS

1. Mix one bottle cap each of sugar and water in a cup. Use a spoon to stir. Pour the mixture into one cap until it is full (Figure 15-26).
2. Do the same with sweetener and water. Use a second cap and cup. Remember to rinse the spoon clean before you stir again.
3. Place both caps close together where there are ants. Mark which cap contains the sugar. Watch what happens.

Figure 15-26

DISCOVERY PROBLEMS

observing   **A.** What do you notice? Which mixture attracts more ants?

observing   **B.** What will happen if you test the sweetener by itself?

observing   **C.** What will happen if you test it with different kinds of ants?

observing   **D.** What will happen if you test different sweeteners?

experimenting   **E.** How can you find out how other insects will act toward artificial sweeteners?

inferring   **F.** Keep a record of your findings. Look it over. How do the responses of these animals help them to stay alive?

TEACHING COMMENT

PREPARATION AND BACKGROUND

You may want to check where students put the caps. They should be equally accessible to the ants.

GENERALIZATION

The ability to respond to a high-energy food can help an animal to survive.

SAMPLE PERFORMANCE OBJECTIVES

Knowledge: The child states that insects are more likely to be attracted to sugar than to low-energy sweeteners.

Process: The child designs ways to test responses of several different insects toward sweeteners.

FOR YOUNGER CHILDREN

You might have younger students first try themselves to discriminate between light solutions of sugar water and sweetener water. Afterward, they can try to fool some ants or other insects.

INVESTIGATION: *THE FRIGHT DISTANCES OF WILD ANIMALS*

One difference between wild and tame animals is how easily they are frightened. How close have you come to a wild bird before it flew off? How about other wild animals?

EXPLORATORY PROBLEM

What are the fright distances of some wild birds?

NEEDED

wild birds
different kinds of bird food (bread crumbs, seeds, bacon bits)
handkerchief
meter stick or yardstick

TRY THIS

1. Go where there are some wild birds.
2. Sprinkle some bread crumbs on the ground at different distances from you.
3. Watch where the birds pick up the crumbs each time. Measure the closest distance the birds dare to come near you.

DISCOVERY PROBLEMS

measuring

A. What is the fright distance of these birds? Is every bird in this group frightened at the same distance? Are other kinds of birds frightened at another distance?

hypothesizing

B. What would be the fright distance if you tried other foods?

hypothesizing

C. Suppose you go to the same place and drop crumbs each day for a week. What do you think the fright distance of the same birds would be then?

measuring

D. How close can you get to different birds without food? Slowly walk toward each perched bird until it flies away. Measure the distance between you and the perch place each time.

experimenting

E. How do different sounds and noises affect fright distance? Different movements?

experimenting and communicating

F. What are the fright distances of other wild animals? Find squirrels, chipmunks, and other animals. Make a record of what happens.

TEACHING COMMENT

PREPARATION AND BACKGROUND

Pupils can usually notice differences in bird species, but they often have trouble communicating what they see. A simple bird identification book can help.

If possible, let children repeat this activity over several days. They will discover that birds and other wild animals typically decrease their fright distances if the same harmless stimulus is presented each time.

Caution: Children should never touch wild animals that approach humans and never feed them by hand. Such animals are abnormal and may be ill.

GENERALIZATION

Fright behavior is an inborn property of wild animals that helps them to survive. Fright distance may decrease when animals become used to objects or events.

SAMPLE PERFORMANCE OBJECTIVES

Knowledge: The child can state that fright distances vary with different species of wild animals.

Process: The child can measure fright distances of animals under several conditions and draw proper inferences from the data.

INVESTIGATION: *BIRD NESTS*

Have you ever seen a bird nest close up? Birds do not have to learn how to make nests. This is an inborn behavior. A nest is used to lay and hatch eggs in. The hatched chicks stay there until they grow up enough to fly. The materials used for the nest may come from many different things. Sometimes the materials birds use are quite surprising.

EXPLORATORY PROBLEM A

How can you find out more about how some birds make nests?

NEEDED

several abandoned bird nests
pencil
tweezers

TRY THIS

1. Look for abandoned bird nests in trees and large bushes. The best time for this is in winter.
2. Collect several nests. Ask a responsible adult to help you.
3. Bring the nests to class.

DISCOVERY PROBLEMS

observing   **A.** What is the size and shape of each nest? How is each made?

observing   **B.** How are the nests alike? different?

observing   **C.** What materials were used to make the nests? Use tweezers and a pencil to help you pick apart the nests.

inferring   **D.** Make a list of the materials. Which seem to come from where the birds live? Which, if any, seem to come from far away? (Keep this list for use next spring.)

inferring   **E.** What kind of bird probably made each kind of nest? Get some bird books from the library. See if they can help you find out.

EXPLORATORY PROBLEM B

Given choices, what materials will some birds pick to make nests?

NEEDED

60-centimeter (2-foot) cardboard square
thread
aluminum foil
large nail
different strings
scissors
different cloth pieces
different-colored yarn
paper strips

TRY THIS

1. Do this activity in early spring, when many birds build nests.
2. Punch many holes in the cardboard with a large nail. Wiggle the nail in each hole to make it larger.

3. Cut narrow pieces of cloth, paper, and foil.

4. Cut small pieces of string and yarn.

5. Thread these materials partway through the cardboard's holes. Label under each hole what is there.

6. Tack the cardboard to a tree where other trees and bushes grow.

7. Check the board each day to see what is missing.

DISCOVERY PROBLEMS

observing   **A.** Which materials were taken first? Replace these materials right away. Will they be taken again before other materials? Check again to see.

experimenting   **B.** How can you change the picked materials to make them less attractive? You might cut longer pieces of yarn, for example, or cut wider cloth strips. How can you make the unpicked materials more attractive?

observing   **C.** What will happen if you move the board to another place? How will your findings compare with those before?

observing   **D.** Make a list of the materials selected. How does it compare with the list of nest materials you made in the winter?

TEACHING COMMENT

PREPARATION AND BACKGROUND

Bird's nests are usually abandoned by winter and are rarely used again. So winter is a good time to collect nests. In the unlikely event that eggs are found, the nest should be left undisturbed. The materials-selection board is best placed off the ground on a tree trunk or low limb away from traffic. However, it should be visible and accessible to the children.

GENERALIZATION

Birds use materials from the environment to build their nests; the ability to build nests has survival value.

SAMPLE PERFORMANCE OBJECTIVES

Knowledge: The child can describe the kinds of materials local birds are likely to use in nest building.

Process: The child can compose two listings of findings and compare them for similarities and differences.

References

American Association for the Advancement of Science. (1993). *Benchmarks for science literacy.* New York: Oxford University Press.

National Research Council. (1996). *National science education standards.* Washington, DC: National Academy Press.

Selected Trade Books: Animal Life and Environment

For Younger Children

Aaseng, N. (1987a). *Meat-eating animals.* Lerner.

Aaseng, N. (1987b). *Prey animals.* Lerner.

Breeden, R. (Ed.). (1974). *Creepy crawley things.* National Geographic Society.

Bruchac, J. (1992). *Native American animal stories.* Fulcrum.

Carle, E. (1987). *The very hungry caterpillar.* Philomel.

Carle, E. (1995). *The very lonely firefly.* Philomel.

Cousins, L. (1991). *Country animals.* Morrow.

Crump, D. (1983). *Creatures small and furry.* National Geographic Society.

Day, J. (1986). *What is a mammal?* Golden Books.

Dreyer, E. (1991). *Wild animals.* Troll Associates.

Fleming, D. (1993). *In the small, small pond.* Henry Holt.

Fowler, A. (1992). *It's best to leave a snake alone.* Children's Press.

Freedman, R. (1980). *Tooth and claw: A look at animal weapons.* Holiday.

Palotta, J. (1992). *The icky bug counting book.* Charlesbridge.

Penn, L. (1983). *Young scientists explore animal friends.* Good Apple.

Pfloog, J. (1987). *Wild animals and their babies.* Western.

Priestly, A. (1987). *Big animals.* Random House.

Savage, S. (1992). *Making tracks.* Lodestar.

Stone, L. M. (1983). *Marshes and swamps.* Children's Press.

Sutton, F. (1983). *The big book of wild animals.* Putman.

Urquhart, J. C. (1982). *Animals that travel.* National Geographic.

Wildsmith, B. (1991). *Animal homes.* Oxford.

Wozmek, F. (1982). *The ABC of ecology.* Davenport.

For Older Children

Bright, M. (1987). *Pollution and wildlife.* Watts.

Dean, A. (1977). *How animals communicate.* Messner.

Dean, A. (1978). *Animal defenses.* Messner.

Earthbooks Staff. (1991). *National Wildlife Federation's book of endangered species.* Author.

Fichter, G. S. (1991). *Poisonous animals.* Watts.

Flegg, J. (1991). *Animal builders.* Newington.

Gallent, R. A. (1986). *The rise of mammals.* Watts.

Grossman, S., & Grossman, M. L. (1981). *Ecology.* Wonder.

Leon, D. (1982). *The secret world of underground creatures.* Messner.

Maynard, T. (1991). *Animal inventors.* Watts.

Penny, M. (1987). *Animal evolution.* Watts.

Pringle, L. (1987). *Home: How animals find comfort and safety.* Macmillan.

Sabin, F. (1985). *Ecosystems and food chains.* Troll Associates.

Sanders, J. (1984). *All about animal migrations.* Troll Associates.

Yamashita, K. (1993). *Paws, wings, and hooves.* Lerner.

Resource Books

Butzow, C. M., & Butzow, J. W. (1989). *Science through children's literature. An integrated approach* (animal reproduction and development topics, pp. 61–65; ducks, ants, spiders, ladybugs, fish, pp. 66–94; animal adaption topics, pp. 102–106). Teacher Ideas Press.

Fredericks, A. D., Meinbach, A. M., & Rothlein, L. (1993). *Thematic units: An integrated approach to teaching science and social studies* (animals and how they grow topics, pp. 111–122). HarperCollins.

LeCroy, B., & Holder, B. (1994). *Bookwebs: a brainstorm of ideas for the primary classroom* (animal activities pp. 30–31). Teachers Ideas Press.

Shaw, D. G., & Dybdahl, C. S. (1996). *Integrating science and language arts. A sourcebook for K–6 teachers* (animal life topics, pp. 57–59). Allyn and Bacon.

HUMAN BODY AND NUTRITION

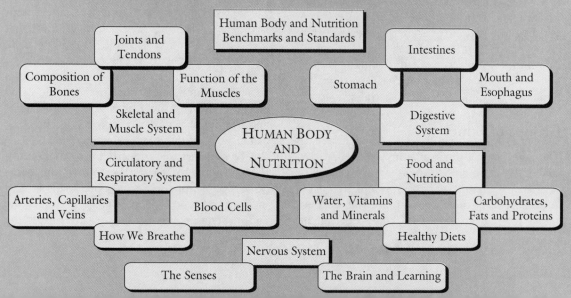

Human Body and Nutrition
Benchmarks and Standards

Joints and
Tendons

Intestines

Composition of
Bones

Function of the
Muscles

Stomach

Mouth and
Esophagus

Skeletal and
Muscle System

Digestive
System

HUMAN BODY
AND
NUTRITION

Circulatory and
Respiratory System

Food and
Nutrition

Arteries, Capillaries
and Veins

Blood Cells

Water, Vitamins
and Minerals

Carbohydrates,
Fats and Proteins

How We Breathe

Healthy Diets

Nervous System

The Senses

The Brain and Learning

By any measure, the human body is a master-piece of organization. It is composed of millions of tiny cells, many of them differing in shape, size, and internal makeup according to the work they do.

Groups of cells that work together are tissues. Examples are the connective tissue that holds the body together, muscle tissue, nerve tissue, blood tissue, and epithelial (skin) tissue. When tissues work together, they are called *organs.* Examples are the lungs, heart, stomach, and eyes. Organs that work together are *systems.*

We will consider several body systems in this chapter, including the skeletal and muscle systems, which support and move the body; the nervous system, which controls the body; the circulatory and respiratory systems, which move the blood and permit breathing; and the digestive system, which fuels the body by breaking down foods into simpler forms. A final section examines *nutrition:* the makeup of foods and how they affect the body.

Skeletal and Muscle System Concepts
(Experiences p. 483)

It is hard to imagine how the human body would look without bones. It has more than 200 bones joined into a skeletal framework that gives the body its overall shape and support. The bones are not all individual, unique pieces that fit together. Rather, there are groups of bones, all well fitted for their specialized work.

Groups of Bones

The main part of the skull consists of eight relatively flat bones joined together into the characteristic helmet-like shape. In children, the joints between the bones are movable. This allows the bones to grow as children get older.

In adults, the skull bones will have grown together into a solid, curved surface with immovable joints. The only head bone we can ever move voluntarily is the jawbone. Chewing and normal conversation depend on this movement.

The skull is joined to a stack of oval and irregular small bones called the *vertebrae,* or spine. The vertebrae permit bending and twisting motions. In between each small bone is a pad of tough, elastic tissue called *cartilage.* The cartilage pads keep the spinal bones from grinding or hitting together as we move. As we age during adulthood, the pads continue to compress, making us shorter. Between 40 and 70, for example, we may lose an inch or more in height.

The spinal bones also have holes in them. This allows the bundle of nerves that make up the spinal cord to run through the length of the protective vertebrae. Side holes in the vertebrae permit nerve branches from the spinal cord to go out to other parts of the body.

Many children think that "standing up straight" means having a straight backbone. This is not so. Although the vertebrae are stacked in a column, the column is curved in a shallow S form. This permits better balance than a vertical backbone.

Attached to the backbone are 12 pairs of ribs. The top 10 pairs curve around and join the breastbone in front. But if you feel your two pairs of bottom ribs, you may notice that they are not joined in front. For this reason, they are called "floating ribs."

The ribs form a flexible cage that protects the heart, lungs, and other organs. The cartilage that fastens the ribs is somewhat elastic, and the ribs are bendable. This is why the chest can expand and contract as we breathe.

The *hipbones* are fastened at the other end of the backbone. With the bottom of the backbone, they form a large and open shallow bowl in front. The bowl helps to support the body and protects some of the organs below the waist. The lowest parts of the hipbones are used for sitting.

The *long bones* of the arms and legs are the levers that allow us to walk, run, and throw. These bones are strong but also light for their size, because they are mostly hollow inside. If they were solid, the increased weight would slow us down considerably. Long bones are thicker at the ends than in the center section and fit the ends of adjoining bones.

Composition of Bones

A soft material called *marrow* is found inside many bones, particularly the long bones. There are two kinds of marrow. *Red* marrow is found at the ends of the bones; these are the sites where red blood cells are manufactured. *Yellow* marrow is stored inside the middle of the bones and is mainly composed of fat.

A newborn baby's skeleton is composed mostly of soft cartilage. As the baby grows, its body continually replaces the cartilage with calcium and other minerals from digested food, so the skeleton continually hardens. Children's bones typically are softer than those of adults because they contain more cartilage. This makes their bones less likely to break under stress. Some cartilage never changes to bone, like the ears, tip of the nose, and several other places.

Movable Joints

A rigid skeletal framework would be of little use. The reason we can move is because many bones are held together by movable joints. Tough, thick cords of elastic tissue, called *ligaments,* make up the material that joins bone to bone. We have several different kinds of movable joints, and each allows different movements. Hinged joints allow us to bend the elbow, knee, and fingers. Notice that the movement is in only one direction.

The thumb is particularly interesting. It has only two hinged joints, yet we can move the thumb so it opposes any finger. A third joint up near the wrist makes this movement possible.

A ball-and-socket joint at the shoulder allows rotary motion of the arm. A similar socket connects the upper leg bone at the hip, but movement in this case is more restricted. Other kinds of joints allow wrist, head, foot, and other motions. In all, we have six different kinds of movable joints.

Muscles

Under the skin, and inside the body, are about 600 muscles, two-thirds of which are *voluntary* muscles. These muscles are connected to bones, and we can move them on command. Some muscles, such as those that move food through the intestines and those that make the heart beat, cannot ordinarily be controlled. These are the *involuntary* muscles.

Muscles can only pull; they work in opposite pairs. This is easiest to see with the jointed leg bones. If you swing a leg forward, muscles in the front part of the thigh and hip contract and pull the leg forward. If you swing the leg back, muscles in the back part of the thigh and hip contract and pull the leg back.

Tendons

Muscles are attached to bone and cartilage by the *tendons.* These are tough, white, twisted fibers of different lengths. Some are cordlike; others are wider and flat. Tendons are enclosed in sleeves of thin tissue that contain a slippery liquid. This permits them to slide back and forth without rubbing.

Tendons are strong and unstretchable. Some that are easy to observe are found inside the elbow and back of the knee. One of the strongest and thickest tendons in the body is the Achilles tendon. It is located just above the heel of the foot. Also easy to observe are the tendons that pull the finger bones as you wiggle your fingers. If you try this and touch the forearm with the opposite hand, you will notice that muscles in the forearm, not muscles in the hand, mainly move the fingers. Children are usually surprised by this.

Makeup of Muscles

How do muscles work? Why do they get tired? Why does exercise make us warm?

A microscope reveals that voluntary muscles are made up of bundles of fibers, each about the size of a human hair, but far stronger. Like the entire muscle, each fiber shortens as it pulls and lengthens as it relaxes. The number of fibers that work depends on how heavily the muscle is strained. Also, not all the fibers work simultaneously. Each is rapidly and continually switched on and off by the nervous system as the muscle works. This allows each fiber some rest and greater overall endurance for the muscle.

The energy to move a muscle comes from a form of sugar called *glycogen*. It is found inside the muscles' cells. About a fourth of the energy released by this sugar goes into moving the muscle. The rest is released as heat. The faster a muscle is used, the more heat is produced. This is why heavy exercise makes us warm.

Sooner or later, heavy exercise fatigues the muscle. Not only is the supply of glycogen consumed, but waste products build up in the cell faster than they can be removed. As the waste products build up, the muscle fibers work more and more slowly.

NERVOUS SYSTEM CONCEPTS
(Experiences p. 485)

Nerves

What happens inside the nervous system when we sense an object and react to it? The central part of the nervous system is composed of the brain and spinal cord. Nerves connected to the brain and spinal cord branch out in ever-smaller tendrils to all parts of the body.

When nerve endings are stimulated in some sense organs, ordinarily an electrical message is zipped through sensory nerves from the receptor to the spinal cord and then to the brain. In turn, the brain flashes back a message along motor nerves, which control muscles. The time between when the brain receives a signal and when it returns a command to the muscles is called one's *reaction time*.

Quick Reflexes

A curious thing happens, however, when a quick reflexive action is required. The brain is bypassed until the reflex action happens. For example, if you should touch a finger to a hot stove, the electrical impulses travel from the finger to the spinal cord. But instead of the signal going to the brain, the spinal cord itself flashes a signal along the motor nerves, which immediately activate muscles to jerk the hand away. Meanwhile, the spinal cord also sends impulses to the brain that cause you to feel pain. The sensation, though, is felt *after* you have already reacted to the danger. This, of course, has survival value.

Brain

The brain is the control center of the body. Instead of a single mass, it is made up of three parts: the *cerebrum,* the *cerebellum,* and the *medulla*. Each has a different job.

The cerebrum is the brain's largest part. It consists of two halves that occupy the top portion of the skull. This is the part that governs the conscious, rational processes and receives signals from the senses. The cerebrum also controls the body's voluntary muscles.

The cerebellum is a far smaller part and is located below and behind the cerebrum. It governs perception of balance and coordinates the voluntary muscles.

The medulla adjoins the top of the spinal column at the base of the skull. It governs the involuntary muscles used for digesting food, coughing or sneezing, breathing, pumping blood, and the like.

Learning

How successfully we adapt to the environment often depends on our ability to learn. We learn in several different ways. At the lowest level is trial-and-error learning. This is how we learn to do handwriting or hit a golf ball. The brain works in combination with the senses and muscles to provide corrective feedback.

Learning increases when we organize the data we deal with. Recognizing patterns, outlining, and drawing diagrams are some ways we improve learning. Learning also increases when we associate something we do not know with something we do know. Using memory devices to learn names or to remember spelling words are examples. Reasoning and problem solving are at the highest levels of learning.

The Senses

We receive most of the sensations our brains turn into perceptions through five organs: the eye, ear, nose, tongue, and skin. How do they work? Let's look at each in turn.

THE EYE. In the eye, as in the other sense organs, are the tiny nerve endings of neurons, or nerve cells. The retina, or back section of the eyeball, contains two kinds of light-sensitive neurons: rods and cones. The cones are clustered in and around the center of the retina and are sensitive to color. The rods are distributed outside the cones and are sensitive to light, but not color. The nerve endings of both rods and cones join into a bundle called the optic nerve, which leads to the brain.

THE EAR. The ear has three parts: outer, middle, and inner. The first two parts pass on sound vibrations to the inner ear, located deep inside the skull. The inner ear contains the cochlea, a spiral passage shaped like a snail's shell. Inside

are sound-sensitive nerve endings and a liquid. When vibrations move into the inner ear, the cochlea's liquid vibrates and stimulates the nerve endings. This instantly transmits electric impulses to the auditory nerve, which then zips them to the brain. At that point, we hear.

If you have ever been seasick, you can probably blame your inner ear. It has an intricate part that controls our sense of balance. The part consists of three tubes, formed in half circles, called the semicircular canals. The tubes contain a thin liquid and are arranged in three different positions relative to each other. These positions correspond to the three ways we move our heads: up and down, sideways tilt, and the turning motion. Each motion of the head sloshes the liquid in one of the canals, stimulating nerve endings inside. The impulses are flashed along a branch of the auditory nerve that leads to the cerebellum rather than to the large cerebrum.

One seasickness theory states that the several motions felt in the inner ear conflict with what we see. This is especially so below deck. The sensory conflict triggers the body reaction.

THE NOSE. The nose has nerve endings in the nasal cavity that are sensitive to chemicals. When breathed into the nose, the chemicals dissolve in the moist film of mucous that covers a membrane in the nasal cavity. There nerve endings are stimulated to send signals to the sensory nerves and brain. Continual exposure to one odor causes the nerve cells to become insensitive to that odor. Yet other odors may be detected very well at the same time.

Nerve cells of the nose seem to sense only four primary odors: burnt, rancid, acid, and fragrant odors. Some scientists think that every other odor may simply be some combination of two or more of the four primary odors.

THE TONGUE. Exactly what we taste is an individual matter, even though our tongues are similarly constructed. The tongue contains clusters of nerve cells in the tiny bumps we call taste buds. Taste buds are sensitive to four flavors:

sweet, sour, salty, and bitter. Most buds are clustered in the tip, on the edges, and in the back of the tongue. The tip tends to be sensitive to sweet and salty flavors, the sides to sour flavors, and the back to bitter flavors. However, the exact places vary with people. The taste buds clump into small mounds called *papillae*. These are connected to a sensory nerve that leads to the brain.

Do you remember how tasteless food is when a head cold causes a stuffy nose? It is easy to confuse the sense of taste with that of smell. As we eat, the odors given off by the food stimulate the sense of smell. So both organs work together.

Sometimes the sense of smell dominates. For example, if you chew a tiny piece of radish while you hold a small fresh piece of apple or onion under your nose, you will believe that you are eating the apple or onion.

THE SKIN.   Our skin contains no fewer than five different kinds of nerve endings, which are sensitive to pressure, touch, pain, heat, and cold. These nerve endings are positioned at various depths in the skin. Pressure, for example, is felt much deeper in the skin than touch.

Our nerve endings are also scattered unevenly. The lips and finger tips have many more endings clustered together than other places such as the back of the neck or arm. This is why they are so sensitive.

CIRCULATORY AND RESPIRATORY SYSTEM CONCEPTS
(Experiences p. 497)

Circulatory System

It would be difficult to design a better system than the human blood system for the same function. Blood is the vehicle that transports food, chemicals, and oxygen to all parts of the body. It picks up wastes from the cells and moves them through organs whose job is to remove them. Blood also protects the body.

The liquid part of blood is a clear, yellowish substance called *plasma*. In the plasma are three kinds of solid materials: *red cells, white cells,* and *platelets*. The red cells are most numerous and give the blood its characteristic color. They carry oxygen from the lungs to the body's cells and carbon dioxide from the cells back to the lungs. White cells are larger and move about freely among the body's cells, attacking and consuming disease germs. Platelets also have an important function. They help to make the blood clot wherever the body is injured and bleeding.

Blood moves in the body because it is pumped by the heart, a powerful muscle about the size of one's fist. It pumps blood by alternately contracting and relaxing. Oxygen-poor blood flows into one side of the heart. Squeezing motions pump this blood into the lungs, where it receives oxygen. The oxygen-rich blood then flows back into the opposite side of the heart from where it is pumped to the rest of the body.

In a sense, the circulatory system is really a combination of two interconnected networks of tubes of various sizes. One network sends the blood from the heart to the lungs and back again to the heart. The other sends blood from the heart to the rest of the body and returns it to the heart.

Oxygen-rich blood flows from the heart to the body through thick tubes called *arteries*. Arteries branch out all over the body, getting progressively narrower until they become extremely fine *capillaries*. Capillaries may be as narrow as one-fiftieth the diameter of a human hair and are threaded throughout the cells. Digested food and oxygen pass through the capillaries into the adjacent cells. Capillaries also take up carbon dioxide and other waste products from the cells. The waste-carrying capillaries join into progressively larger tubes called *veins,* which carry blood back to the heart. The entire trip takes about 1'5 seconds. Note that the veins do not carry "blue" blood as most children's science text illustrations would indicate. Those of us who have donated blood realize that it is a dark red as opposed to the bright red of oxygenated blood found in arteries.

Respiratory System

Body cells use oxygen to oxidize, or "burn," food. This process releases energy. Carbon dioxide and water vapor are by-products of this process, just as they are when a candle burns inside an inverted jar. A candle goes out when the oxygen supply is diminished. Likewise, oxidation of food requires a steady supply of enough oxygen. The job of the respiratory system is to replace the carbon dioxide and water vapor in our blood with oxygen. Let's see how this is done.

As we breathe in air through the nose, it passes through hollow nasal passages above the mouth where it is warmed and filtered. Hair-like, moving cilia inside the passages catch dust and airborne particles. These particles are swept to the mouth and coughed up or swallowed. The membrane lining the passages is coated with mucous, which also traps airborne materials.

The air then moves through the voice box or larynx and down into the throat. Two tubes are found there. One tube channels food into the stomach and is called the gullet, or *esophagus.* A second tube, the *windpipe,* or trachea, is located in front of the esophagus. It goes to the lungs. A flap of tissue, the epiglottis, covers the windpipe automatically when we eat or drink. This usually prevents food or liquids from entering the windpipe.

The windpipe shortly divides into two tubes called *bronchi.* One bronchus is attached to each lung. In the lungs, the bronchi split into progressively smaller branches of tubes. Each of

the tiniest tubes ends in a tiny air sac. Since there are many thousands of these sacs, the lungs have a soft, spongy appearance.

Each sac swells like a tiny balloon when we breathe air into the lungs. Surrounding each sac are many capillaries. Oxygen from breathed-in air in the sac passes through the sac's thin wall into the capillaries. Carbon dioxide and water vapor in the capillaries pass the opposite way into the air sacs. These gases then move up through the branched tubes and are exhaled.

Your students may read that body cells use oxygen to "burn" digested food and that carbon dioxide is one by-product of the process. But don't be surprised if most still assume that the air they breathe out is the same as the air they breathe in (Mintzes, 1984).

To show them the difference, you might get some limewater from a drugstore, two identical balloons and small glass jars, and a bicycle tire pump. (Limewater is an indicator for carbon dioxide.) Pour limewater into each of the two jars until half full. Have a child fill one balloon with the pump and the other using lung power. Release the air from one balloon under the limewater surface of one jar, then do this with the second balloon and jar. The limewater exposed to the lung air should turn milky; the other should stay about the same.

Breathing

Children typically believe that the act of breathing in forces the lungs to draw in air and expand. This is not what happens. Breathing in occurs because of unequal air pressure. Examine the process yourself.

Notice what happens when you take a deep breath: The chest cavity enlarges. It enlarges because rib muscles contract and pull the ribs up and outward. At the same time the *diaphragm,* a thin sheet of muscle between the chest and the abdomen, pulls downward. This further enlarges the chest cavity. Enlarging the chest cavity reduces the air pressure inside the lungs. So the stronger outside air pressure forces air into the air passages and lungs.

When we breathe out, the diaphragm relaxes and moves upward. At the same time, the rib muscles relax, and the ribs move down and inward. This reduces the size of the chest cavity, which forces air out of the lungs.

DIGESTIVE SYSTEM CONCEPTS
(Experiences p. 504)

We can eat food, but when is it inside the body? The answer to this seemingly simple question depends on whose point of view we take.

Most people would say that food is inside the body once it is swallowed. To biochemists, however, any food still within the 9-meter (30-foot) digestive tube they call the *alimentary canal* is considered outside the body. This underlines the uselessness of foods we eat until they are digested, or chemically broken down and dissolved into a form that can be used in the cells. The digestive system (Figure 16-1) is marvelously suited to this function. Let's see how it works.

The Mouth

The digestive process begins when we start chewing food. Our front teeth (incisors and canines) cut and tear the food. Back teeth (molars) crush it into small particles. At the same time, saliva pours into the food from six salivary glands in and near the mouth. Saliva softens the food and begins the chemical breakdown of starches. A gradual, sweetening flavor is experienced when we chew starchy foods such as cooked potato, soda cracker, or bread. The saliva contains an enzyme called ptyalin that reduces large starch molecules into simple sugar molecules. (An enzyme is a catalyst, or chemical that brings about or speeds up chemi-

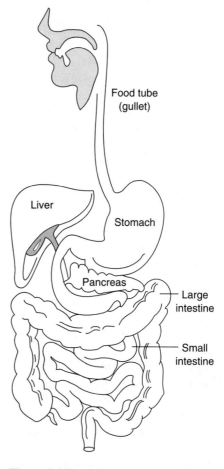

Figure 16-1
The digestive system.

cal reactions without being changed itself.) Besides ptyalin, several other enzymes in the body's digestive system help break down food into usable form.

The Food Tube

Swallowed food passes into the esophagus, or food tube. It is squeezed down into the stomach by regular, wavelike contractions of smooth muscles that surround the esophagus. Similar muscles are located all along the alimentary canal. Because it is muscle action (peristalsis), not gravity, that moves the food inside the canal, it is possible to eat and swallow while standing on our heads.

The Stomach

Peristaltic motions continue in the stomach. The food is churned slowly in gastric juices secreted from the stomach lining. Several enzymes and diluted hydrochloric acid break down most of the proteins. Digestion of starch stops because acid prevents ptyalin from working. Some fats are broken down, but for the most part, fats go through the stomach undigested.

If the stomach's hydrochloric acid is so powerful, why doesn't this corrosive liquid digest the stomach itself? Only in recent years have researchers pinpointed the reason. A small amount of ammonia (this is an alkali or base) is secreted in the lining of the stomach. It effectively neutralizes acid next to the lining without interfering with the acid's digestive action elsewhere in the stomach. We use the same principle of neutralizing an acid when we drink seltzer or soda water to settle a "sour" stomach.

The Intestines

After about two to six hours in the stomach, depending on what and how much has been eaten, the partially digested food materials are pushed into the small intestine. Here, glands within intestinal walls produce digestive juices with enzymes that begin working on the food. Additional digestive juices are secreted into the intestine from small tubes connected to the liver and pancreas.

Throughout the small intestine, peristaltic motion continues as digestive juices complete the breakdown of carbohydrates into simple sugars, proteins into amino acids, and fats into fatty acids and glycerine. At various portions of the small intestine, the sugars and amino acids are absorbed into blood vessels within its lining. Digested fats are first absorbed into the lymph system and then later transported into the blood stream.

Nondigestible material or waste, composed chiefly of cellulose, passes into the large intestine. Much of the water contained in waste material is absorbed into the intestinal walls. The remaining substance is eliminated from the body.

Food products dissolved in the blood are distributed to cells after they are processed by the liver. In the cells, these products are oxidized, changed into protoplasm, or stored as fat.

FOOD AND NUTRITION CONCEPTS
(Experiences p. 505)

We may eat hundreds of foods combined in thousands of ways. But nutritionally speaking, there are four kinds: sugars, starches, fats, and proteins. Some persons would add three more: vitamins, minerals, and water. These seven nutrients may be combined into three groups:

1. Foods for energy—sugars, starches, and fats.
2. Foods for growth and repair of cells—proteins.
3. Food for regulation of body processes—vitamins, minerals, and water.

Carbohydrates

If we heat table sugar in a test tube, the sugar gradually turns black, and water vapor is given off. The black material is carbon. The water is formed as hydrogen and oxygen atoms given off by individual sugar molecules combine. Heat some starch, and again carbon and water appear. Both sugar and starch are *carbohydrates,* a name that means "carbon and water."

Although sugar and starches are composed of the same elements, these elements may appear in various combinations and form relatively small or large molecules. "Simple" sugar molecules, for example, are the smallest carbohydrate molecules. They may be found in grapes and many other fruits. When two simple sugar molecules become attached, a complex sugar, such as table sugar, is formed. A starch molecule is nothing more than a long chain of sugar molecules tightly attached to one another.

In digestion, carbohydrates are broken down into simple sugars. Only in this form are these molecules small enough to pass through cell membranes into the cells, where they "burn" and release energy. The "burning" is a result of *oxidation,* a process in which oxygen chemically combines with fuel—in this case, sugar—and releases heat energy. (Rusting is a form of slow oxidation; fire is very fast oxidation.) The oxygen comes from the air we breathe.

Fats

Analysis shows that fats are also composed of carbon, hydrogen, and oxygen. However, fat molecules have relatively fewer oxygen atoms than carbohydrates. Because they are oxygen "poor," fat molecules can combine with more oxygen atoms and yield about twice as much energy as carbohydrates.

Foods rich in carbohydrates and fats provide our principal source of energy. But when we eat more than we need of these materials, the cells store any excess in the form of fat. Fat storage does not occur uniformly throughout all body cells, as every figure-conscious person knows.

Proteins

The proteins are extremely complex, large molecules. A single molecule may contain thousands of atoms. Like the preceding nutrients, proteins are made up of carbon, hydrogen, and

oxygen. But proteins also contain nitrogen and, typically, sulfur. Proteins are the main source of materials (amino acids) needed for growth and repair of body cells. Excess proteins can be oxidized in cells and so provide energy.

Although all animal and some plant foods (mainly beans, peas, nuts) are rich in proteins, no single plant source contains sufficient amino acids for complete growth and repair of body cells. However, a *combination* of legumes and grains (beans and rice) can furnish all the needed amino acids.

Vitamins

Vitamins are essential to health because they regulate cell activities. These substances permit biochemical processes to take place. Without proper vitamins, the body may suffer from several deficiency diseases, such as scurvy, rickets, and anemia. A balanced diet is usually all that is needed to prevent the disease. But, particularly in the last decade, scientists have found clues that vitamins may play a larger role than previously thought in achieving optimal health and preventing some chronic diseases, such as cancer, decline of the immune system in the aged, heart disease, eye degeneration, and others. This is why some nutritionists recommend a daily multivitamin as "insurance." However, most researchers see the need for more evidence before they can recommend large doses of vitamins aimed at specific diseases or conditions.

Minerals

Several minerals are essential because they help to regulate cell activities. In addition, some minerals are incorporated into body tissue. Calcium and phosphorus form the hard portions of our bones and teeth. Milk is especially rich in these two minerals. Iron and copper help form red blood cells. A proper amount of iodine is needed in the thyroid gland for normal oxidation to take place in cells. Salt is often iodized to prevent goiter, an iodine deficiency. Some minerals cannot be used by cells unless specific vitamins are present. Most fruits and vegetables are rich in vitamins and minerals.

Water

There are many reasons why water is essential to life and good nutrition. It changes chemically to form part of protoplasm. Water is the chief part of blood. It cools the body and carries away accumulated poisons. It is important to digestion and excretion. About two-thirds of the body itself is composed of water.

Besides drinking water directly, we take in much water in the food we eat. For example, celery is about 95 percent water, and fresh bread is about 35 percent water.

Choosing a Healthful Diet

A century ago many Americans were likely to suffer from undernutrition, but today the problem is often the opposite. Most of us eat too much, particularly of foods rich in fat, such as meat and dairy products. This increases the risk of heart disease, stroke, and diabetes, and may also increase the incidence of certain types of cancer. Nutritionists today recommend that we eat far more grains, fruits, and vegetables than has been customary in the American diet.

Many children and adults realize that they must eat a variety of foods to have a proper or "balanced" diet, but are unsure of its makeup. To help us select a healthful combination of nutrients, the U.S. Department of Agriculture has published a food pyramid, with guidelines for five groups of foods (Figure 16-2).

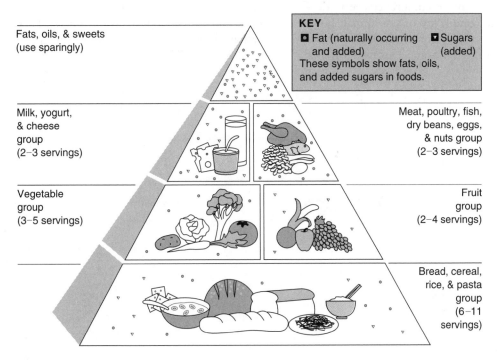

Fats, oils, & sweets (use sparingly)

KEY
◻ Fat (naturally occurring and added) ▼ Sugars (added)
These symbols show fats, oils, and added sugars in foods.

Milk, yogurt, & cheese group (2–3 servings)

Meat, poultry, fish, dry beans, eggs, & nuts group (2–3 servings)

Vegetable group (3–5 servings)

Fruit group (2–4 servings)

Bread, cereal, rice, & pasta group (6–11 servings)

Figure 16-2
Food guide pyramid.

Notice that grains, at the base, get the most servings, while fats, oils, and sweets are to be used only sparingly. In the dairy group, many nutritionists recommend that only nonfat or low-fat products be served. In the meat group, they suggest lean rather than well-marbled meat, skinless poultry, and egg whites rather than whole eggs.

Of course, the pyramid is only a general guide. Size of servings and the number of calories we need to eat depend on our size, age, health, and lifestyle.

HUMAN BODY AND NUTRITION BENCHMARKS AND STANDARDS

As students progress through the elementary years, they gain a more comprehensive understanding of the complexity of the human body and the need to care for it through proper nutrition and exercise. Some examples of specific standards related to the human organism are as follows:

SAMPLE BENCHMARKS (AAAS, 1993).

■ People need water, food, air, and waste removal, and a particular range of temperatures in their environment (by Grades K–2, p. 128).

■ Food provides energy and materials for growth and repair of body parts. Vitamins and minerals, present in small amounts in foods, are essential to keep everything working well (by Grades 3–5, p. 144).

SAMPLE STANDARDS (NRC, 1996).

■ Humans have distinct body structures for walking, holding, seeing, and talking (by Grades K–4, p. 129).

■ The human organism has systems for digestion, respiration, reproduction, circulation, excretion, movement, control, and coordination, and for protection from disease. These systems interact with one another (by Grades 5–8, p. 156–175).

INVESTIGATIONS AND ACTIVITIES

SKELETAL AND MUSCLE SYSTEM EXPERIENCES
(Concepts p. 472)

ACTIVITY: WHAT HAPPENS WHEN MINERALS ARE REMOVED FROM A BONE?

NEEDED

narrow jar and cap
vinegar
two clean matched chicken bones

TRY THIS

1. Put one bone in the jar. Leave the other one outside.
2. Fill the jar with enough vinegar to cover the bone.
3. Cap the jar and wait five days.
4. Remove the bone from the jar and rinse it with water.
   a. Compare the bones. In what ways are the two bones different? How easily does each bone bend? How are the bones still alike?
   b. What difference would it make if your bones had no hard minerals? What foods are rich in minerals?

ACTIVITY: HOW USEFUL ARE YOUR THUMBS?

NEEDED

paper clip
pencil and paper
tape

TRY THIS

1. Make a list of some things you can do now with one or two hands. Which do you think you cannot do without thumbs? Which might you do less well? Which might you do as well?
2. You might record what you think on a chart. You can make a check mark first for what you think, and then an X for what you find out.

Can Do with Thumbs	Without Thumbs		
	Can't Do	Do Less Well	Do as Well
Pick up paper clip	✓	X	
Tie shoelace			
Write my name			
Shake hands			
Button a shirt			

3. Ask someone to tape your thumbs to your hands.

4. Try doing the things on the list without using your thumbs. What surprises, if any, did you find? How do your thumbs help you?

ACTIVITY: *WHAT HAPPENS WHEN YOU OVERWORK YOUR MUSCLES?*

NEEDED

pencil and paper
watch with second hand

TRY THIS

1. Open one hand all the way, then quickly close it to make a tight fist.

2. Open and close it just like that for one minute without stopping. Do it as fast as you can.

3. Count and record what you are able to do during the first and last 30 seconds.

   a. How do the first half and the last half figures compare?

   b. What difference might it make if you change hands?

   c. If you went slower, would you be able to make more fists in one minute?

   d. Can you make as many fists in a second trial? If not, how long must you rest in between to do so?

NERVOUS SYSTEM EXPERIENCES

(Concepts p. 474)

INVESTIGATION: *EYE BLINKING*

When do your eyes blink? Do they blink when something suddenly comes near them? Eye blinking can protect your eyes. Have you also found that your eyes blink at other times? Regular eye blinking wipes your eyes clean and keeps your eyes soft and moist.

EXPLORATORY PROBLEM

How much can you control your protective eye blinking?

NEEDED

clear kitchen wrap
sticky tape
tissue paper
scissors
large file card
partner

TRY THIS

1. You will need to make an eye shield. Cut out the center of a large file card. Leave at least a 2-centimeter (or 1-inch) border.
2. Stick a double layer of clear kitchen wrap to the border with tape.
3. Hold up the shield to your eyes. Look at your partner through the clear wrap (Figure 16-3). Let him *gently* toss a tiny wad of tissue toward it. *Caution:* Closely monitor this activity.

DISCOVERY PROBLEMS

observing

A. Do your eyes blink each time the wad hits the shield? Can you stop your eyes from blinking?

communicating

B. Are you able to control your eye blinking with practice? If so, how much practice? Keep a record.

observing

C. Trade places with some other people. How does their protective eye blinking compare to yours?

observing and inferring

D. How often do a person's eyes blink the regular way? Secretly observe the number of times someone blinks for one minute. Compare the blinking rates of different people. Do their blinking rates change when they know you are observing them?

Figure 16-3

observing

E. How often do some animals blink their eyes? Which animals can you observe?

TEACHING COMMENT

PREPARATION AND BACKGROUND

Blinking is an automatic reflex that children like to investigate. Many children find it hard to prevent the protective blinking reaction when the wad is tossed at the shield. This is good, because the reaction has survival value. Regular blinking, of course, is easily controllable when we are conscious of the act. The rate varies widely among persons and is influenced by a variety of factors.

GENERALIZATION

Eye blinking is a protective reflex action that is partly controllable. The rate of blinking varies among different people.

SAMPLE PERFORMANCE OBJECTIVES

Process: The child can make an accurate record of the blinking rates of different people and order them according to frequency.

Knowledge: The child can explain why automatic eye blinking has greater survival value than conscious blinking.

INVESTIGATION: *YOUR REACTION TIME*

Have you ever had to stop fast when riding your bike? The time between when we sense something and when we act is called our *reaction time*. What people would you expect to have fast reaction times? slower reaction times?

EXPLORATORY PROBLEM

How can you find out about your reaction time?

NEEDED

ruler
paper
partner
pencil

TRY THIS

1. Have your partner hold up a ruler just above your open thumb and forefinger. The ruler's lowest marked number should be facing down. Keep your eye on this ruler end.

2. Have your partner drop the ruler without warning. When you see it drop, close your fingers quickly and catch the ruler (Figure 16-4).

Figure 16-4

3. At what number did you catch the ruler? Read the closest whole number just above your two closed fingers. This is your reaction time number.

DISCOVERY PROBLEMS

hypothesizing and communicating   **A.** What persons in your class may have faster reaction times than yours? slower reaction times? Test these people and your partner. Keep a record.

inferring

B. Will you react to a sound faster than to what you see? Have your partner make a sound just as she drops the ruler. Your eyes should be closed. Catch the ruler when you hear the sound. Compare this reaction time number with the one made when you saw the ruler drop.

inferring

C. Will you react to a touch faster than to sound or sight? Your eyes should be closed. Your partner can touch your head lightly when she drops the ruler. Catch the ruler when you feel her touch. Compare this reaction time with the other times.

experimenting

D. Does the time of day affect your reaction time? Does practice make a difference? Does which hand you use make a difference? How can you find out? What other ideas would you like to try?

TEACHING COMMENT

PREPARATION AND BACKGROUND

For meaningful comparisons, it is important that students do the test in the same way. *Caution:* It is important that the ruler be turned before it is dropped. You want the flat part of the ruler, *not* the ruler edges, to be pinched by the two fingers.

GENERALIZATION

People have different reaction times. The sense signal people react to also makes a difference in their reaction times.

SAMPLE PERFORMANCE OBJECTIVES

Process: The child can measure relative differences in reaction time of people by using a dropped ruler.

Knowledge: The child can state several variables that may influence a person's reaction time.

INVESTIGATION: *HOW PRACTICE IMPROVES LEARNING*

Suppose you learn to do something one way, and then someone says you must learn to do it another way. Why might this be hard to do? How might learning to draw or write backward be a problem? How might practice help?

EXPLORATORY PROBLEM

How can you learn to do mirror drawing or writing?

NEEDED

small mirror
paper
clay
pencil
book
ruler
watch or clock with second hand
graph paper

TRY THIS

1. Draw a triangle on paper, no larger than the one in Figure 16-5.

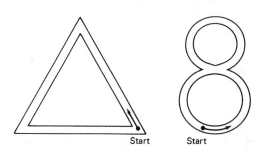

Figure 16-5

2. Arrange the paper, a mirror, and a book as in Figure 16-6. Use two pieces of clay to hold up the mirror.

3. Sit so you must look into the mirror to see the triangle.

4. Place your pencil point on the triangle corner at "start."

5. Observe a watch and notice the time.

6. Draw a line inside and around the whole triangle. Look at the mirror to see what you are doing. Keep the line between the triangle's inside and outside borders. If you go beyond the borders, stop drawing. Start again from the place where you left the border.

7. When you complete the drawing, check the time again. Record in seconds how long it took for this first trial.

Figure 16-6

DISCOVERY PROBLEMS

measuring   **A.** How will practice affect the time needed to draw around the tri-
            angle? How much faster will your second trial be? third trial?
            fourth trial? Make a record like this of what you find out:

NUMBER OF TRIALS   TIME TO FINISH (SECONDS)

NUMBER OF TRIALS	TIME TO FINISH (SECONDS)
1	160
2	140
3	100
4	70

communicating   **B.** Make a graph of your findings. Notice how to do this on the
                graph in Figure 16-7. Suppose it took 160 seconds to finish the
                first trial.

                Put your finger on 1 at the bottom. Follow the line up to and oppo-
                site 160. A dot is placed where the two lines cross. Check to see how
                the other figures are recorded. See how a line has been drawn from
                one dot to the next. This line is called a *curve*. The graph tells about
                learning, so the line may be called a *learning curve*.

predicting   **C.** Study your own learning curve. How fast do you think you can
                draw the triangle after six trials? seven trials? eight trials? nine tri-
                als? ten trials? Record your findings on your graph and complete
                your learning curve.

inferring   **D.** How does your learning curve compare to those of others? Do
                some people learn mirror drawing faster than others?

predicting   **E.** Try a mirror drawing of another figure, such as a large 8 (Figure
                16-5). What shape will your learning curve be for this figure? Will
                people who learned fast before learn fast again?

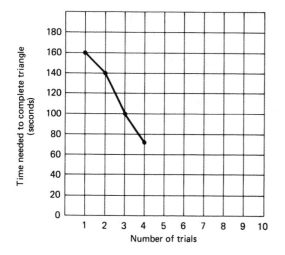

Figure 16-7

hypothesizing **F.** What other problems about learning mirror drawing can you investigate?

TEACHING COMMENT

PREPARATION AND BACKGROUND

You may have to help some students with the line graphs if they lack experience. Also, expect some students to have trouble deciding how many seconds it takes to draw completely around each figure.

GENERALIZATION

An earlier learning may interfere with a later learning. Proper practice can improve one's performance.

SAMPLE PERFORMANCE OBJECTIVES

Process: The child can record data accurately on a graph.

Knowledge: The child can predict when an earlier learning is likely to interfere with later learning.

FOR YOUNGER CHILDREN

This investigation is too abstract for young children in its full form. But if the exploratory problem is presented as a hand–eye coordination activity, young students will enjoy it.

INVESTIGATION: *YOUR SENSE OF TOUCH*

What can you tell about an object by touch? What are some small objects you might know just by touching them?

EXPLORATORY PROBLEM

What objects can you match just by touch?

NEEDED

cloth blindfold
open cardboard box (with a hand-sized hole cut in each side)
matched pairs of small objects
partner

TRY THIS

1. Put a blindfold on your partner. Or, your partner's eyes should be closed. He should not see what you are doing.
2. Put two small, unlike objects inside the box, which should be upside down.
3. Place another small object outside the box. It should match one of the objects inside. Let your blindfolded partner feel it.
4. Next, have your partner feel the objects inside the box. Can he tell which one matches the outside object?
5. Take turns with your partner in playing this game. Use different objects each time. Later use as many objects each time as you can.

DISCOVERY PROBLEMS

observing and inferring
A. Which objects are hard to tell apart? Which are easy? What makes them easy or hard to tell apart?

classifying
B. Can you use touch to put objects in order by size? by roughness? Which objects?

experimenting
C. Is it easier to tell what an inside object is if you can see the outside objects? How can you find out?

experimenting
D. Is it easier to tell what an inside object is with two hands than with one? How can you find out?

TEACHING COMMENT

PREPARATION AND BACKGROUND

Many small objects around the classroom and home may be used in this activity. Among objects easily paired are these: chalk, pencils, leaves, erasers, crayons, nails, coins, washers, rubber bands, cloth of various sizes and textures, paper, foil, and toy figures.

Size, texture, shape, hardness, and, to a minor extent, weight will be the properties used by children to identify objects by touch.

GENERALIZATION

Several properties of an object can be discovered by touch.

SAMPLE PERFORMANCE OBJECTIVES

Process: The child infers the identities of objects and matches them by touch.
Knowledge: The child describes the properties that can be used to identify an object.

FOR OLDER CHILDREN

Try a challenging variation that stresses communication skills. One child holds an object behind her and describes its properties to a partner. The partner touches the several objects inside the box and selects one that matches the description. The described and selected objects are then compared to see if they are identical.

To make the task harder, make the differences among the objects less obvious. Also, put more objects inside the box.

INVESTIGATION: *THE SENSITIVITY OF YOUR SKIN*

Suppose you could not tell if something was touching your skin. How might this change your life?

EXPLORATORY PROBLEM

How can you find out how sensitive your skin is to touch?

NEEDED

ruler
paper and pencil
partner
paper clip

TRY THIS

1. Open up and then bend a paper clip into a U shape.
2. Push the two points together so they meet.
3. Touch the points lightly to the palm of your partner's hand. Eyes should be closed.

4. Ask your partner if he feels two points or one.

5. Separate the two points a short distance. Ask again if he feels two points or one (Figure 16-8).

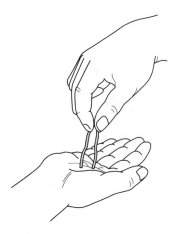

Figure 16-8

6. Keep repeating this action. Each time, move the two points farther apart until your partner feels two points. Then measure the distance between the two points with a ruler.

7. Switch with your partner so you can have your skin tested.

DISCOVERY PROBLEMS

observing, measuring, and communicating   **A.** Where on your skin can you feel the two points soonest? Let your partner measure and make a record such as this one:

BODY PART   DISTANCE BETWEEN THE POINTS

Finger tip

Palm of hand

Back of hand

Back of neck

Lips

inferring and classifying   Look carefully at your completed record. Which seems to be the most sensitive place measured? In what order should the places go if arranged from least to most sensitive?

inferring   **B.** How does your record compare to those of other people? Are some people more sensitive than others? If so, which people? Are certain places on people's skin more sensitive than others? If so, which places?

TEACHING COMMENT

PREPARATION AND BACKGROUND

Many of our nerve ends are found near the skin surface and are distributed unevenly. Typically, our fingertips are more sensitive to touch than other body parts. This is because a high concentration of nerve endings is located there.

It is important that children who are being tested keep their eyes closed. Otherwise, their perception of touch may be altered by what they see. *Caution:* Supervise closely to ensure that the paper clip points are touched *lightly* to the skin.

GENERALIZATION

Some places on our skin are more sensitive to touch than other places; also, some people are more sensitive to touch than others.

SAMPLE PERFORMANCE OBJECTIVES

Process: The child can measure and compare skin sensitivity at several places on the body.

Knowledge: The child can predict which places on a person's skin are more likely to be sensitive to touch.

FOR YOUNGER CHILDREN

Most primary students should be able to do the exploratory section of this investigation and contrast the sensitivity of a fingertip with the palm of the hand.

INVESTIGATION: *YOUR SENSITIVITY TO TEMPERATURE*

Suppose you have two containers of water. One is slightly warmer than another. Could you tell by touch a temperature difference in the water? Does it depend on how much of a difference there is?

EXPLORATORY PROBLEM

How can you find out the smallest temperature difference you can feel?

NEEDED

two cups half-filled with water (one water sample should be warm)
paper and pencil
partner
thermometer (one you can get wet)

TRY THIS

1. Dip a finger into each cup. It is probably easy now for you to tell which cup of water is cooler and which is warmer (Figure 16-9).

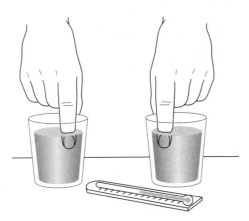

Figure 16-9

2. Let your partner pour a little of the cooler water into the warmer water. You can probably still easily feel the temperature difference.

3. Have your partner continue to reduce the temperature difference between the two cups. She can do this by pouring a little water back and forth between the cups. Keep feeling the water in both cups each time.

4. Stop when you can just barely tell there is a temperature difference. Make sure you are not just imagining this. Close your eyes and let your partner switch around the cups a few times. Tell your partner which cup is cooler or warmer each time. Always keep your eyes closed when the cups are switched.

5. Put the thermometer into each cup for at least half a minute. What is the difference between the two readings?

DISCOVERY PROBLEMS

experimenting   **A.** What is the smallest temperature difference your partner can feel? Get some more warm and cool water and find out.

experimenting **B.** Are some people more sensitive than others? Are people with thin fingers more sensitive than those with thicker fingers? Are toes more sensitive than fingers?

hypothesizing **C.** What questions would you like to investigate?

TEACHING COMMENT

PREPARATION AND BACKGROUND

The beginning temperature difference between the two water samples should be obvious. But it need not be a wide one. If you do not have access to a hot-water tap, warm some water on a hot plate. Or draw two half-cups of tap water and slip an ice cube into one for several minutes.

Children will need the ability to read thermometers to do this investigation. The average child can detect a temperature difference as little as 1.5°C (3°F). Some students will detect an even smaller difference. Eyes are closed for each test.

GENERALIZATION

People differ in their sensitivity to temperature.

SAMPLE PERFORMANCE OBJECTIVES

Process: The child can measure and compare the abilities of different people to detect small differences in water temperature.

Knowledge: The child can state the approximate range of children's differences in detecting water temperature.

CIRCULATORY AND RESPIRATORY SYSTEM EXPERIENCES
(Concepts p. 476)

INVESTIGATION: *PEOPLE'S PULSE BEATS*

Your heart pumps blood through long tubes in your body called arteries. Your arteries are very elastic. They stretch then shrink slightly each time the heart pumps more blood through them. These tiny movements are called *pulse* beats. You can tell how fast your heart pumps by feeling your pulse beats.

EXPLORATORY PROBLEM

How can you feel and measure how fast your pulse beats?

NEEDED

watch or clock with second hand
paper and pencil

TRY THIS

1. Press on the inside part of your wrist with four fingers. (See Figure 16-10.)

Figure 16-10

2. Find where you can best feel your pulse.

3. Count how often your pulse beats in one minute while sitting. The number of pulse beats in one minute is your "resting" pulse rate (this would differ when exercising).

4. Record your pulse rate on paper.

DISCOVERY PROBLEMS

experimenting   **A.** How does what you do change your pulse rate? For example, how does standing affect it? lying down? exercise?

experimenting   **B.** How do your pulse rates compare before and after eating?

observing   **C.** Where else on your body can you feel your pulse? Is the pulse rate there the same as at the wrist?

experimenting   **D.** How do the pulse rates of different people compare? For example, how do the pulse rates of boys and girls compare? How do adults and children compare? How do young and old adults compare? Does how tall a person is make a difference in pulse rate? Does how heavy a person is make a difference?

hypothesizing   **E.** What else do you notice about people, or what they do, that might affect pulse rates?

observing   **F.** How do you think the pulse rates of dogs, cats, and other animals compare with those of humans? How can you find out?

TEACHING COMMENT

PREPARATION AND BACKGROUND

The pulse may also be felt quite easily on each side of the throat just under the chin.

The pulse rate usually slows with age and size. Also, boys have slightly slower rates than girls. Seven-year-olds average around 90 beats per minute, which is almost twice the rate for the very aged. Athletic training also reduces the rate because it develops a larger, stronger heart. These factors similarly influence animal pulse rates, particularly size. An elephant, for example, has a very slow pulse rate.

There are several opportunities to make useful graphs in this investigation. For example, how long does it take for the pulse to return to a resting rate after exercise? What is the effect of eating on the rate? Also, watch for chances to control variables and make operational definitions: What is a tall, young, old, heavy, or tired person? If we are testing for age, how can we control height and weight?

GENERALIZATION

One's pulse rate is a measure of how fast the heart beats in one minute. A variety of conditions may affect it.

SAMPLE PERFORMANCE OBJECTIVES

Process: The child can accurately measure his pulse rate.
Knowledge: The child can describe several conditions that influence the pulse rate.

INVESTIGATION: *THE VOLUME OF AIR YOU BREATHE*

How much air do you breathe in a single breath? How big a container do you think you would need to hold it?

EXPLORATORY PROBLEM

How can you find out how much air you breathe?

NEEDED

large bowl or pail, placed in a sink
masking tape
plastic or glass bottle with cap (1 gallon or 4 liter)
string
rubber tube

ruler
paper sheet
partner
pencil

TRY THIS

1. Stick a strip of tape down the side of the bottle.
2. Mark the strip into 10 equal parts.
3. Partly fill a large bowl or pail with water.
4. Fill the bottle with water and cap it.
5. Put the bottle, upside down, into the bowl.
6. Remove the cap while the bottleneck is underwater.
7. Put one end of the tube into the bottle. (You may have to tip the bottle a little. Have someone hold the bottle so it does not go far over.)
8. Wrap some paper around the other end of the tube (Figure 16-11).

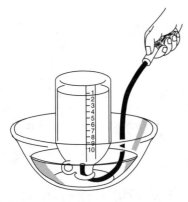

Figure 16-11

9. Take a regular breath. Then blow out the air through the tube. Quickly pinch the tube shut when you finish blowing. Observe how much water is forced out of the bottle. This tells you how much air you blow out.
10. Refill the bottle each time you try a breath test.

DISCOVERY PROBLEMS

measuring

A. By what tape mark is the water level for a regular breath? Make a record, so you can compare it to other marks.

measuring

B. How much more air can you hold when you breathe deeply? Take a deep breath. Blow out all the air you can. Compare the new and old marks.

measuring

C. How much air can other persons blow out in one breath? (Wrap a fresh paper around the tube end each time someone new blows through it.)

communicating

D. Make a graph of your findings. Use each person's chest size, or height, or weight for one part of your graph. Use their water level mark for the other part, as in Figure 16-12.

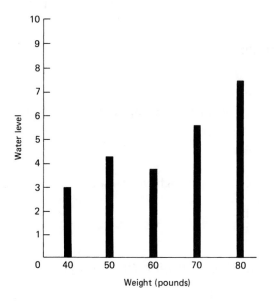

Figure 16-12

predicting

E. Can you use your graph to predict more findings? For example, will two persons who weigh the same get the same results? Will two people with the same height or chest size get the same results?

hypothesizing and communicating

F. What else do you notice about people that might affect how much air they can hold? For example, do athletes have more lung space than others? What is an "athlete"?

TEACHING COMMENT

PREPARATION AND BACKGROUND

A child can measure chest sizes with string. For good hygiene, a fresh, small slip of paper should be wrapped around the tube end each time it is used.

A typical plastic one-gallon container has curved sides and some space for the bottle neck. Therefore, to divide it accurately into 10 parts requires more mathematics than is presently suggested. Students can use a measuring cup to calculate the total number of ounces (or milliliters) in the bottle, and divide by 10. Then they can fill the bottle a tenth at a time to make each mark.

GENERALIZATION

The volume of water displaced by "lung" air is a rough measure of lung capacity. People's lungs vary greatly in air capacity.

SAMPLE PERFORMANCE OBJECTIVES

Process: The child can construct a graph that shows the relationship of weight (or other measurable property) to lung capacity.

Knowledge: The child can explain how the volume of the displaced water is associated with lung capacity.

FOR YOUNGER CHILDREN

Younger students will enjoy and profit from making rough comparisons of their lung capacities.

INVESTIGATION: HOW FAST PEOPLE BREATHE

How many breaths do you take each minute? Does everyone breathe equally fast? What conditions may affect how fast people breathe?

EXPLORATORY PROBLEM

How can you find out how many breaths you take each minute?

NEEDED

watch or clock with second hand
pencil and paper

TRY THIS

1. Count one breath each time you breathe *out* while sitting.

2. Observe the time on a clock. Count the number of times you breathe out in one minute (Figure 16-13).

3. Record the number on a piece of paper.

Figure 16-13

DISCOVERY PROBLEMS

measuring

A. How fast do you breathe after exercise? Bend and touch your toes or do some other easy exercise for one minute. Then count your breaths for one minute.

measuring and communicating

B. How fast do other people breathe while sitting? Compare people who are different in weight, height, and sex. Tell them how to count their breaths. Keep time for one minute. Record each person's name and how fast each breathes.

measuring

C. How fast do other people breathe after exercise? Record your findings.

predicting

D. Can you predict how fast some people will breathe? Study your records and observe the people. What are the people like who are slow breathers? faster breathers? Perhaps other people who are like them will also be fast or slow. Pick a few people you have not tested before and find out.

hypothesizing

E. What else about people, or what they do, might affect
how fast they breathe?

TEACHING COMMENT

PREPARATION AND BACKGROUND

The main purpose of this investigation is to help children record and think about
data. Children will discover a variety of breathing rates, but reasons for these differences will be inconclusive at their level of understanding. You might mention that
there is no single proper breathing rate for everyone. What is natural for one person
may not be for another.

GENERALIZATION

People have different breathing rates; exercise affects one's breathing rate.

SAMPLE PERFORMANCE OBJECTIVES

Process: The child can compare two sets of breathing data and note likenesses and
differences.

Knowledge: The child can predict the approximate average breathing rate of several
classmates who are in sitting positions.

DIGESTIVE SYSTEM EXPERIENCES
(Concepts page 478)

ACTIVITY: *HOW DOES CHANGING STARCH INTO SUGAR HELP THE BODY?*

NEEDED

two small jars or glasses
teaspoon
starch
sugarless soda
cracker
sugar
water

TRY THIS

1. Bite off a piece of sugarless cracker and chew it for at least one minute.

   a. How does the taste of the cracker change as you chew it? A soda cracker is
   made up mostly of starch. The saliva in your mouth starts changing the

starch into a sugar. It is changed the rest of the way in your small intestine. Before food can be used by your body cells, it must be in a *dissolved* form. Does changing a starch into a sugar help it to dissolve? Find out for yourself.

2. Half-fill two small jars with water.

3. Put a teaspoon of sugar in one jar and one of starch in the other. Mix each for a minute.

   b. Which food dissolves? Will more stirring make the undissolved food dissolve?

TEACHING COMMENT

Students will need to know that when a material dissolves it is no longer visible. The solution looks clear.

FOOD AND NUTRITION EXPERIENCES
(Concepts p. 479)

ACTIVITY: *WHICH FOODS HAVE STARCH?*

NEEDED

iodine
piece of white chalk
medicine dropper
cornstarch
tiny pieces of foods (such as white bread, rice, macaroni, cheese, potato, cereals)
teaspoon
waxed paper

TRY THIS

1. Place a bit of cornstarch on waxed paper. Crush a small piece of white chalk next to it with a spoon.

2. Put one drop of iodine on each. Notice how the cornstarch turns purple-black. The chalk should look red-brown. When a food turns purple-black, it has starch.

3. Test your food samples with the iodine. Crush each sample first with the spoon. Wash it off each time.

   a. Which samples seem to have starch? Which do not?

4. Try the starch test on part of an unripe banana. Then test part of a very ripe banana. Taste a little of each.

   b. What difference do you notice? When does a banana seem to have more starch? When does it seem to have more sugar?

ACTIVITY: *WHICH FOODS HAVE FATS?*

NEEDED

brown paper bag
drop of oil
small pieces of different foods (such as bacon, olive, margarine, bread, apple, cheese)
drop of water

TRY THIS

1. Spread a drop of oil on the brown paper. Fat is mostly oil.
2. Spread a drop of water alongside it. Allow it to dry.
3. Hold up the paper to the light. Notice the difference in the two spots. Fat shows as a shiny, oily spot.
    a. Which foods do you think have fat?
4. Make a list and then test the foods you can. Rub each small piece into the brown paper.
    b. Which made an oily stain? How do your findings compare with what you thought?

INVESTIGATION: *SOME PROPERTIES OF POWDERED FOODS*

You eat many different white powders. Cake is made with baking powder. White bread is made with white flour. Cornstarch helps to make gravy. You can even make milk by mixing powdered milk with water.

If you take a quick look at most white powders, they seem alike. But each is really different in several ways.

EXPLORATORY PROBLEM

How can you tell one white powder from another? *Caution:* Do not use taste for this investigation.

NEEDED

white powders (such as baking powder, baking soda, white flour, powdered sugar, cornstarch, powdered milk)
small jar of water
three medicine droppers
teaspoon

small jar of iodine solution
paper towel
small jar of white vinegar
magnifier

TRY THIS

1. Put less than a quarter-teaspoon of one powder on a paper towel. Only a little is needed (Figure 16-14).

Figure 16-14

2. Observe it carefully through a magnifier. How does it look?
3. Feel the powder with your fingers. How does it feel?
4. Put a drop of water on the powder. What happens?
5. Put a drop of iodine solution on the powder. What happens?
6. Put a drop of vinegar on the powder. What happens?

DISCOVERY PROBLEMS

observing and communicating **A.** How does this powder compare to other powders? Test a few more powders. Record what you observe on a chart such as this:

Powder Tested	How It Looks Magnified	How It Feels	Reaction to Water	Reaction to Iodine	Reaction to Vinegar
Cornstarch					
Flour					
Baking soda					

inferring

B. Which test or tests seem most useful to tell the powders apart? least useful?

inferring

C. Can you identify an unknown powder? Ask someone to put a quarter-teaspoon of powder on a fresh paper towel. You should not know what powder it is, but it should be one recorded on your chart. Make some tests and use your chart to identify it.

inferring

D. Can you identify two unknown powders mixed together? Have someone choose two chart powders and mix them. Do the rest as in Problem C.

hypothesizing

E. What other ways can you test white powders? What other powders can you test?

TEACHING COMMENT

PREPARATION AND BACKGROUND

Any material has certain physical properties that may be used to identify it. By performing certain tests, children may learn some of the different properties of similar-looking powdered foods as well as other powders.

Small baby food jars make excellent containers for the powders and test liquids. For the iodine solution, mix two full medicine droppers of iodine in a half-full baby food jar of water.

Children may try additional tests such as heating the powders and mixing them with water. A small cup can be formed from kitchen foil and held over a candle flame with a spring clothespin. *Caution:* Supervise closely for safety. Only a tiny amount of powder need be heated. A powder may also be mixed in water in a clear glass jar and then compared with other water-powder mixtures.

Caution: Students should not taste powders. Explain that some powders they should not eat may get mixed with some powdered foods in this investigation. For example, some nonfoods they may want to test are powdered detergent, white tempera paint powder, crushed white chalk, talcum powder, alum, scouring powder, tooth powder, and plaster of paris.

GENERALIZATION

A material may be identified by tests to reveal its physical properties.

SAMPLE PERFORMANCE OBJECTIVES

Process: The child can infer the identity of several powders by interpreting recorded data.

Knowledge: The child can describe several different physical properties of at least two common powdered foods.

FOR YOUNGER CHILDREN

Younger students can do this activity well with fewer tests and powders. For example, have them observe two powders and make perhaps two tests, such as how they look magnified and how they feel. They can then receive an "unknown" powder and try to match it with one of the two powders tested.

REFERENCES

American Association for the Advancement of Science. (1993). *Benchmarks for science literacy.* New York: Oxford University Press.

Mintzes, J. J. (1984). Naive theories in biology: Children's concepts of the human body. *School Science and Mathematics, 84* (7), 548–55.

National Research Council. (1996). *National science education standards.* Washington, DC: National Academy Press.

SELECTED TRADE BOOKS: HUMAN BODY AND NUTRITION

For Younger Children

Adler, D. A. (1991). *You breathe in, you breathe out.* Watts.

Berger, M. (1983). *Why I cough, sneeze, shiver, hiccup, and yawn.* Harper & Row.

Bishop, P. R. (1991). *Exploring your skeleton.* Watts.

Cole, J. (1989). *The magic school bus inside the human body.* Scholastic.

Hoover, R., & Murphy, B. (1981). *Learning about our five senses.* Good Apple.

Hvass, U. (1986). *How my body moves.* Viking.

Kindersley, D. (1991). *What's inside my body?* Peter Lang.

Parker, S. (1991). *Eating a meal: How you eat, drink and digest.* Watts.

Penn, L. (1986). *The human body.* Good Apple.

Sattler, H. R. (1982). *Noses are special.* Abingdon.

Showers, P. (1982). *You can't make a move without your muscles.* Crowell.

Sproule, A. (1987). *Body watch: Know your insides.* Facts on File.

For Older Children

Allison, L. (1976). *Blood and guts: A working guide to your own little insides.* Little, Brown.

Behm, B. (1987). *Ask about my body.* Raintree.

De Bruin, J. (1983). *Young scientists explore the five senses.* Good Apple.

Gabb, M. (1991). *The human body.* Watts.

Galperin, A. (1991). *Nutrition.* Chelsea House.

Harlow, R., & Morgan, G. (1991). *Energy and growth.* Watts.

Hausherr, R. (1989). *Children and the AIDS virus: A book for children, parents, and teachers.* Clarion.

Klein, A. E. (1977). *You and your body.* Doubleday.

Parker, S. (1991). *Nerves to senses: Projects with biology.* Watts.

Rayner, C. (1980). *The body book.* Barron.

Rutland, J. (1977). *Human body.* Watts.

Simon, S. (1979). *About the foods you eat.* McGraw-Hill.

Taylor, R. (1982). *How the body works.* EMC Publications.

Walpole, B. (1987). *The human body.* Messner.

Ward, B. R. (1991). *Diet and health.* Watts.

Wilson, R. (1979). *How the body works.* Larousse.

Wolf, D., & Wolf, M. L. (Eds.). (1982). *The human body.* Putnam.

Wong, O. (1986). *Your body and how it works.* Children's Press.

Zim, H. S. (1979). *Your skin.* Morrow.

Resource Books

Butzow, C. M., & Butzow, J. W. (1989). *Science through children's literature. An integrated approach* (nutrition topics, pp. 107–111). Teachers Ideas Press.

Fredricks, A. D., Meinbach, A. M., & Rothlein, L. (1993). *Thematic units: An integrated approach to teaching science and social studies* (health topics, pp. 140–145; body system topics, pp. 189–194). HarperCollins.

Shaw, D. G., & Dybdahl, C. S. (1996). *Integrating science and language arts. A sourcebook for K–6 teachers* (circulatory system topic, pp. 65–67). Allyn and Bacon.

THE EARTH'S CHANGING SURFACE

Building Up of
the Land

How Rocks Are
Formed

Earth's Changing Surface
Benchmarks and Standards

Magma and
Volcanoes

Rock Cycle

Faults and
Earthquakes

Fossils

Plate Tectonics

Sedimentary,
Igneous, and
Metamorphic

Weathering and
Erosion

Soil and Its
Makeup

Wind and Water
Erosion

Conservation
Practices

THE EARTH'S
CHANGING
SURFACE

Plant Action

Humus, Loam,
Sand, Silt, and
Clay

Chemical
Weathering

Shifting sand dunes, eroding hillsides, weeds growing on an asphalt playground, and muddy water running in gutters are all evidence that the earth's surface is changing.

This chapter examines some of the forces that wear down and build up the earth and their rock and soil products. Four sections include weathering and erosion, soil and its makeup, the building up of the land, and how rocks are formed.

WEATHERING AND EROSION CONCEPTS
(Experiences p. 525)

Perhaps the only permanent feature about the earth's surface is the continuous process of change it reveals. The forces that weather and erode the land are powerful and ceaseless.

Strictly speaking, *weathering* refers to the breaking down of rocks into smaller parts through the action of agents such as plants, chemicals, frost, and changes of temperature. *Erosion* includes weathering plus the process of transporting weathered material from one location to another, as in the action of running water, wind, and glaciers.

Plant Actions

It is hard for some children to realize at first that plants break down rocks. After all, rocks are "hard" and plants are "soft," they reason. But plants weather rocks in several ways.

Growing roots may wedge deeply into a cracked rock and force it apart. As dry plant seeds absorb water, they swell with surprising force and may perform a similar wedging function. Tiny flat plants called *lichens* grow on bare rock (Figure 17-1). Acids released by these plants decompose and soften the rock. Larger plants may then follow in a long succession, each contributing to the rock's destruction.

Figure 17-1
Lichens play a part in weathering rock.

Chemical Weathering

Oxygen and water in the air combine with rock surfaces to produce "rust." Reddish soils, for example, usually contain oxidized iron compounds.

Falling rain picks up a small amount of carbon dioxide in the air and forms carbonic acid. Although it is well diluted, this substance slowly wears down limestone. Older limestone buildings and statuary have a soft, worn look from the dissolving effect of acidic rainwater. This is especially noticeable in England and in several areas in the northeastern United States, where coal burning has been prevalent. Abnormal quantities of sulfur dioxide released into the air increase the acidic content of rain and hasten weathering. (We will consider acid rain again in the next chapter.)

Rainwater that percolates into the ground may encounter a limestone formation and dissolve some of it, so forming a cave. This is how the Carlsbad Caverns of New Mexico, Luray Caverns of Virginia, and Mammoth Caves of Kentucky were formed. Because the surface appearance of a rock is somewhat altered by chemical weathering, we must often chip or break it to note its natural color.

Expansion–Contraction

Frozen water also contributes to weathering. Many rocks are relatively porous. Water, you may remember, is one of the few substances that expands in freezing. As absorbed water expands, bits of rock are broken off. In addition, ice may wedge apart cracked rocks.

Stones placed around campfires are sometimes cracked because rocks conduct heat poorly. The difference between a hot surface and cooler interior may produce strains that cause parts to flake off. But some of this *exfoliation,* as it is called, may be from expansion due to release of pressure. Rocks formed underground are subjected to great pressures. When they finally appear on the surface, because of erosion or other means, there may be a tendency for these rocks to "unsqueeze" slightly, thus starting some cracks.

Running Water

Moving water is no doubt the most erosive force on earth. Abrasive, waterborne rocks and particles have gradually formed the Grand Canyon over millions of years. Millions of tons of soil daily wash from banks and hills over the world into streams and are eventually carried into the ocean. Ocean waves ceaselessly pound huge cliffs and boulders into sand.

Water running down hills usually forms gullies. As the slope angle increases, water moves more swiftly, so hastening erosion. Rain splashing on near-level fields has a different erosive effect. Broad sheets of soil wash off into lower places without obvious gullying.

Wind Erosion

The effect of wind erosion became dramatically apparent to millions of Americans in the Dust Bowl years of 1934–1935. Prairie lands originally covered by a grassy sod had been broken up for agriculture. A combination of dry weather and marginal farming practices resulted in the most destructive dust storms ever seen in the United States.

Glacial Erosion

Glaciers also contribute to land erosion. Huge snow deposits build up when snowfall exceeds the melting rate. Gradually, some of the underlying snow compacts into ice and the glacier flows slowly downhill, as in the case of mountain valley glaciers.

Continental glaciers are much larger, ranging to thousands of square miles in size. At one time, a large part of North America was buried under snow and ice. Today, much of Greenland and Antarctica are covered by such glaciers. Gravity forces these glaciers to spread out as more and more snow piles on top.

When glaciers move, they scour the land under their tremendous weight, scooping out basins and leveling hills. As they melt, huge deposits of soil and rocks are left at the sides and leading edge. Effects of glaciation may be seen in many parts of our country, particularly in New England and the north central states (Figure 17-2).

SOIL AND ITS MAKEUP CONCEPTS
(Experiences p. 535)

Many children understand that weathering and erosion can wear underlying rock into small particles. But they often do not realize that there is more to productive soil than just rock

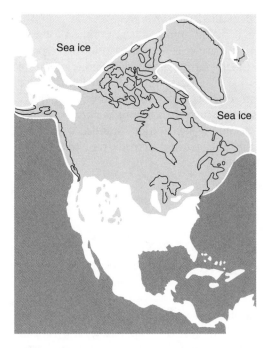

Figure 17-2
About 11,000 years ago, glaciers advanced deeply into what is now the northern United States.

Figure 17-3
A soil profile, or cross section, 3 feet (0.9 meters) deep. Subsoil becomes coarser and contains less humus with depth.

particles. It is not until decomposed plant and animal matter is added (or manufactured chemicals applied) that the soil becomes productive enough to support agriculture (Figure 17-3).

Humus, as this organic matter is called, supplies plants with nitrogen, phosphorus, potassium, and other essential elements. The decomposition of organic material is done by soil bacteria. Acids released in decomposition also dissolve other minerals in the soil particles. Humus retains water well and so keeps soil from drying out rapidly. The darkish color of humus-laden soil absorbs sunlight efficiently, and so it is warmer than light-colored soil. This speeds up plant growth and reduces seed failure.

Earthworms, you may recall, are important to soil for several reasons. They help break up the soil, which permits air, as well as water, to reach the plant roots. Root cells die unless they

absorb sufficient oxygen. And, as earthworms eat through soil, they mix it and leave castings that contain rich fertilizing ingredients.

Soil Makeup

The composition of soil is easily studied if you mix some earth in a water-filled jar and allow the jar to stand several hours. Gravity causes the several materials to settle in order. Heavier, coarser particles like pebbles settle first, followed by sand, silt, and clay. Any humus present floats on the water surface.

The best soil for most plants is *loam,* composed of sand (30 to 50 percent), silt (30 to 50 percent), clay (up to 20 percent), and abundant humus. Silt and clay have small particles that retain water well. Having been eroded from rocks rich in certain minerals, they contain elements plants need for healthy growth. Coarser sand particles make soil porous, enabling air and water to reach plant roots. A soil composed of sand or clay alone lacks the moderate degree of porosity that seems best for watering plant roots.

Soils differ greatly in their degree of acidity and alkalinity. Strawberry plants thrive in acidic soil. Many grasses grow well in alkaline or basic soils. Clover does best in soil that is neither basic nor acidic, but neutral.

Soil Conservation

One of the reasons erosion is a fearsome enemy of the farmer is the time required for good soil to form. It may take up to 500 years for a single inch of good topsoil to be produced by natural means. With a rapidly multiplying world population, topsoil conservation is a serious concern.

Some of the things farmers do to preserve topsoil are shown in Figure 17-4. Each is directed toward a specific problem. *Contour plowing,* for example, is used when plowing hilly land. Plowing straight up or down a hill will cause gullies to form during rain or irrigation. Plowing around the hill reduces gully erosion. *Strip cropping* alternates a row crop that has much bare soil exposed, such as corn, with a ground cover crop, such as clover. This reduces wind erosion. A tree *windbreak* will also help if the field is located where a strong wind usually blows from one direction. *Terracing* may be used to prepare relatively flat areas for growing crops on steep slopes. *Check dams* of stones or logs may be used to slow down water in a stream or prevent a gully from widening.

Perhaps the greatest advance of this century in conserving farm topsoil is a recently adopted practice called *residue management,* which does away with the plow. Even the best plowing practices bare soil to water and wind erosion. Now, many farmers leave the residue or stubble from harvested crops in place to hold soil and moisture. Tractor-pulled machines gouge places for seeds, which then sprout and grow through the decomposing residue. Besides minimizing erosion, the method actually rebuilds the precious topsoil.

BUILDING UP OF THE LAND CONCEPTS
(Experiences p. 539)

Careful geological studies show that the powerful forces of weathering and erosion should have long ago worn down the earth's surface to a low-lying plain. Then why are there mountains? Part of the answer is seen in volcanic activity.

Magma

Fiery molten rock from deep underground, called *magma,* thrusts up through weak spots and cracks in the earth's crust. When this material reaches the surface, it is called *lava.*

Sometimes the accumulation of magma and high-pressure gases is so great that the molten rock shoots up to the surface in a spectacular eruption. This can happen under the ocean, as well as on land. The Hawaiian Islands are the eroded tops of volcanoes, as are the Azores in the Atlantic Ocean.

Sometimes magma may quietly ooze up through great cracks in the crust and spread out over the ground. Large parts of the Pacific Northwest are covered with hardened lava beds to depths of thousands of feet. Similar lava flows have occurred in Iceland.

Figure 17-4
Some ways of preventing erosion: *(a)* contour plowing, *(b)* strip crops, *(c)* terraces,
(d) check dam, *(e)* tree windbreak.

Several types of magmatic activity are not directly visible until erosion has worn away parts of the crust. Magma may stop flowing and cool before it reaches the surface, or it may push up part of the crust, forming a dome, or *laccolith*. Erosion of the surrounding crust makes the dome more prominent (Figure 17-5).

Where does heat energy for volcanoes originate? There are several theories, one of which we will look at now. Some scientists think that radioactive rocks are responsible in some places.

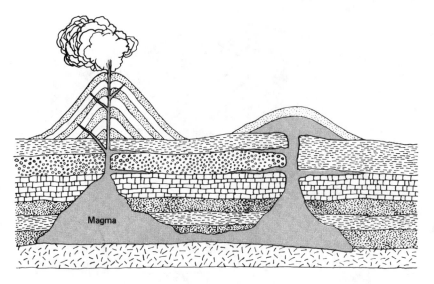

Figure 17-5
A volcano and a laccolith.

One radioactive element is uranium, which continually shoots off helium atoms and changes to lead. In the process, a tiny amount of heat energy is generated. If many rocks of this type become concentrated, it is conceivable that they could bring about enough heat energy to melt rocks. (The known rate of decay of uranium into lead is useful in finding the age of rocks. Since the rate apparently never changes, scientists can figure age by noting the ratio of remaining uranium to lead.)

Earthquakes and Faults

Earthquakes happen when the crust breaks under the strain of its deforming forces. Parts of the crust may move horizontally, diagonally, or vertically along a huge crack, or *fault*. Over a long time, *block mountains* may develop through tilted or vertical movements along a fault line. This seems to be how the Sierra Nevada range was formed.

Other mountains seem to be made through *folding*. Immense forces push parts of the crust into giant wrinkles. The Appalachians are an example.

Plate Theory

How does modern science explain such major changes in the earth's crust? When we look at a world map, certain land masses of the earth, while far apart, seem to fit together like pieces of a jigsaw puzzle. The east coast of South America and the west coast of Africa are examples. Could it be that these and other continents were once joined?

Many modern earth scientists infer this. They think that the earth's thin crust was once solid, but now is fragmented into six to eight immense "plates" and several smaller ones that fit in between. The plates drift on the earth's fiery mantle of molten rock some 100 kilometers (60 miles) or so below. The continents float on the plates like passengers on rafts. Plate edges do not necessarily coincide with the edges of continents. According to *plate tectonics theory,* the plates continually pull apart, collide, grind edges, or partially slide under each other.

Ocean floors, for example, form when two plates drift apart. Magma pushes up from the mantle and fills the ever-widening gap between the plates. When one plate pushes into or under another, folded mountains and block mountains may be formed. A plate edge that thrusts downward under another melts into the fiery mantle below. Some of the magma that results thrusts up through weak spots in the solid crust to form volcanoes. Earthquakes may happen as plates slide past each other in opposite directions. The great friction between the two massive plates may cause the movements to temporarily stop. However, stresses build up until the crust suddenly fractures and the plates grind onward.

Plate movements are surprisingly fast, up to 20 centimeters (8 inches) a year in some locations, given the approximate 5-billion-year age of the earth. Apparently, the force needed to move the rigid plates comes from convection currents in the molten mantle below.

Note the correlation between regions of earthquake and volcanic activity in Figure 17-6. Many scientists infer that these active regions reveal some boundaries of the huge, drifting plates. A Cakequake (Hardy & Tolman, 1991)—which introduces plate tectonics through types of plate movements—makes learning these concepts a fun activity.

HOW ROCKS ARE FORMED CONCEPTS
(Experiences p. 540)

"What are rocks made of?" children often ask. Rocks are made up of *minerals* which are natural inorganic materials that make up most of the earth's crust. Some minerals are composed of a single element, such as copper or carbon. A

beautiful diamond is an example of almost pure carbon formed under enormous pressure underground. Other minerals are compounds of two or more minerals, such as mica or quartz. The chemical makeup of a mineral is the same anywhere it is found on earth. A pure copper or quartz sample is as recognizable in Asia as in North America.

Geologists have developed many ways of identifying minerals. These may include observing its color, hardness, luster, how it splits along a plane, how it breaks, its density, its crystal structure, and how it reacts to chemicals.

Just as a word may be made up of one or more letters of the alphabet, rocks may be composed of one or more minerals. But there are far more known minerals than letters of the alphabet (about 2,000). Most are seldom seen. Fewer than 100 minerals make up the bulk of the earth's crust.

Usually, rocks are given the same name when they contain essentially the same minerals, like granite. Some samples, though, may contain a greater proportion of one or more of the minerals than other samples. So not all granite samples look alike, nor do many other rock samples given a certain name. Although there are many minerals, rocks are formed in just three ways.

Sedimentary Rocks

Sediments from eroded rocks are the raw materials for new sedimentary rocks. The sediments are usually moved and deposited by rivers into coastal trenches and basins. Some rivers deposit sediments into large lakes. Sand, clay, silt, pebbles, and stones are common sedimentary materials. Sediments gradually collect layer upon layer where they are deposited, which makes the layers press harder and harder on the lower sediments. The enormous pressure, plus chemicals dissolved in the water, cement the sediments together. Sand particles

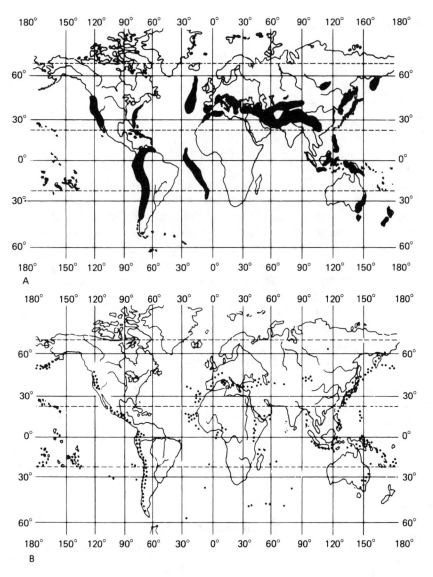

Figure 17-6
Earthquake (A) and volcano (B) regions of the world.

become sandstone, mud or clay becomes shale, and pebbles and rocks and sand combine to form conglomerate.

Not all sediments come from eroded materials. Limestone and chalk are examples of rock formed on the ocean floor from the com-pressed skeletons and shells of billions of ocean animals, including clams, mussels, and corals. Some sedimentary rock may also form from previously dissolved chemicals that deposit out of solution when the water can no longer hold them.

Igneous Rocks

A second way rocks are formed is through the cooling of magma or lava. These are igneous rocks (the word *igneous* means "formed from fire"). A common example of igneous formation happens in domes, or laccoliths. Magma squeezes under a surface rock layer, slowly cools, and becomes solid. When the surface rocks erode away, the underlying rock is exposed. Granite is the most frequently found rock of this kind. Its large crystals reveal that it cooled slowly.

Lava that is blown from a volcano or that flows out of cracks in the crust cools quickly. So it has small crystals or no visible crystals. The light, spongy rock called pumice and the black, glassy rock called obsidian are examples.

Metamorphic Rocks

Sedimentary and igneous rocks may undergo severe pressure and heat as parts of the crust move, fold, thrust deeper under the ground, or are buried under lava flows. This may cause physical and chemical changes in the rocks, making them metamorphic rocks (the word *metamorphic* means "changed in form"). Sedimentary rocks such as limestone become marble, sandstone may become quartzite, and shale becomes slate. Igneous rock such as granite changes to gniess (pronounced "nice") or soft coal changes to hard coal.

Metamorphic rocks are harder than the original rock material. They often have compression bands of different colors. Usually, crystals are small. Still, it is easy to confuse metamorphic rocks with igneous rocks.

Table 17-1 shows 12 kinds of rocks children can use to become acquainted with the three basic types. They are fairly distinctive and easy to obtain. Some, and perhaps all, of these rocks may be included in specimens students bring to school. If not, they may be acquired from local rock collectors, museums, and science supply companies.

Fossils

The remains, or signs, of animals or plants in rock are called fossils. The most likely rocks in which fossils are found are sedimentary. Occasionally, fossils are found in partly metamorphosed sedimentary rocks, but pressure and heat usually destroy fossils.

Fossils are formed in different ways. When some animals died, they were covered by sediments. The soft body parts decomposed, but teeth and skeletons remained, preserved by hardened layers of sediment. In other cases, even the skeletons disintegrated, but before they did, mineral-laden water infiltrated into the bones and replaced bone with minerals. This left a perfect cast replica of the skeleton in many cases. Some trees have left casts in a similar way. This is how specimens of the Petrified Forest in Arizona were formed. Additional fossils have been discovered frozen in ice, found in tar pits, and other places.

The so-called *fossil fuels*—coal, oil, and natural gas—were formed from the remains of plants and animals millions of years ago. Huge masses of organic matter in swampy forests were covered by mud, silt, and other sediments. Gradually, the sediments formed into stony layers. Pressure and heat from immense crustal movements caused physical and chemical changes in the buried organic matter. Some formed into seams of coal trapped between shale and slate. Some deposits changed into thick, black oil and natural gas, often trapped between layers of folded rock.

Rock Cycle

The same processes that formed rocks in the past continue today. Over many thousands of years, rocks change their forms. Even so, there is much evidence that the same mineral materials are

Table 17-1
Igneous, sedimentary, and metamorphic rocks

Igneous Rocks	Description	How Formed
Pumice	Grayish, fine pores, glassy, frothy, light, floats on water.	From rapid cooling of frothy, surface lava containing gases.
Volcanic Breccia	Consolidated fragments of volcanic ash, such as glass, pumice, quartz.	From being exploded high into the air from a volcano and settling.
Obsidian	Black, glassy, no crystals.	From very rapid surface cooling of lava.
Basalt	Dark, greenish-gray, very small crystals, may have some holes.	From rapid cooling of lava close to the surface. Escaping gases form holes.

Table 17-1
Igneous, sedimentary, and metsorphic rocks *(continued)*

Igneous Rocks	Description	How Formed
 Granite	Coarse crystals, white to gray, sometimes pinkish.	From slow, below-surface cooling of molten rock (magma), as when domes are formed.

Sedimentary Rocks	Description	How Formed
 Conglomerate	Rounded pebbles, stones, and sand cemented together.	From loose materials compacted by pressure of overlying sediments and bound by natural cement.
 Sandstone	Sand grains clearly visible, gray, yellow, red.	From sand compacted by pressure of sediment, bound by natural cement.

Table 17-1
Igneous, sedimentary, and metamorphic rocks *(continued)*

Sedimentary Rocks	Description	How Formed
Shale	Soft, smells like clay, fine particles, green, black, yellow, red, gray.	From compacted mud bound by natural cement.
Limestone	Fairly soft, white, gray, red, forms carbon dioxide gas bubbles when touched with acids.	From dead organisms that used calcium carbonate in sea water in making body parts; from evaporation of sea water containing calcium carbonate.

Metamorphic Rocks	Description	How Formed
Marble	Different, mixed colors, may have colored bands, medium to coarse crystals, fizzes if touched with acids.	Formed when pure limestone is subjected to intense heat and pressure.

Table 17-1

Igneous, sedimentary, and metamorphic rocks *(continued)*

Metamorphic Rocks	Description	How Formed
Slate	Greenish-gray, black, red, splits in thin layers, harder than shale.	Formed when shale is subjected to intense heat and pressure.
Quartzite	Very hard, white, gray, pink, indistinct grains, somewhat glassy.	Formed when sandstone is subjected to intense heat and pressure.

used over and over in a kind of rock cycle. Figure 17-7 shows what seems to happen.

All three kinds of rocks erode when exposed on the earth's surface. The resulting sediments, under pressure, form into rock cemented with water-borne chemicals. When these rocks undergo further pressure, torsion, and heat, they metamorphose. The metamorphic rocks turn into magma when heated further. When the magma cools and hardens, it becomes igneous rock. Some of it may metamorphose if folded or twisted or heated again. Some erodes. The cycle continues.

EARTH'S CHANGING SURFACE BENCHMARKS AND STANDARDS

Most children have explored with soil, rocks, and play sand or seen pictures or movies which include volcanoes and earthquakes. Activities in the elementary school should further refine these explorations and discover additional properties about the Earth. Sample Benchmarks and Standards include:

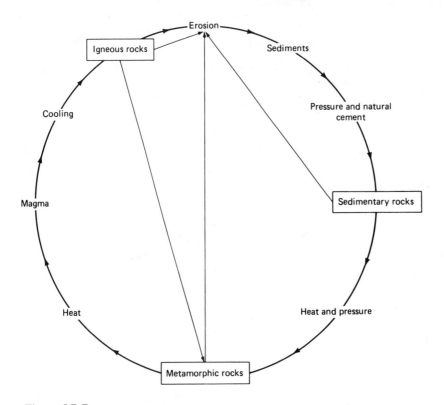

Figure 17-7
The rock cycle.

SAMPLE BENCHMARKS (AAAS, 1993).

■ Chunks of rocks come in many sizes and shapes, from boulders to grains of sand and even smaller (by Grades K–2, p. 72).

■ Waves, wind, water, and ice shape and reshape the Earth's land surface by eroding rock and soil in some areas and depositing them in other areas, sometimes in seasonal layers (by Grades 3–5, p. 72).

SAMPLE STANDARDS, (NRC, 1996).

■ Soils have properties of color and texture, capacity to retain water, and ability to support the growth of many kinds of plants, including those in our food supply (by Grades K–4, p. 134).

■ Some changes in the solid earth can be described as the "rock cycle." (by Grades 5–8, p. 160).

INVESTIGATIONS AND ACTIVITIES

WEATHERING AND EROSION EXPERIENCES
(Concepts p. 511)

ACTIVITY: *HOW CAN SEEDS BREAK UP ROCKS?*

NEEDED

two small topless milk or juice cartons
moist soil
plaster of paris
stick
bean seeds

TRY THIS

1. Soak some bean seeds in water overnight.

2. Plant them in a small carton half-filled with moist soil.

3. Mix some plaster of paris and water in a second carton. Make the mixture like a thick milk shake.

4. Pour the plaster mixture lightly over the soil. Make the cover about 0.5 centimeter (¼ inch) thick.

   a. Will the growing seeds be strong enough to break through the hard cover? If so, how long do you think it will take?

   b. If the seeds do break through, how thick a plaster cover will beans go through?

   c. What examples can you find of plants breaking up rocks and other hard materials? Look for plants growing in cracks in rocks, sidewalks, asphalt, and other paved surfaces.

INVESTIGATION: *HOW WEATHERING BREAKS DOWN MINERALS*

Over time, gases in the air can cause a chemical change in many different minerals in rocks. The process is called chemical *weathering*. A rock that is chemically weathered becomes loose and easily crumbled. Something like this happens when iron or steel breaks down as it rusts. You can learn more about chemical weathering by making things rust.

EXPLORATORY PROBLEM

How can you make an iron nail rust?

NEEDED

plain iron nails
container of dry soil
container of wet soil
steel wool

TRY THIS

1. Rub the nail with steel wool for a few seconds. This will take off any chemical that may have been put on to prevent rusting.

2. Get a container of wet soil. Bury the nail just under the surface. Dig up the nail each day to see if, or how much, it is rusting. Put the nail back in the same way each time. Keep the soil damp (Figure 17-8).

Figure 17-8

DISCOVERY PROBLEMS

observing   **A.** When does rust first appear? How quickly is the whole nail covered with rust?

hypothesizing   **B.** Will a nail rust more quickly on the wet soil's surface than below it? What do you think?

hypothesizing   **C.** What would happen if you put a nail in water?

hypothesizing   **D.** What would happen if you buried a nail in dry soil?

hypothesizing   **E.** Will a piece of steel wool rust faster than a nail?

experimenting   **F.** What are some other materials that might rust? In what other ways can you get them to rust? How can you prevent materials from rusting?

TEACHING COMMENT

PREPARATION AND BACKGROUND

Make sure that any steel wool used is the soapless variety. Plastic margarine or cottage cheese containers are handy to hold soil for this activity. Soil may be dried, if needed, by spreading it on a newspaper and exposing it to sunlight.

Oxygen chemically combines directly with many minerals, as in the rusting process. Carbon dioxide also produces chemical weathering, but indirectly. It dissolves in rainwater to form a weak acid called carbonic acid. This attacks limestone and cementing materials that hold minerals together in some rocks.

GENERALIZATION

Gases in the air may cause chemical weathering in rocks. Rust is an example of chemical weathering.

SAMPLE PERFORMANCE OBJECTIVES

Process: The child can experiment and determine which among several variables are likely to produce rust.

Knowledge: The child can identify several conditions that are likely to produce chemical weathering.

FOR YOUNGER CHILDREN

Younger children should be able to do Try This, Discovery Problem A, and the first question in Discovery Problem F.

ACTIVITY: *HOW DO MINERAL DEPOSITS FORM IN CAVES?*

NEEDED

Epsom salt
two small paper cups
thick, soft string
large paper cup
spoon
two small stones
thick wash cloth or piece of towel

TRY THIS

1. Fill a large paper cup three-fourths full with water. Dissolve as much Epsom salt in it as you can.

2. Pour the solution into the two small paper cups.

3. Tie a small stone to each string end to weigh them down. Put one string end into each small paper cup. Have the string sag between cups.

4. Place the cups on top of the wash cloth. Leave at least 4 centimeters (1½ inches) between the cloth and string. Allow a few days for mineral deposits to form on the string and cloth (Figure 17-9).

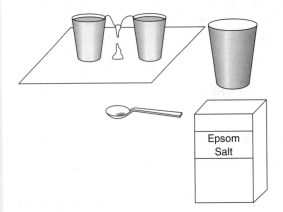

Figure 17-9

In a real cave, water with dissolved minerals in it drips from the cave ceiling to the floor. The water leaves minerals behind as it evaporates at both places. Little by little, the mineral deposits build up to look like "icicles" of stone. Those that hang down are called *stalactites.* Those that point up are *stalagmites.* (To remember them, think of *C* for ceiling and *G* for ground.)

a. In your model where is the stalactite? stalagmite?

b. How does your model work compared to the real thing?

ACTIVITY: *HOW DOES FREEZING WATER BREAK UP ROCKS?*

NEEDED

several porous or cracked rocks
freezer bag

TRY THIS

1. Leave some rocks in water for several hours. Use cracked rocks and those that soak up water. Sandstone and limestone are good to use.

2. Put the rocks in a bag. Place the bag in a freezer overnight. Examine the rocks the next day.

   a. What, if anything, happened to the rocks?

   b. How can you explain your results?

   c. If some rocks broke, maybe the cold alone did it. How can you experiment to be more sure that freezing water broke the rocks in this case?

TEACHING COMMENT

Porous rocks may be detected by placing some rocks in water and looking for those on which bubbles form. Students can be more sure that freezing water cracked their rocks by placing in the freezer another bag that contains similar, unsoaked rocks.

ACTIVITY: *HOW DOES WEATHERING CHANGE A ROCK?*

NEEDED

several different weathered rocks
thick paper bag
soft paper towel or facial tissue
hand lens
empty egg carton
hammer

TRY THIS

1. For safety, to break open a rock, put it into a thick paper bag. Hold the bag against a cement curb or sidewalk. Hit the rock a few times with a hammer through the bag.

2. Look at the weathered and fresh rock surfaces with a hand lens. How are they different? alike?

3. Make a weathered rock display. Take two of the larger pieces of the rock. Wrap one piece in tissue or a soft towel so only the weathered part shows. Wrap the other so only the fresh surface shows. Place them in opposite spaces in an egg carton. Do this with other broken rocks, also, until you fill the carton. What will happen if you shift the rocks around so the samples are not opposite one another? How many of the rocks will your friends be able to match? If someone shifts them for you, how many will *you* be able to match?

INVESTIGATION: *SOIL EROSION*

After a rain have you noticed how water has carried away, or *eroded*, soil? Splashing raindrops and running water are responsible for much soil erosion. But not all places with soil erode, and some places erode much more than others.

EXPLORATORY PROBLEM

How can you test to see what affects soil erosion?

NEEDED

two throw-away pie pans
soil
plastic sauce dishes (two matched)
juice cans (two small matched)
measuring cups
meter stick or yardstick
a small- and a medium-sized nail
hammer

TRY THIS

1. Punch 10 holes in the bottom of 1 juice can with a small nail. Use a medium-sized nail to punch 10 holes in the second can. Both cans should be open at the top.
2. Fill a sauce dish level and to the brim with soil. Put the dish into a pie pan to catch any spilled material.
3. Place a meter stick or yardstick upright behind the dish. Hold the small-hole can 60 centimeters (24 inches) above the dish.
4. Have someone pour a half-cup of water into the juice can. When the can stops "raining," observe the soil and pie pan (Figure 17-10).

DISCOVERY PROBLEMS

observing   **A.** What, if any, signs of erosion can you observe?

observing   **B.** How will a heavier "rain" affect erosion? Fill a second saucer with soil. Use the medium-hole can for rain. Compare the results with the first trial.

observing   **C.** How will loose soil erode compared to tightly packed soil? Prepare two saucers and find out. (Use only one can for the "rain" in Problems C through E.)

observing   **D.** How will tilted soil erode compared to level soil?

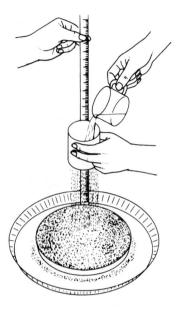

Figure 17-10

observing **E.** How will covered soil erode compared to bare soil? Cover the soil in one dish with several leaves.

inferring **F.** What are some conditions that seem to reduce soil erosion? That seem to increase soil erosion? What examples can you find outdoors that show some or all of these conditions?

TEACHING COMMENT

PREPARATION AND BACKGROUND

All of the preceding conditions are important in affecting soil erosion. But all are not easy to produce reliably with small-scale soil testing. Finding actual samples of erosion, as in Discovery Problem F, is important to achieving full understanding.

GENERALIZATION

Rainfall, soil cover, degree of incline, and compactness affect soil erosion.

SAMPLE PERFORMANCE OBJECTIVES

Process: The child can locate several outdoor examples of soil erosion and infer the conditions that influenced the examples.

Knowledge: The child can state several conditions that affect soil erosion.

INVESTIGATION: *WIND EROSION*

What happens to loose soil on a windy day? The moving of soil or rocks from one place to another is *erosion*. Soil erosion by wind is a big problem in some places.

EXPLORATORY PROBLEM

How can you find out about wind erosion around you?

NEEDED

two rulers
sticky tape
crayon
scissors
empty milk carton (small)
open, unpaved area outdoors
sand or soil
large sprinkling can
windy day

TRY THIS

1. Make a wind erosion recorder. Cut two narrow slots on top of a small milk carton. (See Figure 17-11.)
2. Stick two rulers through the slots.
3. Fill the carton with sand or soil to make it heavy.
4. Cut two 45-centimeter (18-inch) strips of sticky tape.
5. Put one strip evenly over the top of each ruler, *sticky side out*. Fasten the strip ends to each ruler with tape.
6. Draw an arrow on the carton top with crayon.
7. Place your recorder (Figure 17-11) where the wind is blowing loose soil. Point the arrow north. Leave the recorder for 30 minutes. Notice how bits of wind-blown soil collect on the sticky tape.

DISCOVERY PROBLEMS

observing and inferring   **A.** Examine the sticky tape on all four sides. Which side has the most soil? From which direction did the wind blow most?

hypothesizing   **B.** Where do you think there is the most wind erosion around the school? the least wind erosion? Make more recorders. Put one in each place and find out. What reasons can you give for what you find?

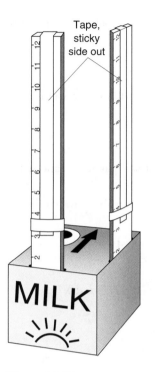

Tape, sticky side out

MILK

Figure 17-11

experimenting

C. What difference in wind erosion is there between grass-covered and bare soil? How can you find out?

experimenting

D. What difference in wind erosion is there between dry and damp soil? How can you find out?

classifying and inferring

E. Collect windblown soil bits each day for a week with your recorder. Change the sticky tape each day. Can you arrange the strips in order from most to fewest soil bits? On what day was there the most wind erosion? the least erosion? Can you tell from which main direction the wind blew each day?

hypothesizing

F. When during the day is there the most wind erosion where you live? How can you find out? What else can you discover with your recorder?

TEACHING COMMENT

PREPARATION AND BACKGROUND

Some children may not realize at first that some variables need to be controlled in this investigation. If two areas are to be tested, two identical recorders must be exposed to wind within equal areas at the same time. When possible, let students discover this for themselves.

GENERALIZATION

Soil erosion by wind depends on how hard the wind blows and how the soil is protected from the wind.

SAMPLE PERFORMANCE OBJECTIVES

Process: The child can place in order, from most to fewest soil particles, tape strips collected during a given time for one week.

Knowledge: The child can state several soil conditions that contribute to wind erosion.

ACTIVITY: *HOW DO GLACIERS CHANGE THE LAND?*

NEEDED

throw-away aluminum pie pan
freezer
stones and pebbles
place with bare soil

TRY THIS

1. Put some rocks and pebbles in a pie pan. Spread them about halfway around the pan's inside edge as shown in Figure 17-12.
2. Put some water into the pan, but let the tops of the rocks stick out of the water.
3. Leave the pan in a freezer overnight.
4. Remove your frozen glacier model from the pan. Turn it over so the rocks sticking out are underneath.

Figure 17-12

5. Place the model flat on some bare dirt. Push it so the stones are forward. Press down at the same time. Push it in a straight line for about 60 centimeters (2 feet).

6. Let your model stay and melt at the end of that distance. Come back to this place several hours later after it has melted. Observe carefully everything that has been left behind.

   a. How can you tell the direction in which the "glacier" moved?

   b. How can you tell how wide it was?

   c. How can you tell where the forward part of the glacier stopped and melted?

SOIL AND ITS MAKEUP EXPERIENCES
(Concepts p. 512)

INVESTIGATION: *THE MAKEUP OF SOILS*

What are some things you eat that grow in soil? How is soil important in your life? What do you think makes up soil?

EXPLORATORY PROBLEM

How can you find out what makes up soil?

NEEDED

fresh soils (two different types)
spoon
three glass jars with caps
newspaper
water
three sheets of white paper
magnifying glass
paper cup

TRY THIS

1. Spread newspaper on a table or desk. Put a sheet of white paper on top.

2. Pour some soil from one bag onto the white paper. What is the color of the soil? (See Figure 17-13.)

3. Spread out the soil with a spoon. Use a magnifier to see better. What animals or animal parts do you see? (Put live animals in a paper cup.) What plant or plant parts do you see? Animal and plant materials in soil are called humus.

4. Feel the soil between your fingers. Rough soil has more large-sized rock bits or particles than smooth soil. Use a magnifier. Can you find three sizes of rock particles? Which size makes up most rock particles in your sample?

Figure 17-13

5. Sort the different humus and rock materials into layers. Here is how. Fill a glass jar half full with the soil you are observing. Fill the rest of the jar with water. Shake the jar and then let it settle for an hour. Where does the humus settle? How much is there? In what order do the different-sized rock particles settle? How much is there of each size?

DISCOVERY PROBLEMS

observing and inferring   **A.** How good a soil detective are you? Can you tell which two soil samples are from the same place? Have a partner pour some soil into three white sheets. Two soil samples should come from one bag and one soil sample from the other bag. (Do not look while this is done.) Try to identify the two soil samples from the same bag. Observe color, humus, and rock particles. Do the shake test, also, if needed.

observing and inferring   **B.** What is the makeup of soil from different places? Get samples of different soils around school and home. How are the soil samples alike and different? How does deeper soil compare with surface soil from the same place? How many soil samples can you match as in Discovery Problem A?

TEACHING COMMENT

PREPARATION AND BACKGROUND

The two bags of soil in the first activity should come from two very different locations. Make sure the materials in each bag of soil are fairly evenly distributed. Otherwise, it will be hard to match soil samples that come from the same bag.

GENERALIZATION

Soil is made up of humus and rock particles; different soils may be identified by the kinds and amounts of these materials.

SAMPLE PERFORMANCE OBJECTIVES

Process: When shown three samples, two of which are the same, the child can observe similarities and differences and match the proper pair.

Knowledge: The child can describe the materials that make up soil and can explain that soils look different because these materials vary in kind and amount.

FOR YOUNGER CHILDREN

Primary students may be less systematic than older students in how they observe soil materials and may need more help in locating soil samples.

INVESTIGATION: *HOW WATER SINKS INTO DIFFERENT SOILS*

Some of the rain that falls on soil runs off it into streams. Some rain also soaks into the ground. This water can help crops grow. If water sinks deep below the surface, it may be pumped to the surface for many uses. How fast water soaks into soil depends on several conditions. You can find out some for yourself.

EXPLORATORY PROBLEM

What can you do to test how fast water sinks into soils?

NEEDED

two matched cans (one with both ends removed)
watch with second hand
water
different outdoor places with soil

TRY THIS

1. One can should be open at both ends. Scratch a mark sideways on the can's side 2.5 centimeters (1 inch) from one end.
2. Go to a place with soil outdoors. Use your foot to press the can into the soil up to the mark.
3. Have the second can filled with water. Pour the water into the first can without spilling any (Figure 17-14). With a watch, check how long it takes for all the water to sink in.

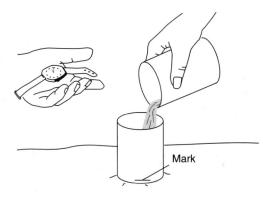

Mark

Figure 17-14

DISCOVERY PROBLEMS

measuring **A.** How much time is needed for the water to sink into the soil?

measuring **B.** Compare the sink times of different soils. How will soil with grass compare to the same kind of soil without grass?

measuring **C.** How will sandy soil compare with sticky soil?

measuring **D.** How will hard-packed soil compare with loose soil?

measuring **E.** How will soil that is usually in the sun compare with soil that is usually in the shade?

measuring **F.** How will soil on a hill compare with soil that is on a flat surface?

inferring **G.** What are some things about soil that seem to make water sink in quickly? slowly?

TEACHING COMMENT

PREPARATION AND BACKGROUND

A steel can is likely to hold up better than an aluminum can for this activity. Some hard soils may require an adult's weight to push the can down to the mark.

GENERALIZATION

Permeable soils tend to be loosely packed and composed of coarse mineral particles with little or no humus.

SAMPLE PERFORMANCE OBJECTIVES

Process: The child can measure and compare the permeability of several different kinds of soils.

Knowledge: The child can explain the conditions that are likely to be found in highly permeable soils.

FOR OLDER CHILDREN

To make this investigation into an experiment for older students, start with Discovery Problem G. Then, after discussing hypotheses, ask, "How can we find out?"

BUILDING UP OF THE LAND EXPERIENCES
(Concepts p. 514)

ACTIVITY: *FORCES ACTING ON THE EARTH'S CRUST*

NEEDED

box lid or tray
round balloon (large)
sand or dry soil
three chocolate sheet cakes (unfrosted)

INTRODUCTION

When rocks melt underground, they form a thick fiery-hot liquid called *magma*. Hot gases and steam, released when the rocks melt, mix with the magma and build up great pressure. This forces the magma to squeeze into cracks or weak places under the earth's crust. Magma may push up and bend rock layers above without coming to the surface. This can make a *dome mountain*. You can make a model of one.

Earthquakes may also change the Earth's surface. There are three types of earthquakes where the crust moves horizontally, diagonally, or vertically.

TRY THIS

1. Spread a thin layer of sand or soil in a box lid or tray.

2. Lay a balloon on the sand. Let its neck stick out over the lid's side.

3. Cover the balloon with about 5 centimeters (2 inches) of sand or soil. Make the "land" surface level.

4. Slowly blow air into the balloon so it is partly filled.

    a. What happens to the land surface?

    b. What in the model is like the magma?

    c. What is like the layers of rock above the magma?

5. Now, holding the first of the 3 cakes with one hand on each side, push the cake together until a "fault" develops in the cake. (This is a fault.)

6. Hold the second cake with both hands on its sides and gently pull the cake apart until a "fault" forms a trench.

7. The final cake is held as above but the left hand pulls toward the body and the right hand pulls away from the body, producing a strike slip fault.

a. Compare and contrast each of the three faults.

b. Look on a raised surface (relief) globe and compare the faults produced to areas of the Earth where similar faults may have occurred.

TEACHING COMMENT

A large, round balloon is recommended. Small balloons are hard to inflate, and the weight of the soil will make this even harder to do. A small plastic bag may also be easily inflated if its opening is tightly wrapped around the end of a drinking straw and fastened with sticky tape.

Thin layers of alternating chocolate and vanilla simulate rock layers when performing the earthquake activity.

HOW ROCKS ARE FORMED EXPERIENCES
(Concepts p. 517)

INVESTIGATION: THE PROPERTIES OF ROCKS

Have you ever heard the saying, "It's as hard as a rock"? Does this mean all rocks are equally hard? What do you think?

EXPLORATORY PROBLEM A

How can you find out the hardness of different rocks?

NEEDED

penny
six different rocks
large iron nail
partner
glass baby food jar
pencil and paper

TRY THIS

1. Study this hardness scale. It can help you to group your rocks.

HARDNESS SCALE	ROCK TEST
Very soft	Can be scratched with your fingernail
Soft	A new penny will scratch it. A fingernail will not.
Medium	A nail will scratch it. A penny will not.
Hard	It will scratch glass. A nail will not scratch it.

2. Test each rock according to this scale.

3. Keep a record of how hard each rock is. One way is to label each rock with a different letter. Write the letter on a slip of paper. Then put the rock on the slip (Figure 17-15). Record each rock's letter and hardness on a sheet of paper.

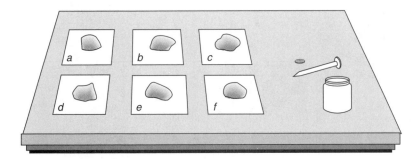

Figure 17-15

DISCOVERY PROBLEMS

observing and classifying **A.** Will someone else who tests your rock agree with you? Let your partner test your rocks. They should be on the lettered paper slips. Have her record each rock's letter and hardness. How much is this record like yours? Are there differences? Why?

classifying **B.** How can you put your six rocks in order from softest to hardest? (*Hint:* How can scratching one rock with another help?)

observing and classifying **C.** What other rocks can you test for hardness? How much will someone else agree with you if they test the same rocks?

EXPLORATORY PROBLEM B

What other properties of rocks can you observe and describe?

NEEDED

same materials as in Exploratory Problem A
vinegar
piece of white tile
new partner
paper cup

TRY THIS

1. *Color:* What is the color of the rock? Some rocks have several mixed colors. The best way to decide color is with a streak test. Rub the rock on the rough side of some tile. What color is the streak? (Figure 17-16.)

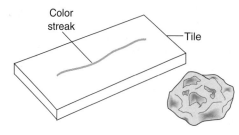

Figure 17-16

2. *Feel:* How does the rock feel to you? Is it rough? smooth? soapy? What else?

3. *Layers:* Does the rock seem to be made up of flat layers pressed together?

4. *Holes:* Does the rock have many small holes in it?

5. *Fizz:* If the rock is placed in a small cup of vinegar, do many tiny bubbles appear?

6. *Fossils:* Can you see tiny parts of sea shells or other such materials?

7. *Heaviness or Density:* How heavy does the rock seem for its size? light? medium? heavy?

8. *Other Properties:* What other properties of your rocks can you observe?

DISCOVERY PROBLEMS

classifying

A. Play a game with a partner. Sort some of your rocks into two groups according to one property (use color, or feel, etc.). Can a partner tell which property you used to sort them?

observing and communicating

B. Play the "I'm-Thinking-of-a-Rock" game with a partner. Place four or more rocks in a row. Think of just one rock and some of its properties. Can your partner find out what rock you have in mind? He must ask you only questions that can be answered by yes or no. Example: "Is it a rough rock?" (Yes.) "Does it have holes?" (No.)

communicating

C. How well can you describe your rocks? Can you make a chart that your partner can use to identify them? Make a chart of all properties you observe about your rocks. Label your rocks and try to remember which rock is which.

Rock	Hardness	Color	Feel	Layers	Holes
A	Medium	Gray	Smooth	No	Yes
B					
C					
D					

Give your completed chart and rocks to your partner. The rocks should be out of order, so he must study your chart to tell which rock is A, B, C, and so on.

inferring

D. Which chart descriptions were helpful? Which confused your partner? How could these be made clearer?

TEACHING COMMENT

PREPARATION AND BACKGROUND

Only about 30 minerals make up most common rocks. So you will observe some of the same minerals many times in different rocks.

GENERALIZATION

Rocks vary in hardness, color, texture, and other properties.

SAMPLE PERFORMANCE OBJECTIVES

Process: The child can classify rocks on the basis of hardness by using a simple hardness scale.

Knowledge: The child can state several properties by which rocks can be described.

FOR YOUNGER CHILDREN

Most younger students should be able to sort rocks by color and by either/or categories: smooth/rough, heavy/light, and holes/no holes.

INVESTIGATION: *CRYSTALS AND HOW THEY GROW*

It is interesting to see the crystals that make up some rocks. Most crystals are formed underground when melted minerals collect and grow in size as they cool. You can learn more about crystals and how they "grow" by making some yourself.

EXPLORATORY PROBLEM

How can you grow crystals?

NEEDED

glass or ceramic saucer
string
hand lens
hot water
table salt
cup
alum (potash)
spoon
borax

TRY THIS

1. Stir as much salt into a half-cup of hot water as will dissolve.

2. Pour the salt solution into a saucer. Put a small string in the solution. Leave part of it outside so you can pick up the string later (Figure 17-17). Put the saucer where it will not be disturbed.

3. Wait several days until most of the salt solution has evaporated. Carefully pour off what is left. Then give the crystals forming on the saucer bottom and string a day to dry.

4. Examine the dry crystals with a hand lens.

DISCOVERY PROBLEMS

observing   **A.** How do the salt crystals look? Study their shape, size, and how they stick together.

Figure 17-17

observing **B.** What do alum and borax crystals look like? Prepare crystals from these materials as you did from salt. Study the crystals carefully with a hand lens.

inferring **C.** Have someone place before you strings of crystals prepared from salt, alum, and borax. Can you tell which is which without being told?

observing **D.** How, if at all, does quickness of cooling affect crystal size? Prepare two solutions of alum in separate saucers. Put one in a refrigerator so it will cool fast. Put the other where it will cool slowly. Examine each solution the next day.

TEACHING COMMENT

PREPARATION AND BACKGROUND

Alum (potash) is sold in drugstores, rather than in grocery stores. Sugar is another substance from which a solution may be prepared for crystal growing. All solutions should be very heavy or saturated for good crystals to form.

A solution that cools quickly forms small crystals. This is like molten rock that cools relatively quickly at or near the earth's surface. A solution that cools more slowly has time to form larger, coarser crystals. This is like molten rock that cools slowly deep underground.

GENERALIZATION

Crystals may form from molten rock or may be grown from mineral solutions. The size of crystals depends on how fast the molten rock and solutions cool.

SAMPLE PERFORMANCE OBJECTIVES

Process: Through observing, the child can determine enough properties of three common minerals to identify them when they are unlabeled.

Knowledge: The child can explain that crystal size depends on the cooling rate of either molten rock or a mineral solution.

REFERENCES

American Association for the Advancement of Science. (1993). *Benchmarks for science literacy*. New York: Oxford University Press.

Hardy, G. R., & Tolman, M. N. (1991). Cakequake! An earthshaking experience. *Science and Children, 29*(1), 18–21.

National Research Council. (1996). *National science education standards*. Washington, DC: National Academy Press.

SELECTED TRADE BOOKS: THE EARTH'S CHANGING SURFACE
For Younger Children

Booth, E. (1985). *Under the ground*. Raintree.

Branley, F. M. (1991). *Earthquakes*. Crowell.

Butler, D. (1991). *First look under the ground*. Gareth Stevens.

Cole, J. (1988). *The magic schoolbus inside the earth*. Scholastic.

Harris, S. (1979). *Volcanoes.* Watts.

Ingoglia, G. (1991). *Look inside the earth.* Putnam.

Leutscher, A. (1983). *Earth.* Dial.

McNulty, F. (1979). *How to dig a hole to the other side of the world.* Harper.

Podendorf, I. (1982). *Rocks and minerals.* Children's Press.

Roberts, A. (1983). *Fossils.* Children's Press.

Schwartz, L. (1991). *My earth book.* Learning Works.

Sipier, P. (1986). *I can be a geologist.* Children's Press.

Williams, L. (1986). *The changing earth.* Wright Group.

Wyler, R. (1987). *Science fun with dirt and mud.* Messner.

For Older Children

Bramwell, M. (1987). *Planet earth.* Watts.

Challand, H. (1983). *Volcanoes.* Children's Press.

Fordor, R. V. (1978). *Earth in motion: The concept of plate tectonics.* Morrow.

Fordor, R. V. (1983). *Chiseling the earth: How erosion shapes the land.* Enslow.

Gallant, R. A. (1986). *Our restless earth.* Watts.

Lampton, C. (1991). *Earthquake.* Millbrook Press.

Lauber, P. (1991). *Volcanoes and earthquakes.* Scholastic.

Levine, S., & Grafton, A. (1992). *Projects for a healthy planet.* Wiley.

Lye, K. (1991). *The earth.* Millbrook Press.

Marcus, E. (1984). *All about mountains and volcanoes.* Troll Associates.

Nixon, H. H., & Nixon, J. L. (1980). *Glaciers: Nature's frozen rivers.* Dodd.

Rickard, G. (1991). *Geothermal energy.* Gareth Stevens.

Ruthland, J. (1987). *The violent earth.* Random House.

Rydell, W. (1984). *Discovering fossils.* Troll Associates.

Selden, P. (1982). *Face of the earth.* Children's Press.

Williamson, T. (1985). *Understanding the earth.* Silver Burdett.

Winner, P. (1986). *Earthquakes.* Silver Burdett.

Resource Books

Butzow, C. M., & Butzow, J. W. (1989). *Science through children's literature. An integrated approach* (volcano, rock, and soil topics, pp. 123–138). Teachers Ideas Press.

Butzow, C. M., & Butzow, J. W. (1994). *Intermediate science through children's literature: over land and sea* (geological topics, pp. 62–88). Teachers Ideas Press.

Fredericks, A. D., Meinbach, A. M., & Rothlein, L. (1993). *Thematic units: An integrated approach to teaching science and social studies* (the changing earth topics, pp. 202–209). HarperCollins.

Shaw, D. G., & Dybdahl, C. S. (1996). *Integrating science and language arts. A sourcebook for K–6 teachers* (rock cycle topic, pp. 78–82; rock topics, pp. 111–130). Allyn and Bacon.

WATER, AIR, AND WEATHER

Water, Air, and
Weather
Benchmarks and
Standards

WATER, AIR,
AND WEATHER

Winds

Air Pressure
and Cyclones

Weather

Humidity

Air
Temperature

Properties of
Water

Water
Conservation

Water

Water
Pollution

Acid Rain

Atmosphere

Composition
of Air

Air and Its
Properties

Air Pressure

Reality of Air

It's easy to take clean air and water for granted. And why not? For most of us, all we need do is breathe easily and turn on a faucet. But experiences of recent years with pollution and water shortages are making people lose their complacency.

In this chapter, we examine some properties of water and air, the importance of a clean supply of both, and some concepts basic to understanding weather, organized under three headings: water, air and its properties, and weather.

■

WATER CONCEPTS
(Experiences p. 562)

Our need for water commands our attention in both direct and indirect ways. Water is vital to life. You saw in another chapter how water transports chemicals to cells, removes waste materials, and performs other vital functions. Although humans may survive for weeks without food, water is needed within a few days. Bathing, cooking, and recreational activities also require water.

Agriculture consumes enormous volumes of water for irrigating plants in rain-poor regions. Industry, too, is a huge user of water. The manufacture of paper, steel, rubber, chemicals, and other products continually requires more water.

Even our future energy resources depend, in part, on having adequate water. For example, coal in the western United States would be most efficiently transported if crushed and sent through pipes after being mixed with water. The extraction of oil from shale rock also requires much water. But there is not enough water in the right places to meet all such needs.

Because water has so many uses, it is important to understand its properties. Let's look at some now.

Some Properties of Water

Water is an excellent solvent. In fact, more substances dissolve in water than in any other common liquid. Some other properties of water basic to our discussion are its molecular attraction, how it exerts pressure, and how it flows.

MOLECULES AND WATER.   You may recall from Chapter 9, "Heat Energy," that there is an attractive force between molecules called cohesion. In a solid, the spaces between molecules are relatively small. So a solid material sticks together, or coheres, well enough to maintain its own shape. Molecules of a liquid are farther apart. Their weaker cohesion causes them to slide about and assume the shape of a container. The cohesion of gas molecules is weaker still since these molecules are even farther apart.

Cohesion of water molecules is central to the process of evaporation. Heat energy must overcome water's cohesive force, as well as the force of air pressing down. If this could not happen, evaporation could not take place. The sun, of course, is the chief source of heat energy. When we spread out a water puddle to make it dry faster, the sun's energy overcomes the cohesive force of more water molecules at one time. So the rate of evaporation increases.

PRESSURE.   The weight of water gives it pressure. The deeper the water, the more pressure. This is one reason a dam is built with a thicker base than top. At any depth, the pressure is exerted in all directions and planes.

Pressure is also involved when something floats. For an object to float, opposing balanced forces work against each other. Gravity pulls down on the object, and the water pushes it up. The key to floating is the object's size relative to its weight. If it is light for its size, it has relatively high volume. That is, it presents a large surface area for the water to push against. This is why a ship made of steel floats. The water displaced by an object that is light for its size pushes up as forcefully as gravity pulls the object down.

An object floats higher in the ocean than in fresh water because ocean water has more minerals dissolved in it, especially salt. Therefore, a cup of ocean water weighs more than a cup of fresh water. Having more weight, it pushes back with greater force on any object that displaces it. This allows a ship to carry a heavier cargo in salt water than fresh water.

WATER FLOW. Gravity is the force that moves water in nature. Water cannot flow higher than its source unless some other force is more powerful. To store their water supply, some towns and small cities pump water into a large tank mounted on a tower. Water then flows by gravity through all pipes connected to the town tank. In some places, buildings are constructed that are taller than the tower. Pumps are installed in the buildings for water to reach the higher floors.

Clean, Adequate Water

Will there be enough water for enough people in enough places in the foreseeable future? A dependable answer to this question seems impossible now. But we can survey what it takes to get a clean and adequate supply of water, beginning with some sources of water.

SOURCES. A look at a globe tells us there is no shortage of water. About 71 percent of the earth's crust is covered with it. Most, though, is in the oceans and is too salty for either land plants or animals. So our immediate sources of fresh water are found elsewhere, in lakes, rivers, reservoirs, and beneath the land surface as groundwater.

Groundwater comes from rainwater that is absorbed into the soil and porous rock. It continues to sink until it reaches a layer of solid, nonporous rock. As more rainwater soaks into the ground, more of the below-surface section becomes saturated. The upper limit of the saturated section is called the *water table*. The table profile often corresponds roughly to that of the surface. When the surface dips below the water table, we see a lake or spring. Groundwater in a location does not always come from rainwater sinking from directly above. Groundwater may percolate through ground and porous rock diagonally or horizontally for some distance before it stops.

To construct a water well, a hole is drilled or dug to some depth below the water table. This helps to ensure a steady supply of water should the water table lower during dry spells.

Ocean water is the main source of evaporating water on earth. So the oceans are the basic source for fresh water. When salt water evaporates, the salt is left behind. Air currents carry the water vapor far inland. There it condenses and falls as rain, hail, or snow.

Over the long run, the water cycle gives what should be a steady supply of groundwater and other water. But several factors today make it hard to find usable fresh water in many places. Increased uses for water, as mentioned earlier, is one reason. Another is pollution.

POLLUTION. Many cities continue to dump partly treated or raw sewage into nearby rivers or lakes, from which drinking water is often drawn. As a result, purification of water is getting harder and more expensive. Factories, too, often discharge wastes into accessible waters. Another major source of pollution is agriculture. Chemical fertilizers and pesticides wash off the land into streams and bays.

An overload of fertilizers or sewage in a lake or other body of water causes an abnormally large population of algae to grow. The algae block sunlight from reaching aquatic plants under the water's surface; so the plants, as well as the animals that feed on them, die. Dead material piles up on the lake bottom. The overcrowded algae also die in time, and the decomposers take over. Eventually, the oxygen supply in the water is largely depleted and the decomposers die, too. They are replaced by bacteria that can live without oxygen. What was once a source of clean water and a complex community of living things is a silted, near-dead, putrescent swamp. A reversal can occur through natural changes of the land surface and a gradual succession of ever-higher forms of life, but this may take centuries or longer.

In recent years, much publicity has been given to a particularly ominous threat to the nation's water supply, hazardous waste dumps. At such sites, poisonous chemicals may leak from storage containers and percolate down through the ground, contaminating groundwater, nearby streams, and lakes. Drinking or swimming in the water, and eating fish whose organs have accumulated the poisons, have been linked to severe health problems, including brain damage, cancer, and birth defects in children.

ACID RAIN. Many waste products are discharged into the air as well as on the ground and into bodies of water. These, also, may end up polluting our water and other natural resources. The burning of fossil fuels in factories, power plants, and automobiles releases sulfur and nitrogen oxides into the atmosphere. When water vapor is present, these gases are converted into sulfuric acid and nitric acid. The rain that falls from a polluted region can be as acidic as vinegar.

Acid rain, including acid sleet, hail, and snow, is contaminating water supplies, killing trees and fish stocks, and corroding water systems. Its effects are easily noticeable where there are large concentrations of coal-burning power plants, heavy industry, and automobiles. But even more damage may result far beyond these places. Winds aloft, especially the prevailing westerlies in our country, sweep the pollutants into large, distant regions. The northeastern United States and adjacent Canadian area have been most affected.

Some progress has been made in reducing the pollutants through the use of chemical filters in industry and pollution control devices for automobile exhaust systems. But large-scale improvements in industrial pollution bear a daunting price tag. Especially nettlesome is the answer to the question: Who pays? When suspected sources of pollution are hundreds of miles away, and thousands of jobs or millions of utility bills are affected, an acceptable answer becomes highly complicated.

CONSERVATION. It seems inevitable that people will need to change certain water-use habits. Many habits were fostered when regional populations were small, pollution was less severe, water uses were fewer, and resources were more abundant. Conservation, or wise use, of water resources is becoming more common because more persons now are aware of the consequences if it is not practiced.

Stricter laws to protect water supplies are continually enacted. More attention is being given to the recycling of industrial wastes and the safe storage of long-lasting, harmful chemicals. Bare slopes are being planted to protect watersheds. Fertilizers and pesticides are being used under more controlled conditions in agriculture. People are learning to use less water in more situations without wasting it. An important by-product of water conservation is energy conservation. A significant amount of the nation's energy is used in pumping water and heating it.

FUTURE WATER SUPPLY. It's possible that even increased conservation measures will fail to meet future needs for water. Where will more usable water come from? Just as some scientists are looking for ways to directly tap the sun's energy, others are investigating methods for directly converting ocean water to fresh water.

One way to remove salt from ocean water is to distill it. The water is heated, changed to a vapor, and condensed, much like in the water cycle. Another method freezes ocean water. The ice that forms at the surface is mostly fresh water. It is removed and melted. There are many other methods now being used and explored. At present, all are too expensive for widespread use. If more economical means can be found, the direct conversion of ocean water to fresh water could bring major changes in many dry regions of the world and in the world's food supply.

AIR AND ITS PROPERTIES CONCEPTS
(Experiences p. 571)

Air has many of the properties of water and may contain much water in gaseous form. However, air also has some unique properties. To better understand some of its specific features, let's first take an overall look at where our immediate air supply comes from: the atmosphere.

The Atmosphere

Space exploration has made us more aware of how dependent we are on our atmospheric environment. Without an air supply, humans cannot survive for more than minutes. Although we may travel in comfort thousands of kilometers across the earth's surface, an ascent of only 5 kilometers into the sky may require special oxygen apparatus.

How far out does the atmosphere extend? No one knows exactly, but meteorologists have identified four roughly separable layers of differing properties: the troposphere, stratosphere, ionosphere, and exosphere (Figure 18-1).

TROPOSPHERE. The troposphere extends to a height ranging from 8 kilometers (5 miles) at

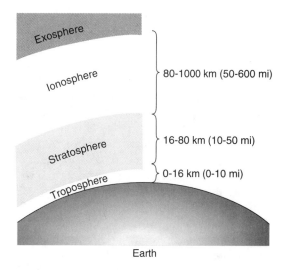

Figure 18-1
The atmosphere has several layers.

the poles to about 16 kilometers (10 miles) at the equator. This is the region where practically all weather conditions take place.

Why the difference in altitudes? Tropospheric air is coldest at the poles and so weighs more per unit than warmer, equatorial air. Also, the earth spins on its axis. The fastest speed of rotation, about 1,600 kilometers (1,000 miles) per hour, is at the equator. This offsets the earth's gravitational pull to some extent. The speed of rotation decreases as distance to the poles decreases, just as a person who runs on an inside track can slowly jog along, while someone on an outside track must run swiftly just to keep abreast. As the rotational speed slows, gravity has an increasing effect. In the troposphere, stable air temperature steadily decreases with altitude.

STRATOSPHERE. Just above the troposphere is the stratosphere, which reaches to about 80 kilometers (50 miles). This is the layer airlines use on some routes for long-range cruising. The cold, thin air is remarkably smooth and clear because vertical movements of warmed air and atmospheric dust particles are largely confined to the layer below. Air travelers may note some pale clouds of ice crystals above cruising altitude, but these are infrequent.

Between the lower reaches of the stratosphere and the troposphere are found winds that vary greatly in force and direction. Most interesting are the *jet streams,* rivers of high-velocity air several kilometers high and more than 150 kilometers wide. They range to thousands of kilometers in length and tend to flow from west to east. A pilot may increase the speed of a plane several hundred kilometers per hour by locating and staying within a jet stream.

In the stratosphere, at an altitude of 16 to 48 kilometers (10 to 30 miles), is a layer of *ozone* that absorbs much of the sun's harmful ultraviolet radiation. The layer is largely composed of molecules that have three atoms of oxygen, rather than the usual two. Certain chemicals released into the atmosphere, called *chlorofluorocarbons* (CFCs), collect unevenly in the ozone layer and destroy the ozone molecules. This greatly reduces the layer's capacity to block ultraviolet rays and so more get through to the earth's surface at various places.

Excess radiation increases the risk of skin cancer, eye damage, and immune system impairment. It can also reduce crop yields and disrupt ocean food chains. International agreements in force require the phasing out of CFCs, widely used in refrigerants, air conditioners, industrial cleaning solvents, and manufacture of some plastics. They are being replaced by less harmful but more expensive chemicals.

IONOSPHERE. Beyond a height of about 80 kilometers (50 miles), the stratosphere gradually blends into the ionosphere. In this region are ions, or electrically charged particles formed when air molecules are hit by high-energy solar and cosmic rays. These harmful rays are largely absorbed at and below this level. Auroras are sometimes visible. Meteors burn to ashes from friction as they strike scattered air molecules.

The ionosphere is an invaluable aid to radio communication on earth. The earth's surface is curved, but radio waves travel in straight lines. One way of overcoming this problem has been to transmit radio waves to the ionosphere, where they are reflected downward to other points on earth. Since solar "storms" frequently disturb the ionosphere and disrupt communication, this has not proved to be a completely satisfactory solution. Radio and television signals reflected from communications satellites are helping to solve this problem.

EXOSPHERE. The exosphere begins at about 1,000 kilometers (600 miles) and extends to an undetermined distance. A few air molecules have been detected beyond where the ionosphere adjoins the exosphere and it is probable that others are scattered thousands of kilometers beyond. For practical purposes, this region may be considered the beginning of interplanetary space.

Although scientists estimate the entire weight of our atmosphere at an enormous 4.5 quadrillion metric tons, more than half of all air molecules are concentrated below a height of 5.6 kilometers (3.5 miles). The combination of this enormous pressure and the unimaginably small size of air molecules results in the presence of air in practically everything on or near the earth's surface. Air is found in most soils, water, and even in some rocks. Consider now more effects of this pressure.

Air Pressure

Because the average weight of air is about 1 kilogram per square centimeter, or 14.7 pounds per square inch, at sea level, there are tons of air pressing against the human body. Why, then, are we not crushed? There are two basic reasons. Like water, air at a given level presses with equal force in all directions. Because there is a counteractive force for every force, the pressure is neutralized. Counteractive pressure also takes place in our bodies. Air molecules are so tiny that they dissolve in the blood stream, besides occupying space in our lungs and other body cavities.

Unlike free air, the air in our bodies lags somewhat in building up or reducing counteractive back pressure as atmospheric pressure changes. Have you noticed your ears "pop" while rising quickly in an elevator of a tall building? This happens because air pressure in the inner ear tends to remain the same while the outside air pressure decreases with increased altitude. The result is an uncomfortable outward pushing sensation behind the eardrums. A slow elevator gives more opportunity for inner ear pressure to be adjusted through the Eustachian tube, which connects the inner ear to the nasal passages and mouth.

A similar but much more dangerous situation is faced by deep-sea divers. As they descend into the water, air is pumped under increasing pressure into the diving helmet and suit to counteract increasing water pressure. After working for 20 to 30 minutes, the diver's circulatory system contains an abnormal amount of air. If the diver ascends rapidly to the surface, a region of much lower air pressure, air in the blood may expand and form bubbles. This causes a very painful and possibly fatal condition known as "the bends."

The lag in adjusting to outside atmospheric pressure may also be why some persons complain of aches and pains just before rainy weather. Outside air pressure usually lessens before a storm. If the body's blood pressure remains the same, the blood will now press outward a little more forcibly than usual against body joints and tissues. It is possible that the slight extra pressure may cause discomfort.

Makeup of Air

There are so many references to the earth's "ocean of air" that it is easy for us to get the impression that pure air is a uniform compound, such as pure water. Actually, the air we breathe is a mixture of several separate and distinct gases, of which the three most important to survival are oxygen, nitrogen, and carbon dioxide.

Oxygen makes up about 21 percent of the air, and nitrogen 78 percent. Oxygen is essential to us because it combines readily with sugars in our body cells and releases heat energy. Oxygen is also essential to burning.

Nitrogen is essential to survival because it is necessary for plant growth. It also dilutes the oxygen we breathe. Continual breathing of pure oxygen speeds up metabolic processes to the point where the body cannot get rid of waste products fast enough to survive. The small amount of carbon dioxide in the air, about $3/100$ of 1 percent, is needed for photosynthesis in green plants. Besides these gases, there is less than 1 percent of such gases as argon, krypton, helium, neon, radon, and xenon. All these atmospheric gases are remarkably well mixed by winds up to a height of 8 to 10 kilometers, or 5 to 6 miles.

But this is not all we breathe. As hay-fever sufferers know, there are other substances mixed in the air. Besides the troublesome pollens, there are dust, smoke, salt particles, water vapor, chemicals, spores, bacteria, and viruses.

The Reality of Air

Because pure air has no taste, color, or odor, its study for children, especially primary level students, has an elusive quality not present in many other areas. So it is usually good to begin with activities that bring out the tangibility of air.

Like other material objects such as automobiles, houses, books, and people, air is a real thing. Children can feel it and see it move things in the form of wind. A blown-up balloon or a soap bubble shows that air takes up space. A slowly falling parachute demonstrates that air resists motion. A can that is crushed when some inside air is removed shows that air has weight.

Sipping liquid through a straw shows this, too. Since many children are confused about how a straw works, consider it for a moment.

When we sip some air out of a straw, the air pressure in the straw is reduced. Since the atmosphere now has more relative pressure, it presses down on the liquid's surface and pushes it up inside the straw's space once occupied by the air.

If you are skeptical, try the following experiments. Place two straws in your mouth, but leave one *outside* the pop bottle or glass. You will find it is now practically impossible to drink the liquid. Why? Air traveling inward through the outside straw restores the pressure in your mouth and drinking straw to normal. For the second experiment, fill a flask with water and seal it tightly with a one-hole stopper containing a glass tube. No matter how hard you sip, no water goes up the tube. There is no air pressing down on the water. With a *two*-hole stopper, though, normal drinking is possible. Air pressure is exerted through the second hole.

As with drinking straws, the events we associate with "suction" are really due to removing or reducing air pressure from one part of a device. Air pressure on all other parts then pushes and performs the work. In vacuum cleaners, for example, the motor whirls a reversed fan that reduces air pressure at the cleaning nozzle. The surrounding air then *pushes* dirt particles into the nozzle. A "suction" cup works in a similar way. By pressing down on the pliable rubber cup, most of the air inside is forced out. Air from all other sides pushes against the cup's exterior and holds it fast to whatever surface it has been pressed.

WEATHER CONCEPTS
(Experiences p. 584)

Weather is the condition of the lower atmosphere at a given time and place. If you have been rained on while expecting a sunny afternoon, you know how quickly it can change. Weather changes happen because changes in temperature, moisture, pressure, and other variables alter the way air "behaves." We'll examine some of these variables next, one at a time.

Causes of Winds

At early morning off an African coast, hundreds of fishing boats point out to sea as a fresh land breeze fills their colorful lateen sails. The boats return in the afternoon with sails taut from a sea breeze blowing in the opposite direction. You have probably experienced a similar shift of winds at the seashore or by a large lake. How does this happen? (See Figure 18-2.)

TEMPERATURE DIFFERENCES. You may recall from the heat energy chapter that warmed air expands and is pushed up by denser, colder air that rushes in and replaces it. Winds are caused by the unequal heating and cooling of the earth's surface. During the day, solar radiation is absorbed by the sea and land. The land heats up much faster. One reason is that sunlight penetrates only a short distance below the land's surface, but penetrates more deeply into water. Another reason is the higher heat capacity of water.

After a short period of sunlight, air immediately above the earth is heated by the ground and begins expanding. Cooler, heavier air from the sea rushes in and pushes the lighter air upward. The reverse occurs at night and until the following morning. During this period, the land cools quickly and stays cool, while the sea remains relatively warmer. As air warmed by contact with the water expands, it is pushed upward by cooler air rushing in from the cooler land.

These air movements are not confined to land and sea settings. The same basic air movements take place between any surfaces that have a temperature difference. As temperature differ-

Day   Night

Figure 18-2
Winds are caused by unequal heating and cooling of the earth's surface.

ences increase, the resulting wind force increases. This is one reason why a large fire is so destructive. It creates a powerful, localized wind that fans and spreads the flames.

PREVAILING WINDS. The world's prevailing winds are caused by the same unequal heating of the earth's surface on a grand scale. But the earth's rotation adds a factor. If the earth did not rotate, heavy, cold air at the poles would simply flow due south and north, and push up warmed, expanding equatorial air. The rotation (named the *Coriolis effect*) results in a wind deflection to the *right* in the northern hemisphere. A deflection to the *left* occurs in the southern hemisphere.

You can see why this happens with a globe and some chalk. Rotate the globe from west to east. While it is moving, draw a line from the North Pole due south toward the equator. Note that the line curves to the right. Draw a line from the South Pole and the curve is reversed. (We will return to the Coriolis effect in a later section.)

WINDS ALOFT. Detailed understanding of wind patterns requires much more background than can be given here. For example, we have briefly discussed jet streams. There are, however, other winds aloft. It is possible for an airplane pilot to meet a wind blowing from one direction at one altitude and another blowing from another direction higher up. You will not want to explore this subject in detail at the elementary level. Still, it will be worthwhile to help students learn that wind direction aloft may differ from surface wind direction.

To calculate winds aloft, meteorologists use measuring instruments to observe small, helium-filled balloons as they rise to various altitudes. A cruder method is to observe cloud movements with a *nephoscope,* a circular mirror marked with the points of a compass. Properly aligned, this instrument can show children the direction of cloud movement as the cloud reflection moves across the mirror.

Air Temperature

In parts of Southern California and Mexico, it is sometimes possible in winter to observe snowy mountain peaks while lying on a warm, sunny beach. Children are curious about conditions like this ("Aren't the mountain peaks closer to the sun?"). Most adults know that air is colder at higher altitudes. But why?

TEMPERATURE AND ALTITUDE. One reason air is colder at higher altitudes is the varying distance of air molecules from the earth's surface. Air molecules closest to the earth are warmed more easily by conduction and heat waves radiated from the earth's surface than those farther away.

Second, as we get closer to sea level, more and more molecules are piled up. This increased weight compresses the air. With reduced space for movement, there is more energy exchange among molecules as they collide. So the heat energy in the denser molecule "population" is concentrated into a relatively low, dense layer.

There is also a third reason. As warmed air is pushed up, it expands and cools as it meets lower air pressure with the increased altitude. Whatever heat energy is contained in the original air parcel is dissipated throughout an ever-larger volume.

The combined effect of these causes makes pushed-up air cool about 2°C for each 300 meters, or 3.5°F for each 1,000 feet. As pushed-down air is compressed, the opposite happens.

TEMPERATURE AND POLLUTION. As you saw, the atmosphere is a gigantic greenhouse that slows the loss of heat received from solar radiation. Fortunately, the earth loses and gains about the same amount of heat each day. A narrow temperature range enables life to continue. Since the Industrial Revolution, though, conditions have been developing that may upset this delicate balance.

Most scientists think the lower atmosphere is gradually becoming slightly warmer through increased carbon dioxide from the burning of fuels such as coal and oil. As light waves from the sun warm the earth's surface, heat waves going from the surface into the atmosphere are partly blocked by carbon dioxide. Some of the heat energy cannot escape into space. This causes the atmosphere to lose slightly less heat than it gains from solar radiation. Recent data seem to support a global warming trend.

Yet a few scientists say it is also possible that the trend may be reversing. To them, the data suggest that the earth's atmosphere is cooling very gradually. In recent years, there has been a large increase in air pollution throughout the world. The greater number of suspended pollutants in the air may be causing more and more sunlight to be reflected away from the earth *before* it reaches the earth's surface. If true, this could overcome the effect of the increased carbon dioxide.

Although not everyone agrees about what is happening to the air temperature, a definite trend in either direction could bring trouble. An average increase of a few degrees could turn huge, fertile land areas into semi-deserts, and an average temperature drop of 4° to 5°C could launch another ice age.

Evaporation and Humidity

Many students understand in a limited way the concepts of evaporation and humidity, but may not understand how the two are related. This section can help deal with these concepts.

EVAPORATION. In an earlier chapter, you saw that heat and atmospheric pressure affect an evaporating liquid. Increased heat energy increases the speed of molecules. Additional speed enables molecules to overcome the cohesive forces of nearby molecules, and greater numbers leave the liquid's surface than before. Any decrease of atmospheric pressure also affects evaporation because it tends to "take the lid off." The counterforce of air molecules pressing down on the surface of an evaporating liquid becomes weaker, and more evaporation takes place. This is a reason mountain climbers must be so careful with dehydration.

It is easy to see why increasing a liquid's surface area increases the rate of evaporation. There is greater exposure to the air above and a higher probability of more molecules escaping. This is why you have to add water more often to a rectangular aquarium than to a fish bowl of equal volume.

The wind, too, speeds up evaporation. When air just above the surface of an evaporating fluid becomes quickly saturated, the wind blows it away and replaces it with drier air.

HUMIDITY. Another factor influencing evaporation is *humidity* which is the amount of moisture already present in the air. On humid days, we feel sticky and uncomfortable because our perspiration evaporates very slowly. We may turn on an electric fan to feel more comfortable. Moving air from a fan cools us because it speeds up evaporation of perspiration from the skin.

Without an evaporating liquid, *a fan has no cooling effect at all.* You can see this by putting a thermometer in front of a whirling electric fan. There is no difference in the before and after readings. But dampen some cotton and stick it to the thermometer bulb. The rapidly evaporating water will now cause a noticeable drop in temperature.

The moisture content of air changes considerably from time to time. The capacity of air to hold moisture depends on its temperature, so warm air holds more moisture than cooler air. The percentage of moisture in air at a certain temperature, compared to all it could hold at that temperature, is called its *relative humidity.* During a period of low relative humidity, our skin moisture evaporates more quickly than it can be effectively replaced. This results in dry, chapped skin.

One reason we have more colds in winter may be directly related to the relative humidity of air in our homes. The cool air of winter holds comparatively little moisture. As it is warmed by heaters, it expands and becomes even drier. Unless the home heating system is equipped to give additional moisture, the air becomes increasingly dry. The protective mucous film that coats the delicate nasal membrane evaporates, and we become more open to infections.

Relative humidity is often measured with a wet-and-dry bulb thermometer apparatus called a *hygrometer.* Two identical thermometers are placed next to each other. The bulb of one instrument is enclosed in a wet cotton wick that is immersed in water. The wet-bulb thermometer is fanned rapidly until its reading steadies at some lower point. As water evaporates from the wick, it is continually replaced by water traveling upward through the wick by capillary action. Any difference in thermometer readings is translated into the percentage of relative humidity by consulting a reference table.

Condensation

DEW. Many mornings we see dew drops glistening on lawns, parked automobiles, spider webs, and other surfaces. When the ground cools during the night, its temperature may fall below that of the surrounding air. As the surrounding air loses some heat energy, its molecules slow down. Water vapor molecules in the air slow enough to be attracted to, and condense on, a cool nearby surface. The same thing happens when water droplets form on a cold pop bottle or cold water pipe.

Remember, relative humidity varies with air temperature. Any parcel of air containing some water vapor becomes saturated if cooled enough. The loss of heat energy slows down molecular speed and reduces the range of molecular movement. The attractions of water molecules for one another now draw them together into visible drops.

DEW POINT. The temperature at which condensation takes place is called the *dew point.* In very humid air, as in a steamy shower room, water vapor condenses on walls and mirrors although they may be only several degrees cooler than the air. Comparatively dry desert air may have to be cooled much more before reaching its dew point.

FOG. We may see fog when the surface temperature is low enough to cool air that is a short distance above the ground to its dew point. In this case, water vapor condenses on tiny specks of airborne dust and remains suspended.

Sometimes fog results from the unequal cooling of land and water. Such fog is common over a lake in summer. Cool air from the land flows over warm, moist air just above the lake. As the warmer air cools to its dew point, condensation occurs and we see fog. Fog can be considered a low cloud.

CLOUDS AND CLOUD TYPES. Clouds at higher altitudes are formed in several ways, but all involve a parcel of air that is cooled to its saturation, or dew, point. In one method, wind may blow moist air up a mountain slope. As the air rises, it expands because of decreasing air pressure, cools, and condenses on airborne dust particles. If the dew point is below freezing, tiny ice crystals may form.

Sometimes air is pushed aloft when two huge air masses merge. The cooler, heavier air mass will push under the warmer, lighter mass. Again, expansion, cooling, and condensation take place.

A third method of cloud formation happens when heat from the ground develops convection currents. The affected air near the ground is heated and is pushed up by heavier, cooler surrounding air. The rising air finally cools and its moisture condenses.

When enough moisture is present, the tiny, constantly moving droplets within a cloud collide from time to time and form larger drops. These may fall as rain. In freezing temperatures, ice crystals collect and fall as snow.

Knowing the air temperature and its dew point can enable you or upper-grade students to roughly calculate cloud heights. Here is how it is done. Suppose the outdoor air temperature is now 88°F. Stir a thermometer around in a metal can of ice water. At the exact instant water droplets occur on the can, read the temperature of the immersed thermometer. This is the dew point. Say it reads 74°F, which makes a difference of 14°F between the two figures. Rising air cools at about 3.5°F for each 1,000 feet of altitude. Dividing 14 by 3.5 gives a quotient of 4. Multiply this figure by 1,000. The bases of nearby clouds should be about 4,000 feet above you. (With metric measures, use 2°C for 3.5°F and 300 meters for 1,000 feet.)

Although experts have invented more than 200 cloud classifications, young children can be taught to recognize three basic cloud forms. *Cirrus* clouds are high, wispy formations of ice crystals. *Cumulus* clouds are white, fluffy, and usually associated with clear visibility and fair weather. *Stratus* clouds are lower, darker formations that appear as a dense layer. These clouds may blanket the entire sky and precipitate rain within a short time. (See Figure 18-3.)

WATER CYCLE. You can see that condensation is the opposite of evaporation. Together, they form the water cycle. Powered by the sun, an immense but finite volume of water over the earth constantly evaporates, condenses, and falls without apparent end.

Air Masses and Cyclones

At one time, it was thought that air pressure over any one point was always the same. We now know otherwise. Huge masses of air are continually on the move over the earth, bringing changes in pressure and weather.

AIR MASSES. An air mass is a huge volume of air that picks up distinctive temperature and humidity conditions from the surface underneath. These conditions are fairly uniform throughout the mass, which may cover thousands of square kilometers or miles.

An ocean air mass is typically moist. Air over land is drier. Air near the polar regions is cold, while that near the equator is warm. So four different kinds of air masses are possible: cold

Figure 18-3
Three basic cloud forms: *(a)* cirrus, *(b)* cumulus, *(c)* stratus.

and dry, cold and moist, warm and dry, and warm and moist. Figure 18-4 shows the origins of four kinds of air masses that often move into the continental United States.

Cold air is heavier than warm air. Dry air is heavier than moist air. Just as water flows from a high point to a lower one, air flows from a region of relatively high pressure to one of lower pressure. But because of the earth's rotation, the flow is not in a straight line.

CYCLONES AND ANTICYCLONES. The Coriolis effect causes air masses and the general circulation of air to move in gigantic spirals called *cyclones* and *anticyclones*. (Cyclones should not be confused with tornadoes, which are small, violent, twisting air currents that come from a mixture of super-heated and cold air.) A cyclone is a larger area of relative lower pressure with the point of lowest pressure in the center; it is also called a *low*. An *anticyclone* is a large area of relatively high pressure with the highest pressure in the center; it is also called a high.

Figure 18-4
Four common air masses.

In the northern hemisphere, air movements spiral counterclockwise toward the center of a low. In a high, they spiral clockwise away from the center of highest pressure. These movements are reversed in the southern hemisphere. Highs and lows may move hundreds of kilometers a day. A typical pattern of movement in the United States is from west to east.

Lows often bring bad weather. This is because cold or dry heavier air moves in and pushes up warm or moist lighter air. The moisture condenses when the air rises to its dew-point altitude and falls as rain or snow.

Highs usually bring more pleasant weather. As cool or dry heavier air spirals downward from the center of a high, it warms about 2°C (3.5°F) for each 300 meters (1,000 feet) loss of altitude. As it warms, the mass of air is able to hold more and more moisture without it condensing. The result is usually clear, sunny weather.

Figure 18-5
Aneroid barometer.

Measuring Pressure

Highs and lows are detected by noting changes in cloud, temperature, and wind patterns. However, the most important changes observed are those in air pressure. An instrument used for measuring air pressure is the *barometer*. There are two kinds.

In a *mercurial* barometer, a glass tube about 90 centimeters (36 inches) long and closed at one end is filled with mercury and inverted into a dish of mercury. While some of the liquid runs out, a column of about 76 centimeters (30 inches) remains. This tells the force of air pressing on the liquid's surface. As air pressure increases, the column rises higher into the vacuum above. The reverse takes place with reduced pressure.

Since mercurial barometers are easily broken and cumbersome, most weather observers use the *aneroid* barometer (Figure 18-5). This consists of a thin, flexible, metal box from which air has been largely removed. As air pressure presses on it with varying degrees of force, the

box moves in and out accordingly. A cleverly linked leverage system transfers these movements to a movable needle on a dial.

Because air pressure also changes with altitude, aneroid barometers are used in many airplanes to indicate altitude. This is done by merely changing the dial to read in a unit of height rather than one of pressure. Such a barometer is called an altimeter.

■

WATER, AIR, AND WEATHER BENCHMARKS AND STANDARDS

Weather, water, and air are popular topics in the elementary grades. Students frequently complete daily weather logs and journal descriptions of the changing weather patterns, often including pictures of what they see. Representative Benchmarks and Standards related to water, air, and weather include:

SAMPLE BENCHMARKS (AAAS, 1993).

■ Water left in an open container disappears, but water in a closed container does not disappear (by Grades K–2, p. 67).

■ Some events in nature have a repeating pattern. The weather changes day to day, but things such as temperature and rain (or snow) tend to be high, low, or medium in the same months every year (by Grades K–2, p. 67).

SAMPLE STANDARDS (NRC, 1996).

■ Weather changes from day to day and over the seasons. Weather can be described in measurable quantities such as temperature, wind direction and speed, and precipitation (by Grades K–4, p. 134).

■ The atmosphere is a mixture of nitrogen, oxygen, and trace gasses that include water vapor (by Grades 5–8, p. 160).

INVESTIGATIONS AND ACTIVITIES

WATER EXPERIENCES
(Concepts p. 548)

INVESTIGATION: *HOW WATER AND OTHER LIQUIDS STICK TOGETHER*

Suppose you fill a glass with water to the very top. What do you think will happen if you add more water?

EXPLORATORY PROBLEM

How high can you fill a container of water before it spills?

NEEDED

three small plastic vials
spoon
two matched medicine droppers
newspaper
water
liquid soap or detergent
paper clips
rubbing alcohol
paper cup
meter stick or yardstick

TRY THIS

1. Fill a small container to the top with water.
2. Gently drop paper clips into the container one at a time. (See Figure 18-6.)
3. Watch how the water "heaps" higher in the container. Count the number of clips it takes for the water to spill. Make a record.

DISCOVERY PROBLEMS

observing   **A.** How high can you heap other liquids? Try soapy water and alcohol. How do these liquids compare with water? Put the three containers side by side and see. How many paper clips does it take for soapy water and alcohol to spill?

observing   **B.** How large are the drops of different liquids? Take up water in one medicine dropper and alcohol in another. Hold up the droppers

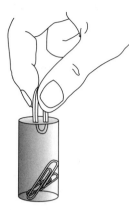

Figure 18-6

side by side. Slowly squeeze each bulb until a drop forms at each open end. How do the drop sizes compare? Try soapy water also.

observing **C.** Which liquid—water, soapy water, or alcohol—has the largest drops? the smallest drops? Here is another way to find out. Put 100 drops of each liquid into separate, matched, small containers. Compare how high each liquid is inside.

observing **D.** What kinds of drop prints do different liquids make on newspaper? (See Figure 18-7.) Hold a meter stick or yardstick upright over newspaper. Squeeze a drop of water from a medicine dropper held near and about halfway up the stick. What does the drop print look like on the newspaper? How large is it? Let a drop fall from the top of the stick. How does the print look now? Try drops of soapy water and alcohol, too.

inferring **E.** Can you match up a liquid with its drop print? Can you tell from how high each drop fell? Ask a partner to make drop prints as you did. Do not watch as the prints are made.

hypothesizing **F.** What other liquids can you test? How do you think they will compare with your first liquids?

TEACHING COMMENT

PREPARATION AND BACKGROUND

Any liquid has the property of cohesion, which is the tendency for its molecules to stick together. The cohesion of water is strong compared with some other liquids. This is why water forms a bulge that rises above the rim of an overly full glass. Soap weakens the cohesive power of water, so the bulge of slightly soapy water is noticeably lower. That of alcohol is lower still; its cohesion is relatively weak. This is one reason it evaporates so fast.

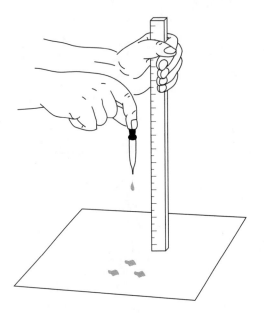

Figure 18-7

GENERALIZATION

Some liquids seem to stick together more strongly than others.

SAMPLE PERFORMANCE OBJECTIVES

Process: The child can observe and compare the relative sizes of drops of water, soapy water, and alcohol.

Knowledge: The child can predict the relative sizes of drops of two liquids after first observing how high each bulges in the filled container.

FOR YOUNGER CHILDREN

Most younger students are successful in manipulating the materials and making observations.

INVESTIGATION: *HOW TO MEASURE VOLUME WITH WATER*

Rocks and other solid objects have many different shapes. Sometimes it is hard to tell which of two different-shaped objects is larger; that is, takes up more space. (The amount of space an object takes up is its volume.)

EXPLORATORY PROBLEM

How can you compare the volumes of small solid objects?

NEEDED

five different-shaped rocks (small)
ruler
oil-base modeling clay
large jar with straight sides
small lead fishing sinker
water
masking tape and pencil
fork or spoon

TRY THIS

1. Fasten a strip of masking tape on a jar the long way.
2. Half-fill the jar with water.
3. Put one rock into the jar. Mark the water level on the tape with a pencil.
4. Remove the rock with a fork or spoon.
5. Put a second rock into the jar. Compare the new water level with the pencil mark (Figure 18-8).

DISCOVERY PROBLEMS

classifying

A. How can you put the rocks in order from smallest to largest?

Figure 18-8

inferring
    B. Make a clay ball the size of some rock. Where will the water level be if you put it into the jar? Mark the tape to show your estimate, then test your hypothesis.

inferring
    C. Suppose you form the same clay ball into another shape. Where do you think the water level will be? Try many different shapes.

inferring and observing
    D. Suppose you break the same clay piece into two parts. Where do you think the water level will be? What happens to the water level when you break the clay into more than two parts?

inferring
    E. Will a heavy clay ball make the water level rise higher than a lighter one? Make two clay balls the same size, but have a lead weight in the middle of one ball. Try each ball and find out.

measuring
    F. How much larger is one rock compared to another? With a ruler and pencil, make evenly spaced marks on the jar's tape strip. Call each pencil mark one "unit." Compare the difference in water-level units before and after a rock is put in the jar. How much difference in units is there between your smallest and largest rock?

predicting
    G. Get other small objects. How well can you predict the volume of each in units?

TEACHING COMMENT

PREPARATION AND BACKGROUND

This investigation may help some of your students learn to conserve volume as measured by displaced water. That is, the space an object takes up is determined by its overall surface, rather than shape, weight, or number of parts.

GENERALIZATION

The volumes of different-shaped solid objects may be compared by the water each displaces.

SAMPLE PERFORMANCE OBJECTIVES

Process: The child can measure the difference in volume between two rocks by using "water-level units."

Knowledge: The child can explain that the volume of water an object displaces is determined by the volume of space the object occupies.

FOR YOUNGER CHILDREN

The Exploratory Problem and Problems A through D may be used as readiness experiences.

INVESTIGATION: *THINGS THAT FLOAT IN WATER*

Can you tell, just by looking at an object, whether it will float in water? What kinds of objects float? What kinds of objects sink?

EXPLORATORY PROBLEM

How can you find out which small objects will float?

NEEDED

plastic bowl
salt
bag of small objects to test
ruler
oil-base modeling clay
spoon
large washers
paper towels
kitchen foil (15 centimeters or 6 inches square)

TRY THIS

1. Half-fill a plastic bowl with water.
2. Empty the bag of small objects on your desk. Put those you think will float into one group. Put those you think will sink in another group.
3. Place all the objects from one group into the water. Observe what happens, then remove the objects. Do the same thing with the other group of objects.

DISCOVERY PROBLEMS

inferring **A.** How many objects did what you thought? What are the objects like that floated? sank?

experimenting **B.** What can you do to sink the objects that floated?

experimenting **C.** What can you do to float the objects that sank?

experimenting **D.** In what ways can you get a piece of foil to float? sink?

experimenting **E.** How can you make a foil boat?

experimenting **F.** How many washers can your foil boat carry? What can you do to make it carry more washers?

experimenting **G.** How can you get a piece of clay to float?

inferring **H.** Make a clay boat the same size as your foil boat. Which do you think will carry more washers?

measuring   **I.** Can you make two foil boats that will carry, from the first try, exactly the same weight? two clay boats that will carry the same weight from the first try?

experimenting   **J.** What can you get to float in salt water that cannot float in fresh water?

inferring   **K.** Can you find anything that will float in fresh water and sink in salt water?

TEACHING COMMENT

PREPARATION AND BACKGROUND

Children can develop some understanding in this investigation about the buoyancy of different objects in water and how the density of water affects buoyancy. You might also want children to explore liquids other than water.

A bag of small objects to test for floating might include a wooden checker, pencil, key, marble, plastic objects, pieces of leather, rubber eraser, and small toy figures. The children can bring in many more.

Uniform objects other than large washers may be used to measure the weight-carrying capacity of children's boats. Identical marbles, pennies, or small pieces of ceramic tile work well. To avoid rust, be sure all steel washers are dried before they are stored.

GENERALIZATION

Objects that are light for their size float; adding salt to water makes floating easier.

SAMPLE PERFORMANCE OBJECTIVES

Process: Through measuring, the child can construct two near-identical boats with near-identical weight capacities.

Knowledge: When shown some new objects, the child can predict which will float.

FOR YOUNGER CHILDREN

Activities A through G have been done successfully by primary students. The other activities that involve careful measuring and counting may be difficult and are not recommended.

ACTIVITY: *WHAT HAPPENS TO WATER PRESSURE WITH DEPTH?*

NEEDED

empty milk carton (tall)
nail (or sharp pencil)
sink
water

TRY THIS

1. Punch a nail hole in the carton's side, halfway up, from the inside out.
2. Punch another hole above it and a third hole below it, from the inside out.
3. Cover all three holes tightly with three fingers. Fill the carton with water. Keep it in the sink.
   a. If you take away your fingers, what do you think will happen?
4. Remove your fingers quickly from the three holes.
   b. What happened? In what part of the carton was the water pressure the greatest?

TEACHING COMMENT

Sometimes the torn edges of the holes will impede the flow of water. Punching the holes from the inside out makes this less likely.

ACTIVITY: *HOW HIGH CAN WATER FLOW COMPARED TO ITS ORIGIN?*

NEEDED

rubber tube (1 meter or 1 yard long)
container of water
funnel that fits the tube
sink

TRY THIS

1. Stick the funnel end tightly into a tube end. Do this activity in a sink.
2. Hold up the funnel. Have someone pour water into it.
3. When water comes out of the tube, pinch it off.
4. Have someone fill the funnel with water. Keep the tube end pinched off. How high will you be able to hold the tube end and still have water come out? Higher than the funnel? as high? lower?
5. Let go of the tube end. Try holding it at different heights. What did you find?

INVESTIGATION: *THE FILTERING OF POLLUTED WATER*

Most cities have water treatment plants to clean, or *purify,* their drinking water. The unclean water is first pumped to a large settling tank, where it stays for a while. Some of the dirt and other polluting particles in the water settle to the bottom. The cleaner water on top then goes into a filtering tank, which has thick layers of sand and gravel. Sometimes there is a layer of charcoal between these layers. As the water filters through, still more polluting materials are left behind.

It's not easy to clean polluted water, even by filtering. You can find out more about this yourself.

EXPLORATORY PROBLEM

How can you clean polluted water by filtering?

NEEDED

cut-off pint milk carton
clean sand
charcoal briquette
cotton
small glass jar
nail
jar of soil water
small paper bag

TRY THIS

1. Punch some holes with a nail in the bottom of a cutoff milk carton.
2. Spread some cotton inside on the carton bottom. Add some clean sand.
3. Put crushed charcoal on top of the sand. (To crush charcoal, put a briquette into a small bag. Pound it with a rock.) Then add another layer of sand.
4. Place the filter on top of a small glass jar.
5. Pour some *clean tap water* into your filter. (This will pack the materials more tightly together.)
6. Prepare a jar of soil water. Put a handful of soil into a jar of water and mix. Let the water settle for a half hour.
7. Pour some soil water from the top of the jar into the filter. Watch the filtered water trickle into the small jar (Figure 18-9).

DISCOVERY PROBLEMS

observing **A.** How clean is the filtered water compared to the soil water?

observing **B.** How clean would the water get with fewer filtering materials? with just one filtering material?

observing **C.** Will your filter remove ink or food coloring?

observing **D.** Does the order in which you have your filter materials matter?

experimenting **E.** Would more or other materials work better? How else could you improve your filter?

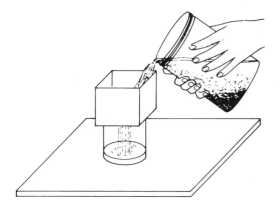

Figure 18-9

Teaching Comment

PREPARATION AND BACKGROUND

Caution students not to drink their filtered water. They should know that a chemical is added to filtered water in city water plants to kill germs that survive filtering.

Your students may enjoy having a contest to determine the best filter. They may need to be reminded that everyone should filter samples of the same polluted water.

GENERALIZATION

Some water pollutants may be removed by filtering the water through layers of different permeable materials.

SAMPLE PERFORMANCE OBJECTIVES

Process: The child can experiment to find ways to improve the efficiency of a simple water filter.

Knowledge: The child can make a water filter with simple materials that removes larger particles from polluted water.

AIR AND ITS PROPERTIES EXPERIENCES
(Concepts page 551)

INVESTIGATION: *WHERE AIR CAN BE*

Air is found everywhere on the earth. Air can go into tiny places. But can air get inside everything? What things do you think have some air inside? do not have air inside?

EXPLORATORY PROBLEM

How can you find out what things have some air inside?

NEEDED

plastic bowl (half-filled with water)
orange peel
sand
coin
stone
cracker
piece of brick
leather
soft wood
several kinds of fabrics

TRY THIS

1. Put a piece of brick into a bowl of water (Figure 18-10).

Figure 18-10

2. Watch for tiny bubbles on the brick. These are air bubbles. This shows there was some air inside the brick.

3. Put a coin into the water. You will probably see no bubbles. This shows the coin probably had no air inside.

DISCOVERY PROBLEMS

observing	**A.** Does a piece of cloth have air in it? Do some kinds of cloth have more air in them than others?
observing	**B.** Does leather have air in it? Can a soft piece of wood have air in it?
observing	**C.** Does a cracker have air in it? does an orange peel?
observing	**D.** Can a stone have air in it? Try several different kinds.
experimenting	**E.** Does sand have air in it? How can you find out?
inferring	**F.** What else do you think might have air in it? What else might not have air in it?

Teaching Comment

PREPARATION AND BACKGROUND

Some soft materials show dramatically that they contain air if squeezed under water. Soft pine, balsa wood, and leather are examples. Pliers or tongs may serve as squeezers, if needed.

The spaces between sand or soil particles commonly contain much air. Surface air bubbles may easily be seen if water is poured into a small jar with sand inside. (While water also usually contains air, the volume is small compared to that found in the spaces between sand particles.)

GENERALIZATION

Air can be found almost everywhere. Most porous materials contain some air.

SAMPLE PERFORMANCE OBJECTIVES

Process: The child can infer which objects are likely to contain air by observing their physical properties.

Knowledge: The child can describe the properties of objects that contain or do not contain some air.

FOR OLDER CHILDREN

Older children can be challenged to detect if water contains air. They may look for bubbles in the water that rise to the surface and break. This can be seen in standing water, but is more quickly observable as water becomes heated.

Also, let them boil some aquarium water in a teakettle to remove most of the air. After the boiled water cools again to the aquarium temperature, a goldfish may be placed in the water. Have them compare the more rapid gill movements of the fish with those observed before in the aquarium. Return the fish to the aquarium after several minutes to avoid harming it.

INVESTIGATION: *Soap Bubbles*

Have you ever blown soap bubbles? If so, how big was your biggest bubble? how small was your smallest bubble?

EXPLORATORY PROBLEM

How can you blow soap bubbles? What is it like inside a bubble?

NEEDED

paper cup of bubble liquid
soda can with ends removed

bendable plastic straw
paper cup half full of water
small piece of cardboard
liquid detergent or soap
scissors
glycerin
thin wire (6 inches)
spoon
child's plastic swimming pool
hula-hoop
small wooden box or stool

TRY THIS

1. Cut the straw end into four parts. Use the end that bends.

2. Push back the four parts as shown in the drawing (Figure 18-11).

3. Bend the straw into a J shape.

4. Dip the cut end into the bubble liquid.

5. Put the other straw end into your mouth and blow gently.

6. Place a mixture of dish soap (32–64 ounces), glycerine (10 tablespoons), and water in a child's plastic pool. Set a small wooden box or stool in the center (above the water line).

7. Place a student on the stool and then quickly pick the hula-hoop straight up from the bottom of the pool to above the student's head. A bubble will form

Figure 18-11

and surround the child. Larger amounts of glycerin and/or dish soap will make longer-lasting bubbles.

DISCOVERY PROBLEMS

observing   **A.** What different kinds of bubbles can you blow? How big a bubble can you make? how small?

observing   **B.** How many bubbles can you blow with one dip of your pipe? How few?

observing   **C.** What do you see when you look at a bubble? when you look through the large bubble around you?

predicting   **D.** What will happen if you catch a bubble in your hand? What will happen if your hand is soapy?

experimenting **E.** How can you make a bubble floating in air stay up? Move to your left? right? up? (*Hint:* How might a piece of cardboard help you?)

experimenting **F.** Bend pieces of wire into loops and other shapes. Dip them into the liquid and blow. What kinds of bubbles do they make?

experimenting **G.** Make extra-large bubbles. Take a soda can that has no top or bottom. Dip one end into bubble liquid. How big a bubble can you make?

experimenting **H.** Can you make a better bubble liquid? Mix a capful of liquid detergent or soap in a half-cup of water. How does it work? Will adding some glycerin make bigger bubbles? How much works best?

TEACHING COMMENT

PREPARATION AND BACKGROUND

Use either a commercial bubble-blowing liquid or prepare your own from liquid detergent. Many teachers have gotten excellent results from Dawn™ or Joy™ liquid detergent. Both products contain a high glycerin content. A 1-part detergent to 16-parts water mix works well. Add some glycerin (sold at drugstores) for even bigger bubbles. Mix thoroughly.

This investigation is done best outdoors. However, when students try to steer their bubbles in a certain direction by waving a piece of cardboard, a near-windless condition is needed. On a windy day this activity can be done indoors in a more limited way. Students can discover that a bubble stays up best if the cardboard or hand is waved rapidly from side to side *over* the bubble. This decreases the air pressure over the bubble and so the surrounding air rushes in, holding up the bubble. Likewise, for lateral motion, a bubble will "follow" a waved cardboard.

GENERALIZATION

A soap bubble is made up of air inside and soap outside; big bubbles have more air inside than small ones. Moving air can make soap bubbles move.

SAMPLE PERFORMANCE OBJECTIVES

Process: When given the materials, the child can vary the mixture of a bubble liquid to produce larger bubbles.

Knowledge: The child can explain that a large bubble contains more air than a smaller one.

FOR OLDER CHILDREN

Older students enjoy and profit from an experimental approach to this investigation. Have them test the relative effectiveness of several commercial preparations or their own bubble preparations: Which one makes the biggest bubbles? Which one makes bubbles last the longest? Let them change the proportions of your prepared mixture or substitute other ingredients. For example, adding glycerin to bubble mix makes giant, long-lasting bubbles.

Invite them to compare several kinds of commercial bubble pipes and plastic rings ("wands") for making bubbles. Or, encourage them to invent their own devices. Challenge them to land soap bubbles inside a designed target area outdoors. To do so, they will have to consider wind velocity, the height from which they release bubbles, and bubble sizes.

INVESTIGATION: *PARACHUTES*

How does a parachute help someone who jumps from an airplane? What makes a parachute fall slowly? You can learn more about real parachutes by making small ones.

EXPLORATORY PROBLEM

How can you make a small parachute?

NEEDED

thin plastic (clothes covers from dry cleaners)
sticky tape
thin cloth (scrap cotton)
scissors
string
modeling clay

TRY THIS

1. Cut a square the size of a handkerchief from thin plastic.
2. Cut a small hole in the center of the plastic.
3. Cut four strings the same size.

4. Tie one string end to each corner of the plastic.

5. Tie the other string ends together in a knot.

6. Shape a small ball of clay around the knot (Figure 18-12).

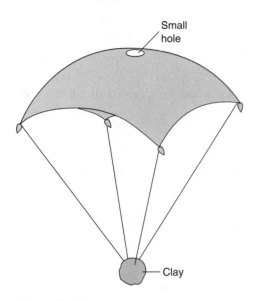

Figure 18-12

DISCOVERY PROBLEMS

observing   **A.** Try out your parachute on the playground. Drop it from the top of the play slide. Then roll it up loosely and throw it into the air. Does rolling make it work better?

hypothesizing   **B.** Suppose you cover the hole with sticky tape. What difference might this make?

hypothesizing   **C.** Suppose you make the hole larger. What difference might this make?

hypothesizing   **D.** Suppose you add more clay to the ball. What difference might this make?

experimenting   **E.** How can you make a parachute that will fall slower than the one you have now?

experimenting   **F.** How can you get a small and large parachute to fall equally fast?

experimenting   **G.** What is the smallest parachute you can make that will work correctly?

experimenting   **H.** What other materials can you use to make parachutes?

TEACHING COMMENT

PREPARATION AND BACKGROUND

Learning about parachutes allows children to thoughtfully manipulate several variables. In doing so, they learn to think of air as a tangible, material substance.

The thin plastic clothes bags dry cleaners use are excellent material for chutes. *Caution:* Remind students that a plastic bag should never be placed over the head.

GENERALIZATION

A parachute is built to catch the air as it falls; it can be changed to fall faster or slower.

SAMPLE PERFORMANCE OBJECTIVES

Process: When comparing the performance of two model parachutes, the child drops them from the same height at the same time.

Knowledge: The child can describe how to make a model parachute fall faster or slower.

FOR OLDER CHILDREN

Older students can construct parachutes with improved performance. In addition, they may invent rubber-band launchers (slingshot type, for example) to zip a rolled-up parachute into the air. Ask them to predict the effect of wind drift on their parachutes. Some may be able to predict direction and distance well enough to hit a named target area.

ACTIVITY: *HOW CAN YOU SHOW THAT AIR TAKES UP SPACE?*

NEEDED

deep glass bowl (large)
water
two small glasses
paper towels

TRY THIS

1. Fill the bowl three-fourths full with water.
2. Hold a glass with the open end down. Push it straight down into the water.
3. Put a second glass in the water sideways, so it fills with water.

4. Now tip the first glass. Try to "pour" the air up from the first glass into the second glass (Figure 18-13).

   a. What happens to the water in the higher glass?

   b. What happens in the lower glass?

   c. How can you get the air back into the first glass?

   d. Suppose you put a crushed paper towel in the bottom of a glass. How could you put the open glass underwater without getting the towel wet?

Figure 18-13

TEACHING COMMENT

If no air bubbles are lost in the process, the air may be transferred from one glass to the next indefinitely. Because air is lighter than water, the air-filled glass will always need to be below the water-filled glass during the transfer.

ACTIVITY: *HOW CAN YOU TELL IF AIR IN A BALLOON WEIGHS ANYTHING?*

NEEDED

two matched balloons
meter stick or yardstick
scissors
sticky tape
string

TRY THIS

1. Hang a meter stick evenly from a doorway or other place. Use a string and tape.

2. Attach a string loosely to each of the two deflated balloons.

3. Tape each string to an *end* of the stick. Be sure the stick is level after the balloons are hung. If not, place a partly open paper clip on the stick where needed to balance it (Figure 18-14).

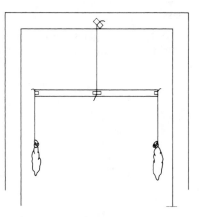

Figure 18-14

a. What will happen if you blow up one balloon and rehang it?

b. In what ways can you make the stick level again? The strings must stay at the ends of the stick.

TEACHING COMMENT

Be sure the balloon strings are always affixed to the stick *ends* to help assure balance. In **b,** the deflated balloon can be blown up like the inflated one. Or the inflated balloon may be slowly deflated by puncturing it at the neck with a pin.

INVESTIGATION: *AIR NEEDED FOR BURNING*

What are some ways you can stop a candle from burning? How important is air for a candle to keep burning?

EXPLORATORY PROBLEM

How long do you think a candle will burn inside a closed jar?

NEEDED

small candles
matches

modeling clay
four different-sized wide-mouth glass jars
clock or watch with second hand
metal pie pan
pencil and paper
paper towels
graph paper
measuring cup

TRY THIS

1. Stick some clay to the middle of a pie pan.
2. Stand a candle upright in the clay.
3. Light the candle. Put the used match in the pan.
4. Pick up your next-to-smallest jar. Put it upside down over the candle (Figure 18-15).

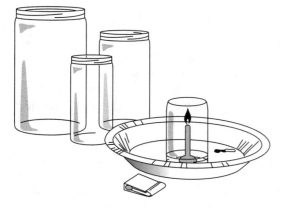

Figure 18-15

5. Look at a clock that has a second hand. How long does it take for the candle to go out? Record this time.
6. Remove the jar. Move a wad of several paper towels in and out of the jar a few times. This will clear out the bad air inside.

DISCOVERY PROBLEMS

measuring and communicating   **A.** How long will the candle burn a second time? a third time? Be sure to remove the bad air after each trial. Record the trial times and the average time like this:

Jar Size	Time for Each			Average Time	Predicted Time
Smallest					
Next Smallest	30	34	32	32	—
Next to Largest					
Largest					

measuring and predicting

B. How long do you think the candle will burn in the smallest jar? in the next-to-largest jar? Write your predicted times on the chart. Use three trials for each jar. Record the trial times and the average times on your chart. Compare the average and predicted times.

observing and predicting

C. How much larger than the other jars is your largest jar? Compare your jars and then study your chart. How long do you think the candle will burn in the largest jar?

communicating

D. You can make better predictions. Get different jars. Use a measuring cup to discover how much water each jar holds. Find out burning times for the smallest and largest jars. Then make a graph. Mark the average burning times of the smallest and largest jars. Draw a light line in between.

predicting

E. How closely can you predict the burning times for other jars? Find the jar size column on the bottom of the graph. Follow the column up until you reach the drawn line. Then, look straight across to the left at the burning time. (See Figure 18-16.) How will recording more jar times make it easier to predict more accurately?

hypothesizing

F. What difference will it make in burning times if you change the candle? For example: Does candle size make a difference? Does the flame's closeness to the jar top make a difference? Will two candles die out twice as fast as one?

observing

G. Does the shape of the jar make a difference in burning times? Compare pairs of matched jars with different shapes and find out.

experimenting

H. How can you make a candle burn longer in a *small* jar than in a larger jar? Can you think of several ways?

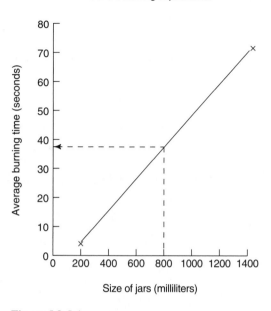

Figure 18-16

TEACHING COMMENT

PREPARATION AND BACKGROUND

A candle flame dies out in a closed container after it uses a certain percentage of the oxygen in the air. The flame burns longer in a large jar than in a smaller one because of the larger oxygen supply.

Provide at least four different-sized, wide-mouth glass jars with straight sides for the investigation. You might try half-pint, pint, quart, and half-gallon sizes, or 200-, 400-, 800-, and 1,600-milliliter sizes. These exact capacities are not critical.

If you wish to stress the graphing activity in Problem D, you might begin with it and continue through the sequence. If you believe your students are not ready for it, omit this activity. If many points are plotted on this graph, the line drawn between them will resemble a curve rather than a straight line. Use this finding to demonstrate that using more data allows more accurate predictions. More than four jars will be needed to do Problem D.

Caution: Some schools restrict the use of matches or an open flame to responsible adults. In any event, it is wise to closely supervise their use.

GENERALIZATION

A flame needs air to burn; how long a flame burns depends, in part, on how much air it has.

SAMPLE PERFORMANCE OBJECTIVES

Process: When given minimal data, the child can construct a graph to predict the burning times of candles in different-sized containers.

Knowledge: The child can explain why a candle will burn longer in a large closed container than in a smaller one.

FOR YOUNGER CHILDREN

Supervise this investigation closely and omit the measuring and graphing activities. It is simpler to compare pairs or sets of jars in each activity than it is to time each candle-burning event. When done this way, most of the activities should be interesting and understandable. Only you should handle burning materials.

WEATHER EXPERIENCES
(Concepts p. 554)

ACTIVITY: *HOW FAST DOES SOIL HEAT AND COOL COMPARED TO WATER?*

NEEDED

two matched glass jars
sunshine
soil
water

TRY THIS

1. Fill one jar with soil and the other with water.
2. Leave the jars in a shady place for an hour.
3. Touch the soil and water surfaces to see if both are about the same temperature. If not, wait a while. If they are, then put both jars in the sun for an hour.
4. Touch both surfaces again.
   a. Which feels warmer, the soil or water surface?
   b. Which will cool faster if you put both back in the shade?

TEACHING COMMENT

This activity is useful when teaching how the unequal heating of the earth's surface causes winds.

INVESTIGATION: *EVAPORATION*

Many persons hang wet clothes on a clothesline. After a while, the clothes are dry. What do you think happens to the water? When water disappears into the air, we say it *evaporated*. You can find out more about evaporation by drying wet paper towels.

EXPLORATORY PROBLEM

How can you get a paper towel to dry? How long will it take?

NEEDED

plastic bowl of water
piece of cardboard
paper towels
two aluminum pie plates

TRY THIS

1. Put a paper towel underwater to soak it.
2. Bunch the wet towel in your fist. Squeeze out all the water you can.
3. Open the towel and lay it on a pie plate (Figure 18-17).
4. Leave the plate on your desk. Check the time.
5. Every so often feel the towel to see if it is dry. Check the time again when it is all dry.

DISCOVERY PROBLEMS

predicting

A. Suppose you put one wet towel where it is shady and cool, and another where it is sunny and warmer. Which wet towel do you think will dry first?

Figure 18-17

communicating   **B.** What can you do to show that a dried-out towel is completely "dry"? How many others agree with you?

predicting   **C.** Suppose that, to make it windy, you fan one wet towel with cardboard. You do not fan a second wet towel. Which towel do you think will dry first?

predicting   **D.** Suppose you spread out one wet towel and leave another bunched like a ball. Which towel do you think will dry first?

predicting   **E.** Suppose you leave one wet towel on top of a plate. You leave a second wet towel under another plate. Which towel do you think will dry first?

experimenting   **F.** Play a game with a friend. Who can dry a wet paper towel faster? How can you make the game fair?

experimenting   **G.** What is the longest you can keep a wet paper towel from drying?

TEACHING COMMENT

PREPARATION AND BACKGROUND

The foregoing sequence gives several chances for children to manipulate conditions that affect the evaporation rate of water. The last two activities encourage them to manipulate these conditions creatively. Discovery Problem C calls for fanning one wet towel with cardboard to simulate a windy condition. Clipping the towel to the pie plate with several paper clips will keep it from blowing off the plate.

GENERALIZATION

Wind, heat, and an uncovered and spread-out condition all help to make a wet paper towel dry faster.

SAMPLE PERFORMANCE OBJECTIVES

Process: The child can vary and control at least one condition to increase the drying rate of a wet paper towel.

Knowledge: The child can state at least one condition that will change the drying rate of a wet paper towel.

FOR OLDER CHILDREN

Invite older children to do the activities with more precision. For example, they might attempt to predict the drying times in each of the activities.

Have them calculate the drying *rate* of a wet towel or sponge by using a beam balance. Let them suspend a wet towel from one end of the beam, and clay or another object on the other end to achieve a balance. Then, as the towel dries and lightens, the beam will begin to tilt up. Students can add water to the towel with an eyedropper, one drop at a time, to keep the beam level.

Ask questions such as: "How many drops evaporate in one minute?"; "Does spreading out the drops you add make a difference in the evaporation rate?"; and "Will half of a wet towel have half the evaporation rate of a whole towel?" If you do not have a beam balance, just suspend a meter stick or dowel from a string. Your students will be delighted at the dramatic effect of the evaporation rate. It takes only a few minutes, under usual conditions, for it to be noticeable.

INVESTIGATION: *RELATIVE HUMIDITY*

Can you remember times when the air has felt very dry? very moist, or *humid*? The amount of moisture, or water vapor, in the air often changes. Warm air can hold more moisture without raining than cold air. The percent of moisture now in the air compared to what it can hold at the present temperature is the *relative humidity*. You can make an instrument to measure the relative humidity. It is called a hygrometer.

EXPLORATORY PROBLEM

How can you make a hygrometer?

NEEDED

two matched Fahrenheit thermometers
cardboard
narrow cotton strip or thick cotton shoelace
two rubber bands
quart milk carton
paper clip

TRY THIS

1. Fasten two thermometers to the sides of an empty milk carton. Use rubber bands to hold them in place.
2. Use a pencil to punch a hole in the carton under one thermometer.
3. Put about 2.5 centimeters (1 inch) of water into the carton. Close the top with a paper clip. This will keep the water from evaporating quickly.
4. Wet a strip of cotton with water.
5. Stick one end of the strip through the punched hole into the water inside. Fasten the other end to the bulb of the thermometer above (Figure 18-18).
6. To use your hygrometer, fan the thermometers with some cardboard for three minutes in a shady place. Read the temperatures of each thermometer.
7. Use the relative humidity table (Figure 18-19) to find the percent of moisture in the air. At the left, mark the wet bulb temperature lightly with pencil. At the top,

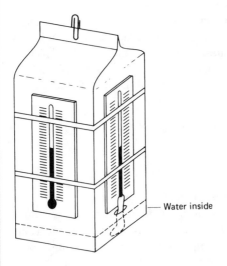

Water inside

Figure 18-18

lightly mark the dry bulb temperature. Move one finger across the row and another down the column from the marked spots. Notice the percent of relative humidity where your two fingers meet.

DISCOVERY PROBLEMS

measuring   **A.** What is the relative humidity now?

hypothesizing **B.** How, if at all, might relative humidity change from day to day? How, if at all, does it change?

observing   **C.** How well can you use your senses to tell if the air is drier or moister from day to day? Use your hygrometer to check how well you do.

measuring   **D.** How does the relative humidity outdoors compare to that indoors?

hypothesizing **E.** What would you expect the relative humidity to be outdoors on a rainy day? Measure it in some partly sheltered place and see.

inferring   **F.** How do your relative humidity measurements compare with those of the local weather bureau?

Teaching Comment

PREPARATION AND BACKGROUND

When no difference appears between the wet and dry bulb temperatures, the relative humidity is 100 percent. This condition is unlikely to be recorded outdoors unless there is dense fog or rain.

Dry bulb temperature (°F)

Wet bulb temperature (°F)	56	58	60	62	64	66	68	70	71	72	73	74	75	76	77	78	79	80	82	84
38	7	2																		
40	15	11	7																	
42	25	19	14	9	7															
44	34	29	22	17	13	8	4													
46	45	38	30	24	18	14	10	6	4	3	1									
48	55	47	40	33	26	21	16	12	10	9	7	5	4	3	1					
50	66	56	48	41	34	29	23	19	17	15	13	11	9	8	6	5	4	3		
52	77	67	57	50	43	36	31	25	23	21	19	17	15	13	12	10	9	7	5	3
54	88	78	68	59	51	44	38	33	30	28	25	23	21	19	17	16	14	12	10	7
56		89	79	68	60	53	46	40	37	34	32	29	27	25	23	21	19	18	14	12
58			89	79	70	61	54	48	45	42	39	36	34	31	29	27	25	23	20	16
60				90	79	71	62	55	52	49	46	43	40	38	35	33	31	29	25	21
62					90	80	71	64	60	57	53	50	47	44	42	39	37	35	30	26
64						90	80	72	68	65	61	58	54	51	48	46	43	41	36	32
66							90	81	77	73	69	65	62	59	56	53	50	47	42	37
68								90	86	82	78	74	70	66	63	60	57	54	48	43
70									95	91	86	82	78	74	71	67	64	61	55	49
72											95	91	86	82	79	75	71	68	61	56
74													96	91	87	83	79	75	69	62
76															96	91	87	83	76	69
78																	96	91	84	76
80																			92	84
82																				92

Percent of relative humidity

Figure 18-19

Students may notice a marked difference between indoor and outdoor readings. This is most likely in winter. As the room is heated, the air is able to hold more moisture, so the relative humidity goes down.

GENERALIZATION

A hygrometer can be used to measure the relative humidity. This is the percent of moisture that air holds compared to what it can hold at a given temperature.

SAMPLE PERFORMANCE OBJECTIVES

Process: The child can measure the relative humidity by using a hygrometer and consulting a table.

Knowledge: The child can describe conditions when high and low humidity are likely.

ACTIVITY: HOW CAN YOU "COLLECT" AND SEE WATER VAPOR IN THE AIR?

NEEDED

shiny can (clean)
thermometer
ice cubes

TRY THIS

1. Half-fill the can with water. Add five or six ice cubes.
2. Put a thermometer inside the can of ice water.
3. Watch for tiny drops on the can's sides. When they first appear, record the water temperature. (This is called the *dew point*. It tells the temperature at which water vapor will change from a gas to a liquid and *condense* on objects.)

    a. At what temperature was the dew point?

    b. Will the dew-point temperature be different in a smaller or larger container?

    c. Can an ice-water mixture get colder than the dew point?

    d. How, if at all, will the dew-point temperature change from day to day?

ACTIVITY: *HOW CAN YOU MEASURE CHANGES IN AIR PRESSURE?*

NEEDED

glass jar
balloon
rubber band
scissors
straw
file card
glue

TRY THIS

1. Make a *barometer*. Cut out a large part of a balloon. Stretch it tightly over the jar opening. Use a rubber band to hold it fast.
2. Pinch one straw end flat. Cut a point with scissors at this end.
3. Glue the straw's other end to the center of the stretched balloon.
4. Fasten a file card to a wall. Place the barometer by it. Have the straw pointer centered on the card and almost touching.
5. Make a mark on the card where the straw points each day for a week (Figure 18-20).

    a. On what day was the air pressure the highest? lowest?

    b. When, if at all, was there no change in air pressure?

TEACHING COMMENT

Increased air pressure pushes down harder on the balloon diaphragm. This makes the straw pointer go up. Decreased air pressure causes the higher pressure inside the

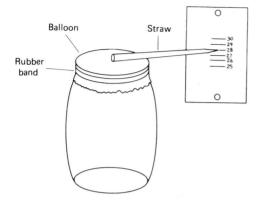

Figure 18-20

jar to push up on the diaphragm, so the pointer goes down. The movement can be increased a bit by gluing a piece of matchstick under the straw at the jar rim. You might challenge students to calibrate their barometers. They can note the daily barometric pressure in the newspaper or phone the weather bureau. After a week or so of recording the official pressure next to their own recordings, they may be able to predict roughly the official pressure from their own barometers. Place this kind of barometer where it will have the least change of temperature. Otherwise, the air in the jar may expand and contract so much that the effects of changing air pressure will be obscured.

REFERENCES

American Association for the Advancement of Science. (1993). *Benchmarks for science literacy.* New York: Oxford University Press.

National Research Council. (1996). *National science education standards.* Washington, DC: National Academy Press.

SELECTED TRADE BOOKS: WATER, AIR, AND WEATHER

For Younger Children

Ardley, N. (1983). *Working with water.* Watts.

Branley, F. M. (1987). *Air is all around you.* Harper & Row.

Carle, E. (1996). *Little Cloud.* Philomel.

Cole, J. (1986). *The magic schoolbus at the waterworks.* Scholastic.

Eden, M. (1982). *Weather.* Merrimack.

Gibbons, G. (1987). *Weather forecasting.* Macmillan.

Greene, C. (1991a). *Caring for our air.* Enslow.

Greene, C. (1991b). *Caring for our water.* Enslow.

Kalan, R. (1991). *Rain.* Morrow.

Kirkpatrick, R. K. (1985). *Look at weather.* Raintree.

Leutscher, A. (1983). *Water.* Dutton.

Llewellyn, C. (1991). *First look in the air.* Gareth Stevens.

Lloyd, D. (1983). *Air.* Dial Books.

Maki, C. (1993). *Snowflakes, sugar, and salt.* Lerner.

Martin, C. (1987). *I can be a weather forecaster.* Children's Press.

Otto, C. (1992). *That sky, that rain.* Harper.

Palazzo, J. (1982). *What makes the weather?* Troll Associates.

Pluckrose, H. (1987). *Think about floating and sinking.* Watts.

Seixas, J. S. (1987). *Water—what it is, what it does.* Greenwillow.

Smeltzer, P., & Smeltzer, V. (1983). *Thank you for a drink of water.* Winston.

Swallow, S. (1991). *Air.* Watts.

Taylor, K. (1992). *Flying start science series: Water; light; action; structure.* Wiley.

Webb, A. (1987). *Water.* Watts.

Webster, V. (1982). *Weather experiments.* Children's Press.

For Older Children

Arnov, B. (1980). *Water: Experiments to understand it.* Lothrop.

Branley, F. M. (1982). *Water for the world.* Harper & Row.

Bright, M. (1991). *Polluting the oceans.* Watts.

Cosner, S. (1982). *Be your own weather forecaster.* Messner.

De Bruin, J. (1983). *Young scientists explore the weather.* Good Apple.

Dickinson, J. (1983). *Wonders of water.* Troll Associates.

Flint, D. (1991). *Weather and climate.* Watts.

Ford, A. (1982). *Weather watch.* Lothrop.

Frevert, P. (1981). *Why does the weather change?* Creative Education.

Gallant, R. A. (1987). *Rainbows, mirages, and sundogs.* Macmillan.

Jeffries, L. (1983). *Air, air, air.* Troll Associates.

Kiefer, I. (1981). *Poisoned land: The problem of hazardous waste.* Atheneum.

Miller, C., & Berry, L. (1987). *Acid rain.* Messner.

Murata, M. (1993). *Science is all around you: Water and light.* Lerner.

Pollard, M. (1987). *Air, water, and weather.* Facts on File.

Riley, P. D. (1986). *Air and gases.* David & Charles.

Seymour, P. (1985). *How the weather works.* Macmillan.

Smith, H. (1983). *Amazing air.* Lothrop.

Snodgrass, M. E. (1991). *Environmental awareness: Water pollution.* BSP Publications.

Steele, P. (1991). *Wind: Causes and effects.* Watts.

Walpole, B. (1987). *Water.* Watts.

Ward, A. (1986). *Experimenting with surface tension and bubbles.* David & Charles.

Wu, N. (1991). *Planet earth: Life in the oceans.* Little, Brown.

Resource Books

Butzow, C. M., & Butzow, J. W. (1989). *Science through children's literature. An integrated approach* (water topics, pp. 150–157; weather topics, pp. 200–205). Teachers Ideas Press.

Butzow, C. M., & Butzow, J. W. (1994). *Intermediate science through children's literature: over land and sea* (weather topics, pp. 24–36; ocean and lake topics, pp. 131–169). Teachers Ideas Press.

Fredericks, A. D., Meinbach, A. M., & Rothlein, L. (1993). *Thematic units: An integrated approach to teaching science and social studies* (weather topics, pp. 153–160). HarperCollins.

LeCroy, B., & Holder, B. (1994). *Bookwebs: A brainstorm of ideas for the primary classroom* (air activities pp. 97–98). Teachers Ideas Press.

Shaw, D. G., & Dybdahl, C. S. (1996). *Integrating science and language arts. A sourcebook for K–6 teachers* (water cycle topic, pp. 73–78). Allyn and Bacon.

CHAPTER
19

THE EARTH IN SPACE

THE EARTH IN SPACE

The Earth in Space
Benchmarks and Standards

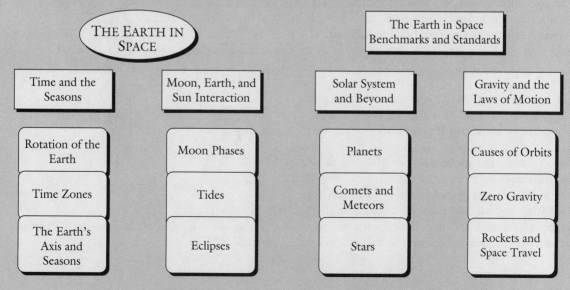

Time and the Seasons	Moon, Earth, and Sun Interaction	Solar System and Beyond	Gravity and the Laws of Motion
Rotation of the Earth	Moon Phases	Planets	Causes of Orbits
Time Zones	Tides	Comets and Meteors	Zero Gravity
The Earth's Axis and Seasons	Eclipses	Stars	Rockets and Space Travel

The sky's the limit.

What goes up must come down.

Even tricycle riders today smile at these clichés. Television, magazines, and space missions have given children a beyond-the-earth outlook unknown to most previous generations.

But outside of school, few children learn the basic ideas and physical laws that give meaning to the motions of objects in space. We'll concentrate on several of these ideas and laws in this chapter as we examine how the earth's motions in space cause time and seasonal changes; how the relative motions of sun, earth, and moon bring about moon phases, eclipses, and tides; how to measure size and distance in the solar system and beyond; and how gravity and the laws of motion affect the movements of planets, satellites, and rockets.

TIME AND THE SEASONS CONCEPTS
(Experiences p. 608)

Because the earth is so large compared to the size of a person, it is hard at first to visualize the earth's motions in space. One remedy is to make the earth small compared to a person. That is what a globe model of the earth does.

Globe and Shadows

If you put a globe in the sun, the sunlight shines on one-half of the globe, as it does on one-half of the earth. If you position your town or city so it is upright, and north on the globe faces north, the globe will face the sun as the earth does.

How will you know this is so? You can test it. Stick a small nail through a piece of sticky tape and fasten the nail head down to your town on the globe. Be sure the nail is vertical.

(You may have to prop up the globe base with a book or two.) Then look at the nail's shadow. You'll find it identical in direction and proportional to shadows of other objects around you. Leave the globe in place during the day, and the nail shadow will move and change length like the other shadows do as the earth rotates. Or, if you want a preview of what shadows the earth objects will make, you can rotate the globe and watch the nail's shadow.

Rotation and Time

Most upper-grade children know the earth rotates, but few can tell in which direction. The sun rises in a generally eastern direction and sets in a generally western direction, with opposite shadows. Therefore it is a west-to-east rotation.

Figure 19-1 shows how persons on the east coast of the United States move into the sunlight. To them, it looks as though the sun is rising from the horizon and climbing higher as time goes by. Six hours from the time they first

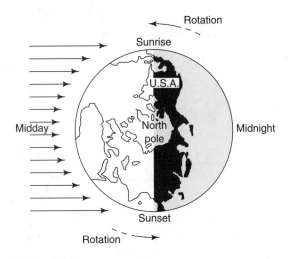

Figure 19-1

The apparent motion of the sun is caused by the earth's rotation.

observe "sunrise," the sun is closest to being directly overhead. This is midday, or the exact middle of the daylight period. Gradually, they continue to rotate counterclockwise. Shadows grow longer. Around 6:00 p.m., it is almost twilight, and the sun appears to sink into the western horizon. The next 12 hours they spend in darkness, until once again the sun appears to rise. A complete rotation takes 24 hours, or one complete day. Of course, most of the time people in New York (or elsewhere) do not have equal parts of daylight and darkness. You know that summer days are longer than winter days, for example. We shall discuss why shortly.

Expect some trouble with the term *day* because it has two meanings: the hours during which it is light, and the time for one complete rotation. You might use the terms *complete day* and *daylight* to separate the two.

Time Zones

It would be extremely inconvenient to judge time by where the sun is overhead. Every location a few kilometers east or west of another location would have a different noon time as the sun reached its midday position, for example. Though this was not a problem in the days of slow-moving transportation, it became intolerable when railroads were established.

The problem was solved in 1833 by creating four standard time zones in the United States.

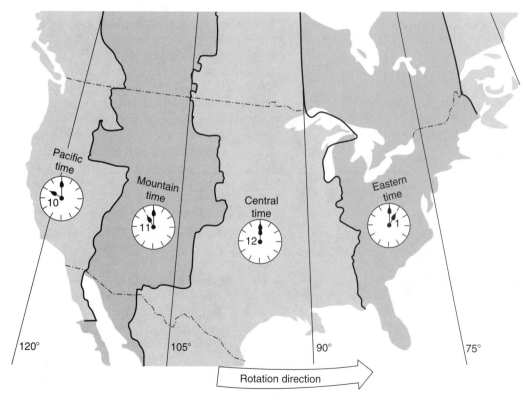

Figure 19-2
The continental United States has four time zones.

Figure 19-2 shows those in use today in the continental United States. We set our watches ahead going eastward and back going westward. The entire globe is now divided into 24 time zones, 15° apart. (The 15° separations came from dividing 360° by 24 hours, since the earth is a near sphere.)

The practical effect of having the same time zone for three cities hundreds of kilometers or miles apart is shown in Figure 19-3. Notice that only one city can experience midday at a given moment, although it is noon at all three cities.

Seasons

Persons in New York on December 21st experience about 9 hours of daylight and 15 hours of darkness. Six months later, the reverse happens. An even greater difference is found at a higher latitude, such as near Seattle, Washington (50th parallel). To see why, first examine Figure 19-4. Notice that the earth's axis is tilted 23° from the plane of the earth's orbit around the sun. As the earth revolves about the sun, its axis continues to point in the same direction—toward the north star. Check the winter position. Because of the tilt, the northern hemisphere is in darkness longer than it is in daylight. You can see this by checking the length of the parallels of latitude shown. In the summer position, you see the reverse. Now the same latitude is exposed to sunlight for a much longer period. At the "in between" periods of spring and fall, day and night periods are more nearly equal.

Also observe that the southern hemisphere has opposite conditions to those in the northern hemisphere. While New York shivers in December, the beaches in sunny Rio de Janeiro are crowded with swimmers and sun bathers enjoying their summer.

However, besides the increased length of the days, there is another reason why summers are warmer than winters. The sun's rays are more nearly overhead during summer than at other times. Note the words *more nearly overhead*. Because the earth's axis is tilted, at noon the sun can never be completely vertical (at a 90° angle) north of the Tropic of Cancer or south of the Tropic of Capricorn.

If you ask students to explain why it is warmer in summer than it is in winter, don't be surprised if one replies, "The earth is closer to the sun." This is entirely logical, even though it is wrong. In fact, the opposite is true. The earth's path (orbit) around the sun is a slightly elongated circle, or ellipse, as are nearly all the orbits of celestial bodies. In winter, we are almost 5 million kilometers (3 million miles) closer to the sun than in summer. But because this distance is small compared to the average distance, about 150 million kilometers (93 million miles), the effect is negligible.

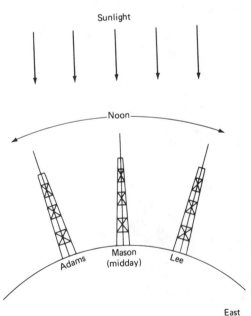

Figure 19-3
Midday at one city and noon at three cities in the same time zone. (Not to scale.)

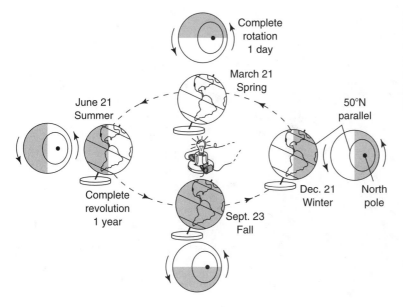

Complete
rotation
1 day

June 21
Summer

March 21
Spring

50°N
parallel

Complete
revolution
1 year

Sept. 23
Fall

Dec. 21
Winter

North
pole

Figure 19-4
The seasons. Outside figures as viewed from above. Note the unequal periods of daylight at the 50th parallel except on March 21 (spring equinox) and September 23 (fall equinox).

MOON, EARTH, AND SUN INTERACTION CONCEPTS
(Experiences p. 615)

Why does the moon seem to change its shape? Why does the ocean have tides? What causes eclipses? Children are curious about these things. This section presents some ways the sun, earth, and moon interact. We'll consider moon phases first.

Moon Phases

You know that the moon, like our earth, receives and reflects light from the hot, glowing sun. Also, the moon revolves around the earth in about 28 days. Study Figure 19-5 for a moment. The drawings on the right show the earth and moon as seen from far out in space. The drawings of the moon on the left show how it looks to us when the moon is in each of eight different positions.

Imagine standing on the earth in the center of this illustration. Look at Position 1. This is the *new moon* position. The moon's face is now dark to us. Slowly, the moon moves on in its orbit. At Position 2, we see a *new crescent moon;* at Position 3, a *first-quarter moon.* At Position 4, we see a *new gibbous moon;* one side is now almost fully illuminated. At Position 5, there is a *full moon.* The other positions reverse the sequence of phases from old gibbous, last quarter, old crescent, to new moon.

As the moon moves from the new to full positions, more and more of it appears to be shining; it is said to be *waxing.* But from full to new moon positions, less and less of its lighted part is visible from earth, so it is said to be *waning.* Try the moon phase investigation on pages 615-617. Compare the phases you see with those in Figure 19-5.

Tides

The interaction of sun, moon, and earth also results in tides. How do they happen? The law

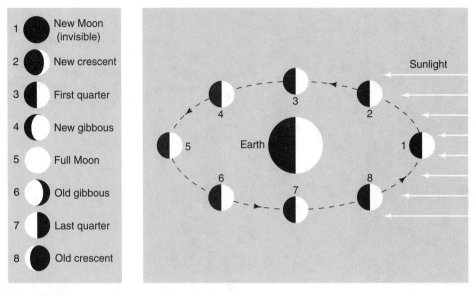

Figure 19-5
Moon phases as seen from the earth (left).

of universal gravitation, first formed by the great eighteenth-century philosopher and scientist, Sir Isaac Newton, provides much of the answer. Briefly stated, *every object in the universe attracts each other; the force of this attraction depends on the mass of each object and the distance between them.* ("Mass" is the amount of matter that makes up the object.)

As shown in the Figure 19-6, the mutual attraction between earth and moon causes the ocean to bulge at Position 1. This is a *direct high tide.* An *indirect high tide* appears at Position 3 because it is most distant from the moon, so gravitational attraction is weakest here. (We will add a refinement to this statement shortly.) Also, the land surface is pulled slightly away from this region. Positions 2 and 4 have low tides because these are areas of weak attraction that furnish the extra water making up the high tides.

What causes the tide to rise and fall? Put yourself in Position 1. As you rotate on the earth toward Position 2, the tide will seem to ebb, or fall. You experience a low tide. Moving

from Position 2 into 3, you gradually come into the bulge. It seems as though the tide is "coming in." You experience a high tide. Rotating onward, you have another low tide before once again arriving at the direct high-tide area. In other words, the oceans tend to bulge continually in the moon's direction and opposite point, as the earth rotates. The continual bulges create the illusion that the tides are moving in and out independently.

Since the earth's rotation takes about 24 hours, high tides happen about every 12 hours. (Remember, there is one direct and one indirect high tide simultaneously.) Six hours elapse between low and high tides. Actually, these times are a little longer because the moon itself moves some distance in its orbit while the earth rotates. Because the tidal bulge moves in alignment with the moon as it advances, the earth must rotate an extra 52 minutes each 24 hours before it is again in the direct high-tide zone.

Twice monthly, unusually high and low tidal ranges occur called *spring* tides. High tides are

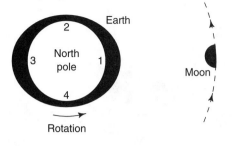

Figure 19-6
Mutual attraction between earth and moon causes ocean tides.

very high and low tides are very low. (Incidentally, there is no connection between *spring* tides and the season. Perhaps the name arose because these tides appear to "spring up" so fast.) A week later, there is much less variation from high to low tides. Tides during this period are called *neap* tides.

Figure 19-7 shows how these tides take place. When the sun and moon are aligned *(a)*, the sun's added gravitational attraction causes very high spring tides. This happens when the moon is in either the full or new moon phase. Because the sun is so far away, its tremendous mass adds only one-third to the force of gravitational attraction. When the sun and moon pull at right angles *(b)*, we have neap tides. This happens when the moon is in its first- and last-quarter phases.

Interestingly, besides water tides, there are also huge atmospheric tides and tiny land tides. All happen through the same interaction of sun, moon, and earth. Accurate measurements show that some land portions of the earth rise and fall more than 30 centimeters (one foot) with the tides.

Eclipses

Causes of eclipses are seen in Figure 19-8. Both earth and moon cast conelike shadows. When the moon is in Position 1, the tip of its shadow barely reaches the earth. Persons in this small, shadowy area see a *solar eclipse*. A total eclipse is never more than 272 kilometers (170 miles) across. Sunlight is cut off except for a whitish halo, called the *corona*. The shadow moves quickly over the ground, because both the earth and moon are in motion. Sunlight is never blocked for more than eight minutes.

In Position 2, the moon is eclipsed when it revolves into the earth's large shadow. Practically everyone on the earth's dark side can see a *lunar eclipse*, which may last for two hours before the moon revolves out of the earth's shadow. There are several partial lunar and solar eclipses each year.

Notice that eclipses happen in the full and new moon positions. Why, then, don't they occur every few weeks? The reason is that the

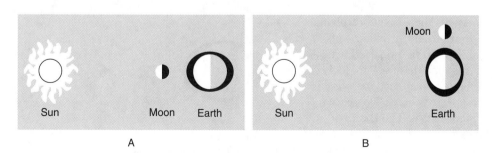

A   B

Figure 19-7
The sun also affects tidal flows.

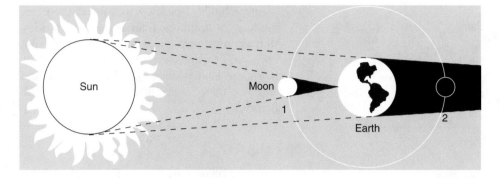

Figure 19-8
Causes of solar (1) and lunar (2) eclipses.

moon's plane of orbit is tilted about 5° from the earth's orbital plane around the sun. This usually causes the moon to pass above and below positions required for eclipses.

A 5° tilt would be only a minor deviation from the earth's orbital plane in Figure 19-8, hardly enough to make a difference. But in proper scale, this small deviation is quite significant. With a scale of 2.5 centimeters to 1,600 kilometers (1 inch to 1,000 miles), the earth's diameter is 20 centimeters (8 inches), and the moon's is 5 centimeters (2 inches). Their distance apart is 6 meters (20 feet). The sun's diameter and distance at this scale are even more surprising. Imagine a sun model 22 meters (72 feet) across, 2.4 kilometers (1½ miles) away!

The Earth–Moon System

We normally think of the moon revolving around the earth, but strictly speaking, this is not quite the case. The gravitational attraction of these two objects is such that they are locked together in a revolving system that has a common center of mass (barycenter). To see why this is so, look at Figure 19-9. The large ball of clay represents the earth, and the small one is the moon. A short wire joins the two to simulate their gravitational attraction. If you suspend System A from the middle with a string, the much

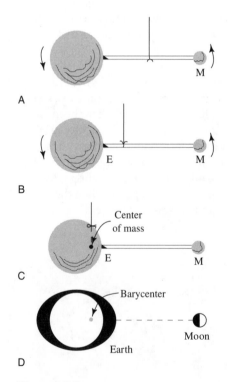

Figure 19-9
The earth–moon system has a common point of balance, or center of mass, called the barycenter. (Distance not to scale.)

heavier earth goes down and the moon goes up. The same thing would happen if a heavy adult and a small child got on a seesaw with the fulcrum in the middle. In System B, the balance is improved but much the same thing happens. In System C, though, a balance is found. If you spin each model system with a twisted string, System A and B will wobble and sway unevenly; but System C revolves uniformly and simulates the motion of the earth–moon system.

Now for the refinement on the cause of indirect tides, as promised earlier. In any spinning system such as this, there is a tendency for the two objects to fly apart. The gravitational attraction between the two prevents this from happening. In System D, the side of the earth facing the moon is strongly attracted to the moon. The water moves more easily than the solid earth, so it flows strongly toward the near side and becomes a high tide. The earth's opposite side is attracted less because it is farther away. So the tendency of this far side of the spinning system to fly apart is countered only weakly by the weakened gravitational pull. The result is an indirect high tide.

Our model is imperfect in several ways. The earth's mass is about 80 times greater than the moon's. Also, the distance scale is wrong. If we were to use the proper scale, our short wire connector would need to be at least several feet long.

The Moon's Orbit

From an earth reference position, it is natural to regard the moon as revolving in a circular path around the earth (or, more accurately, the barycenter). But motion is relative to the observer. If we could see the moon's path from far out in space, it would not look circular. Instead, it would weave in and out in a shallow, alternating pattern along the earth's orbit. (See Figure 19-10.) Since the sun is in motion, a similar pathway is woven by the earth. Is it wrong, then, to say the moon *revolves* around the earth and the earth around the sun? Not at all. It is just another way of looking at the same set of facts.

SOLAR SYSTEM AND BEYOND CONCEPTS
(Experiences p. 621)

Planets

The earth is one of nine planets revolving around a medium-sized star, the sun. How did the solar system begin? Scientists are not sure. One prominent theory holds that the sun and planets may have been formed from an enormous swirling cloud of dust and gases. Slowly, gravitational attraction caused these materials to come closer together. The speed of rotation increased more and more. As rotating dust and gas particles rubbed together, much friction and heat developed. A large mass in the center became so hot that it formed into the sun. Gradually, most of the remaining materials spread out as a result of their spinning and began revolving around the

Figure 19-10
The earth and moon orbits drawn to scale.

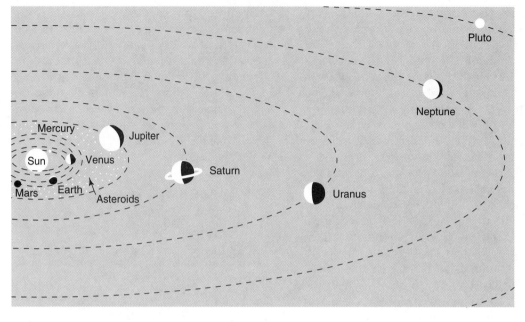

Figure 19-11
The solar system. (Not to scale.)

sun. They slowly shrank and cooled into nine separate masses, which became planets (see Figure 19-11).

Mercury is the closest planet to the sun. It rotates very slowly, only two-thirds around to one complete revolution around the sun, which takes only 88 days. Its small mass results in a surface gravity too weak to retain an atmosphere.

Venus, next in order from the sun, is enveloped in a dense atmosphere of mostly carbon dioxide. This reflects sunlight so well that, except for the sun and moon, Venus is the brightest object in the sky. Its surface temperature, too, is very high.

After the earth is *Mars.* It has an unusual reddish appearance and polar ice caps that advance and recede with the seasons. It is more like the earth than the other planets, but its very thin atmosphere and severe weather make it unlikely that living things are on this planet. In 1976, two remotely controlled space vehicles landed on Mars, but their instruments detected no forms of life. Two tiny natural satellites, or moons, revolve speedily around Mars.

Between Mars and the next planet, *Jupiter,* is an unusually large gap containing several thousand irregularly shaped chunks of stone and metal called *asteroids* (tiny "stars"). Some astronomers think these may be the remains of a planet that came too close to huge Jupiter and disintegrated under its powerful gravitational attraction. Ranging from about 1.6 to 800 kilometers (1 to 500 miles) in diameter, they are invisible to the unaided eye.

Jupiter and *Saturn* are by far the largest *outer planets.* Jupiter's diameter is 11 times greater than that of the earth. Saturn is conspicuous because of its many rings, believed to be composed of ice particles. *Uranus* and *Neptune* are nearly the same size, about three and one-half times the earth's diameter. *Pluto* is so small and distant that it was not discovered until 1930. Its orbital plane is tilted sharply from those of other planets, and its orbit is so elliptical that at times the planet is closer to the sun than Neptune.

Ancient sky-watchers were so puzzled by the changing appearance of the planets that they named them "wanderers." Long ago all such objects were thought to be stars, which ordinarily seem fixed in space. We realize now that their differences in brightness and position from time to time occur because they revolve at different distances and speeds in their orbits around the sun.

Today, astronomers are finding new planets and discovering more about distant bodies through the use of the Hubble Space telescope and other space probes. For an up-to-date account of new findings, students should be encouraged to log onto NASA's web pages on the Internet (http://spacelink.msfc.nasa.gov/).

Comets and Meteors

Comets are huge, unstable bodies apparently composed of gases, dust, ice, and small rocks. A few are briefly visible as they occasionally sweep near the sun and far out again in immense, highly elliptical orbits. They have so little mass that the pressure of sunlight causes a long streamer, or "tail," to flow from the comet head always in a direction opposite the sun. Like the planets, comets may have originated from the gases and dust of the solar nebula over 4 billion years ago.

Most children have seen "shooting stars." These are fragments of rock and metal, probably from broken-up asteroids and parts of comets, that hurtle through interplanetary space at high speeds. Although most are no larger than a grain of sand, some weigh tons. It is estimated that billions of such *meteors,* as they are called, plunge daily into the earth's atmosphere and burn into extinction from the heat of air friction. The few that do penetrate to the earth in solid form other than dust are called meteorites.

Is there any danger of being struck by a meteorite? Not much. There are only a few instances of anyone ever being injured. One such event happened in 1954. An Alabama woman was grazed by a 10-pound meteorite that crashed through her roof. In 1982, a 6-pound meteorite smashed through the roof of a home in Connecticut. No one was injured.

Size and Distances

By far the most difficult ideas in astronomy for children to grasp are the distances and sizes of objects in space. It would be helpful to their thinking if a large section of the playground could be used for scaled distance activities. Yet even a very large area can be inadequate to demonstrate both distance and size on the same scale. At 2.54 centimeters to 12,000 kilometers (1 inch to 8,000 miles), for example, Pluto would need to be located about 11 kilometers (7 miles) away!

Distances are even more astounding as we move beyond the solar system. Now, the kilometer or mile is too tiny as a unit of measurement for practical purposes. You will want to acquaint students with the light-year, defined as the distance a beam of light travels in one year. At 300,000 kilometers (186,000 miles) per second, this is almost 9.5 trillion kilometers (6 trillion miles).

The Stars

When we view the stars, some seem to group into a pattern, or constellation. People commonly think such stars are about the same in size and distance from the earth. But the only thing stars in a constellation typically share is a common direction. If we could view constellations from other angles (we can, very slightly, as the earth orbits the sun), most constellation patterns would disappear.

The light from the nearest star, the sun, takes about eight minutes to reach the earth. In contrast, a distance of 4.3 *light-years* separates us from the next nearest star, *Proxima Centauri*. These stars have over a hundred billion companions clustered in an immense aggregation of stars and filmy clouds of gas and dust called the *Milky Way galaxy*. The shape of our galaxy is like a pocket watch, with a thickened center, standing on end (Figure 19-12). It is thought to be about 100,000 light-years long and 12,000 light-years thick. The galaxy seems to be slowly rotating about its center, where the stars are most thickly concentrated.

Our galaxy is but one of millions more strewn throughout space at incomprehensible distances, containing further stars beyond reliable calculation.

GRAVITY AND THE LAWS OF MOTION CONCEPTS
(Experiences p. 625)

Nobody knows what caused the planets to begin moving, but the reason they keep moving is readily understandable: There is almost nothing in space to stop them. But why do they circle the sun? You have already been introduced

to Newton's law of gravitation. Equally important to understand is Newton's law of *inertia*. Briefly stated, *any object at rest or in motion remains at rest or continues in motion in a straight line unless acted on by some outside force.*

Anyone who has ever tried to push a heavy, stalled automobile knows how hard it is to move a heavy body at rest. It has much inertia. Anyone who has ever tried to stop a heavy, rolling automobile by pushing against it knows how difficult *this* is. A body in motion has the inertia of motion (momentum). The more momentum it has, the harder it is to stop it.

Causes of Orbits

Figure 19-13 shows how the laws of gravitation and inertia combine to keep objects in orbit. Although a natural satellite, the moon, is shown in this case, the same laws operate with all bodies that orbit other bodies in space.

If the moon were unaffected by our earth's powerful gravitational force, it would follow a straight path owing to its inertial momentum.

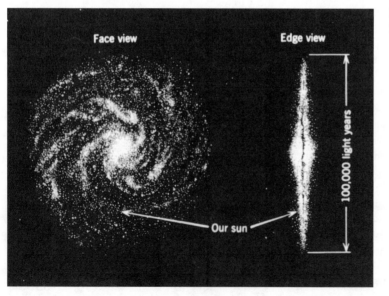

Figure 19-12
The Milky Way galaxy.

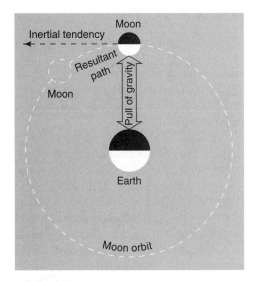

Figure 19-13
A balance between gravity and inertia keeps a satellite in orbit.

Because it is affected, the moon follows a path that is a result of each factor countering the other.

A common example of this countering effect happens when a ball rolls swiftly off a table. Instead of falling straight down, the ball's inertia of momentum keeps it going nearly sideways for an instant until gravity forces it to the floor. The resultant path of its fall is an arc.

In our illustration, gravity and inertia are equally powerful. If this were not so, the moon would either be drawn into the earth or pull away from it. This is what happens to an artificial satellite that moves too slowly or too fast. Clearly, getting a space satellite into a sustained orbit is tricky business. Its velocity and angle of entry into orbit must be calculated closely. Since perfection in these matters is nearly impossible, most orbits are markedly elongated (elliptical).

Because gravity weakens with distance, the speed of the orbiting body must be slower as the distance from its parent body increases.

This is necessary in order to maintain balance of the two forces. At 35,680 kilometers (22,300 miles) from the earth, for example, the proper orbital speed for a satellite results in one complete orbit each 24 hours. Because this is the period of the earth's rotation, a satellite positioned above the equator always stays in the same relative position. With several of these satellites properly spaced, television and radio signals are relayed to any place on earth.

Zero Gravity

When astronauts circle the earth in a satellite, they have no sensation of weight. This is because the pull of gravity is balanced exactly by the counteracting inertia of motion. We sometimes experience this *weightless,* or *zero gravity,* condition on earth for an instant when an elevator starts rapidly downward or an automobile goes too fast over the crown of a steep hill.

In one science lesson not long ago, a bright child asked her teacher an astute question: "If we would be weightless in an orbiting satellite, why wouldn't we be weightless on the moon?" The teacher had her reconsider the law of gravitation, especially the part that says ". . . this attraction depends on the *mass* of each object and the distance between them."

Because the moon has a much smaller mass than the earth, its surface gravity is only about one-sixth that of the earth's. An 81-kilogram (180-pound) astronaut weighs a mere 13.5 kilograms (30 pounds) on the moon. However, the moon's mass is almost infinitely greater than that of a space vehicle. The tiny mass of a space vehicle has practically no gravity at all.

Since prolonged periods of weightlessness seem detrimental to astronauts' health, attempts are being made to design space vehicles that create a gravity-like condition. This may be done by rotating the vehicle at a carefully calculated speed. The astronauts' inertia gives them a feeling of gravity as they are slightly pressed against the spaceship's interior. An analogy is the small ball that remains stationary on the rim of a roulette wheel until it stops turning.

Rockets

Through the ages, people have always yearned to explore what mysteries lie beyond the earth. But until recently, our technology has not been as advanced as our ambitions. Early devices and inventions designed for space travel included hitching a flock of geese to a wicker basket, hand-cranking propellers attached to hot-air balloons, and festooning a box with crude rockets containing gunpowder. Occasionally, such contraptions were personally occupied by their daring inventors—and some did depart from this earth, although not in the manner intended.

Because space is a near vacuum, no engine that draws oxygen from the air to burn its fuel can serve in a propulsion system. Instead, rocket engines are used; these carry their own oxygen supply. Rockets work because *for every action there is an equal and opposite reaction* (another law of motion by Newton). When a rocket pushes hot gases out of its combustion chamber (action), the gases push back (reaction) and thrust the rocket ahead.

Most rockets today are composed of multiple stages fastened together in a cluster or a tandem arrangement. The main rocket propels all the stages to a point where the rocket's fuel is expended and then it drops off. The remaining stages reach even higher velocities as the process continues, lightening the load each time. The speed of the last stage represents the accumulated sum of speeds attained by each stage. Perhaps future rockets will be efficient enough to reduce or eliminate the necessity for present cumbersome staging techniques.

Problems in Space Travel

Although modern rocketry provides the means to reach beyond the earth, travel for astronauts poses some difficult problems. As the rocket blasts off in a terrifying surge of power, the rapid acceleration pins the astronauts' bodies to the seats with crushing force.

Once beyond the earth's atmosphere, they need oxygen and sufficient pressure to keep their bodies working normally. They need some means of temperature control. Without air conduction of heat energy, the side of the spaceship facing the sun gets very hot, and the dark side grows freezing cold. Because of their weightless condition, the astronauts may eat and drink from plastic squeeze bottles.

To prevent the space vehicle from being burned to a cinder as it enters the atmosphere, the angle and speed of reentry must be exactly right. These are only some of the problems of space travel.

With so many difficulties, why do people venture into space? Although our curiosity is one answer, of course, there are many advantages to be gained from continued space efforts. Some benefits are improved communications, surveys of earth resources, long-range weather forecasting and possible weather control, astronomers' observation posts beyond the annoying interference of the earth's atmosphere, possible answers to how the universe was formed, and improved mapping and navigation. All these benefits may help us understand and solve problems here on Earth.

Eventually, there will be the most important reason of all. Someday, perhaps three to five billion years from now, the sun's nuclear fuel will be largely depleted. The sun should gradually expand and engulf the inner planets in an unimaginable inferno of extinction before it finally collapses and dies out. Perhaps by then our descendants will have found a comfortable haven among the stars.

THE EARTH IN SPACE
BENCHMARKS AND STANDARDS

Students who observe the sun, moon, stars, and planets will begin to find patterns in their behavior. Seasons, tides, phases of the moon, and day and night are all relevant topics as indicated below in the sample Standards and Benchmarks.

SAMPLE BENCHMARKS (AAAS, 1993).

■ Like all planets, the earth is approximately spherical in shape. The rotation of the earth on its axis every 24 hours produces the night-and-day cycle (by Grades 3–5, p. 68).

■ We live on a relatively small planet, the third from the sun (by Grades 6–8, p. 68).

SAMPLE STANDARDS (NRC, 1996).

■ Objects in the sky have patterns of movement. The sun, for example, appears to move across the sky in the same way every day, but its path changes slowly over the seasons (by Grades K–4, p. 134).

■ Most objects in the solar system are in regular and predictable motion. Those motions explain such phenomena as the day, the year, phases of the moon, and eclipses (by Grades 5–8, p. 160).

INVESTIGATIONS AND ACTIVITIES

TIME AND THE SEASONS EXPERIENCES
(Concepts p. 594)

INVESTIGATION: *THE WAY THE EARTH ROTATES*

Each day, the sun seems to follow a pattern in the sky. It seems to rise in one direction, move across the sky, and then set in the opposite direction. But the sun is relatively still. We know that it only seems to move because the earth rotates. In which direction does the earth rotate? You can find out for yourself by using a globe and then the earth itself.

EXPLORATORY PROBLEM

How can you find out the direction in which the earth rotates?

NEEDED

globe
sunshine
small nail with large head
hammer
sticky tape
stick (1 meter or 1 yard long)

TRY THIS

1. Get a small nail. Push the nail point through the sticky side of a small piece of tape. Fasten the nail head down to the place on the globe where you live.
2. Take the globe, hammer, and stick out in the sunshine. Pound the stick upright into the ground.
3. Notice the shadow made by the stick. Position the globe so the nail is upright and makes a shadow exactly in the same direction. (You may have to slip a book under the globe's base to keep the nail upright.)
4. Rotate the globe from west to east as shown in Figure 19-14.

DISCOVERY PROBLEMS

observing   **A.** What happens to the nail shadow if you rotate the globe a little from west to east? Make a record of the direction and length of the shadow.

observing   **B.** What happens to the nail shadow if you rotate the globe a little from east to west? Make a record.

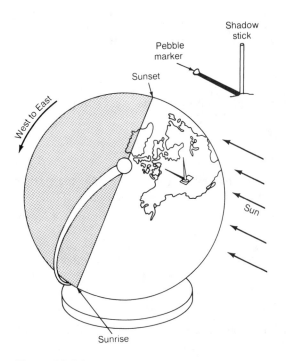

Figure 19-14

observing   **C.** Put a pebble marker at the tip of your stick's shadow. Look at the shadow again 5 minutes later. In which direction did the shadow move?

inferring   **D.** In which direction does the earth rotate?

inferring   **E.** Notice other shadows around you. How does their direction compare to the direction of the stick's shadow? How does that help you with Problem D? Where will their shadows be in an hour? in 3 hours?

TEACHING COMMENT

PREPARATION AND BACKGROUND

Some students may need to be shown directions outdoors and on the globe. You might help them to understand that north always runs from where they are to the north pole and the south runs from there to the south pole.

For the best shadow, the stick needs to be reasonably upright. A plumb bob, made of string tied to a piece of chalk, can help students align the stick if needed. You may substitute a tetherball pole for the stick. The nail, also, should be upright. If needed, something can be slipped under the globe base to make the nail vertical.

Perhaps you can borrow briefly some globes from other teachers. If so, you might want to do this activity with your entire class divided into small groups.

GENERALIZATION

Daily shadows on earth move from west to east; this shows that the earth rotates the same way.

SAMPLE PERFORMANCE OBJECTIVES

Process: The child can infer from globe and shadow data the direction of the earth's rotation.

Knowledge: The child can explain why the sun seems to rise in the east and set in the west.

INVESTIGATION: *A Shadow Clock*

Before people had clocks, one way they told time was by watching shadows on sunny days. You can do that, too. But now you can use a clock to check how well you can keep time using shadows.

EXPLORATORY PROBLEM

How can you keep time with shadows?

NEEDED

blank file card (large)
pencil
nail
clock or watch
sunny day

TRY THIS

1. Lay the card in a sunny place. Put the nail, pointing up, in the center of the card. Trace a small circle around the nail head. If the nail falls over, be sure to replace it inside the circle.

2. Each hour you can, trace the nail shadow with a pencil, and then check a clock. Record the hour by the tip of the pencil tracing (Figure 19-15). It is all right to carry your shadow clock back and forth, but always put it back in the same way and place.

3. Plan to check your shadow clock on the next sunny day.

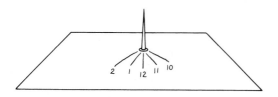

Figure 19-15

DISCOVERY PROBLEMS

observing **A.** Check the shadow clock each hour, or when you can. Notice where the shadow is. How well can you keep time by the hour?

observing **B.** Can you tell the right time on the half hour? Can you tell when it is 15 minutes before the hour? 15 minutes after the hour?

observing **C.** How long will your shadow clock keep the right time? a week? longer than a week?

observing **D.** Do the nail shadows slowly change? If so, how?

inferring **E.** Compare a regular clock with a shadow clock. What are some advantages and disadvantages of each?

TEACHING COMMENT

PREPARATION AND BACKGROUND

It is essential that students align their shadow clocks exactly the same way each time. Otherwise, their pencil recording may not coincide with additional shadows. A chalk outline or piece of tape to align an edge can be a helpful reminder.

Within a week, or sooner, children will detect a difference in the shadow alignments. This happens because the tilted earth continues to move around the sun. The same event is responsible for changes of seasons.

GENERALIZATION

It is possible to keep track of the time in a general way with a shadow clock. It gets less accurate as time goes on.

SAMPLE PERFORMANCE OBJECTIVES

Process: Within several days the child observes discrepancies between the first shadow and following shadows made by a shadow clock.

Knowledge: The child is able to make and estimate the approximate time with a shadow clock.

FOR YOUNGER CHILDREN

Try the basic activity. But have younger children record shadows for only one or two times: "How can the shadow clock tell us when it's time for lunch?" "Time to go home?" (Taping paper over the classroom clock will add interest.)

ACTIVITY: *How Warm Is Slanted Versus Direct Sunshine?*

NEEDED

cardboard
two matched thermometers
black paper
stapler
scissors
books

TRY THIS

1. Cut two same-sized pieces of cardboard.
2. Staple black paper to each piece. Staple a pocket for each thermometer as shown in Figure 19-16. Slip a thermometer in each pocket.
3. Lay one thermometer flat in the sun. It will get slanted sunshine. Prop up the other thermometer with some books so the sun strikes it directly.
4. Look at each thermometer carefully. Be sure neither thermometer rises so high that it breaks. After a few minutes, take out the thermometers and check the temperatures.

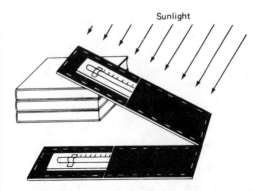

Figure 19-16

a. Which has the higher temperature?

b. Which seems to give more heat, slanted or direct sunshine?

TEACHING COMMENT

Your students may be unsure about how high they must prop up the direct-sunlight thermometer. You might have them tape a nail head down to the cardboard. They then can tilt the cardboard until the nail no longer makes a shadow, indicating relatively vertical sunlight.

INVESTIGATION: *WHY WE HAVE SEASONS*

Suppose you could see the earth from outer space as it circles the sun each year. This would help you to understand why we have seasons. But you might have to wait a long time to do that. You can use a globe and light to find out now.

EXPLORATORY PROBLEM

How can a model earth (globe) and sun (lighted bulb) be used to show seasons?

NEEDED

tilted globe
unshaded table lamp
small nail with large head
pencil and paper
sticky tape
ruler

TRY THIS

1. Get a tilted globe. The earth rotates on a make-believe pole. The pole's north end always points toward the North Star as the earth circles the sun. (That is why globes are tilted.)

2. Label one wall "north." (You will need to keep the globe tilted toward that wall.)

3. Tape a nail head down to the place on the globe where you live.

4. Set up the globe and lamp as you see in Figure 19-17. Darken the room.

5. Begin at the summer position. Center the nail in the "sunshine" and point the north pole toward north. Look at the nail shadow where you live. Measure and record how long it is. Notice how much daylight there is east and west of where you live.

6. Repeat Step 5 at each of the other three positions.

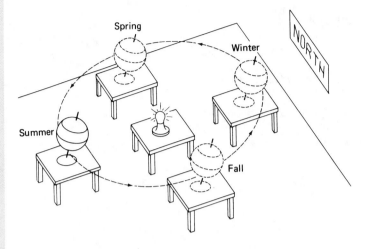

Figure 19-17

DISCOVERY PROBLEMS

observing   **A.** During what season do you see the shortest shadow where you live? the longest shadow where you live? (A short shadow shows strong, direct sunshine. A long shadow shows weak, slanted sunshine.)

inferring   **B.** When is the longest period of sunshine where you live? When is the shortest period of sunshine? (The longer the sun shines, the warmer it gets where you live.)

inferring   **C.** During which seasons will the periods of daylight and darkness be about the same?

inferring   **D.** Where and when north of you is it possible to have 24 hours of darkness? 24 hours of daylight? When and where can this happen south of you?

Teaching Comment

PREPARATION AND BACKGROUND

If four globes are available, all four can be set up and used at the same time with four groups of students. Each group can rotate to a new position after a few minutes for observation and measurement. The best place from which to observe the amount of daylight and darkness at one's latitude is just above the globe's north pole.

GENERALIZATION

The earth's tilted axis and revolution about the sun cause seasonal changes.

SAMPLE PERFORMANCE OBJECTIVES

Process: The child can measure and compare shadow lengths and contrasting areas of daylight and darkness on the globe.

Knowledge: The child can explain that without a tilted axis and the earth's revolution around the sun there would be no seasons.

MOON, EARTH, AND SUN INTERACTION EXPERIENCES
(Concepts p. 597)

INVESTIGATION: *MOON PHASES*

Have you ever watched the moon over one or two weeks? If so, you know its shape seems to go through changes, or *phases.* You can predict what phase will show when you understand why the moon's appearance changes. Working with a *moon model* can help. A ball can be the moon, and your head can be the earth. Light from a bright window can be the sun.

EXPLORATORY PROBLEM

How can a model be used to show moon phases?

NEEDED

white ball (tennis or volleyball)
bright window
daytime moon

TRY THIS

1. Draw all the classroom shades except for one bright window.
2. Hold the ball above eye level and face the window (Figure 19-18). See the dark or shadowy side of the model. This is a *new moon.* (A real new moon cannot be seen from the earth.)
3. Turn the model moon to the left. Stop when you are sideways to the window. This is a *first-quarter* moon. The moon has gone a quarter, or one-fourth, of the way around the earth.
4. Make another quarter turn to the left. Stop when your back is to the window. Now all of the moon facing you is lighted by the sun. This is a *full* moon.
5. Move a quarter turn left until you are sideways to the window. This is a *last-quarter* moon. Compare it to the first-quarter moon. Notice that the opposite part shines now.

Figure 19-18

6. Move the last quarter turn to your left. This is the new moon again. From one new moon to the next takes about four weeks.

DISCOVERY PROBLEMS

inferring   **A.** Figure 19-19 shows eight moon phases out of order. Using your moon model, can you figure out the correct order? Start with the new moon.

observing   **B.** Go outside in the sun. Point your model toward the real moon. Notice where the sun shines on the real moon. Notice where it shines on the model. How does the real-moon phase compare to the model phase?

experimenting   **C.** How can you move your model in the sun to make other phases? (*Caution:* Never look at the sun. It may harm your eyes.)

predicting   **D.** Observe the moon now and then for a few days. Notice how its appearance changes. Keep a record. Can you predict what it will look like in a week? two weeks? Draw what you think and then find out.

Figure 19-19

TEACHING COMMENT

PREPARATION AND BACKGROUND

If a bright window is unavailable, use the light from a filmstrip projector in a dark room. To do Problem B, a daytime moon must be visible. Consult the detailed weather section of your local newspaper for moonrise and moonset times during a period when a daytime moon is visible.

GENERALIZATION

Moon phases appear because one-half of the moon is lighted by sunshine as it revolves around the earth.

SAMPLE PERFORMANCE OBJECTIVES

Process: The child can predict an upcoming sequence of moon phases after observing the moon for a week.

Knowledge: The child can demonstrate with a ball and sunshine how moon phases occur.

INVESTIGATION: *AN EARTH–MOON MODEL*

Astronauts have now walked on the moon several times, so it is easy to think that the moon is close to earth. However, the moon is far away. One way to show its distance is to make a scale model.

EXPLORATORY PROBLEM

How can you make a scale model of the earth and moon?

NEEDED

basketball
string
tennis ball
ruler
scissors
clay

TRY THIS

1. You will need a large ball for the earth and a smaller one for the moon. The earth is about four times as wide as the moon. Measure the width of a ball by putting it between two books. Use a ruler to find the distance between the books. A basketball is about four times wider than a tennis ball.

2. The moon is about 30 earth widths away, or 10 times farther away than the distance around the earth. Wrap a string 10 times around the basketball. Cut off what is left.

3. Stretch the string between the "earth" and "moon" (Figure 19-20). This scale model shows sizes and distance compared to the real earth.

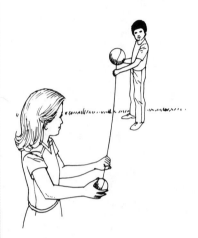

Figure 19-20

DISCOVERY PROBLEMS

measuring **A.** How can you make a scale model that is half this size?

measuring **B.** Suppose you had a ball 10 centimeters (4 inches) wide to use as the earth. How large would the moon need to be? How far apart should the earth and moon be? (*Hint:* Check Steps 1 and 2 again.)

measuring **C.** Suppose you had a ball 5 centimeters (2 inches) wide to use as the moon. How large would the earth need to be? How far apart should the earth and moon be?

measuring **D.** Suppose you wanted your whole model to be no longer than a meter stick or yardstick. How large would you make your earth and moon? How far apart would you place them?

TEACHING COMMENT

PREPARATION AND BACKGROUND

The sequence is designed to help children gain an understanding of proportion without the mathematics of proportion. After these experiences, most students should have a realistically scaled view of the earth–moon system. If you want to, you might proceed directly with figures they can scale: earth diameter 12,800 kilometers (8,000 miles), moon diameter 3,200 kilometers (2,000 miles), and average distance between them 384,000 kilometers (240,000 miles).

GENERALIZATION

Relative sizes and distance in the earth–moon system may be shown in a scale model.

SAMPLE PERFORMANCE OBJECTIVES

Process: Given one measure, the child can derive the two other measures needed to make a scale model of the earth–moon system.

Knowledge: The child can make a scale model of the earth–moon system.

INVESTIGATION: *Eclipses of the Sun and Moon*

Sometimes the earth, moon, and sun are in a straight line in space. Then, something interesting may happen: The moon may block off, or eclipse, the sunlight, or the earth may block, or eclipse, the moon. You can learn how eclipses work with a model of the sun, moon, and earth.

EXPLORATORY PROBLEM

How can you use a volleyball, a tennis ball, and a projector to show eclipses?

NEEDED

volleyball or basketball
filmstrip projector
tennis ball
sticky tape
string

TRY THIS

1. Set up the materials as shown in Figure 19-21. Put a basketball or volleyball on a table. This will be the "earth."
2. Fasten a short string to a tennis ball with sticky tape. This will be the "moon."
3. Darken the room. Turn on the projector "sun." Point it toward the earth.
4. Holding the string, move the moon around the earth. Notice the shadows made by the moon and the earth.

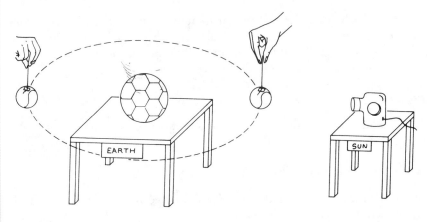

Figure 19-21

DISCOVERY PROBLEMS

observing   **A.** At what position does the moon make a shadow on the earth? (This is an eclipse of the sun.)

observing   **B.** How much of the earth is covered by the moon's shadow?

observing   **C.** At what position does the earth make a shadow on the moon? (This is an eclipse of the moon.)

observing   **D.** How much of the moon is covered by the earth's shadow?

inferring   **E.** Would more people on earth be able to see a sun eclipse or a moon eclipse? Why?

inferring   **F.** Move the moon around the earth again, but now have it go just above or below the earth. Do you see eclipses now? Why or why not?

TEACHING COMMENT

PREPARATION AND BACKGROUND

Some students may wonder why there are not a solar eclipse and a lunar eclipse every month. You might use Problem F to help them understand that the plane of the moon's orbit around the earth is somewhat tilted. Also, the two bodies are relatively much farther apart than in the model, so usually the moon's shadow misses the earth, and the earth's shadow misses the moon. The distance between the two bodies also means that the moon's shadow on earth in solar eclipses is much smaller than found in Problem B.

   Caution: Children (or adults) should never look at the sun during a solar eclipse. The sun can quickly injure eyes.

GENERALIZATION

A lunar eclipse happens when the earth's shadow falls on the moon. A solar eclipse happens when the moon's shadow falls on the earth.

SAMPLE PERFORMANCE OBJECTIVES

Process: The child can infer from observing a model whether a solar or lunar eclipse is more likely to be viewed from the earth.

Knowledge: The child can describe the relative positions of the sun, moon, and earth during a lunar eclipse and solar eclipse.

SOLAR SYSTEM AND BEYOND EXPERIENCES
(Concepts p. 601)

INVESTIGATION: *SIZE AND DISTANCE IN THE SOLAR SYSTEM*

The solar system is huge. You cannot make a model that shows both size and distance at the same time. It would be too big to fit in the classroom or playground.

But you can make a scale model of part of the system—the sun and earth. It can help you to understand more about distance and size in the solar system.

EXPLORATORY PROBLEM

How can you make a scale model of the sun and earth?

NEEDED

yellow construction paper
clay
meter stick or yardstick
straight pin
sticky tape
playground
scissors

TRY THIS

1. Make a clay ball 1 centimeter (⅜ inch) wide for the earth.
2. The sun is 108 times wider than the earth, so cut out a circle 108 centimeters (43 inches) wide from yellow construction paper. (You may need to tape some sheets together.)
3. The sun is about 150 million kilometers (93 million miles) from the earth, so the 2 models will need to be about 116 meters (383 feet) apart.

4. Practice taking giant steps. Try to make each step a meter (or yard) long. Then step off the sun–earth distance on the playground (Figure 19-22).

5. Have someone hold up the model sun at one end. Hold up your tiny model earth, stuck on a pin, at the other end. Notice how far away the sun is?

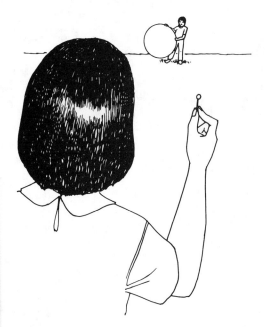

Figure 19-22

DISCOVERY PROBLEMS

measuring   **A.** The planet Jupiter is five times farther away from the sun than the earth. How far away (meters or feet) would Jupiter be with your model?

measuring   **B.** Uranus is almost 18 times farther from the sun than the earth. How far away would Uranus be with your model?

measuring   **C.** Pluto, the farthest planet, is more than 39 times farther away. How far would Pluto be with your model?

measuring   **D.** The largest of the solar system's nine planets is Jupiter. It is 11 times wider than the earth. How large would Jupiter be with your model?

measuring   **E.** The smallest planet is Pluto. It is only about one-third as wide as the earth. How large would it be with your model?

TEACHING COMMENT

PREPARATION AND BACKGROUND

A large circle may be drawn with a pencil tied to a string. Its radius with the present sun model would be 54 centimeters (21 inches).

Many students will enjoy being challenged to extend their solar system model on a local map. Pluto will need to be placed several kilometers or miles away!

GENERALIZATION

The large distances among planets in the solar system make it difficult to scale planet sizes and distances together in a model.

SAMPLE PERFORMANCE OBJECTIVES

Process: The child can measure and calculate size and distance in constructing a model of the solar system.

Knowledge: The child states that either size or distance may be scaled in a partial solar system model, but not both, if the model is to fit into a classroom.

INVESTIGATION: *CONSTELLATIONS*

Most people have seen the group, or *constellation*, of stars called the Big Dipper. The stars make a pattern that looks like an old-fashioned water dipper. There are many more constellations of stars. But while they seem to make a pattern, they may be very different in size and millions of kilometers from each other. Seen from another angle, they may not look at all like constellations. You can find out more about what constellations are like by making a model.

EXPLORATORY PROBLEM

How can you make a model of a constellation?

NEEDED

cardboard box
aluminum foil
scissors
black thread
black paint or paper
sticky tape

TRY THIS

1. Cut off the top and one side of a cardboard box.

2. Cover the side and back inside with black paint or paper.

3. Snip different-sized pieces of black thread to hold your "stars."

4. Make different-sized stars from pieces of foil. Wrap each piece around a thread end. Squeeze each into a ball shape.

5. Ask someone to use tape and hang your stars in some pattern different from the one shown in Figure 19-23. (Notice that in the front view, this constellation looks like a *W*, but from the side it looks like an upside-down *V*. If the box's side was as long as the playground, you could put the stars even farther apart. Then you would see no pattern at all from the side.)

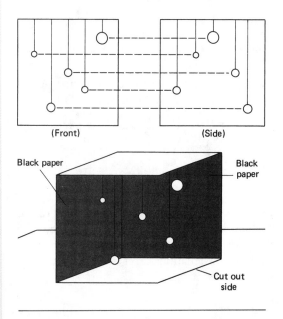

Figure 19-23

DISCOVERY PROBLEMS

observing   **A.** Look at the constellation your partner has made from the front view from 15 steps away. Can you draw its shape?

observing   **B.** At what distances from you are the stars? Which is closest, or next closest? Record what you think from left to right.

inferring   **C.** What do you think the constellation looks like from the side? Draw what you think.

observing **D.** Ask your partner to twist the box around very slightly. How, if at all, does this help you to tell distances and the side pattern? How much more must the box be twisted around to tell?

inferring **E.** Play a game with your partner. Each person hangs a different constellation. How many stars can you order properly by distance from you? How many side patterns can you tell from front patterns?

TEACHING COMMENT

PREPARATION AND BACKGROUND

It is essential that students first view the constellation model directly from the front and from some distance. Otherwise, the activity may be less effective. The foil balls may quickly be suspended, and shifted as needed, by affixing each thread end to the box top inside with a bit of tape.

GENERALIZATION

Stars of a constellation share a common direction, but they may vary greatly in size and distance from each other.

SAMPLE PERFORMANCE OBJECTIVES

Process: The child can infer a "side" pattern of stars by observing the constellation from a slight angle. (The degree of skill is related to the size of the angle needed to make a correct inference.)

Knowledge: The child states that the pattern of a constellation depends on the position of the observer in space.

GRAVITY AND THE LAWS OF MOTION EXPERIENCES
(Concepts p. 604)

ACTIVITY: WHY DOESN'T THE SUN'S GRAVITY PULL IN THE NEAR PLANETS?

NEEDED

strong string (2 meters or 6 feet long)
partner
rubber ball
watch with second hand
sewing thread spool
outdoor place

TRY THIS

1. Tie one end of the string tightly to the ball. Slide the other end through the hole of a sewing spool.

2. You will be the "sun." The ball "planet" will revolve around you on the string. Hold the spool in one hand. Whirl the planet by moving the spool around. Hold the string with your other hand to keep it from slipping through the spool (Figure 19-24). (You could mark the string below the spool to easily see any slip.)

3. Feel how the ball pulls on the string. Have someone count the number of times your planet circles the sun in 15 seconds. Try to keep the string length above the spool the same.

4. Try it a second time. Keep the string length the same as before, but now pull harder on the string below the spool. This increases the pull of "gravity" on your planet. If the planet is to stay at the same distance, what must happen to its speed?

5. Have someone count again the number of orbits your planet makes in 15 seconds. How do the first and second counts compare? What do you think makes it possible for the closer planets not to be pulled into the sun?

Figure 19-24

ACTIVITY: *WHAT MAKES A ROCKET WORK?*

NEEDED

sausage-shaped balloon
sticky tape

string (6 meters or 20 feet long)
paper clip
soda straw
five pennies

TRY THIS

1. Thread one end of the string through a straw. Fasten that end low on a table leg. Fasten the other end high on a wall. The string should be tight.

2. Blow up the balloon. Fold over the small, open end and fasten it with a paper clip.

3. Fasten the balloon to the straw with tape (Figure 19-25).

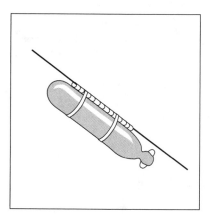

Figure 19-25

4. Hold the balloon near the floor end of the string. Quickly remove the paper clip and let go. What happens to the balloon? How can you explain what happens?

5. Have a contest with teams of classmates to see whose balloon rocket can lift the most weight to a "space station." Tie one end of each string to a light fixture or other high place. Fasten pennyweights to each balloon with sticky tape. Make some fair rules: The lower end of each string and rocket must touch the floor when the rocket is released. Each team gets two turns; the first is for practice. Observe carefully what the best rockets look like during the first trial. Use this information to prepare for the second trial. No team can change its rocket once the second trials begin. To win, here are some things to think about.

   ■ How much air should be in the balloon? (If it breaks, you're out of the contest.)

   ■ How long should the straw be? How should it be attached to the balloon?

■ Should the string be upright or at a slant? What kind of string is best?

■ How many pennies should be stuck on the balloon? Where is it best to put them for balance?

TEACHING COMMENT

When air rushes out of the balloon, there is an equal and opposite push inside, so the balloon moves. In a rocket engine, burned fuel forms hot gases that push out the open back of the engine. An equal and opposite push inside moves the rocket forward.

REFERENCES

American Association for the Advancement of Science. (1993). *Benchmarks for science literacy.* New York: Oxford University Press.

National Research Council. (1996). *National science education standards.* Washington, DC: National Academy Press.

SELECTED TRADE BOOKS: THE EARTH IN SPACE

For Younger Children

Bendick, J. (1991a). *Artificial satellites: Helpers in space.* Millbrook Press.

Bendick, J. (1991b). *Comets and meteors: Visitors from space.* Millbrook Press.

Branley, F. M. (1986). *What makes day and night.* Harper & Row.

Branley, F. M. (1987a). *The moon seems to change.* Harper & Row.

Branley, F. M. (1987b). *The planets in our solar system.* Harper & Row.

Branley, F. M. (1987c). *Rockets and satellites.* Harper & Row.

Branley, F. M. (1988). *The sun, our nearest star.* Crowell.

Branley, F. M. (1991). *The big dipper.* Harper Collins.

Calmenson, S. (1982). *My book of the seasons.* Golden Press.

Cole, J. (1990). *The magic school bus lost in the solar system.* Scholastic.

Fradin, D. (1984). *Spacelab.* Children's Press.

Friskey, M. (1982). *Space shuttles.* Children's Press.

Gorey, E., & Neumeyer, P. (1982). *Why we have day and night.* Capra Press.

Hamer, M. (1983). *Night sky.* Watts.

Jackson, K. (1985). *The planets.* Troll Associates.

Jay, M. (1987). *Planets.* Watts.

Weimer, T. E. (1993). *Space songs for children.* Pearce–Evetts.

For Older Children

Adams, R. (1983). *Our wonderful solar system.* Troll Associates.

Adler, I. (1980). *The stars: Decoding their messages.* Crowell.

Alexander, K. (1990). *The kid's book of space flight.* Running Press.

Asimov, I. (1990). *Projects in astronomy.* Gareth Stevens.

Asimov, I. (1991). *Ancient astronomy.* Dell.

Bendick, J. (1982). *Space travel.* Watts.

Berger, M. (1983). *Bright stars, red giants and white dwarfs.* Putnam.

Branley, F. M. (1987). *Star guide.* Harper & Row.

Cabellero, J. A. (1987). *Aerospace projects for young children.* Humanics.

Couper, H., & Henbest, N. (1987). *The moon.* Watts.

Fichter, G. S. (1982). *Comets and meteors.* Watts.

Furniss, T. (1987). *Let's look at outer space.* Watts.

Gallant, R. A. (1983). *Once around the galaxy.* Watts.

Gardner, R. (1988). *Projects in space science*. Messner.

Harris, A., & Weissman, P. (1990). *The great voyager adventure: A guided tour through the solar system*. Messner.

Kelch, J. (1990). *Small worlds: Exploring the 60 moons of our solar system*. Messner.

Lauber, P. (1982). *Journey to the planets*. Crown.

Lewellen, J. (1981). *Moon, sun and stars*. Children's Press.

Myring, L. (1982). *Sun, moon and planets*. EDC Press.

Richard, G. (1987). *Spacecraft*. Watts.

Ridpath, I. (1991). *Space*. Watts.

Riley, P. D. (1986). *The earth and space*. David & Charles.

Simon, S. (1982). *The long journey from space*. Crown.

Simon, S. (1984). *The moon*. Four Winds.

Vogt, G. (1982). *Mars and the inner planets*. Watts.

Vogt, G. (1987). *Space laboratories*. Watts.

Wood, R. (1991). *Thirty-nine easy astronomy experiments*. Tab Books.

Resource Books

Butzow, C. M., & Butzow, J. W. (1989). *Science through children's literature: An integrated approach* (astronomy and outer space topics, pp. 158–168). Teachers Ideas Press.

Fredericks, A. D., Meinbach, A. M., & Rothlein, L. (1993). *Thematic units: An integrated approach to teaching science and social studies* (earth, sun, and moon topics, pp. 161–167; space exploration, pp. 210–217). HarperCollins.

Shaw, D. G., & Dybdahl, C. S. (1996). *Integrating science and language arts. A sourcebook for K–6 teachers* (rocket and space travel topics, pp. 213–230). Allyn and Bacon.

PROFESSIONAL BIBLIOGRAPHY

GENERAL SOURCES OF ACTIVITIES

Bybee, R., Peterson, R., Bowyer, J., & Butts, D. (1984). Activities for teaching about science and society. Upper Saddle River, NJ: Merrill/Prentice Hall. (Activities that relate to social needs and problems.)

DeVito, A., & Krockover, G. H. (1991). *Creative sciencing: Ideas and activities for teachers and children*. Glenview, IL: Scott, Foresman (Good Year). (About 160 activities designed to stimulate creativity.)

Freidl, A. E. (1997). *Teaching science to children, an inquiry approach*. New York: Random House. (A large array of hands-on activities for children, including many discrepant events.)

Lowery, L. F., & Verbeeck, C. (1987). *Explorations* (3 volumes: *earth science, physical science, life science*). Carthage, IL: Fearon. (48 process-oriented activities for grades 1–3.)

Strongin, H. (1991). *Science on a shoestring*. Reading, MA: Addison-Wesley. (Easy-to-do investigations with readily found, inexpensive materials.)

Van Cleave, J. P. (1989–1991). *Science for Every Kid* (5 volumes: *biology, chemistry, earth, astronomy, physics*). New York: Wiley. (Each volume has 101 activities for grade three and beyond, many of which are suitable for science fair projects.)

TEACHER PERIODICALS

Discover, Time, Inc., 3435 Wilshire Blvd., Los Angeles, CA 90010. (Monthly. Interesting, up-to-date information about developments in science.)

Frontiers, National Science Foundation, 4201 Wilson Blvd., Arlington, VA 22230. (Newsletter of the National Science Foundation).

Journal of Elementary Science Education, contact Joseph Peters, Editor, The University of West Florida, 11000 University Parkway, Pensacola, FL 32514. (Practical and theoretical articles related to elementary science teaching and learning.)

Journal of Research in Science Teaching, contact Arthur White, National Association for Research in Science Teaching Executive Secretary, The Ohio State University, 1929 Kenny Rd., Columbus, OH 43210-1015. (Scholarly articles on research and practice.)

Journal of Science Teacher Education, contact Joseph Peters, Association for the Education of Teachers in Science Executive Secretary, The University of West Florida, 11000 University Parkway, Pensacola, FL 32514. (Practical and scholarly articles related to teacher preservice, teacher inservice, and science teaching.)

Natural History, American Museum of Natural History, Central Park West at 79th St., New York, NY 10024. (Monthly, 10 issues a year. Interesting articles on a variety of natural subjects, including ecology.)

School Science and Mathematics, contact Donald Pratt, School Science and Mathematics Association Executive Secretary, Curriculum and Foundations, Bloomsburgh University, Bloomsburgh, PA 17815-1301. (Monthly, nine issues a year. Includes articles on methods and research.)

Science, American Association for the Advancement of Science, 1515 Massachusetts Ave., N.W., Washington, DC 20005. (Monthly, except bimonthly Jan./Feb. and July/Aug. Accurate, up-to-date nontechnical information about developments in science.)

Science Activities, Science Activities Publishing Company, Skokie, IL 60076. (Ten issues a year. Useful activities for teachers of the upper grades and beyond.)

Science and Children, National Science Teachers Association, 1840 Wilson Blvd., Arlington, VA 22201-3000. (Monthly, eight issues a year. Articles of interest and practical value to elementary school teachers.)

Science Education, John Wiley and Sons, Inc., 605 Third Ave., New York, NY 10158. For individual subscriptions contact Joseph Peters, Association for the Education of Teachers in Science Executive Secretary, The University of West Florida, 11000 University Parkway, Pensacola, FL 32514. (Reports of research and essays on the teaching of elementary and secondary school science.)

Science News, Science Service, 1719 N Street, N.W., Washington, DC. (Weekly. Brief, easy-to-read reports on current findings of scientific research.)

CHILDREN'S PERIODICALS

Digit, P.O. Box 29996, San Francisco, CA 94129. (Six issues a year. Computer games, ideas, challenges. Upper elementary.)

Enter, One Disk Drive, P.O. Box 2686, Boulder, CO 80322. (Ten issues a year. Computer games, ideas, challenges from the producers of the Children's Television Workshop. Upper elementary.)

National Geographic World, National Geographic Society, Department 00481, 17th and M Streets, N.W., Washington, DC 20036. (Monthly. Articles on environmental features of interest to children.)

Odyssey, AstroMedia Corp., 625 E. St. Paul Ave., P.O. Box 92788, Milwaukee, WI 53202. (Bimonthly. Full-color astronomy and space magazine for children 7 to 13.)

Ranger Rick's Nature Magazine, National Wildlife Federation, 1412 Sixteenth St., N.W., Washington, DC 20036. (Monthly, for children of elementary school age. Interesting stories and pictures on natural subjects, including ecology. *Your Big Backyard,* also 10 issues, is for preschool and primary-level children.)

Scienceland, 501 Fifth Ave., Suite 2102, New York, NY 10017. (Monthly, eight softcover booklets issued a year. Well-received magazine for children, preschool to third grade.)

Science Weekly, P.O. Box 70154, Washington, DC 20088. (Twenty issues a year. Current science developments for children in grades one through six.)

3–2–1 Contact, Children's Television Workshop, P.O. Box 2933, Boulder, CO 80322. (Ten issues a year. Experiments, puzzles, projects, and articles for children 8 to 14.)

PROFESSIONAL TEXTS

Abruscato, J. (1996). *Teaching children science.* Englewood Cliffs, NJ: Allyn & Bacon. (Methods, activities, and content for elementary school science.)

Barba, R. H. (1995). *Science in the multicultural classroom: A guide to teaching and learning.* Needham Heights, MA: Allyn & Bacon. (Elementary science methods.)

Blough, G. O., & Schwartz, J. (1990). *Elementary school science and how to teach it.* New York: Holt, Rinehart and Winston. (Methods and comprehensive coverage of subject matter content.)

Cain, S. E., & Evans, J. M. (1990). *Sciencing: An involvement approach to elementary science methods.* Upper Saddle River, NJ: Merrill/Prentice Hall. (A methods text organized into six broad units to develop teaching competencies.)

Carin, Arthur A. (1997). *Teaching science through discovery.* Upper Saddle River, NJ: Merrill/Prentice Hall. (Methods and activities, with emphasis on discovery teaching.)

Esler, W. K., & Esler, M. K. (1996). *Teaching elementary science.* Belmont, CA: Wadsworth. (Methods and subject matter. Exemplifies and applies three kinds of lessons.)

Gabel, D. (1993). *Introductory science skills.* Prospect Heights, IL: Waveland Press. (A laboratory approach to learning science and mathematics skills, and basic chemistry.)

Good, R. G. (1977). *How children learn science.* New York: Macmillan. (Research on children's mental development and recommendations for teaching science.)

Harlan, J. (1992). *Science experiences for the early childhood years.* Upper Saddle River, NJ: Merrill/Prentice Hall. (Everyday science activities for younger children.)

Howe, A. C., & Jones, L. (1993). *Engaging children in science*. Upper Saddle River, NJ: Merrill/Prentice Hall. (Elementary science methods.)

Jacobson, W. J., & Bergman, A. B. (1991). *Science for children*. Upper Saddle River, NJ: Prentice Hall. (Methods and content of elementary-school science.)

Lind, K. K. (1996). *Exploring science in early childhood: A developmental approach*. Albany, NY: Delmar Publishers. (Elementary science methods.)

Martin, D. J. (1997). *Elementary science methods: A constructivist approach*. Albany, NY: Delmar Publishers. (Elementary science methods.)

Martin, R. E., Jr., Sexton, C., Wagner, K., & Gerlovich, J. (1994). *Teaching science for all children*. Needham Heights, MA: Allyn & Bacon. (Methods and content of elementary school science.)

Peterson, R., Bowyer, J., Butts, D., & Bybee, R. (1984). *Science and society: A source book for elementary and junior high school teachers*. Upper Saddle River, NJ: Merrill/Prentice Hall. (Content and comprehensive methods. Emphasizes science's impact on society.)

Renner, J. W., & Marek, E. A. (1988). *The learning cycle and elementary school science teaching*. Portsmouth, NH: Heinemann. (Emphasizes methods that match children's cognitive processes for successful science teaching.)

Sprague, C., Fiel, R. L., & Funk, H. J. (1995). *Learning and assessing science process skills*. Dubuque, IA: Kendall Hunt. (Process skill development and assessment.)

Tolman, M. N., & Hardy, G. R. (1995). *Discovering elementary science: Method, content, and problem-solving activities*. Needham Heights, MA: Allyn & Bacon. (Elementary science methods and content.)

Victor, E., & Kellough, R. (1997). *Science for the elementary and middle school*. New York: Macmillan. (Methods, content, and activities. Features an extensive scope of subject matter in outline form.)

Wassermann, S., & Ivany, J. W. G. (1988). *Teaching elementary science*. New York: Harper & Row. (Stresses informal, inquiry-type science experiences for children.)

AGENCIES AND SOCIETIES[1]

Association for the Education of Teachers in Science, 11000 University Parkway, Pensacola, FL 32514, email:jpeters@uwf.edu, http: // science.coe.uwf.edu/aets/aets.html

Computer Learning Foundation, P.O. Box 60007, Palo Alto, CA 94306-0007, http://www.thejournal.com/clf/support.html/

ERIC Clearinghouse for Science, Mathematics, and Environmental Education (ERIC/CSMEE), 1929 Kenny Rd., Columbus, OH 43210-1080., http://www.erisce.org/

ERIC Clearinghouse on Disabilities and Gifted Education, The Council for Exceptional Children, 1920 Association Dr., Reston, VA 22091-1589, (703) 264-9474, fax (703) 264-9494.

ERIC Clearinghouse on Elementary and Early Childhood Education (ERIC/EECE), University of Illinois at Urbana–Champaign, 805 W. Pennsylvania Ave., Urbana, IL 61801-4897.

Foundation for Science and Disability, E.C. Keller, Jr., Treasurer, 236 Grand St., Morgantown, WV 26505-7509.

Franklin Institute Science Activity Kits for Grades 1–4, Science Kit & Boreal Laboratories, Elementary Science Division, 777 East Park Dr., Tonawanda, NY 14150-6784, 1-800-828-7777.

International Council of Associations for Science Education (ICASE), Jack B. Holbrook, Executive Secretary, ICASE, P.O. Box 6138, Limassol, Cyprus.

International Council of Associations for Science Education (ICASE), Stepping Into Science Project, Homerton College, Cambridge, CB2 2PH, England, http://sunsite.anu.edu.au/icase/

National Audubon Society, A Teacher's Resource Manual, 700 Broadway, New York, NY 10003-9562, (212) 979-3000, fax: (212) 979-3188.

National Energy Foundation, 5225 Wiley Post Way, Suite 170, Salt Lake City, Utah 84116.

National Science Foundation, 4201 Wilson Blvd., Arlington, VA 22230, http://stis.nsf.gov/

National Weather Service, 1325 East West Highway, Silver Spring, MD 20910, http://tgsvs.nws.naaa.gov/

---

[1]For an updated list of agencies and their electronic addresses, see http://science.coe.uwf.edu/.

Office of Indian Education Programs, Bureau of Indian Affairs, U.S. Dept. of the Interior, 1951 Constitution Ave., N.W., Washington, DC 20240.

Society for Advancement of Chicanos and Native Americans in Science (SACNAS), University of California, 1156 High St., Santa Cruz, CA 95064, 408-459-4272, fax (408) 459-3156, email:sacnas@cats.ucsc.edu

TERC, 2067 Massachusetts Ave., Cambridge MA 02140, (617) 547-0430, fax (617) 349-3535, http://www.terc.edu/

U.S. Environmental Protection Agency, Headquarters Service Branch, Public Information Center, 401 M. St., S.W. (3406), Washington, DC 20460, (202) 260-2080, fax: (202) 260-7762, public-access@epamail.epa.gov.

U.S. Geological Survey, Information Services, P.O. Box 25286, Denver, CO 80225-9916., http://www.usgs.gov/

SCIENCE CURRICULUM PROJECTS

ACTIVITIES FOR INTEGRATING MATHEMATICS AND SCIENCE (AIMS)

Grades K–8. This program, developed at Fresno (California) Pacific College, was originally funded by the National Science Foundation to train a group of teachers in the rationale and methods for integrating science and mathematics in Grades 5–8. The classroom testing of written materials produced such positive results that a full-fledged writing project was launched to develop additional teaching booklets. Materials are now available for K–8. The rationale for AIMS includes these points: (1) Math and science are integrated outside the classroom and so should also be integrated inside it; (2) as in the real world, a whole series of math skills and science processes should be interwoven in a single activity to create a continuum of experience; (3) the materials should present questions that relate to the student's world and arouse their curiosity; (4) the materials should change students from observers to participants in the learning process; (5) the investigations should be enjoyable because learning is more effective when the process is enjoyed.

For more information, write to AIMS Education Foundation, P.O. Box 8120, Fresno, CA 93747-8120. http://www.AIMSedu.org/

EDUCATION DEVELOPMENT CENTER INSIGHTS

Grades K–6. The Education Development Center is in Newton, MA. The program con-

tains 17 activity-based modules that can be used separately within another science curriculum or as a full curriculum within the life, earth, and physical science areas. Each module is organized around four phases of instruction: Getting Started, Exploring and Discovering, Organizing and Processing for Meaning, and Applying and Extending Ideas. Six major science themes are incorporated into the program: systems, change, structure and function, diversity, cause and effect, and energy. Content and process skills are balanced across the curriculum. Material from other school subjects is integrated into many activities to give an overall understanding of how they normally relate.

The activities, often open-ended, focus on experiences that draw on the urban environment. Playground apparatus, toys, and the students themselves may serve as resources for learning science concepts. Instructional materials are designed for both the inexperienced teacher and the veteran who seeks innovative strategies to develop critical and creative thinking in students.

An advisory group of teachers from seven major urban areas continually gave feedback to program developers about the quality of learning and assessment activities.

The commercial distributor is Improving Urban Elementary Science Project, Education Development Center, Inc. 55 Chapel St., Newton, Massachusetts 02158; phone: 617-969-7100, extension 2430.

ELEMENTARY SCIENCE STUDY (ESS)

Grades K–6. ESS was begun in the 1960s as a curriculum improvement project of the Education Development Center, a nonprofit organization devoted to generating new ideas for education.

The program consists of 56 units of instruction that cover a wide range of science subjects. Each unit has a teacher's manual, and most units have an accompanying kit of materials. No fixed master plan exists for scope and sequence. The developers felt that each school district was best qualified to assemble its own curriculum from the units to meet local conditions.

ESS is intentionally child centered. Activities are designed to reflect the wonder, curiosity, and natural play of childhood. While the teacher guide for each unit suggests an overall structure, the students help determine the direction the activities take and how much time is spent on each activity. Most classroom procedures are exploratory and open-ended. ESS believes that learning happens best when children are free to use their own styles without over-structuring and premature closing from adults.

Materials are available from Delta Education, Inc., P.O. Box 915, Hudson, NH 03051. http://www.delta-ed.com/

FULL OPTION SCIENCE SYSTEM (FOSS)

Grades K–6. This program is designed to serve both regular and most special education students in a wide cross-section of schools. Developed at the Lawrence Hall of Science, Berkeley, California, the program features several modules at each grade level that include science lesson plans in the earth, life, and physical sciences, and extension activities in language, computer, and mathematics applications.

The laboratory equipment includes several package options, from complete kits to individual items. Materials assembly directions show how teacher and students can gather and construct equipment for many activities. A correlation table tells how to integrate activities with other programs and state department of education guidelines for science.

Much care is taken to have a suitable match between activities and students' ability to think at different ages. Further work has been done to make the program easy to instruct and manage. Provisions for preparation time, ease of giving out and retrieving materials, cleanup, storage, and resupply have continually guided program developers.

The commercial distributor of FOSS is the Encyclopedia Britannica Educational Corporation, 310 South Michigan Avenue, Chicago, IL 60604.

GREAT EXPLORATIONS IN MATH AND SCIENCE (GEMS)

Grades Preschool–9. Gems is a growing resource for activity-based science and mathematics. Developed at the University of California at Berkeley's Lawrence Hall of Science and tested in thousands of classrooms nationwide, over 50 GEMS Teacher's Guides and Handbooks offer a wide spectrum of learning opportunities from preschool and kindergarten through tenth grade. GEMS guides can be integrated into your curriculum or stand on their own as a stimulating way to involve students.

The GEMS series interweaves a number of educational ideas and goals. GEMS guides encompass important learning objectives summarized on the front page of each guide, under the headings of skills, concepts, science themes, mathematics strands, and the nature of science and mathematics. Taken together, these headings help summarize the objectives of the unit. These objectives can be directly and flexibly related to science and mathematics curricula, local and district guidelines, state frameworks, benchmarks, and the national standards. For more on flexible ways to build your own curricula using GEMS, contact the University of California, GEMS, Lawrence Hall of Science, Berkeley, CA 94720-5200.

NATIONAL GEOGRAPHIC KIDS NETWORK

Grades 4–6. The National Geographic Kids Network is a program that has children gather data on real science problems and then use a computer network to share their data with a scientist and children in other locations. The developer is the Technical Education Resource Center (TERC) in partnership with the National Geographic Society, which publishes and distributes the program.

Each of the instructional units is six weeks long and focuses on a central science problem. Children learn to ask questions and gather data in scientifically acceptable ways. The data are transmitted to an interested scientist who analyzes the data, answers children's questions, and then sends back an overview of all the collected information from cooperating schools.

Curriculum materials include children's handbooks that have background information on the topic of study, teacher guides, and computer software. The software is made up of a word-processing program, data charts, and a computer map of North America, all of which are used to ready and transmit data.

For details, write National Geographic Society Educational Services, 17th & M Streets, Washington, DC 20036.

NUFFIELD SCIENCE 5–13

Grades K–8. Science 5–13 is a series of reference and resource publications for the teacher that suggests an open-ended, child-centered approach to elementary science. ("5–13" signifies the age span of the children served.) This program was begun as a curriculum project at the Nuffield Education Foundation of Great Britain.

The basic set of teaching units is composed of 20 volumes. Some unit titles are: "Working with Wood"; "Science, Models, and Toys"; "Structure and Forces"; "Children and Plastics"; "Trees"; and "Ourselves." An additional set of six titles in environmental education complements the basic program.

A major contribution of Science 5–13 is how it takes children's beginning experiences with everyday things and freely extends them in many directions. All the while, children's intellectual development is carefully considered. In the United States, the distributor is Macdonald-Raintree, Inc., 205 W. Highland Ave., Milwaukee, WI 53203.

OUTDOOR BIOLOGY INSTRUCTIONAL STRATEGIES (OBIS)

Ages 10–15. Developed at the Lawrence Hall of Science, University of California (Berkeley), OBIS is designed for use with community youth organizations and schools that want to offer outdoor laboratory experiences. Four activity packets offer a broad selection of interesting, firsthand activities for studying ecological relationships in different environments: desert, seashore, forest, pond and stream, city lots, and local parks.

Each activity card consists of background information for the leader, description of materials needed and any advance preparation required, a lesson plan, and several follow-up suggestions. Each activity can be used alone or as part of a developmental sequence. The commercial distributor is: Delta Education, Box 915, Hudson, NH 03051.

SCIENCE FOR LIFE AND LIVING

Grades K–6. The full name for this curriculum is "Science for Living: Integrating Science, Technology, and Health." The developer is the BSCS Group, a nonprofit foundation for science education.

After readiness activities at the kindergarten level, these concepts and skills form the main curriculum structure: order and organization (Grade 1); change and measurement (Grade 2); patterns and prediction (Grade 3); systems and analysis (Grade 4); energy and investigation (Grade 5); and balance and decisions (Grade 6). Children build their own understanding of an integrated world of science, technology, and health as they work through activities that bring out the concepts and skills.

Each complete lesson contains five consecutive phases: (1) An *engagement* activity begins the lesson. Children connect what they know to the present material and reveal their prior knowledge, including misconceptions. (2) *Exploration* follows, in which students explore the materials or environment and form a common base of experience. (3) Next, an *explanation* phase gives students a chance to describe what they are learning, and the teacher is given an opportunity to state the intended learning. (4) *Elaboration* then provides activities that extend understandings and give further chances to practice skills. (5) The last phase, *evaluation,* allows students and teacher to assess what has been learned.

Published materials are available from the Kendall/Hunt Publishing Company, 2460 Kerper Blvd., Dubuque, IA 52001.

SCIENCE AND TECHNOLOGY FOR CHILDREN (STC)

Grades 1–6. The developer of this curriculum project is the National Science Resources Center, established in 1985 by the National Academy of Sciences and the Smithsonian Institution to improve the teaching of science and mathematics in the nation's schools. The project's mission is to significantly increase the number of schools that offer hands-on science programs to children, and to interest more females and minority members in science.

Teaching units include such titles as *Weather and Me* (Grade 1), *The Life Cycle of Butterflies* (2), *Plant Growth and Development* (3), *Electric Circuits* (4), *Microworlds* (5), and *Magnets and Motors* (6). They are designed to focus on easy-to-use materials and integrate science with other areas of the curriculum. Each unit includes a teacher's guide; pupil activity booklet; a description of needed materials; and annotated lists of recommended trade books, computer software, and audiovisual materials.

The developers sought to make the management of materials and activities as practical as possible. In the field testing of units, evaluation procedures monitored how well the units worked under a wide variety of classroom conditions.

For details, contact the National Science Resources Center, Arts and Industries Building, Room 1201, Smithsonian Institution, Washington, DC 20560.

SCIENCE—A PROCESS APPROACH (SAPA)

Grades K–6. SAPA has a unique structure. It uses process skills rather than subject-matter content as the base for its scope and sequence. Subject matter is used mainly as an aid to developing the skills, although much content is presented.

Eight "basic" processes are taught in Grades K–3: observing, using space/time relationships, using numbers, measuring, classifying, communicating, predicting, and inferring. In Grades 4–6, five "integrated" processes are taught that build on and extend the basic processes: formulating hypotheses, controlling variables, interpreting data, defining operationally, and experimenting. The method used to organize the development of the skills was to identify the process behaviors of scientists, and then to logically break down the behaviors into sequences through which they could be learned by children.

SAPA II, a more recent version of this program, has a more flexible structure than the first edition. Alternate procedures have been provided to allow the teacher more leeway in meeting students' individual differences and organizing teaching.

The commercial supplier is Delta Education, Inc., P.O. Box 915, Hudson, NH 03051.

SCIENCE CURRICULUM IMPROVEMENT STUDY (SCIS)

Grades K–6. SCIS is organized on a base of powerful and modern science concepts. Each of 12 instructional units features a central concept, with supporting subconcepts and process skills integrated into the activities.

Lessons have three parts: exploration, invention, and discovery. In the exploratory part, children are given objects to observe or manipulate. At times these observations are guided by the teacher; otherwise, the children observe and manipulate the objects as they wish.

Explorations allow firsthand contact with the material under study and provide a basis for children to use language. At the same time, the need arises for an explanation to make sense out of what has been observed. This is taken up in the second part of the lesson sequence. After discussion, the teacher gives a definition and a word for the new concept.

This "invention" of a concept sets up the third part of the lesson. Now, the children are given a variety of further experiences within which they discover many applications of the concept. These extend and reinforce their knowledge and skills.

An updated version of this program, *SCIS3*, is available from Delta Education, Inc., P.O. Box 915, Hudson, NH 03051.

SCIENCE IN A NUTSHELL

Grades K–8. Real fun with real science. Discover how exciting real science can be with Delta's new Science in a Nutshell mini-kit series. Introduce or enhance specific science content areas in the classroom, at home, in a resource room, or in an after-school program. Clearly written, hands-on activities challenge young scientists aged 6–12 to investigate their world. Mini-kits are suitable for use with individuals or with small groups of two to three. Contact Delta Education, P.O. Box 3000, Nashua, NH 03061, 1-800-442-5444, fax 1-800-282-9560.

UNIFIED SCIENCES AND MATHEMATICS (USMES)

Grades K–8. The Unified Sciences and Mathematics for Elementary Schools project was funded by the National Science Foundation to develop and try out interdisciplinary units of instruction involving science, mathematics, social sciences, and language arts. The units are centered on long-range investigations of real and practical problems geared to the local environment. The units, 26 in all, may be used by local school planners to design different curricula to meet their needs and reflect a problem-solving approach.

Several kinds of materials are provided for planners and teachers: an introductory guide to USMES, a teacher resource book for each major problem, background papers, a design lab manual (that tells how to set up and make needed apparatus), and a curriculum correlation guide.

More information may be obtained from ERIC Clearinghouse for Science, Mathematics, and Environmental Education (ERIC/CSMEE), 1929 Kenny Rd., Columbus, OH 43210–1080.

WONDERSCIENCE

Wonderscience offers hands-on science activities for elementary school teachers and students. Wonderscience is published monthly from October through May as a joint effort of the American Chemical Society, 1155 Sixteenth St., NW, Washington, DC 20036, and the American Institute of Physics, One Physics Ellipse, College Park, MD 20740. The single-copy subscription price is $6.00/eight issues plus $3.50 handling for each address. For subscription information call toll-free 1-800-333-9511 or write to Wonderscience at the ACS address.

COMMERCIAL SCIENCE SUPPLIERS

The following classifications of suppliers may not be entirely accurate, because suppliers often change offerings with business conditions. A current catalog should reveal the full scope of materials for sale in each case. Use school stationery when requesting free elementary-level catalogs. An annual, comprehensive listing of suppliers accompanies each January issue of *Science and Children*.

GENERAL SUPPLIES

Carolina Biological Supply Company
2700 York Road
Burlington, NC 27215
http://www.carosci.com/

Connecticut Valley Biological Supply
 Company
Valley Road
Southampton, MA 01073

Delta Education, Inc.
P.O. Box 915
Hudson, NH 03051
http://www.delta-ed.com/

Edmund Scientific Company
101 E. Gloucester Pike
Barrington, NJ 08007

Frey Scientific Company
905 Hickory Lane
Mansfield, OH 44905

Learning Things, Inc.
68A Broadway
Arlington, MA 02174

Ward's Natural Science Establishment
5100 West Henrietta Road
P.O. Box 92912
Rochester, NY 14692

BOTTLE BIOLOGY

Wisconsin Fast Plants
University of Wisconsin-Madison
College of Agricultural and Life Sciences
Dept. of Plant Pathology
1630 Linden Dr.
Madison, WI 53706
1-800-462-7417
fastplants@calshp.cals.wisc.edu
http://fastplants.cals.wisc.edu

BALANCES

Ohaus Scale Corporation
29 Hanover Road
Florham Park, NJ 07932

MICROSCOPES AND MICROPROJECTORS

American Optical Corporation
Eggert and Sugar Roads
Buffalo, NY 14215

Bausch & Lomb, Inc.
1400 North Goodman Street
Rochester, NY 14602

Brock Optical
414 Lake Howell Road
Maitland, FL 32751-5907

Ken-A-Vision Manufacturing Company
5615 Raytown Road
Raytown, MO 64133

Swift Instruments, Inc.
P.O. Box 95016
San Jose, CA 95016

AQUARIA, TERRARIA, CAGES

Carolina Biological Supply Company
2700 York Road
Burlington, NC 27215

Jewel Aquarium Company
5005 West Armitage Avenue
Chicago, IL 60639

Science Kit, Inc.
777 E. Park Drive
Tonawanda, NY 14150

KITS AND MODELS

Delta Education, Inc.
P.O. Box 915
Hudson, NH 03051

Denoyer-Geppert Company
5235 N. Ravenswood Avenue
Chicago, IL 60640

NASCO Company
901 Janesville Avenue
Fort Atkinson, WI 53538

Science Kit, Inc.
777 E. Park Drive
Tonawanda, NY 14150

SOFTWARE

Scholastic Software & Multimedia
2931 East McCarty St.
Jefferson City, MO 65101
1-800-724-6527

Sunburst Educational Software
Dept. EG53, 101 Castleton St.
P.O. Box 100
Pleasantville, NY 10570
1-800-321-7511
http://www.nysunburst.com

ENVIRONMENTS AND NUTRITION FOR CLASSROOM ANIMALS[1]

Animal	Environment	Nutrition[2]
Ants	Glass terrarium or large jar with dirt (covered with black paper)	Small food scraps or dead insects
Birds	Bird cage (ensure cage is large enough for bird to move freely)	Birdseed (nutritional mix from pet store—not wild bird seed)
Butterflies & Moths	Butterfly "tent" (sold in kits) or large jar with wire screen on top with small branches	Sugar water solution
Caterpillars	Medium-sized jar with holes in lid; include a small branch	Leaves (preferably near to where they were found)
Chameleons & Lizards	Aquarium with screened top; dirt, stones, and branches on bottom	Mealworms or live insects
Fish	Aquarium with gravel and filter (dechlorinate water before use)	Fish food from pet store (do not overfeed); brine shrimp
Frogs & Toads	Aquarium with shallow water and rocks to climb out of the water	Mealworms, small caterpillars, or live insects
Fruit Flies	Small jars with fine mesh covering	A small amount of overly ripe fruit
Guinea Pigs & Rats	Large animal cage with secure openings and an exercise wheel	Guinea pig food; small amounts of fresh fruit and vegetables
Hamsters, Gerbils, & Mice	Medium or large animal cage with secure openings and an exercise wheel	Hamster or gerbil food; small amounts of fresh fruit and vegetables

(continues on next page)

---

[1]Contact the National Science Teachers Association (1840 Wilson Blvd., Arlington, VA 22201-3000) for the Guidelines for Responsible Use of Animals in the Classroom.

---

[2]All animals require plenty of fresh water. To remove the chlorine from water, leave it standing overnight.

(continued)

Mealworms	Wide jar or plastic bucket with screen or mesh cover	Oatmeal and small slices of fresh apple
Newts & Salamanders	Aquarium with shallow water and rocks rising above water line	Mealworms and live insects
Rabbits	Large animal cage (rabbits will chew on cage, so avoid wood)	Rabbit pellets, fresh vegetables (avoid too much lettuce)
Snakes	Terrarium with secure openings; heating device (contact pet shop)	Live mice or insects (contact pet shop for specifics)
Spiders	Glass jar covered with screen	Live insects
Tadpoles	Aquarium ¼ filled with water and rocks above the water line	Small insects or finely chopped meat
Turtles (land)	Terrarium with non-poisonous plants and water pool	Mealworms, insects, earthworms; finely chopped vegetables
Turtles (aquatic)	Aquarium which is mostly water-covered, but with small land area	Mealworms, insects, earthworms; finely chopped vegetables

APPENDIX

E

SUMMARY OF CHILDREN'S THINKING[3]

Thought Process	Intuitive Thought[4]	Concrete Operations	Formal Operations
Cause and Effect	Logic often contradictory, unpredictable. Events may occur by magic or for human convenience.	Contradictions avoided. Physical objects are linked to show cause and effect. Common-sense explanations may be wrong but logical.	Can separate logic from content. Systematic control of variables possible, as well as hypothetical "thought experiments," to test ideas.
Relative Thinking	Egocentric perceptions and language. Little grasp of how variables interrelate. Physical properties viewed in absolute, not relative, ways.	Perceptions of position and objects more objective. Aware of others' views. Some understanding of interrelated variables, when connected to concrete objects and pictures.	Understand relative position and motion. Can define and explain abstract concepts with other concepts or analogies. May temporarily show some egocentricity in propositions.
Classifying and Ordering	Sort one property at a time. Little or no class inclusion. Trial-and-error ordering in early part of stage.	Understand class inclusion principle. More consistent seriation with diverse objects. Can follow successive steps, less discrete thinking.	Can recombine groups into fewer, more abstract categories. Can form hierarchical systems.
Conservative Thinking	Mostly do not conserve. Perceptions dominate thinking. Center attention on one variable and do not compensate. Little or no reverse thinking.	Can reverse thinking, consider several variables and compensate. Conserve most of the Piagetian test concepts.	Conserve all of the Piagetian test concepts, with displaced and solid volume usually last.

---

[3]Based on a format suggested by Robert Mele.

[4]Intuitive thought is the last period of the preoperational stage.

STATE EDUCATION AGENCIES

Alabama
Alabama State Dept. of Education
Gordon Persons Bldg.
Montgomery, AL 36130

Alaska
State of Alaska
Dept. of Education
801 W. 10th St., Ste. 200
Juneau, AK 99801-1894

Arizona
Arizona Dept. of Education
1535 West Jefferson St.
Phoenix, AZ 85007

Arkansas
Arkansas Dept. of Education
4 State Capitol Mall
Little Rock, AR 72201

Bureau of Indian Affairs
Dept. of Interior, BIA
1849 C Street, NW
Mail Stop 3525, Code 521
MIB
Washington, DC 20240

California
State Dept. of Education
721 Capitol Mall, 3rd Floor
Sacramento, CA 95814

Colorado
Colorado Dept. of Education
201 East Colfax Ave.
Denver, CO 80203

Connecticut
State Dept. of Education
P.O. Box 2219, Rm. 369
Hartford, CN 06145

Delaware
State Dept. of Public Instruction
Townsend Bldg.
P.O. Box 1402
Dover, DE 19903

District of Columbia
Education Program
D.C. Public Schools
415 12th St., NW, Rm. 1004
Washington, DC 20004

Florida
Florida Dept. of Education
Florida Education Center, Ste. 522
Tallahassee, FL 32399

Georgia
Georgia Dept. of Education
1862 Twin Towers East
Atlanta, GA 30334

Hawaii
Education Program
189 Lunalilo Home Rd., 2nd Floor
Honolulu, HI 96825

Idaho
LaRon Smith, Mathematics and Science Coordinator
Idaho State Dept. of Education
650 W. State St.
P.O. Box 83720
Boise, ID 83720-0027
(208) 332-6943
lsmith@sde.state.id.us

Illinois
Illinois State Board of Education
100 North First St.
Springfield, IL 62777-0001

Indiana
Indiana Dept. of Education
Rm. 229 State House
Indianapolis, IN 46204-2798

Iowa
W. Tony Heiting, Ph.D.
Consultant, Science Education
Bureau of Instructional Services
State of Iowa
Department of Education
Grimes State Office Building
Des Moines, IA 50319-0146
(515) 281-3249

Kansas
Kansas Dept. of Education
120 East 10th St.
Topeka, KS 66612-1103

Kentucky
Kentucky Dept. of Education
Capitol Plaza Tower, 500 Mero St.
Frankfort, KY 40601

Louisiana
State Dept. of Education
P.O. Box 94064
Baton Rouge, LA 70804-9064

Maine
Maine State Dept. of Education
State House Station #23
Augusta, ME 04333

Maryland
Maryland State Dept. of Education
200 West Baltimore St.
Baltimore, MD 21201-2595

Massachusetts
Massachusetts Dept. of Education
350 Main St.
Malden, MA 02148-5023
(617) 388-3300

Michigan
Michigan Dept. of Education
P.O. Box 30008
Lansing, MI 48909

Minnesota
Minnesota Dept. of Education
Capitol Square Bldg., Rm. 922
St. Paul, MN 55101

Mississippi
State Dept. of Education
Walter Sillers Bldg., Ste. 501
P.O. Box 771
Jackson, MS 39205-0771

Missouri
Missouri Dept. of Education
Dept. of Elementary & Secondary Education
P.O. Box 480
Jefferson, MO 65102

Montana
Office of Public Instruction
State Capitol Bldg.
Helena, MT 59620

Nebraska
Nebraska Dept. of Education
301 Centennial Mall South
P.O. Box 84987
Lincoln, NE 68509-4987

Nevada
Nevada Dept. of Education
Capitol Complex
Carson City, NV 89710

New Hampshire
New Hampshire Dept. of Education
1010 Pleasant St.
Concord, NH 03301

New Jersey
New Jersey Dept. of Education
Division of Standards and Assessment
CN 500
Trenton, NJ 08625-0500

New Mexico
State of New Mexico
Dept. of Education
300 Don Gaspar
Santa Fe, NM 87501-2786
(505) 827-6516

New York
New York State Education Dept.
Bureau of Professional Career
Opportunity Programs
Empire State Plaza
Cultural Education Center
Rm. 5C64
Albany, NY 12230

North Carolina
Dept. of Public Instruction
116 West Edenton St.
Raleigh, NC 27603-1712

North Dakota
Dept. of Public Instruction
State Capitol
Bismark, ND 58505

Ohio
Ohio Dept. of Education
65 South Front St.
Columbus, OH 43266-0208

Oklahoma
State Dept. of Education
Sandy Garrett
State Superintendent of Public Instruction
2500 North Lincoln Blvd.
Oklahoma City, OK 73105-4599
(405) 521-3301
fax: (405) 521-6205

Oregon
Oregon Dept. of Education
700 Pringle Parkway, S.S.
Salem, OR 97310

Pennsylvania
G. Kip Bollinger, Ed.D.
Science Education Adviser
Division of Arts and Science
Bureau of Curriculum and Instruction
Pennsylvania Department of Education
8th Floor, 333 Market Street
Harrisburg, PA 17126-0333
(717) 783-6598
TDD (717) 783-8445
pa@panet.mste.org

Puerto Rico
Office of Education
Office 809
Dept. of Education
Hato Rey, PR 00919

Rhode Island
Dr. Dennis Cheek
Coordinator of Mathematics,
Science & Technology
Rhode Island Department of Education
255 Westminster Street
Providence, RI 02902-3400
(401) 277-4600

South Carolina
South Carolina Dept. of Education
Curriculum Section
801 Rutledge Bldg.
Columbia, SC 29201

South Dakota
Paula L. Lind
Administrative Assistant
Department of Education
and Cultural Affairs
700 Governors Drive
Pierre, SD 57501-2291
(605) 773-3426
FAX: (605) 773-6139

Tennessee
Tennessee Dept. of Education
4th Floor Northwing
Cordell Hull Bldg.
Nashville, TN 37243-0388

Texas
J. W. Collins
Director of Science
Texas Education Agency
1701 N. Congress
Austin, Texas 78701

Utah
Utah Dept. of Education
250 East 500 South
Salt Lake City, UT 84111

Vermont
Vermont State Dept. of Education
120 State St.
Montpelier, VT 05602

Virginia
James Firebaugh, Jr.
Science Specialist
Virginia Dept. of Education
P.O. Box 2120
Richmond, VA 23218-2120
(804) 225-2651
fax (804) 786-1703
jfirebau@pen.k12.va.us

Washington
David Kennedy
Program Supervisor for Science
Office of Superintendent of Public Instruction
P.O. Box 47200
Olympia, WA 98504-7200

West Virginia
West Virginia Dept. of Education
1900 Kanawha Blvd., East, Rm. B-252
Charleston, WV 25305

Wisconsin
Dept. of Public Education
125 South Webster St.
P.O. Box 7841
Madison, WI 53707-7841

Wyoming
State Dept. of Education
241 Hathaway Bldg.
Cheyenne, WY 82002-0050

INDEX